America

A CONCISE HISTORY

Volume 1
TO 1877

CANADA

MINNESOTA
Duluth
L. Superior
St. Paul
Minneapolis
Sioux Falls
Mississippi R.
WISCONSIN
Madison
Milwaukee
MICHIGAN
L. Michigan
L. Huron
Lansing
Detroit
L. Erie
MAINE
Augusta
Burlington
Portland
Montpelier
VT. N.H.
Concord
Manchester
Boston
Albany
MASS.
Providence
R.I.
Hartford
CONN.
NEW YORK
Buffalo
L. Ontario
St. Lawrence R.

IOWA
Des Moines
Omaha
Lincoln
Illinois R.
Chicago
Gary
Wabash R.
OHIO
Wheeling
Toledo
Cleveland
Harrisburg
Pittsburgh
PENNSYLVANIA
Newark
New York
Trenton
NEW JERSEY
Philadelphia
Dover
DELAWARE

ILLINOIS
Springfield
INDIANA
Indianapolis
Columbus
Cincinnati
Frankfort
W. VA.
VIRGINIA
Washington, D.C.
MD.
Baltimore
Annapolis

Topeka
Kansas City
Jefferson City
St. Louis
Louisville
KENTUCKY
Ohio R.
Charleston
Richmond
Roanoke R.
Norfolk
MISSOURI
Wichita
Cumberland R.
APPALACHIAN MOUNTAINS
Raleigh
NORTH CAROLINA
Knoxville
Nashville
Charlotte
TENNESSEE
SOUTH CAROLINA
Columbia

Tulsa
Oklahoma
ARKANSAS
Arkansas R.
Memphis
Tennessee R.
Santee R.

Canadian R.
Little Rock
Atlanta
GEORGIA
Charleston
Birmingham
MISS.
ALABAMA
Alabama R.
Ocmulgee R.
Savannah

Fort Worth
Dallas
LOUISIANA
Jackson
Montgomery

Trinity R.
Sabine R.
Red R.
Mississippi R.
Mobile
Tallahassee
Jacksonville

Houston
Baton Rouge
New Orleans
FLORIDA
Tampa

Gulf of Mexico

Atlantic Ocean

Elevation
Feet	Meters
9,843	3,000
6,562	2,000
3,281	1,000
1,640	500
656	200
0	0

Miami

BAHAMAS

67° 66°
Atlantic Ocean
San Juan
18°
PUERTO RICO
Ponce
Caribbean Sea
0   50
Miles

CUBA

250   500
Miles

95°   85°   80°   75°

Michael P. Conzen
University of Chicago
Advisory Editor for Cartography

America

A CONCISE HISTORY

Volume 1
TO 1877

James A. Henretta
University of Maryland

David Brody
University of California, Davis

Lynn Dumenil
Occidental College

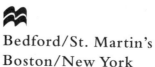
Bedford/St. Martin's
Boston/New York

Executive editor: Paul Shensa
History editor: Katherine E. Kurzman
Development editor: Jennifer E. Sutherland
Production editors: Elizabeth Geller/Shuli Traub
Production supervisors: Stacey B. Alexander/Scott Lavelle
Art director: Lucy Krikorian
Text design: Design Associates
Graphic arts manager: Demetrios Zangos
Photo research: Photosearch
Cover art: Crockett Street Looking West by Herman Lungkwitz. Courtesy of The
  Witte Museum.
Cartography: Mapping Specialists, Ltd.
Composition: TSI Graphics
Printing and binding: R.R. Donnelley & Sons Company

Library of Congress Catalog Card Number: 97-62266

Manufactured in the United States of America.

4 3 2 1 0 9
f e d c b

For information, write: Bedford/St. Martin's, 75 Arlington Street,
Boston, MA 02116   (617) 426-7440

ISBN: 1-57259-401-2

For Our Teachers and Students

PREFACE

*A*merica: *A Concise History* presents a succinct overview of the American experience in a handy, low-cost format while preserving the structure, balance, and inclusive vision of *America's History*, Third Edition, by James A. Henretta, W. Elliot Brownlee, David Brody, Susan Ware, and Marilynn S. Johnson. Designed as a single-column paperback, the text feels and reads less like a traditional course book and will prove more inviting to the average undergraduate.

Through an intensive development process, we've created an original text in *America: A Concise History*, narrated in a lively style and filled with new insights. Lynn Dumenil, professor of history at Occidental College, has brought her expertise as a cultural historian of twentieth-century America to the author team and has taken prime responsibility for the decades since 1914. James Henretta has rewritten all the chapters through the Civil War (Chapters 1–15), and David Brody revisits Chapters 16–22.

To write a text that would be forty percent shorter than our comprehensive survey while maintaining a strong narrative line, we decided to focus each part of *America: A Concise History* around a few themes and to link our discussions so that students could trace developments over the entire span of U. S. history. We give special emphasis to the evolution of political institutions and policies, the changing character of social groups, the increasing complexity of cultural life, and the interaction between people and their environment. This selective thematic approach provides students with a coherent overview of American history, which instructors can enrich with supplemental readings.

Most important, *America: A Concise History* presents a *balanced* narrative of our nation's past. In our discussions of government and politics, diplomacy and war, we show how they affected—and were affected by—ethnic groups and economic conditions, intellectual beliefs and social change, and religious and moral values of the times. Our text integrates social and political history, probing the lives of the rich diversity of people who have become Americans and analyzing the institutions—political, economic, and religious—that represent a common national identity.

FEATURES

To assist students while they read, *America: A Concise History* has a clear chronology and a strong conceptual framework. Each volume is divided into three parts, with each corresponding to a distinct phase of development. Every part begins at a crucial turning point, such as the Cold War, and emphasizes the dynamic forces at work. Part openers contain **Thematic Timelines** that highlight key developments and brief **Part Essays** that focus on the crucial engines of historical change that created new conditions of life. This part organization will help students understand the major themes in each period of American history, to see that bits and pieces of historical data acquire significance as part of a larger pattern of development.

Throughout the main text we have tried to mix quotations from ordinary Americans into the narrative to create a vivid account. Moving students further back into the context of the historical moment, each chapter includes two **American Voices**, first-person excerpts from letters, diaries, autobiographies, and public testimony that paint a striking picture of the social or political life of the time. These selections, virtually all newly selected and edited for *America: A Concise History*, bring history alive and remind students that the past is much more than a chronicle of the great and powerful.

Each chapter is enhanced by a selection of maps and contemporary illustrations and concludes with a **Timeline** listing important events. Finally, the Documents section reprints the Declaration of Independence and the Constitution of the United States, and the appendix lists statistical information. Also included is a comprehensive list of suggestions for further reading, organized by the headings in each chapter.

SUPPLEMENTS

Users of *America's History* have always cited the ancillary package as a key to the book's success in the classroom. We thus felt it very important to make all the materials for the big book available to adopters of *America: A Concise History*. The *Instructor's Resource Manual* provides an abundance of material to aid instructors in planning the course and enhancing student involvement, including specially commissioned Historiographic Essays and Documents Modules that focus on native Americans, African-Americans, Latino-Americans, women, and constitutional and diplomatic history. One hundred and ten full-color transparencies reproduce maps and figures from the textbook, as well as a selection of fine art and historic photographs. The *Who Built America?* CD-ROM, called "a truly exciting, high-quality electronic book" by *The Wall Street Journal*, covers the period from 1876 to World War I.

In addition, however, several key ancillaries have been specially prepared to support teaching with the concise book; the *Instructor's Resource Manual, Test Bank, Student Guides*, and *Documents Collection* have all been rewritten to take account of the important changes in coverage and approach. Finally, a new ancillary is available for people who use a brief text as a core around which to array a variety of supplements; *Using The Bedford Series in History and Culture with* America: A Concise History provides concrete suggestions for using two dozen volumes from this highly regarded series in conjunction with our text.

American History: A Concise Documents Collection, Volumes 1 and 2

by Douglas Bukowski

For instructors who like to use a variety of brief primary sources in class, a set of readings has been prepared to accompany *America: A Concise History*. For each chapter in the text, a corresponding chapter in this collection includes five to seven excerpts from important sources in political, social, economic, and cultural history. For each reading a helpful headnote gives students context on the author and selection. A series of three to five questions follow the reading to help students think critically about the source. At the end of each chapter, additional questions tie the readings together, inviting students to think about how this diverse set of pieces reflects the complex tenor of the time.

Student Guide, Volumes 1 and 2

Vol. 1 by Stephen J. Kneeshaw (College of the Ozarks); Timothy R. Mahoney (University of Nebraska–Lincoln); Linda Gies (Eastern New Mexico University); and Barbara M. Posadas (Northern Illinois University); Vol. 2 by Thomas R. Frazier (Baruch College, emeritus)

Specially prepared for *America: A Concise History*, the *Student Guide* will help conscientious students improve their performance in the course by developing better learning skills and study habits. The guide begins with an introduction by Gerald J. Goodwin (University of Houston) on how to study history, which is followed by discrete sections for each chapter that reinforce major themes and test on the book's coverage. Each chapter includes a summary of the essential facts and ideas of the text chapter, with fill-in questions; the timeline from the textbook with short explanations of the significance of each event; a glossary; skill-building exercises based on a map, table, or figure; exercises for the American Voices; and a self-test.

Instructor's Resource Manual, Volumes 1 and 2

Vol. 1 by Timothy R. Mahoney (University of Nebraska–Lincoln) and Linda Gies (Eastern New Mexico University); Vol. 2 by Thomas R. Frazier (Baruch College, emeritus), Stephen J. Kneeshaw (College of the Ozarks), and Linda Gies

The *Instructor's Resource Manual* contains materials to aid instructors in teaching *America: A Concise History* and enhance student involvement. For each chapter of the textbook the resources include a list of chapter themes, a brief summary, an annotated timeline from the textbook with additional information, lecture suggestions, class discussion starters, topics for writing assignments, and suggested topics for research. In addition, the *Instructor's Resource Manual* includes nine historiographic essays by outstanding scholars on topics like populism, a guide to writing about history by Gerald J. Goodwin (reprinted in the Student Guide), and a film and video guide by Stephen J. Kneeshaw.

Using The Bedford Series in History and Culture with *America: A Concise History*

by Scott Hovey

Recognizing that many instructors use a brief core text to provide a backbone around which to array supplements, Bedford/St. Martin's has made the Bedford series volumes available at a discount to adopters of *America: A Concise History*. This short guide by Scott Hovey gives practical suggestions for using a dozen volumes from the Bedford series with each volume of this concise text, providing links between text and supplement as well as ideas for starting discussions focused on a single primary-source volume.

Test Bank, Volumes 1 and 2

by Thomas L. Altherr and Adolph Grundman (Metropolitan State College of Denver), and James Miller

The *Test Bank* provides 80 to 110 questions for each chapter of *America: A Concise History*, including multiple-choice questions, fill-ins, and short and long essay questions. Computerized test-generation systems are also available for IBM-compatible and Macintosh platforms.

ACKNOWLEDGMENTS

The scholars and teachers who reviewed our manuscript saved us from many mistakes and made suggestions that enhanced the cogency of our interpretations. All have used concise texts in their courses, and their classroom experience has helped us create a book that will meet the needs of today's diverse students. Special thanks are due to: Thomas Blantz, University of Notre Dame; John Buenker, University of Wisconsin–Parkside; Emmett Essin, East Tennessee State University; David Huehner, University of Wisconsin–Washington County; John Johnson, University of Northern Iowa; Stephen Kneeshaw, College of the Ozarks; Chana Lee, Indiana University; Robert Martin, University of Northern Iowa; Carl Moneyhon, University of Arkansas–Little Rock; John S. Nader, State University of New York at Delhi; Steven Reiss, Northeastern Illinois University; and Kenneth Scherzer, Middle Tennessee State University.

As the authors of *America: A Concise History*, we know better than anyone else how much this book is the work of other hands and minds. We are grateful to Paul Shensa, who helped us to conceive this book, and to Jennifer Sutherland who, as always, held us to the highest scholarly standards as she masterfully edited our text. We also thank our editorial and production team for their dedicated efforts: Stacey B. Alexander, Elizabeth Geller, Lawrence Guerra, Cindy Joyce, Fernando Quinones, Shuli Traub, and Demetrios Zangos. Finally, we want to express our appreciation for the invaluable assistance of Patricia Deveneau, Lawrence Peskin, and Norman Cohen, whose work contributed in many ways to the intellectual vitality of *America: A Concise History*.

James A. Henretta
David Brody
Lynn Dumenil

CONTENTS

LIST OF MAPS

ABOUT THE AUTHO

James A. Henretta is Priscilla Alden Burke Professor o   , at
the University of Maryland, College Park. He received h.   ..uate education at Swarthmore College and his Ph.D. from Harvarc   ..versity. He has
taught at the University of Sussex, England; Princeton University; UCLA;
Boston University; as a Fulbright lecturer in Australia at the University of
New England; and at Oxford University as the Harmsworth Professor of
American History. His publications include *The Evolution of American Society,
1700–1815: An Interdisciplinary Analysis; "Salutary Neglect": Colonial Administration under the Duke of Newcastle; Evolution and Revolution: American Society,
1600–1820; The Origins of American Capitalism*; and important articles in early
American and social history. He recently completed a fellowship at the
Woodrow Wilson Center working on a study of *The Transformation of the Liberal State in America, 1800–1970.*

David Brody is Professor Emeritus of History at the University of California, Davis. He received his B.A., M.A., and Ph.D. from Harvard University. He
has taught at the University of Warwick in England, at Moscow State University in the former Soviet Union, and at Sydney University in Australia. He is
the author of *Steelworkers in America; Workers in Industrial America: Essays on the
20th Century Struggle*; and *In Labor's Cause: Main Themes on the History of the
American Worker.* He has been awarded fellowships from the Social Science
Research Council, the Guggenheim Foundation, and the National Endow-
ment for the Humanities. He is past president (1991–92) of the Pacific Coast
Branch of the American Historical Association. His current research is on industrial labor during the Great Depression.

Lynn Dumenil is Professor of History at Occidental College in Los Angeles.
She is a graduate of the University of Southern California and received her
Ph.D. from the University of California, Berkeley. She has written *The Modern
Temper: American Culture and Society in the 1920s* and *Freemasonry and American
Culture: 1880–1930.* Her articles and reviews have appeared in *Journal of Amer-
ican History; Journal of American Ethnic History; Reviews in American History*; and
American Historical Review. She has been a historical consultant to several doc-
umentary film projects and has served on committees of the Organization of
American Historians, the American Studies Association, and the Immigration
History Society. Her current work is on World War I, citizenship, and the state.

America

A CONCISE HISTORY

Volume 1
TO 1877

THEMATIC TIMELINE

	ECONOMY From Subsistence to Prosperity	GOVERNMENT From Monarchy to Republic	RELIGION From Hierarchy to Pluralism	SOCIETY The Evolution of Cultures
1450	Native American subsistence economy Europeans fish off North American coast	Rise of monarchical states in Europe	Protestant Reformation (1517)	Spanish confront Pueblo peoples of New Mexico
1600	First staple crops: furs and tobacco	James I rules by "divine right" Virginia House of Burgesses (1619)	English Puritans and Catholics found colonies in America	Calvinism and freehold ideal in New England White servitude and African slavery in Chesapeake colonies
1640	New England trade with sugar islands Mercantilism: First Navigation Act (1651)	Puritan Revolution Stuart restoration (1660) Bacon's rebellion (1675)	Religious liberty in Rhode Island Anglicanism is state church in Virginia	Eastern Woodland Indians retreat inland Aristocratic ideal in Chesapeake
1680	Tobacco trade stagnates Rice cultivation expands	Dominion of New England (1686–89) Glorious Revolution	Quakers create religious liberty in Pennsylvania Rise of toleration	African-American languge and culture
1720	Mature farm economy in North Imports from Britain increase	Rise of the assembly Challenge to "deferential" politics	German and Scots-Irish pietists arrive First Great Awakening	Cultural diversity in Mid-Atlantic colonies Franklin and the American Enlightenment
1760	Trade boycotts encourage manufacturing	Tenant and yeoman uprisings Ideas of popular sovereignty	Evangelical Baptists Quebec Act protects Catholicism (1774)	Sense of American identity

PART 1

THE CREATION OF AMERICAN SOCIETY

1450–1775

For thousands of years the first Americans lived isolated from the rest of the world, developing a rich diversity of societies adapted to the different environments of the continent. The coming of Europeans tore the fabric of these societies to shreds. European settlers transplanted their own societies to the New World—their economic practices, their political systems, their cultures, their religions. But in learning to live in the new land, the men and women who came to England's North American colonies eventually created distinctly new societies.

First, thanks to the abundant resources of eastern North America, the settlers compiled a record of economic achievement. Plenty replaced poverty as the settlers created a bustling economy and, in New England and the Mid-Atlantic colonies, prosperous communities of independent farm families. In the southern colonies the price of prosperity for a few was oppression and captivity for the rest—indentured servitude for many whites and, later, slavery for almost all blacks.

Second, white men of property created an increasingly free and competitive political system. The first English settlers brought authoritarian institutions to America, but arbitrary rule gradually gave way to new kinds of local government that included representative assemblies with real power.

Third, the diversity of religious belief among the settlers eroded support for an established church and promoted the new ideal of religious toleration.

Finally, conditions in the English colonies fostered the creation of new social identities. Many had a unique outlook or language, such as the cultures created by African-Americans and German-Americans. But after 1720 the values and the practices of the European settlers—English, Scots, Scots-Irish, Dutch, German—converged as a result of the religious revivals of the Great Awakening and the dissemination of Enlightenment thought. The result was a new American identity based on the English language, British legal and political institutions, and shared experiences.

WORLDS COLLIDE: EUROPE AND AMERICA

- Native American Worlds
- Traditional European Society in 1450
- Europe and the World, 1450–1550
- The Protestant Reformation and the Rise of England, 1500–1630

In 1492 the peoples of Europe and America lived in separate worlds, unaware of each other's existence. An estimated 70 million native Americans, the descendants of migrants from Asia, populated the vast continents of the Western Hemisphere. Across the Atlantic Ocean another 70 million people inhabited the much less extensive lands of Western Europe. Around 1450 a few Europeans, hungry for the trade and riches of Asia, began to venture far from their native shores. Within a few decades Christopher Columbus, an Italian navigator in the service of Spain, encountered the lands and peoples of the Americas, setting off a collision of cultures that changed the course of world history. The subsequent arrival in the Western Hemisphere of enslaved Africans—first in the West Indies and by 1550 in Brazil—added another dimension to the unfolding story.

How did Europeans become leaders in world trade and extend their influence across the Atlantic? What was the character of the native Americans' life and culture, and what made their societies vulnerable to conquest by European adventurers? How did England, an insignificant nation in 1492, acquire the political will and economic resources to establish colonies in North America? And what led to the transatlantic trade in enslaved Africans? In the answers to these questions lie the origins of the United States.

NATIVE AMERICAN WORLDS

When the Europeans arrived, the great majority of native Americans—probably 40 million—lived in Mesoamerica (present-day Mexico and Guatemala) and another 10 million resided in lands to the north (present-day United States and Canada). Some lived in simple agricultural communities, but the majority resided in societies ruled by warrior-kings and priests. In Mesoamerica and Peru, Indian peoples created civilizations whose art, religion, society, and economy were as complex as those of Europe and the Mediterranean.

The First Americans

The first people who lived in the Western Hemisphere were migrants from Asia. Some might have come by water, but most probably came by land. Strong archaeological evidence suggests that during the last Ice Age, which began about 30,000 years ago, small bands of hunters followed herds of game across a land bridge between Siberia and Alaska. A tale of the Tuscarora Indians, who lived in present-day North Carolina, tells of a famine in the old world and a journey over ice toward where "the sun rises," a trek that brought their ancestors to a lush forest with abundant food and game. Most anthropologists believe that this migratory stream continued for about 20,000 years, until the glaciers melted and the rising ocean waters submerged the land bridge. Then the people of the Western Hemisphere, who by that time had moved as far south as the tip of South America and as far east as the Atlantic coast of North America, were cut off from the rest of the world for 400 generations.

For another 3,000 years the first Americans lived as hunter-gatherers, subsisting on the abundant wildlife and vegetation. But about 3000 B.C. some native American peoples began to develop horticulture, most notably in present-day Mexico. These inventive farmers planted avocado, chili peppers, and cotton and learned how to breed maize, or Indian corn, as well as tomatoes, potatoes, and manioc, crops that would eventually enrich the food supply of the entire world. Over the centuries the Indian peoples bred corn into a much larger, extremely nutritious plant that was hardier, had more varieties, and had a higher yield per acre than wheat, barley, and rye, the staple cereals of Europe. They also learned to cultivate beans and squash and plant them together with corn; this provided a nutritious diet and preserved soil fertility, allowing intensive farming and high yields. The resulting agricultural surplus laid the economic foundation for populous and wealthy societies in Mexico, in Peru, and for a time in the Mississippi Valley.

The Maya and the Aztecs

The flowering of civilization in Mesoamerica began among the Mayan peoples of the Yucatan Peninsula of Mexico and the neighboring rain forests of

Chacmool Statue
Striking statues of a reclining man, called Chacmools, were prominent features of many Mayan temples. Priests placed sacrifices and gifts to the gods on the Chacmools' flat stomachs.

Guatemala. The Maya built large religious centers, urban communities with elaborate systems of water storage and irrigation. By A.D. 300 the Mayan city of Tikal had at least 20,000 inhabitants, mostly farmers who worked the nearby fields and whose labor was used to build huge stone temples. An elite class claiming descent from the gods ruled Mayan society, living in splendor on goods and taxes extracted from peasant families. Drawing on traditions that stretched back to the Olmec people, who had lived along the Gulf of Mexico around 700 B.C., skilled Mayan artisans decorated temples and palaces with art depicting warrior-gods and complex religious rituals. Mayan astronomers created a calendar that recorded historical events and predicted eclipses of the sun and the moon with remarkable accuracy. The Maya also developed hiero-glyphic writing to record royal lineages and noteworthy events, including wars.

Beginning around A.D. 800, Mayan civilization declined. Some evidence suggests that a two-century-long dry period caused a decline in population and an economic crisis which prompted overtaxed peasants to desert the temple cities and retreat into the countryside. By A.D. 900 many religious centers had been abandoned, but other Mayan city-states lasted until the Spanish invasion, and emigrants may have carried Mayan technology and culture into the Mississippi Valley.

As the Mayan empire flourished in the Yucatan, a second major Mesoamerican civilization developed in the central Valley of Mexico around the city of Teotihuacán, with its magnificent Pyramid of the Sun. At its zenith about A.D. 500 Teotihuacán had more than 100 temples, about 4,000 apartment buildings, and a population of at least 100,000. By A.D. 800 Teotihuacán had also declined, probably because of a long-term drop in rainfall and recurrent invasions by seminomadic peoples. Eventually the militant Toltecs from the deserts of northern Mexico took control of Teotihuacán and created a great empire, only to be overtaken by another warrior tribe, the Aztecs.

The Aztecs entered the Valley of Mexico from the north and settled on an island in Lake Texcoco. There, in A.D. 1325, they began to build a new city, Tenochtitlán (present-day Mexico City). They learned the settled ways of the resident peoples, mastered their complex irrigation systems, and established an elaborate culture with a hierarchical social order. Priests and warrior nobles ruled over twenty clans of free Aztec commoners who farmed communally owned land, and the nobles used huge numbers of non-Aztec slaves and serfs to labor on their private estates. Artisans worked in stone, pottery, cloth, leather, and especially obsidian (hard volcanic glass used to make sharp-edged weapons and tools).

The Aztecs remained an aggressive tribe and soon subjugated most of central Mexico. Their rulers demanded both economic and human tribute from scores of subject tribes, gruesomely sacrificing untold thousands of men and women to the god of war. Aztec merchants, organized in a hereditary guild, created far-flung trading routes and imported furs, gold, textiles, food, and obsidian. By A.D. 1500 Tenochtitlán had grown into a great metropolis with splendid palaces and temples and over 200,000 inhabitants. The Aztecs' wealth, strong institutions, and military power posed a formidable challenge to any adversary, at home or from afar.

The Indians of the North

The Indians who lived north of the Rio Grande were much fewer in number and less formidable in military strength. In A.D. 1500 and for most of the preceding centuries these Indians lived in hundreds of dispersed communities of a few thousand people (see Map 1.1). Most were organized in self-governing tribes composed of *clans*—groups of related families that had a common identity and a real or legendary common ancestor. They were led by local chiefs who, aided by the clan elders, led ceremonies and regulated personal life. For example, elders encouraged individuals to share food and other scarce goods, promoting an ethic of reciprocity rather than one of accumulation. Elders banned marriage between members of the same clan, a rule that helped prevent inbreeding, and granted families use-rights over certain planting grounds and hunting areas, since the concept of private ownership of land was virtually unknown in Indian culture. Clan leaders also resolved personal feuds, disciplined individuals who violated customs, and decided whether to go to war.

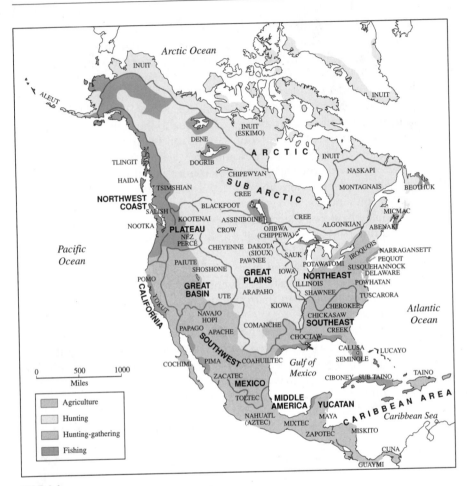

MAP 1.1

Native American Peoples, 1492

Native Americans populated the entire Western Hemisphere at the time of Columbus's arrival, having created diverse cultures that ranged from the centralized agriculture-based empires of the Maya and the Aztecs to seminomadic tribes of hunter-gatherers. The sheer diversity among Indians—of culture, language, tribal identity—inhibited united resistance to the European invaders.

However, their power was far less than that of the Mayan and Aztec nobles, because their kinship-based system of government was locally based and worked by consensus, not by coercion.

Over the centuries some of these tribes exerted influence over neighboring peoples through trade or conquest. The earliest expansive Indian culture appeared in the eastern woodlands of North America as the inhabitants increased the food supply by domesticating plants, settled in large villages, and exchanged goods. By A.D. 100 the vigorous Hopewell people of present-day Ohio had spread their influence through trade from present-day Wisconsin to

Louisiana. They built large burial mounds and surrounded them with extensive circular, rectangular, or octagonal earthworks that in some cases still survive. The Hopewell people buried their dead with art: copper beaten into elaborate designs, crystals of quartz, mica cut into the shapes of serpents and human hands, and stone pipes carved to represent frogs, hawks, bears, and other animals. For unknown reasons, their elaborate trading network gradually collapsed around A.D. 400.

A second complex culture developed in the Southwest. By A.D. 600 farming peoples in present-day Arizona were using irrigation to grow two crops a year, fashioning fine pottery, and worshiping their gods on platform mounds. In New Mexico, the Mogollon peoples developed large multiroom stone structures after A.D. 1000, while the Anasazi built residential-ceremonial villages in steep cliffs as well as devising a road system and various astronomical devices. But these cultures gradually collapsed after A.D. 1250 as long periods of drought and invasions by the Navajos and the Apache disrupted food production. The descendants of these Pueblo peoples—including the Zuni and the Hopi—later built strong but smaller and more dispersed village societies.

Casas Grandes Pot
The artistically and architecturally talented Mogollon and Anasazi peoples of Arizona and New Mexico took utilitarian objects—such as this ordinary pot—and decorated them with black-on-white designs. Their cultures flourished from 1000 to 1250, after which they slowly declined.

The last large-scale culture to emerge north of the Rio Grande was the Mississippian civilization. Beginning about A.D. 800, the advanced farming technology of Mesoamerica spread into the Mississippi River Valley, perhaps carried by emigrants fleeing from warfare among the Maya. New strains of maize and beans, planted on productive river bottomland, provided a protein-rich diet for the resident peoples and created an agricultural surplus. A robust culture based on small fortified temple cities quickly emerged. By A.D. 1150 the largest city, Cahokia (near present-day St. Louis), had a population of 10,000 and more than 100 temple mounds. As in Mesoamerica, the tribute paid by peasant cultivators supported a privileged class of nobles and priests who patronized skilled artisans. However, by A.D. 1350 this Mississippian civilization was in rapid decline, undermined by urban diseases such as tuberculosis and warfare over the fertile bottomlands.

The values and institutions of Mississippian civilization endured for centuries and accounted for the fierce resistance by the Indians of this region to Spanish and French invaders. As late as 1700 French traders and priests who encountered the Natchez people found a society rigidly divided among hereditary chiefs, two intermediate groups of nobles and honored people, and a bottom class of peasants. Undoubtedly influenced by Mesoamerican rituals, the Natchez practiced human sacrifice; the death of a chief called for the sacrifice of his wives and the enlargement of a ceremonial mound to bury their remains. Because of their stratified social order, eighteenth-century British settlers would call the Mississippian peoples (the Choctaw, Creeks, Chickasaw, Cherokee, and Seminole) the Five Civilized Tribes.

The most important legacy of the Mississippian civilization was its agricultural practices. Although farming in Mesoamerica was the province of both sexes, among the eastern Woodland peoples it became the work of women. Over the centuries Indian women became adept horticulturalists, using flint hoes and superior strains of corn, squash, and beans to reduce the dependence of their peoples on gathering and hunting. In the summer many tribes lived in semipermanent villages of domed wigwams where women cultivated fields, passing the right to use them to their daughters. Because of the importance of farming, a matrilineal inheritance system developed among many eastern Indians, including the Five Nations of the Iroquois. The ritual lives of these peoples also focused on religious ceremonies related to the agricultural cycle, such as the Iroquois green corn and strawberry festivals. While Indians ate better as a result of these advances in farming, they enjoyed few material comforts. Their lives were harsh, and their populations grew slowly.

In A.D. 1500 most Indians north of the Rio Grande had resided on the same lands for generations, but there were no great Indian empires and no major cities or religious centers. And because the peoples spoke many different languages (no fewer than sixty-eight east of the Mississippi River), there were few alliances among tribes. Neither their social organization nor their historical experience prepared them to deal collectively with the European invaders.

Women and Agriculture
As a Dutch traveler reported, Indian women planted corn by making "heaps like mole hills, each about two and a half-feet from the others" into which they put "five or six seeds." By planting two acres, a woman typically harvested 60 bushels of shelled corn, half the calories required by five persons for a year. Because of their economic contribution, women had a high status among many eastern Woodland peoples.

TRADITIONAL EUROPEAN SOCIETY IN 1450

In A.D. 1450 few observers would have predicted that the European peoples would become the overlords of the Western Hemisphere. A thousand years after the fall of the Roman empire Europe remained a backward society. Most Europeans, like most native Americans, were exploited peasants or poor farmers who had little knowledge of the wider world. Their lives and those of their descendants who would migrate to the Americas were shaped by the cultural and religious values of the traditional rural world.

The Peasantry

There were only a few large cities in Western Europe before A.D. 1450: Rome, Paris, Amsterdam, London, the city-states of northern Italy. More than 90 percent of the population consisted of peasants living in small rural communities. Usually families owned or leased a small dwelling in the village center and had the right to farm strips of land in the surrounding fields. The fields were not divided by fences or hedges, making cooperative farming a necessity. Each year the male householders decided which crops to plant and how many cows and sheep each family could graze on the commonly used meadows. Because there were few merchants or good roads, most families exchanged surplus grain and meat with their neighbors or bartered their farm products for the services of local millers, weavers, and blacksmiths. Most peasants yearned to be yeomen, under no obligation to a landlord and owning enough land to support a family in comfort, but relatively few achieved that goal. Most men and women lived hard, unvarying lives in the towns or regions of their birth.

Sustenance required unremitting labor. Other than water- or wind-powered mills for grinding grain, raw muscle was the major source of energy. While horses and oxen strained to break the soil with primitive wooden plows, men staggered as they guided them from behind. At harvest time workers cut hay, wheat, rye, and barley with hand sickles, but output was at most one-tenth of a modern yield.

As among the native Americans, nearly all aspects of European peasant life followed a seasonal pattern. The agricultural year began in March or April, when the ground thawed and dried, allowing the villagers to begin the exhausting work of spring plowing and planting. Peasants cut the first crop of hay in June and stored it as winter fodder for their livestock. During these busy spring months men sheared the thick winter wool of their sheep, which the women washed and spun into yarn. In the summer life became more relaxed. Families could mend their fences or repair their barns and houses. August and September often were marked by grief as infants and old people succumbed to epidemics of fly-borne dysentery. Fall brought the strenuous harvest time, but once the crops were in, people celebrated with solemn feasts of thanksgiving and riotous bouts of merrymaking. As winter approached, peasants slaughtered excess livestock and salted or smoked the meat. During the cold months they completed the tasks of threshing grain and weaving textiles and had time to visit friends and relatives in nearby villages. Many rural people died in January and February, victims of the cold and viral diseases. Then, just before the agricultural cycle began again in the spring, rural residents held carnivals to celebrate with drink and dance the end of the long winter night.

For most peasants the margin of existence was thin, and this situation corroded family relations. About half of all peasant children died before the age of twenty-one. Malnourished mothers fed their babies sparingly, calling them "greedy and gluttonous" little beasts, and many newborn girls were "helped to die" so that their older brothers would have enough to eat. To relieve overcrowding at home and instill discipline, English parents commonly sent their children to live as servants in other households, where they often were mistreated. Violence—assault, murder, rape—was much more prevalent than in the modern world, and hunger and disease were constant companions. "I have seen the latest epoch of misery," a French doctor reported as famine and plague struck. "The inhabitants . . . lie down in a meadow to eat grass, and share the food of wild beasts."

Often destitute, usually exploited and dominated by landlords and aristocrats, many peasants simply accepted their condition, but others did not. It would be the deprived rural classes of England and Western Europe, hoping for a better life for themselves and their children, who would supply the majority of white migrants to the Western Hemisphere.

Hierarchy and Authority

In the traditional European social order, as in the Aztec and Mayan empires, authority came from above. Kings and princes owned vast tracts of land and lived in splendor off the labor of the peasantry. Monarchs sought to extend their power by levying royal taxes, creating law courts, and conscripting men for military service. Yet they were far from supreme, given the power of the nobles, each of whom also owned large estates and controlled hundreds of peasant families. Collectively, these noblemen had the power to challenge royal authority. They had their own legislative institutions, such as the French *parlements* and the English House of Lords, and enjoyed special privileges, such as the right to a trial before a jury of their peers. Because nobles had direct control over the peasantry, monarchs had little choice but to appoint them as local judges and militia officers. But after 1450 kings began to undermine the power of the nobility and create more centralized states, laying the basis for overseas expansion.

Just as kings and nobles ruled the polity, the men in peasant families ruled their women and children. The man was the head of the house, his power justified by the teachings of the Christian Church. As one English clergyman put it, "The woman is a weak creature not embued with like strength and constancy of mind"; law and custom consequently "subjected her to the power of man." Upon marriage, an English woman assumed her husband's surname and usually moved to his village. She was required (under the threat of legally sanctioned physical "correction") to submit to her husband's orders. Moreover, she surrendered to her husband the legal right to all her property, including her clothes. Upon his death she received only a dower, usually the use during her lifetime of one-third of the family's land and goods.

A father controlled the lives of his children with equal authority, demanding that they work for him until their middle or late twenties. Then a landowning peasant would provide land to sons and dowries to daughters and choose marriage partners of appropriate wealth and status for them. In many regions fathers bestowed most of the land on the eldest son in the inheritance practice known as *primogeniture* (preference to the firstborn male). Custom called for landless brothers and sisters to work on their brother's farm in return for food and shelter, but the small size of most peasant holdings forced many younger children to join the ranks of the roaming poor.

In this world of scarcity the individual had to submit to the discipline of superiors or to the consensus of the village community. As among the eastern Woodland Indians, local authorities strictly regulated individual behavior for the common good; for example, in Germany they granted marriage licenses only to couples with enough property to support a family. Officials also imposed limits on what could be charged for the staff of life: a loaf of bread, a sack of flour or grain. Fearful of change, they made tradition the measure of existence. "After a thing had been practiced for so long that it becomes a Custom," an English clergyman proclaimed, "that Custom is Law." In such a society few men—and even fewer women—had much personal freedom or individual identity.

Hierarchy and authority prevailed in the traditional European social order both because of the power of established institutions and because, in a violent and unpredictable world, they offered ordinary people a measure of security. These values, which migrants carried with them to America, would shape the character of family life and the social order there well into the eighteenth century.

The Power of Religion

The Roman Catholic Church served as the great unifying force in Western European society. By A.D. 1000 Christianity had converted virtually all of pagan Europe. The pope, as head of the Catholic Church, directed a vast hierarchy of cardinals, bishops, and priests. Latin, the language of scholarship, was preserved by Catholic priests and monks, and Christian dogma provided a common understanding of God, the world, and human history. Equally important, the Church provided another bulwark of authority and

Christ's Crucifixion
This graphic portrayal of Christ's death on the cross by the German painter Grünewald sought to remind believers of the reality of death and the need for repentance. [Mathias Grünewald, Isenheim Altarpiece (central panel), Colmar, Musée Unterlinden, Giraudon/Art Resource]

discipline in society. Every village had a church, and holy shrines dotted the byways of Europe.

Christian doctrine penetrated deeply into the everyday lives of peasants. Over the centuries the Church had adopted a religious calendar that followed the agricultural cycle and transformed pagan festivals into Christian holy days. Thus the winter solstice, which for pagans marked the return of the sun and the victory of light over darkness, became the feast of Christmas. This merging of the sacred and the agricultural cycle endowed all worldly events with meaning. Few Christians believed that events occurred by chance; they were the result of God's will. To avert famine and plague, peasants turned to priests for spiritual guidance and offered prayers to Christ and the saints. God's presence in the world was renewed continually through the sacrament of Holy Communion. According to Catholic doctrine, priests had the power to change sacramental bread and wine into the body and blood of Christ. By consuming the bread of the Host, peasants could partake in the divine.

The Church taught that Satan constantly challenged God by tempting people into evil. If prophets spread unusual doctrines, they were surely the tools of Satan. If a devout Christian fell mysteriously ill, the sickness might be the result of an evil spell cast by a witch in league with Satan. Crushing other religions and suppressing false doctrines (heresies) among Christians was an obligation of rulers and a principal task of the new orders of Christian knights. Between A.D. 1096 and 1291 successive armies of Christians, led by European kings and nobles, embarked on a series of Crusades to expel Muslims from the Holy Land where Jesus had lived.

The Crusaders succeeded in gaining control of much of Palestine, but the impact on Europe was more profound. Religious warfare reinforced and intensified its Christian identity, resulting in renewed persecution of Jews and their expulsion from many European countries. Many Jewish refugees went to Germany, only to be driven farther east, to Poland, over the next few centuries. The Crusades also broadened the intellectual and economic horizons of the privileged classes of Western Europe, bringing them into contact with the advanced Muslim peoples of the Mediterranean region who controlled the trade among Europe, Asia, and Africa and led the world in scholarship.

EUROPE AND THE WORLD, 1450–1550

Around A.D. 1450 Europeans shook off the lethargy of their traditional agricultural society with a major revival of learning, the Renaissance. Inspired by new knowledge and a new optimism, the rulers of Portugal and Spain commissioned Italian navigators to find new trade routes to India and China. These maritime adventurers soon brought Europeans into direct contact with the peoples of Africa, Asia, and the Americas, beginning a new era in world history.

Renaissance Beginnings

Stimulated by the wealth and learning of the Arab world, first Italy and then the countries of northern Europe experienced the rebirth of learning and cultural life now known as the Renaissance. Arab traders had access to the fabulous treasures of the East, such as silks and spices, and Arab societies had acquired magnetic compasses, water-powered mills, and mechanical clocks. In great cultural centers such as Alexandria and Cairo in Egypt, Arab scholars carried on the legacy of Christian Byzantine civilization, which had preserved the great achievements of the Greeks and Romans in religion, medicine, philosophy, mathematics, astronomy, and geography. Through Arab learning, the peoples of Europe reacquainted themselves with their own classical heritage.

The Renaissance had the most profound impact on the upper classes. Merchants from the Italian city-states of Venice, Genoa, and Pisa dispatched ships to Alexandria, Beirut, and other eastern Mediterranean ports, where they purchased goods from China, India, Persia, and Arabia and sold them throughout Europe. The enormous profits from this commerce created a new class of merchants, bankers, and textile manufacturers who conducted trade, lent vast sums of money, and spurred technological innovation in silk and wool production. This moneyed elite ruled the republican city-states of Italy and created the concept of civic humanism, an ideology that celebrated public virtue and service to the state and would profoundly influence European and American conceptions of government.

Drawing inspiration from classical Greek and Roman (rather than Christian) sources, Renaissance intellectuals were optimistic in their view of human nature and celebrated individual potential. Embracing the confident psychology of the Renaissance, they saw themselves not as prisoners of blind fate or victims of the forces of nature but as many-sided individuals with the capacity to change the world.

This energetic view appealed to Renaissance rulers. In *The Prince* (1513), Niccolò Machiavelli, inspired by the state-building activities of the ambitious monarchs of France and Western Europe, provided unsentimental advice on how monarchs could increase their political power. Kings followed his advice, creating royal law courts and bureaucracies to reduce the power of the landed classes and seeking alliances with merchants and manufacturers. Monarchs allowed merchants to trade throughout their realms and granted privileges to artisan guilds, encouraging both domestic manufacturing and foreign trade. In return, these rulers extracted taxes from towns and loans from merchants to support their armies and officials. This alliance of monarchs, merchants, and royal bureaucrats challenged the power of the agrarian nobility, while the increasing wealth of the monarchical nation-state propelled Europe into its first age of expansion.

Portugal Penetrates Africa and Asia

Under the direction of Prince Henry (1394–1460), Portugal led the great surge of expansion. Henry was a many-sided individual, at once a Christian warrior and a Renaissance humanist. As a general of the Crusading Order of Christ, he had fought the Muslims in North Africa, an experience which reinforced his desire to extend the bounds of Christendom—and Portuguese power. As a humanist, Henry patronized Renaissance thinkers and relied on Arab and Italian geographers for the latest knowledge about the shape and size of the continents. Imbued with the spirit of the Renaissance, he tried to fulfill the predictions of his horoscope: "to engage in great and noble conquests and to attempt the discovery of things hidden from other men."

Because Arab and Italian merchants dominated trade in the Mediterranean, Henry sought an ocean route to the wealth of Asia. In the 1420s he established a center for exploration and ocean mapping and sent out ships to sail the African coast. His seamen soon discovered and settled the islands of Madeira and the Azores. By 1435 Portuguese sea captains were roaming the coast of West Africa, seeking ivory and gold in exchange for salt, wine, and fish. By the 1440s they were trading in humans as well, the first Europeans to engage in the African slave trade. For centuries Arab merchants had conducted a brisk overland trade in slaves, buying sub-Saharan Africans captured during local ethnic conflicts and selling them throughout the Mediterranean region. At first the Portuguese transported enslaved West Africans to sugar estates in Madeira and the Azores. Later they would carry hundreds of thousands of slaves to toil and die on the sugar plantations of Brazil and the West Indies.

After Henry's death in 1460 Portuguese adventurers continued to look for a direct ocean route to Asia. In 1488 Bartholomeu Dias rounded the Cape of Good Hope, the southern tip of Africa, and ten years later Vasco da Gama reached India. Although the Arab, Indian, and Jewish merchants who controlled the trade along India's Malabar Coast tried to exclude him, da Gama acquired a highly profitable cargo of cinnamon and pepper (used to flavor and preserve meat). To capture this commerce for Portugal, da Gama returned to India in 1502 with twenty-one fighting vessels, which outmaneuvered and outgunned the Arab fleets. The plunder-hungry Portuguese burned cities and seized the property of rival traders. Soon the Portuguese government set up fortified trading posts for its merchants at key points around the Indian Ocean and opened trade routes from Africa to Indonesia and up the coast of Asia to China and Japan. Portuguese merchants could undersell Arab traders because their ships held more and traveled faster than overland caravans. In a momentous transition, Portuguese replaced Arabs as the leaders in world commerce and the trade in African slaves.

Spain and America

Spain quickly followed Portugal's example. As Renaissance rulers, King Ferdinand of Aragon and Queen Isabella of Castile saw national unity and commerce as the keys to power and prosperity. Married in their teens in an arranged match, the young rulers (1474–1516) combined their kingdoms and completed the centuries-long campaign (the *reconquista*) to oust the Moors (Arabs) from their realm. In 1492 their armies reconquered Granada, the last outpost of Islam in Western Europe. Continuing their effort to use the Catholic religion to build a sense of "Spanishness," Ferdinand and Isabella launched a brutal Inquisition against suspected Christian heretics and expelled or forcibly converted thousands of Jews. Simultaneously they sought new opportunities for trade and empire.

Because Portugal controlled the southern, or African, approach to Asia, Isabella and Ferdinand listened with interest to proposals for a western route to the riches of the East. Its main advocate was Christopher Columbus, a forceful Genoese sea captain who, after many failed ventures, was determined to become rich and famous. Misinterpreting the findings of Italian geographers, Columbus persuaded the Spanish monarchs that the Atlantic Ocean, long feared by Arab sailors as an endless "green sea of darkness," was little more than a narrow channel of water separating Europe from Asia. Dubious at first, Ferdinand and Isabella finally agreed to arrange financial backing from Spanish merchants and charged Columbus not only to discover a new trade route to China but also to carry Christianity to other peoples.

Columbus set sail with three small ships on August 3, 1492. Six weeks later, after a voyage of 3,000 miles, he finally found land, disembarking on one of the islands of the present-day Bahamas on October 12, 1492. Although surprised by the rude living conditions of the natives, Columbus expected them to be quickly "delivered and converted to our holy faith." With ceremony and solemnity, he claimed the islands for Spain and for Christendom.

Believing he had reached Asia—"the Indies," in fifteenth-century parlance—Columbus called the native inhabitants "Indians" and labeled the islands "the West Indies." He then explored the Caribbean islands, demanding gold from the local Tainos and Arawak peoples. Buoyed by the natives' stories of rivers of gold lying "to the west," Columbus left forty men on the island of Hispaniola and returned triumphantly to Spain, taking several Tainos to display to Isabella and Ferdinand.

The Spanish monarchs were sufficiently impressed by his discovery to support three more voyages over the next twelve years. During those expeditions Columbus began the transatlantic slave trade, carrying a few hundred Indians to bondage in Europe and importing black slaves from Africa to work as artisans and farmers in the Spanish settlements. However, he failed to find either golden treasures or great kingdoms, and his death in 1506 went virtually unrecognized. Ignoring Columbus, a German geographer gave the new continents the name of a Florentine merchant, Amerigo Vespucci, who traveled to South America around 1500 and called it a *nuevo mundo*, a New World. For its part, the Spanish Crown was determined to make it a Spanish world.

Columbus's First Impressions of Native Americans

*A*s *a well-traveled mariner, Columbus knew the world and its peoples. But he was clearly puzzled by the first "Indians" he encountered: their lack of clothes and iron weapons, skin color, and painted bodies. To maintain his belief that he had reached Asia, he visualized a more advanced civilization on the mainland.*

Because I knew that they were a people to be delivered and converted to our holy faith rather by love than by force, [I] gave to some among them some red caps and some glass beads, which they hung around their necks, and many other things of little value. At this they were greatly pleased and became so entirely our friends that it was a wonder to see. . . .

They all go naked as their mothers bore them, and the women also, although I saw only one very young girl. . . . Their hair is coarse almost like the hairs of a horse's tail and short; they wear their hair down over their eyebrows, except for a few strands behind, which they wear long and never cut. Some of them are painted black, and they are the colour of the people of the Canaries, neither black nor white, and some of them are painted white and red. . . .

They do not bear arms or know them, for I showed to them swords and they took them by the blade and cut themselves through ignorance. They have no iron. Their spears are certain reeds, without iron, and some of these have a fish hook at the end, while others are pointed in various ways. . . . I saw some who bore marks of wounds on their bodies . . . and they indicated to me that people came from other islands, which are near, and wished to capture them, and they defended themselves. And I believed and still believe that they come here from the mainland to take them for slaves. They should be good servants and of quick intelligence, . . . and I believe that they would easily be made Christians, for it appeared to me that they had no creed.

SOURCE: Bartolomé de Las Casas, *The Journal of Christopher Columbus* (1847/70), trans. by Cecil Jane, rev. and annotated by L. A. Vigneras (London: Hakluyt Society, 1960), pp. 39–41.

The Conquest

Although Columbus had found no gold, rumors of riches to the west encouraged Spanish adventurers to follow in his footsteps. Most of these men were not explorers or merchants but hardened veterans of the Moorish wars who were eager to get rich. The Spanish Crown offered them plunder, estates in the conquered territory, and titles of nobility in return for creating an empire. After subduing the Arawak and Tainos on Hispaniola, these military adventurers explored the mainland in search of booty. Juan Ponce de León searched for gold and slaves along the coast of Florida in 1513 and gave the peninsula its name. Vasco Núñez de Balboa crossed the Isthmus of Darien

(Panama) in 1513, not finding gold but becoming the first European to see the Pacific Ocean.

The first great success of the Spanish *conquistadors* (conquerors) occurred in Mexico (see Map 1.2). In 1519 Hernando Cortés landed on the Mexican coast with 600 men and marched toward the Aztec capital of Tenochtitlán. Fortuitously, Cortés arrived in the very year in which Aztec mythology had predicted the return of the god Quetzalcoatl to his earthly kingdom. Believing that Cortés might be the returning god, Moctezuma, the Aztec ruler, acted indecisively. After the failure of an ambush against the conquistadors, he allowed Cortés to proceed without challenge to Tenochtitlán and received him with great ceremony, only to become his captive. When Moctezuma's forces attempted to expel the invader, they were confronted by superior European military technology. The sight of the Spaniards in full armor, with cannon that shook the heavens, made a deep impression on the Aztecs, who had learned how to purify gold and fashion it into ornate religious objects but did not produce iron tools or weapons. Moreover, the Aztecs had no wheeled carts or cav-

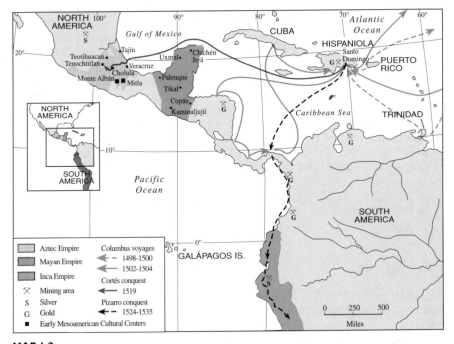

MAP 1.2
The Spanish Conquest
The Spanish first invaded the islands of the Caribbean. Rumors of a magnificent golden civilization led to Cortés's attack on the Aztec empire in 1519. Thanks to the devastating impact of European diseases on Indian peoples, Spanish conquistadors soon conquered the Mayan temple cities and the Inca empire in Peru, completing one of the great conquests in world history.

Aztec Elders Describe the Spanish Conquest

During the 1550s Friar Bernardino de Sahagún published the Florentine Codex: General History of New Spain, *in which the Aztecs described their reaction to the invading Europeans and the devastating impact of smallpox.*

Moctezuma enjoyed no sleep, no food, no one spoke to him. Whatsoever he did, it was as if he were in torment. . . . And when he had so heard what the messengers reported, he was terrified, he was astounded. . . . Especially did it cause him to faint away when he heard how the gun, at [the Spaniards'] command, discharged: how it resounded as if it thundered when it went off. It indeed bereft one of strength; it shut off one's ears. And when it discharged, something like a round pebble came forth from within. Fire went showering forth; sparks went blazing forth. And its smoke smelled very foul. . . .

All iron was their war array. In iron they clothed themselves. With iron they covered their heads. Iron were their swords. Iron were their crossbows. Iron were their shields. Iron were their lances. And those which bore them upon their backs, their deer [horses], were as tall as roof terraces.

And their bodies were everywhere covered; only their faces appeared. They were very white; they had chalky faces; they had yellow hair, though the hair of some was black. . . . And when Moctezuma so heard, he was much terrified. It was as if he fainted away. His heart saddened; his heart failed him. . . .

[Soon] there came to be prevalent a great sickness, a plague. It was in Tepeilhuitl that it originated, that there spread over the people a great destruction of men. Some it indeed covered [with pustules]; they were spread everywhere, on one's face, on one's head, on one's breast. There was indeed perishing; many indeed died of it. No longer could they walk; they only lay in their abodes, in their beds. . . . There was much perishing. Like a covering, covering-like, were the pustules. Indeed, many people died of them, and many just died of hunger. There was death from hunger; there was no one to take care of another; there was no one to attend to another.

SOURCE: Friar Bernardino de Sahagún, *Florentine Codex: General History of New Spain,* trans. by Arthur J. O. Anderson and Charles E. Dibble (Salt Lake City: University of Utah Press, 1975), Book 12, pp. 17–20, 26, 83.

alry, and their warriors, fighting on foot with flint- or obsidian-tipped spears and arrows, were no match for mounted Spanish conquistadors, wielding steel swords and protected by heavy armor.

Still, the vast population of the Aztec empire could easily have crushed the European invaders if the Indian peoples had remain united and healthy. But Cortés exploited the widespread resentment against the Aztecs, forming military alliances and raising thousands of troops from subject peoples who had seen their wealth expropriated by Aztec nobles and their people sacrificed to the Aztec sun god. The Aztec empire collapsed, the victim not of superior Spanish military technology but of a vast internal rebellion of Indian peoples.

As the Spanish sought to impose their dominion over these peoples, they had a silent ally—disease. Separated from Eurasia for thousands of years, the inhabitants of the Western Hemisphere had no immunities to common European diseases. Smallpox, influenza, and measles ravaged the native American peoples, killing tens of thousands of warriors, depriving the people of leaders, and sapping the morale of the survivors. Exploiting this demographic weakness, Cortés quickly extended Spanish rule over the entire Valley of Mexico, and his lieutenants subdued the rest of the highland peoples and then moved against the Maya in the Yucatan Peninsula, eventually conquering them as well.

In the late 1520s Francisco Pizarro led a new military expedition to the mountains of Peru, home of the rich and powerful Inca empire. By the time Pizarro reached Peru, half the population had died from European diseases, which had been spread by Indian traders. Weakened militarily and fighting over succession to the throne, the Inca nobility was easy prey for Pizarro's army. In little more than a decade Spain had become the master of the wealthiest and most populous regions of the Western Hemisphere.

In their ceaseless quest for gold Spanish adventurers were the first Europeans to see large sections of the southern and western United States (see Map 2.1 and the accompanying discussion on page 31). But despite many years and thousands of miles of exploration, they found no gold and few other riches, and so Spanish settlement was limited to Mesoamerica and South America.

Nonetheless, the Spanish invasion and European diseases changed life forever throughout the Western Hemisphere. Virtually the entire Indian population of Hispaniola—some 1 million people—was wiped out by disease and warfare. In Mesoamerica as a whole in 1500 there were probably 40 million Indians; by 1650 that region had only 3 million native Americans. In Peru the population plummeted from 9 million in 1533 to fewer than half a million a century later. The Pueblo peoples of the Southwest and the Mississippian chiefdoms of Florida and the Southeast may have suffered equally catastrophic losses from diseases introduced by the expeditions led by Francisco Vázquez de Coronado and Hernando de Soto.

In Mesoamerica, Spanish overlords ruthlessly exploited the surviving native Americans, forcing them to work on vast plantations to raise crops for local consumption and cattle whose hides were exported to Europe. The Spaniards also altered the natural environment by introducing grains and grasses which supplanted the native flora. Horses, first brought over by Cortés, gradually spread throughout the Western Hemisphere and in the following centuries dramatically changed the way of life of many Indian peoples, especially on the Great Plains of the United States.

The food products of the Western Hemisphere—maize, tomatoes, potatoes, manioc—had an equally great impact on Europe and Africa, increasing agricultural yields and stimulating the growth of populations. Also, the gold and silver that had honored Aztec gods now flowed into the countinghouses of Spain and into the treasury of its monarchs, making that nation the most powerful in Europe for more than a century.

By that time, the once magnificent civilizations of Mexico and Peru lay in ruins and the surviving native Americans had lost much of their cultural identity. Spanish priests suppressed their traditional gods and converted them to Catholicism; as early as 1531 an Indian convert reported a vision of a dark-skinned Virgin Mary, later known as the Virgin of Guadalupe. Soon Spanish bureaucrats imposed taxes and supervised the lives of the Indians, and 500,000 Spanish migrants eventually settled on their lands. Because nearly 90 percent of the Spanish settlers were men and took Indian women as wives or mistresses, the result was a substantial *mestizo* (mixed-race) population. Around 1800, at the end of the colonial era, Spanish America had about 17 million people: 7.5 million Indians, 3.2 million Europeans, 1 million Africans, and 5.5 million people of mixed race and a mixed cultural heritage.

Indians resisted assimilation by retreating into the mountains, but they never had the numbers or the power to oust the Spanish invaders or their descendants. Today only a single Indian tongue, Guarani in Paraguay, is a recognized national language, and no native American state sits in the United Nations. For the original Americans the consequences of the European intrusion in 1492 were tragic and irreversible.

THE PROTESTANT REFORMATION AND THE RISE OF ENGLAND, 1500–1630

Christian fervor had played an important role in the expansionary policies of Portugal and Spain, but now it divided Europe into opposing camps of Catholics and Protestants. A Protestant rebellion in the Spanish Netherlands drained the newfound wealth of the Spanish Crown even as England was undergoing a major economic transformation, giving it the resources to expand into North America and bringing about a new collision of European and Indian peoples.

The Protestant Movement

Over the centuries the Catholic Church had become a large and wealthy institution, controlling vast resources throughout Europe. Renaissance popes and cardinals were among the leading patrons of the arts, but some also misused the Church's wealth. Pope Leo X (1513–1521) was the most notorious, receiving half a million ducats a year from the sale of religious offices. In England, Cardinal Thomas Wolsey set an equally poor example by giving church positions to his relatives. Ordinary priests and monks sometimes used their authority to obtain economic or sexual favors. One English reformer denounced the clergy as a "gang of scoundrels" who should be "rid of their vices or stripped of their authority," but he was ignored. Other reformers, such as Jan Hus of Bohemia, were tried and executed as heretics.

In 1517 Martin Luther, a German monk and professor at the university in Wittenberg, nailed his famous Ninety-five Theses to the door of the castle church. That widely reprinted document condemned the sale of *indulgences*—church certificates that pardoned a sinner from punishments in the afterlife. Luther argued that redemption could come only from God through grace, not from the church for a fee. He was excommunicated by the pope and threatened with punishment by King Charles I of Spain, who in 1519 became head of the Holy Roman Empire, which embraced most of Germany. Northern German princes (with their own grudges against the emperor) embraced Luther's doctrines and protected him from arrest.

Luther broadened his attack, articulating positions that differed from Roman Catholic doctrine in three major respects. First, Luther rejected the doctrine that Christians could win salvation through good deeds, arguing that people could be saved only by grace, which came as a gift from God. Second, he downplayed the role of clergymen as mediators between God and the people, proclaiming, "Our baptism consecrates us all without exception and makes us all priests." As a consequence he also rejected the exclusive authority of the pope to interpret Scripture. Third, Luther said that believers must look to the Bible (not church doctrine) as the ultimate authority in matters of faith. So that everyone could read the Bible, he translated it from Latin into German. Embracing Luther's views, most princes in northern Germany broke from Rome, in part because they wanted the power to appoint bishops and control the Church's property.

Peasants as well as princes heeded Luther's attack on authority and, to his dismay, mounted protests of their own. In 1524 some German peasants rebelled against their manorial lords and were ruthlessly suppressed. Fearing social revolution, Luther urged obedience to established political institutions. Ten years later a group of Anabaptists (so called because they rejected infant baptism) seized control of the city of Münster. They established polygamy, abolished most rights to private property, and placed political power in the hands of "Saints"—those who felt God had saved them through grace. Catholic and Lutheran troops joined together to quell the Anabaptists, who became a symbol to conservatives of the dangers of religious dissent.

For his part, Emperor Charles dispatched armies to Germany to restore his political authority and Catholicism, unleashing a generation of warfare. Eventually the Peace of Augsburg (1555) restored order by allowing princes to decide whether their subjects were to be Catholic or Protestant. Most southern German rulers installed Catholicism as the official religion, while those in the north made Lutheranism the state creed.

The most rigorous Protestant doctrine was established in Geneva, Switzerland, under the leadership of the French theologian John Calvin. Even more than Luther, Calvin stressed the omnipotence of God and the corruption of human nature. His *Institutes of the Christian Religion* (1536) depicted God as an awesome and absolute sovereign who governed the "wills of men so as to move precisely to that end directed by him." Calvin preached the doctrine of *predestination*—the idea that God had chosen certain people for salvation even before they were born, condemning the rest to eternal damnation. In Geneva he set up a model Christian community, eliminating bishops and placing spiritual power in the hands of ministers chosen by the members of each congregation. For Geneva's Calvinists the state had the duty to remake society into a disciplined religious community. Accordingly, ministers and pious laymen ruled the city, prohibiting frivolity and luxury.

Despite widespread persecution, Calvinists won converts all over Europe. Calvinism was adopted by the Huguenots in France, by reformed churches in Belgium and Holland, and by Presbyterians in Scotland.

In England, King Henry VIII (1509–1547) initially opposed the spread of Protestantism in his kingdom. But when the pope denied his request for a divorce from Catherine of Aragon, Henry broke with Rome and made himself the head of a national Church of England (which granted his divorce). Henry made few changes in doctrine, organization, and ritual. But after the reign of his daughter, Queen Mary (1553–1557), who briefly restored Catholicism as the state religion and executed 300 Protestant clergymen, there was growing sentiment against Catholic beliefs and rituals.

Henry's younger daughter, Queen Elizabeth I (1558–1603), sought a middle way. She approved a Protestant confession of faith that incorporated both the Lutheran doctrine of salvation by grace and the Calvinist belief in predestination. To mollify traditionalists Elizabeth retained the Catholic ritual of Holy Communion—now conducted in English rather than in Latin—as well as the hierarchy of bishops and archbishops.

Elizabeth's compromises angered radical Protestants, who condemned the power of bishops as "anti-Christian and devilish and contrary to the Scriptures" and called for major changes in church organization. Many reformers took inspiration from the presbyterian system pioneered in Calvin's Geneva and developed fully by John Knox for the Church of Scotland; there, local congregations elected lay elders (presbyters), who assisted ministers in running the church. By 1600, 500 ministers in the Church of England wanted to eliminate bishops and install a presbyterian form of church government.

By this time many English Protestants were calling themselves "unspotted lambs of the Lord" or (embracing a term initially devised to insult them) "Puritans." To a greater extent than most Protestants they wanted to purify the church of "false" teachings and practices. Following radical Calvinist principles, Puritans condemned many traditional religious rites, such as Holy Communion, as magical or idolatrous; instead, their services were focused on a carefully argued sermon on ethics or dogma. Puritans also placed special emphasis on the idea of a "calling," the duty to serve God in one's work. To ensure that all men and women had access to God's commands, they encouraged everyone to read the Bible, thus promoting widespread literacy. Finally, most Puritans wanted authority over spiritual and financial matters to rest primarily with the local congregation, not with bishops or even presbyterian synods. Eventually a stream of Puritan migrants would carry these radical Protestant doctrines to America.

The Dutch and the English Challenge Spain

Luther's challenge to Catholicism came just two years before Cortés conquered the Aztec empire, and the two events remained linked. Gold and silver from Mexico and Peru made Spain the wealthiest nation in Europe and King Philip II (1556–1598) its most powerful ruler. In addition to Spain, Philip presided over wealthy states in Italy, the commercial and manufacturing provinces of the Spanish Netherlands (Holland and Belgium), and, after 1580, Portugal and all its possessions in America, Africa, and the East Indies.

Philip, an ardent Catholic, tried to root out Protestantism in the Netherlands, which had become wealthy from trade with the vast Portuguese empire and from the weaving of wool and linen. To protect their Calvinist faith and political liberties, the Dutch and Flemish provinces revolted in 1566, and in 1581 the seven northern provinces declared their independence, becoming the Dutch Republic (or Holland). When Elizabeth I of England dispatched 6,000 troops to assist the Dutch cause, Philip found a new enemy. In 1588 he sent the Spanish Armada—130 ships and 30,000 men—against England. Philip planned to reimpose Catholicism in England and then wipe out Calvinism in Holland. But the Armada failed utterly, as English ships and a fierce storm destroyed the Spanish fleet. Nor was this the end of Spanish disasters. Philip had spent much of his American gold on foreign wars, undermining the Spanish economy and prompting the migration of hundreds of thousands of Spaniards to America. By the time of his death in 1598, Spain was in serious decline.

As Spain faltered, Holland prospered. Amsterdam emerged as the financial capital of northern Europe, and the Dutch Republic replaced Portugal as the dominant European power in Asia and coastal Africa. The Dutch also looked across the Atlantic, investing in sugar plantations in Brazil and the Caribbean and establishing fur-trading posts in North America.

England also emerged as an important European state, its economy stimulated by a rise in population from 3 million in 1500 to 5 million in 1630. An equally important factor was the state-supported expansion of the merchant community. English merchants had long supplied high-quality wool to European weavers and, around 1500, created a domestic system of manufacturing. In this *outwork* (or *putting-out*) system merchants bought wool and provided it to landless peasants, who spun and wove the wool into cloth. The merchants then sold the finished product in English and foreign markets.

The government helped merchant capitalists expand production by setting low rates for wages. To increase exports, Elizabeth I awarded bonuses to manufacturers who sold goods in foreign markets and granted special privileges to merchant groups such as the Muscovy Company, providing it with a monopoly

Elizabeth I (1558–1603)
Attired in richly decorated clothes, Queen Elizabeth I celebrates the destruction of the Spanish Armada (pictured in background) and proclaims her nation's imperial ambitions. The queen's hand rests on a globe, asserting England's claims in the Western Hemisphere.

on the export of English cloth to Russia. Similar charters were granted to the Levant Company (Turkey) in 1581, the Guinea Company (Africa) in 1588, and the East India Company in 1600.

This system of state-supported manufacturing and trade became known as *mercantilism*. English monarchs, like the rulers of many European states, used mercantilist policies to increase exports and reduce imports, thus obtaining a favorable balance of trade. Gold and silver flowed into the country in payment for English manufactures, stimulating further economic expansion and enriching the merchant community. Increased trade also meant higher revenues from import duties, which swelled the royal treasury and enhanced the power of the national government. By 1600 the success of these merchant-oriented policies made overseas colonization possible. The English (as well as the Dutch) now had the merchant fleets and economic wealth to challenge Spain's monopoly in the Western Hemisphere.

Social Change and the Puritan Exodus

Other economic changes in England (as well as continuing religious conflict) provided a large body of willing settlers. The massive expenditure of American gold and silver by Philip II of Spain had doubled the money supply of Europe and sparked a major economic transition—known today as the Price Revolution—which brought about profound social changes.

In England, the nobility were the first casualties of the price revolution. Aristocrats had customarily rented out their estates on long leases for fixed rents, gaining a secure income and plenty of leisure. As one English nobleman put it, "We eat and drink and rise up to play and this is to live like a gentleman." Then inflation struck. In two generations the price of goods tripled, but the nobility's income barely increased.

As the wealth and status of the aristocracy declined, that of the yeomen and the gentry rose. The *gentry* (substantial landholders who lacked the titles and legal privileges of the aristocracy) had smaller but more efficiently managed estates than the nobility. They kept pace with inflation by renting land on short leases at higher rates. *Yeomen*, described by a European traveler as "middle people of a condition between gentlemen and peasants," owned small amounts of land which they worked with family help. Since their labor costs remained constant, yeomen's sale of wheat—which now sold for two or three times its traditional price—brought increasing profits, which they used to build substantial houses and provide land for their children.

Economics influenced politics. As aristocrats lost wealth, their branch of Parliament, the House of Lords, declined in influence. At the same time, members of the rising gentry entered the House of Commons and, supported by yeomen, demanded new rights and powers for that house, such as control of taxation. Thus the price revolution encouraged the rise of governing institutions in which rich commoners and small property owners had a voice, a development with profound consequences for English—and American—political history.

Peasants and farm laborers made up three-fourths of the population of England, and their lives also were transformed by the price revolution. Many of these rural folk lived in open-field settlements, but the rise of domestic manufacturing increased the demand for wool, prompting profit-minded landlords and wool merchants to persuade Parliament to pass enclosure acts. These acts allowed owners to fence in open fields and put sheep to graze on them. Thus dispossessed, peasant families lived on the brink of poverty by spinning and weaving wool or by working as wage laborers on large estates.

Wealthy men had "taken farms into their hands," an observer noted in 1600, "and rent them to those that will give most, whereby the peasantry of England is decayed and become servants to gentlemen."

These changes set the stage for a substantial migration to America. As land prices continued to rise, thousands of yeomen families looked across the Atlantic for land for their children. The enclosure movement created an even greater number of impoverished peasants, who were prepared to go to America as indentured servants.

And now there were enterprising men ready to establish a permanent English presence in America. The first attempts, all failures, occurred in the 1580s. Sir Humphrey Gilbert's settlement in Newfoundland collapsed for lack of financing, and Sir Ferdinando Gorges's colony along the coast of Maine foundered because of inadequate supplies and the harsh climate. Sir Walter Raleigh's three expeditions to North Carolina ended in disaster when the famous "lost" colony of Roanoke vanished without a trace. After these failures, merchants replaced minor gentry as the leaders of the colonization movement. To provide adequate funding, they formed *joint-stock companies*, which sold shares of stock to many investors. A royally chartered joint-stock venture, the Virginia Company of London, founded the first permanent English settlement in America at Jamestown (Virginia) in 1607. The investors hoped to grow rich by finding gold and exploiting the labor of the natives to mine it. In any event, they prospered by transporting tens of thousands of English indentured servants to the new colony.

While English merchants promoted settlement in Virginia, thousands of English men and women contemplated migration to America to escape a new wave of religious conflict. Elizabeth's successor, King James I (1603–1625), rejected most Puritan and Presbyterian reforms. He remarked bitterly that Presbyterians favoring representative institutions of church government "agreeth as well with a monarchy as God with the Devil." Like other European monarchs, James maintained that kings drew their authority directly from God and thus had a "divine right" to rule. As for the congregationalist-minded Puritans, James threatened to "harry them out of the land, or else do worse."

Radical Protestants took the king at his word and began to flee, first to the Dutch Republic and then to New England and the West Indies. Religious intolerance also drove English Catholics to America. Thousands of other settlers accompanied the Catholics and Puritans, fleeing poverty or hoping for greater prosperity.

These migrations from England would bring about a new collision between the European and native American worlds. Just as the intrusion of the Spanish into Mesoamerica around 1500 had changed forever the history of that region, the coming of the English—and Dutch and French—to eastern North America a century later would produce a similar spectacle of disease and war and cultural conflict.

CHAPTER I TIMELINE

30,000–10,000 B.C.	Settlement of the Americas
3000–2000 B.C.	Cultivation of maize begins
A.D. 100–400	Hopewell culture in Mississippi Valley
300	Rise of Mayan civilization
500	Zenith of Teotihuacán civilization
700–1100	Spread of Arab Muslim civilization
800–1350	Mississippian culture
1096–1291	Crusades bring Europeans into contact with Islamic civilization
1212–1492	Spanish *reconquista*
1325	Aztecs establish capital at Tenochtitlán
1415–1500	Portuguese establish maritime empire
1450–1550	Italian Renaissance
1492	Christopher Columbus's first voyage to America
1513	Juan Ponce de León explores Florida
1517	Martin Luther starts Protestant Reformation
1519	Hernando Cortés leads Spanish conquest of Mexico
1534	Henry VIII establishes Church of England
1536	John Calvin's *Institutes of The Christian Religion*
1550–1630	Price revolution English mercantilism Enclosure movement
1556–1598	Philip II, king of Spain
1558–1603	Elizabeth I, queen of England
1560s	English Puritan movement begins
1603–1625	James I, first Stuart king of England

CHAPTER 2

THE INVASION AND SETTLEMENT OF NORTH AMERICA, 1550–1700

- Imperial Conflicts and Rival Colonial Models
- The Chesapeake Experience
- Puritan New England
- The Indians' New World

Establishing colonies in distant lands was not for the faint of heart. First came a long voyage in small ships over uncharted waters. Then the migrants, weakened by weeks of travel, spoiled food, and shipboard diseases, faced the challenge of life in an alien land inhabited by potentially hostile peoples. The risks were great and the rewards uncertain, yet tens of thousands of Europeans crossed the Atlantic during the seventeenth century, driven by poverty and persecution at home or drawn by the lures of the New World: land, wealth, and—as one group of pious settlers put it—advancing the "gospell of the Kingdome of Christ in those remote parts."

For native Americans, European invasion and settlement were nothing short of catastrophic. Whether they came as missionaries, fur traders, or settlers, the white-skinned people spread havoc. European diseases, sporadic warfare, and religious conversion threatened Indian peoples with the loss of their lives, lands, and age-old cultures. European-style warfare "slays too many men," protested the Narragansett. The first century of cultural contact foretold the course of North American history: the advance of the invaders and the dispossession of the Indian peoples.

IMPERIAL CONFLICTS AND RIVAL COLONIAL MODELS

New Spain represented the first colonial model in America: the Spanish regime forced the Indians to convert to Catholicism and work digging gold

29

and farming large estates for Spanish overlords. This coercive model was much less effective in the less densely populated lands north of the Rio Grande, where other Europeans founded different types of colonies and interacted in different ways with the Indians. New France and New Netherland developed as huge fur-trading empires, while the English built thriving settler colonies in New England and the Chesapeake. Each of these four colonial models had a distinctive character and goal.

Spanish Supremacy Challenged

By the 1560s few Spanish officials still dreamed of finding rich Indian empires north of Mexico. Now their main goal was to prevent other European nations from establishing settlements from which they could attack the Spanish treasure fleet. Roving English "sea dogs" were already plundering Spanish possessions in the Caribbean, and French corsairs were attacking Spanish treasure ships, halving the Spanish Crown's revenue. Equally ominously, French Protestants began to settle in Florida, long claimed by Spain. In response King Philip II ordered that the Frenchmen in Fort Caroline, Florida, be "cast . . . out by the best means," and Spanish troops massacred 300 members of the "evil Lutheran sect."

To safeguard Florida, in 1565 Spain established a fort at St. Augustine, the first permanent European settlement in the future United States. It also founded a dozen other military outposts and religious missions, one as far north as Chesapeake Bay, but these were soon destroyed by Indian attacks.

These military setbacks prompted the Spanish Crown to adopt a new policy toward native Americans. The Comprehensive Orders for New Discoveries, issued in 1573, placed the "pacification" of new lands primarily in the hands of missionaries, not conquistadors. Franciscan friars promptly established missions in the Pueblo world visited by Coronado two generations before, naming the area *Nuevo México* (see Map 2.1). But in 1598 Juan de Oñate led an expedition of 500 soldiers and settlers into New Mexico to establish a fort and a trading villa. Oñate's men seized corn and clothing from the Pueblo peoples and murdered or raped those who resisted. When Indians of the Acoma pueblo killed 11 Spanish soldiers, the remaining troops destroyed the pueblo, killing 500 men and 300 women and children. Faced by now-hostile Indian peoples, most of the settlers withdrew.

Meanwhile, Spain confronted a new threat in the Atlantic. In 1586 the English sea captain Sir Francis Drake sacked the important port city of Cartagena (in present-day Colombia) and nearly wiped out St. Augustine. These attacks, along with the settlement of Virginia in 1607 and that of French Quebec in 1608, alarmed the Spanish authorities. To maintain its claim to the entire continent, the Spanish Crown reinforced the garrison at St. Augustine and revived the Franciscan missions in New Mexico. However, Spanish officials decided that an outpost in California would not be worth the cost, delaying permanent European occupation of that area until 1769.

MAP. 2.1

New Spain Looks North, 1513–1610

The quest for gold drew Spanish adventurers deep into North America. Cortés himself dispatched the first expeditions along the Pacific coast, and in the 1540s Hernando de Soto and Francisco Vázquez de Coronado led expeditions that penetrated as far north as Kansas and Tennessee. In 1565 the Spanish founded a permanent settlement at St. Augustine in present-day Florida; in 1610, after the explorations of Juan de Oñate, they settled Santa Fe in New Mexico.

New Spain: Territory and Missions

The Catholic Church was Spain's primary colonizer north of the Rio Grande, although the Crown also granted large tracts of land to a few influential settlers. Franciscan friars established missions in Georgia, northern Florida, and especially New Mexico. The friars built their missions and churches near existing Indian pueblos and villages and often learned Indian languages. Protected by Spanish soldiers, they smashed the religious idols of the native Americans and, to win their allegiance to the Christian god, dazzled them with rich vestments, gold crosses, and silver chalices.

For the Franciscans, religious conversion and cultural assimilation went hand in hand. They introduced the European practice of having men instead of women grow most of the crops and encouraged the Indians to talk, cook, dress, and walk like Spaniards. Sexual sinners and spirit worshipers were punished, usually by whipping. Most native Americans tolerated the Franciscans out of fear of military reprisals or in hopes of learning their spiritual secrets.

Conversion in New Mexico
Franciscan friars introduced Catholicism to the Indian peoples north of the Rio Grande, assisted by nuns of various religious orders. This 1631 engraving shows La V. M. María de Jesús de Agreda preaching to a nomadic people (*los chichimecos*) in New Mexico.

But when Christian prayers failed to prevent European diseases and soldiers from devastating their communities, many Indians returned to their ancestral religions.

Spanish rule was hardly benevolent. Monks and settlers alike systematically exploited Indian labor, ignoring laws intended to protect the native peoples. Franciscan missions depended on Indian workers, who grew the crops and carried them to market, often on their backs. Privileged Spanish landowners collected tribute from the native population, usually in goods but often through forced labor. They also "ransomed" native American women and children who had been captured by nomadic Indian peoples and forced them to work as slaves.

By 1680 years of forced tribute, drought, and raids by Navajos and Apache threatened many pueblos in New Mexico with extinction. Led by Popé, an Indian *shaman* (priest), the peoples of two dozen pueblos mounted a carefully coordinated rebellion, killing over 400 Spaniards and forcing the remaining 2,000 colonists to flee 300 miles down the Rio Grande to El Paso. The Pueblo peoples desecrated churches and tortured and killed twenty-one missionaries. Reconquered a decade later, they rebelled again in 1696, only to be subdued. Exhausted by war but now able to practice their own religion and avoid forced labor, the Pueblo peoples accepted their dependent position, joining with the Spanish to defend their lands against attacks by nomadic Indians.

New France: Furs and Souls

In the 1530s Jacques Cartier had claimed the lands bordered by the Gulf of St. Lawrence for France, but the first permanent settlement came only in 1608, with the founding of Quebec. Even then, few French men and women migrated to America. Many French peasants held strong legal rights to their village lands, and few had been displaced by the enclosure of common fields. Moreover, the French government wanted an ample supply of farm laborers and military recruits and offered few incentives to migrants. Finally, the Catholic monarchs barred Huguenots (French Protestants) from Quebec, fearing that they would undermine state interests. Consequently, New France did not develop as a settler colony. In 1698 its European population was only 15,200, compared with the 100,000 settlers in the English colonies.

Instead, New France became a vast fur-trading enterprise, and French explorers traveled deep into the continent to seek new suppliers and claim new lands (see Map 2.2). In 1673 Jacques Marquette reached the Mississippi River in present-day Wisconsin and traveled as far south as Arkansas. Exploration of the majestic river was completed in 1681 by Robert de La Salle, who sought fortune as well as fame. As a French priest noted with disgust, La Salle's expedition hoped "to buy all the Furs and Skins of the remotest Savages, who, as they thought, did not know their Value; and so enrich themselves in one single voyage." To honor Louis XIV, the Sun King, La Salle named the region Louisiana; soon it included the thriving port of New Orleans on the Gulf of Mexico.

Despite their small numbers, French traders and explorers had a disastrous impact on native Americans living near the Great Lakes. By introducing European diseases, they unwittingly triggered epidemics that killed 25 to 90 percent of the native population, and by providing a market for deerskins and beaver pelts, they set in motion a devastating series of Indian wars. Beginning in the 1640s, the New York Iroquois seized control of the fur trade by launching aggressive wars against the Huron and many Algonquin peoples, forcing them to migrate to the north and west.

While French traders amassed furs, French priests sought converts among both the dispossessed Huron and the belligerent Iroquois. Between 1625 and 1763 hundreds of Jesuit priests lived among the Indians and, to a greater extent than the Spanish Franciscans, came to understand their values. One Jesuit reported a Huron belief that "our souls have desires which are inborn and concealed, yet are made known by means of dreams" and used it to explain the Christian doctrines of immortality and salvation. Indians at first welcomed the "Black Robes" as powerful spiritual beings with magical secrets, such as the ability to forge iron, but skepticism grew when prayers to the Christian

MAP 2.2

Eastern North America in 1660

Four European nations had permanent settlements in eastern North America by 1660, but only England had substantial numbers of settlers—some 25,000 in New England and another 15,000 in the Chesapeake. The English settlements hugged the coastline, leaving most of the land in the hands of native American peoples.

god did not protect them from disease, famine, and enemy attack. A Peoria chief charged that "His fables are good only in his own country; we have our own, which do not make us die as his do."

Unlike the Spanish Franciscans, the French missionaries did not use Indians for forced labor, and they prevented brandy from becoming a bargaining item in the French fur trade as rum had become in the English. Moreover, the French Jesuits won converts by addressing Indian needs. In the 1690s young Illinois women embraced the cult of the Virgin Mary because they could use its emphasis on chastity to assert the Algonquin belief that unmarried women were "masters of their own body." Still, most Indians who had the choice found it more satisfying to hold on to their traditional values than to adopt European religious beliefs.

New Netherland: Commerce

Unlike the French and Spanish, the Dutch in North America had little interest in religious conversion. Their eyes were fastened on commerce, for the Dutch Republic was the trading hub of Europe. Henry Hudson, an Englishman employed by the Dutch East India Company, found and named the Hudson River in 1609, and a few years later the Dutch established fur-trading posts on Manhattan Island and at Fort Nassau (present-day Albany). In 1621 the Dutch government chartered the West India Company, giving it a trade monopoly in West Africa and exclusive authority to establish outposts in America. The company set up new trading stations in Connecticut, New Jersey, Delaware, and Pennsylvania and in 1624 "purchased" Manhattan Island from the Indians, founding the town of New Amsterdam as the capital of New Netherland.

These wilderness outposts attracted few Dutch settlers, and their small size made them vulnerable to invasion from New England or New France. To encourage migration, the West India Company granted huge estates along the Hudson River to wealthy Dutchmen, stipulating that each proprietor settle fifty tenants on his land within four years or lose it; by 1646 only one proprietor, Kiliaen Van Rensselaer, had succeeded. The population in Dutch North America remained small, reaching only 1,500 at the time of the English conquest in 1664.

Although New Netherland failed as a settler colony, it flourished briefly as a fur-trading enterprise. In the 1640s the Dutch seized prime farming land from the Algonquin peoples and took over their trading network, in which corn and wampum from Long Island were exchanged for furs from Maine. The Algonquin responded with force. By the end of a bloody two-year war more than two hundred Dutch residents and a thousand Indians had been killed, many in brutal massacres of women, children, and elderly men. After the war the Dutch West India Company largely ignored its crippled North American settlement, concentrating instead on the profitable importation of African slaves to its sugar plantations in Brazil.

Moreover, Dutch officials in New Amsterdam ruled shortsightedly. Governor Peter Stuyvesant rejected the demands of English settlers on Long Island for a representative system of government, alienating the colony's increasingly diverse population of Dutch, English, and Swedish migrants. Consequently, in 1664, during an Anglo-Dutch war, the population of New Amsterdam offered little resistance to an English invasion and subsequently accepted English rule. For the rest of the century the renamed towns of New York and Albany remained small fur-trading centers, Dutch-English outposts in a region still dominated by native Americans.

The English Model: Land and Settlers

The first English settlement in North America was also an economic venture. In 1606 the ambitious merchant stockholders of the Virginia Company of

London received a charter from James I that granted them the right to exploit North America from present-day North Carolina to southern New York. To honor the memory of Elizabeth I, the "Virgin Queen," the company's directors named the region Virginia. They promised to settle the land and "propagate the *Christian* religion" among the "infidels and Savages."

But trade for gold and other valuable goods was the main goal, and the first expedition in 1607 included no settlers, ministers, or women. The company retained ownership of all the land in Virginia and appointed a governor and a small council to direct the migrants, who were its employees or "servants." They were expected to procure their own food and ship anything of value—gold, exotic crops, and Indian merchandise—back to England.

The traders were unprepared for the challenges they would face. Some were young gentlemen with personal ties to the shareholders of the Virginia Company but no experience in living off the land: a bunch of "unruly Sparks, packed off by their Friends to escape worse Destinies at home." The rest were cynical adventurers bent on conquering the Indians for their gold or turning a quick profit from trade. Like the company's directors, they expected to find established towns with ample supplies of food and labor and Indians with gold to trade for English cloth and tinware.

Arriving in Virginia after a hazardous four-month voyage, the newcomers settled on a swampy peninsula on a river. They named both their new home (Jamestown) and the waterway (James River) after their sovereign. The traders found forty different Indian peoples who willingly exchanged corn for English goods but had little else to offer and no interest in working for them. Unfortunately, the settlers did not want to plant crops and raise food for themselves. All they wanted, one of them noted, was to "dig gold, refine gold, load gold."

But there was no gold and not much food, only illness and disease. Of the 120 Englishmen who embarked on the expedition, only 38 were alive nine months later. Although the Virginia Company had sent 1,200 settlers to Jamestown, by 1611 fewer than half remained. "Our men were destroyed with cruell diseases, as Swellings, Fluxes, Burning Fevers, and by warres," one of the leaders reported, "but for the most part they died of meere famine."

Powhatan, the leading chief of some two dozen tribes near Jamestown, was prepared to trade with the English if they supported him against his Indian rivals. But when desperate traders raided Indian villages for food and the new governor demanded that he acknowledge the sovereignty of James I, Powhatan accused the English of coming "not to trade but to invade my people and possess my country." Nevertheless, the Indian chief, whom Governor John Smith described as a "grave majestical man," sought peace with the English, giving his daughter Pocahontas in marriage to the adventurer John Rolfe in 1614.

Rolfe played a leading role in the colony until his death in 1622. After importing seeds from the West Indies, he began to cultivate tobacco, which was already popular in England as a result of imports from Spanish America. Soon tobacco became the basis of economic life in Virginia, cultivated primarily by hundreds of poor white English laborers. Then, as Rolfe noted in 1619, "a Dutch man of warre . . . sold us twenty Negars." Those black workers were the first Africans in English North America and, in a sense, the first African-Americans.

As hopes for the Indian trade declined and tobacco exports rose, the Virginia Company instituted a new and far-reaching set of policies. In 1617 it allowed individual settlers to own land, granting 100 acres to every freeman in Virginia, and established a *headright* system in which every incoming head of a household had a right to 50 acres of land and 50 additional acres for every adult family member or servant. The company also approved a system of representative government. The House of Burgesses, which first convened in Jamestown in 1619, had the authority to make laws and levy taxes, although its legislative acts could be vetoed by the governor or nullified by the company. By 1622 these incentives of land ownership and local self-government had attracted about 4,500 new English recruits. Virginia was about to become a settler colony.

A second tobacco-growing settler colony developed in neighboring Maryland, but it had very different roots. Maryland was owned by an aristocrat, Cecilius Calvert, who carried the title Lord Baltimore. In 1632 Charles I, the successor to James I, gave Baltimore a charter that made him the proprietor of the territory bordering the vast Chesapeake Bay. Baltimore could sell, lease, or give this land away as he wished. He also had the authority to appoint public officials and to found churches and appoint ministers.

Baltimore wanted Maryland to become a refuge from persecution for his fellow English Catholics. He therefore devised a policy of religious toleration intended to minimize confrontations between Catholics and Protestants, instructing the governor (his brother, Leonard Calvert) to allow "no scandall nor offence to be given to any of the Protestants" and to "cause All Acts of Romane Catholicque Religion to be done as privately as may be." In 1634, 20 gentlemen (mostly Catholics) and 200 artisans and laborers (mostly Protestants) established St. Mary's City overlooking the mouth of the Potomac River. The population grew quickly, for the Calvert family carefully planned and supervised the colony's development, hiring skilled artisans and offering ample grants of land to wealthy migrants.

The booming European market for tobacco ensured Maryland's economic future, but political and religious conflict threatened its stability. When Governor Leonard Calvert tried to govern without the "Advice, Assent, and Approbation" of the freemen of the colony, as the charter specified, a representative assembly elected by the freemen insisted on the right to initiate legislation, which Lord Baltimore grudgingly granted. Uprisings by Protestant settlers also threatened Maryland's religious mission. To protect his Catholic coreligionists, who remained a minority, Lord Baltimore managed to persuade the Assembly to enact a Toleration Act (1649) that granted religious freedom to all Christians. By midcentury England had populated the lands near Chesapeake Bay with thousands of settlers.

THE CHESAPEAKE EXPERIENCE

The English colonies in the Chesapeake Bay region were an economic success for some but a social and moral disaster for many more. Settlers forcefully dispossessed Indians of their lands, and prominent families ruthlessly exploited the labor of white indentured servants and enslaved laborers from Africa, pursuing their dreams of wealth by ruling the society by deceit and force of arms.

Settling the Tobacco Colonies

In Virginia the influx of settlers sparked all-out war with the Indians. The land-hungry farmers coveted land that the native Americans had cleared and were using. The English demands alarmed Opechancanough, Powhatan's brother and successor. After forming an alliance with other Chesapeake tribes, in 1622 the chief launched a surprise attack, killing nearly a third of the white population and vowing to drive the rest into the ocean. The English retaliated by burning the Indians' cornfields to deprive them of food, a strategy that secured the safety of the colony by the late 1620s.

The cost of the war was high. The Indians killed many settlers and burned property, but their own losses were even worse. The time of coexistence was past. As one English militiaman put it, "[we now felt we could] by right of Warre, and law of Nations, invade the Country, and destroy them who sought to destroy us; whereby wee shall enjoy their cultivated places . . . possessing the fruits of others' labour."

Distressed by the Indian uprising, James I dissolved the Virginia Company, accusing its directors of mismanagement, and created a royal colony. Now the king and his ministers appointed the governor and a small advisory council. The House of Burgesses was retained, but any legislation it enacted required ratification by the king's Privy Council. James also legally established the Church of England in Virginia, so that all property owners had to pay taxes to support the clergy. These institutions—a royal governor, an elected assembly, and an established Anglican church—became the model for royal colonies throughout English America.

Tobacco was the primary factor shaping the early history of the Chesapeake colonies. Indians had long used tobacco leaves as a medicine and a stimulant. By the 1620s English men and women began to crave tobacco and the nicotine it contained, smoking, chewing, and snorting it with abandon. Initially James I condemned the use of this "vile Weed" and warned that its "black stinking fumes" were "baleful to the nose, harmful to the brain, and dangerous to the lungs." But his attitude changed as revenues from a tobacco duty, or import tax, filled the royal coffers.

European demand for tobacco set off a forty-year economic boom in the Chesapeake, and thousands of profit-hungry migrants flocked to the region. "All our riches for the present do consist in tobacco," a planter remarked in

The Tobacco Economy

Tobacco provided a bare livelihood for family farmers but brought wealth to those who exploited the labor of indentured servants and slaves. The workers cured the tobacco stalks by hanging them for several months in a well-ventilated shed; then they stripped the leaves and packed them tightly into large barrels, or "hogsheads," for shipment to Europe.

1630. Exports rose from about 3 million pounds in 1640 to 10 million pounds in 1660. Planters moved up the river valleys, establishing large farms (plantations) that were distant from one another but easy to reach by water. The scarcity of towns meant a much weaker sense of community than existed in the open-field villages of rural England.

Unfortunately, mosquitoes flourished in the mild Chesapeake climate, spreading malaria and weakening people's resistance to other diseases. Pregnant women were especially hard hit. Many died after bearing a first or second child, and so settler families were small. Malaria, smallpox, fever, and dysentery took such a toll that while more than 15,000 settlers arrived in Virginia between 1622 and 1640, the population rose only from 2,000 to 8,000.

For most of the seventeenth century life in the Chesapeake colonies remained harsh and short. Most men never married because there were few women. Families often were disrupted by early death; rarely did both parents survive to see their children grow to adulthood. As a result, unmarried young men and orphaned children accounted for a substantial portion of the population, making Chesapeake society very different from that in England.

Servants and Masters

Despite the dangers, by 1700 over 80,000 English settlers had moved to Virginia and another 20,000 had arrived in Maryland. English shipping registers provide insight into their motivation. Three-quarters of the 5,000 migrants from Bristol were men, mostly under twenty-five years old; many had traveled hundreds of miles searching for work. Once in Bristol, these penniless sojourners were persuaded by merchants and sea captains to sign labor contracts called *indentures* and embark for the Chesapeake. The indentures bound them to work in return for room and board for a period of four or five years (or, in the case of younger servants, until age twenty-one).

For merchants, servants represented valuable cargo because their contracts fetched high prices in the labor-starved Chesapeake. For plantation owners, they were an incredible bargain. During the tobacco boom a male indentured servant could produce five times his purchase price in a year. Furthermore, servants were counted as household members, and so planters in Virginia received 50 acres of land for each one they imported.

Most masters ruled their servants with an iron hand, beating them for bad behavior and withholding permission to marry. If a servant ran away or became pregnant, a master went to court to increase the term of service. Female servants were especially vulnerable to abuse. As a Virginia law of 1692 stated, "dissolute masters have gotten their maids with child; and yet claim the benefit of their service." Uncooperative servants had their contracts sold to new masters. As an Englishman remarked in disgust, in Virginia "servants were sold up and down like horses."

For most indentured servants this ordeal did not provide the hoped-for escape from poverty. Half the men died before receiving their freedom, and another quarter remained poor; only a quarter acquired some property and respectability. Surviving female servants generally fared better because men in the Chesapeake had grown "very sensible of the Misfortune of Wanting Wives." Many married their masters or other well-established men. By migrating to the Chesapeake, these few—and very fortunate—men and women escaped a life of landless poverty in England.

The Seeds of Revolt

During the boom years of the 1620s tobacco sold for twenty-four pence a pound; forty years later it was fetching barely one-tenth as much. Overproduction in the Chesapeake caused a collapse of the tobacco market.

Political decisions made in England contributed to the decline. In 1651, in an effort to exclude Dutch ships and merchants from England's overseas possessions, Parliament passed an Act of Trade and Navigation. Revised and

Hard Times in Early Virginia

The lot of an indentured servant in Virginia was always hard, especially before 1630, when food was scarce and Indians were a constant danger. In 1623 Richard Frethorne begged his parents to buy out the remaining years of his labor contract so that he could return to England.

Loving and kind father and mother . . . this is to let you understand that I your child am in a most heavy case by reason of the nature of the country . . . it causes much sickness, as the scurvy and the bloody flux [severe dysentery], and diverse other diseases, which make the body very poor and weak, and when we are sick there is nothing to comfort us. For since I came out of the ship, I never ate anything but peas and loblollie [gruel]. As for deer or venison I never saw any since I came into this land. There is indeed some fowl, but we are not allowed to go and get it, but must work hard both early and late for a mess of water gruel and a mouthful of bread and beef.

People cry out day and night, Oh that they were in England without their limbs and would not care to lose any limb to be in England again . . . we live in fear of the enemy every hour. . . . We are in great danger, for our plantation is very weak, by reason of the dearth, and sickness of our company. . . .

I have nothing to comfort me, nor there is nothing to be gotten here but sickness and death, except that one had money to lay out in some things for profit; but I have nothing at all, no not a shirt to my back, but two rags nor no clothes, but one poor suit, nor but one pair of shoes . . . my cloak is stolen by one of my own fellows, and to his dying hours would not tell me what he did with it, but some of my fellows saw him have butter and beef out of a ship, which my cloak [no] doubt paid for. . . .

SOURCE: Susan M. Kingsbury, ed., *The Records of the Virginia Company of London* (Washington, D.C., Library of Congress, 1935), vol. 4, pp. 58–60.

extended in 1660 and 1663, the Navigation Acts permitted only English or colonial-owned ships to enter American ports. They also required the colonists to ship certain "enumerated articles," including tobacco, only to England. Because the king imposed ever higher import duties, the English market grew slowly. Moreover, Chesapeake planters could no longer legally trade with Dutch merchants, who paid the highest prices. As a result, by the 1670s planters got only one penny a pound for their crop.

Nonetheless, the number of planters in Virginia and Maryland grew and tobacco exports continued to increase, from 20 million pounds annually in the 1670s to 41 million pounds between 1690 and 1720. But profit margins were thin, and the Chesapeake ceased to be a land of upward social mobility.

Yeomen families earned just enough to scrape by or fell into debt and had to sell their land. Even harder hit were newly freed indentured servants, who were entitled to 50 acres of land. Low tobacco prices made it nearly impossible for them to pay the necessary claim fees or buy the tools and seed needed to plant tobacco. Most ex-servants had to sell their labor again, signing new indentures or becoming wage workers or tenant farmers.

Gradually the economic life of the Chesapeake colonies came to be dominated by an elite of planter-landlords and merchants. Established landowners prospered by dividing their ample estates and leasing small plots to the growing army of former servants. They also lent money at high interest rates to hard-pressed yeomen families. Some well-to-do planters became commercial middlemen, setting up small retail stores or charging a commission for storing the tobacco of their poorer neighbors and selling it to English merchants. In Virginia this elite accumulated nearly half the land by soliciting favors from royal governors and filing fictitious headright claims. In Maryland wealthy planters controlled labor with equal success; in one county they owned about 40 percent of the work force through the indenture system.

As these aggressive entrepreneurs confronted a growing number of young landless laborers, social divisions intensified, reaching a breaking point during the corrupt regime of Governor William Berkeley. Berkeley first served as governor of Virginia between 1642 and 1652, when he won fame by putting down a major Indian revolt. As governor again beginning in 1660, he made large land grants to himself and to members of his council, who exempted their own lands from taxation and appointed friends as county judges and local magistrates. Berkeley suppressed dissent in the House of Burgesses by assigning land grants to friendly legislators and appointing their relatives to the posts of sheriff, tax collector, and justice of the peace. Once his favorites were in power, the governor refused to call new elections.

Social and political unrest increased when the corrupt Burgesses changed the voting system to exclude landless freemen, who constituted half the adult white male population. Property-holding yeomen retained the vote but were unhappy about falling tobacco prices, rising taxes, and political corruption. The Virginia elite—unlike the English aristocracy and gentry—was too newly formed and crudely ambitious to command the respect of the lower orders.

Bacon's Rebellion

In 1675 a new Indian conflict sparked a social revolution. By this time the Indians in Virginia were few and weak, their numbers having dwindled from about 30,000 in 1607 to a mere 2,000. Most lived on lands guaranteed by treaty that were coveted by some of the 40,000 whites now in Virginia. Most wealthy planters lived in the coastal districts and opposed armed expansion into Indian territory, as did the planter-merchants who traded with the native Americans for furs. But poor freeholders and aspiring tenants who wanted cheap land insisted that the Indians be expelled or exterminated.

Fighting broke out when Virginia militiamen murdered thirty Indians. Defying orders from Governor Berkeley, a larger force of 1,000 militiamen then surrounded a fortified Susquehannock village and killed four chiefs. The outraged Susquehannock retaliated by killing eighty whites in raids on outlying plantations. Berkeley did not want war, which would disrupt the fur trade, and proposed a defensive military policy, asking the House of Burgesses in March 1676 to raise money to build a series of frontier forts. Western settlers dismissed this strategy as useless, a plot by the "grandees," as one freeman called them, to impose high taxes on the yeomen and to take "all our tobacco into their own hands."

Nathaniel Bacon emerged as the leader of the westerners. A wealthy and bold man, he had recently arrived from England and settled on a frontier estate. Although he was only twenty-eight, Bacon commanded the respect of his neighbors because of his high status—Berkeley had made him a member of the governor's council—and vigor. When Berkeley refused to grant Bacon a military commission, Bacon marched his frontiersmen against the Indians anyway, slaughtering some of the peaceful Doeg people and triggering a political upheaval that overshadowed the Indian question.

Condemning the frontiersmen as "rebels and mutineers," Berkeley expelled Bacon from the council and placed him under arrest. Then, realizing the rebel leader's military power, the governor reinstated him, agreed to legislative elections, and accepted the far-reaching political reforms enacted by the new House. The Burgesses, who now included influential supporters of Bacon, curbed the powers of the governor and the council and cut their patronage powers by converting many local offices into elected posts. The legislature also restored voting rights to landless freemen.

Those much-needed reforms did not end the rebellion. Bacon was bitter at Berkeley, and the poor farmers, indentured servants, and blacks in his army were resentful of exploitation by the "grandees" and eager to flaunt their power. Backed by 400 armed men, Bacon seized control of the colony and issued a "Manifesto and Declaration of the People," demanding the death or removal of all Indians and an end to the rule of wealthy "parasites." "The poverty of the country," Bacon proclaimed, "is such that all the power and sway is got into the hands of the rich." In the bloody civil war that followed Bacon's army burned Jamestown to the ground and plundered the plantations of Berkeley's allies. When Bacon died suddenly from dysentery in October 1676, the governor took his revenge, dispersing the rebel army, seizing the estates of well-to-do rebels, and hanging twenty-three men.

Bacon's rebellion was a pivotal event. Although planter-merchants continued to dominate the colony, they no longer tolerated rule by a corrupt oligarchy. They limited the governor's authority and found public positions for substantial and politically ambitious property owners like Bacon. The planter-merchant elite also appeased the lower social orders by cutting their taxes and supporting an expansionist military policy that promised them access to Indian lands.

The uprising also contributed to the emergence of a new labor system: African slavery. Slavery in the Chesapeake had grown because of a scarcity of English indentured servants, but now its expansion was fueled by the elite's desire to forestall another rebellion by freed white servants. To maintain their privileged class position, the leaders of Virginia and Maryland committed themselves and their descendants to a social system based on the exploitation of enslaved blacks.

PURITAN NEW ENGLAND

The Puritan exodus to America was both a worldly quest for land and a moral effort to preserve the "pure" Christian faith. This blend of realism and idealism gave a distinctive character to the Puritans' experiment. Even as the migrants to New England went about the task of creating a society of independent property-owning farm families, they continued to promote a spiritual vision, giving a moral dimension to American history.

The Puritan Migration

From the beginning New England differed from other European settlements. New Spain and Jamestown were populated initially by unruly male adventurers, and New France and New Netherland by commercial-minded fur traders. By contrast Plymouth, the first permanent community in New England, was settled by women and children as well as men, most of whom were members of pious Protestant families—the Pilgrims.

The Pilgrims were radical Protestants who had separated completely from the Church of England, thus earning the name "Separatists." Seeking freedom to practice their creed, the Pilgrims left England and settled among like-minded Dutch Calvinists in Holland. Subsequently, thirty-five of them decided to migrate to America, where they hoped to maintain their English identity. Led by William Bradford and joined by sixty other migrants from England, they founded the Plymouth colony in 1620.

Before sailing to America aboard the *Mayflower*, the Pilgrims organized themselves into a joint-stock corporation and secured financial backing from sympathetic Puritan merchants. Their stated intention was to settle in the territory granted to the Virginia Company, but by accident or design they landed on the coast of New England. There, outside the jurisdiction of Virginia and lacking a charter from King James I, they created their own covenant of government, the Mayflower Compact, to "combine ourselves together into a civill body politick." This document was the first "constitution" adopted in North America. It translated into political terms the Pilgrims' long-standing belief in the autonomy of the religious congregation and, while recognizing the sovereignty of the king, produced a system of self-government based on the rule of law.

The first winter in America tested the Pilgrims. As in Jamestown, hunger and disease took a heavy toll; of the 100 migrants who arrived in November, only half survived until the spring. Thereafter the Plymouth colony—unlike Virginia—became a healthy and thriving community because the cold climate inhibited the spread of mosquito-borne diseases and the religious discipline established a strong work ethic. Unlike the gold-hungry adventurers in Virginia, the Pilgrims quickly built solid houses and planted ample crops. Their numbers grew rapidly, to 3,000 by 1640, prompting the creation of ten new towns with extensive powers of self-government. A new legal code (1636) provided for a colonywide system of representative government and a rudimentary bill of rights.

The Pilgrims were devout Christians and tried to live according to the laws and ethics of the Bible, which in their view required limiting the power of the state over religion. As "Separatists," they had cut themselves off from the Church of England and believed that each congregation should be self-governing, free from control by either a religious or a political hierarchy. In that sense they anticipated the "separation of church and state."

Meanwhile, England was plunging deeper into religious turmoil. King Charles I (1625–1642) reaffirmed his father's support for the Church of England but personally repudiated some Protestant doctrines, such as justification by faith. The Puritans, who had gained many seats in Parliament, accused the king of "popery." Charles's response was to dissolve Parliament in 1629. For the next decade he ruled by "divine right," raising money through royal edicts, customs duties, and the sale of monopolies. The king's arbitrary rule struck at the dignity of the landed gentry, who expected to exercise authority through the House of Commons. The merchant community, a stronghold of Puritanism, was also displeased as higher tariffs ate away at their profits. Then, in 1633, the king chose William Laud, who loathed Puritans, to head the Church of England. Laud removed hundreds of Puritan ministers, forcing Anglican rituals on their congregations and prompting thousands of Puritans to seek refuge in America.

In 1630, 900 Puritans boarded eleven ships and sailed across the Atlantic under the leadership of John Winthrop, a well-educated and highly regarded country squire. Using a corporate (trading) charter granted by the king for use in England, the Puritans established the Massachusetts Bay colony in the area around Boston. Like the Pilgrims, the Puritans envisioned a reformed Christian society, a genuinely "new" England. However, rather than break with the Church of England, they hoped to reform it (hence, they were "non-Separatists"). Many Puritans saw themselves as central actors in a great drama, a "saving remnant" chosen by God to preserve the true faith in America. The Lord "has sifted a whole nation," a Puritan minister declared, "that he might send choice grain over into this Wilderness."

Winthrop believed that England was morally corrupt and "overburdened with people." He sought land and opportunity for his children and a place in history for his people. "We must consider that we shall be as a City upon a Hill," Winthrop told his fellow passengers aboard the ship *Arbella* in 1630. "The eyes of all people are upon us." Once in America, Winthrop and his associates transformed their joint-stock business corporation, the General Court of shareholders, into a colonial legislature. Over the next decade about 10,000

Puritans migrated to the Massachusetts Bay colony, along with 10,000 others fleeing hard times in England.

The Puritans created representative political institutions that were locally based, with the governor as well as the assembly and council elected by the colony's freemen. However, to ensure rule by the godly, the Puritans limited the right to vote and hold office to men who were Puritan church members. Eschewing the religious toleration of the Pilgrims, they established Puritanism as the state-supported religion and barred members of other faiths from conducting services. Massachusetts Bay became a religious commonwealth with the Bible as the legal as well as spiritual guide. For example, following a biblical rule, Puritans divided inheritances among all children, with a double portion going to the oldest son. "Where there is no Law," the government advised local magistrates, they should rule "as near the law of God as they can."

Puritans and Pequots

Seeing themselves as God's chosen people, the Puritans viewed their intrusions on native American lands from a moral perspective. "By what right or warrant can we enter into the land of the Savages," they asked themselves while still in England, "and take away their rightfull inheritance from them and plant ourselves in their places?" John Winthrop thought that a disastrous smallpox epidemic of 1633 that killed hundreds of Indians provided a clear answer to that question. "If God were not pleased with our inheriting these parts," he pointed out, "Why doth he still make roome for us by diminishing them as we increase?" Citing the Book of Genesis, the magistrates of Massachusetts Bay declared that because the Indians had not "subdued" most of their land by plowing or fencing it, they had no "just right" to it.

Imbued with moral righteousness, the Puritans often treated native Americans with a brutality equal to that of Spanish conquistadors and Nathaniel Bacon's frontiersmen. In 1637 Pequot warriors attacked Puritan farmers who had begun to intrude onto their lands in the Connecticut River Valley. As sporadic violence escalated into war, Puritan militiamen and their Indian allies led a surprise attack on a Pequot village and massacred about 500 men, women, and children. "God laughed at the Enemies of his People," one soldier boasted, "filling the Place with Dead Bodies." The survivors were ruthlessly tracked down and sold into slavery in the Caribbean. In the end the Pequot people were virtually exterminated.

Like most Europeans, English Puritans viewed the Indians as "savages," culturally inferior people who did not deserve civilized treatment. But the Puritans were not racist as the term is understood today. To them, native Americans were neither genetically inferior nor members of a different race—they were white people with sun-darkened skins. "Probably the devil" delivered these "miserable savages" to America, wrote the Puritan minister Cotton Mather, "in hopes that the gospel of the Lord Jesus Christ would never come here to destroy or disturb his absolute empire over them."

This interpretation inspired attempts at conversion. John Eliot, a Puritan minister, translated the Bible into Algonquian and undertook missions to Indians outside Boston and on Cape Cod. Because Puritans demanded that Indians conform to English customs and master Puritan theology, only a few native Americans became full members of Puritan congregations. However, the Puritans created "praying towns" that, like the Spanish Franciscans' missions in New Mexico, attempted to control the Indian population. Within a generation more than a thousand Indians lived under Puritan supervision in fourteen special mission towns. They were forbidden to practice their native religion, required to conform to the laws of Massachusetts, and initially denied the right to own the land on which they lived. Thus, a combination of European diseases, military force, and Christianization pacified most of the Algonquin peoples who lived along the seacoast of New England, guaranteeing, at least temporarily, the safety of the white settlers.

Religion and Society, 1630–1670

By eliminating bishops and elaborate rituals, the Puritans were seeking to recreate the simplicity of the first Christians. They devised a democratic church structure controlled by the *laity*—the ordinary members of the congregation— hence their name, *Congregationalists*. Influenced by John Calvin, Puritans embraced predestination, believing that God had chosen a few "elect" men and women (the Saints) for salvation and had condemned the rest to damnation. Consequently, the Saints set extraordinarily high standards for church membership, rigorously examining those who applied. Even the Saints lived in great anxiety, for they could never be sure that they were really among the elect.

Puritans dealt with the uncertainties of divine election in three ways. Some congregations stressed the conversion experience: when God infused a soul with grace, the person was "born again" and *knew* that salvation was at hand. Other Puritans stressed "preparation," the confidence in redemption that came from years of spiritual guidance and church discipline. Still others believed that God had entered into a *covenant*, or contract, with them, promising to treat them as a divinely "chosen people" as long as they ordered their lives in accordance with His laws.

To maintain God's favor, Puritan magistrates purged their society of religious dissidents. One target was Roger Williams, the minister of Salem. Williams preferred the Pilgrims' separation of church and state and condemned the legal establishment of Congregationalism in Massachusetts Bay. He taught that political magistrates should have authority over only the "bodies, goods, and outward estates of men," not their spiritual lives. Moreover, he questioned the Puritans' right to seize (rather than buy) Indian lands. The Puritan magistrates banished him from Massachusetts Bay.

Williams and his followers resettled in Rhode Island in 1636, founding the town of Providence on land acquired from the Narragansett Indians. Other religious dissidents founded Portsmouth and Newport. In 1644 these towns

Changing Images of Death
Death—sudden and arbitrary—
was a constant presence in the
preindustrial world. Pre-1700 New
England gravestones often depicted
death as a frightening skull, warning people to repent of their sins.
After 1700 a smiling cherub
adorned many gravestones, suggesting a more optimistic view of
the afterlife.

obtained a corporate charter from the English Parliament that granted them
full authority "to rule themselves." In Rhode Island there was no legally established church; every congregation was autonomous, and individual men and
women could worship God as they pleased.

Puritan magistrates also felt threatened by Anne Hutchinson, the wife of a
merchant and a mother of seven who worked as a midwife. Hutchinson held
weekly prayer meetings in her house—often attended by as many as sixty
women—in which she accused certain Boston clergymen of placing undue emphasis on church laws and good behavior. In words that recalled Martin Luther's
rejection of indulgences, Hutchinson argued that salvation was not something
that people could earn; there was no "covenant of works." Instead, salvation was
bestowed by God through the "covenant of grace." Hutchinson accepted the importance of revelation: the direct communication of truth by God to the individual believer. Since this doctrine diminished the role of ministers and, indeed, of all
established authority, Puritan magistrates found it heretical.

The magistrates also resented Hutchinson because of her sex. Like other Christians, Puritans believed in the equality of souls: both men and women could be saved. When it came to the governance of church and state, however, women were seen as being clearly inferior to men. As the Pilgrim minister John Robinson put it, women "are debarred by their sex from ordinary prophesying, and from any other dealing in the church wherein they take authority over the man." Puritan women could never be ministers, lay preachers, or even voting members of the congregation.

In 1637 the Massachusetts Bay magistrates put Hutchinson on trial for heresy, accusing her of believing that inward grace or truth frees an individual from the rules of the church. Hutchinson defended her views with great skill and tenacity, and even Winthrop admitted that she was "a woman of fierce and haughty courage." But the judges found her guilty and berated her for not attending to "her household affairs, and such things as belong to women." Banished, she followed Roger Williams into exile in Rhode Island, settling eventually in New York, where she was killed in an Indian raid in 1643.

The coercive policies of the magistrates, along with the desire for better land, prompted some Puritans to leave Massachusetts Bay. In 1636 Thomas Hooker led a hundred settlers to the Connecticut River Valley, where they established the town of Hartford. Others followed, settling along the river at Wethersfield and Windsor. In 1639 the Connecticut Puritans adopted the Fundamental Orders, a plan of government that included a representative assembly and a popularly elected governor. Connecticut was patterned after Massachusetts Bay, with a firm union of church and state and a congregational system of church government, but voting rights were extended to most property-owning men—not just church members.

As Puritans established themselves in America, England fell into a religious war. When Archbishop Laud imposed a new prayer book on Presbyterian Scotland, a Scottish Presbyterian army invaded England. Thousands of English Puritans—including scores of Puritans who had returned from America—rose up in revolt, demanding greater authority for Parliament and an end to arbitrary royal rule. After four years of civil war the Parliamentary forces led by Oliver Cromwell were victorious. In 1649 Parliament executed Charles I, proclaimed a republican commonwealth, and imposed a presbyterian system of governance on the Church of England.

The Puritan triumph was short-lived. Popular support for the commonwealth quickly ebbed, especially when Cromwell took dictatorial control of the government in 1653. After his death a repentant Parliament summoned Charles I's son, Charles II, to the throne. In 1660 the monarchy was restored, and bishops reclaimed their authority in the Church of England. For many Puritans, Charles II's accession represented the victory of the Antichrist—the false prophet described in the last book of the New Testament.

The outlook in New England seemed hardly less grim, for many younger Puritans had not experienced conversion and become full church members. Their "deadness of soul" threatened the Puritan experiment, since they could not present their own children for baptism. To preserve Puritanism, ministers devised the Halfway Covenant in 1662; it altered traditional Calvinist dogma by allowing unconverted Puritans to baptize their children. Not conversion but birth became the key to church membership. Thus, in the First Church of Milford, Connecticut, in the period 1639–1770, 72 percent of the members belonged to the thirty-six families who had established the original congregation.

The Halfway Covenant began a new phase of the Puritans' "errand into the wilderness." They had come to New England to preserve the "pure" Christian church, expecting to return in triumph to a Europe ready to receive the true Gospel. Since that sacred mission had been dashed by the Restoration in England, Puritan ministers articulated a new vision: they exhorted their congregations to create a new society in America based on their faith and ideals.

Richard Mather (1596–1669)
Mather migrated to New England in 1635 after Archbishop Laud stripped him of his pulpit. His son Increase Mather was a leading Boston clergyman, as was his grandson Cotton Mather, the author of *Magnalia Christi Americana*, an epic of the Puritan adventure in New England.

The Puritan Imagination and Witchcraft

Like the native Americans they encountered in New England, the Puritans believed that the physical world was full of supernatural forces. This faith in "spirits" stemmed in part from Christian teachings, such as the Catholic belief in miracles and the Protestant faith in the powers of "grace." Devout Christians saw signs of God's (or Satan's) power in blazing stars, deformed births, and other unusual events. Noting that "more Ministers' Houses than others proportionably had been smitten with Lightning," Samuel Sewell, a prominent Massachusetts minister, wondered "what the meaning of God should be in it."

The respect for spiritual "forces" reflected certain pagan assumptions that were held by both ordinary people and highly educated individuals. When Sewell moved into a new house, he tried to fend off evil spirits by driving a metal pin into the floor. And thousands of Puritans followed pagan astrological charts printed in farmers' almanacs to determine the best times to plant crops, marry off their children, and make other important decisions.

Zealous ministers attacked many of these beliefs and practices and condemned "cunning" individuals who claimed to have special powers as healers or prophets. Many ordinary Christians looked on folk doctors or conjurers as "wizards" or "witches" who acted at the command of Satan. Between 1647 and 1662 civil authorities in Massachusetts and Connecticut hanged fourteen people for witchcraft, mostly older women who, their accusers claimed, were "double-tongued," "had an unruly spirit," or in some way challenged prevailing customs.

The most dramatic episode of witch-hunting took place in Salem, Massachusetts, in 1692. The causes were complex and involved group rivalries and deception. Poor and resentful farmers in a rural area of Salem apparently sought to retaliate against certain wealthier church members by bringing charges of witchcraft against their families and friends. Things got out of hand when judges allowed the introduction of dubious evidence. Massachusetts authorities arrested 175 people and executed 20, 19 of them women. Fear and suspicion spread into the neighboring village of Andover. Its people "were much addicted to sorcery," claimed one observer, and "there were forty men in it that could raise the Devil as well as any astrologer."

The Salem episode, together with the imposition of royal government in Massachusetts in 1692, marked a turning point for New England. The intense religiosity of the first two generations of Puritans was dealt a blow by popular revulsion against the mass executions at Salem; there would be no more legal prosecutions for witchcraft. The European Enlightenment which began around 1675 also promoted a more rational view of the world. Increasingly, educated people explained accidents and sudden deaths with theories about natural forces, not with religion, satanism, astrology, or witchcraft. Unlike Samuel Sewell (who died in 1730), well-read men of the next generation, such as Benjamin Franklin, would conceive of lightning not as a supernatural sign but as a natural phenomenon.

A Freeholding Society

In creating New England communities, Puritans consciously avoided the worst features of traditional Europe. They did not wish to live in a society dominated by a few wealthy landowners or under a distant government that levied oppressive taxes.

Local rule and freehold property were essential to the Puritans' concept of a God-fearing "just society." To fashion a world of independent communities and landowning families, New England governments relied on land-distribution policies. The General Courts of Massachusetts Bay and Connecticut did not adopt the Chesapeake headright system, which favored wealthy planters, or give thousands of acres of land to favored individuals. Instead, they bestowed the title to a township on a group of settlers, or proprietors, who distributed the land among themselves. The title was given in *fee simple*, which meant that the proprietors' families held the land outright, free from manorial obligations or feudal dues; they could sell, lease, or rent it as they pleased.

Widespread ownership of land did not imply equality of wealth or status. Like most Europeans of that time, Puritans embraced a social and economic hierarchy that provided order and security in an uncertain world. "God had Ordained different degrees and orders of men," proclaimed the wealthy Boston merchant John Saffin, "some to be Masters and Commanders, others to be Subjects, and to be commanded." Consequently, town proprietors normally bestowed the largest plots of land on men of high social status, who often became political leaders. However, all male heads of families received some land and had a voice in the town meeting, the main institution of local government.

Local communities in New England had much more political power than did most peasant villages in Europe. Each year the town meeting chose selectmen to manage town affairs. It also levied taxes; enacted ordinances regarding fencing, lot sizes, and road building; and regulated the use of common fields for grazing livestock and cutting firewood. Beginning in 1634, each town in Massachusetts Bay elected its own representatives to the General Court. As the number of towns increased, the representative assembly gained authority at the expense of the governor and magistrates, further enhancing local control.

The rough economic equality in the farming communities of New England gradually declined. The larger proprietors owned enough land to divide among all their sons, usually three or four. Smallholders could provide land for only some of their sons, the rest of whom became landless. Newcomers who lacked the rights of proprietors were the least well off, for they had to buy land or work as tenants or laborers. By 1702, in Windsor, Connecticut, landless sons and newcomers accounted for no less than 30 percent of the male taxpayers. It would take years of saving or migration to a new town for these men and their families to become freeholders.

Despite these inequalities, nearly all New Englanders had an opportunity to acquire property, and even those at the bottom of the social scale enjoyed some economic security. When he died in the 1690s, Nathaniel Fish was one of the poorest men in Barnstable, Massachusetts, yet he owned a two-room cottage, 8 acres of land, an ox, and a cow. For him and thousands of other settlers New England had proved to be the promised land, a new world of opportunity.

THE INDIANS' NEW WORLD

Native Americans on the eastern seaboard were also living in a new world, but for them it was a bleak, dangerous, and conflict-ridden place. They responded to European invasion and settlement in a variety of ways: banding together in new tribes, retreating to the Appalachian Mountains, and on occasion doing battle with the Europeans.

Metacom's War

By the 1670s the white population of New England had reached 55,000 while the Indian population continued to decline from an estimated 120,000 in 1570, to 70,000 in 1620, to barely 16,000 in 1670. Like Opechancanough in Virginia and Popé in New Mexico, Metacom, leader of the Wampanoag

Metacom (King Philip), Chief of the Wampanoag

The Indian uprising of 1675 left an indelible mark on the historical memory of New England. This painting of 1850 was used by traveling performers to tell the story of King Philip's War and was done on semitransparent cloth so that it could be lit from behind for dramatic effect. (Shelburne Museum)

The Unredeemed Captive

A decade and a half after Metacom's War, Indians mounted new attacks against Massachusetts frontier settlements. In 1704 Mohawk Indians attacked the town of Deerfield and took back to French Canada 112 prisoners, including seven-year-old Eunice Williams. Most of the captives were returned or ransomed, and in 1713 Peter Schulyer, an Albany fur trader, sought the return of Eunice Williams, who was now sixteen.

I arrived from Albany at Mont Reall [Montreal] on ye 15th of April. . . . Monsr. De Vaudruille [Vaudrieuil], Governor and Chief of Canada . . . gave me all the Encouragement I could immagine for her to go home. . . . Accordingly I went to the ffort of Caghenewaga [Kahnawake] being accompanied by one of the Kings officers and a ffrench Interpreter [and] likewise another of the Indian language. . . .

I thought fitt first to apply mySelf to the priests . . . And [as I] was informed before that this infant (As I may say) was married to a young Indian, I therefore proposed to know the Reason why this poor captive should be Married to an Indian being a Christian born . . . said he they came to me to Marry them. . . . And if he would not marry them they matter'd not, for they were resolved never to leave on the other. . . . He sent for her, who presently came with the Indian She was married to both together. She looking very poor in body, bashfull in the face, but proved harder than Steel in her breast. . . .

I first Spoak to her in English, Upon wch she did not Answr me; And I believe She did not understand me, she being very Young when she was taken. . . . I Imployed my Indian Languister to talk to her . . . but could not get one word from her. . . . And I could not prevail wth her to go home . . . that she might only go to see her father, And directly return hither again. . . .

And these two words ["Jaghte oghte, a plaine denyall"] were all we could gett from her; in allmost two hours time that we talked with her . . . and the time growing late and I being very Sorrowfull, that I could not prevail upon nor get one word more from her I took her by the hand and left her in the priest's house.

[Eunice Williams remained among the Mohawk, bore two daughters, twice visited her English brothers and sisters, and died in Canada in 1785, aged eighty-nine.]

SOURCE: John Demos, *The Unredeemed Captive: A Family Story from Early America* (New York, Knopf, 1994), pp. 101–108.

tribe, concluded that only united resistance could stop the advance of the Puritans. Forging a military alliance with the Narragansett and Nipmuck peoples in 1675, Metacom attacked white settlements throughout New England. Bitter fighting continued into 1676, ending only when Metacom was killed.

The war was a deadly affair. The Indians burned 20 percent of the English towns in Massachusetts and Rhode Island and killed 5 percent of the adult white population. But their own losses—from famine and disease as well as battles—were much larger, perhaps 25 percent of the population. Many survivors were sold into slavery in the Caribbean, including Metacom's wife and nine-year-old son.

Subsequently, most New England Indians accepted their dependent status, surviving as a separate group on the margins of white society. They had suffered a double tragedy, losing both their land and the integrity of their traditional cultures.

The Fur Trade and the Inland Peoples

The Indian peoples in the interior of North America remained independent, but few were able to maintain their customary way of life. Epidemics and drunkenness sapped the vitality of many peoples. As tribes exchanged furs for iron utensils and cloth blankets, they lost their traditional artisan skills—making fewer flint hoes, clay pots, and skin garments. After two or three generations some eastern Indians had to rely on European manufacturers for many basic goods. To the west of the Appalachians traditional subsistence activities remained strong because canoes could carry only small quantities of imported goods.

The greatest threat to the cultures of the inland peoples was the fur trade. Eager for European trade goods, Indian families and villages began to claim exclusive hunting and trapping rights over an area, undermining clan unity. More important, conflict between tribes increased as rival bands of hunter-warriors competed to control the trade in furs. The Iroquois peoples of New York were the most successful. Organized in large towns of 500 to 2,000 persons and united in a great "longhouse" confederation (the Five Nations), the Iroquois virtually destroyed the neighboring Eries and the Neutrals and forced the Huron to move north of the Great Lakes. Then they pushed a dozen Algonquian-speaking peoples—Ottawa, Fox, Sauk, Kickapoo, Miami, Illinois—out of their traditional lands north of the Ohio River. The Algonquin crowded into a newly formed multitribal region west of Lake Michigan (present-day Wisconsin). Commitment to battle increased the influence of those who made war, and so the balance of power shifted from elders to headstrong young warriors.

The fur trade also transformed the Indians' relationship with the natural world. Native Americans were animists in religion, believing that everything—animals, trees, rocks—had a living spirit that demanded respect. Each clan in a tribe venerated an animal as its *totem*, or symbol, often considering themselves descendants of that animal. Tribesmen could hunt those totem animals only if they followed certain customs. As they skinned beavers or butchered deer for food and clothing, they thanked their spirits by offering prayers or burning tobacco and respectfully burying the carcasses and entrails. As they killed more and more animals for their fur, the Indians sensed the displeasure of the natural world. The epidemics that swept their communities confirmed their fears: the spirits of the animals were taking their revenge. The warriors of the Micmac of Nova Scotia confessed that they no longer knew "whether the beavers are among our friends or our enemies."

America had become a new world for its Indian peoples. All the invaders—Dutch and French fur traders no less than Spanish conquistadors and English settlers—had undermined traditional native American societies, forcing their members to fashion new ways of life.

CHAPTER 2 TIMELINE	
1565	Spain establishes St. Augustine, Florida
1573	Spanish Comprehensive Orders for New Discoveries
1598	Acoma War in New Mexico
1607	English adventurers settle Jamestown, Virginia
1608	Samuel de Champlain founds Quebec
1619	First Africans arrive in Chesapeake Virginia House of Burgesses convened
1620	Pilgrims found Plymouth colony
1620–1660	Tobacco boom in Chesapeake colonies
1621	Dutch West India Company chartered
1622	Opechancanough's uprising; Virginia becomes a royal colony (1624)
1625	Jesuits begin missionary work in Canada
1630	Puritans found Massachusetts Bay colony
1634	Maryland settled
1636	Roger Williams settles Rhode Island
1637	Pequot War Anne Hutchinson banished
1640s	Five Iroquois Nations go to war over fur trade
1649–1660	Puritan Commonwealth in England
1660–1678	William Berkeley, governor of Virginia
1660–1720	Poor tobacco market Indentured servitude declines
1664	English conquer New Netherland
1675–1676	Bacon's rebellion Metacom's uprising
1680	Popé's Rebellion in New Mexico
1692	Salem witchcraft trials

THE BRITISH EMPIRE IN AMERICA, 1660-1750

- The Politics of Empire, 1660–1713
- The Imperial Slave Economy
- The New Politics of Empire, 1713–1750

By 1660 English traders and settlers had pushed aside the native Americans and founded two clusters of colonies along the eastern coast of North America. The pace of settlement quickened as British officials encouraged the migration of tens of thousands of English men and women to the mainland and the importation of even greater numbers of enslaved Africans to grow sugar on the islands of the West Indies. As the American colonies grew in size, numbers, and wealth, they changed in character, becoming crucial parts of a transatlantic system of trade and forming the first British Empire.

The British Empire was the product of calculated policy, not chance. To protect their increasingly valuable colonies from European rivals—the Dutch in New Netherland, the French in Quebec and the West Indies, and the Spanish in Florida—English officials expanded the navy and repeatedly went to war. As a result, imperial warfare was a major factor in the century between 1660 and 1750.

A long struggle over imperial administrative control emerged as a second significant theme. To profit from the products and commerce of the American settlements, the home government attempted to control their trade through strict mercantilist economic regulations and to subordinate local political institutions to imperial direction. While never completely successful, these policies worked well enough to create a prosperous empire and make England a dominant power in Europe.

THE POLITICS OF EMPIRE, 1660–1713

In the first decades of settlement the Chesapeake and New England colonies were governed in a haphazard fashion. Taking advantage of the upheaval produced by civil war in England, local oligarchies of Puritan magistrates and tobacco-growing planters governed as they wished. With the restoration of the monarchy in 1660, royal bureaucrats tried to impose order on the unruly settlements.

The Restoration Colonies

In 1660 Charles II ascended to the English throne. A generous but extravagant man who was always in debt, Charles rewarded his aristocratic supporters and paid his creditors with millions of acres of American land. In 1663 he gave the Carolinas, an area long claimed by Spain and populated by thousands of Indians, to eight friends. The next year all the territory between the Delaware and Connecticut rivers went to his brother James, the duke of York. James took possession of the conquered province of New Netherland, renaming it New York after himself, and passed on the ownership of New Jersey to two of the Carolina proprietors.

In one of the great land grabs in history, a few English aristocrats had won title to vast provinces. Like Maryland, their new colonies were proprietorships; they owned all the land and could rule as they wished as long as the laws conformed broadly to those of England. Most proprietors sought to create a traditional social order presided over by a gentry class and a legally established Church of England. Thus, the Fundamental Constitutions of Carolina (1669) prescribed a manorial system with a powerful nobility and a mass of serfs.

This aristocratic scheme was pure fantasy. The first settlers in North Carolina, poor families from Virginia, refused to work on large manors and chose to live on modest farms, raising grain and tobacco. Indeed, farmers in Albemarle County, angered by taxes on tobacco exports and by the annual *quitrents* (small payments that acknowledged the lordship of the proprietors), rebelled in 1677. After deposing the governor, they forced the proprietors to abandon most of their financial claims.

The colonists of South Carolina, many of whom had come from Barbados (by then an overcrowded sugar island), refused both the Fundamental Constitutions and the payment of quitrents. The settlers from Barbados brought their African slaves and used them to raise cattle and food crops for export to the West Indies. They also opened a lucrative trade with native Americans, exchanging English manufactured goods for furs and Indian slaves. The market in Indian slaves encouraged slave-raiding attacks on Franciscan missions in Florida, threatening war with Spain and in 1715 prompting a violent war with the resident Yamasee people. South Carolina remained an ill-governed, violence-ridden frontier settlement until the 1720s.

In stark contrast to the Carolinas, the proprietary colony of Pennsylvania (which included present-day Delaware) pursued a pacifistic policy toward native Americans and became prosperous. In 1681 Charles II bestowed the colony on William Penn in payment of a large debt owed to Penn's father. Born to wealth and destined for courtly pursuits, the younger Penn converted to the Society of Friends (Quakers), a radical Protestant sect, and used his prestige to spread its influence. Pennsylvania, his greatest achievement, was designed as a refuge for Quakers, who were persecuted in England because they refused to serve in the army and pay taxes to support the Church of England.

Like the Puritans, the Quakers wanted to restore the simplicity and spirituality of early Christianity. But Quakers were not Calvinists, who restricted salvation to a small elect. Quakers followed the teachings of their founders George Fox and Margaret Fell, who argued that all men and women could be saved because God had imbued each person with an inner "light" of grace or understanding. In Quaker meetings for worship there was no minister or sermon; members sat in silence until moved to speak by the inner light.

Penn's Frame of Government (1681) was a radical document for its time because it guaranteed political liberty and religious freedom and allowed Christians of all denominations to vote and hold office. Thousands of Quakers, primarily from the middling classes of northwestern England, settled along the Delaware River in or near the city of Philadelphia, which Penn himself planned. The proprietor sold land at low prices—and in fee simple—and, to attract other Protestant settlers, advertised in Dutch and German. In 1683 migrants from the German province of Saxony founded Germantown (just outside Philadelphia) and were soon joined by thousands of other Germans attracted by fertile land and the prospect of freedom from religious warfare. Ethnic diversity, pacifism, and freedom of conscience made Pennsylvania the most open and democratic Restoration colony.

From Mercantilism to Dominion

Beginning in the 1650s, the English government extended to America the mercantilist policies used to control its foreign trade. To oust Dutch merchants from the English colonies, the Navigation Act of 1651 required that goods imported into England or its American settlements be carried on English-owned ships. New acts in 1660 and 1663 strengthened the ban on foreign merchants and stipulated that colonial sugar, tobacco, and indigo could be shipped only to England. To provide more business for English merchants, the acts also required that European exports to America pass through England. To enforce these laws and raise money, the Revenue Act of 1673 imposed a "plantation duty" on sugar and tobacco exports and created a staff of customs officials to collect it.

The English government backed its mercantilist policy with force. "What we want," declared the duke of Albemarle, "is more of the trade the Dutch now have." In three commercial wars between 1652 and 1674 the English navy drove the Dutch from New Netherland and ended Dutch supremacy in the West African slave trade. Meanwhile, English merchants expanded their fleets and dominated Atlantic commerce.

Many Americans resisted the mercantilism of Charles II as burdensome and intrusive. Edmund Randolph, a customs official in Massachusetts, reported that the Puritan-dominated government took "no notice of the laws of trade," welcoming Dutch merchants, importing goods from the French sugar islands, and claiming that its royal charter exempted it from most of the new regulations. Outraged, Randolph called for English troops to "reduce Massachusetts to obedience." The Lords of Trade and Plantations (the committee that managed colonial affairs) pursued a punitive legal strategy instead. In 1679 they denied the claim of Massachusetts Bay to the adjoining province of New Hampshire, creating a separate colony with a royal governor. To bring the Puritan colony directly under English control, in 1684 the Lords persuaded the English Court of Chancery to annul the charter of Massachusetts Bay on the grounds that its government had virtually outlawed the Church of England and violated the Navigation Acts.

The accession to the throne of James II (1685–1688), an admirer of France's despotic Louis XIV and of "divine right" monarchy, prompted the Lords of Trade to create a centralized imperial system in America. Backed by the king, in 1686 the Lords revoked the corporate charters of Connecticut and Rhode Island and merged them with the Massachusetts Bay and Plymouth colonies to form a new royal province, the Dominion of New England. Two years later they added New York and New Jersey to the Dominion, creating a single colony from the Delaware River to Maine.

These actions went far beyond mercantilism, which had respected the political autonomy of the various colonies while regulating their trade, and extended to America the authoritarian model of colonial administration practiced in Ireland. James II appointed Sir Edmund Andros, a former military officer, as governor of the Dominion, empowering him to abolish the existing legislative assemblies and rule by decree. In Massachusetts Andros advocated public worship in the Church of England, offending Puritan Congregationalists, and banned town meetings, angering villagers who prized local self-rule. Even worse, he challenged all land titles granted under the original Massachusetts charter. He offered to provide new deeds, but not in fee simple; title holders would be required to pay an annual quitrent. The Puritans protested to the king, but James refused to restore the old charter.

The Glorious Revolution of 1688

James II angered English political leaders as much as Andros alienated the Americans. The king revoked the charters of many English towns, rejected the advice of Parliament, and aroused popular opposition by openly practicing Roman Catholicism. In 1688, when James's Spanish Catholic wife gave birth to a son, the prospect of a Catholic heir to the throne ignited a quick and

The Target of the Glorious Revolution
The stance and facial expression of James II (1685–1688) suggest his arrogant personality. The king's arbitrary actions and Catholic sympathies prompted rebellions in England and America and cost him the throne.

bloodless coup known as the Glorious Revolution. Backed by popular protests and the army, Protestant parliamentary leaders forced James into exile and enthroned Mary, his Protestant daughter by his first wife, and her Dutch husband, William of Orange. Queen Mary II and King William III agreed to rule as constitutional monarchs, accepting a Declaration of Rights that limited royal prerogatives and increased personal liberties and parliamentary powers.

The coup leaders felt a need to justify their substitution of one monarch for another. John Locke provided that justification in his *Two Treatises on Government* (1690), which rejected divine right theories of monarchial rule and argued that the legitimacy of government rests on the consent of the governed and that individuals have inalienable natural rights to life, liberty, and property. Locke's celebration of individual rights and representative government had a lasting influence in America, where many political leaders wanted to increase the powers of the colonial assemblies.

More immediately, the Glorious Revolution sparked popular rebellions in Massachusetts, Maryland, and New York. When the news of the coup reached

Boston in April 1689, Puritan leaders seized Governor Andros and shipped him back to England. William and Mary agreed to break up the Dominion of New England, creating the new royal colony of Massachusetts (which included Plymouth and Maine), but refused to restore all the Puritans' powers. According to the new charter of 1692, the king would appoint the governor (and naval officers to enforce customs regulations), all male property owners (not just Puritan church members) would have the vote, and members of the Church of England would enjoy religious freedom.

The uprising in Maryland had both religious and economic causes. Since 1660 tobacco prices has been falling, threatening the livelihoods of smallholders, tenant farmers, and former indentured servants, most of whom were Protestant. They resented the rising taxes and the high fees imposed by wealthy proprietary officials, who were primarily Catholics. When Parliament ousted James II in England, a Protestant Association quickly removed the officials appointed by the Catholic Lord Baltimore. The Lords of Trade suspended Baltimore's proprietorship, imposed royal government, and established the Church of England as the colony's official church. This settlement lasted until 1715, when Benedict Calvert, the fourth Lord Baltimore, converted to the Anglican faith and the Crown restored the proprietorship to the Calvert family.

In New York the rebellion against the Dominion of New England was supported by both English settlers angered by James's prohibition of representative institutions and Dutch Protestants who welcomed Queen Mary and her Dutch husband to the English throne. Dutch artisans in New York City helped oust Lieutenant Governor Nicholson, an Andros appointee and an alleged Catholic sympathizer, and rallied behind a new government led by Jacob Leisler, a migrant German soldier who had married into a prominent Dutch merchant family. At first Leisler found supporters among all classes and ethnic groups, but when he freed debtors from prison and championed a more democratic town-meeting form of government, most wealthy merchants (who had traditionally controlled the city government) turned against him. In 1691 a new royal governor took control of New York, restored the representative assembly, and supported the wealthy classes against the Dutch artisans. Leisler was indicted for treason, convicted by an English jury, hanged, and then decapitated. A new merchant-dominated Board of Aldermen passed ordinances that lowered artisans' wages. Conflict between the Leislerian and anti-Leislerian factions continued until the 1710s.

In both America and England the Glorious Revolution of 1688–1689 began a new phase in imperial history. The uprisings in Boston and New York toppled the authoritarian Dominion and restored internal self-government, while in England the new constitutional monarchy enhanced the political power of financiers and merchants, who reestablished a mercantile empire based on trade, rejecting James II's plan for an imperial dominion based on bureaucratic rule. This policy gave free rein to enterprising merchants and to the emerging American representative assemblies. Although Parliament created a new Board of Trade (1696) to supervise the American settlements, it had little success. Settlers and proprietors resisted the Board's attempt to install royal governors in all the colonies, as did many English political leaders, who feared an increase in royal power. Consequently, the empire remained diverse, an odd mixture of corporate governments (Connecticut and Rhode Island) and proprietary institutions (Pennsylvania, Maryland, the Carolinas) in colonies that were of minor economic importance and royal governments in the great staple-producing settlements (the West Indies, Virginia) and elsewhere (Massachusetts, New York, New Jersey).

Imperial Warfare

Beginning in 1689, Britain and France fought a century-long series of wars to determine which nation would be dominant in Western Europe. The first of these conflicts to have a major impact in the Western Hemisphere was the War of the Spanish Succession (1702–1713), which pitted Britain against France and Spain. In North America the British tried to protect their growing settlements in the Carolinas by launching an attack against Spanish Florida. An expedition from South Carolina burned St. Augustine but failed to capture the fort. Then the Carolinians armed Creek and Chickasaw warriors and Indians who had fled from forced labor at Spanish missions. This Indian army destroyed the remaining Franciscan missions in northern Florida, attacked the Spanish settlement at Pensacola, and massacred the Apalachee who remained loyal to the Spaniards. To preserve control of Florida and protect Havana in nearby Cuba, the Spanish reinforced St. Augustine and launched unsuccessful attacks against Charleston, South Carolina.

Native Americans also took part in the fighting in the Northeast between the French in Quebec and the Puritan colonies in New England. To halt the expansion of English settlement, French officials provided supplies and arms to pro-French Abenaki and Mohawk warriors, who destroyed English settlements along the coast of Maine and in 1704 attacked the western Massachusetts town of Deerfield, where they killed 48 residents and carried 112 into captivity (see American Voices, p. 54). New England responded to these raids by launching attacks against French settlements, joining with British troops to seize Port Royal. However, in 1710 a major British-American expedition against the French stronghold at Quebec failed miserably.

The New York frontier remained quiet because France and England did not want to disrupt the lucrative fur trade and because most of the Iroquois nations had adopted a new policy of "aggressive neutrality." The Five Iroquois peoples—the Mohawk, Oneida, Onondaga, Cayuga, and Seneca—had long lived in a strong political confederation and during the 1670s had entered into a "covenant chain" of alliances with the English governors of New York and the Algonquin tribes of New England. However, during the 1690s pro-British and pro-French factions among the Iroquois fought one another in a devastating "beaver war." Subsequently the Five Nations adopted a neutralist stance, exploiting their central location by trading with the English and the French but refusing to fight for either side. The Delaware leader Teedyuscung explained this strategy by showing his people a pictorial message from the Iroquois: "You see a Square in the Middle, meaning the Lands of the Indians; and at one End, the Figure of a Man, indicating the English; and at the other End, another, meaning the French. Let us join together to defend our land against both."

Stymied militarily in America, Britain used victories in Europe to win major territorial and commercial concessions in the Treaty of Utrecht (1713). From France, Britain obtained Newfoundland, Acadia (Nova Scotia), the Hudson Bay region of northern Canada, and access to the western Indian trade (see Map 3.1). From Spain, Britain acquired the strategic fortress of Gibraltar at the entrance to the Mediterranean and commercial privileges in Spanish America. These gains solidified Britain's commercial supremacy and brought peace to eastern North America for a generation.

MAP 3.1
Britain's American Empire, 1713
Britain's West Indian colonies were small in size—mere dots on the Caribbean Sea—but large in economic importance. Their sugar plantations brought wealth to England and provided markets for the farm products of northern mainland colonies.

In the Southwest the Spanish established permanent settlements in Texas, beginning at San Antonio in 1718, to protect the silver mines in northern New Spain from attacks from French Louisiana. This expansion of Spanish influence was opposed by the prosperous town-dwelling Caddo peoples, one of whose confederacies, the "Kingdom of Tejas," would give Texas its name. The Caddo had expelled the Spanish Franciscans in 1693, blaming them for a fatal smallpox epidemic. A generation later the Tejas refused baptism (believing "that the [holy] water kills them") and successfully resisted Spanish control by turning to the French for firearms and trade goods. Like the Iroquois, the Caddo peoples had learned how to turn European rivalries and warfare to their own advantage.

THE IMPERIAL SLAVE ECONOMY

Britain's interest in American affairs reflected the increasing importance to its trade of the staple crops of sugar, tobacco, and rice. Using land seized from native Americans, European merchants and planters had created a new agricultural and commercial order which historians call the South Atlantic system. At the core of the new system of production stood enslaved labor from Africa.

The African Background

Vast and diverse, West Africa stretches from present-day Senegal to Cameroon and then extends southward to Congo and Angola. In 1500 tropical rain forest covered much of the coast, but a series of great rivers—the Senegal, Gambia, Volta, Niger, and Congo—provided relatively easy access to the woodlands, plains, and savanna of the interior.

Most residents farmed small plots and lived in extended families in small villages. Normally, men cleared the land and women planted and harvested the crops. On the plains of the savanna, millet, cotton, and livestock were the primary products, while the forest peoples grew yams and harvested oil-rich palm nuts. Forest dwellers exchanged kola nuts, a mild stimulant, for the textiles and leather goods produced by savanna dwellers. Similarly, salt produced along the seacoast was traded for iron or gold mined in the hills of the interior.

Most West Africans spoke related languages but were divided into hundreds of distinct cultural and political groups. A majority of the people lived in hierarchical, socially stratified societies ruled by princes. Others resided in stateless societies organized by family and lineage (much like those of the Woodland Indians of eastern North America). Both women and men had secret societies that cut across lineage and clan loyalties in stateless cultures and checked the powers of rulers in princely states. These societies provided sexual education for the young, conducted adult initiation ceremonies, and, by shaming individuals and officials, enforced a code of public conduct and private morality.

Spiritual beliefs varied greatly. Although some West Africans had been converted to the Muslim faith and believed in a single god, most recognized a variety of deities ranging from a remote creator-god who seldom interfered in human affairs to numerous spirits that lived in the earth, animals, and plants. Male blacksmiths (who had mastered the secrets of iron making) and female potters (who had transformed the basic elements of earth, water, and fire) captured these spiritual powers in amulets, "power generators" that protected those who wore them. Africans also paid homage to their ancestors, who were believed to inhabit a spiritual world from which they could intercede in behalf of their descendants. Royal families paid elaborate homage to their ancestors in an attempt to give themselves an aura of divinity.

At first European traders had a positive impact on life in West Africa by introducing new plants and animals. Portuguese merchants carried coconuts from East Africa, oranges and lemons from the Mediterranean, and pigs from Western Europe. From the Americas traders brought sweet potatoes, peanuts, papaya, pineapples, and tobacco. American maize and cassava (manioc) gradually displaced millet and yams as staples in the West African diet; in many areas their higher yields promoted population growth.

Portuguese merchants expanded existing trade networks, stimulating the African economy. European iron bars and metal products joined kola nuts and salt moving inland; grain, gold, ivory, and cotton textiles flowed to the coast to provision European ships. This inland trade remained in the hands of Africans because of disease; Europeans were quickly stricken by yellow fever, malaria, and dysentery, and their death rate was more than 50 percent a year.

Europeans soon joined in the trade in humans. Unfree status had existed for many centuries in West Africa. Some people were held in bondage as security for debts; others were sold into servitude by their kin, often in return for food in times of famine; still others were war captives. Although treated as property and exploited as agricultural laborers, slaves usually were considered members of the society that had enslaved them and sometimes were treated as kin. Most retained the right to marry, and their children were often free. A small proportion of unfree West Africans were "trade slaves," sold from one kingdom to another or carried overland to the Mediterranean region, mostly by Arab traders. Thus, the first Portuguese in Senegambia found that the Wolof king

> supports himself by raids which result in many slaves from his own as well as neighboring countries. He employs these slaves in cultivating the land allotted to him; but he also sells many to the Azanaghi [Arab] merchants in return for horses and other goods, and also to the Christians, since they have begun to trade with these blacks.

The demand for labor in the Western Hemisphere gradually transformed the scale and nature of African slavery (see Map 3.2). Between 1440 and 1550 Portuguese traders carried a few thousand Africans each year to sugar plantations

SLAVE DESTINATIONS	
SOUTH AMERICA	
Brazil	3,650,000
Dutch America	500,000
WEST INDIES	
British	1,660,000
French	1,660,000
CENTRAL AMERICA	
Spanish	1,500,000
NORTH AMERICA	
British Colonies	500,000
EUROPE	175,000
TOTAL	9,645,000

MAP. 3.2

The Atlantic Slave Trade

West Africa was home to scores of peoples and dozens of kingdoms. Some states, such as Dahomey, became aggressive slavers, taking tens of thousands of war captives and selling them to European traders. About 15 percent of these enslaved Africans died on the transatlantic voyage, the brutal "middle passage"; most of the survivors labored on sugar plantations in Brazil and the British and French West Indies.

in Madeira and the Azore Islands. Between 1550 and 1700, Portuguese and Dutch merchants annually transported about 10,000 Africans across the Atlantic to Brazil and the Caribbean. Then English and French merchants took over this trade in humans, developing African-run slave-catching systems that extended far into the interior. Between 1700 and 1810 they carried about 7 million Africans—800,000 in the 1780s alone—to toil and die in the Americas, primarily on sugar estates in the West Indies.

The South Atlantic System

Sugar was the cornerstone of the South Atlantic system, its cultivation fueled by a new European craving for sweetness, which previously had been available only from honey and fruit juices. Imitating Dutch and Portuguese planters in Brazil, English and French merchants developed sugar plantations in the West Indies, beginning with Barbados around 1650. By 1700 they were investing heavily in the Leeward Islands and Jamaica; by 1750 Jamaica had 700 large sugar plantations worked by more than 105,000 enslaved Africans.

Sugar production required fertile land, many laborers to plant and cut the cane, and heavy equipment to process it into raw sugar and molasses. Because only wealthy merchants or landowners had the capital to outfit a plantation, a planter–merchant elite developed in the sugar industry. As the Scottish economist Adam Smith declared in his famous treatise *The Wealth of Nations* (1776), sugar was the most profitable crop in Europe and America.

The South Atlantic system brought wealth to the entire English economy. Most West Indian planters lived as "absentees" in England, spending their profits there. Moreover, the Navigation Acts required that American sugar be sold to English consumers or sent through England to continental markets; by 1750 reexports of sugar and tobacco accounted for half of all British exports. Substantial profits also came from the trade in slaves, for the Royal African Company sold male slaves in the West Indies for five times what it paid for them in Africa. To transport slaves (and machinery and settlers) to America, shipyards built hundreds of vessels. Thousands of English and Scottish men and women worked in related industries: building port facilities and warehouses, refining sugar and tobacco, distilling rum from molasses (a by-product of sugar), and manufacturing textiles and iron products for the growing markets in Africa and America. Commercial expansion also provided a supply of experienced sailors, helping to make the Royal Navy the most powerful fleet in Europe.

The South Atlantic system was an economic and human tragedy for West Africa and the parts of East Africa, such as Madagascar, where slavers also preyed. Between 1550 and 1870 the Atlantic slave trade uprooted about 15 million Africans, diminishing the wealth and population of the continent. Overall, the iron, tinware, rum, and cloth that entered the African economy in exchange for slaves was worth from one-tenth (in the 1680s) to one-third (by the 1780s) as much as the goods those slaves produced.

In addition, the slave trade changed the nature of West African society by encouraging centralized states and military conquest. In 1739 an observer noted that "whenever the King of Barsally wants Goods or Brandy . . . the King goes and ransacks some of his enemies' towns, seizing the people and selling them." War and slaving became a way of life in Dahomey, where the royal house made the sale of slaves a state monopoly and used the resulting access to European guns to create a military despotism. Dahomey's army, which included a contingent of 5,000 women, systematically raided the interior for captives, exporting thousands of slaves each year. The Asante kings also used the firearms and wealth acquired through the Atlantic trade to create a bureaucratic empire of 3 million to 5 million people. Yet slaving remained a choice, not a necessity. The old and still powerful Kingdom of Benin, famous for its cast bronzes and carved ivory, resolutely opposed the slave trade, prohibiting the export of male slaves for over a century (see American Voices, p. 70).

The trade in humans changed many aspects of African life. Class divisions hardened as people of noble birth sold those of lesser status. Gender relations shifted as well. Men constituted two-thirds of the slaves sent across

An African King
This striking bronze plaque from Benin, an important kingdom in West Central Africa, depicts a mounted king, his attendants, and (probably) his children.

the Atlantic both because European planters paid more for men and because African traders directed women captives into local slave markets. The resulting imbalance between the sexes allowed some African men to take several wives, changing the nature of marriage. Most important, the Atlantic trade prompted harsher forms of slavery in Africa, eroding the dignity of human life there as well as on the plantations of the Western Hemisphere.

The Slave Trade in Africa

The demand for black laborers in the Americas disrupted African society, encouraging wars among peoples and forever changing millions of lives. The narrative of Venture Smith describes how this affected many Africans.

I was born at Dukandarra, in Guinea, about the year 1729. My father's name was Saungm Furro, Prince of the tribe of Dukandara. My father had three wives. Polygamy was not uncommon in that country, especially among the rich, as every man was allowed to keep as many wives as he could maintain. By his first wife he had three children. The eldest of them was myself, named by my father, Broteer. . . .

The first thing worthy of notice which I remember was, a contention between my father and mother, on account of my father marrying his third wife without the consent of his first and eldest, which was contrary to the custom generally observed among my countrymen. In consequence of this rupture, my mother left her husband and country, and travelled away with her three children to the eastward. I was then five years old . . .; [a year later] the difference between my parents had been made up . . . and I was once more restored to my paternal dwelling in peace and happiness. . . .

[Shortly afterwards] my father learned that the place had been invaded by a numerous army, from a nation not far distant, . . . instigated by some white nation who equipped them [with guns] and sent them to subdue and possess the country. . . . The army of the enemy was large, I should suppose consisting of about six thousand men. Their leader was called Baukurre. After destroying the old prince [my father], they decamped and immediately marched towards the sea, lying to the west, taking with them myself and the women prisoners. . . .

All of us were then put into the castle, and kept for market. On a certain time I and other prisoners were . . . rowed to a vessel belonging to Rhode Island. . . . I was brought on board by one Robertson Mumford, steward of said vessel, for four gallons of rum, and a piece of calico, and called VENTURE, on account of his having purchased me with his own private venture. Thus I came by my name. All the slaves that were bought for that vessel's cargo, were two hundred and sixty.

SOURCE: John Bayles, ed., *Black Slave Narratives* (New York: Macmillan, 1970), pp. 36–44.

Slavery and Society in the Chesapeake

The first Africans arrived in Virginia in 1619, but for the next forty years their numbers remained small and they were not legally enslaved. English common law acknowledged indentured servitude but not *chattel slavery*—the ownership of one human being by another. If planters wanted legalized slavery, they would have to create it. In the West Indies and South Carolina they did exactly that, enacting statutes permitting chattel slavery in the first decade of settlement.

The law of slavery developed more slowly in the tobacco colonies of Maryland and Virginia. About 400 Africans were living in the Chesapeake colonies in 1649, making up 2 percent of the population; by 1670 the proportion of blacks had reached only 5 percent. Africans were forced to work hard and were ill fed and ill clothed, but so were most English indentured servants. A significant number of black workers received their freedom by completing a term of service or converting to Christianity. Some African Christian freemen even purchased slaves or bought the labor contracts of English servants, suggesting that religion and personal initiative were as important as race in determining social status at this time. By becoming a Christian and a planter, an enterprising African could aspire to near equality with the English settlers.

Beginning in the 1660s, for unclear reasons, legislatures in the Chesapeake colonies enacted laws that lowered the status of Africans. Perhaps the English-born elite grew more conscious of race as the number of Africans increased. By 1671 the Virginia House of Burgesses had forbidden Africans to own guns or join the militia. It had also barred them—"tho baptized and enjoying their own Freedom"—from buying the labor contracts of white servants and specified that conversion to Christianity did not qualify Africans for eventual freedom. Being black was becoming a mark of inferior legal status, and being a slave was becoming a permanent and hereditary condition.

Subsequently African slavery expanded not because it was "necessary"—white families and English indentured servants could have continued to grow tobacco and could have cultivated rice and sugar as well—but because it was profitable. After Bacon's rebellion of 1675–1676, planters imported thousands of Africans, primarily because the growing slave trade made them less expensive than white indentured servants (who were in short supply and thus more costly) but also because slaves had few legal rights and could be disciplined more strictly. A law of 1692 prohibiting sexual intercourse between English and Africans was intended to separate white and black workers and create a racially divided society. Finally, in 1705, a Virginia statute explicitly defined virtually all resident Africans as slaves: "All servants imported or brought into this country by sea or land who were not Christians in their native country shall be accounted and be slaves." The Chesapeake elite had chosen to create a society based on enslaved black laborers, who numbered 10 percent of the Chesapeake population by 1700 and 20 percent by 1720.

These years witnessed significant changes among whites as well. As settlement moved inland after 1675, away from the disease-ridden lowlands, English migrants lived long enough to form stable families and communities. When death rates had been high, many husbands had named their wives as executors of their estates and legal guardians of their children. Now they bestowed those powers on their male kin. Reaffirming the primacy of male heirs, they also limited widows' portions to the traditional one-third share during their lifetimes. Men reassumed their customary control of family property.

The reappearance of strict patriarchy within the family mirrored larger social developments. The planter elite now stood at the top of a rural social hierarchy, exercising authority over a small yeoman class, a large group of white tenant farmers, and a growing host of enslaved black laborers. Wealthy planters used Africans to grow food as well as export tobacco; build houses, wagons, and tobacco casks; and make shoes and clothes. By increasing their self-sufficiency, the planter elite survived the depressed tobacco market between 1680 and 1720. Small-scale planters who used family labor to grow tobacco fared less well, falling deeper into debt.

However, the Virginia gentry paid attention to the concerns of middling and poor whites, reducing their taxes and allowing them to vote. The strategy of the leading families—the Carters, Lees, Randolphs, Robinsons—was to curry favor with the voters at election time, bribing them with rum, money, and the promise of favorable legislation. In return, yeomen planters were expected to elect their wealthy neighbors to political office and defer to their authority. This political horse trading enhanced the power of the planter elite at the expense of the royal governor. It also created solidarity among whites, as did the spread of African slavery; by 1770 there were 500,000 slaves in the southern mainland colonies, roughly one-third of the population, and 60 percent of the English families in the Chesapeake owned at least one slave.

As time passed, affluent Chesapeake planters modeled themselves after the English aristocracy. Between 1720 and 1750 they replaced their modest wooden houses with brick mansions. They and their wives read English journals, imported English clothes, and dined in the English fashion. Planters hired English tutors to teach etiquette to their daughters and sent their sons to London to be educated as gentlemen. Most of these young men returned to America, married, and followed in their fathers' footsteps, managing plantations and participating in politics. Gentry women deferred to their husbands' authority, reared pious children, and maintained elaborate social networks. Using the profits of the South Atlantic system, the planter-merchants of the Chesapeake formed an increasingly well-educated, refined, and stable ruling class.

The Expansion of Slavery

For the enslaved Africans at the bottom of the social scale, the South Atlantic system was an unrelieved tragedy. Torn from their village homes, captives were marched in chains to coastal ports. From there they made the perilous "middle passage" to the New World in hideously overcrowded ships. Some Africans jumped overboard, choosing to drown rather than endure more suffering. Nearly a million (15 percent of the 8 million who crossed the Atlantic between 1700 and 1810) died on the journey, mostly from dysentery, smallpox, or scurvy.

Africans who toiled in the sugar islands faced the harshest conditions. Planting and harvesting sugarcane required intense labor under a tropical sun, with a pace set by the overseer's whip. With sugar prices high and the cost of slaves low, many planters worked slaves to death and then imported more. Between 1708 and 1735 about 85,000 Africans were brought into Barbados, but the black population increased only from 42,000 to 46,000.

Conditions were less severe in Maryland and Virginia, where many slaves lived relatively long lives. Tobacco was a less physically demanding crop than sugar, and epidemic diseases did not spread as easily because the plantations were small and dispersed. Also, because tobacco profits were low, planters could not constantly buy new slaves and therefore treated those they had less harshly. Tobacco planters attempted to increase their work force through reproduction, purchasing higher numbers of female slaves and encouraging large families. In 1720 women made up about a third of the African population of Maryland, and the black population had begun to increase naturally. One absentee owner instructed his plantation agent "to be kind and indulgent to the breeding wenches, and not to force them when with child upon any service or hardship that will be injurious to them." By midcentury American-born slaves constituted a majority among Chesapeake blacks.

The most oppressive conditions for slaves existed in South Carolina. The colony had grown slowly until Africans from rice-growing cultures turned rice into a profitable export crop around 1700. To expand production, white planters imported tens of thousands of Africans, who by the 1710s made up a majority of the colony's population and 80 percent of those living in the rice-growing lowlands. Mosquito-borne epidemic diseases took thousands of African lives, while overwork killed many more slaves, for moving tons of dirt to build irrigation works was brutally hard. As in the West Indies, there were many deaths and few births.

Community and Resistance

Slaves regarded each other not as Africans but as members of a specific people: Mende, Hausa, Ibo, Yoruba. To prevent slave revolts, white planters consciously enhanced this sense of cultural diversity. "The safety of the Plantations," declared a widely read English pamphlet, "depends upon having Negroes from all parts of Guiny, who do not understand each other's languages and Customs and cannot agree to Rebel."

Africans found it in their interest to transcend this cultural diversity. The largely African-born population of the South Carolina lowlands created a new and widely understood language, the Gullah dialect, using English and African words in an African grammatical structure. In the Chesapeake, where there were more American-born blacks and a less concentrated slave population, a European visitor in the mid-eighteenth century reported that "all the blacks spoke very good English." A common language was one prerequisite

Hulling Rice in Georgia
In this early twentieth-century photograph, the descendants of enslaved women use traditional African mortar-and-pestle technology to separate the hard outer shell from grains of rice.

for the creation of African-American communities. The growth of stable family and kin networks was another. A high death rate inhibited the creation of multigenerational families in South Carolina, but after 1725 blacks in the Chesapeake were able to establish enduring families and extended kin networks.

African-Americans gradually developed a culture of their own, passing on family names, traditions, and knowledge to the next generation. Aspects of the slaves' African heritage could be seen in wood carvings, the giant wooden mortars and pestles used to hull rice, and the design of shacks. Many African-Americans retained traditional Muslim religious beliefs or relied on the spiritual powers of conjurers. Others adopted Protestant Christianity, reshaping its doctrines, ethics, and rituals to fit their needs and creating a spiritually rich and long-lasting religious culture.

However, slaves had few opportunities for education and accumulated few material goods. A well-traveled European who visited a slave hut in Virginia in the late eighteenth century found it to be

more miserable than the most miserable of the cottages of our peasants. The husband and wife sleep on a mean pallet, the children on the ground; a very bad fireplace, some utensils for cooking. . . . They work all week, not having a single day for themselves except for holidays.

African Culture in South Carolina
The dance and the musical instruments are of Yoruba origin, the contribution of Africans from the Niger River–Slave Coast region (the homeland of the Yoruba), an area that accounted for one-sixth of the slaves imported into South Carolina before 1770.

AMERICAN VOICES

Sadism under Slavery

Planters relied on various incentives to extract work from their African slaves. A few used rewards, providing cooperative laborers with food, leisure, and better treatment. Many more relied on force, extracting work by whipping recalcitrant laborers. Some went further, as described by Philip Fithian, a Princeton graduate employed as tutor by a Virginia planter.

When I am on the Subject, I will relate further, what I heard Mr George Lees Overseer, one Morgan, say the other day that he himself had often done to Negroes, and found it useful; He said that whipping of any kind does them no good, for they will laugh at your greatest Severity; But he told us he had invented two things, and by several experiments had proved their success.—For Sulleness, Obstinacy, or Idleness, says he, Take a Negro, strip him, tie him fast to a post; take then a sharp Curry-Comb, + curry him severely til he is well scrap'd; + call a Boy with some dry Hay, and make the Boy rub him down for several Minutes, then salt him, & unlose him. He will attend to his Business (said the inhuman Infidel) afterwards!—But savage Cruelty does not exceed His next diabolical Invention—To get a Secret from a Negro, says he, take the following Method—Lay upon your Floor a large thick plank, having a peg about eighteen Inches long, of hard wood, & very Sharp, on the upper end, fixed fast in the plank—then strip the Negro, tie the Cord to a staple in the Ceiling, so as that his foot may just rest on the sharpened Peg, then turn him briskly round, and you would laugh (said our informer) at the Dexterity of the Negro, while he was releiving his Feet on the sharpen'd Peg!

SOURCE: Philip Vickers Fithian, *Journals and Letters, 1767–1774* (Williamsburg, Va.: Colonial Williamsburg Press, 1934), pp. 50–51.

Slaves resisted the rigorous work routine at their peril. To punish slaves who disobeyed, refused to work, or ran away, planters resorted to the lash and the amputation of fingers, toes, and ears. Declaring the chronic runaway Ballazore an "incorrigible rogue," Robert "King" Carter of Virginia ordered all his toes cut off: "nothing less than dismembering will reclaim him." Thomas Jefferson, who witnessed such cruelty on his father's plantation in mid-eighteenth-century Virginia, noted that each generation of whites was "nursed, educated, and daily exercised in tyranny," for the relationship "between master and slave is a perpetual exercise of the most unremitting despotism on the one part, and degrading submission on the other."

White violence was related to the size and density of the slave population. English planters in the predominantly African West Indies routinely branded troublesome slaves with hot irons. In South Carolina the outnumbered whites maintained authority by imposing strict regulations. Black workers were forbidden to leave the plantation without special passes, and rural patrols enforced those regulations.

Slaves dealt with their plight in a variety of ways. Some bargained with their owners, agreeing to do extra work in return for better food and clothes. Others resisted by working slowly or stealing. Still others attacked their owners or overseers even though this was punishable by mutilation or death. A successful rebellion was nearly impossible because whites were armed and, outside of coastal South Carolina, more numerous than Africans. Some newly arrived slaves without ties to African-American culture escaped to the frontier, where they tried to establish African villages or, more often, married into Indian tribes. Others, especially those fluent in English, fled to towns, where they tried to pass as free blacks.

The largest slave uprising of the eighteenth century, the Stono rebellion, occurred in the late 1730s, when the governor of Spanish Florida promised freedom and land to slaves who ran away from South Carolina. At least sixty-nine slaves reportedly escaped to St. Augustine, and rumors circulated "that a Conspiracy was formed by Negroes in Carolina to rise and make their way out of the province." When war between England and Spain broke out in 1739, seventy-five Africans killed a number of whites near the Stono River, stole guns and ammunition, and marched south toward Florida. Unrest swept the countryside, but the white militia killed many of the Stono rebels and dispersed the rest, preventing a general uprising. Frightened whites tightened plantation discipline and imported fewer new slaves. For Africans the price of active resistance was high.

The Northern Maritime Economy

The South Atlantic system encompassed nonslaveholding farmers in the northern mainland colonies because the sugar islands provided a ready market for bread, lumber, fish, and meat. As a West Indian explained in 1647, planters in the islands "had rather buy food at very dear rates than produce it by labour, so infinite is the profit of sugar works." By 1700 the economies of the West Indies and New England were tightly interwoven. After 1720 farmers and merchants in New York, New Jersey, and Pennsylvania entered this trade, shipping wheat, corn, and bread to the sugar islands.

The South Atlantic system tied the whole British Empire together. In return for sugar exports to England, West Indian planters received *bills of exchange* (credit slips) from London merchant houses. The planters used those bills to buy slaves and reimburse American merchants for the crops produced by northern farmers. Farmers and merchants then exchanged the bills for British manufactures, completing the cycle.

American merchants in Boston, Philadelphia, and New York invested some of their profits in new ships and factories. In Boston, Newport, and Providence they refined raw sugar into finished loaves (previously imported from England) and distilled West Indian molasses into rum. By the 1740s Boston distillers were exporting more than half a million gallons of rum annually. In addition, merchants in smaller ports, such as Salem and Marblehead, built a major fishing industry, providing mackerel and cod to feed the slaves of the sugar islands and to export to southern Europe. Southern merchants transformed Baltimore into a major port by developing a bustling trade in wheat, while Charleston traders exported deerskins, indigo, and rice to European markets.

The expansion of commerce in the eighteenth century fueled rapid growth in American port cities and coastal towns. By 1750 Newport, Rhode Island, and Charleston, South Carolina, had nearly 10,000 residents apiece, Boston 15,000, and New York almost 18,000. The largest port was Philadelphia, whose population reached 30,000 by 1776, the size of a large European provincial city. Smaller coastal towns were centers of the shipbuilding and lumber industries. By the 1740s seventy sawmills dotted the Piscataqua River in New Hampshire, providing low-cost wood for homes, warehouses, and especially shipbuilding. Taking advantage of the Navigation Acts, which allowed colonists to build and own trading vessels, scores of shipwrights turned out oceangoing ships, while hundreds of other artisans made ropes, sails, and metal fittings for the new fleet. Shipyards in Boston and Philadelphia launched about 15,000 tons of oceangoing vessels annually; eventually colonial-built ships made up about a third of the British merchant fleet.

The impact of the South Atlantic system extended into the interior of North America. A small fleet of trading vessels sailed back and forth between Philadelphia and the villages along the Delaware Bay, exchanging cargoes of European goods for barrels of flour and wheat. In the 1750s hundreds of professional teamsters in Maryland moved to market 370,000 bushels of wheat and corn and 16,000 barrels of flour annually—over 10,000 wagon trips. To service this traffic entrepreneurs and artisans set up taverns, livery stables, and barrel-making shops in small towns along the wagon roads, providing additional jobs. The prosperous interior town of Lancaster, Pennsylvania, boasted more than 200 artisans, both German and English. The South Atlantic system thus provided not only markets for farmers (by far the largest group of northern residents), but also opportunities for merchants, artisans, and workers in country towns and seaport cities.

At the top of seaport society stood a small group of wealthy landowners, who lived off their rents, and prosperous merchants. By 1750 about forty merchants controlled over 50 percent of Philadelphia's trade and had taxable assets averaging £10,000, a huge sum at the time. Like the Chesapeake gentry, these prosperous northern merchants imitated the British upper classes, importing design books from England and building Georgian-style mansions to showcase their wealth. Their wives created a genteel culture, decorating their houses with fine furniture and entertaining guests at elegant dinners.

Artisan and shopkeeper families formed the middle ranks of seaport society and numbered nearly half the population. Innkeepers, butchers, seamstresses, shoemakers, weavers, bakers, carpenters, masons, and dozens of other specialists socialized among themselves, formed mutual-help societies, and worked to gain a *competency*—an income sufficient to maintain their families in modest comfort and dignity. Wives and husbands often worked as a team, teaching the "mysteries of the craft" to their children. The most prosperous owned their own houses and shops (sometimes run by widows continuing a family business). Some artisans aspired to wealth and status, an entrepreneurial ethic that prompted them to hire apprentices and expand production. Most craft workers were not well-to-do, however; these middling people had taxable assets averaging about £300. Many of them were quite poor; a tailor was lucky to accumulate £30 worth of property in his lifetime.

Laboring men and women formed the lower ranks of urban society. Boston, Philadelphia, and New York needed hundreds of dockworkers to unload manufactured goods and molasses from inbound ships and reload the ships with barrels of wheat, fish, and rice for export; these demanding jobs often were filled by black slaves and white indentured servants. Hundreds of merchant seamen lived in the poor wards of port cities, along with unskilled men who worked for wages. Poor women—whether single, married, or widowed—could eke out a living by washing clothes, spinning wool, or working as servants or prostitutes. To make ends meet, most laboring families sent their children out to work at an early age. Indispensable to the economy yet without homes of their own, these bound laborers, wage earners, and merchant seamen lived in crowded tenements in back alleys. In good times hard work brought family security or enough money to drink cheap New England rum in waterfront taverns.

Periods of stagnant commerce affected everyone, threatening merchants with bankruptcy and artisans with irregular work. For laborers and seamen, whose household budgets left no margin for sickness or unemployment, depressed trade meant hunger, dependence on charity handed out by town-appointed overseers of the poor, and—for the most desperate—a life of petty thievery. Involvement in the South Atlantic system between 1660 and 1750 brought uncertainty as well as opportunity to northern workers and farmers.

THE NEW POLITICS OF EMPIRE, 1713–1750

The triumph of trade changed the politics of empire. British ministers, pleased with the prosperous commerce in staple crops, were content to rule the colonies with a gentle hand. The colonists enjoyed a significant degree of self-government and economic autonomy, allowing them to challenge the rules of the mercantilist system.

The Rise of the Assembly

Before 1689 political affairs in most colonies were dominated by proprietors, royal governors, and authoritarian elites, reflecting the view that "Authority should Descend from *Kings* and *Fathers* to *Sons* and *Servants*," as a royalist political philosopher put it. In the Glorious Revolution of 1688 the English political faction known as the Whigs challenged that outlook, winning the fight for a constitutional monarchy that limited the authority of the Crown. Their ideal government would divide power among the monarchy, the aristocracy, and the commons. Whigs did not advocate democracy but did believe that nonnoble property owners should have some political power, especially over the levying of taxes. When Whig politicians forced William and Mary to accept a Declaration of Rights in 1689, they strengthened the powers of the House of Commons at the expense of the Crown.

American representative assemblies copied the English Whigs and insisted on maintaining their authority over taxes, refusing to fund military projects and other programs advocated by royal governors. Gradually the legislatures won partial control of patronage and the budget, angering imperial bureaucrats and absentee proprietors. "The people in power in America," complained the proprietor William Penn during a struggle with the Pennsylvania Assembly, "think nothing taller than themselves but the Trees." In Massachusetts during the 1720s the assembly refused repeatedly to obey the king's instructions to provide a permanent salary for the royal governor; subsequently legislatures in North Carolina, New Jersey, and Pennsylvania declined to pay their governors any salary for several years.

The Rise of an American Gentry
George Wyllys (1710–1796) came from a family of political leaders in Connecticut and served as secretary of the colony from 1730 to 1796. The emergence of capable and well-educated men such as Wyllys (note the books in his library) bolstered the growing power of the American representative assemblies.

The rise of the assembly created an elitist rather than a democratic political system. Although most property-owning white men had the right to vote after 1700, only men of considerable wealth and status stood for election. In Virginia in the 1750s seven members of the influential Lee family sat in the House of Burgesses and, along with other powerful Virginia families, dominated its major committees. In New England descendants of the original Puritans had intermarried and formed a core of political leaders. "Go into every village in New England," John Adams said in 1765, "and you will find that the office of justice of the peace, and even the place of representative, have generally descended from generation to generation, in three or four families at most."

Neither elitist assemblies nor wealthy property owners could impose unpopular edicts on the people. The crowd actions that had overthrown the Dominion of New England in 1689 were a regular part of political life in England and America and were used to achieve social and economic aims. Mobs upheld community values: in New York they closed houses of prostitution, while in Salem, Massachusetts, they ran people with infectious diseases out of town. Other mobs had economic motives, rioting to prevent merchants from exporting grain from Boston during a wartime shortage in 1710 and proprietors from forcing their tenants from disputed lands in New Jersey in the 1730s and 1740s. When officials in Boston tried to restrict the sale of farm produce to a designated public marketplace, a crowd destroyed the building and defied the authorities to arrest them. "If you touch One you shall touch All," an anonymous letter warned the sheriff, "and we will show you a Hundred Men where you can show one."

Such expressions of popular power, combined with the growing power of the assemblies, undermined the old authoritarian system. By the 1750s most colonies had representative political institutions that were broadly responsive to popular pressure and increasingly immune from British control.

Salutary Neglect

British colonial policy during the reigns of George I (1714–1727) and George II (1727–1760) contributed significantly to the rise of American self-government. Royal bureaucrats relaxed their supervision of internal colonial affairs, focusing instead on defense and trade. Two generations later the British political philosopher Edmund Burke would praise this strategy as "salutary [healthy] neglect."

Salutary neglect was a by-product of the political system developed by Sir Robert Walpole, leader of the Whigs in the House of Commons between 1720 and 1742. Using appointments, pensions, and gifts, Walpole transformed the formerly antagonistic relationship between king and Parliament into one of cooperation. But his tactics offended the self-described Real (or Radical) Whigs, who argued that by using patronage and bribery to create a strong Court (or Crown) party, Walpole had betrayed the constitutional monarchy

established by the Glorious Revolution. A Country party of landed gentlemen warned that high taxes, a bloated royal bureaucracy, and a standing army
threatened the liberties of the people.

The arguments of the Radical Whigs and the Country party appealed to
Americans who wanted to enhance the power of the provincial assemblies. In
their eyes the royal governors in America still had too much arbitrary power;
they pointed to Governor William Cosby of New York, whose salary demands
and selling of offices threw the province into political chaos for a decade.
American Whigs warned that colonial governors, emulating Walpole, would
use land grants and political appointments to control the assemblies.

Walpole's patronage policies weakened the imperial system in a more direct fashion by filling the Board of Trade with men of little talent. These
"placemen" did little, weakening the morale of more capable imperial officials. When Governor Gabriel Johnson went to North Carolina in the 1730s,
determined to "make a mighty change in the face of affairs" by curbing the
assembly, he was soon discouraged by the lack of support from other British
officials. Forsaking reform, he decided "to do nothing which can be reasonably blamed, and leave the rest to time, and a new set of inhabitants."

Salutary neglect did not "cause" Americans to seek independence; in fact,
in the short run mild rule under Walpole strengthened the colonists' allegiance to Britain (as did the increasing popularity of British goods and culture). But the legislative autonomy allowed by salutary neglect did encourage
Americans to expect a position of political equality within the empire.

Consolidating the Mercantile System

Walpole's main preoccupation during the years of salutary neglect was to protect British commercial interests from foreign threats. One of his major initiatives was the new colony of Georgia. In the early 1730s General James
Oglethorpe and a group of social reformers successfully petitioned King
George II for land south of the Carolinas. They named the new colony in
honor of the king and planned it to be a refuge for Britain's poor. Envisioning
a society of small farms worked by independent landowners and white indentured servants, the trustees of Georgia limited most land grants to 500 acres
and, unlike other British colonies, initially outlawed slavery.

Walpole arranged for Parliament to subsidize Georgia because he wanted
to protect the valuable rice colony of South Carolina from Spanish Florida.
Spain had long resented the British presence in Carolina and was outraged by
the expansion into Georgia, where Spanish Franciscans had Indian missions.
In addition, English merchants had steadily increased their trade in slaves and
manufactured goods to Spain's colonies in Mesoamerica, eventually controlling two-thirds of that trade, and Spanish officials wanted to resist this often illegal commercial imperialism. In 1739 Spanish naval forces sparked the
so-called War of Jenkins' Ear by mutilating Robert Jenkins, an English sea captain who was trading illegally with the Spanish West Indies.

Walpole jumped on this provocation to begin the first significant military conflict in America in a generation. In 1740 British regulars commanded by Governor Oglethorpe, together with provincial troops from South Carolina and Georgia and some Indian allies, launched an unsuccessful expedition against St. Augustine, which was defended by Spanish soldiers and escaped African slaves. Later that year the governors of the other mainland colonies raised 2,500 volunteers, who joined a British naval force in an assault on the Spanish seaport of Cartagena (in present-day Colombia). The attack failed, and instead of enriching themselves with Spanish booty, hundreds of colonial troops died of tropical diseases.

The War of Jenkins' Ear became part of a general European conflict, the War of the Austrian Succession. The British and French navies clashed in the West Indies, but initially there was little fighting along the long frontier between the Anglo-American colonies and French Canada. Then, in 1745, more than 3,000 New England militiamen, supported by a British naval squadron, captured the powerful French naval fortress of Louisbourg, which protected the entrance into the St. Lawrence River. The Treaty of Aix-la-Chapelle (1748) returned Louisbourg to France, but the war secured the territorial integrity of Georgia by reaffirming British military superiority in that region.

An unexpected threat to British economic ascendancy in North America was American competition, which British officials were determined to eliminate. According to the mercantilist Navigation Acts, colonies could produce only agricultural goods and raw materials; the more profitable manufacturing of goods and the provision of commercial services were reserved for the home country. In 1699 Parliament had prohibited Americans from marketing colonial-made textiles; in 1732 the ban was extended to the sale of hats, and in 1750 to iron products such as plows, axes, and skillets.

However, the Navigation Acts had a major loophole because they allowed Americans to own ships and transport goods. Colonial merchants exploited those provisions, securing 95 percent of the commerce between the mainland and the West Indies and 75 percent of the trade in manufactures shipped from London and Bristol. Quite unexpectedly, British mercantilism had created a dynamic and wealthy community of colonial merchants.

The flour, fish, and meat produced by the rapidly growing mainland colonies raised another set of problems for the British authorities. By the 1720s the British sugar islands could not absorb these goods, and so colonial merchants sold them in the French West Indies. These supplies helped French planters produce low-cost sugar, undercutting British sales in Europe. When American rum distillers began to prefer cheap French molasses to the British product, planters petitioned Parliament for help. The resulting Molasses Act of 1733 permitted the mainland colonies to export fish and farm products to the French islands but, to enhance the competitiveness of British molasses, placed a high tariff on French molasses. American merchants and public officials protested that the act would cut farm exports and cripple their distilling industry, making it more difficult for colonists to purchase British goods. When

Parliament ignored their petitions, American merchants continued importing French molasses and bribed customs officials to ignore the new tax. Luckily, sugar prices rose in the mid-1730s, and the act was not enforced.

The lack of adequate currency in the colonies led to another confrontation. American merchants sent most of the specie and bills of exchange they earned in the West Indian trade to Britain to pay for manufactured goods, draining the domestic money supply. To remedy this problem, the assemblies of ten colonies established land banks which lent paper money to farmers, taking their land as collateral. Farmers used the paper money to buy tools or livestock or to pay their creditors, thereby stimulating trade. But some assemblies, such as that of Rhode Island, issued large amounts of currency, causing it to fall in value, and required merchants to accept it. Creditors, especially English merchants, rightly complained that they were being forced to accept worthless currency. In 1751 Parliament passed a Currency Act that prevented all the New England colonies from establishing new land banks and prohibited the use of public currency to pay private debts.

These economic conflicts angered a new generation of British political leaders, who believed that the colonies already had too much autonomy. In 1749 Charles Townshend of the Board of Trade charged that American assemblies had assumed many of the "ancient and established prerogatives wisely preserved in the Crown." Townshend and other officials were determined to replace salutary neglect with a more rigorous system of imperial control.

CHAPTER 3 TIMELINE

1651	First Navigation Act
1660	Restoration of Charles II
1660s	Barbados becomes sugar island Virginia moves toward slave system New Navigation Acts
1664	New Netherland captured; becomes New York
1669	Fundamental Constitutions of Carolina
1681	William Penn founds Pennsylvania
1686–1689	Dominion of New England
1688–1689	Glorious Revolution in England and rebellions in Massachusetts, Maryland, and New York
1696	Board of Trade created
1705	Virginia statute defines slavery
1714–1750	British policy of "salutary neglect" Rise of American assemblies
1718	Spanish missions and garrison in Texas
1720–1742	Sir Robert Walpole chief minister
1720–1750	Dahomey becomes "slaving" state Black natural increase in Chesapeake Rice exports from Carolina soar Africans in Carolina create Gullah language Planter aristocracy in southern colonies Expansion of seaport cities on mainland
1732–1733	Georgia colony chartered Molasses Act
1739	Stono rebellion War of Jenkins' Ear
1750	Iron Act
1751	Currency Act

CHAPTER 4

GROWTH AND CRISIS IN AMERICAN SOCIETY, 1720–1765

- Freehold Society in New England
- The Mid-Atlantic: Toward a New Society, 1720–1765
- The Enlightenment and the Great Awakening, 1740–1765
- The Midcentury Challenge: War, Trade, and Land, 1750–1765

By 1720 Britain's North American settlements were well established. The early dangers were past. The Indians in coastal areas had been expelled or pacified and the colonists produced enough food to feed themselves and send a surplus to markets in Europe and the West Indies. Steady immigration, the slave trade, and natural increase had brought the population to 400,000.

During the next 45 years, natural increase more than doubled the population of New England, while the mid-Atlantic colonies, with their promise of freehold land, political liberties, and religious tolerance, drew hundreds of thousands of new migrants from Europe. In addition, tens of thousands of enslaved Africans were imported into the southern settlements. By 1765 the mainland population had grown fivefold, to almost 2 million people.

As the new arrivals and the landless younger children of long-settled families moved west in search of opportunities, they fought with each other and reignited conflict with native peoples and with the other European powers contesting for dominance of North America, France and Spain.

FREEHOLD SOCIETY IN NEW ENGLAND

In the 1630s the Puritans had migrated from a country where a handful of nobles and gentry owned 75 percent of the arable land and farmed it by using servants, leaseholding tenants, and wage laborers. In their new home they had created a long-lived yeoman society in which farm families owned 70 percent of the land as *freeholders*—without feudal dues or leases.

Farm Families: Women's Place

The Puritans' egalitarianism did not extend to the family, which by law and custom remained a patriarchy. Men claimed power in the state and authority in the family. The Reverend Benjamin Wadsworth of Boston advised women in his pamphlet *The Well-Ordered Family* (1712) that being richer, more intelligent, or of higher social status than their husbands mattered little: "Since he is thy Husband, God has made him the head and set him above thee." Their duty, Wadsworth concluded, was "to love and reverence him."

Throughout their lives women saw at firsthand that their role was a subordinate one. Small girls watched their mothers defer to their fathers. As young adults they learned that their marriage portions were inferior in kind and size to those of their brothers; daughters received not land but money, livestock, or household goods. Ebenezer Chittendon of Guilford, Connecticut, for example, left all his land to his sons, decreeing that "Each Daughter have half so much as Each Son, one half in money and the other half in Cattle."

Throughout New England women were raised to be dutiful helpmeets (helpmates) to their husbands. Farmwives spun thread and yarn from flax or wool and wove it into shirts and gowns. They knitted sweaters and stockings, made candles and soap, churned milk into butter and pressed curds into cheese, brewed malt into beer, preserved meats, and mastered dozens of other household tasks. The most exemplary or "notable" practitioners of these domestic arts won praise from the community, for their labor was crucial to the rural household economy.

Reproduction—being a mother—was no less central a task. Most women married in their early twenties; by their early forties they had given birth to six or seven children, usually delivered with the aid of midwives. A large family sapped a woman's emotional strength, focusing her energies on domestic activities for about twenty of her most active years. A Massachusetts mother explained that she had no time for religious activities because "the care of my Babes takes up so large a portion of my time and attention."

In long-settled communities a gradual reduction in farm size prompted many couples to have fewer children. After 1750 women in Andover, Massachusetts, bore an average of only four children and thus gained the time and energy to pursue other tasks. Farm women made extra yarn, cloth, or cheese to exchange with neighbors or sell to shopkeepers, enhancing their families' standard of living. Or, like Susan Huntington of Boston (who had the good fortune to be rich), they spent more time in "the care & culture of children, and the perusal of necessary books, including the scriptures."

Yet women's lives remained tightly bound by a web of legal and cultural restrictions. While ministers often praised the piety of the women in their

Tavern Culture
By the eighteenth century many taverns were run by women, such as this "Charming Patroness," who needed all her charm to deal with the raucous clientele. It was in taverns, declared the puritanical John Adams, that "diseases, vicious habits, bastards, and legislators are frequently begotten."

congregations, they excluded them from church governance. Thus, after Hannah Heaton questioned the authority of her Congregationalist minister, thinking him unconverted and a "blind guide," she quit her husband's church and sought out one of the few sects (mostly Quaker or Baptist) that welcomed questioning women and allowed them to become spiritual leaders. But Heaton was an exception. Most women in New England remained constrained by the conventional view that, as Timothy Dwight put it, women should be "employed only in and about the house and in the proper business of the sex."

Farm Property: Inheritance

As the base of early American economic life, land was much prized. "The hope of having land of their own & becoming independent of Landlords is what chiefly induces people into America," an official reported in the 1730s. But acquiring a farmstead was only the first step toward independence, because most migrating Europeans also wanted to provide for the next generation. Parents who were propertyless or poor indentured their sons and daughters to more prosperous households, where they would have enough to eat and could learn the ways of the world. When the indentures ended at age eighteen or twenty-one, the more ambitious young men would begin the slow ten- to twenty-year climb up the agricultural ladder, from servant to laborer to tenant and finally to freeholder. Luckier sons and daughters in successful farm families received a marriage portion when they reached marriageable age—usually twenty-three to twenty-five.

The *marriage portion*—land, livestock, or farm equipment—served several purposes, both repaying children for their labor and ensuring their loyalty during their parents' old age. It also allowed parents to choose their children's partners, which they did not hesitate to do because everyone's future prosperity depended on a wise choice. Normally, children had the right to refuse an unacceptable match, but they did not have the luxury of "falling in love" with whomever they pleased.

Marriage under English common law was hardly a contract between equals. A bride relinquished to her husband the legal ownership of her land and personal property. After her husband's death, she received the right to use (but not to sell) a third of the family's estate. Death or remarriage canceled this use-right, and her portion was divided among the children. In this way the widow's property rights were subordinated to those of the family "line," which stretched, through the children, across the generations.

To preserve the ideal of a freehold society based on family property, some fathers willed the farm to a male child, specifying that it remain undivided and in the family forever. These fathers provided their other children with money, apprenticeship contracts, or frontier tracts with which to become freeholders in other communities. Other parents required the oldest son to pay money or goods to the younger children in return for the family farm. Finally, some yeomen moved to frontier regions, where life was hard but land for the children was cheap and abundant. "The Squire's House stands on the Bank of the Susquehannah," the traveler Philip Fithian reported from the Pennsylvania backcountry. "He tells me that he will be able to settle all his sons and his fair Daughter Betsy on the Fat of the Earth."

The historic accomplishment of these farmers was the creation of whole communities composed of independent property owners. A French visitor remarked on the sense of personal worth and dignity in this rural world, which contrasted sharply with European peasant life. Throughout the northern colonies, he wrote, he had found "men and women whose features are not marked by poverty, by lifelong deprivation of the necessities of life, or by a feeling that they are insignificant subjects and subservient members of society."

The Crisis of Freehold Society

With each generation the population of New England doubled, mostly as a result of natural increase. The Puritan colonies had about 100,000 people in 1700, 200,000 in 1725, and almost 400,000 in 1750. In long-settled areas farms had been divided and subdivided, leaving parents in a quandary. In the 1740s the Reverend Samuel Chandler of Andover, Massachusetts, was "much distressed for land for his children," seven of whom were boys. By the 1750s in the neighboring town of Concord, about 60 percent of farmers owned less land than their fathers had.

Because parents had less to give their children, they had less control over their lives. The system of arranged marriages broke down as young people engaged in premarital sex and then used pregnancy to win their fathers' permission to marry. Throughout New England the number of firstborn children conceived before marriage rose spectacularly, from about 10 percent in the 1710s to 30 percent or more in the 1740s. Given another chance, young people "would do the same again," an Anglican minister observed, "because otherwise they could not obtain their parents' consent to marry."

New England families met the threat to the freeholder ideal through a variety of strategies. Many parents chose to have smaller families by using primitive methods of birth control. Others joined with neighbors to petition the provincial government for new land grants. As they moved inland—eventually into New Hampshire and the future Vermont—they hacked new communities out of the forest. Still others used their small plots in established communities more productively, replacing the traditional English crops of wheat and barley with high-yielding potatoes and Indian corn. Corn offered a hearty food for humans, and its leaves furnished feed for cattle and pigs, which in turn provided milk and meat. In time New England developed a livestock economy, becoming the major supplier of salted and pickled meat to the West Indies. By 1770 preserved meat accounted for about 5 percent of the value of all exports from the mainland colonies.

Finally, New England farmers compensated for their smaller plots by exchanging goods and labor, developing the full potential of what one historian has called the "household mode of production." Men lent each other tools, draft animals, and grazing land. Women and children joined other families in spinning yarn, sewing quilts, and shucking corn. Farmers plowed fields owned by artisans and shopkeepers, who repaid them with shoes, furniture, or store credit. Typically, no money changed hands; instead, farmers, artisans, and shopkeepers recorded their debts and credits in personal account books and every few years "balanced" the books by transferring small amounts of cash. The system allowed households—and the entire economy—to achieve maximum output, preserving the freehold ideal.

THE MID-ATLANTIC: TOWARD A NEW SOCIETY, 1720–1765

Unlike New England, which was settled mostly by English Puritans, the mid-Atlantic colonies of New York, New Jersey, and Pennsylvania became home to peoples of differing origins, languages, and religions. Strong ethnic and linguistic ties bound German settlers to one another, as did deep sectarian loyalties among Scots-Irish Presbyterians, English and Welsh Quakers, German Lutherans, and Dutch Reformed Protestants.

Opportunity and Equality

Ample fertile land and a long growing season attracted migrants to the mid-Atlantic, and profits from wheat financed its settlement. Between 1720 and 1770 wheat prices doubled because of a population explosion in Western Europe. By 1770 the value of the wheat, corn, flour, and bread shipped from the middle colonies to Europe and the West Indies amounted to over 15 percent of all mainland exports. This prosperity helped the combined population of New York, New Jersey, and Pennsylvania surge from 50,000 in 1700 to 120,000 in 1720 and 350,000 in 1765.

As the population rose, so did the demand for land. Nonetheless, many migrants refused to settle in New York's Hudson River Valley, which, unlike the predominantly freehold colonies of Pennsylvania, New Jersey, and New England, was inhabited primarily by tenant farmers. There, long-established Dutch families presided over manors created by the Dutch West India Company and wealthy English families, such as the Morris and Heathcote clans, dominated vast tracts granted by early English governors (see Map. 4.1). These propertied families sought to live like European gentry, but few migrants were interested in becoming their tenants. In 1714 only 82 tenants lived on the vast manor of Rensselaerswyck. But as freehold land became scarce in eastern New York, more families were forced to accept tenancy leases. Manorial lords attracted tenants by granting them long leases and the right to sell any improvements they made to the next tenant. Thus, Rensselaerswyck had 345 tenants in 1752 and nearly 700 by 1765.

Most tenant families hoped that with hard work and luck they could acquire freehold farmsteads. But though these grain-growing farmers prospered, they rarely became rich because preindustrial technology limited their output. One worker with a hand sickle could reap only half an acre a day; any ripe uncut grain promptly sprouted and became useless. The cradle scythe, an agricultural tool introduced during the 1750s, doubled or tripled the amount of grain a worker could cut. Even so, a family with two adult workers could not harvest more than about 15 acres of wheat in a growing season, a yield of perhaps 150 to 180 bushels of grain. After family needs were met, the remaining surplus might be worth £15—enough to buy salt and sugar, tools, cloth, and perhaps a few acres of land.

Unlike New York, rural Pennsylvania was initially a land of equality. In Chester County the original migrants arrived with approximately equal resources. They lived simply in small houses with one or two rooms, a sleeping loft, a few benches or stools, some wooden trenchers (platters), and a few wooden noggins (cups). Only the wealthiest families ate off pewter or ceramic plates imported from England or Holland. The rise of the wheat trade and an influx of poor settlers introduced marked social divisions. By the 1760s some Chester County farmers had grown wealthy by hiring propertyless laborers to raise large quantities of wheat for market sale. Others had become successful entrepreneurs, providing newly arrived settlers with land, equipment, goods, and services. Gradually a new class of wealthy agricultural capitalists—large-scale

MAP 4.1

The Hudson River Manors
Dutch and English manorial lords
dominated the fertile eastern
shores of the Hudson River Valley, leasing small farms to German
tenant families and refusing to sell
land to migrants from overcrowded New England. This
powerful elite produced leading
American families, such as the
Roosevelts.

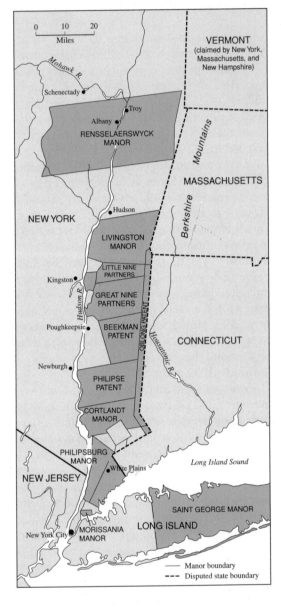

farmers, rural landlords, speculators, storekeepers, and gristmill operators—accumulated estates that included mahogany tables, four-poster beds, couches, table
linen, and imported Dutch dinnerware.

At the bottom of the social order nearly half of all white men were propertyless. Some landless men, the sons of property owners, would eventually in-
herit at least part of the family estate, but just as many were Scots-Irish
inmates—single men or families "such as live in small cottages and have no

taxable property, except a cow." In the predominantly German settlement of Lancaster, Pennsylvania, a merchant noted an "abundance of Poor people" who "maintain their Families with great difficulty by day Labour." Although Scots-Irish and German migrants hoped to become tenants and eventually landowners, a sharp rise in land prices prevented many from realizing their dreams.

Merchants and artisans took advantage of the ample supply of labor by organizing a putting-out system. They bought wool or flax from large-scale producers and paid propertyless workers and subsistence farmers to spin it into yarn or weave it into cloth. An English traveler reported in the 1760s that hundreds of Pennsylvanians had turned "to manufacture, and live upon a small farm, as in many parts of England." Indeed, in many places the colonies had become as crowded and socially divided as rural England (see American Voices, p. 94), and many farm families feared—with good reason—a return to the lowly status of the European peasant.

Ethnic Diversity

The middle colonies were not a melting pot in which European cultures blended into a homogeneous "American" outlook; they were a patchwork of ethnically and religiously diverse communities. A traveler in Philadelphia in 1748 found no fewer than twelve religious denominations, including Anglicans, Quakers, Swedish and German Lutherans, Scots-Irish Presbyterians, and even Roman Catholics. Large communities of German sectarians, such as the Moravians in Bethlehem and Nazareth, Pennsylvania, added to this diversity.

Migrants usually kept their ethnic identities, often by marrying within their own groups or maintaining the customs of their native lands. The major exception were the Huguenots, Calvinists expelled from France who settled in New York and various seacoast cities; they gradually lost their French ethnic identity by intermarrying with other Protestants. More typical were the Welsh Quakers. Seventy percent of the children of the original Welsh migrants to Chester County, Pennsylvania, married other Welsh Quakers, as did 60 percent of the third generation.

Members of the Society of Friends (Quakers) became the dominant social group in Pennsylvania, at first because of their numbers and later, despite a huge influx of new migrants after 1720, because of their wealth and influence. Quakers controlled Pennsylvania's representative assembly until the 1750s and exercised considerable power in New Jersey. Pacifists, they avoided war with native Americans. In 1682 William Penn negotiated a treaty with the Delaware Indians; later the Pennsylvania government purchased land from the Indians rather than seizing it by force. These conciliatory policies enabled Pennsylvania to avoid a major Indian war until the 1750s, unlike the other British colonies. Some Quakers extended their egalitarian values to their relations with blacks. After 1750 most Quaker meetings condemned the institution of slavery, and some expelled members who continued to keep slaves.

The Distress of an Indentured Servant

Between 1720 and 1775 thousands of poor Europeans came to the mainland colonies as indentured servants and were sold to the highest bidder. "They sell the servants here as they do their horses, and advertise them as they do their beef and oatmeal," wrote an astonished British officer. James Revel, a servant sold to a planter in the Virginia backcountry, described his ordeal in verse.

Some view'd our limbs, and other's turn'd us round,
Examining like Horses, if we're sound,
What trade are you, my Lad, says one to me,
A Tin-man, Sir, that will not do, says he.
    Some felt our hands and view'd our legs and feet,
And made us walk, to see we were compleat; . . .
    If any like our look, our limbs, our trade,
The Captain then a good advantage made. . . .

Down to the harbour I was took again,
    On board of a sloop, and loaded with a chain;
Which I was forc'd to wear both night and day,
For fear I from the sloop should get away. . . .
    And when the sloop with loading home was sent
An hundred mile we up the river went
The weather cold and very hard my fare,
My lodging on the deck both hard and bare,
    At last to my new master's house I came,
At the town of Wicoccomoco call'd by name,
Where my Europian clothes were took from me,
Which never after I again could see.
    A canvas shirt and trowsers then they gave,
With a hop-sack frock in which I was to slave:
No shoes nor stocking had I for to wear,
Nor hat, nor cap, both head and feet were bare.
    Thus dress'd into the Field I must next go,
Amongst tobacco plants all day to hoe,
At day break in the morn our work begun,
And so held to the setting of the Sun.

SOURCE: Bernard Bailyn, *Voyagers to the West* (New York: Knopf, 1986), pp. 327, 348.

The Quaker vision of a "peaceable kingdom" attracted many Europeans seeking freedom and opportunity, including Germans who fled from war, religious persecution, and poverty in their homeland. First to arrive, in 1683, was a group of Mennonites attracted by a pamphlet promising religious freedom. In the 1720s religious upheaval and population growth in southwestern Germany and Switzerland stimulated a wave of migrants. "Wages were far better," Heinrich Schneebeli reported to his friends in Zurich after an exploratory trip to Pennsylvania, and "one also enjoyed there a free unhindered exercise of religion." Beginning in 1749, thousands of Germans and Swiss fled their overcrowded and war-torn societies; by 1756, 37,000 of these migrants had landed in Philadelphia.

German settlements soon dominated certain areas of Pennsylvania, while other groups moved down the Shenandoah Valley into the western parts of Maryland, Virginia, and the Carolinas. Some Germans and Swiss came to America as *redemptioners*—a type of indentured servant—but many more came with some resources, determined to improve the lives of their children.

Most German migrants were content to live in a British-defined political community, for few came from the governing classes and many rejected political activism on religious grounds. They slid easily into the status of loyal subjects of the German-born (and German-speaking) king of England, engaging in politics only to protect their religious liberty and property

A Quaker Meeting for Worship
Quakers met for worship in plain, unadorned buildings and sat in silence, waiting for inspiration by the "inner light." In this British work, entitled *Quaker Meeting*, an elder (his hat hung on a peg above his head) speaks to the congregation. Women spoke frequently, an experience that prepared Quaker women to play a leading role in the nineteenth-century women's rights movement. (Museum of Fine Arts, Boston)

rights—insisting, for example, that as in Germany, married women should have property rights. Moreover, they guarded their language and cultural heritage carefully, encouraging their American-born children to take marriage partners of their own ancestry. A minister in North Carolina admonished his congregation "not to contract any marriages with the English or Irish," explaining that "we owe it to our native country to do our part that German blood and the German language be preserved in America." Thus, these migrants and their descendants spoke to each other and read newspapers in German, conducted church services in German, and preserved German agricultural practices. English visitors to the middle colonies remarked that German women were "always in the fields, meadows, stables, etc. and do not dislike any work whatsoever."

The Scots-Irish formed the largest group of eighteenth-century migrants from Europe, some 150,000 in number. They were the descendants of Presbyterian Scots who around 1650 had been sent to Ireland to bolster English control of its Catholic population. Once in Ireland, however, the Scots had faced discrimination and economic regulation by the English. The Test Act of 1704 excluded Scottish Presbyterians as well as Irish Catholics from holding public office in Ireland. English mercantilist regulations placed heavy import duties on the woolen goods Scots-Irish weavers produced, and Scots-Irish farmers were heavily taxed. "Read this letter, Rev. Baptist Boyd," a New York settler wrote back to his minister, "and tell all the poor folk of ye place that God has opened a door for their deliverance . . . all that a man works for is his own; there are no revenue hounds [tax collectors] to take it from us here." Lured by such reports, after 1720 thousands of Scots-Irish sailed for Philadelphia and then migrated to central Pennsylvania and southward down the Shenandoah Valley into Maryland and Virginia. Like the Germans, the Scots-Irish were determined to keep their culture. They held to their Presbyterian faith and promoted marriage within the church.

A Pluralistic Society

In Western Europe religious pluralism was condemned, and even in America most ministers remained committed to an established church and government enforcement of religious rules. Throughout Pennsylvania "the preachers do not have the power to punish anyone, or to force anyone to go to church," complained the minister Gottlieb Mittelberger. As a result, "Sunday is very badly kept. Many people plough, reap, thresh, hew or split wood and the like." Thus, Mittelberger concluded, "Liberty in Pennsylvania does more harm than good to many people, both in soul and body."

However, religious sects in Pennsylvania enforced moral behavior among their members through communal self-discipline. For example, each Quaker family attended a weekly worship meeting and a monthly discipline meeting. Four times a year a committee met with each family to make certain the children were receiving proper religious instruction. The committee also reported on the moral behavior of adults; a Chester County meeting disciplined one of its members "to reclaim him from drinking to excess and keeping vain company." Permission to marry was granted only to couples with sufficient land, livestock, and equipment to support themselves and their future children. The children of well-to-do Friends received ample marriage portions and usually married within the sect, while those who lacked resources remained unmarried or married non-Quakers. In Chester County about two-thirds of the young men and women who married outside the faith were barred from Quaker meetings. Thus, communal sanctions effectively sustained a self-contained and prosperous Quaker community.

In the 1750s Quaker dominance in Pennsylvania finally came under attack. Scots-Irish Presbyterians on the frontier challenged the pacifism of the Quaker-dominated assembly, demanding a more aggressive Indian policy. Many of the newer German migrants also opposed the Quakers; they wanted laws that respected their inheritance customs and representation in proportion to their numbers in the provincial assembly. As an observer noted, Scots-Irish Presbyterians, German Baptists, and German Lutherans had begun to form "a general confederacy" against the Quakers; but they found it difficult to unite because of "a mutual jealousy, for religious zeal is secretly burning."

During the 1760s and again during the War for Independence, latent religious and ethnic passions would break out, yet the mid-Atlantic experiment in freedom and diversity would survive. In the centuries to come cultural pluralism, an open political order, and passionate ethnic and social conflicts would characterize much of American society.

THE ENLIGHTENMENT AND THE GREAT AWAKENING, 1740–1765

Two great European cultural movements reached America between the 1730s and the 1760s: the Enlightenment and Pietism. The *Enlightenment*, which emphasized the power of human reason to shape the world, appealed especially to better-educated men and women from merchant or planter families and to urban artisans. *Pietism*, an emotional, evangelical religious movement that stressed a Christian's relation to God, attracted many social groups, especially farmers and urban laborers. The two movements promoted independent thinking in different ways; together they transformed American intellectual and cultural life.

The Enlightenment in America

Most early Americans relied on religious precepts or folk wisdom to explain the workings of the natural world. Thus, Swedish settlers in Pennsylvania attributed magical powers to the great white mullein, a common wildflower.

When they had a fever, a traveler reported, they would "tie the leaves around their feet and arms." Even educated people believed that events occurred for reasons that today would be considered magical. When a measles epidemic struck Boston in the 1710s, the Puritan minister Cotton Mather tried to contain it by "getting the Blood of the Great Passover sprinkled on our Houses." Like most Christians, Mather believed that the earth stood at the center of the universe and that God intervened directly in human affairs.

Early Americans held to these beliefs despite the Scientific Revolution, which had challenged both traditional Christian and folk world views. As early as the 1530s the astronomer Copernicus had observed that the earth traveled around the sun, rather than vice versa, implying a more modest place for humans in the universe. Other scholars had conducted experiments using empirical methods—actual observed experience—to learn about natural phenomena. Eventually the English scientist Isaac Newton, in his *Principia Mathematica* (1687), used mathematics to explain the movement of the planets around the sun. Newton's laws of motion and concept of gravity described how the universe could operate without God's constant intervention, undermining traditional Christian explanations of the cosmos.

In the century between the publication of Newton's book and the outbreak of the French Revolution in 1789, the philosophers of the European Enlightenment applied scientific reasoning to all aspects of life, including social institutions and human behavior. Enlightenment thinkers believed that human beings could observe, analyze, understand, and improve their world. They advanced four fundamental principles: the lawlike order of the natural world, the power of human reason, the natural rights of individuals (including the right to self-government), and the progressive improvement of society.

In his *Essay Concerning Human Understanding* (1690), John Locke emphasized the impact of environment, experience, and reason on human behavior, proposing that the character of individuals and societies was not fixed by God's will but could be changed through education and purposeful action. His *Two Treatises on Government* (1690) advanced a revolutionary theory: political authority was not divinely ordained but sprang from "*social compacts*" people made to preserve their "natural rights" to life, liberty, and property. In Locke's view, not princes but people conferred political legitimacy, so that governments might change through the decision of a majority.

The Enlightenment ideas of Locke and others came to America with books and travelers and quickly affected educated colonists' conceptions of religion, science, and politics. As early as the 1710s the Reverend John Wise of Ipswich, Massachusetts, combined Locke's political principles with Calvinist theology to defend the decision of Congregational churches to vest power in lay members. Wise argued that just as the "social compact" formed the basis of political society, the religious covenant made the congregation—not bishops or monarchs, as in the Church of England—the interpreter of spiritual authority. When a smallpox epidemic threatened Boston in the 1720s, Cotton Mather sought a scientific rather than a religious remedy, joining with a prominent Boston physician to support the new technique of inoculation.

Enlightenment Philanthropy: The Philadelphia Hospital
This imposing structure, built in 1753, embodied two Enlightenment principles: purposeful action could improve society, and the world should express reason and order, exhibited here in the symmetrical facade. Etchings such as this one, *A Southeast Prospect of the Pennsylvania Hospital,* c. 1761, by John Streeper and Henry Dawkins, bolstered Philadelphia's reputation as the center of the American Enlightenment.

The epitome of the Enlightenment in America was Benjamin Franklin. Born in Boston in 1706 to a devout Calvinist family and apprenticed to a printer as a youth, Franklin became a self-made, self-taught man. As a tradesman, printer, and journalist in Philadelphia, he formed "a club of mutual improvement" which met weekly to discuss "Morals, Politics, or Natural Philosophy." Franklin's imagination was shaped by Enlightenment literature, not by the Bible. In fact, as he explained in his *Autobiography,* "from the different books I read, I began to doubt of Revelation itself."

Like many urban artisans, wealthy Virginia planters, and affluent seaport merchants, Franklin became a *deist.* Influenced by Enlightenment science, deists believed that God had created the world but allowed it to operate in accordance with the laws of nature. The deists' God was a rational being, a divine "watchmaker" who did not intervene directly in history or in people's lives. Rejecting the authority of the Bible, deists relied on people's "natural reason" to define a moral code. Adherence to the code, they believed, would be rewarded by God after death.

Franklin popularized the practical outlook of the Enlightenment—in *Poor Richard's Almanac,* which was read by thousands—and contributed to it himself. In 1743 he helped found the American Philosophical Society, an institution devoted to "the promotion of useful knowledge"; he invented bifocal lenses for eyeglasses, an improved stove (the Franklin stove), and the lightning rod. Franklin's book on electricity, first published in England in 1751, was praised by the English scientist Joseph Priestley as the greatest contribution to science since Newton.

Franklin's city, Philadelphia, became the showplace of the American Enlightenment, boasting a circulating library filled with the latest scientific treatises from Europe and the first American medical school (1765). Quaker and Anglican merchants built a Hospital for the Sick Poor in 1751 and in 1767 added a Bettering House to shelter the aged and disabled and offer employment to the poor. In Philadelphia and other American cities ambitious printers published newspapers and gentleman's magazines, the first significant nonreligious publications to appear in the colonies. Thus, the European Enlightenment added a secular dimension to colonial intellectual life, preparing the way for American contributions to republican political theory during the Revolutionary Era.

Pietism in America

As a few Americans—mostly urban artisans and merchants and wealthy Virginia planters—turned to deism, many other Americans embraced the European devotional movement known as Pietism. Forsaking theological arguments, Pietists emphasized devout, or "pious," behavior, emotional church services, and striving for a mystical union with God. Their teachings came to America with German migrants in the 1720s and sparked a religious revival among many farmers, artisans, and laborers. In Pennsylvania and New Jersey the Dutch minister Theodore Jacob Frelinghuysen moved from church to church, preaching rousing, emotional sermons to German settlers. In private prayer meetings he harnessed their enthusiasm and encouraged lay members to preach a message of spiritual urgency to growing congregations. A decade later William Tennent and his son Gilbert, Presbyterian clergymen who copied Frelinghuysen's approach, led revivals among Scots-Irish migrants in the same area.

Simultaneously, an American pietistic movement was born in Puritan New England. Puritanism had begun in England during the 1580s as part of an earlier pietistic upsurge, but over the decades many Puritan congregations had lost their religious zeal. In the 1730s the minister Jonathan Edwards sought to restore spiritual commitment to the Congregational churches in the Connecticut River Valley. A philosopher as well as an effective preacher, Edwards urged his hearers—especially young men and women—to commit themselves to a life of piety and prayer.

George Whitefield, a young English evangelist, transformed the local revivals into a "Great Awakening" that spanned the mainland settlements. Whitefield had experienced conversion after reading German pietistic tracts and was influenced by John Wesley, the founder of English Methodism, who combined enthusiastic preaching with disciplined "methods" of worship. Whitefield carried Wesley's style to America and enjoyed equally great success, preaching throughout the mainland colonies from 1739 to 1741.

From Georgia to Massachusetts huge crowds of "enthusiasts" greeted the young preacher. "Religion is become the Subject of most Conversations," the *Pennsylvania Gazette* reported. "No books are in Request but those of Piety and Devotion." The usually skeptical and restrained Benjamin Franklin was so impressed by Whitefield's oratory that when the preacher asked for contributions, Franklin emptied his pockets "wholly into the collector's dish, gold and all." By the time the evangelist reached Boston, the Reverend Benjamin Colman reported, the people were "ready to receive him as an angel of God."

Whitefield owed his appeal partly to his compelling personal presence. "He looked almost Angelical; a young, slim, slender Youth . . . Cloathed with Authority from the Great God," wrote a Connecticut farmer (see American Voices, page 102). Like most evangelical preachers, Whitefield did not read his sermons but spoke from memory, as if inspired, raising his voice for dramatic effect, gesturing eloquently, and making striking use of biblical metaphors. The young preacher evoked a deep emotional response when he impressed on his listeners that they had all sinned and must seek salvation. Hundreds of men and women suddenly felt the "new light" of God's grace within them. Afterward, strengthened and self-confident, these New Lights were prepared to follow in Whitefield's footsteps.

Religious Upheaval in the North

Like all cultural explosions, the pietistic revival was controversial. Conservative ministers such as Charles Chauncy of Boston condemned (and feared) the "cryings out, faintings and convulsions" produced by emotional preaching. These "Old Lights" persuaded the Connecticut legislative assembly to prohibit traveling preachers from speaking to established congregations without the ministers' permission. When Whitefield returned to Connecticut in 1744, he found many pulpits closed to him. But the New Lights won repeal of the law in 1750, resisting attempts by civil authorities to silence them. "I shall bring glory to God in my bonds," a dissident preacher wrote from jail. Dozens of farmers, women, and artisans roamed the countryside, condemning the Old Lights as "unconverted" sinners.

During the Great Awakening both New Lights and Baptists questioned government involvement in religion. In New England many New Lights left the established Congregational Church; by 1754 they had founded 125 "separatist" churches. Other dissidents joined Baptist congregations, which favored a greater separation of church and state. According to the Baptist preacher Isaac Backus, "God never allowed any civil state upon earth to impose religious taxes." In New York and New Jersey the Dutch Reformed Church split in two, as New Lights resisted conservative church authorities in the Netherlands.

The Awakening also challenged the authority of ministers, whose education and biblical knowledge had once commanded respect. Gilbert Tennent questioned those qualifications in an influential pamphlet, *The Dangers of an Unconverted Ministry*, maintaining that not theological training but conversion

AMERICAN VOICES

The Power of a Preacher

George Whitefield's reputation as an inspired preacher drew thousands to his sermons, including Nathan Cole and his wife, a Connecticut farm couple.

Now it please God to Send Mr. Whitefield into this land; and my hearing of his preaching at Philadelphia, like one of the old apostles . . . I felt the Spirit of God drawing me by conviction; I longed to see and hear him and wished he would come this way. . . . Then of a sudden, in the morning about 8 or 9 of the clock there came a messenger and said Mr. Whitefield . . . is to preach at Middletown this morning at ten of the clock.

And when we came within about half a mile of the road that comes down . . . to Middletown, on high land I saw before me a cloud or fog rising . . . [and] a noise something like a low rumbling thunder and presently found it was the noise of horses' feet coming down the road, and this cloud was a cloud of dust made by the horses' feet . . . and as I drew nearer it seemed like a steady stream of horses and their riders. . . . And when we got to Middletown old meeting house there was a great multitude, it was said to be 3 or 4000 of people, assembled together. . . .

When I saw Mr. Whitefield come upon the scaffold, he looked almost Angelical; a young, slim, slender Youth before some thousands of people with a bold undaunted countenance. And my hearing how God was with him everywhere as he came, it solemnized my mind and put me into a trembling fear before he began to preach; for he looked as if he was cloathed with Authority from the Great God, and a sweet solemnity sat upon his brow, and my hearing him preach gave me a heart wound. By God's blessing my old foundation was broken up, and I saw that my righteousness would not save me.

SOURCE: Merrill Jensen, ed., *American Colonial Documents to 1776* (*English Historical Documents*, vol. 9) (New York: Oxford University Press, 1955), pp. 544–545.

qualified ministers to hold office. Reasserting Luther's commitment to the priesthood of all believers, Tennent suggested that anyone who had experienced the saving grace of God could speak with ministerial authority. Not long afterward, the Baptist Isaac Backus celebrated this spiritual democracy, noting that "the common people now claim as good a right to judge and act in matters of religion as civil rulers or the learned clergy."

By joining in religious revivals, farm families reaffirmed a cooperative work ethic and questioned economic competition and the pursuit of wealth. "In any truly Christian society," Tennent explained, "mutual *Love* is the *Band and Cement*"—not the mercenary values of the marketplace. Suspicious of merchants and land speculators and dismayed by the erosion of traditional morality, Jonathan Edwards spoke for many rural Americans when he charged that a "private niggardly spirit" was more suitable "for wolves and other beasts of prey, than for human beings."

As religious enthusiasm spread, churches founded new colleges to educate their youth and train ministers. New Light Presbyterians established the College of New Jersey (Princeton) in 1746, and New York Anglicans founded King's College (Columbia) in 1754. Baptists set up the College of Rhode Island (Brown); the Dutch Reformed Church subsidized Queen's College (Rutgers) in New Jersey. The true intellectual legacy of the Awakening, however, was not education for the few but a new sense of religious authority among the many.

Social and Religious Conflict in the South

In the southern colonies religious conflict took an intensely social form, especially in Virginia. Although the established Church of England was supported by public taxes, it had never ministered to most Virginians. African-Americans (about 40 percent of the population) were generally ignored by the church, and landless whites (another 20 percent) attended irregularly. Middling white freeholders, who accounted for about 35 percent of the population, formed the core of most Anglican congregations. But prominent planters and their families (5 percent of the population) held real power in the church and used their control of parish finances to discipline Anglican ministers. One clergyman complained that dismissal awaited any minister who "had the courage to preach against any Vices taken into favor by the leading Men of his Parish."

The Great Awakening challenged both Anglicanism and the power of elite planters. In 1743 the bricklayer Samuel Morris, inspired by his reading of George Whitefield's sermons, led a group of Virginia Anglicans out of the established church. Seeking a more vital religious experience, Morris and his followers invited New Light Presbyterian ministers from Scots-Irish settlements along the Virginia frontier to lead their prayer meetings. Soon these local revivals spread across the backcountry and into the so-called Tidewater region along the Atlantic coast, threatening the social authority of the Virginia gentry. Planters and their well-dressed families were used to arriving at Church of England services in elaborate carriages drawn by well-bred horses. Some routinely flaunted their power by marching in a body to their seats in the front pews. These potent reminders of the gentry's social superiority would vanish if freeholders attended New Light Presbyterian rather than Church of England services. Moreover, religious pluralism would threaten the gentry's ability to tax the masses to support the established church.

To prevent the spread of New Light doctrines, Virginia's governor denounced the "false teachings," and Anglican justices of the peace closed down Presbyterian meetinghouses. Their harassment kept most white yeomen families and poor tenants within the Church of England, as did the fact that most Presbyterian ministers were highly educated and sought converts mainly among skilled workers and propertied farmers.

By contrast, the evangelical Baptist preachers who came to Virginia in the 1760s drew their congregations primarily from the poor, offering solace and hope in a troubled world. Their central ritual was adult baptism, often by complete immersion in water. Once men and women had experienced the infusion of grace—had been "born again"—they were baptized in an emotional public ceremony that celebrated the Baptists' shared fellowship. During the 1760s thousands of yeomen and tenant farm families in Virginia were drawn to revivalist meetings by the enthusiasm and democratic ways of Baptist preachers.

Even slaves were welcome at Baptist revivals. As early as 1740 George Whitefield had openly condemned the brutality of slaveholders and urged that Africans be brought into the Christian fold. In South Carolina and Georgia a handful of New Light planters took up this challenge, but the hostility of the white population and the commitment of many Africans to their ancestral religions kept the number of converts low. The first sizeable conversion of slaves took place in the 1760s among second- and third-generation African-Americans in Virginia. Hundreds of those slaves, who knew English and English ways, joined Baptist churches run by ministers who taught that all people were equal in God's eyes.

The ruling gentry reacted violently to the Baptists, who posed a threat to their dominance. The Baptists courted blacks and poor whites and emphasized equality by calling one another "brother" and "sister." Baptist preachers urged their followers to work hard and lead virtuous lives and condemned customary pleasures of Chesapeake men such as gambling, drinking, whoring, and cockfighting. In response, Anglican sheriffs and justices of the peace broke up Baptist services by force. In Caroline County, Virginia, an Anglican posse attacked one Brother Waller, who was attempting to pray when, a fellow Baptist reported, "he was violently jerked off the stage; they caught him by the back part of his neck, beat his head against the ground, and a gentleman gave him twenty lashes with his horsewhip." Despite such attacks, about 20 percent of Virginia's whites and hundreds of enslaved blacks had joined Baptist churches by 1775. In the South as in the North, Protestant revivalism was on the way to becoming a dominant American religious tradition.

Although Anglican slaveholders retained their economic and political power in Virginia, the revival gave meaning to the lives of poor families. Through membership in more democratic churches, white yeomen and tenant farmers asserted their economic interests. Moreover, as Baptist ministers spread Christianity among slaves, the cultural gulf between blacks and whites shrank, undermining one justification for slavery and giving blacks a new sense of spiritual identity. Within a generation African-Americans would develop their own versions of Protestant Christianity.

THE MIDCENTURY CHALLENGE: WAR, TRADE, AND LAND, 1750–1765

In 1745 Governor Shirley of Massachusetts predicted that within a century the population of Britain's mainland colonies would equal that of France and "lay a foundation for a Superiority of British power upon the continent of Europe." In fact, this shift in the balance of diplomatic power began within two decades when the colonists joined in a Great War for Empire that undermined French influence not only in Europe but in Asia and America as well.

The French and Indian War

In 1750 the interior of North America was still inhabited by Indians, who intended to remain in control. Most French settlers lived along the St. Lawrence River, near the fur-trading centers of Montreal and Quebec (see Map 4.2). The more numerous British inhabitants had not ventured across the Appalachian Mountains, both because the lands to the west offered few natural transportation routes and because of Indian resistance. For a generation native Americans had bargained for guns and subsidies from British and French officials and firmly resisted the intrusion of white settlers. However, their strategy of playing off the French against the British was breaking down as European governments refused to pay the rising cost of the "gifts" the Indians demanded as part of the "play-off" system. Along the Ohio River the Delaware and Shawnee declared their independence from the Iroquois, creating more instability. To shore up England's alliance with the Six Nations, the Board of Trade called for a great intercolonial meeting with the Iroquois at Albany, New York, in June 1754.

A central issue was the Anglo-American demand for Indian lands, the result of population growth in New England and the South, and the huge migration of Europeans to the middle colonies. In an unsuccessful bid to settle Scottish migrants west of Albany, British agents bestowed manufactured goods on the Mohawk. To the south, Governor Dinwiddie of Virginia and a group of prominent planters organized the Ohio Company in 1749. Supported by influential London merchants, they obtained a royal grant of 200,000 acres along the upper Ohio River, with the promise of 300,000 more. These intrusions infuriated the Iroquois, who complained, "We don't know what you Christians, English and French intend; we are so hemmed in by both, that we have hardly a hunting place left."

Britain's movement into the Ohio Valley alarmed the French, who countered by constructing Fort Duquesne at the point where the Monongahela and Allegheny rivers join to form the Ohio (present-day Pittsburgh). The confrontation escalated in 1754 when Dinwiddie dispatched an expedition led by Colonel George Washington, a young planter eager to speculate in western lands, to support the claims of the Ohio Company. In July 1754 French troops seized Washington and his men, prompting expansionists in Virginia and Britain to demand war. But the British prime minister, Henry Pelham, urged calm: "There is such a load of debt, and such heavy taxes already laid upon the people, that nothing but an absolute necessity can justifie our engaging in a new War."

William Pitt, a rising British statesman, and Lord Halifax, the new head of the Board of Trade, strongly advocated a policy of expansionism in the

MAP 4.2
European Spheres of Influence, 1754
France laid claim to vast areas of North America and tried to counter the numerical superiority of British settlers through alliances with Indian peoples. For their part, native Americans
played off one European power against another. By expelling the French from North America,
the Great War for Empire disrupted this system, leaving Indian peoples on their own in resisting Anglo-American settlers.

colonies. Even before news of the fighting reached London, the Board of Trade had considered a proposal for a "union between ye Royal, Proprietary, & Charter Governments," but decided instead to dispatch a military governor-general and ask the colonial assemblies to finance a series of defensive forts. For their part, the Anglo-American delegates to the intercolonial meeting in Albany, New York, responded to the French threat by devising a Plan of Union. Primarily the work of Benjamin Franklin, the Albany Plan proposed that the colonies send delegates to a continental assembly that would assume responsibility for all western affairs: trade, Indian policy, and defense. But the proposed union, which was to be presided over by a royal governor-general, never materialized because the provincial assemblies wanted to preserve their authority and the imperial government feared the consequences of convening the great assembly.

Instead, Halifax and Pitt persuaded the ministry to dispatch naval and military forces to America, where they joined with colonial militia in attacking French forts. In June 1755 British and New England troops captured Fort Beauséjour in Nova Scotia (Acadia) and deported 6,000 Acadians, some of whom eventually settled in Louisiana. In July, as 1,400 British regulars and 450 Virginia militiamen advanced on Fort Duquesne, they were surprised by a small force of French and a larger group of Delaware and Shawnee, who had decided to side with the French. In the ensuing battle the British commander, General Edward Braddock, lost his life and half his troops. "We have been beaten, most shamefully beaten, by a handfull of Men," Washington complained bitterly as he led the survivors back to Virginia.

The Great War for Empire

In 1756 the fighting in America had spread to Europe, where the conflict later became known as the Seven Years' War. Britain and Prussia aligned themselves against France and Austria. When Britain decided to mount major offensives in India and West Africa as well as in North America and the West Indies, the conflict quickly became a Great War for Empire. Britain had reaped unprecedented profits from its overseas trading empire and was determined to crush France, the main obstacle to further expansion.

William Pitt, who was appointed Secretary of State in 1756, was the grandson of the East Indies merchant "Diamond" Pitt and a committed expansionist. Pitt was a haughty man constantly at odds with his colleagues. "I know that I can save this country," he declared, "and that I alone can." Indeed, Pitt was a master of strategy, both commercial and military, and his goal was to cripple France by attacking its colonies. In planning the critical campaign against New France, Pitt exploited a demographic advantage: on the North American mainland, Britain's 2 million subjects outnumbered the French 14 to 1. To mobilize the colonists, Pitt agreed to pay half the cost of their troops and supply them with arms and equipment. He then committed a major British fleet and thousands of British regulars to the American conflict, appointing three young officers—James Wolfe, Jeffrey Amherst, and William Howe—as the top commanders.

In 1758 the British forced the French to abandon Fort Duquesne, which they renamed Fort Pitt, and then captured Louisbourg. The following year Wolfe attacked Quebec; after several failed attacks, 4,000 British troops scaled the high cliffs protecting the city and overwhelmed the French. Quebec's fall was the turning point of the war. The Royal Navy prevented French reinforcements from crossing the Atlantic; when British forces captured Montreal in 1760, the conquest of Canada was complete.

Indian peoples from New York to Michigan grew increasingly concerned as British armies and traders occupied French forts, curtailed their "gifts" and supplies of gunpowder, and used rum to cheat them out of furs. Fearing an influx of Anglo-American settlers, the Ottawa chief Pontiac sought to restore the old French alliance, declaring, "I am French, and I want to die French." Neolin, a Delaware prophet, went further, urging a repudiation of all Europeans and a return to native American traditions. In 1763 Pontiac led a group of loosely confederated tribes in a major uprising, capturing nearly every British garrison west of Fort Niagara and besieging the fort at Detroit. But the Indian alliance gradually weakened, and British military expeditions defeated the Delaware near Fort Pitt and broke the siege of Detroit. In the peace settlement that followed, Pontiac and his allies accepted the British as their new political "fathers." In return, the British addressed the Indians' concerns by temporarily barring Anglo-Americans from settling west of the Appalachians by establishing the Proclamation Line of 1763.

Elsewhere the British went from success to success. Fulfilling Pitt's dream, the East India Company captured French commercial outposts and took control of trade in large sections of India. British forces seized French Senegal in West Africa, the French sugar islands of Martinique and Guadeloupe, and the Spanish colonies of Cuba and the Philippine Islands. When the war ended, Pitt was no longer in office, but his maritime strategy had extended British power around the world.

The Treaty of Paris of 1763 confirmed the triumph, granting Britain sovereignty over half the continent of North America, including French Canada, all French territory east of the Mississippi River, and Spanish Florida. Spain received Louisiana west of the Mississippi, along with the restoration of Cuba and the Philippines. The French empire in North America was reduced to a handful of sugar islands in the West Indies and two rocky islands off the coast of Newfoundland. The transatlantic British empire was at the height of its power.

British Economic Growth

Britain owed its triumph in large part to its unprecedented economic resources. Since 1700, when it had wrested control of many oceanic trade routes from the Dutch, Britain had been the dominant commercial power. By 1750 it was becoming the first country to undergo the Industrial Revolution. New

Pontiac
This portrait depicts Pontiac as both an Indian, symbolized by the necklace
of bear claws, and as a European-style ruler with a regal demeanor and a
flowing robe. Pontiac did indeed partake of two worlds, absorbing French
culture as he asserted his Indian identity.

technology and work discipline made Britain the first—and for over a century the most powerful—nation in the world.

New machines and new business practices were enabling Britain to produce more wool and linens, more iron tools, paper, chinaware, and glass than
ever before—and to sell those goods at lower prices. British artisans had designed and built water- and steam-driven machines that powered lathes for
shaping wood, jennies and looms for spinning and weaving textiles, and ham-
mers for forging iron. The new machines produced goods far faster than

human hands could. Furthermore, the entrepreneurs who ran the new factories drove their employees hard, forcing them to keep pace with the machines and work long hours. To market these products, English and Scottish merchants launched aggressive campaigns in the rapidly growing mainland colonies, extending a full year's credit instead of the traditional six months to American traders. Soon Americans were purchasing 20 percent of all British exports.

This first "consumer revolution" raised the living standard of many Americans. Colonial merchants and storekeepers stocked larger inventories (on credit) and offered credit to their customers, allowing settlers to buy equipment and household goods for their farms. Americans paid for those goods by increasing their agricultural exports. Scottish merchants helped Virginia planters and Scots-Irish migrants settle the Piedmont, a region of plains and rolling hills just inland from the Tidewater counties. They granted the settlers ample credit to purchase land, slaves, and equipment and took their tobacco crop in payment, exporting it to expanding markets in France and central Europe. By the 1760s South Carolina planters were sending indigo valued at £117,000 a year to English textile factories and exporting about 65 million pounds of rice a year to Holland and southern Europe. New York, Pennsylvania, Maryland, and Virginia became the breadbasket of the Atlantic world, supplying Europe's exploding population with wheat at ever increasing profits. In Philadelphia wheat prices jumped almost 50 percent between 1740 and 1765.

This first American spending binge, like most subsequent splurges, landed many consumers in debt. Even during the boom times of the 1750s and 1760s exports paid for only 80 percent of imported British goods. The remaining 20 percent—millions of pounds—was financed by the British merchants who extended credit. Moreover, the boom ended when the war in America wound down and Britain slashed its troop levels and military expenditures. The loss of military markets, contracts, and cash subsidies made it more difficult for Americans to purchase British goods. Merchants looked anxiously at their overstocked warehouses and feared bankruptcy. "I think we have a gloomy prospect before us," a Philadelphian noted in 1765, "as there are of late some Persons failed, who were in no way suspected." The increase in transatlantic trade had raised living standards but also had made Americans more dependent on overseas creditors and international economic conditions.

Land Conflicts and Western Uprisings

In good times or bad the colonial population continued to grow, and that (combined with the shortage of arable land in long-settled areas) caused political conflict over land rights. With each new generation the problem got worse. In 1738 families who traced their American ancestry back four generations had founded the town of Kent, Connecticut, at the generally accepted western boundary of the colony. The next generation had to find somewhere else to go. In 1749 Connecticut farmers formed the Susquehannah Company, and a few years later petitioned the legislature to assert jurisdiction over the

Wyoming Valley in northeastern Pennsylvania, where some of them had settled. But the Penn family reaffirmed its proprietary rights over the valley and issued its own land patents. Soon rival land claimants were burning down one another's houses. To avert further violence the governments of Pennsylvania and Connecticut referred the dispute to the authorities in London, where it remained undecided at the time of independence.

Land disputes also broke out along the imprecise border between New York and Massachusetts, when hundreds of yeomen families from New England moved into the disputed territory and refused to accept tenancy leaseholds from manorial landlords. Instead, the migrants purchased freehold titles from land speculators in Massachusetts and encouraged long-settled Dutch and German tenants to rebel against the landlords. In 1766 New England migrants and tenant farmers in Westchester, Dutchess, and Albany counties refused to pay rent and used mob violence to close the courts. At the behest of the royal governor, General Thomas Gage and two British regiments joined local sheriffs and manorial bailiffs to suppress the tenant uprising and evict the squatters.

Simultaneously, in New Jersey and the southern colonies, resident landowners and English aristocrats revived long-dormant seventeenth-century land charters. Judges supported most of their legal claims. For example, court decisions upheld the right of Lord Granville, an heir of one of the original Carolina proprietors, to collect quitrents in North Carolina and awarded ownership of the entire northern neck of Virginia (along the Potomac) to Lord Fairfax.

This revival of proprietary power underscored the growing strength of the landed gentry and the increasing resemblance between rural societies in Europe and America. High-quality land east of the Appalachians was getting more expensive, and much of it was controlled by English aristocrats, manorial landlords, and wealthy speculators. Tenants and even yeomen farmers feared they soon might be reduced to the status of European peasants.

As farmers moved west in search of cheap freehold land, they found themselves in the middle of disputes over Indian policy, political representation, and debts. In Pennsylvania, Scots-Irish migrants who lived along the frontier wanted to push the Indians out of the colony, but pacifistic Quakers prevented such military action. In 1763 a band of Scots-Irish farmers, the Paxton Boys, took matters into their own hands and massacred twenty native Americans. When Governor John Penn tried to bring the murderers to justice, about 250 armed Scots-Irish advanced on Philadelphia. Benjamin Franklin intercepted the angry mob at Lancaster and arranged a compromise, narrowly averting a battle. Prosecution of the accused men failed for lack of witnesses. Although the Scots-Irish dropped their demand for the expulsion of the Indians, the episode left a legacy of racial hatred and political resentment. A decade later the Scots-Irish would take their revenge against the Indians in the west and the Quaker and Anglican elite in the east.

Violence broke out in the backcountry of South Carolina as well, where land-hungry whites and Cherokee had clashed repeatedly during the war

A Backcountry Road
The first settlers in interior valleys lived in small, crude log cabins that were strung out along the road. Loneliness and desolation, suggested here by a solitary rider, were overcome by concerted efforts to build social communities, often through church-centered activities.

with France. After the war ended in 1763 a group of vigilantes, the Regulators, tried to impose order on outlaw bands of whites roaming the countryside. The Regulators whipped people suspected of poaching or stealing property. They also demanded that the eastern-controlled government provide more local courts, fairer taxes, and greater local representation in the provincial assembly. The eastern-dominated assembly, wanting to suppress the Regulators but fearing slave revolts on lowland rice plantations, refused to send troops to the backcountry. The assembly therefore compromised, creating locally controlled courts in the west and reducing fees for legal documents but refusing to reapportion the legislature or lower western taxes. Eventually a rival group, the Moderators, raised an armed force of its own and forced the Regulators to accept the authority of the colonial government. Like the Paxton Boys in Pennsylvania, the South Carolina Regulators attracted attention to western needs but ultimately failed to wrest power from the eastern elite.

Another political controversy arose in the newly settled backcountry of North Carolina. After the Great War for Empire tobacco prices plummeted, carrying many farmers into debt and into court. Eastern judges directed sheriffs to seize the property of bankrupt farmers and auction it off to pay creditors and court costs. Backcountry farmers resented merchants' lawsuits, not just because they generated high fees for lawyers and court officials but also because they violated local custom. As in rural New England, farmers were used to making loans among neighbors on the basis of mutual trust and often allowed the loans to remain unpaid for years.

To save their farms, North Carolina debtors created their own Regulator movement. They intimidated judges, closed down courts, and broke into jails to free their comrades. But the Regulators also proposed a coherent program of democratic reforms. Their leader, Herman Husband, told his followers not to vote for "any Clerk, Lawyer, or Scotch merchant. We must make these men subject to the laws or they will enslave the whole community." The Regulators demanded passage of a law allowing them to pay their taxes in the "produce of the country" rather than in cash. They also wanted legal fees reduced and (like the South Carolina Regulators) greater legislative representation and fairer taxes so that each person would be taxed "in proportion to the profits arising from his estate." In 1771 the royal governor mobilized the eastern militia and defeated a large Regulator force at the Alamance River; seven insurgent leaders were summarily executed. Not since Leisler's revolt in New York in 1689 had political conflict caused so much bloodshed in America.

In 1771 as in 1689, colonial conflicts became intertwined with imperial politics. In far-off Connecticut the Reverend Ezra Stiles defended the Regulators. "What shall an injured & oppressed people do," he asked, when faced with "Oppression and tyranny (under the name of Government)?" Stiles's remarks reflected growing resistance to British imperial control, a result of the changes that had occurred in the mainland colonies between 1720 and 1765. America was still a dependent society closely tied to Britain by trade, culture, and politics, but it was also an increasingly complex society with the potential for an independent existence. British policies would determine the direction the maturing colonies would take.

CHAPTER 4 TIMELINE

1700s	Freehold ideal in rural communities Arranged marriages common Woman's "place" as subordinate helpmate
1700–1714	New Hudson River manors created
1720s	Germans and Scots-Irish settle in middle colonies
1730s	Enlightenment ideas spread to America Tennents lead Presbyterian revivals Jonathan Edwards preaches in New England
1739	George Whitefield and the Great Awakening
1740–1760s	Population pressure in New England Ethnic pluralism in middle colonies Rising grain and tobacco prices Increasing rural inequality
1740s	Old Lights versus New Lights New colleges founded
1743	Franklin founds American Philosophical Society
1749	Ohio Company; Susquehannah Company
1750s	Industrial Revolution begins in England "Consumer revolution" raises American debt Indian "play-off" system breaks down
1754	French and Indian War begins Albany Congress
1755	French Acadians deported
1759	Fall of Quebec
1760s	New York and New England border conflicts Regulator movements in the Carolinas Evangelical Baptists in Virginia
1763	Treaty of Paris ends Great War for Empire Pontiac leads Indian uprising Paxton Boys in Pennsylvania

TOWARD INDEPENDENCE: YEARS OF DECISION, 1763–1775

- The Reform Movement, 1763–1765
- The Dynamics of Rebellion, 1765–1766
- The Growing Confrontation, 1767–1770
- The Road to War, 1771–1775

As the Great War for Empire ended, the American colonists rejoiced over the triumph of British arms. But twelve years later many of them were angry and had themselves taken up arms to resist British authority. How had it happened, asked the president of King's College in New York, that such a "happily situated" people had decided to "hazard their Fortunes, their Lives, and their Souls, in such a Rebellion"?

Unlike other colonial peoples of the time, Americans lived in a prosperous, stable society with a strong tradition of representative government. This unique historical circumstance created experienced leaders and a self-confident populace capable of supporting an independence movement. When the home government made a determined attempt to reform the imperial system, Americans rebelled. The long overdue but disastrous reforms prompted a violent response which began a downward spiral of political conflict and ideological debate that ended in civil war.

This course of events was hardly predictable in 1765, when the Americans were indeed a "happily situated" people. And it was far from inevitable, for Britain and its colonies had lived for decades in a peaceful and prosperous union. Purposeful British statecraft could have saved the empire. Instead, passionate Patriot agitation brought about its demise.

THE REFORM MOVEMENT, 1763–1765

The Great War for Empire had a mixed legacy. By driving the French out of Canada, Britain had achieved dominance over eastern North America (see Map 5.1). But the cost of the triumph was high: a mountain of debt that prompted the British ministry to impose new taxes on its American possessions and, more fundamentally, to redefine the empire as one not of mercantilist regulation but of imperial dominion.

BRITISH COLONIES		
Royal	Proprietary	Corporate

| | Population | | Average Annual | Exports |
	White (in 1770)	Black	Exports (in 1770)	per White (shillings)*
West Indian Islands	40,000	330,000	£1,856,000	928s.
Southern Mainland	600,000	394,000	£1,703,776	57s.
Northern Mainland	1,092,000	45,000	£1,105,376	21s.

*(20 shillings = 1£, 1 shilling = about $3.60.)

MAP 5.1

Britain's American Empire in 1763

In 1763 Britain was dominant in the West Indies and controlled all of eastern North America. British troops occupied the conquered colonies of Florida and Quebec and sought to prevent Anglo-American settlement west of the Proclamation Line.

The Legacy of War

The war made visible the differences between British and colonial society, for the fighting brought thousands of British troops to the mainland colonies. Many Americans were shocked by the arrogance of upper-crust British officers. British soldiers, a Massachusetts militiaman wrote in his diary, "are but little better than slaves to their officers." The hostility was mutual. General James Wolfe complained that colonial troops were drawn from the dregs of society and that "there was no depending on them in action."

The war also exposed the weakness of British administrative control, especially that of the royal governors. In theory governors had extensive political powers, including command of the provincial militia, but in reality they had to share power with the colonial assemblies. Britain's Board of Trade complained that in Massachusetts "almost every act of executive and legislative power is ordered and directed by votes and resolves of the General Court." This situation, British officials agreed, had to change.

Imperial authorities began by enforcing the Navigation Acts strictly. Before the war American merchants had routinely bribed customs officials to circumvent the Molasses Act of 1733. To curb such corruption, in 1762 Parliament passed a Revenue Act that prohibited English customs appointees from leasing their positions to deputies, who often accepted bribes. In addition, the ministry instructed the Royal Navy to stop the flourishing wartime trade between the mainland colonies and the French islands. The fact that French armies attempting "to Destroy one English province, are actually supported by Bread raised in another" was absurd, declared an outraged British politician.

This more restrictive policy culminated in 1763 with the deployment of a large peacetime army of about 10,000 men in North America. The decision stemmed from a variety of motives. First, the ministry wanted to discourage rebellion by the 60,000 French residents of the newly captured province of Quebec and to protect Florida, which Spain wanted back. Second, Pontiac's rebellion had underscored the need for a substantial military garrison along the frontier both to awe the Indians and to deter land-hungry whites from settling west of the Proclamation Line of 1763. Finally, some British politicians feared that with the French gone from Canada, Americans would seek greater freedom from imperial control. As Henry Knox, a Treasury official who once had served the Crown in Georgia, put it: "The main purpose of Stationing a large Body of Troops in America is to secure the Dependence of the Colonys on Great Britain." By stationing an army in America, the British ministry was indicating its willingness to use force to preserve its authority.

A more immediate problem was Britain's national debt, which had nearly doubled as a result of the war, from £75 million in 1754 to £133 million in 1763. To pay the rising interest charges, Lord Bute, the new prime minister, would have to raise taxes. Treasury officials advised against increasing the land tax, at an all-time high and paid by the propertied classes, whose support the government needed. Bute therefore imposed higher import duties on tobacco and sugar, which manufacturers passed on to British consumers in the form of higher prices. The ministry also increased *excise levies*—essentially sales taxes— on goods such as salt, beer, and distilled spirits, passing along the costs of the war to the king's ordinary subjects.

To collect these taxes and duties, the British government doubled the size and increased the powers of its bureaucracy. Customs agents and informers patrolled the coasts of southern Britain, arresting smugglers and seizing tons of goods, such as French wines and Flemish textiles, on which import duties had not been paid. Convicted smugglers faced heavy penalties, including death or "transportation" to America as indentured servants.

Thus, the price of empire abroad had turned out to be debt and a more powerful government at home—developments that confirmed the worst fears of the opposition, the Radical Whigs and Country Party landlords, who had long emphasized the dangers of a big and expensive government. The Treasury, they charged, was now at the mercy of the "monied interest," the banks and financiers who were reaping millions of pounds in interest from government bonds. The bureaucracy, they protested, was bloated, filled with thousands of "worthless *pensioners* and *placemen*." Worried by this corruption, reformers demanded that Parliament be made more representative. The Radical Whig John Wilkes demanded an end to "rotten boroughs"—tiny districts whose voters were controlled by wealthy aristocrats and merchants. In domestic affairs as in colonial policy, the war had transformed political life, creating a more active and arguably a more oppressive government.

British Reform Strategy

This political transformation was particularly apparent in colonial affairs. A new generation of British officials was determined to reform the imperial system. The first to take action was George Grenville, who became prime minister in 1763. The following year Grenville won enactment of a Currency Act, which protected the financial interests of British merchants by banning the use of paper money as legal tender throughout the colonies. Then he introduced a new Navigation Act, the Sugar Act of 1764, to replace the widely evaded Molasses Act of 1733. Treasury officials had looked closely at the pattern of colonial trade and had convinced Grenville that the mainland settlers had to sell some of their wheat, fish, and lumber in the French islands. Without the molasses, sugar, and bills of exchange those sales brought, the colonists would lack the funds to buy British manufactured goods. Therefore, Treasury officials resisted demands from British sugar planters to cut off trade between the mainland and the French islands by reviving the duty of 6 pence per gallon on French molasses. Instead, they recommended a smaller duty of 3 pence per gallon, arguing that it would allow British molasses to compete with the cheaper French product without destroying the mainland's export trade or distilling industry.

This carefully crafted policy garnered little support among American merchants and manufacturers, however. Many New England traders, such as John

Hancock of Boston, had made their fortunes by smuggling French molasses and thus had never paid the duty. Their profits would be cut severely by the new regulations. These merchants, joined by New England distillers, who feared a rise in the price of molasses, orchestrated a political campaign against the Sugar Act. Publicly, they protested that the new tax would wipe out trade with the French islands. Privately, they vowed to evade the duty by smuggling or by bribing officials. Merchants and their allies also raised constitutional objections to the new legislation. The speaker of the Massachusetts House of Representatives argued that the duties constituted a tax, so that the Sugar Act was "contrary to a fundamental Principall of our Constitution: That all Taxes ought to originate with the people."

The Sugar Act of 1764 raised other constitutional issues as well. To enforce the duties, the act extended the jurisdiction of *vice-admiralty courts*—maritime tribunals composed only of a judge—denying the accused a hearing before a common-law jury. For half a century colonial legislatures had vigorously opposed vice-admiralty courts; to limit their power, lawmakers had extended the jurisdiction of colonial courts to cover customs offenses occurring in the seaports or coastal waters. As a result, merchants charged with violating the Navigation Acts often were tried in common-law courts and acquitted by local juries. By extending the jurisdiction of vice-admiralty courts to all customs offenses wherever they occurred, the Sugar Act closed this loophole.

The powers given to the vice-admiralty courts revived old American fears and raised new constitutional objections. An influential Virginia planter charged that the courts illegally discriminated against British subjects living in America: the colonists "were not sent out to be the Slaves but to be the Equals of those that remained behind," he asserted. John Adams, a young Massachusetts lawyer who was defending John Hancock on a charge of smuggling, took a similar position. "Is there not in this Clause a Brand of Infamy, or Degradation, and Disgrace, fixed upon every American?" Adams demanded to know. "Is he not degraded below the rank of an Englishman?"

Although the logic of these arguments was compelling, some of the facts were wrong. The new vice-admiralty legislation did not discriminate against Americans but simply extended British legal practices to America. Vice-admiralty courts had long played a major role in Britain, where they were unpopular among both smugglers and political leaders who feared unbridled royal power. The real issue was the growing authority of the British state. Having lived for decades under a policy of salutary neglect, Americans knew that the new British policy challenged the existing constitutional structure of the empire. As a committee of the Massachusetts House put it, the Sugar Act and other British edicts "have a tendency to deprive the colonies of some of their most essential Rights as British subjects."

For their part, British officials insisted on Parliament's supremacy and denied that the colonists could claim the privileges inscribed in their royal charters or the traditional rights of Englishmen. When Royal Governor Francis Bernard of Massachusetts heard that the Massachusetts assembly had objected to the Sugar Act, claiming no taxation without representation, he asserted that Americans did not have that constitutional right. "The rule that a *British* subject shall not be bound by laws or liable to taxes, but what he has consented to by his representatives," Bernard argued, "must be confined to the inhabitants of Great Britain only." In the eyes of most British officials and politicians, Americans were second-class subjects of the king, their rights limited by the Navigation Acts and the national interests of the British state, as determined by Parliament.

The Stamp Act

The issue of taxation brought about the first great imperial crisis. When Grenville introduced the Sugar Act, he also announced his intention to seek a stamp tax to cover part of the cost of keeping 10,000 British troops in America—some £200,000 per year (about $15 million today). The new tax would raise revenue by requiring stamps (similar to modern postage stamps) on court documents, land titles, contracts, playing cards, newspapers, and other printed items. A similar English tax that had been levied since 1694

George Grenville, Architect of the Stamp Act
As prime minister from 1764 to 1766, Grenville assumed leadership of the movement for imperial reform and taxation. But most British politicians believed that the colonies should be better regulated and share the cost of the empire.

was yielding an annual revenue of £290,000; Grenville hoped the American levy would raise at least £60,000 a year. The prime minister knew that some Americans would object to the tax on constitutional grounds, and so he asked explicitly whether any member of the House of Commons doubted "the power and sovereignty of Parliament over every part of the British dominions, for the purpose of raising or collecting any tax." No one rose to object.

Confident of Parliament's support, Grenville vowed to impose a stamp tax in 1765. This challenge threw the London agents of the colonial legislatures into confusion. They all agreed that the assemblies could not apportion their defense budget among themselves; the colonies had met together only once, at the Albany Congress of 1754, and not a single assembly had accepted that body's proposals.

Benjamin Franklin, representing the Pennsylvania assembly, countered Grenville's initiative with an innovative proposal for American representation in Parliament. "If you chuse to tax us," he suggested to a British friend, "give us Members in your Legislature, and let us be one People." But with the exception of William Pitt, British politicians rejected Franklin's radical idea. They argued that the colonists were "virtually" represented in the home legislature by the merchants who sat in Parliament and by other members with interests in America. Colonial leaders were equally skeptical of Franklin's plan; Americans were "situate at a great Distance from their Mother Country," the Connecticut assembly declared in a printed pamphlet that was quickly sent to London, and therefore "cannot participate in the general Legislature of the Nation." Influential merchants in Philadelphia, worried that a handful of colonial delegates would be powerless in Parliament, warned Franklin "to beware of any measure that might extend to us seats in the Commons."

The way was clear for Grenville to introduce the Stamp Act both to raise revenue and to assert a constitutional principle, "the Right of Parliament to lay an internal Tax upon the Colonies," as his chief assistant observed. The ministry's plan worked smoothly. The House of Commons refused to accept American petitions opposing the act and passed the new legislation by an overwhelming vote of 205 to 49. At the request of General Thomas Gage, commander of British military forces in America, Parliament also passed a Quartering Act that directed colonial governments to provide barracks and food for the British troops stationed in the colonies. Finally, Parliament approved Grenville's proposal that violations of the Stamp Act be tried in vice-admiralty courts.

The design was complete. Using the doctrine of Parliamentary supremacy, Grenville had begun to fashion a genuinely imperial administrative system, run by British officials without regard for the American assemblies. He thus provoked a constitutional confrontation not only on the specific issues of taxation, jury trials, and quartering of the military but on the fundamental question of representative self-government.

THE DYNAMICS OF REBELLION, 1765–1766

Grenville had thrown down the gauntlet to the Americans. Although the colonists had often opposed unpopular laws and arbitrary governors, they had never before faced a reform-minded ministry and Parliament. But Patriots— as the defenders of American rights came to be called—took up Grenville's challenge, organizing to protest the acts, rioting in the streets, and delivering speeches that bordered on treason.

The Crowd Rebels

In May 1765 the eloquent young Virginian Patrick Henry addressed the House of Burgesses and blamed the legislation on the new king, George III (1760–1820). Comparing George to the tyrannical Charles I, Henry seemed to call for a new republican revolution. Dismayed by Henry's nearly treasonous remarks, the Burgesses nonetheless endorsed his attack on the Stamp Act, declaring that any attempt to tax the colonists without their consent "has a manifest Tendency to Destroy American freedom." In Massachusetts, James Otis, another republican-minded firebrand, persuaded the House of Representatives to call for a general meeting of all the colonies in New York in October to consider a "loyal and humble representation" to the king and Parliament "to implore Relief" from the act.

Nine colonial assemblies sent delegates to the Stamp Act Congress, which devised a set of Resolves protesting strongly against the loss of American "rights and liberties," especially trial by jury. The delegates contested the constitutionality of the Stamp and Sugar acts, declaring that only the colonists' elected representatives could impose taxes on them. They also rejected, because of their distance from Britain and their local interests, direct representation in the House of Commons. Then, assuring Parliament that Americans "glory in being subjects of the best of Kings having been born under the most perfect form of government," the delegates humbly petitioned for repeal of the Stamp Act. Other influential Americans advocated nonviolent resistance through a boycott of British goods.

Popular resentment was not so easily contained. When the act went into effect on November 1, disciplined mobs led by men who called themselves the Sons of Liberty demanded the resignation of newly appointed stamp-tax collectors, most of whom were native-born colonists. In Boston the Sons of Liberty made an effigy of the collector Andrew Oliver, which they beheaded and burned; then they destroyed a new brick building that Oliver owned. Two weeks later Bostonians attacked the house of Lieutenant Governor Thomas Hutchinson, a defender of social privilege and imperial authority, breaking the furniture, looting the wine cellar, and burning the library (see American Voices, p. 124).

In nearly every colony similar crowds of angry people—the "rabble," as their detractors called them—intimidated royal officials. Near Wethersfield, Connecticut, 500 farmers and artisans confronted the locally prominent tax

A British View of American Mobs
The cartoonist depicts the Sons of Liberty as sadists, subjecting a British
excise officer to physical abuse, and as wanton destroyers of property,
dumping tea into the harbor. The Liberty Tree in the background raises
the question: Does Liberty mean Anarchy?

collector, Jared Ingersoll, and forced his resignation. One rioter "lookt upon
this as the Cause of the People," he shouted, and would not "take Directions
about it from any Body." In New York nearly 3,000 shopkeepers, artisans, laborers, and seamen marched through the streets, breaking street lamps and
windows and crying "Liberty!"

The Threat of Mob Rule

To Josiah Quincy, Jr., a Boston gentleman, the destruction of the house of Chief Justice Thomas Hutchinson in August 1765 raised the prospect of popular tyranny and "lawless despotism."

There cannot, perhaps, be found in the records of time a more flagrant instance to what a pitch of infatuation an incensed populace may arise than the last night afforded. . . . The populace of Boston . . . assembled in King's Street; where, after having kindled a fire, they proceeded, in two separate bodies, to attack the houses of two gentlemen of distinction . . . and did great damage in destroying their houses, furniture, &c., and irreparable damage in destroying their papers. Both parties . . . then unitedly proceeded to the Chief-Justice's house, who, not expecting them, was unattended by his friends who might have assisted, or proved his innocence. . . .

This rage-intoxicated rabble . . . beset the house on all sides, and soon destroyed every thing of value. . . . The destruction was really amazing. . . .

The distress a man must feel on such an occasion can only be conceived by those who the next day saw his Honor the Chief-Justice come into court . . . with tears starting from his eyes, and a countenance which strongly told the inward anguish of his soul.

GENTLEMEN [he said]: There not being a quorum of the court without me, I am obliged to appear. Some apology is necessary for my dress: indeed, I had no other. Destitute of every thing. . . .

I call my Maker to witness, that I never, in New England or Old, in Great Britain or America, neither directly nor indirectly, was aiding, assisting, or supporting—in the least promoting or encouraging—what is commonly called the Stamp Act; but, on the contrary, did all in my power, and strove as much as in me lay, to prevent it. . . .

Who, that marks the riotous tumult, confusion, and uproar of a democratic . . . state [would not fly] . . . to that best asylum, that glorious medium, the British Constitution? . . . May ye never lose it through a licentious abuse of your invaluable rights. . . .

SOURCE: Reprinted from *Proceedings of the Massachusetts Historical Society*, 1st ser., 1791–1883 (20 vols., 1879–1884), Vol. 4 (1858–1860), pp. 47–51.

Although the strength of the Liberty mobs was surprising, crowd actions were a fact of life in both Britain and America. Every November 5 Protestant mobs on both sides of the Atlantic celebrated Guy Fawkes Day by burning the pope in effigy to mark the failure of a Catholic uprising in 1605. Colonial mobs regularly destroyed houses used as brothels and rioted to protest the impressment of merchant seamen by the Royal Navy. The Stamp Act crowds were simply acting according to tradition.

The leaders of the Sons of Liberty were mostly minor merchants or skilled artisans who knew each other from their jobs, churches, or neighborhoods. The mobs they led were composed of a diverse mixture of established artisans, struggling journeymen, and poor laborers and seamen. Many were drawn into the streets by economic issues. Imports of low-priced British shoes and other manufactured goods threatened the livelihood of some artisans, and so they opposed a stamp tax that would lower their declining standard of living. Unlike "the Common people of England," a well-traveled colonist observed, "the people of America . . . never would submit to be taxed that a few may be loaded with palaces and Pensions and riot in Luxury and Excess, while they themselves cannot support themselves and their needy offspring with Bread."

Other crowd members were moved by the religious passions aroused by the Great Awakening. These evangelical Protestants led disciplined, hardworking lives and resented the arrogance and immorality of British military officers and the corruption of royal bureaucrats. Still other crowd members had imbibed from their parents and grandparents the antimonarchical sentiments of the seventeenth-century Puritan revolution. A letter sent to a Boston newspaper promising to save "all the Freeborn Sons of America" from "tyrannical ministers" was signed "Oliver Cromwell." Finally, a substantial portion of many mobs included apprentices, journeymen, day laborers, and unemployed sailors—young men seeking adventure and excitement who, when fortified by drink, were ready to resort to violence.

Throughout the colonies popular resistance nullified the Stamp Act, lending a democratic cast to the emerging American Patriot movement. "Nothing is wanting but your own Resolution," a New York Son of Liberty declared during the upheaval, "for great is the Authority and Power of the People." On Guy Fawkes Day (November 5, 1765), New York Lieutenant Governor Cadwallader Colden, fearing an assault on Fort George, where the stamps were stored, called on General Gage to use his small military force against the crowd. Gage refused. "Fire from the Fort might disperse the Mob, but it would not quell them," he told Colden, "and the consequence would in all appearances be an Insurrection, the Commencement of Civil War." Frightened collectors distributed few stamps, and angry Americans coerced officials into accepting legal documents without them.

Slow communication across the Atlantic meant that the ministry's response to this resistance would not be known until the following spring. But royal officials clearly could no longer count on the deferential political behavior that had ensured stability in the colonies for three generations. "What can a Governor do without the assistance of the Governed?" the Philadelphia customs collector lamented.

Ideological Roots of Resistance

The American resistance movement began in the seaport cities because urban residents were directly affected by British policies. The Stamp Act taxed goods used by merchants and lawyers, such as newspapers and legal documents; the Sugar Act raised the cost of molasses to urban merchants and distillers; and the Currency Act complicated everyone's trade and financial transactions. Moreover, British firms had begun selling low-cost manufactured goods directly to colonial shopkeepers, threatening the livelihood of American artisans and merchants. All in all, an official in Rhode Island reported, the interests of Britain and the colonies were increasingly "deemed by the People almost altogether incompatible in a Commercial View."

At first the colonists framed their protests narrowly in terms of economic and political self-interest. One pamphleteer complained that colonists were being compelled to give the British "our money, as oft and in what quantity they please to demand it." Other writers alleged that the British had violated particular "liberties and privileges" embodied in colonial charters. But American Patriots gradually broadened the terms of debate by defining "liberty" as an abstract ideal—as a "natural right" of all people—rather than a set of historical privileges. Pamphlets of remarkable political sophistication circulated throughout the colonies, providing the resistance movement with both an intellectual rationale and a political agenda.

As Patriot merchants and lawyers formulated their arguments, they drew on three intellectual traditions. The first was English *common law*—the centuries-old body of legal rules and procedures that protected the king's subjects against arbitrary acts by the government. In 1761 the Boston lawyer James Otis had cited English legal precedent in the famous Writs of Assistance case, in which he disputed the constitutionality of a general search warrant permitting customs officials to inspect the property and possessions of any and all persons. Similarly, in demanding a jury trial for John Hancock, John Adams invoked common-law tradition. "This 29th Chap. of Magna Charta," Adams argued, referring to an ancient English document that had established the right to trial by jury, "has for many Centuries been esteemed by Englishmen, as one of the noblest Monuments, one of the firmest Bulwarks of their Liberties." Adams and other lawyers protested again when the terms of appointment for colonial judges were altered from "during good behavior" to "at the pleasure" of the royal governor, arguing that the change in wording compromised the independence of the judiciary. Customary legal practices and common-law rights, they maintained, could not be abridged by bureaucratic edict or even parliamentary statute.

A second major intellectual resource for educated Americans was the rationalist thought of the Enlightenment. Unlike common-law attorneys, who valued precedent and venerated the ways of the past, Enlightenment philosophers such as David Hume and Frances Hutcheson questioned the past and relied on reason to discover and correct social ills. The urban elite also was influenced by the political philosopher John Locke, who argued that all individuals possessed certain "natural rights," such as life, liberty, and property, which government was responsible for protecting. And they celebrated French theorists such as Montesquieu, who devised institutional curbs to prevent the arbitrary exercise of political power.

The republican and Whig strands of the English political tradition provided the third ideological basis for the American Patriot movement. In some places, particularly Puritan New England, Americans had long venerated the Commonwealth era—the brief period between 1649 and 1660 when England was a republic. After the Glorious Revolution of 1688 many colonists had welcomed the constitutional restrictions placed on the monarchy by English Whigs, such as the ban on royally imposed taxes. Later, many educated Americans absorbed the arguments of Radical Whig spokesmen who denounced political corruption. "Bribery is so common," John Dickinson of Pennsylvania had complained during a visit to London in the 1750s, "that there is not a borough in England where it is not practiced." These republican and Radical Whig sentiments predisposed many Americans to distrust imperial reform. Joseph Warren, a Boston physician and Patriot, reported that many townspeople thought the Stamp Act was intended "to force the colonies into rebellion," after which the ministry would use "military power to reduce them to servitude."

Thus, the ideology of Enlightenment thinkers, common-law attorneys, and Radical Whig critics of ministerial policy endowed colonial opposition to British control with high moral significance, turning a series of tax protests into a broad resistance movement.

The Informal Compromise of 1766

In Britain, Parliament was in turmoil, with different political factions advocating radically different responses to the American challenge. George III had replaced Grenville with a new prime minister, Lord Rockingham, who led a group of tradition-minded politicians (labeled Old Whigs by one historian) that opposed Grenville's policies toward the colonies. But hard-liners in Parliament, outraged by the popular rebellion in America, demanded that imperial reform continue. They wanted to dispatch British soldiers to the seaport cities to suppress the riots and force the Americans to submit to the constitutional supremacy of Parliament. "The British legislature," declared Chief Justice Sir James Mansfield, "has authority to bind every part and every subject, whether such subjects have a right to vote or not."

Rockingham tried to reconcile the various factions to a common policy. Three groups were willing to repeal the Stamp Act, but for very different reasons. The Old Whigs advocated repeal because they believed that America was important not as a source of tax revenue but as a source of "flourishing and increasing trade" that added to the national wealth. Some Old Whigs even agreed with the colonists that the new tax was unconstitutional. British merchants also favored repeal, because an American boycott of British goods had caused a drastic fall in their sales. In January 1766 the leading commercial centers of London, Liverpool, Bristol, and Glasgow deluged Parliament with petitions, pointing out the threat to British prosperity. "The Avenues of Trade are all shut up," a Bristol merchant with large inventories on hand complained. "We have no Remittances and are at our Witts End for want of Money to fulfill our Engagements with our Tradesmen." Finally, former Prime Minister William Pitt demanded that "the Stamp Act be repealed absolutely, totally, and immediately" because it was a failed policy. Pitt's view of the constitutional issues was ambiguous; he argued both that Parliament could not tax the colonies and that British authority over America was "sovereign and supreme, in every circumstance of government and legislation whatsoever."

Rockingham gave each side just enough to claim victory. To assist British merchants and mollify colonial opinion, he repealed the Stamp Act and ruled out the use of troops against colonial crowds. He also modified the Sugar Act, reducing the duty on French molasses from 3 pence to 1 penny a gallon but extending it to British molasses as well. Thus, the revised Sugar Act not only regulated foreign trade, which most American politicians accepted, but taxed a British product, which some colonists saw as unconstitutional. Finally, Rockingham pacified imperial reformers and hard-liners with the Declaratory Act of 1766, which explicitly reaffirmed the British Parliament's "full power and authority to make laws and statutes . . . to bind the colonies and people of America . . . in all cases whatsoever."

Because the Stamp Act crisis ended quickly, it might have been forgotten quickly. In 1766 the constitutional status of the American provinces remained uncertain, but political positions had not yet hardened. Leaders of goodwill could still hope to work out an imperial relationship that was acceptable to both sides.

Mixing Business and Politics, 1766
Hurt by the colonists' trade boycott, British manufacturers campaigned for repeal of the Stamp Act. To celebrate repeal—and expand the market for its teapots in America—the Cockpit Hill factory in Derby quickly produced a commemorative design.

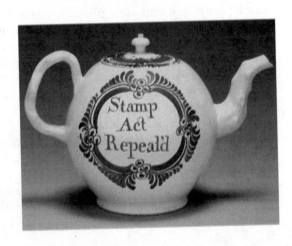

THE GROWING CONFRONTATION, 1767–1770

The compromise of 1766 was short-lived. Within a year political rivalries in Britain sparked a new and more prolonged struggle with the American provinces. On both sides of the Atlantic economic self-interest and ideological rigidity aggravated the conflict, resurrecting the passions and violence of 1765 and dashing prospects for a quick resolution of the crisis.

The Townshend Initiatives

Often the course of history is changed by a small event—a leader's illness, a personal grudge, a chance remark. So it was in 1767, when Rockingham's Old Whig ministry collapsed and George III named William Pitt to head the new ministry. Pitt, the master strategist of the Great War for Empire, was chronically ill with gout and frequently missed cabinet meetings and Parliamentary debates, leaving Chancellor of the Exchequer Charles Townshend in command. Pitt was sympathetic toward America; Townshend was not. Since his service on the Board of Trade in the 1750s, Townshend had favored imperial reform; at last he had the power to push it through. When Townshend presented the military budget to Parliament in 1767, his longtime rival Lord Grenville rose to demand again that the colonists pay for the British troops in America. On the defensive, Townshend made an unplanned, fateful policy decision. Convinced of the necessity of imperial reform and eager to reduce the English land tax, he promised that he would find a new source of revenue in America.

The new tax legislation, known as the Townshend Act of 1767, was intended to free royal officials from financial dependence on the American legislatures, enabling them to enforce Parliamentary laws and royal directives. The tax imposed duties on paper, paint, glass, and tea imported into the colonies and was expected to raise about £40,000 a year. To pacify Grenville, part of the revenue would defray military expenses, but the major part would be used to pay the salaries of governors, judges, and other imperial officials. To enhance further the power of the royal bureaucracy, Townshend devised the Revenue Act of 1767. The new act created a Board of American Customs Commissioners in Boston and vice-admiralty courts in Halifax, Boston, Philadelphia, and Charleston. These administrative innovations were far-reaching, and posed a greater threat to American autonomy than did the small sums raised by the import duties.

New York gave Townshend another chance to challenge the colonial assemblies when it refused to comply with the Quartering Act of 1765. Fearing an unlimited drain on its treasury, the New York legislature first denied General Gage's requests for barracks and supplies and then limited its assistance. Unsatisfied, the British ministry instructed New York to assume complete financial responsibility for its defense against Indian attacks. If the assembly refused, some members of Parliament threatened that an extra port duty would be imposed on New York imports and exports to raise the needed funds. The earl of Shelburne, the new secretary of state, went even further, suggesting the appointment of a military governor with authority to seize funds from New York's treasury to pay for quartering the troops and "to act with Force or Gentleness as circumstances might make necessary." Townshend decided on a less provocative measure, the so-called Restraining Act of 1767, which suspended the New York assembly until it submitted to the Quartering Act. Faced with the loss of self-government, New Yorkers appropriated the required funds.

The Restraining Act was of great significance because it threatened Americans with the loss of their representative governments. The British Privy Council had always supervised the assemblies, invalidating about 5 percent of all colonial laws (such as those establishing land banks or vesting new powers in the assemblies). Townshend's Restraining Act went much further by declaring American governmental institutions to be completely dependent on Parliamentary favor.

America Again Resists

The Townshend Duties revived the constitutional debate over taxation. During the Stamp Act crisis some Americans had suggested that "external" duties on trade (which Britain had always regulated) were acceptable but that direct or "internal" taxes (which had never before been levied) were not. Townshend thought this distinction between internal and external taxes "perfect nonsense," but told Parliament that "since Americans were pleased to make that distinction, he was willing to indulge them [and] . . . to confine himself to regulations of Trade." Most colonial leaders refused to accept the legitimacy of Townshend's measures, however. They agreed with John Dickinson, author of *Letters from a Farmer in Pennsylvania* (1768), that the real issue was not whether the tax was internal or external but the intention of the legislation. Because the Townshend duties were not designed to regulate trade but to bring revenue to the imperial government, they amounted to taxes imposed without consent.

Americans debated the wisdom of a new boycott of British goods. In February 1768 the Massachusetts House of Representatives sent a letter to the other assemblies condemning the Townshend Act for taxing the colonists and thereby infringing on their "natural & constitutional Rights." In April Boston merchants began a new boycott of British imports, and New York traders followed in August. Philadelphia merchants, sailors, and dockworkers, who were more heavily involved in direct trade with Britain, refused to join the movement, believing they had too much to lose. Nonetheless, public support for nonimportation gradually spread to smaller port cities, such as Salem, Newport, and Baltimore, and into the countryside. In Puritan New England, ministers and public officials supported the boycott by condemning "luxury and dissipation" and the use of "foreign superfluities" and promoted the domestic manufacture of necessities such as paper and cloth.

American women, ordinarily excluded from playing a prominent role in public affairs, became crucial to the nonimportation movement through their production of "homespun" textiles. During the Stamp Act crisis, groups of young women with ties to Patriot leaders had underscored their support for the cause by increasing their output of yarn and cloth. The contest over the Townshend duties elicited support from a much broader group of women, including many pious farmwives who assembled to spin yarn at the homes of their ministers. Some gatherings were openly patriotic, such as one in Berwick, Maine, where the spinners, "as true Daughters of Liberty," celebrated American goods, "drinking rye coffee and dining on bear venison." Many more women's groups combined their support for nonimportation with charitable work by spinning flax and wool to donate to the needy.

Newspapers celebrated these women, prompting thousands of others to redouble their efforts at the spinning wheel and loom. One Massachusetts town proudly claimed an annual output of 30,000 yards of cloth; East Hartford, Connecticut, reported 17,000 yards. Although this surge in domestic production did not compensate for the loss of British imports, which had averaged about 10 million yards a year, it inspired support for nonimportation in hundreds of communities.

Indeed, the boycott as well as new crowd actions united thousands of Americans in a common political movement. The Sons of Liberty published the names of merchants who imported British goods, broke their store windows, and harassed their employees. Many merchants deeply resented the crowds' attacks on their reputations and property. Fearing mob rule, they condemned nonimportation and stood by the royal governors. Still, in March 1769 most Philadelphia merchants finally responded to public pressure and joined the nonimportation movement. Two months later the members of the Virginia House of Burgesses agreed not to buy dutied articles, British luxuries, or slaves. "The whole continent from New England to Georgia seems firmly fixed," the *Massachusetts Gazette* proudly announced; "like a strong, well-constructed arch, the more weight there is laid upon it, the firmer it stands; and thus with America, the more we are loaded, the more we are united." Reflecting colonial self-confidence, Benjamin Franklin called for a return to the pre-1763 mercantilist system. "It is easy to propose a plan of conciliation," Franklin declared: "*repeal* the laws, *renounce* the right, *recall* the troops, *refund* the money, and *return* to the old method of requisition."

British patience was exhausted. When a copy of the Massachusetts House's letter opposing the Townshend duties reached London in the late spring of 1768, Lord Hillsborough, the secretary of state for American affairs, branded it as "unjustifiable opposition to the constitutional authority of Parliament." He instructed Governor Francis Bernard to dissolve the House if it refused to rescind its action. To strengthen the "Hand of Government" in Massachusetts and assist the Commissioners of the Customs, who had been forced by a mob to take refuge on a British naval vessel, Hillsborough dispatched four regiments of troops to Boston.

Hillsborough's goal was to prepare for an armed showdown with the radical Boston Patriots. By the end of 1768 a thousand British regulars were encamped in Boston, and military coercion was a very real prospect. General Gage accused public leaders in Massachusetts of "Treasonable and desperate Resolves" and advised the ministry to "Quash this Spirit at a Blow." Parliament responded by threatening to appoint a special commission to hear evidence of treason, and King George supported Hillsborough's plan to repeal the Townshend duties in all the colonies except Massachusetts. Once the rebellious New Englanders were isolated, the British army would bring them to their knees.

The stakes had risen. In 1765 American resistance to taxation had provoked a Parliamentary debate. In 1768 it produced a plan for military coercion.

The Second Compromise

At this critical moment the British ministry's resolve faltered. A food shortage in Britain caused riots across the countryside; in the highly publicized "Massacre of Saint George Fields," troops killed seven demonstrators. The Radical Whig John Wilkes, supported by associations composed of merchants, tradesmen, and artisans, stepped up his attacks on government corruption and won election to Parliament. Overjoyed, American Patriots drank toasts in Wilkes's honor and purchased thousands of teapots and drinking mugs emblazoned with his picture. Riots in Ireland over the growing military budget there added to the ministry's difficulties.

The American trade boycott also began to hurt. Normally the mainland colonies had an annual trade deficit of £500,000, but in 1768 they imported less from Great Britain, cutting the deficit to £230,000. In 1769 the boycott had a major impact. By continuing to export tobacco, rice, fish, and other goods to Britain while refusing to buy its manufactured goods, Americans accumulated a trade surplus of £816,000. To revive their flagging fortunes, British merchants and manufacturers petitioned Parliament for repeal of the Townshend duties. Government revenues, nearly 70 percent of which came from excise taxes and duties on imported goods, had also suffered. By late 1769 merchants' petitions had persuaded some ministers that the Townshend duties were a mistake, and the king had withdrawn his support for Hillsborough's plan.

Early in 1770 Lord North became prime minister and arranged a new compromise. Arguing that it was foolish to tax British exports to America (raising their price and decreasing consumption), North persuaded Parliament to repeal the duties on glass, paper, paint, and other manufactured items. But he retained the tax on tea as a symbol of Parliament's supremacy. Gratified, merchants in New York and Philadelphia rejected pleas from Patriots in Boston to continue the boycott. Indeed, most Americans did not insist on strict adherence to their constitutional principles and did not contest the symbolic levy on tea. Instead, they simply avoided paying the tax by drinking smuggled tea.

Even violence in New York City and Boston did not rupture the compromise. During the boycott New York artisans and workers had taunted British troops, mostly with words but occasionally with stones and fists. In retaliation the soldiers tore down a Liberty Pole (a Patriot flagpole), setting off a week of street fighting. In Boston friction between the townsmen and British soldiers over constitutional principles, in particular the legitimacy of the occupation of the town by a Standing Army, and everyday issues, such as competition for part-time jobs, sparked the "Boston Massacre." In March 1770, menaced by a mob of laborers and seamen, a group of soldiers fired into the crowd, killing five men, including one of the leaders, Crispus Attucks, an escaped slave who was working as a seaman. A Radical Whig pamphlet accused the British of deliberately planning the massacre.

Although most Americans remained loyal to the empire, five years of conflict over taxes and constitutional principles had significantly altered their sentiments. In 1765 American public leaders had accepted Parliament's authority; the Stamp Act Resolves had opposed only certain "unconstitutional" legislation. By 1770 the most outspoken Patriots—Benjamin Franklin in Pennsylvania, Patrick Henry in Virginia, and Samuel Adams in Massachu-

Patrick Henry, a Great Orator
Henry drew on evangelical Protestantism to create a new mode of political oratory. "His figures of speech . . . were often borrowed from the Scriptures," a contemporary noted, while his style and speech conveyed "the earnestness depicted in his own features." (Shelburne Museum, Shelburne, Vt. Photograph by Ken Burris)

setts—had repudiated Parliamentary supremacy, claiming equality for their assemblies. Franklin wanted to redefine the empire to make Britain and the colonies "distinct and separate states" united under "the same Head, or Sovereign, the King." His proposal horrified Thomas Hutchinson, the American-born royal governor of Massachusetts, who rejected the idea of "two independent legislatures in one and the same state." For Hutchinson, the British Empire was a whole, its sovereignty indivisible. "I know of no line," he told the Massachusetts House of Representatives, "that can be drawn between the supreme authority of Parliament and the total independence of the colonies."

There the matter rested. The British had twice tried to impose taxes on the colonies, and American Patriots had twice forced them to retreat. If Parliament insisted on exercising its claim to sovereignty, at least some Americans would have to be subdued by force. Fearful of civil war, the ministry hesitated to take the final fateful step.

THE ROAD TO WAR, 1771–1775

The repeal of the Townshend duties in 1770 restored harmony to the British Empire. For the next three years most disputes were resolved peacefully. Yet below the surface lay strong fears and passions and mutual distrust. Suddenly, in 1773, those undercurrents erupted, overwhelming any hope for compromise. In less than two years the Americans and the British stood on the brink of war.

The Tea Act

Radical Boston Patriots who wanted greater rights for the colonies continued to warn Americans of the dangers of imperial domination. In November 1772 Samuel Adams persuaded the Boston town meeting to establish a Committee of Correspondence "to state the Rights of the Colonists of this Province." Within a few months eighty Massachusetts towns had similar committees. Other colonies copied the practice when the British government set up a royal commission to investigate the burning of the *Gaspée*, a British customs vessel, in Rhode Island. The commission's powers, particularly its authority to send Americans to Britain for trial, first aroused the Virginia House of Burgesses, which created a Committee of Correspondence "to communicate with the other colonies" about the situation in Rhode Island. By July 1773 committees had sprung up in Connecticut, New Hampshire, and South Carolina.

Parliament's passage of a Tea Act in May 1773 initiated the chain of events that led directly to civil war. Lord North had designed the act to provide financial relief for the British East India Company, which was deeply in debt because of military expeditions undertaken to extend British trade in India. The Tea Act provided the company with a government loan and, more important, eliminated the customs duties on the company's tea as it passed through Britain.

Lord North failed to understand how unpopular the Tea Act would be in America. Since 1768, when the Townshend Act had placed a duty of 3 pence a pound on tea, American traders had been importing Dutch tea illegally. By the 1770s about 90 percent of the tea consumed in the colonies was contraband. However, the Tea Act was designed to make the East India Company's tea cheaper than Dutch tea. Radical Patriots accused the ministry of bribing Americans to give up their principles; as an anonymous woman wrote in the *Massachusetts Spy*, "the use of tea is considered not as a *private* but as a *public* evil . . . a handle to introduce a variety of . . . oppressions amongst us." One such oppression was the East India Company's decision to distribute the tea directly to shopkeepers, a tactic that would eliminate most colonial merchants from the trade. "The fear of an Introduction of a Monopoly in this Country," General Haldimand reported from New York, "has induced the mercantile part of the Inhabitants to be very industrious in opposing this Step and added Strength to a Spirit of Independence already too prevalent."

The Committees of Correspondence took the lead in organizing resistance to the Tea Act. They held public bonfires at which they persuaded their fellow citizens (sometimes gently, sometimes not) to consign British tea to the flames. The Sons of Liberty also prevented East India Company ships from landing new supplies. By forcing the Company's captains to return the tea to Britain or store it in public warehouses, the Patriots effectively nullified the legislation.

Governor Thomas Hutchinson of Massachusetts, determined to uphold the Tea Act, hatched a scheme to land the tea and collect the tax. When a shipment of tea arrived on the *Dartmouth*, he had the ship passed through customs immediately, after which it could not depart without paying the tax. If the tea duty were not paid within twenty days, by law customs officials could seize the cargo, land it with the help of the British army, and sell the tea at auction. But Patriots foiled the governor's plan by raiding the *Dartmouth*: a group of artisans and laborers disguised as Indians boarded the ship, broke open the 342 chests of tea (valued at about £10,000, or roughly $800,000 today), and threw them into the harbor (see American Voices, p. 136). "This destruction of the Tea is so bold and it must have so important Consequences," John Adams wrote in his diary, "that I cannot but consider it as an Epoch in History."

The British Privy Council was outraged, as was the king. "Concessions have made matters worse," George III declared. "The time has come for compulsion." Early in 1774 Parliament decisively rejected a proposal to repeal the duty on American tea and instead enacted four Coercive Acts to force Massachusetts into submission. A Port Bill closed Boston Harbor until the East India Company received payment for the destroyed tea. A Government Act annulled the Massachusetts charter and prohibited most local town meetings. A new Quartering Act required the colony to build barracks or accommodate

Mob Discipline at the Boston Tea Party

George Robert Twelves Hewes, a poor Boston shoemaker, became a Patriot in part because a British soldier had refused to pay him for a pair of shoes. His account of the Tea Party describes the discipline imposed by the Sons of Liberty both on their followers and on other citizens.

It was now evening, and I immediately dressed myself in the costume of an Indian, equipped with a small hatchet. . . . After having painted my face and hands with coal dust in the shop of a blacksmith, I repaired to Griffin's wharf, where the ships lay that contained the tea. When I first appeared in the street . . . I fell in with many who were dressed, equipped and painted as I was . . . and marched in order to the place of our destination. . . . The name of him who commanded the division to which I was assigned, was Leonard Pitt. . . .

As soon as we were on board the ship, [Pitt] appointed me boatswain, and ordered me to go to the captain and demand of him the keys to the hatches. . . . We then were ordered by our commander to open the hatches, and take out all the chests of tea and throw them overboard . . . first cutting and splitting the chests with our tomahawks. . . .

Several attempts were made by some of the citizens of Boston and its vicinity, to carry off small quantities of [the tea] for their family use. . . . One Captain O'Conner, whom I knew well, came on board for that purpose . . . filled his pockets, and also the lining of his coat. . . . We were ordered to arrest him. . . . I seized him by the skirt of his coat, and . . . tore it off. . . .

The next day we nailed the skirt of his coat . . . to the whipping post in Charlestown, the place of his residence, with a label on it, commemorative of the occasion which had thus subjected the proprietor to the popular indignation.

SOURCE: James Hawkes, *A Retrospect of the Boston Tea-Party.* . . . (Boston: 1834), pp. 37–41.

soldiers in private houses. To protect royal officials from Massachusetts juries, a Justice Act allowed the transfer of trials for capital crimes to other colonies or to Britain.

In response, Patriot leaders throughout the mainland condemned these "Intolerable Acts" and rallied support for Massachusetts. In far-off Georgia, a Patriot warned the "Freemen of the Province" that "every privilege you at present claim as a birthright, may be wrested from you by the same authority that blockades the town of Boston." "The cause of Boston," George Washington declared from Virginia, "now is and ever will be considered as the cause of America." The activities of the Committees of Correspondence had created a firm sense of unity.

In 1774 Parliament passed the Quebec Act, which heightened the Americans' sense of common danger. The law extended the boundaries of Quebec into the Ohio River Valley, threatening to restrict the western boundaries of Virginia and other seaboard colonies. It also gave legal recognition to Roman Catholicism—a humane concession to French Canadians but one that aroused old religious hatreds, especially in New England, where Puritans associated Catholicism with arbitrary royal government. Although the ministry had not intended the Quebec Act as a coercive measure, many colonial leaders saw it as another demonstration of Parliament's power to intervene in American domestic affairs.

The Continental Congress Responds

American leaders called for a new all-colony assembly, the Continental Congress. The newer colonies—Florida, Quebec, Nova Scotia, and Newfoundland—did not attend, but delegates chosen by all the other mainland assemblies (except Georgia, whose legislature was effectively controlled by a royal governor) met in Philadelphia in September 1774. New England delegates to the First Continental Congress advocated political union and defensive military preparations. Southern leaders, fearing a British plot "to overturn the constitution and introduce a system of arbitrary government," favored a new economic boycott. But many delegates from the middle colonies held out for a political compromise.

Led by Joseph Galloway of Pennsylvania, these men of "loyal principles" outlined a scheme for a new imperial system that resembled the Albany Plan of Union of 1754. Under Galloway's proposal, America would have a legislative

Religion and Rebellion
Many American Protestants hated bishops and the ecclesiastical power they represented. This cartoon warned that the Quebec Act of 1774, which allowed the practice of Catholicism in Canada, was part of a plot by the Church of England to impose bishops on the American colonies.

council selected by the colonial assemblies and a president-general appointed by the king. The new council would have veto power over Parliamentary legislation that affected America. Despite this feature, however, the delegates refused to endorse Galloway's plan. With British troops occupying Boston, it was thought to be too conciliatory.

Instead, the First Continental Congress passed a Declaration of Rights and Grievances that condemned the Coercive Acts and demanded their repeal. It also repudiated the Declaratory Act of 1766, which had proclaimed Parliament's supremacy over the colonies, and demanded that Britain restrict its supervision of American affairs to matters of external trade. Finally, the Congress began a program of economic retaliation, beginning with nonimportation and nonconsumption agreements that would take effect in December 1774. If Parliament did not repeal the Intolerable Acts by September 1775, all colonial exports to Britain, Ireland, and the West Indies would be cut off. Thus, ten years of constitutional conflict had culminated in all-out commercial warfare.

Even at this late date a few British leaders continued to hope for compromise. In January 1775 the earl of Chatham (William Pitt) asked Parliament to give up its claim to tax the colonies and recognize the Continental Congress as a lawful body. In return for these and other concessions, he suggested, the Congress should acknowledge Parliamentary supremacy and grant a continuing revenue to help defray the British national debt.

But the British ministry had backed down twice; a third retreat was impossible. The honor of the nation was at stake. The ministry rejected Chatham's plan, branding the Continental Congress an illegal assembly. It also dismissed a proposal by Lord Dartmouth, the colonial secretary, to send commissioners to America to negotiate a settlement. Instead, Lord North set stringent terms: Americans must pay for their own defense and administration and acknowledge Parliament's authority to tax them. To put teeth in these demands, North imposed a naval blockade on American trade with foreign nations and ordered General Gage to suppress dissent in Massachusetts. "Now the case seemed desperate," the prime minister told former Governor Thomas Hutchinson, who was living in exile in London. "Parliament would not—could not—concede. For aught he could see it must come to violence."

The Rising of the Countryside

Ultimately, the success of the urban-led Patriot movement would depend on support from the large rural population. At first most farmers had little interest in imperial issues. Their lives were deeply rooted in the soil, and their prime allegiance was to family and community. But the French and Indian War had taken their sons away and raised their taxes. In Newtown, Long Island, for example, farmers had paid an average of 10 shillings a year in taxes until 1754; by 1756 their taxes had jumped to 30 shillings a year to cover military expenses. Peace brought them only slight relief; the Quartering Act cost each Newtown resident 20 shillings in taxes in 1771. Rural Americans found these increases onerous, though in fact they paid much lower taxes than did most Britons.

The urban-led nonimportation movements of 1765 and 1769 also raised the political consciousness of many rural Americans. When the Continental Congress declared a new economic boycott of British goods in 1774, it easily established a network of local Committees of Safety and Inspection to support it. Appealing to rural thriftiness, the Congress condemned those who wore expensive imported clothes to funerals, approving only "a black crape or ribbon on the arm or hat for gentlemen, and a black ribbon and necklace for ladies." In Concord, Massachusetts, eighty percent of male heads of families and a number of single women signed a Solemn League and Covenant vowing support for nonimportation.

Patriots also appealed to the yeoman tradition of agricultural independence, which was everywhere under attack. Arable land had become scarce and expensive in long-settled regions; in many new communities merchants were seizing farmsteads for delinquent debts. The new demands of the British government would further drain "this People of the Fruits of their Toil," complained the town meeting of Petersham, Massachusetts. "The duty on tea," added a Patriot pamphlet, "was only a prelude to a window-tax, hearth-tax, land-tax, and poll-tax, and these were only paving the way for reducing the country to lordships." By the 1770s many northern yeomen felt personally threatened by British imperial policy.

Despite their higher standard of living, southern slaveowners had similar fears. Many Chesapeake planters had fallen deeply into debt to British merchants. Accustomed to being masters on their plantations, they resented their financial dependence and feared the prospect of political dependence raised by the Coercive Acts. Influential planters worried that once Parliament had subdued Massachusetts, it might seize control of Virginia's county courts and House of Burgesses, depriving the gentry of the political power it had enjoyed so long. This threat moved Patriot planters to action. "The spark of liberty is not yet extinct among our people," one planter declared, "and if properly fanned by the Gentlemen of influence will, I make no doubt, burst out again into a flame."

While many wealthy planters and affluent merchants supported the Patriot cause, other prominent Americans worried that resistance to Britain would destroy respect for all political institutions, ending in mob rule. When the Sons of Liberty turned to violence to enforce nonimportation, their fears increased. One well-to-do New Yorker complained, "No man can be in a more abject state of bondage than he whose Reputation, Property and Life are exposed to the discretionary violence . . . of the community."

Other social groups also refused to support the resistance movement. In regions where many wealthy landlords became Patriots, such as the Hudson Valley of New York, tenant farmers often favored the maintenance of imperial authority. Similar social divisions prompted some backcountry Regulators in North Carolina and farmers on the eastern shore of Chesapeake Bay in Maryland to oppose the policies advocated by the local Patriot gentry. Ethnic and religious conflicts in the middle colonies prompted thousands of ordinary colonists to remain loyal to the king. Many Quakers and Germans in

Pennsylvania and New Jersey tried to remain neutral because of pacifist religious principles or from fear of political change.

Beginning in 1774, prominent Americans of "loyal principles"—mostly royal officials, merchants with military contracts, clergy of the Church of England, and well-established lawyers—denounced the Patriot movement, accusing it of seeking independence. They coalesced in a small but articulate pro-British party. But in most areas they failed to organize potential supporters and were therefore unable to affect the course of events. A Tory Association started by Governor Wentworth of New Hampshire drew only fifty-nine members, fourteen of whom were the governor's relatives. At this crucial juncture Americans who favored resistance to British rule commanded the allegiance—or at least the acquiescence—of the majority of white Americans.

The Failure of Compromise

When the Continental Congress met in September 1774, New England was already openly defying British authority. In August 150 delegates from neighboring towns had gathered in Concord, Massachusetts, for a Middlesex County Congress. The illegal convention had advised Patriots to close the royal courts of justice and transfer their political allegiance to the popularly elected House of Representatives. Armed crowds had prevented judges appointed by the royal governor from holding court and had harassed supporters of the imperial regime.

General Thomas Gage, by then the military governor of Massachusetts, tried desperately to maintain imperial power. In September 1774 he ordered British troops in Boston to seize Patriot armories and storehouses at Charlestown and Cambridge. In response, 20,000 colonial militiamen mobilized to safeguard military supply depots in Concord and Worcester. The Concord town meeting voted to raise a defensive force, the famous Minutemen, to "Stand at a minutes warning in Case of alarm." Increasingly, Gage's authority was limited to Boston, where it rested primarily on the bayonets of his 3,500 troops. Meanwhile, the Massachusetts House met on its own authority, issued regulations for the collection of taxes, strengthened the militia, and assumed the responsibilities of government.

Even before the news of Massachusetts's defiance reached London, the colonial secretary, Lord Dartmouth, had proclaimed Massachusetts to be in a state of "open rebellion." Declaring that "force should be repelled by force," he ordered Gage to march quickly against the "rude rabble." On the night of April 18, 1775, Gage dispatched 700 soldiers to capture colonial leaders and supplies at Concord. But Paul Revere and two other Bostonians warned the Patriots, and at dawn on April 19 local militiamen met the British first at Lexington and then at Concord. The skirmishes took a dozen lives. As the British retreated along the narrow roads to Boston, they were repeatedly ambushed by militiamen from neighboring towns. By the end of the day, 73 British soldiers were dead, 174 wounded, and 26 missing. British fire had killed 49 American militiamen and wounded 39. Thus, twelve years of conflict over taxes and constitutional principles had ended in civil war.

CHAPTER 5 TIMELINE

1754–1763	Salutary neglect ends
	British national debt doubles
1760	George III becomes king
1762	Revenue Act reforms customs service
1763	Proclamation Line restricts western settlement
	Peacetime army in America
	Grenville becomes prime minister
1764	Currency Act
	Sugar Act
	Colonists oppose vice-admiralty courts
	Franklin proposes American representation in Parliament
1765	Stamp Act
	Quartering Act
	Stamp Act Congress and riots
1765–1766	First nonimportation movement
1766	First Compromise: Rockingham repeals Stamp Act and enacts Declaratory Act
1767	Townshend duties
	"Restraining Act" in New York
1768	Second nonimportation movement begins
	Daughters of Liberty make homespun cloth
	British army occupies Boston
1770	Second Compromise: North repeals most Townshend duties
	Boston Massacre
1772	*Gaspée* burned in Rhode Island
	Colonial Committees of Correspondence
1773	Tea Act
	Boston Tea Party
1774	Coercive Acts punish Massachusetts
	Quebec Act
	First Continental Congress
	Third nonimportation movement
	Loyalists organize
1775	British ministry orders Gage to suppress rebellion
	Battles of Lexington and Concord

THEMATIC TIMELINE

	GOVERNMENT Creating Republican Institutions	ECONOMY Expanding Commerce and Manufacturing	SOCIETY Defining Liberty and Equality	CULTURE Pluralism and National Identity
1775	State constitutions written Independence declared (1776)	Wartime expansion of manufacturing	Gradual emancipation in North Murray, "On the Equality of the Sexes" (1779)	Paine's *Common Sense* (1776) calls for an American republic
1780	Articles of Confederation (1781) U.S. Constitution (1787)	Bank of North America (1781) Commercial recession (1783–89)	Virginia Statute of Religious Freedom (1786) Idea of republican motherhood	Land ordinances create national domain Webster defines American English
1790	Bill of Rights (1791) First national parties: Federalists and Republicans	First Bank of the United States (1791–1811) States charter business corporations Outwork system expands	Sedition Act limits press freedom (1798)	Indians form Western Confederation Regional differences—New England, South, Mid-Atlantic—persist
1800	Revolution of 1800 Activist state legislatures Chief Justice Marshall asserts judicial power	Cotton economy expands into Old Southwest Farm productivity improves Embargo encourages domestic manufacturing	New Jersey ends woman suffrage (1807) U.S. ends legal importation of African slaves (1808)	African-Americans absorb Protestant Christianity Tecumseh develops Indian identity
1810	Triumph of Republican party State constitutions democratized	Second Bank of the United States (1816–1836) Supreme Court protects contracts and corporations	Expansion of suffrage for white men End of established churches in New England (1820s)	War of 1812 tests national unity Second Great Awakening shapes American identity

PART 2

THE NEW REPUBLIC
1775–1820

The American war is over, Benjamin Rush declared in 1787, "but this is far from being the case with the *American revolution*. . . . It remains yet to establish and perfect our new forms of government." The job was even greater than Rush imagined, for the republican revolution of 1776 challenged traditional values and institutions in many spheres of life.

The first and most fundamental challenge was to create a republican system of government. In 1775 no one in America knew what powers the central and state governments should have or how they should be organized. It took time and experience to find out; the state constitutions and the U.S. Constitution of 1787 were great experiments in self-rule. One unexpected result was the appearance of political parties, new institutions that initially threatened to divide the nation.

Second, Americans had to achieve economic independence, a task that involved the creation of new systems of banking, manufacturing, and transportation and the extension of the national economy into the vast lands of the trans-Appalachian West.

Third, the new nation needed to define the meaning of liberty and equality. Resisting demands from some women and African-Americans that the new republic guarantee equal rights for all, American leaders restricted full citizenship and social equality to white men. A few prominent Americans did suggest a political role for women as "republican mothers" who would train their sons as patriots, while others advocated marriages based on the principle of equality. The impact of republican ideas was more dramatic in religion, as most states abolished established churches and many citizens flocked to democratically organized denominations.

The final challenge was to create a national identity from a diversity of peoples and regions. Gradually political institutions began to unite Americans, as did their increasing participation in the market economy and evangelical Protestant churches.

WAR AND REVOLUTION, 1775–1783

- Toward Independence, 1775–1776
- The Perils of War and Finance, 1776–1778
- The Path to Victory, 1778–1783
- Republicanism Defined and Challenged

The battles at Lexington and Concord transformed American Patriots into rebels willing to use military force to achieve their political ends. Although only a minority of Patriots demanded independence, the outbreak of fighting gave the advantage to the most intrepid. By the end of 1775 radicals dominated local meetings, provincial assembles, and the Continental Congress and demanded a complete break from Britain. "To know whether it be the interest of the continent to be independent," declared Thomas Paine, "we need only ask this easy, simple question: Is it the interest of a man to be a boy all his life?" Responding to such sentiments, on July 4, 1776, Patriot leaders formally severed American ties to Great Britain by agreeing to a Declaration of Independence.

More momentously, the rebels became revolutionaries, as they created new republican state governments. "From subjects to citizens the difference is immense," remarked the South Carolina physician and Patriot David Ramsey. "Each citizen of a free state contains, within himself, by nature and the constitution, as much of the common sovereignty as another." Repudiating aristocratic and monarchical rule, the Patriots placed sovereignty in the people, launching the age of democratic revolutions.

TOWARD INDEPENDENCE, 1775–1776

The Battle of Concord was fought on April 19, 1775, but fourteen months would elapse before the rebels formally broke with Britain. In the meantime, Patriot legislators in most colonies threw out their royal governors and created the two essentials for independence: a government and an army.

Civil War

Armed struggle in Massachusetts lent urgency to the Second Continental Congress, which met in Philadelphia in May 1775. Soon after the Congress opened, more than 3,000 British troops attacked new American fortifications on Breed's Hill and Bunker Hill, overlooking Boston. Three assaults, at the cost of 1,000 British casualties, finally dislodged the Patriot militia. Inspired by his countrymen's valor, John Adams exhorted the Congress to rise to the "defense of American liberty" by calling for volunteers and creating a Continental army headed by George Washington of Virginia. More cautious delegates and those with Loyalist sympathies opposed these measures, warning that they would lead to more violence and commit the colonists irretrievably to rebellion. After bitter debate, Congress approved the proposals—but as Adams lamented, only "by bare majorities."

Despite the blood that had been shed, a majority in Congress still hoped for reconciliation with Britain. Led by John Dickinson of Pennsylvania, these moderates passed an Olive Branch petition, expressing loyalty to George III and asking him to seek the repeal of oppressive Parliamentary legislation. But zealous Patriots such as Samuel Adams of Massachusetts and Patrick Henry of Virginia tried to mobilize anti-imperial sentiment by winning passage of a Declaration of the Causes and Necessities of Taking Up Arms. Americans dreaded the "calamities of civil war," it asserted, but were "resolved to die Freemen rather than to live [as] slaves." The king decided the issue by refusing to receive the petition.

Instead, in August 1775 George III issued a Proclamation for Suppressing Rebellion and Sedition. The following month the Congress launched an invasion of Canada, hoping to unleash a popular uprising and add a fourteenth colony to the rebellion. Patriot forces easily took Montreal, but in December they failed to capture Quebec. To aid the Patriot cause American merchants waged financial warfare, implementing the Congress's resolution to cut off all exports to Britain and its West Indian possessions. By cutting the trade in tobacco and disrupting the production of sugar, they hoped to undermine the British economy. Parliament retaliated at the end of 1775 with a Prohibitory Act that outlawed all trade with the rebellious colonies.

Meanwhile, the fighting in Massachusetts sparked skirmishes between Patriots and Loyalists in Virginia. In June 1775 the Patriot-dominated

House of Burgesses forced the royal governor, Lord Dunmore, to take refuge on a British warship in Chesapeake Bay. Branding the Patriots "traitors," the governor organized two military forces—one white, the Queen's Own Loyal Virginians, and one black, the Ethiopian Regiment. Then, in November, Dunmore issued a controversial proclamation of his own, offering freedom to slaves and indentured servants who joined the Loyalist cause. Faced with the possibility of black uprisings as well as military attack, Patriot planters threatened runaway slaves with death and called for a final break with Britain.

In North Carolina, demands for independence grew more insistent in response to British military threats. Early in 1776 North Carolina's royal governor, Josiah Martin, tried to reestablish imperial authority with a force of 1,500 Scottish Highlanders from the Carolina backcountry. But the Patriot militia in the low country quickly mobilized and in February defeated Martin's army at the Battle of Moore's Creek Bridge, capturing more than 800 troops. As the violence escalated, radical Patriots transformed the assembly into an independent Provincial Congress; in April that body instructed its representatives in Philadelphia "to concur with the Delegates of other Colonies in declaring Independency, and forming foreign alliances." Virginia followed suit. In May, led by George Mason, James Madison, Edmund Pendleton, and Patrick Henry, Patriots called a special convention at which they resolved unanimously to support independence.

Common Sense

The break with Britain did not come easily, for most Americans retained a deep loyalty to the Crown. Joyous crowds had toasted the health of George III after the repeal of the Stamp Act; even as the imperial crisis worsened, Benjamin Franklin had proposed that the king rule over autonomous American assemblies. Americans had condemned tax legislation enacted by Parliament, not the king or the institution of monarchy.

The very structure of American society supported their loyalty. Americans used the same metaphors of age and family to describe imperial rule and social authority. They often pictured the colonies as the dependent offspring—the children—of Britain, the "mother country." Just as the settlers respected male elders in town meetings, churches, and families, so they obeyed the king as the father of his people. Denial of the king's legitimacy might threaten all paternal authority and weaken the hierarchical social order. Nonetheless, by 1775 many Americans were accusing George III of actively supporting oppressive legislation and ordering military retaliation against them.

Surprisingly, agitation against the king became especially intense in Philadelphia, the largest but hardly the most tumultuous seaport city. Because Philadelphia merchants harbored Loyalist sympathies, the city had been slow to join the boycott against the Townshend duties. But artisans, who accounted for about half the city's population, were destined to become a powerful force in the Patriot movement. Worried that British imports threatened their small-scale manufacturing enterprises and that Parliament was attempting to abolish their "just Rights and Privileges," they organized a Mechanics Association. By February 1776 forty artisans sat with forty-seven merchants on the Philadelphia Committee of Resistance, the extralegal body that enforced the latest trade boycott.

The artisans acted out of both economic self-interest and religious ideology. Some artisans, and even more of the city's laborers, were Scots-Irish Presbyterians who had left northern Ireland to escape the hard times created by British mercantilist policies. Many Scots-Irish were also followers of Gilbert Tennent and other New Light ministers. As pastor of Philadelphia's Second Presbyterian Church, Tennent had told his congregation that all men and women were equal before God. Translating that assertion into political terms, New Light Presbyterians shouted in street demonstrations that they had "no king but King Jesus." Republican ideas derived from the European Enlightenment also circulated freely in Pennsylvania. Well-educated scientists and statesmen such as Benjamin Franklin and Benjamin Rush questioned not only the wisdom of George III but the idea of monarchy itself.

At this pivotal moment, with popular sentiment in flux, a single pamphlet tipped the balance. In January 1776 Thomas Paine published *Common Sense*, a call for independence and republicanism phrased in language the general public could understand and respond to. Paine, a minor bureaucrat in England, had been fired from the Customs Service for wage agitation. In 1774, with a letter of introduction from Benjamin Franklin, he had migrated to Philadelphia, where he met Benjamin Rush and others who shared his republican sentiments. In *Common Sense* Paine called George III "the hard hearted sullen Pharaoh of England" and blasted the British system of "mixed government," which yielded only "monarchical tyranny in the person of the King and aristocratical tyranny in the persons of the peers." *Common Sense* went through twenty-five editions and reached hundreds of thousands of homes. Its message was clear: reject the arbitrary powers of king and Parliament and create independent republican states. "A government of our own is our natural right," Paine concluded. "'TIS TIME TO PART."

Independence Declared

Throughout the colonies, Patriot conventions, inspired by Paine's arguments and escalating military conflict with Loyalists, called urgently for a break from Britain. In June 1776 Richard Henry Lee presented the Virginia Convention's resolution to the Continental Congress: "That these United Colonies are, and of right ought to be, free and independent states . . . absolved from all allegiance to the British Crown." Faced with certain defeat, staunch Loyalists and anti-independence moderates withdrew from the Congress, leaving committed Patriots to take the fateful step. On July 4, 1776, the Congress approved a Declaration of Independence.

Affirming the Declaration of Independence
The mood in the room is solemn as Congress formally declares independence from Great Britain. The delegates were now traitors to their country and king, their fortunes and even lives hinging on the success of Patriot arms.

The main author of the Declaration was Thomas Jefferson, a young Virginia planter and legislative leader who had mobilized resistance to the Coercive Acts with the pamphlet *A Summary View of the Rights of British America*. Now Jefferson sought to legitimize the colonies' independence by blaming the rupture on the king. To persuade domestic critics and foreign observers, he condemned the imperial acts that had oppressed Americans, heaping most of the blame on George III: "He has plundered our seas, ravaged our coasts, burned our towns, and destroyed the lives of our people. . . . A prince, whose character is thus marked by every act which may define a tyrant, is unfit to be the ruler of a free people."

Jefferson, who was steeped in the ideas and rhetoric of the European Enlightenment, preceded these accusations with a proclamation of "self-evident" truths: "that all men are created equal"; that they possess the "unalienable rights" of "Life, Liberty, and the pursuit of Happiness"; that government derives its "just powers from the consent of the governed" and can rightly be overthrown if it "becomes destructive of these ends." In linking these doctrines of individual liberty and popular sovereignty with independence, Jefferson established revolutionary republicanism as a defining value of the new nation.

For Jefferson as for Paine, the pen would prove mightier than the sword. Almost overnight many halfhearted Americans became republican revolutionaries. In rural hamlets and seaport cities, crowds celebrated the Declaration by burning George III in effigy; in New York City, they toppled a huge statue of the king. These acts of destruction broke the Patriots' psychological ties to the mother country and the father monarch. Americans were ready to create *republics*, state governments that would derive their authority from the people.

THE PERILS OF WAR AND FINANCE, 1776–1778

The Declaration of Independence prompted Britain to launch a full-scale military assault against the Patriots. For the next two years British forces outfought the Continental army commanded by George Washington, winning nearly every battle. A few inspiring American victories kept the rebellion alive, but in late 1776 and during the winter of 1777–1778 at Valley Forge, the Patriot cause hung in the balance.

War in the North

When the British decided to use military force to crush the American revolt, few observers gave the rebels a chance. Great Britain had 11 million people, compared with the colonies' population of 2.5 million, nearly 20 percent of whom were slaves. The British also had a profound economic advantage because of the immense profits from the South Atlantic system and the emerging Industrial Revolution. These financial resources paid for the most powerful navy in the world, a standing army of 48,000 men, and thousands of German mercenaries. Moreover, British military officers had been tested in combat, and their soldiers were well armed. The imperial government also had the support of tens of thousands of Loyalists in America as well as many Indian tribes hostile to white expansion.

By contrast, the rebellious Americans were militarily weak. They had no navy, and General Washington's poorly trained army consisted of about 18,000 troops, mostly short-term militiamen hastily recruited by state governments in Virginia and New England. The Patriots could field thousands more militiamen, but only for short periods and only near their own farms and towns. Although many American officers were capable veterans of the French and Indian War, even the most experienced had never commanded a large force or faced a disciplined army capable of the intricate maneuvers of European warfare.

To exploit this advantage Britain's prime minister, Lord North, acted swiftly after the unexpected American invasion of Canada in 1775. He ordered an ambitious military mobilization and replaced the ineffective General Gage with a new commander, General William Howe. Howe had served in the colonies during the French and Indian War and had distinguished himself in the siege of Quebec. North ordered him to capture New

York City and seize control of the Hudson River, actions that would isolate the radical Patriots in New England from the other colonies. In July 1776, as the Continental Congress was declaring independence in Philadelphia, Howe was landing 10,000 troops—British regulars and German mercenaries—outside New York City. By August the British army in New York had swollen to 32,000 soldiers, supported by a fleet of thirty warships and 10,000 sailors.

British superiority was immediately apparent. On August 27, 1776, Howe attacked the Americans in the Battle of Long Island and forced their retreat to Manhattan Island. There Howe outflanked Washington's troops, nearly trapping them on several occasions. Outgunned and outmaneuvered, the Continental army again retreated, first to Harlem Heights, then to White Plains, and finally across the Hudson River to New Jersey. By December the British army had pushed the rebels out of New Jersey and across the Delaware River into Pennsylvania, forcing Congress to flee from Philadelphia to Baltimore.

From the Patriots' perspective, winter came just in time, for in the eighteenth century military campaigns were customarily halted during the cold months. The overconfident British let down their guard, allowing the Americans to score a few triumphs. On Christmas night in 1776, Washington crossed the Delaware River and staged a surprise attack on Trenton, New Jersey, forcing the surrender of a thousand German mercenaries (Hessians). Then, in early January 1777, the Continental army won a small engagement at nearby Princeton. The two victories raised sagging Patriot morale and allowed the Continental Congress to return to Philadelphia. Bright stars in a dark night, these momentary triumphs could not mask British military superiority. These are the times, wrote Tom Paine, that "try men's souls."

Armies and Strategies

Instead of following up his victories with a ruthless pursuit of the retreating Americans, Howe was content to demonstrate his superior power, hoping to convince the Continental Congress that resistance was futile. He had opposed the Coercive Acts of 1774 and hoped to negotiate a compromise with the rebels. Howe's caution also reflected the conventions of eighteenth-century warfare, which prescribed outmaneuvering the opposing forces and winning their surrender rather than destroying them. The British general was well aware that his troops were 3,000 miles from supplies and reinforcements. In case of a major defeat, replenishing his force would take six months. Although Howe's tactics were understandable, they cost the British the opportunity to nip the rebellion in the bud.

Howe's failure to win a decisive victory was paralleled by Washington's success in avoiding a major defeat. He too was cautious, challenging Howe on occasion but retreating in the face of superior strength. As Washington advised Congress, "On our Side the War should be defensive." His strategy was to draw the British away from the seacoast, extend their lines of supply, and sap their morale while keeping the Continental army intact as a symbol and instrument of American resistance.

Congress had promised Washington a regular force of 75,000 men, but the Continental army never reached half that number. Yeomen militiamen preferred to serve in local units rather than join the Continental forces. Consequently, the army drew recruits from the lower ranks of society. General William Smallwood of Maryland commanded soldiers who were either poor American-born youths or older foreign-born men—British ex-convicts and former indentured servants. Such men enlisted not for reasons of patriotism but for a bonus of $20 in cash (about $200 today) and the promise of 100 acres of land. Molding these recruits into a fighting force took time. In the face of a British artillery bombardment or flank attack, many men panicked; hundreds of others deserted, unwilling to submit to the discipline and danger of military life. The soldiers who stayed resented the contemptuous way Washington and other American officers treated the camp followers—the women who came along with the recruits and took care of their material and emotional needs.

Such support was crucial, for the Continental army was poorly supplied and faintly praised. Radical Whig Patriots had long viewed a peacetime standing army as a threat to liberty; even in wartime they preferred the militia to a professional force. Consequently, the Continental army lacked adequate supplies and pay. General Philip Schuyler of New York complained that his troops were "weak in numbers, dispirited, naked, destitute of provisions, without camp equipage, with little ammunition, and not a single piece of cannon." Given these handicaps, Washington was fortunate not to have suffered an overwhelming defeat in the first year of the war.

Victory at Saratoga

Howe's failure to achieve a decisive victory surprised and dismayed Lord North and his colonial secretary, Lord George Germain, who now realized that restoration of the empire would require a long-term military commitment. Accepting the challenge, the government increased the British land tax to finance the war and prepared to mount a major campaign in 1777.

The isolation of New England remained the primary British goal and was to be achieved by a three-pronged attack on Albany, New York. General John Burgoyne was to lead a large contingent of British regulars from Quebec to Albany. A second, smaller force of Iroquois warriors (who had allied themselves with the British to protect their land from American settlers) would attack from the west under Colonel Barry St. Leger. To reinforce Burgoyne from the south, Germain ordered Howe to dispatch a force northward from New York City (see Map 6.1).

Howe wanted to attack Philadelphia, the home of the Continental Congress and the Continental army, and end the rebellion with a single victory. With Germain's apparent approval, Howe set his forces in motion. Rather than

MAP 6.1
The War in the North
In 1776 the British drove Washington's army across New Jersey into Pennsylvania. The Americans counterattacked at Trenton and Princeton and camped for the winter at Morristown. In 1777 General Howe captured Philadelphia from the south; Colonel St. Leger and General Burgoyne launched invasions from Canada but were defeated at Oriskany, Bennington, and then Saratoga, the turning point of the war.

march overland through New Jersey, the troops sailed south from New York and then up Chesapeake Bay to approach Philadelphia from the southwest. Howe's troops easily outflanked the American positions along Brandywine Creek, forcing Washington to withdraw. On September 26 the British marched triumphantly into Philadelphia, half assuming that the capture of the rebels' capital would end the uprising. But the Continental Congress fled into the interior, determined to continue the struggle.

The British paid a high price for Howe's decision to attack Philadelphia, for it contributed directly to Burgoyne's defeat. Initially Burgoyne's troops had sped across Lake Champlain, overwhelming the American defenses at Fort Ticonderoga and driving toward the upper reaches of the Hudson River. Then they stalled, for Burgoyne—"Gentleman Johnny," as he was called—fought with style, not speed, weighed down by comfortable tents and ample stocks of food and wine. Burgoyne's progress was further impeded by General Horatio Gates, whose troops felled trees across the crude wagon trail Burgoyne was following and raided his long supply lines to Canada.

By the end of the summer Burgoyne's army—6,000 regulars (half of them German mercenaries) and 600 Loyalists and Indians—was in trouble, bogged down in the wilderness near Saratoga, New York. In August, 2,000 American militiamen left their farms to fight a bitter battle at nearby Bennington, Vermont, depriving British raiders of much-needed supplies of food, horses, and oxen. Meanwhile, Patriot militiamen in the Mohawk Valley forced St. Leger and the Iroquois to retreat. Because Howe needed additional troops to occupy Philadelphia, the British commander in New York City recalled the troops he had sent toward Albany. While Burgoyne waited for help, thousands of Patriot militiamen from Massachusetts, New Hampshire, and New York joined Gates's forces. They "swarmed around the army like birds of prey," an alarmed English sergeant wrote in his journal, and on October 17, 1777, forced Burgoyne to surrender.

The battle at Saratoga proved to be the turning point of the war. The Americans captured 5,000 British troops and their equipment. More important, their victory virtually assured the success of American diplomats in Paris, who were seeking a military alliance with France. Patriots on the home front were delighted, though their joy was muted by wartime difficulties.

Wartime Trials

The war exposed tens of thousands of civilians to deprivation, displacement, and death. "An army, even a friendly one, are a dreadful scourge to any people," a Connecticut soldier wrote from Pennsylvania. "You cannot imagine what devastation and distress mark their steps." New Jersey was particularly hard hit by the fighting, as British and American armies marched back and forth across the state. Those with reputations as Patriots or Loyalists fled their homes to escape arrest—or worse—as soldiers and partisans looted farms, seeking food or political revenge. Wherever the armies went, drunk and disorderly troops harassed or raped women and girls. Families lived in fear of their approach.

Indeed, the War of Independence became a civil war. In New England mobs of Patriot farmers beat suspected Tories or destroyed their property. "Every Body submitted to our Sovereign Lord the Mob," a Loyalist preacher lamented. Patriots organized Committees of Safety to collect taxes, send food and clothing to the Continental army, and impose fines or jail sentences on those who failed to support the cause. "There is no such thing as remaining neutral," declared the Committee of Farmington, Connecticut.

The new state governments were not politically secure, and many teetered on the brink of bankruptcy. To finance the war they borrowed gold, silver, or British currency from wealthy individuals. When those funds ran out, they had to find a new means of feeding, clothing, and paying the troops. Since opposition to taxation had fueled the independence movement, Patriot officials were reluctant to increase taxes. Instead, the states created a new monetary system based on the dollar (not the English pound) and issued $260 million in currency and transferable bonds. Theoretically, the new notes could be redeemed at a stated time in gold or silver, but since they were printed in huge quantities and were not backed by tax revenues or mortgages on land, many Americans refused to accept them at face value. North Carolina's paper money came to be worth so little, even the state government refused it.

The monetary system created by the Continental Congress collapsed too, despite the efforts of the Philadelphia merchant Robert Morris, the "financier of the Revolution." The Congress was completely dependent on funds requisitioned from the states, which frequently paid late or not at all. To raise money Congress depended on loans, but with no revenue of its own, it could not assure creditors they would be repaid. Congress therefore borrowed $6 million from France, which it used as security to encourage wealthy Americans to purchase $27 million in Continental loan certificates. When those funds and other French and Dutch loans were exhausted, Congress followed the lead of the states and financed the war by printing bills of credit. Between 1775 and 1779 it issued $191 million in bills, which were used as currency. By 1780 tax revenues from the states had retired only $3 million, and the value of the bills fell dramatically.

The excess of currency created the worst inflation in American history. The amount of goods available for purchase—both domestic foodstuffs and foreign manufactures—had shrunk significantly because of the fighting and the British naval blockade, while the amount of money in circulation had multiplied. Because more currency was chasing fewer goods, prices rose rapidly. In Maryland, for example, a bag of salt that had cost $1 in 1776 sold for $3,900 a few years later. Unwilling to accept worthless currency, hardpressed farmers refused to sell their crops, even to the Continental army. To supply their own needs, farmers used barter—trading wheat for tools or clothes—or sold goods only to those who could pay in gold or silver. Women, distressed by the high prices for sugar, tea, and bread, formed mobs and seized the goods they needed from storekeepers. Civilian morale and social cohesion crumbled, causing some Patriot leaders to doubt that the rebellion could succeed.

A Flood of Paper Currency
The Continental Congress issued this bill in 1776, declaring it to be worth "SIX Spanish Milled DOLLARS" or the equivalent in gold or silver, but by 1780 most Americans no longer had confidence in the currency and its value collapsed to virtually nothing, giving rise to the phrase "not worth a continental."

Fears reached their peak during the winter of 1777–1778. Howe camped in Philadelphia and with his officers partook of the finest wines, foods, and entertainment the city could offer. Washington's army retreated to Valley Forge, some 20 miles to the west, where about 12,000 soldiers and hundreds of camp followers suffered horribly. "The army . . . now begins to grow sickly," a surgeon confided to his diary. "Poor food—hard lodging—cold weather—fatigue—nasty clothes—nasty cookery. . . . Why are we sent here to starve and freeze?" Nearby farmers refused to help. Some were pacifists—Quakers and German sectarians—unwilling to support either side. Others were self-interested, hoarding their grain in hopes of higher prices in the spring or willing to accept only the gold and silver offered by British quartermasters. "Such a dearth of public spirit, and want of public virtue," Washington complained—but to no effect. By spring, a thousand of his hungry soldiers had vanished into the countryside and another 3,000 had died from malnutrition and disease, along with scores of camp followers. One winter at Valley Forge took as many American lives as had two years of fighting against General Howe.

AMERICAN VOICES

The Ordeal at Valley Forge

The Patriots nearly lost their army—and their struggle for independence—during the winter of 1777–1778. Of the 12,000 soldiers camped at Valley Forge, 3,000 died. The memoir of James Sullivan Martin, a private from Connecticut, describes the beginning of their ordeal.

While we lay here [en route to Valley Forge] there was a Continental thanksgiving ordered by Congress, and the army had all the cause in the world to be particularly thankful, if not for being well off, at least that it was no worse, and we were ordered to participate in it. We had nothing to eat for two or three days previous, except what the trees of the fields and forests afforded us. But we must now have what Congress said—a sumptuous thanksgiving. . . . And what do you think it was, reader? Guess. You cannot guess. . . . I will tell you: it gave each and every man *half a gill* [about one-fourth cup] of rice and a *tablespoon full* of vinegar! . . .

We arrived at Valley Forge in the evening: it was dark. There was no water to be found, and I was perishing with thirst. I searched for water till I was weary and came to my tent without finding any. Fatigue and thirst, joined with hunger, almost made me desperate. I felt at that instant as if I would have taken victuals or drink from the best friend I had on earth by force. . . . Two soldiers, whom I did not know, passed by; they had some water in their canteens. . . . I tried to beg a draught of water from them, but . . . at length I persuaded them to sell me a drip for three pence, Pennsylvania currency, which was every cent of property I could then call my own, so great was the necessity I was then reduced to.

SOURCE: Linda R. Monk, ed., *Ordinary Americans: U.S. History through the Eyes of Everyday People* (Alexandria, VA: Close Up Publications, 1994), pp. 32–33.

THE PATH TO VICTORY, 1778–1783

The Patriots' prospects improved dramatically in 1778, when the United States formed a military alliance with France, the most powerful nation on the European continent. The alliance brought the Americans money, troops, and supplies and changed the conflict from a colonial rebellion to an international war.

The French Alliance

France and America were unlikely partners. France was Catholic and a monarchy; the United States, largely Protestant and a federation of republics. The two peoples had been on opposite sides in wars from 1689 to 1763. But

France was intent on avenging its defeat in the French and Indian War and its loss of Canada. In 1776 the comte de Vergennes, the French foreign minister and an early supporter of American independence, persuaded King Louis XVI to extend a secret loan to the rebellious colonies and supply them with gunpowder. Early in 1777 Vergennes opened commercial and military negotiations with Benjamin Franklin and two other American diplomats, Arthur Lee and Silas Deane. When news of the American victory at Saratoga reached Paris in December 1777, Vergennes urged the king to approve a formal alliance with the Continental Congress.

Franklin and his associates craftily exploited the rivalry between France and Britain, using the threat of a negotiated settlement with Britain to win an explicit French commitment to American independence. The Treaty of Alliance of February 6, 1778, specified that once France had entered the war against Great Britain, neither partner would sign a separate peace before the "liberty, sovereignty, and independence" of the United States were assured. The American diplomats pledged that their government would recognize any French conquests in the West Indies.

The alliance with France gave new life to the Patriots' cause. With access to military supplies and European loans, the American army soon strengthened and hopes soared. "There has been a great change in this state since the news from France," a Patriot soldier reported from Pennsylvania; farmers— "mercenary wretches," he called them—"were as eager for Continental Money now as they were a few weeks ago for British gold."

With renewed energy and purpose, the Congress addressed the demands of the officer corps for pensions. Most officers came from the upper ranks of society and used their own funds to equip themselves and sometimes their men as well. In return they demanded pensions for life at half pay. John Adams condemned the petitioners as "Mastiffs, scrambling for rank and pay like apes for nuts," but General Washington urged Congress to grant the pensions, warning the lawmakers that "the salvation of the cause depends upon it." Congress agreed to grant the officers half pay after the war, but only for seven years.

Meanwhile, the war was becoming increasingly unpopular in Britain. Radical agitators and republican-minded artisans supported American demands for greater rights and campaigned for political reform at home, including broadened voting rights and more equitable representation for cities in Parliament. The landed gentry and urban merchants protested against continuing increases in the land tax and the stamp duty as well as new levies on carriages, wine, and imported goods. "It seemed we were to be taxed and stamped ourselves instead of inflicting taxes and stamps on others," a British politician complained.

But George III remained determined to crush the rebellion. If America won independence, he warned Lord North, "the West Indies must follow them. Ireland would soon follow the same plan and be a separate state, then this island would be reduced to itself, and soon would be a poor island indeed."

Worried about a possible Franco-American alliance, however, the king allowed North to seek a negotiated settlement. In February 1778 Parliament repealed the Tea and Prohibitory acts and, in an amazing concession, renounced its right to tax the colonies. North appointed a commission headed by Lord Carlisle to negotiate with the Continental Congress and offer a return to the constitutional "condition of 1763," before the Sugar and Stamp acts. But the gesture was too little too late. The Patriots, now allied with France, rejected the overture.

War in the South

The French alliance expanded the war but did not rapidly conclude it. When France entered the conflict in June 1778, it was hoping to capture a rich sugar island and therefore concentrated its naval forces in the West Indies. Spain, which joined the war in 1779, also had its own agenda: in return for naval assistance to France, it wanted to regain Florida and Gibraltar.

The British ministry, beset by war on many fronts, settled on a modest strategy. It would use its army to recapture the rich tobacco- and rice-growing colonies of Virginia, the Carolinas, and Georgia and then rely on local Loyalists to hold and administer them. The British knew that Scottish Highlanders in North Carolina retained an especially strong allegiance to the Crown and hoped to recruit other Loyalists from the ranks of the Regulators, the enemies of the low-country Patriot planters. The ministry also hoped to take advantage of southern racial divisions. In 1776 over 1,000 slaves had fought for Lord Dunmore under the banner "Liberty to Slaves!"; thousands more might support a new British offensive. At the least, racial divisions would undermine the Patriots' military efforts. Because African-Americans formed 30 to 50 percent of the population, whites were afraid to arm them. For the same reason many planters refused to allow their sons or white overseers to join the Continental forces, fearing that their absence would encourage slave revolts.

Implementing this southern strategy became the responsibility of Sir Henry Clinton, who replaced the discredited Howe. In June 1778 Clinton ordered the main British army to evacuate Philadelphia and move to more secure quarters in New York. In December he launched his southern campaign, capturing Savannah, Georgia, and mobilizing hundreds of blacks to build barricades and unload supplies. Then Clinton moved inland, capturing Augusta early in 1779. By the end of the year, with the help of local Loyalists, the British had reconquered Georgia, and 10,000 troops were poised for an assault on South Carolina. To counter this threat, the Continental Congress suggested that South Carolina raise 3,000 black troops, but the state assembly overwhelmingly rejected the proposal.

During most of 1780 British forces marched from victory to victory (see Map 6.2). In May Clinton forced General Benjamin Lincoln and his 5,000 troops to surrender at Charleston, South Carolina. Shortly afterward Lord Cornwallis assumed control of the British forces and sent out expeditions to

MAP 6.2
The Campaign in the South

The British ministry's southern strategy started well. British forces captured Savannah in December 1778 and Charleston in May 1779. Brutal guerrilla warfare raged in the interior over the next eighteen months. When Cornwallis carried the battle into Virginia in late 1781, a French and American army surrounded his forces at Yorktown, aided by the French fleet under Admiral de Grasse.

secure the countryside. In August Cornwallis routed an American force commanded by General Horatio Gates, the hero of Saratoga, at Camden. Only about 1,200 Patriot militiamen joined Gates at the battle in Camden—a fifth of the number at Saratoga. Many of them panicked and fled without firing a shot, handing the British control of South Carolina. Hundreds of enslaved African-Americans fled to freedom in Florida, while hundreds more sought protection behind British lines, providing labor for the invading army.

James Lafayette
Born into slavery in Virginia, in 1781 James Lafayette served as a spy for the American army commanded by the marquis de Lafayette, receiving his freedom as a reward and adopting Lafayette's surname. The two Lafayettes met again in 1824, when the Frenchman visited the United States.

Then the tide of battle turned. The Dutch declared war against Britain, completing its diplomatic isolation, and France dispatched troops to America. The French decision was partly the work of the marquis de Lafayette, a republican-minded aristocrat who had offered his services to the American cause long before the alliance of 1778. In 1780 Lafayette persuaded Louis XVI to send General comte de Rochambeau and 5,500 men to Newport, Rhode Island.

General Washington replaced Gates with Nathanael Greene, who devised a new military strategy to recapture the Carolinas. To make the best use of Patriot militiamen, many of whom were "without discipline and addicted to plundering," Greene divided them into small groups commanded by strong leaders and directed them to harass the larger but less mobile British forces. In October 1780 a militia force of Patriot farmers defeated a regiment of Loyalists at King's Mountain, North Carolina, taking about a thousand prisoners. Led by the "Swamp Fox," General Francis Marion, American guerrillas won a series of small but fierce battles in South Carolina, while General Daniel Morgan led another band to a bloody victory at Cowpens, North Carolina, in January 1781. But Loyalist garrisons and militia remained powerful, assisted by the well-organized Cherokee, who hoped to protect their lands by attacking American settlers and troops. "We fight, get beaten, and fight again," General Greene declared doggedly. In March 1781 Greene's soldiers fought Cornwallis's seasoned army to a draw at North Carolina's Guilford Court House.

Weakened by this war of attrition, Cornwallis decided to concede the southernmost states to Greene and seek a decisive victory in Virginia. Aided by reinforcements from New York, the British general invaded Virginia's Tidewater region. There Benedict Arnold, the infamous traitor to the Patriot cause, led Cornwallis's troops up and down the James River, where they met only slight resistance from a small American force commanded by Lafayette. Then, in May 1781, as the two armies sparred near the York Peninsula in Virginia, France ordered its large fleet from the West Indies to North America.

Emboldened by the ample forces at his disposal, Washington launched a well-coordinated attack. Feinting an assault on New York City, he secretly marched General Rochambeau's army from Rhode Island to Virginia, where it joined his own troops. Simultaneously, the French fleet massed off the coast of Virginia, establishing control of Chesapeake Bay. By the time the British discovered Washington's audacious plan, Cornwallis was surrounded, his 9,500-man army outnumbered two to one on land and cut off from reinforcement or retreat by sea. Abandoned by the British navy, Cornwallis surrendered at Yorktown on October 19, 1781.

The Franco-American victory at Yorktown broke the resolve of the British government, which lacked the will or resources to fight a long war of attrition. "Oh God! It is all over!" Lord North exclaimed when he heard the news. The combined French and Spanish fleet menaced the British sugar islands, Dutch merchants were capturing European markets from British traders, and a newly formed group of European states—the League of Armed Neutrality—was demanding an end to Britain's commercial blockade of France. Isolated diplomatically in Europe, stymied militarily in America, and lacking public support at home, the British ministry gave up active prosecution of the war.

The Patriot Advantage

Angry members of Parliament demanded an explanation. How could mighty Britain, victorious in the Great War for Empire, be defeated by a motley group of colonists? The ministry blamed the military leadership, pointing with some justification to a series of blunders. Why had Howe not been more ruthless in pursuing Washington's army in 1776? How could Howe and Burgoyne have failed to coordinate the movement of their armies in 1777? Why had Cornwallis marched deep into the powerful state of Virginia in 1781?

While historians have been critical of the military command, they also have noted the high odds against British success, given broad-based American support for the rebel cause. Although only a third of the white population zealously supported the Patriots, another third was supportive enough to pay the taxes imposed by state governments. Moreover, unlike most revolutionaries, the Patriots were led by experienced politicians who commanded public support. And even though the Continental army had to be built from scratch and was never very large, it was fighting on its own territory with the assistance of thousands of militiamen. The more than 55,000 Tories and thousands of native Americans who fought for the British could not offset these advantages. Once the rebels had the financial and military support of France, they could reasonably hope for victory. A charismatic leader such as William Pitt

Patriot Soldiers at Yorktown, 1781
A French observer captured the diversity of the American forces: a black infantryman from Rhode Island, a French soldier, a buckskin-clad rifleman from Virginia, and (holding the gunnery torch) an artilleryman from the Continental army.

might have suppressed the rebellion, but ordinary politicians and mediocre generals were destined to fail.

Americans, by contrast, had the inspired leadership of George Washington as commander of the Continental army. Washington deferred to the civil authorities, winning respect and support from the Congress and the state governments alike. Confident of his own abilities, he recruited outstanding military officers such as the Prussian Baron von Steuben to instill discipline in the ranks of the fledgling Continental army and turn it into a respectable fighting force.

Washington had a greater margin for error than the British generals, because Patriots controlled local governments and could mobilize the militia to intervene at crucial moments. Thousands of militiamen had besieged General Gage in Boston in 1775, surrounded Burgoyne at Saratoga in 1777, and forced Cornwallis from the Carolinas in 1781. In the end the American people decided the outcome of the conflict. Preferring Patriot rule, they refused to support Loyalist forces or accept imperial control in British-occupied areas. Consequently, while the British won many military victories, they achieved little, and their defeats at Saratoga and Yorktown proved catastrophic.

Diplomatic Triumph

After Yorktown diplomats took two years to conclude the war. Peace talks began in Paris in April 1782, but the French and Spanish stalled for time, hoping for a major naval victory or territorial conquest. Their delaying tactics infuriated the American diplomats—Benjamin Franklin, John Adams, and John Jay—who feared that drawn-out negotiations would tempt France to sacrifice American interests. For this reason the Americans negotiated secretly with the British; if necessary they were prepared to cut their ties to France and sign a separate peace. The British ministry also was eager to obtain a quick settlement. Many members of Parliament no longer supported the war, and ministers feared the loss of a rich West Indian sugar island. Once again Franklin and his colleagues exploited the rivalry between Britain and France.

In the bipartite Treaty of Paris, signed on September 3, 1783, Great Britain formally recognized American independence. Britain retained Canada, which now had a southern boundary at the Great Lakes. All the land south of the lakes between the Appalachian Mountains and the Mississippi River, which Britain had wrested from France just twenty years before, was ceded to the new American republic. Although this territory was still the domain of undefeated native Americans, Britain did not secure its allies' rights to the land by insisting on a separate Indian territory. Leaving the Indians to their fate, negotiators promised to withdraw British garrisons from the region "with all convenient speed." As an Indian of the Wea people complained, "In endeavouring to assist you it seems we have wrought our own ruin." Other treaty provisions granted Americans fishing rights off Newfoundland and Nova Scotia, forbade the British from "carrying away any negroes or other property," and guaranteed freedom of navigation on the Mississippi to British subjects and American citizens "forever." In its only concessions, the American government promised not to hinder British merchants from recovering prewar debts and to recommend to the state legislatures that they return property that had been confiscated from Loyalists and treat them as equal citizens.

In the Treaty of Versailles, signed at the same time as the Treaty of Paris, Britain made peace with France and Spain. Neither American ally gained very much. Spain reclaimed Florida from Britain but failed in its main objective of retaking Gibraltar. France had the pleasure of reducing British power, but its only territorial gain was the Caribbean island of Tobago. Moreover, the war had quadrupled France's national debt; only six years later cries for tax relief and political liberty at home would spark the French Revolution. Only the Americans profited handsomely from the treaties, which gave them independence and opened up the interior of the North American continent for settlement.

REPUBLICANISM DEFINED AND CHALLENGED

From the moment they became revolutionary republicans, Americans began to define the character of their new social order. In the Declaration of Independence Thomas Jefferson had turned to John Locke, the philosopher of *private* liberty, when he declared a universal human right to "Life, Liberty, and the pursuit of Happiness." But Jefferson and many other Americans also lauded "republican virtue," an enlightened quest for the *public* interest. As the New Hampshire constitution phrased it, "Government [was] instituted for the common benefits, protection, and security of the whole community." The tension between self-interest and public interest would shape the new nation's future.

Republican Ideals and Wartime Pressures

Simply put, a republic is a state without a monarch. Yet for many Americans republicanism was not just a political system but a social philosophy. "The word *republic*" in Latin, wrote Thomas Paine, "means the *public good*," which citizens have a duty to secure. "Every man in a republic is public property," asserted the Philadelphia Patriot Benjamin Rush (who eventually extended the notion to include women as well). "His time and talents—his youth—his manhood—his old age—nay more, life, all belong to his country."

Reflecting this concern with public virtue, the Continental Congress praised the self-sacrifice of the militiamen who fought and fell at Lexington and Concord, Saratoga and Camden. It condemned as a "total loss of virtue," as Henry Laurens of South Carolina put it, the wartime demand by Continental officers for lifetime pensions. Raised as gentlemen, officers were supposed to be exemplars of virtue who gave freely to the republic.

But as the war continued, military self-sacrifice diminished. During the winters of 1779 and 1780 Continental troops stationed at Morristown, New Jersey, mutinied, unwilling to endure low pay and sparse rations. To restore authority, Washington ordered the execution of several leaders of the revolt but urged Congress to use monetary incentives—back pay and new clothing—to pacify the recruits. Later in the war, unrest among officers erupted at Newburgh, New York, where Washington had to use his personal authority to thwart a potentially dangerous challenge to the Congress's policies.

Economic distress also tested the republican virtue of ordinary citizens. The British naval blockade had nearly destroyed the New England fishing industry and had cut off the supply of European manufactured goods. British occupation of Boston, New York, and Philadelphia had also cut domestic trade and manufacturing. As unemployed shipwrights, dock laborers, masons, coopers, and bakers left the cities and drifted into the countryside, New York City's population declined from 21,000 residents in 1774 to less than half that by the war's end. In the Chesapeake the British blockade deprived tobacco planters of European markets, forcing them to turn to the cultivation of grain, which could be sold at home.

Everywhere the scarcity of goods brought a sharp rise in prices and widespread appeals for government regulation. Hard-pressed consumers decried merchants and traders as "enemies, extortioners, and monopolizers." But when, in 1777, a convention of New England states limited price increases to 75 percent above the prewar level, many farmers and artisans refused to sell their goods at the set prices. In the end, a government official admitted, consumers had to pay the market price "or submit to starving."

The struggle over regulation came to a head in Philadelphia. After the British withdrawal in 1778, severe food shortages and soaring prices prompted a sharp conflict over regulated versus free trade. Artisans and laborers persuaded a town meeting to establish a Committee on Prices, which set wholesale and retail prices for thirty-two commodities, and justified this regulation by invoking the traditional concept of the "just price." But merchants, led by the financier Robert Morris, condemned the price controls and espoused the "classical liberal" ideas of free trade and enlightened self-interest. Regulation, Morris noted, would only encourage farmers to store their crops, whereas allowing prices to rise would bring goods to market and relieve scarcity. Most farmers agreed with Morris, as did members of the Continental Congress, including Benjamin Franklin, who condemned price controls as "contrary to the nature of commerce."

Nonetheless, most Philadelphians favored "fair" trade rather than "free" trade. At a second town meeting in August 1779, 2,115 Philadelphians voted for regulation, and only 281 against it. In practice, however, many artisan-republicans—shoemakers, tanners, and bakers—found that they could not support their families on fixed prices and did not abide by them. In civilian life as in the military, self-interest tended to triumph over republican virtue.

In those difficult times Patriot women contributed to both the war effort and the well-being of their families by increasing their production of homespun cloth. One Massachusetts town produced 30,000 yards of homespun, while women in Elizabeth, New Jersey, promised "upwards of 100,000 yards of linnen and woolen cloth." Other women assumed the burdens of farm production while their men were away at war. Some went into the fields, plowing, harvesting, and loading grain, while others supervised hired laborers or slaves, in the process acquiring a taste for decision making. "We have sow'd our oats as you desired," Sarah Cobb Paine wrote to her absent husband; "had I been master I should have planted it to Corn." Taught from childhood to act selflessly—to value the welfare of their fathers, brothers, and husbands above their own—most Patriot women did not experience a conflict between republican virtue and self-interest. Their contribution to the war effort boosted their self-esteem and prompted some to claim greater rights in the new republican society. It also sparked an increase in farm household productivity that would soon create a dynamic rural economy.

Spiraling inflation posed the most severe challenge to American families and the notion of public virtue. By 1778 so much currency had been printed that a family needed $7 in Continental bills to buy goods worth $1 in gold or silver. The ratio increased to 42 to 1 in 1779 and 100 to 1 in 1780. When the rate of exchange between Continental currency and specie reached 146 to 1 in 1781, not even the most virtuous Patriots would accept paper money. To restore its value, the Continental Congress asked the states to assess taxes that could be paid at the rate of 40 paper dollars to every silver dollar. This plan redeemed $120 million in Continental bills but enriched speculators who had bought Continental bills at a rate of 100 to 1.

War Mobilization
A few American women actually fought in the war, and thousands more trav-
eled with the Continental army, providing the troops with food and support.
This 1779 woodcut, which illustrated a poem by a "Daughter of Liberty," was
meant to symbolize the wartime contributions of the women of Marblehead,
Massachusetts. (Collection of The New-York Historical Society)

At the end of the war speculators still held $71 million in Continental
notes, hoping they could eventually redeem the currency at an even greater
profit. "Private Interest seemed to predominate over the public weal," a
leading Patriot complained.

Ultimately, the sacrifices made by hundreds of thousands of ordinary
Americans financed the struggle for independence. Farmers and artisans who
had received Continental bills for supplies and soldiers who had taken them
as pay sacrificed the most. The currency literally depreciated in their pockets.

Individually the losses were small, amounting to a tiny "currency tax" every time an ordinary citizen received a paper dollar, kept it a week, and then spent it. Collectively they paid the huge cost of the war.

The Loyalist Exodus

As the war turned in favor of the Patriots, more than 100,000 Loyalists, fearing for their lives, emigrated to the West Indies, Britain, and Canada. The exodus disrupted the established social order, for some of the Loyalists were wealthy and politically powerful merchants, lawyers, and landowners. Although some Patriots wanted to seize the property the "traitors" left behind, most public officials thought that confiscation would be contrary to Patriot principles. For example, the Massachusetts Constitution of 1780 declared that every citizen should be protected "in the enjoyment of his life, liberty, and property, according to the standing laws"; Massachusetts officials extended those rights to most Loyalists.

Thus, there was no government-led social revolution. Most states seized only a limited amount of Loyalist property and sold it to the highest bidder, usually a wealthy Patriot rather than a yeoman or foot soldier. In a few cases confiscations did produce a democratic result. In North Carolina, about half the new owners of Loyalist lands were small-scale farmers. And on the former Philipse manor in New York, Patriot tenants successfully converted their leases into fee-simple ownership. But in general the revolutionary upheaval did not drastically alter the structure of rural society.

Social turmoil was greater in the cities, as Patriot merchants replaced Tories at the top of the economic ladder. In Massachusetts the Lowell, Higginson, Jackson, and Cabot families moved their trading enterprises to Boston to fill the vacuum created by the departure of the Hutchinsons and Apthorps. In Philadelphia, small-scale traders stepped into the vacancies created by the collapse of Anglican and Quaker mercantile firms. In the countinghouses as on the battlefield, Patriots emerged triumphant. The War of Independence replaced a tradition-oriented economic elite—one that invested its profits from trade in real estate, becoming *rentier* landlords—with a group of entrepreneurial-minded republican merchants who promoted new trading ventures and domestic manufacturing.

The Problem of Slavery

During the war thousands of southern slaves had sought freedom by fleeing behind British lines. Two neighbors of Richard Henry Lee, the Virginia Patriot, lost "every slave they had in the world." When the British army evacuated Charleston, more than 6,000 former slaves went with them; another 4,000 left from Savannah. Hundreds of black Loyalists settled permanently in Canada. Over 1,000 others, poorly treated and settled on inferior land in Nova Scotia, sought a better life in the abolitionist settlement in Sierra Leone, West Africa.

Thousands of African-Americans also served the Patriot cause. Free blacks from New England enrolled in Patriot units such as the First Rhode Island

Company and the Massachusetts "Bucks." In Maryland, Patriots recruited a large number of slaves for military service and later freed them, a policy rejected by other southern states. But many slaves struck informal bargains with their Patriot masters, trading loyalty in wartime for a promise of eventual liberty. In 1782 the Virginia assembly passed an act allowing *manumission* (liberation); within a decade planters had freed 10,000 slaves.

Slavery revealed a contradiction in the Patriots' republican ideology. "How is it that we hear the loudest *yelps* for liberty among the drivers of Negroes?" the British author Samuel Johnson chided. Some white Patriots took his point to heart. "I wish most sincerely there was not a Slave in the province," Abigail Adams wrote to her husband, John, as Massachusetts went to war. "It always appeared a most iniquitous Scheme to me—to fight ourselves for what we are daily robbing and plundering from those who have as good a right to freedom as we have."

The Quakers, whose belief in religious equality had made them sharp critics of many social inequities, took the lead in condemning slavery. Beginning in the 1750s, the Quaker evangelist John Woolman had urged Friends to free their slaves; during the war many North Carolina Quakers did so. Other rapidly growing pietistic groups, notably the Methodists and the Baptists, also advocated emancipation and admitted both enslaved and free blacks to their congregations. In 1784 a conference of Virginia Methodists declared that slavery was "contrary to the Golden Law of God on which hang all the Law and Prophets."

Enlightenment philosophy also played a role in the debate. John Locke had argued that ideas were not innate but stemmed from a person's impressions and experiences in the world. Accordingly, Enlightenment thinkers suggested that the oppressive conditions of slavery, not inherent inferiority, accounted for the debased situation of Africans in the Western Hemisphere. As one American put it, "A state of slavery has a mighty tendency to shrink and contract the minds of men." Anthony Benezet, a Quaker philanthropist who funded a school for blacks in Philadelphia, defied popular opinion in declaring that African-Americans were "as capable of improvement as White People."

By 1784, Massachusetts had abolished slavery outright and three other states—Pennsylvania, Connecticut, and Rhode Island—had provided for its gradual termination. Within another twenty years every state north of Delaware had implemented a policy of gradual emancipation. The laws gave priority to white property rights, for they required blacks to endure a few more years of unpaid labor. Thus, the New York Emancipation Edict of 1799 granted freedom only to enslaved children—not their parents—and only at age twenty-five. As late as 1810, 30,000 blacks in the northern states—nearly a fourth of their African-American population—were still enslaved. Whites moved slowly toward emancipation because they feared that freed blacks would compete with them for jobs and housing. More menacing was the possibility of race melding. In 1786 Massachusetts reenacted a colonial-era law that prohibited whites from marrying blacks, Indians, or mulattoes.

Benjamin Banneker Tests Jefferson's Commitment to Natural Rights

In Notes on Virginia (1785) Jefferson suggested the inherent inferiority of the black race. In this letter of 1791 Benjamin Banneker, a free African-American farmer and mathematician who authored an almanac and helped survey the District of Columbia, asks Jefferson to reconsider.

I suppose it is a truth too well attested to you, to need a proof here, that we are a race of Beings who have long laboured under the abuse and censure of the world . . . considered rather as brutish than human, and Scarcely capable of mental endowments. . . .

I hope . . . you will readily embrace every opportunity to eradicate that train of absurd and false ideas and opinions which so prevail with respect to us, and that your Sentiments are concurrent with mine, which are that the one universal Father has given to us all . . . the Same Sensations, and endued us all with the same faculties. . . . Sir I freely and Chearfully acknowledge, that I am of the African race, and, in that colour which is natural to them of the deepest dye. . . .

Sir, Suffer me to recall to your mind that time in which the Arms and tyranny of the British Crown were exerted with very powerful effort in order to reduce you to a State of Servitude. . . . This, Sir, was a time in which you clearly saw into the injustice of a State of Slavery [and] . . . that you publickly held forth this true and invaluable doctrine . . . : "We hold these truths to be Self evident, that all men are created equal . . ."; but Sir how pitiable it is to reflect, that . . . in detaining by fraud and violence so numerous a part of my brethren under groaning captivity and cruel oppression . . . you would at the Same time be found guilty of that most criminal act, which you professedly detested in others, with respect to yourselves.

SOURCE: John J. Patrick, ed., *Founding the Republic: A Documentary History* (Westport, CT: Greenwood Press, 1995), pp. 102–105.

The tension between the republican values of liberty and property was greatest in the South, where slaves, who made up 30 to 60 percent of the population, represented a huge financial investment. Some planters, moved by religious principles or oversupplied with workers on declining tobacco plantations, allowed blacks to buy their freedom through paid work as artisans or laborers. By 1810 manumission and self-purchase had raised the number of freed blacks in Maryland to about a third of the African-American population. But emancipation was never seriously considered in the rice-growing areas of South Carolina and Georgia. The North Carolina legislature condemned Quaker manumissions as "highly criminal and reprehensible" and ordered that free blacks be reenslaved or expelled from the state. In 1792 the Virginia legislature made manumission more difficult. Following the lead of Thomas Jefferson, who owned more than a hundred slaves, the Chesapeake gentry argued that slavery was a "necessary evil" required to maintain white supremacy and the luxurious planter life style.

The southern debate over emancipation ended in 1800 when Virginia authorities thwarted a slave uprising planned by the free black Gabriel Prosser, who was hanged with about thirty of his followers. "Liberty and equality have brought the evil upon us," a letter to the *Virginia Herald* proclaimed in the aftermath, for such doctrines are "dangerous and extremely wicked in this country, where every white man is a master, and every black man is a slave."

A Republican Religious Order

Political revolution broadened the appeal of religious liberty, forcing Patriot lawmakers to devise a new relationship between church and state. Before 1776 only the Quaker- and Baptist-controlled colonies of Pennsylvania and Rhode Island had repudiated the idea of an established church. The most dramatic change came in Virginia, where the Church of England had been the established church. There most Anglicans renounced allegiance to the king, the titular head of the Church of England, and in 1778 reorganized themselves as the Protestant Episcopal Church of America. To win support for the war, the Episcopalians accepted the legitimacy of Presbyterian and Baptist churches, undermining the idea of an established church. Leading Virginia Patriots who embraced the Enlightenment also questioned the wisdom of state-supported churches. In 1776 James Madison and George Mason persuaded the Virginia convention to issue a Declaration of Rights that would guarantee the "free exercise of religion" to all Christians.

After the Revolution an established church and compulsory religious taxes were no longer the norm. Baptists in particular opposed the use of taxes to support religion. In Virginia their political influence prompted lawmakers to reject a bill supported by George Washington and Patrick Henry, which would have imposed a general tax to fund all Christian churches. Instead, in 1786 the Virginia legislature enacted Thomas Jefferson's Bill for Establishing Religious Freedom, which made all churches equal before the law and granted direct financial support to none. In New York and New Jersey the sheer number of churches—Episcopalian, Presbyterian, Dutch Reformed, Lutheran, and Quaker, among others—prevented legislative agreement on an established church or compulsory religious taxes.

Still, many Americans argued that a firm union of church and state would promote morality and respect for authority. "Pure religion and civil liberty are inseparable companions," a group of North Carolinians advised their minister. "It is your particular duty to enlighten mankind with the unerring principles of truth and justice, the main props of all civil government." Accepting this premise, most state governments provided churches with indirect aid by exempting their property and ministers from taxation. Thus the separation of church and state came slowly, especially in New England, where Congregationalist ministers who had strongly supported the independence movement were able to preserve a legally established church until the 1830s. But even there religious taxes could now be used to support Baptist and Methodist churches as well as the established Congregationalists.

Freedom of conscience proved equally controversial. In Virginia, Jefferson's Bill for Establishing Religious Freedom instituted the principle of liberty of conscience by outlawing religious requirements for political and civil posts. However, other states enforced religious criteria for voting and office holding, penalizing individuals who dissented from the doctrines of Protestant Christianity. The North Carolina constitution of 1776 disqualified from public office any citizen "who shall deny the being of God, or the Truth of the Protestant Religion, or the Divine Authority of the Old or New Testament." New Hampshire's constitution contained a similar provision until 1868.

Americans who were influenced by Enlightenment values condemned such restrictions on freedom of conscience. Leading American Patriots, including Thomas Jefferson and Benjamin Franklin, argued that God had given human beings the power of reason so that they could determine moral truths for themselves. To protect society from "ecclesiastical tyranny," they demanded complete freedom of expression.

Many evangelical Protestants also favored freedom of conscience, but their main goal was to protect their churches from state control. The New England minister Isaac Backus warned Baptists not to incorporate their churches or accept state funding because that might lead to state control. In Connecticut a devout Congregationalist welcomed "voluntarism" (the voluntary funding of churches by their members) because it allowed the laity to control the clergy, furthering "the principles of republicanism." In religion as in politics, Americans had begun to create a new republican order.

CHAPTER 6 TIMELINE

1775	Second Continental Congress meets in Philadelphia Battle of Bunker Hill Olive Branch petition Lord Dunmore's proclamation to slaves American invasion of Canada
1776	Patriots skirmish with Loyalists in South Thomas Paine's *Common Sense* Declaration of Independence (July 4) General Howe defeats Washington in New York
1777	Patriot women assist war economy Howe occupies Philadelphia Gates defeats Burgoyne at Saratoga Continental army suffers at Valley Forge Paper currency creates inflation
1778	Franco-American alliance (February 6) Lord North seeks negotiated settlement British begin "southern" strategy by capturing Savannah
1780	General Clinton captures Charleston French army lands in Rhode Island
1781	Cornwallis invades Virginia; surrenders at Yorktown Large-scale Loyalist emigration
1782	Slave manumission act in Virginia (reversed in 1792)
1783	Treaty of Paris (September 3)
1786	Virginia Bill for Establishing Religious Freedom
1800	Gabriel Prosser's rebellion in Virginia

CHAPTER 7

THE NEW POLITICAL ORDER,
1776 – 1800

- Creating New Institutions, 1776–1787
- The Constitution of 1787
- The Political Crisis of the 1790s

Many revolutions end in political chaos or military rule, but the new American republic escaped those unhappy fates. The Loyalist exodus ended support for the monarchy, and most Continental army officers supported civilian rule. Still, General George Washington stunned the world in 1783 when he voluntarily left public life to return to his plantation. "Tis a Conduct so novel," the painter Jonathan Trumbull reported from London, "so inconceivable to People [here], who, far from giving up powers they possess, are willing to convulse the empire to acquire more." Washington's retirement left power in the hands of the Patriot leaders, who were committed to representative government.

Fashioning republican institutions absorbed the energy and intellect of an entire generation. Between 1776 and 1800 Americans not only wrote new state and federal constitutions but also devised a system of politics that was responsive to the popular will. When a bill was introduced into a state legislature, grumbled Ezra Stiles, the conservative president of Yale College, every elected official "instantly thinks how it will affect his constituents," not the public good. What Stiles disparaged as an excess of democracy, most ordinary Americans welcomed. For the first time their interests were represented in the halls of government.

173

CREATING NEW INSTITUTIONS, 1776–1787

The Revolution of 1776 was both a struggle for home rule (independence) and, in the words of the historian Carl Becker, a conflict over "who should rule at home." Who would control the new republican institutions, traditional elites or ordinary citizens? Where would power reside, in the national government or the states?

The State Constitutions: How Much Democracy?

In May 1776 the Continental Congress had urged Americans to suppress royal authority and establish new governing institutions. Most states quickly complied. Within six months Virginia, Maryland, North Carolina, New Jersey, Delaware, and Pennsylvania had written new constitutions and Connecticut and Rhode Island had transformed their colonial charters into republican constitutions by deleting references to the king.

The Declaration of Independence had stated the principle of popular sovereignty: governments derive "their just powers from the consent of the governed." In the heat of revolution, many Patriots gave this clause a democratic twist. In North Carolina the backcountry farmers of Mecklenburg County instructed their delegates to the state's constitutional convention to "oppose everything that leans to aristocracy or power in the hands of the rich and chief men exercised to the oppression of the poor." Voters in Virginia elected a new assembly that "was composed of men not quite so well dressed, nor so politely educated, nor so highly born," an observer remarked. Delaware's constitution declared that "the Right of the People to participate in the Legislature, is the Foundation of Liberty and of all free government."

This outlook received its fullest expression in Pennsylvania, where a coalition of Scots-Irish farmers, Philadelphia artisans, and Enlightenment-influenced intellectuals created the most democratic government in America or Europe. Pennsylvania's constitution abolished property owning as a test of citizenship, granting all men who paid taxes the right to vote and hold office. It also created a *unicameral* (one-house) assembly with complete legislative power. No council or upper house was reserved for the wealthy, and no governor exercised veto power. Other constitutional provisions mandated an extensive system of elementary education, protected citizens from imprisonment for debt, and called for a society of economically independent freemen.

Pennsylvania's democratic constitution alarmed many leading Patriots, who believed that voting and officeholding should be restricted to "men of learning, leisure and easy circumstances." Jeremy Belknap of New Hampshire insisted that "the people be taught . . . that they are not able to govern themselves." He and other conservative Patriots feared that popular rule would lead to the tyranny of legislative majorities, allowing ordinary citizens to use their numerical advantage to tax the rich.

From Boston, John Adams denounced Pennsylvania's unicameral legislature as "so democratical that it must produce confusion and every evil work." To counter its appeal, Adams composed his *Thoughts on Government* and sent the treatise to friends at constitutional conventions in other states. Adams adapted the British Whig theory of mixed government (in which power was shared by the king, lords, and commons) to a republican society. To preserve liberty, he recommended dispersing authority by assigning the different functions of government—lawmaking, administering, and judging—to separate branches. Thus, legislatures would make the laws, which would be enforced by the executive and the judiciary. Adams also called for a *bicameral* (two-house) legislature in which men of property in the upper house would check the excesses of popular majorities in the lower house. As a further curb on democracy, he proposed an elected governor with the power to veto laws and an appointed—not elected—judiciary to review them. Adams argued that this plan was republican because the people would elect both the chief executive and the legislature.

Leading Patriots endorsed Adams's scheme both because they feared democracy and because it resembled the governments of the colonial period. Most states adopted constitutions that provided for bicameral legislatures in which membership in both houses was elective. Recalling the arbitrary conduct of royal governors, most also reduced the powers of the executive; only three gave veto power to the governor. Many states retained property qualifications for voting, however. Thus, in New York, while 90 percent of white men could vote in assembly elections, only 40 percent could vote for the governor and the upper house. The most flagrant use of property to maintain the power of the elite occurred in South Carolina, where the 1778 constitution required candidates for governor to have a debt-free estate of £10,000 (about $600,000 today), senators to be worth £2,000, and assemblymen to own property valued at £1,000. These provisions ruled out officeholding for about 90 percent of white men.

Nonetheless, post-Revolutionary politics had a democratic tinge. State constitutions apportioned seats in the lower houses of the legislatures on the basis of population, giving farmers in western areas the representation they had long demanded. Indeed, backcountry residents were able to transfer state capitals from merchant-dominated seaports such as New York City and Philadelphia to inland cities such as Albany and Harrisburg. Even conservative South Carolina moved its seat of government inland, from Charleston to Columbia.

Most of the state legislatures were filled by new sorts of political leaders. After the war, noted one observer, ordinary voters were less likely to elect their social "betters" to office and chose men of "middling circumstances" who knew "the wants of the poor." By the mid-1780s, middling farmers and urban artisans controlled the lower houses in most northern states and formed a sizable minority in southern assemblies. These "middling men" took the lead in opposing the collection of back taxes and other measures that tended "toward the oppression of the people."

The political legacy of the Revolution was complex. Only in Pennsylvania and Vermont were radical Patriots able to take power and create democratic

An Attack on Patrick Henry's Social Policies

Even before the war ended, democratic-minded state legislators advanced policies
designed to assist ordinary voters. In Virginia, Patrick Henry spoke for yeomen
farmers and debtors in seeking to reduce the burden of military service, cut taxes,
and allow debts to be paid in depreciated paper currency. Such measures were con-
demned by privileged representatives, as in this letter from J. P. (Jack) Custis to his
stepfather, George Washington.

Patrick Henry, who possesses the most unbounded influence over the House,
is, in my opinion, the most absurd politician in the world. He moved, the other
day, that the [military] draft, which has taken place in many counties . . .
should be reduced from eighteen months to twelve months. Absurd as this
motion must appear to every reasonable man, it did not want espousers,
though, fortunately, the number was too small, and the motion was lost. . . .

He [Patrick Henry] is also desirous that half of the tax which was laid, to
furnish bounties for the recruits should be remitted; although half of the State,
or two thirds, have paid it, or are prepared to do so. This matter is not yet determined, and I am afraid he will succeed. . . . By this means, all authority will
be lost, and the State thrown into the greatest confusion.

A law was passed yesterday, making all the money that hath been emitted,
by Congress or this State, a legal tender, in discharge of all debts and Contracts whatsoever; except specific contracts, expressing the contrary. It is also
proposed to emit ten million more. This tender act, iniquitous as it is, was carried by a majority of two to one, and will forever cast a reflection on the justice of the State.

SOURCE: J. P. Custis to George Washington, March 16, 1781, reprinted in the *William and Mary Quarterly*, 3rd ser.,
43 (April 1986), 288–289.

governmental institutions. Yet everywhere, the day-to-day politics of electioneering and interest-group bargaining became much more responsive to the
demands of ordinary citizens.

Equally important, the extraordinary excitement of the Revolutionary Era
tested the dictum that only men could engage in politics. While men continued to control all public institutions—legislatures, juries, government offices—
upper-class women entered into political debate, filling their letters and diaries
(and undoubtedly their conversations) with opinions on public issues. "The
men say we have no business [with politics]," Eliza Wilkinson of South Carolina complained in 1783, "but I won't have it thought that because we are the
weaker sex as to bodily strength we are capable of nothing more than domestic
concerns. They won't even allow us liberty of thought, and that is all I want."

American women did not demand complete equality with men, but they did want to end discriminatory customs and legal rules. Abigail Adams demanded equal legal rights for married women, pointing out that under existing common law they could not own most forms of property and could not enter into a contract or initiate a lawsuit without their husbands' action. "Men would be tyrants" if they continued to hold such power over women, Adams declared to her husband, criticizing him and other Patriots for "emancipating all nations" from monarchical despotism while "retaining absolute power over Wives."

Although men paid some attention to women's requests, they were generally unwilling to question their own dominant position. Most husbands remained patriarchs; even young men who embraced the republican ideal of "companionate" marriage did not support a public role for their wives and daughters. With the partial exception of New Jersey, which granted the vote to unmarried and widowed women of property until 1807, women remained second-class citizens, unable to participate directly in American political life.

The republican belief in the need for an educated citizenry provided an avenue for the most important advances made by American women. In her 1779 essay "On the Equality of the Sexes" (published in 1790), Judith Sargent Murray compared the intellectual faculties of men and women, arguing that women had an equal capacity for memory and superior imagination. Murray conceded that most women were inferior to men in judgment and reasoning,

Judith Sargent (Murray), Age 19
The well-educated daughter of a Massachusetts merchant, Judith Sargent endured a difficult seventeen-year marriage to John Stevens, during which she wrote "On The Equality of the Sexes." After Stevens's death, she wed the Reverend John Murray, who became a leading Universalist. Her portrait, painted around 1771 by John Singleton Copley, captures Murray's skeptical view of the world, which enabled her to question customary gender roles.

but only because of a lack of training: "We can only reason from what we know," and most women had been denied "the opportunity of acquiring knowledge." In the 1790s the attorney general in Massachusetts persuaded a jury that girls had an equal right to schooling under the state constitution. With greater access to public elementary schools and new female academies, many young women became literate, knowledgeable, and intellectually prepared for a role in public life. By 1850 as many women as men in the northeastern states would be able to read and write, and literate women would challenge their subordinate legal and political status.

The Articles of Confederation

As the Patriots moved toward independence in 1776, they envisioned a central government with limited powers. Carter Braxton of Virginia thought the Continental Congress should have the power to "regulate the affairs of trade, war, peace, alliances, &c." but "should by no means have authority to interfere with the internal police [governance] or domestic concerns of any Colony."

This outlook informed the Articles of Confederation, passed by Congress in November 1777. The first national constitution provided for a loose confederation in which "each state retains its sovereignty, freedom, and independence" as well as all powers and rights not "expressly delegated" to the United States. The Articles gave the confederation the authority to declare war and peace, make treaties with foreign nations, adjudicate disputes between the states, borrow and print money, and requisition funds from the states "for the common defense or general welfare." These powers were to be exercised by a central legislature, the Congress, in which each state had one vote regardless of its wealth or population. There was no separate executive branch or judiciary. Important laws needed approval by at least nine of the thirteen states, and changes in the Articles required unanimous consent.

Because of disputes over western lands, the Articles were not ratified by all the states until 1781. States with no claims to land in the West, such as Maryland and Pennsylvania, refused to ratify the Articles until Virginia and other states that did have such claims (based on royal charters in which boundaries stretched to the Pacific Ocean) agreed to relinquish them to Congress to create a common national domain in the West. Threatened by Cornwallis's army in 1781, Virginia finally agreed to give up its land claims (see Map 7.1 for the dates of the actual cessions), and Maryland, the last holdout, then ratified the Articles.

Formal ratification of the Articles was anticlimactic, because the Congress had been exercising de facto constitutional authority for four years, raising the Continental army and negotiating with foreign nations. The Confederation's weakness stemmed primarily from its limited fiscal powers. Lacking the authority to impose taxes, the Congress had to requisition funds from the state legislatures and hope they would pay, which they usually failed to do. Faced with the prospect of the Confederation's bankruptcy in 1780, General

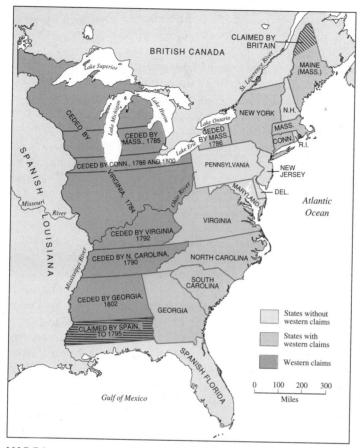

MAP 7.1

Western Land Claims

The Confederation Congress resolved conflicting claims by the states by creating a "national domain." Between 1781 and 1802 all the seaboard states with western land claims ceded them to the national government. The Confederation Congress divided the domain into territories, opening them to citizens from all states and providing them with self-governing in-stituitions and the prospect of statehood.

Washington called urgently for a national system of taxation, warning Patriot leaders that otherwise "our cause is lost."

In response, nationalist-minded members of Congress sought to expand the Confederation's authority. Robert Morris, who became superintendent of finance in 1781, persuaded Congress to charter the Bank of North America, a private institution in Philadelphia, hoping to use its notes to sta-bilize the inflated Continental currency. Morris also developed a compre-hensive financial plan that apportioned some war expenses among the states in proportion to their landed wealth while centralizing control of army expenditures and foreign debt. He hoped that the existence of a national debt would draw attention to the Confederation's need for the power to impose an import duty.

But the nationalists were largely stymied by resistance to an increase in the Confederation's powers, which required the unanimous consent of the states. In 1781 Rhode Island rejected Morris's proposal for an import duty of 5 percent. Two years later New York refused to accept a similar plan, pointing out that it had opposed British import duties and would not accept them from Congress. Rather than send funds to Congress (which might use them to repay debt-holding citizens of other states), some states paid interest directly to their own citizens. By 1786 Pennsylvania, Maryland, New York, and New Jersey had assumed nearly one-third of the domestic debt, showing that the Confederation was essentially a league of states rather than an effective central government.

Despite its limited powers, the Congress successfully planned the settlement of the trans–Appalachian West. The Congress needed to assert the Confederation's title to this great treasure in order to sell it and raise revenue for the government. Thus, in 1783 Congress began to negotiate with Indian tribes, hoping to persuade them that the Treaty of Paris had extinguished their land rights. The Congress also bargained with white squatters, allowing them to stay only if they paid for their lands. Congress wanted to secure an orderly settlement of western lands and their eventual admission to the Union. Given the natural barrier of the Appalachian Mountains, many members of Congress feared that westerners might establish separate republics or even link up with Spanish Louisiana. The danger was real: in 1784 thousands of settlers—"white savages," John Jay called them—set up a new state, Franklin, in what is now eastern Tennessee. To preserve its authority over the West, Congress refused to recognize Franklin or consider its application to join the Confederation. Instead, the delegates directed the states of Virginia, North Carolina, and Georgia to administer the process of creating new states south of the Ohio River.

To the north of the Ohio, Congress established a national domain, issuing three ordinances for the settlement and administration of the Northwest Territory. The Ordinance of 1784, written by Thomas Jefferson, called for the admission of states carved out of the territory as soon as their populations equaled that of the smallest existing state. To deter squatters, the Land Ordinance of 1785 established a grid surveying system and specified that the lands be surveyed before settlement (see Map 7.2). Land was to be sold in fee simple and mostly in large blocs, a provision that favored large-scale investors and speculators.

Finally, the Northwest Ordinance of 1787 provided for the creation of three to five territories, which would eventually become the states of Ohio, Indiana, Illinois, Michigan, and Wisconsin. Reflecting the Enlightenment social philosophy of Jefferson and other Patriots, the ordinance prohibited slavery in those territories and earmarked funds from the sale of some land for the support of schools. Each new territory would be ruled by a governor and

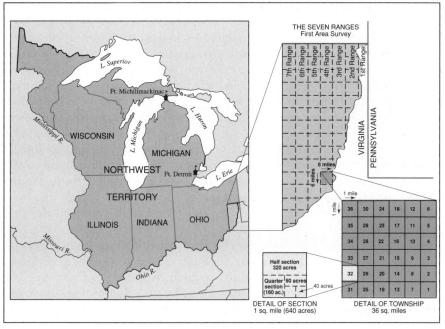

THE SEVEN RANGES
First Area Survey

7th Range | 6th Range | 5th Range | 4th Range | 3rd Range | 2nd Range | 1st Range

VIRGINIA

PENNSYLVANIA

6 miles

6 mile

1 mile

1 mile

36	30	24	18	12	6
35	29	23	17	11	5
34	28	22	16	10	4
33	27	21	15	9	3
32	26	20	14	8	2
31	25	19	13	7	1

Half section
320 acres

Quarter
section
(160 ac.)

80 acres

40 acres

DETAIL OF SECTION
1 sq. mile (640 acres)

DETAIL OF TOWNSHIP
36 sq. miles

L. Superior

Ft. Michilimackinac

Mississippi R.

L. Huron

WISCONSIN

L. Michigan

MICHIGAN

NORTHWEST   Ft. Detroit

L. Erie

TERRITORY

ILLINOIS | INDIANA | OHIO

Missouri R.

Ohio R.

MAP 7.2
Land Divisions in the Northwest Territory
The ordinances of 1785 and 1787 divided the Northwest Territory into uniform sections or townships. The townships were about the same size as New England communities, 36 square miles, and were divided into thirty-six sections of 1 square mile, or 640 acres, surveyed in a grid pattern. The ordinances favored speculators over yeomen by requiring that half the townships be sold in single blocks of 23,040 acres.

judges appointed by Congress. Once the number of free adult men reached 5,000, settlers could elect their own legislature. When the population grew to 60,000, residents could write a republican constitution and apply to join the Confederation. Once admitted, a new state would enjoy all the rights and privileges of the existing states.

The land ordinances of the 1780s were a great and enduring achievement. They provided for the orderly settlement of the West while reducing the prospect of secessionist movements and preventing the emergence of dependent "colonies." The ordinances also added a new "western" dimension to the national identity. The United States was no longer confined to thirteen governments on the eastern seaboard; it had space to expand.

The Postwar Crisis

Whatever the future of the West, postwar conditions in the East were grim. Peace had brought a recession rather than a return to prosperity. The war had destroyed many American merchant ships and cut the export of tobacco and other farm goods. The British Navigation Acts, which once had nurtured colonial commerce, now barred Americans from trading with the British West Indies. And low-priced British manufactures flooded American markets, driving many artisans and wartime textile firms out of business.

State governments emerged from the war with large debts and worthless currencies. Speculators—wealthy merchants and landowners—who had purchased state debt certificates for far less than face value advocated high taxes so that the bonds could be redeemed quickly at full value. But yeomen farmers and artisans, hard hit by the postwar recession, demanded tax relief. To assist debtors, many states enacted laws allowing them to pay creditors in installments. Other states printed more paper currency in an effort to extend credit. Although wealthy men deplored these actions as destructive of "the just rights of creditors," the stopgap measures probably prevented a major social upheaval.

In Massachusetts, the lack of debtor-relief legislation provoked the first armed uprising in the new nation. Merchants and creditors had persuaded the legislature to impose taxes to repay the state's war debt rather than to issue more paper currency. When cash-strapped farmers could not pay their debts, creditors hauled them into court, saddling them with high legal fees. In 1786 residents of central and western counties called extralegal meetings to protest the taxes and property seizures, and bands of angry farmers closed the courts by force. The resistance gradually grew into a full-scale revolt led by the former Continental army captain Daniel Shays.

A struggle against taxes imposed by a nonlocal government, Shays's Rebellion resembled colonial resistance to the Stamp Act. "The people have turned against their teachers the doctrines which were inculcated to effect the late revolution," complained the conservative Massachusetts political leader Fisher Ames. But even the Radical Patriots of 1776 condemned the crowd actions as antirepublican. "Those Men, who ... would lessen the Weight of Government lawfully exercised must be Enemies to our happy Revolution and Common Liberty," charged Samuel Adams. To preserve its authority, the Massachusetts legislature passed a Riot Act outlawing illegal assemblies. Governor James Bowdoin, supported by eastern merchants, equipped a strong fighting force to put down the rebellion and called for additional troops from the Continental Congress. Shays's army dwindled during the winter of 1786–1787, falling victim to freezing weather and inadequate supplies, and Bowdoin's military force easily dispersed the rebels.

The collapsed rebellion provided graphic proof that the costs of war and the fruits of independence were not being shared evenly. Many of those who had suffered while fighting for independence felt they had exchanged one tyranny for another. Massachusetts voters turned Governor Bowdoin out of office, and farmers in New York, northern Pennsylvania, Connecticut, New Hampshire, and Vermont (admitted as a state in 1791) closed courthouses, demanding economic relief. As British officials in Canada predicted the imminent demise of the United States, many Americans feared for the fate of their republican experiment. In these dire times nationalists redoubled their efforts to create a central government equal to the challenges facing the new republic.

An Anti-Shaysite Interviews the Rebels

After Shays's Rebellion, both sides sought to justify their cause. This clever piece, purportedly written by a neutral observer, suggests the rebels' grievances but subtly emphasizes their selfish motives, portraying the "mobility" as anarchists intent on destroying all authority.

What influenced them to thus rise and oppose government? What did they aim at thereby. . . . As therefore I was present with them at the late rising . . . I inquired of an old plough jogger the confessed aim of the people of that assembly. He said, "To get redress of grievances." I asked, "What grievances?"

He said, "We have grievances enough; I can tell you mine. I have labored hard all my days, and fared hard. I have been greatly abused, been obliged to do more than my part in the war, been loaded down with [many taxes:] class-rates, town-rates, province-rates, continental-rates, and all rates, lawsuits, and have been pulled and hauled by sheriffs, constables, and collectors, and had my cattle sold for less than they were worth. I have been obliged to pay, and nobody will pay me . . . and the great men are going to get all we have, and I think it is time for us to rise and put a stop to it, and have no more courts, nor sheriffs, nor collectors, nor lawyers. I design to pay no more. . . ."

I next asked a pert lad . . . [who] made a long harangue upon governors, and jobbers, and lawyers and judges . . . and salaries, and fees, and pensions, and such has ten times too much, and such has five times too much, and . . . the great men pocket up all the money and live easy, and we work hard, and we can't pay it, and we won't pay it. . . .

Thus I went from rank to rank, through all the mobility. . . . I got the secrets of their hearts.

SOURCE: Linda R. Monk, ed., *Ordinary Americans: U.S. History through the Eyes of Everyday People* (Alexandria, VA: Close Up Publications, 1994), pp. 42–43.

THE CONSTITUTION OF 1787

From the moment of its creation, the Constitution was a controversial document. This principled and innovative statement of republican political theory, written in a time of crisis, also embodied the values and interests of men with a personal stake in its outcome.

The Rise of a Nationalist Faction

Men who had served the Confederation during the war—as military officers, diplomats, and officials—had acquired a "national" outlook. General Washington, the financier Robert Morris, and the diplomats Benjamin Franklin, John

Jay, and John Adams became advocates of a stronger central government with the power to control foreign commerce and impose tariffs. They knew that without tariff revenue, Congress would be unable to pay the interest on the foreign debt and the nation's credit would collapse. But southern planters opposed tariffs on cheap British textiles and ironware, and key commercial states in the North—New York, Massachusetts, Pennsylvania—had devised their own trade policies, involving subsidies to local merchants as well as tariffs on imported goods.

By 1786 the nationalists were also worried about the creditworthiness of the state governments. Legislatures in Virginia and other southern states had granted tax relief to various groups of citizens, diminishing public revenue and delaying the redemption of state debts. Taxpayers were being led to believe they would "never be compelled to pay," lamented Charles Lee of Virginia, a wealthy bondholder. Moreover, state governments had jeopardized the integrity of private debts by providing legislative relief to debtors. "While men are madly accumulating enormous debts, their legislators are making provisions for their nonpayment," a South Carolina creditor complained.

Nationalists took the initiative in 1786, when James Madison persuaded the Virginia legislature to call a special convention to discuss tariff and taxation policies. Twelve men representing only five states met in Annapolis, Maryland; after their discussion, they called for another meeting in Philadelphia to undertake a broad review of the Confederation. Nationalists in Congress, frightened by Shays's Rebellion, secured a resolution supporting the Philadelphia convention, calling for a revision of the Articles of Confederation "adequate to the exigencies of government and the preservation of the Union." "Nothing but the adoption of some efficient plan from the Convention," a fellow nationalist wrote to James Madison, "can prevent anarchy first & civil convulsions afterwards."

The Philadelphia Convention

In May 1787, fifty-five delegates arrived in Philadelphia, representing every state except Rhode Island, whose legislature opposed any increase in central authority. Some delegates, such as Benjamin Franklin of Pennsylvania, had been leaders of the independence movement. Others, including George Washington and Robert Morris, had become prominent during the war. Several famous Patriots missed the convention. John Adams and Thomas Jefferson were in Europe, serving as the American ministers to Britain and France. The radical Samuel Adams had not been chosen as a delegate by the Massachusetts legislature, while the firebrand Patrick Henry refused to attend because he favored a limited national government. Their places were taken by capable younger men such as James Madison and Alexander Hamilton.

Most delegates to the Philadelphia convention were merchants, slaveholding planters, or "monied men." There were no artisans, backcountry settlers, or tenants and only a single yeoman farmer. Consequently, most delegates supported creditors' property rights and favored a central government that would protect the republic from "the imprudence of democracy," as Hamilton put it.

The delegates began by electing Washington as the presiding officer. To forestall popular opposition, they decided to deliberate behind closed doors. They agreed that each state would have one vote, as in the Confederation, and that a majority of states would decide an issue. Then the delegates exceeded their mandate to revise the Articles of Confederation by agreeing to consider the Virginia Plan, a scheme for a truly national government devised by James Madison. Madison had arrived in Philadelphia determined to fashion a new political order that would ensure government by men of high character. A graduate of Princeton, he had read classical and modern political theory and served in both the Confederation Congress and the Virginia assembly. His experience in Virginia had convinced him of the "narrow ambition" and lack of public virtue of many state political leaders.

Madison's Virginia Plan differed from the Articles of Confederation in three crucial respects. First, it rejected state sovereignty in favor of the "supremacy of national authority." The central government would have the power to overturn state laws and "legislate in all cases to which the separate States are incompetent." Second, the plan called for a *national* republic that drew its authority directly from all the people and had direct power over them. As Madison explained, the new central government would bypass the states, operating directly "on the individuals composing them." Third, the plan created a three-tier national government with a lower house elected by voters, an upper house elected by the lower house, and an executive and judiciary chosen by the entire legislature.

From a political perspective, Madison's plan contained a fatal flaw. By assigning great power to the lower house, whose composition was based on population, it would have increased the influence of the larger states dramatically. Consequently, delegates from the less populous states rejected the plan, fearing, as a Delaware delegate put it, that the states with many inhabitants would "crush the small ones whenever they stand in the way of their ambitious or interested views."

Delegates from the small states rallied behind the New Jersey Plan devised by William Paterson. This plan strengthened the Confederation by giving the central government the power to raise revenue, control commerce, and make binding requisitions on the states. But it preserved the equality of the states by limiting each state to one vote in a unicameral legislature, as in the Confederation. Delegates from the larger states would not accept this provision. However, after a month of debate a bare majority of the states voted to accept the Virginia Plan as the basis for further discussion.

This decision raised the prospect of a dramatically new constitutional system. During the hot, humid summer of 1787 the delegates met six days a week, debating high principles and considering a multitude of technical details.

Experienced and realistic politicians, they knew that their plan had to be acceptable to existing political factions and powerful social groups. Pierce Butler of South Carolina invoked a classical Greek precedent: "We must follow the example of Solon, who gave the Athenians not the best government he could devise but the best they would receive."

Representation remained the central problem. To satisfy both large and small states, the Connecticut delegates suggested amending the Virginia Plan so that the upper house, the Senate, would always seat two members from each state, while seats in the lower chamber, the House of Representatives, would be apportioned on the basis of population. The size of the states' delegations would be determined every ten years on the basis of a national census. This "Great Compromise" was accepted, but only after bitter debate; to some it seemed less a compromise than a victory for the smaller states.

Other state-related matters were quickly settled. One delegate objected to establishing national courts within the states, warning that "the states will revolt at such encroachments." The convention therefore defined the judicial power of the United States in broad terms, vesting it "in one supreme Court" and leaving the new national legislature to decide whether to establish lower courts within the states. The convention also decided against a uniform freehold property qualification for voting. "Eight or nine states have extended the right of suffrage beyond the freeholders," George Mason of Virginia pointed out. "What will people there say if they should be disfranchised?" In another attempt to appease the states, delegates placed the selection of the president in the hands of an *electoral college* that would be chosen on a state-by-state basis. And they specified that state legislatures, not the voters at large, would elect members of the Senate. By giving state governments an important role in the new constitutional system, the delegates hoped to encourage them to accept a reduction in their sovereignty.

Although slavery was not a prominent issue in the debates, discussion of the subject revealed important regional divisions. While no one proposed the abolition of slavery, Gouverneur Morris of New York spoke for many northern delegates in condemning slavery as "a nefarious institution." George Mason, reflecting the outlook of many Chesapeake planters, who already had ample numbers of slaves, argued for prohibition of the Atlantic slave trade. But delegates from the rice-growing states of South Carolina and Georgia insisted that slave imports continue, warning that otherwise their states "shall not be parties to the Union."

For the sake of national unity, the delegates decided to treat slavery as a political rather than a moral issue. To protect the property of slaveowners, they agreed to a "fugitive" clause that would enable masters to reclaim enslaved blacks (or white indentured servants) who had taken refuge in other states. At the insistence of Georgia and South Carolina, they denied Congress the power to regulate slave imports for twenty years. To mollify the northern states, the delegates agreed not to mention slavery explicitly in the Constitution (referring instead to citizens and "all other Persons"), thus denying the institution national legal status. They also refused southern demands to count slaves and citizens equally in determining states' representation in Congress, accepting a compromise proposal in which a slave would be counted as three-fifths of a free person for purposes of representation and taxation.

Having allayed the concerns of small states and slave states, the delegates proceeded to create a powerful, procreditor national government. The finished document declared that the Constitution and all national legislation and treaties made under its authority would be the "supreme" law of the land. It gave the national government broad powers over taxation, military defense, and external commerce as well as the authority to make all laws "necessary and proper" to implement those and other provisions. To establish the fiscal reputation of the central government and protect creditors, the Constitution mandated that the United States honor the existing national debt. Finally, it restricted the ability of state governments to assist debtors by forbidding them to issue money or enact any "Law impairing the Obligation of Contracts."

The proposed Constitution was not a "perfect production," Benjamin Franklin admitted on September 17, 1787, as he urged the forty-one delegates still present to sign it. Yet the great diplomat confessed his astonishment at finding "this system approaching so near to perfection as it does." His colleagues apparently agreed; all but three signed the document.

The Debate over Ratification

The delegates hesitated to submit the Constitution to the state legislatures for their unanimous consent, as required by the Articles of Confederation, because they knew that Rhode Island (and perhaps a few other states) would reject it. Instead, they specified that the Constitution would go into effect upon ratification by special conventions in at least nine of the thirteen states. The Confederation Congress, because of its nationalist sympathies, winked at this extralegal procedure.

A great national debate immediately began, in which the nationalists seized the initiative with two bold moves. First, they called themselves "Federalists," a term that suggested a loose, decentralized system of government and partially obscured their quest for a strong central authority. Second, they launched a coordinated political campaign, publishing dozens of pamphlets and newspaper articles in support of the proposed Constitution.

The opponents of the Constitution, who became known as Antifederalists, came from diverse backgrounds and were less organized than the Federalists. Some, like Governor George Clinton of New York, enjoyed power in a state and feared losing it. Others were rural democrats who pointed out that the Constitution, unlike most state constitutions, lacked a bill of rights; they feared the power of a central government controlled by merchants and creditors. "These lawyers and men of learning and monied men expect to be managers of this Constitution," worried a Massachusetts farmer, "and get all the power and all the money into their own hands and then they will swallow up all of us little folks . . . just as the whale swallowed up Jonah."

Well-educated Americans with a traditional republican outlook also opposed the new system. To keep government "close to the people," they wanted the nation to remain a collection of small sovereign republics tied together only for trade and defense—not the "United States" but the "States United." Citing the French political philosopher Montesquieu, Antifederalists argued that republican institutions were best suited to cities or small states. Melancton Smith of New York warned that the large electoral districts prescribed by the Constitution would give power to a few wealthy upper-class men, whereas "a representative body, composed principally of respectable yeomanry, is the best possible security to liberty." Patrick Henry foresaw a return to the worst features of British rule: high taxes, an oppressive bureaucracy, a standing army, and a "great and mighty President . . . supported in extravagant munificence."

In New York, where ratification was hotly contested, James Madison, John Jay, and Alexander Hamilton countered these arguments in a series of newspaper articles collectively called *The Federalist*. They stressed the need for a strong government to conduct foreign affairs and insisted that central authority would not foster domestic tyranny. Citing Montesquieu's praise for "mixed government" (and drawing on John Adams's *Thoughts on Government*), the authors of *The Federalist* pointed out that national authority would be divided among a president, a bicameral legislature, and a judiciary. Each branch of government would "check and balance" the others, thus preserving liberty.

Indeed, in *The Federalist*, No. 10, Madison maintained that the size of the national republic would be its greatest protection against tyranny. It was "sown in the nature of man," Madison wrote, that individuals would seek power and form factions to advance their interests. Indeed, "a landed interest, a manufacturing interest, a mercantile interest, a moneyed interest, with many lesser interests, grow up of necessity in civilized nations." He argued that the government of a free society should not suppress those groups but instead prevent any one of them from becoming dominant—an end best achieved in a large republic. "Extend the sphere," Madison concluded, "and you take in a greater variety of parties and interests; you make it less probable that a majority of the whole will have a common motive to invade the rights of other citizens."

Unlike the men at the Philadelphia convention, the delegates who met at the state ratifying conventions between December 1787 and June 1788 represented a wide spectrum of Americans, from untutored farmers and middling artisans to well-educated gentlemen. Generally, delegates from the backcountry were Antifederalists, whereas those from the seacoast were Federalists. A coalition of merchants, artisans, and commercial farmers from Philadelphia and its vicinity spearheaded an easy Federalist victory in Pennsylvania. Other early Federalist successes came in the less populous states of Delaware, New Jersey, Georgia, and Connecticut, where delegates counted on a strong national government to offset the power of their larger neighbors.

The Constitution's first real test came in January 1788 in Massachusetts, one of the most populous states and a hotbed of Antifederalist sentiment (see Map 7.3). Influential Patriots, including Samuel Adams and Governor John Hancock, opposed the new constitution, as did Shaysite sympathizers in the west. But Boston artisans, who wanted tariff protection from British imports, supported ratification. Astute Federalist politicians finally won over wavering delegates by warning of political chaos and promising a national bill of rights. By a close vote of 187 to 168, the Federalists carried the day.

Spring brought new Federalist victories in Maryland and South Carolina. When New Hampshire ratified in June, the required nine states had

MAP 7.3

Ratifying the Constitution

In 1907 the geographer Owen Libby discovered that most delegates from seaboard or commercial farming districts favored the Constitution while those from backcountry areas opposed it. Subsequent research has confirmed Libby's socioeconomic interpretation in North and South Carolina and Massachusetts; however, other factors influenced delegates in some states with frontier districts, such as Georgia, where the Constitution was ratified unanimously.

approved the Constitution. Nonetheless, the essential states of Virginia and New York had not yet acted. Madison, Jay, and Hamilton, writing in *The Federalist*, used their superb rhetorical skills to win support in those states. Leading Federalists reiterated their promise to amend the Constitution with a bill of rights, addressing a powerful Antifederalist argument. In the end the Federalists won narrowly in Virginia, 89 to 79, and that success carried them to victory in New York by the even smaller margin of 30 to 27. North Carolina and Rhode Island ratified only in 1789 and 1790, respectively.

The Federalists, working against great odds, had created a national republic that reestablished the political authority of the traditional elite. The Revolutionary Era, which had enhanced the power of yeomen and other ordinary Americans, had come to an end.

Federalist Gentry
A prominent New England Federalist, Oliver Ellsworth served as Chief Justice of the United States (1796–1800), while Abigail Wolcott Ellsworth was the daughter of a governor of Connecticut. In 1792 the artist Ralph Earl captured the aspirations of the Ellsworths by giving them an aristocratic demeanor and prominently displaying their mansion (in the window). (Wadsworth Atheneum)

The Constitution Implemented

The Constitution expanded the dimensions of American political life, allowing voters to fill national as well as local and state offices. The Federalists swept the election of 1788, placing forty-four supporters in the first Congress; only eight Antifederalists were elected. The Constitution had specified that electors chosen in the states would select the president and vice-president, and as expected, the electors chose George Washington as president. John Adams received the second highest number of electoral votes and became vice-president. The two men took up their posts in New York City, the temporary home of the national government.

Washington, the military savior of his country, became its political father as well. At fifty-seven, he was a man of great personal dignity and influence. Instinctively cautious, he generally followed the administrative practices of the Confederation, asking Congress to reestablish the existing executive departments: Foreign Affairs (State), Finance (Treasury), and War. The president had the power to appoint major officials with the consent of the Senate; Washington insisted on his authority to remove them as well, an approach that ensured the chief executive's control over the bureaucracy. To head the Department of State, Washington chose Thomas Jefferson, a fellow Virginian and an experienced diplomat. For secretary of the Treasury he turned to Alexander Hamilton, a lawyer and wartime military aide. The new president designated Jefferson, Hamilton, and Secretary of War Henry Knox as his *cabinet*, or advisory body.

The new national charter had created a Supreme Court but left the establishment of the court system to Congress. Because the Federalists wanted national institutions to act directly on individual citizens, the Judiciary Act, passed by Congress in 1789, created a hierarchical federal court system with thirteen *district courts*, one for each state, and three *circuit courts* to hear appeals. As the Constitution specified, the Supreme Court had the final say. Moreover, the Judiciary Act permitted appeals to the Supreme Court of constitutional matters that arose in the state courts, ensuring that national judges would decide contested issues.

The Federalists kept their promise to add amendments to the Constitution. Drawing on lists of rights submitted by the states' ratifying conventions, James Madison, who had been elected to the House of Representatives, submitted nineteen amendments to the first Congress. Twelve received legislative approval, of which ten were ratified by the states by December 1791. The amendments, which became known as the Bill of Rights, both mandated certain legal procedures, such as trial by jury, and safeguarded certain fundamental individual rights, such as freedom of speech and religion. Citizens were guaranteed the right to bear arms so that they might serve in the militia and defend their liberties. The Tenth Amendment limited the authority of the national government by reserving nondelegated powers to the states or the people. In addressing Antifederalists' concerns through the Bill of Rights,

Congress secured the legitimacy of the new government and ensured broad political support for the Constitution.

THE POLITICAL CRISIS OF THE 1790s

The final decade of the century brought fresh political challenges. The Federalists split into two irreconcilable factions over financial policy, and the French Revolution widened rifts over political ideology. In the course of these struggles, Alexander Hamilton and Thomas Jefferson defined contrasting views of the American future.

Hamilton's Program

One of George Washington's most important decisions was his choice of Alexander Hamilton as secretary of the Treasury. An ambitious self-made man, Hamilton had come to the mainland from the West Indies in 1772 and enrolled at King's College in New York. During the war Hamilton's military abilities and personal charm had impressed Washington, who had chosen him as his personal aide. In the 1780s, Hamilton had married the daughter of a wealthy Hudson River landowner and become a leading lawyer in New York City. At the Philadelphia convention Hamilton had condemned the "amazing violence and turbulence of the democratic spirit," calling for an authoritarian government headed by a president with nearly monarchical powers.

As Treasury secretary, Hamilton devised bold policies that enhanced the authority of the national government and favored his immediate acquaintances, many of them financiers and seaport merchants. He outlined his plan in three pathbreaking and interrelated reports to Congress: on public credit (January 1790), a national bank (December 1790), and manufactures (December 1791).

The financial and social implications of Hamilton's "Report on the Public Credit" made it instantly controversial. Congress was to redeem at face value the millions of dollars in securities issued by the Confederation, a *redemption* and *funding* plan that would bolster the government's credit but also provide windfall profits to speculators. For example, the merchant firm of Burrell & Burrell had paid about $600 for Confederation notes with a face value of $2,500; their redemption at face value would bring an enormous profit of $1,900. Hamilton proposed to pay off the Burrells and other noteholders with new government securities, which would pay interest at about 6 percent. He hoped that investors, attracted by the relatively high interest rate, would hold (and not speculate with) the new securities, keeping their value high and enhancing the government's credit.

Hamilton's plan for a *permanent* national debt funded by monied men reawakened Radical Whig and republican fears of scheming British financiers and governmental favoritism. Speaking for the Virginia House of Burgesses, Patrick Henry declared that "to erect, and concentrate, and perpetuate a large monied interest, must prove fatal to the existence of American liberty." Challenging the morality of Hamilton's proposal, James Madison sought to assist the thousands of shopkeepers, farmers, and soldiers who had accepted government securities during the dark days of the war and then sold them to speculators. Madison proposed giving the present bondholders only "the highest price which has prevailed in the market" and distributing the remaining funds to the original owners. But identifying the original owners would have been difficult, and nearly half the members of the House of Representatives owned Confederation securities and stood to profit from Hamilton's plan. Melding practicality with self-interest, the House rejected Madison's proposal by a solid margin and approved Hamilton's plan.

Hamilton then advanced a second proposal that favored wealthy creditors, a plan by which the national government would take over the war debts of the states. This *assumption* plan unleashed the flurry of speculation and governmental corruption that critics of redemption had feared. Before Hamilton announced it, Assistant Secretary of the Treasury William Duer used insider knowledge to buy up the depreciated war bonds of southern states. By the end of 1790 Duer and other northern speculators owned more than half the war bonds of Virginia and the Carolinas, which they sold after the announcement of Hamilton's assumption plan caused bond values to rise.

Concerned members of Congress noted that some states, such as Virginia and Maryland, had already levied high taxes to pay off their war debts; under Hamilton's plan they would be taxed to pay the debts of other states as well. To win congressional support for assumption, Hamilton agreed to repay those states and back their bid to locate the national capital along the banks of the Potomac. In return, Maryland and Virginia gave Hamilton the votes he needed in the House of Representatives.

In December 1790, Hamilton, bolstered by the passage of his redemption and assumption bills, asked Congress to charter a national financial institution, the Bank of the United States. The bank, to be jointly owned by private stockholders and the national government, would make loans to merchants, handle government funds, and issue financial notes. Thus, it would provide a respected medium of exchange for the specie-starved American economy and make the new national debt easier to fund. These considerable benefits persuaded a majority of both houses to enact Hamilton's bill and send it to the president for approval.

At this critical juncture, Secretary of State Thomas Jefferson joined ranks with Madison against Hamilton. Jefferson had condemned the shady dealings in southern war bonds and the "corrupt squadron of paper dealers" who had arranged them. Now he charged that Hamilton's scheme for a national bank was unconstitutional. "The incorporation of a Bank," Jefferson told President Washington, was not "delegated to the United States by the Constitution." In a *strict interpretation* of the national charter, Jefferson maintained that the central government had only the limited powers explicitly assigned to it in the Constitution. In response, Hamilton articulated a *loose interpretation*, noting that Article 1, Section 8, empowered Congress to make "all Laws which shall be necessary and proper" to carry out the Constitution's provisions. In Hamilton's view, "if the *end* be clearly comprehended within any of the specified powers, and if the measure is not forbidden by any particular provision of the Constitution, it may safely be deemed to come within the compass of national authority." Washington agreed and signed the legislation creating the bank.

Hamilton turned now to the final element of his financial system: a national revenue that would be used to pay the interest on the national debt. At Hamilton's insistence, in 1792 Congress imposed a variety of domestic excise taxes, including a duty on whiskey distilled in the United States. But the revenue from those taxes was too small. Although his "Report on Manufactures" (1791) had envisioned an economically powerful nation that was self-sufficient in manufactured goods, the Treasury secretary could not ask for high "protective" tariffs that would help American industries by excluding foreign products. Such tariffs would cut trade, depriving the government of needed revenue. Therefore, Hamilton asked Congress for only a modest increase in customs duties, a tariff for "revenue."

Hamilton's carefully designed plan worked brilliantly. As American trade increased, customs revenue rose steadily (providing about 90 percent of the national government's income from 1790 to 1820), allowing him to fund his redemption and assumption programs. In less than two years he had devised a strikingly modern fiscal system that provided the new national government with financial stability.

Jefferson's Vision

Hamilton paid a high price for this success. By the time Washington began his second four-year term in 1793, Hamilton's financial measures had split the Federalists into irreconcilable factions. Most northern Federalists, in both Congress and the states, adhered to the political alliance led by Hamilton, and most southerners to a rival group headed by Madison and Jefferson. By the elections of 1794 the two factions had acquired names. Hamilton's supporters retained their original name: Federalists; Madison's and Jefferson's supporters were called Democratic-Republicans or simply Republicans.

The southern planters and western farmers who became Republicans rejected Hamilton's economic and social philosophy. Thomas Jefferson, a man of great learning, spoke for them. Well read in architecture, natural history, scientific farming, and political theory, Jefferson embraced the optimistic spirit of the Enlightenment, declaring his belief in the "improvability of the human race." But he knew that progress was not inevitable and deplored both the traditional speculative practices of merchants and financiers and the emerging social divisions of an urban industrial economy. Having visited the manufacturing regions in Britain and seen the masses of propertyless laborers there, Jefferson had concluded that workers who depended on wages lacked the economic independence required to sustain a republic.

Jefferson's vision of the American future was agrarian and democratic. Although he had grown up a privileged slaveowner, he understood the needs of yeomen farmers and other ordinary white Americans. His vision took form in his *Notes on the State of Virginia* (1785): "Those who labor in the earth are the chosen people of God," he declared. When Jefferson drafted the Ordinance of 1784, he had pictured a West settled by productive yeomen farm families. Their grain and meat would feed European nations, which "would manufacture and send us in exchange our clothes and other comforts."

During the 1790s, Jefferson's vision moved closer to reality as turmoil in Europe created new opportunities for American farmers. The French Revolution began in 1789; four years later the French republican government went to war against a British-led coalition of monarchical states. As warfare disrupted European farming, wheat prices leapt from 5 to 8 shillings a bushel and remained high for twenty years. Chesapeake and Middle Atlantic farmers increased their grain exports, reaping substantial profits. A boom in cotton exports, fueled by the mechanization of cloth production in Britain and the invention of the cotton gin at home, boosted the economy of the Lower South. As Jefferson had hoped, European markets brought prosperity to American farmers and planters.

Two Visions of America
Thomas Jefferson and Alexander Hamilton confront each other in these portraits, as they did during the 1790s. Jefferson was pro-French; Hamilton, pro-British. Jefferson favored farmers and artisans; Hamilton supported merchants and financiers. Jefferson believed in democracy and rule by legislative majorities; Hamilton argued for a strong executive and for judicial review.

War and Politics

American merchants profited even more handsomely from the European war. President Washington issued a Proclamation of Neutrality that enabled U.S. citizens to trade with both sides. As neutral carriers, American ships could pass through the British naval blockade along the French coastline; they soon took over the lucrative trade between France and its West Indian sugar islands. The American merchant fleet became one of the largest in the world, increasing from 355,000 tons in 1790 to more than 1.1 million tons in 1808. Commercial earnings rose spectacularly, averaging $20 million annually in the 1790s—twice the value of cotton and tobacco exports. To keep up with demand, shipowners invested in new vessels, providing work for thousands of shipwrights, sail makers, laborers, and seamen. Hundreds of carpenters, masons, and cabinetmakers found work building warehouses and elegant Federal-style town houses for newly affluent merchants. In the 1790s the assessed value of property in New York City soared from $5.8 million to $20.7 million.

At the same time, the passions of the European struggle convulsed the new republic. Many Americans had welcomed the French Revolution of 1789 because it abolished feudalism and established a constitutional monarchy. But the creation of the more democratic French republic in 1792 and the execution of King Louis XVI the following year divided public opinion. On one side artisans praised the egalitarianism of the French republicans: in Boston, Royal Alley became Equality Lane. Like the radical French Jacobins, artisans addressed each other as "citizen" and founded political clubs, most of which were strongholds of Jefferson's Republican party. On the other side the wealthy and those with strong Christian beliefs denounced the Terror (the executions of Louis XVI and his aristocratic supporters) and condemned the new French regime for abandoning Christianity in favor of atheism.

These ideological conflicts sharpened the debate over Hamilton's economic policies and even helped foment a domestic insurrection. In 1794 farmers in western Pennsylvania mounted the Whiskey Rebellion to protest Hamilton's excise tax on spirits, which had raised the price—and thus cut the demand—for the corn whiskey they sold locally and bartered for eastern manufactures. Like the Sons of Liberty of 1765 and the Shaysites of 1786, the Whiskey rebels attacked both local tax collectors and the authority of a distant government. But these protesters also waved banners proclaiming the French revolutionary slogan "Liberty, Equality, and Fraternity!" To uphold national authority (and deter secessionist movements along the frontier), President Washington raised an army of 12,000 troops that soon suppressed the rebels.

Britain's maritime strategy also widened the growing political divisions in the United States. In November 1793 the Royal Navy began to prey on American ships bound for France from the West Indies, seizing more than 250 vessels and confiscating their sugar cargoes. To avoid war, President Washington sent John Jay to Britain to negotiate a broad series of issues. Jay returned with a treaty that required the U.S. government to make "full and complete compensation" to British merchants for all pre–Revolutionary War debts owed by American citizens. The treaty also acknowledged Britain's right to remove French property from neutral ships, overturning the American merchants' claim that "free ships make free goods." In return, the agreement allowed American merchants to submit claims of illegal seizure to arbitration and required the British to end their aid to the western Indians and remove six military garrisons from the Old Northwest. Although Jefferson and his Republican followers denounced Jay's Treaty as too conciliatory, the Senate ratified it by the bare two-thirds majority required by the Constitution. As long as Hamilton and his Federalist allies were in power, the United States would have a pro-British foreign policy.

The Rise of Parties

The appearance of rival political parties marked a new stage in American politics. Although colonial legislatures had often divided into temporary factions based on family alliances, ethnicity, or regional concerns, they lacked well-organized parties. The new state and national constitutions made no provision for organized political bodies. The framers of the various constitutions considered parties unnecessary and dangerous; following classical republican principles, they wanted voters and legislators to act independently and in the public interest.

But the revolutionary ideology of popular sovereignty had drawn ordinary citizens into politics, and the appearance of economic and ideological interest groups sparked the appearance of a competitive party system. Merchants and creditors favored Federalist policies, as did wheat-exporting slaveholders in the Tidewater districts of the Chesapeake. The emerging Republican coalition was more diverse and drew supporters from across the social spectrum. By the mid-1790s it included not only southern planters and western farmers but also artisans in the seaport cities, German and Scots-Irish settlers, and smallholding eastern farmers.

Party identity crystallized during the election of 1796. To prepare for the election, Federalist and Republican leaders called legislative caucuses in Congress and conventions in the states to discuss policies, nominate candidates, and mobilize supporters. On election day voters selected candidates for local, state, and national office not only on their individual merits but as representatives of parties that stood for distinct principles.

Federalist candidates triumphed in the 1796 election, winning a majority in Congress and the electoral college. The new president, John Adams, continued Hamilton's pro-British foreign policy. When the French navy began to seize American merchant ships and agents of Prince Talleyrand, the French foreign minister, solicited a loan and a bribe from American diplomats, Adams urged Congress to prepare for war. To overcome Republican objections, he charged that Talleyrand's agents, whom he dubbed X, Y, and Z, had insulted the honor of the United States. The Federalist-controlled Congress responded by cutting off trade with France and authorizing American privateers to seize French ships. Party conflict, which had begun over Hamilton's domestic policies, now extended to foreign affairs.

The Crisis of 1798–1800

For the first but not the last time in American history a controversial foreign policy prompted domestic protest and governmental repression. With the United States fighting an undeclared war against France, pro-Republican immigrants from Ireland viciously attacked Adams's foreign policy. Some Federalists responded in kind: "Were I president, I would hang them for otherwise they would murder me," declared a Philadelphia pamphleteer. To silence its critics, the administration pushed a series of coercive measures through Congress in 1798. The Naturalization Act increased the residency requirement for citizenship from five to fourteen years; the Alien Act authorized the deportation of foreigners; and the Sedition Act prohibited the publication of ungrounded or malicious attacks on the president or Congress. "He that is not for us is against us," thundered the Federalist *Gazette of the United States*. Prosecutors arrested more than twenty Republican newspaper editors and politicians, accused them of sedition, and imprisoned some of them.

Republicans assailed this legislation and charged that the Sedition Act contradicted the First Amendment's prohibition against "abridging the freedom of speech, or of the press." Although the Sedition Act was probably unconstitutional, Republicans did not appeal to the Supreme Court partly because the Court's power to review congressional legislation had not been established and partly because the Court was packed with Federalists.

Madison and Jefferson took the fight to the state legislatures instead. At their urging, in 1798 the Kentucky legislature declared the Alien and Sedition acts to be "unauthoritative, void, and of no force." State legislators justified their rejection of a congressional law by arguing that the national government owed its existence to a compact among the states, which meant that "each party has an equal right to judge by itself." The Virginia legislature passed a similar resolution, establishing the legal theory for a "states' rights" interpretation of the Constitution.

The debate over the Sedition Act set the stage for the election of 1800. Jefferson, once opposed in principle to political parties, now saw them as a valuable way "to watch and relate to the people" the activities of the government. Republicans strongly supported Jefferson's bid for the presidency, pointing to the wrongful imprisonment of newspaper editors and championing states' rights. President Adams responded to their attacks by reevaluating his foreign policy. Rejecting the advice of Hamilton and others who wanted to intensify the undeclared war with France (so that Federalists would benefit from an upsurge in patriotism), Adams put country ahead of party and entered into diplomatic negotiations which brought an end to the war.

Federalists branded Jefferson an irresponsible pro-French radical, "the archapostle of irreligion and free thought," but their strategy failed. Voters protested against the undeclared foreign war—and the special national tax on land and houses that Congress had imposed to pay for it—by giving Republicans a majority in both houses of Congress and a narrow edge in the electoral college. But the electors gave Jefferson the same number of votes as Aaron Burr of New York (Jefferson's choice for vice-president), throwing the presidential election into the House of Representatives. (The Twelfth Amendment, ratified in 1804, would remedy the constitutional defect that caused the deadlock by requiring electors to vote separately for president and vice-president.)

Ironically, as the era of Federalism and its aristocratic outlook came to an end, Alexander Hamilton ushered in a more democratic era. For thirty-five ballots Federalists in the House of Representatives blocked Jefferson's election. Then the former Treasury secretary intervened. Calling Burr an "embryo Caesar" and the "most unfit man in the United States for the office of president," Hamilton persuaded key Federalists to permit his longtime rival's selection. The Federalists' concern for political stability also played a role. As Senator James Bayard of Delaware explained, "it was admitted on all hands that we must risk the Constitution and a Civil War or take Mr. Jefferson."

Jefferson called the election the "Revolution of 1800," and so it was. The bloodless transfer of power demonstrated that governments elected by the people could be changed in an orderly way, even in times of bitter partisan conflict. In his inaugural address in 1801, Jefferson praised this achievement, declaring: "We are all Republicans, we are all Federalists." The new republican constitutional order of 1776 had survived a quarter-century of domestic conflict and foreign crisis.

CHAPTER 7 TIMELINE

1776	Pennsylvania's democratic constitution John Adams, *Thoughts on Government* Propertied women vote in New Jersey (changed in 1807)
1777	Articles of Confederation (ratified 1781)
1779	Judith Sargent Murray, "On the Equality of the Sexes"
1780s	Postwar commercial recession Creditor-debtor conflicts in states
1781	Bank of North America chartered by Congress
1784	Ordinance outlines policy for new states
1785	Jefferson's *Notes on the State of Virginia*
1786	Annapolis commercial convention Shays's Rebellion
1787	Northwest Ordinance Philadelphia constitutional convention
1787–1788	Ratification conventions *The Federalist* (Jay, Madison, Hamilton)
1789	Judiciary Act establishes federal court system
1790	Hamilton's program: redemption and assumption
1791	Bill of Rights ratified
1793	Democratic-Republican party founded
1794	Whiskey Rebellion
1795	Jay's Treaty
1798	Alien, Sedition, and Naturalization acts Kentucky and Virginia resolutions
1800	Jefferson elected in "Revolution of 1800"

CHAPTER 8

TOWARD A CONTINENTAL NATION, 1790–1820

- Westward Expansion
- Republican Policy and Diplomacy
- Regional Diversity and National Identity

When the thirteen colonies declared independence in 1776, the new nation was confined to a narrow strip of land along the Atlantic seaboard. But the peace treaty of 1783 extended the domain of the United States as far west as the Mississippi River, more than doubling the size of the new republic and adding millions of acres of fertile, well-watered land. Taking advantage of this bonanza, land-hungry eastern farmers and ambitious entrepreneurs streamed across the Appalachian Mountains.

Just as this vast migration began, President Thomas Jefferson doubled the nation's size again with the Louisiana Purchase of 1803. "[No] territory can be too large," declared David Ramsey of South Carolina, "for a people, who multiply with such unequaled rapidity." With extraordinary self-confidence, tens of thousands of ordinary Americans accepted the challenge of settling the interior of the continent, trekking hundreds of miles by foot and wagon, confronting angry Indian peoples, and turning dense forests into productive farmland. By 1820 two million white and black Americans—a number almost equal to the nation's total population in 1776—were living in nine new states and three territories west of the Appalachians. The United States was on its way to becoming a truly "continental" republic.

Settlers Move West through Pennsylvania
Thomas Birch captured the optimistic spirit of migrating families in his 1816 painting *Conestoga Wagon on the Pennsylvania Turnpike*. The woman's arm points to the West, suggesting both her family's destination and the course of national development.

WESTWARD EXPANSION

Westward movement transformed the lives of all Americans. In the East the departure of large numbers of young men and women disrupted long-established communities, while in the West hundreds of thousands of Indians faced forced removal from their ancestral lands.

Native American Resistance

In the Treaty of Paris, Great Britain had relinquished its claims to the trans-Appalachian region and its peoples to the United States. Although native Americans rejected American control, pointing out that they had not signed the treaty and had never been conquered, the Confederation Congress used military threats to force the Iroquois from most of their lands in New York and Pennsylvania. Soon the once-powerful Iroquois were confined to relatively small reservations. In 1785 American negotiators used similar tactics to force the Chipewyan, Delaware, Ottawa, and Wyandot to sign away most of the future state of Ohio. This time the tactic did not work, as these tribes repudiated the agreement and joined the Miami, Shawnee, and Potawatomi in a confederacy to defend their lands. Led by Little Turtle, the Western Confederacy defeated American expeditionary forces in 1790 and 1791.

Fearing an alliance between the Western Confederacy and the British in Canada, President Washington doubled the size of the army to 5,000 men and ordered General "Mad Anthony" Wayne to lead a new expedition. In August 1794 Wayne defeated the Indian allies in the Battle of Fallen Timbers and negotiated a settlement. In the Treaty of Greenville (Ohio) in 1795, the United States acknowledged Indian ownership of the lands in the trans-Appalachian West but successfully asserted the nation's sovereignty over the region. The Indians agreed to place themselves "under the protection of the United States, and no other Power whatever" (see Map 8.1). The agreement was also significant because it increased the likelihood that Britain would comply with its obligation (reaffirmed in Jay's Treaty of 1795) to withdraw its garrisons from the region. Indian resistance had slowed but not stopped the advance of American settlement.

Settlers and Speculators

As the fighting subsided, migrants from the North and the South poured across the Appalachians. Tenant farmers and struggling yeomen families in the Chesapeake region headed for Kentucky and Tennessee, fleeing the depleted soils and planter elite of the Tidewater region. As more than 225,000 migrants moved west, a worried landlord complained in the *Maryland Gazette* that "boundless settlements open a door for our citizens to run off and leave us, depreciating all our landed property and disabling us from paying taxes."

The new settlers flocked through the Cumberland Gap into Kentucky and along the Knoxville Road into what would become Tennessee, confident that they would prosper by growing cotton and hemp, which were in great demand. But first they had to gain title to their land. The migrants based their claims on "the ancient cultivation law" governing frontier tracts, invoking the argument of the North Carolina Regulators (see Chapter 4) that the poor had a customary right "from time out of Mind" to occupy "back waste vacant

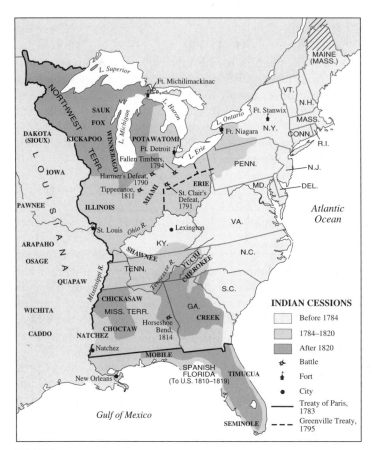

MAP 8.1

Expansion: Military and Diplomatic

On the basis of the peace treaty of 1783, the United States claimed sovereignty over the trans-Appalachian West. When the Indians of the Western Confederacy contested that claim, the American government upheld it by force. Armed diplomacy forced native American peoples to cede by treaty most of their lands east of the Mississippi River.

Lands" sufficient "to provide a subsistence for themselves and their posterity." The Virginia government (which administered the Kentucky territory) allowed "actual settlers" to purchase up to 1,400 acres but allowed twenty-one wealthy individuals and partnerships to acquire handsome tracts averaging 100,000 acres. When Kentucky became a state in 1792, a handful of speculators held title to one-fourth of the land, while half the adult white men owned none and lived as squatters or tenants.

Another wave of migrants flowed out of New England into New York State and beyond, planting new yeomen farm communities in the Great Lakes region. Even though some New England farmers had moved north into New

Hampshire and Vermont and east along the coast of Maine in search of land, many New England communities remained overcrowded. Seeking to provide farmsteads for their children, thousands of New England parents hitched their oxen and horses to wagons and carried tools, plows, and household goods to the fertile plains and rolling hills of upstate New York. By 1820, 800,000 migrants were living in a string of settlements stretching from Albany to Buffalo. Thousands more had pressed on to Ohio.

This vast migration was organized not by governments or joint-stock companies but by the people themselves. To lighten the economic and emotional burdens of migration, many settlers moved in large family groups. As a traveler reported from central New York: "The town of Herkimer is entirely populated by families come from Connecticut. We stayed at Mr. Snow's who came from New London with about ten male and female cousins." Members of Congregational churches often migrated together, transplanting the strong religious and cultural traditions of New England to western communities.

As in Kentucky, much land in New York was snapped up by politically well-connected speculators. In the 1780s the financier Robert Morris acquired 1.3 million acres in the Genesee region of central New York for $75,000—about 6 cents an acre. Speculation drove up the price of farms, making it difficult for yeomen families to realize their dream of landed independence. Thousands of settlers signed lease-purchase agreements with the Dutch-owned Holland Land Company only to become mired in debt because of high interest rates and the difficulty of transporting goods to market. Soon the number of tenants far surpassed the number of freeholders in the counties west of the Genesee River. Having fled declining prospects in the East, these farmers found themselves at the bottom of the economic ladder in the West.

The massive exodus drained eastern towns of money and workers, forcing established farmers to plant different crops and improve their equipment. In New England farmers turned to potatoes, a nutritious, high-yielding crop. In the wheat-growing Middle Atlantic states enterprising farmers replaced metal-tipped wooden plows with cast-iron models that dug a deeper furrow and required a single yoke of oxen instead of two or three. Cast-iron plows reduced the cost of livestock and labor, enabling farmers to maintain production levels even if their sons and daughters had gone west.

Eastern farmers also took advantage of the progressive farming methods advocated by British agricultural reformers. Wealthy "improvers" rotated their crops to maintain the soil's fertility, ordering workers or tenants to plant nitrogen-rich clover and follow it with wheat, corn, wheat, and then clover. In Pennsylvania crop rotation increased the average wheat yield from 12 to 25 bushels per acre. Yeomen diversified their output by raising sheep and selling the wool to textile manufacturers. And they adopted a year-round planting cycle, sowing wheat in the winter and planting corn in the spring to provide fodder for their milk cows. Farm women and girls milked the cows and made butter and cheese to sell in the growing towns and cities.

The "Onion Maidens" of Wethersfield, Connecticut
Founded in 1634 and densely settled by 1750, Wethersfield remained prosperous through agricultural innovation, turning after 1790 to market gardening. Women played a dominant role in this intensive horticulture,
which made Wethersfield the "onion capital" of the United States.

Rural families were now laboring twelve months a year. But whether they
were hacking fields out of western forests or carting manure to replenish eastern
soils, their labor was rewarded by higher output and income. Westward migration
boosted the entire American economy as it improved the quality of rural life.

The Transportation Bottleneck

The geography of the American continent remained an obstacle to economic
advancement. In America as in Europe, the patterns of settlement and trade

had long been determined by water routes. Farmers without access to rivers had to haul their crops by oxcart over narrow dirt trails that turned to mudholes during the wet season. Even in dry weather, ox-drawn carts moved slowly and carried only small loads. They were expensive, too, costing 30 cents a ton-mile, or roughly five times as much as water transport. Incredibly, Pennsylvania farmers paid as much to send wheat and corn 30 miles overland to Philadelphia as merchants did to ship it from Philadelphia to London. Consequently, settlers paid premium prices for land along navigable streams and speculators bought up likely sites for towns along the Ohio, Tennessee, and Mississippi rivers, on which farmers floated their produce to New Orleans. Without access to waterways or good roads, western settlers could not afford to send goods to distant markets.

The enhancement of inland trade became a high priority for the new state governments, which actively encouraged transportation ventures. Between 1793 and 1812, the Pennsylvania legislature granted corporate charters to fifty-five private turnpike companies and Massachusetts chartered over a hundred. The turnpike companies charged tolls for the use of the level gravel roads they built, but the roads cut travel time significantly. State governments and private entrepreneurs also dredged rivers to make them navigable and constructed short canals, mostly to bypass waterfalls or rapids. By 1816 the United States had about 100 miles of canals, but only three were more than 2 miles long and none breached the great Appalachian barrier.

Despite these transportation bottlenecks, white Americans continued to migrate westward. They knew it would take a generation to clear land; build houses, barns, and roads; and plant orchards. But they were confident that their sacrifices would yield future security—a farmstead and an independent livelihood for themselves and their children. Slowly, thousands of yeomen and tenant families turned forests into farms, transforming the landscape of the trans-Appalachian West.

REPUBLICAN POLICY AND DIPLOMACY

Between 1801 and 1825 three Republicans from Virginia—Thomas Jefferson, James Madison, and James Monroe—each served two terms as president. Supported by voters in the new western states and by strong majorities in Congress, the Virginia Dynasty reversed many Federalist policies, completing what Jefferson called the Revolution of 1800.

The Jeffersonian Presidency

Thomas Jefferson was perhaps the most accomplished and versatile statesman in American history. A seasoned diplomat and an insightful political philosopher, he was also a superb politician. On becoming president in 1801, Jefferson won over some of his Federalist opponents by appointing them to major government posts; he used other patronage positions to bolster the Republican party in New England. But the new president still faced a government filled with his opponents, especially in the judiciary. The most important Federalist judge was the formidable John Marshall of Virginia, who had been appointed chief justice of the United States by John Adams in January 1801 (he would serve until 1835). Moreover, the outgoing Federalist-controlled Congress had passed a Judiciary Act in 1801, creating sixteen new judgeships, six additional circuit courts, and a variety of patronage posts, which Adams had filled in a series of "midnight appointments" just before leaving office. The Federalists "have retired into the judiciary as a stronghold," Jefferson complained, "and from that battery all the works of Republicanism are to be beaten down and erased."

Republicans in Congress fought back by repealing the Judiciary Act and impeaching two Federalist judges for their partisan political activities, winning the removal of one. For his part, James Madison, the new secretary of state, refused to deliver the commission of one of Adams's midnight appointees, prompting the famous case of *Marbury v. Madison* (see Chapter 9). Subsequently, Jefferson pursued a conciliatory policy, judging each Federalist bureaucrat on the basis of his ability. During eight years as chief executive, he removed only 109 of 433 Federalist officeholders.

Nonetheless, Jefferson and his party were determined to reverse Federalist policies and shrink the national government to what they considered its proper constitutional size and shape. When the Alien and Sedition acts expired, the Republican Congress did not reenact them, seeing them as politically motivated and unconstitutional. Jefferson also abolished all internal taxes, including the excise tax that had sparked the Whiskey Rebellion of 1794, and reduced the size of the army and navy. He reluctantly accepted the Bank of the United States, which he had condemned as unconstitutional in 1791, because of its importance to the nation's economy. But Jefferson was still opposed to a large public debt, and so he appointed Albert Gallatin, a brilliant Swiss-born fiscal conservative, as Treasury secretary. By cutting expenditures and using customs revenues to redeem government bonds, Gallatin reduced the debt from $83 million in 1801 to $45 million in 1808. With Jefferson and Gallatin at the helm, the nation was no longer run in the interest of northeastern creditors and merchants.

Jefferson and the West

Long before he became president Jefferson had championed the settlement of the West. He had celebrated the yeoman farmer in *Notes on the State of Virginia* (1785), helped compose the Confederation's land ordinances, and strongly supported Pinckney's Treaty of 1795, which allowed westerners to ship crops down the Mississippi for export through Spanish-held New Orleans.

As president, Jefferson had a new opportunity to encourage western settlement. The ordinance of 1785, which had set land policy for the national domain, had favored speculators over yeomen. It specified that half the land be sold in blocs of 23,040 acres at a minimum price of $1 per acre, making direct purchase impossible for all but the wealthy (see Map 7.2, page 181). The other half was to be divided into parcels of 640 acres, but even those were prohibitively expensive for many migrants, who lacked the cash to buy high-quality or well-located land. Poorer settlers demanded better terms, but the Federalist-dominated Congresses of the 1790s instead doubled the minimum price to $2 per acre. Many Federalist politicians were eastern landlords who were determined not to lose their tenants to cheap land in the West.

Because Jefferson wanted to see the West populated with yeomen farm families, the Republicans in Congress won the passage of new laws in 1800 and 1804 reducing the minimum allotment to 320 and then 160 acres and allowing payment in installments over four years. Eventually the Land Act of 1820 reduced the minimum purchase to 80 acres and the price to $1.25 per acre, enabling a farmer with only $100 in cash to buy a western farm.

But international events challenged Jefferson's vision for the West. In 1799 the daring general Napoleon Bonaparte seized power in revolution-torn France and began an ambitious campaign to establish a French empire in both Europe and America. In 1800 Napoleon coerced Spain into signing a secret treaty returning Louisiana to France; two years later Spanish officials began restricting American access to New Orleans. Meanwhile, Napoleon had mobilized an expeditionary force to restore French rule in Haiti (or Saint-Domingue), a rich sugar island that had been seized by rebellious black slaves led by Toussaint L'Ouverture.

Napoleon's actions prompted Jefferson to question his party's traditionally pro-French foreign policy. Trade down the Mississippi River, guaranteed by Pinckney's Treaty of 1795 with Spain, was crucial to the West; any nation that denied Americans access to New Orleans, Jefferson declared, must be "our natural and habitual enemy." To avoid crossing swords with Napoleon, Jefferson instructed Robert R. Livingston, the American minister in Paris, to purchase New Orleans.

Jefferson's diplomacy yielded a magnificent prize: the entire territory of Louisiana. In 1802 the French invasion of Haiti was faltering, the victim of yellow fever and spirited black resistance, and a new war was threatening to break out in Europe. Acting with characteristic decisiveness, Napoleon gave up his dream of an empire in America and in April 1803 offered to sell Louisiana. For about $15 million ($180 million today), Livingston and James Monroe, the American ambassador to Britain, concluded what became known as the Louisiana Purchase (see Map 8.3, page 227). "We have lived long," Livingston remarked to Monroe, "but this is the noblest work of our lives."

The magnitude of the Louisiana Purchase forced the president to reconsider his interpretation of the Constitution. Jefferson had always been a strict constructionist, arguing that the national government possessed only the powers "expressly" delegated to it in the Constitution. But there was no provision in the Constitution for adding new territory. Given his dreams for the West, Jefferson was pragmatic: adopting a loose interpretation, he used the treaty-making powers granted by the Constitution to complete the deal with France.

A scientist as well as a statesman, Jefferson wanted detailed information about the physical features of the new territory and its plant and animal life. In 1804 he sent his personal secretary, Meriwether Lewis, to explore the region along with William Clark, an army officer. Aided by Indian guides, Lewis and Clark traveled up the Missouri River, across the Rocky Mountains, and (venturing beyond the Purchase) down the Columbia River to the Pacific Ocean. After two years they returned with the first maps of the immense wilderness and vivid accounts of its natural resources and native American inhabitants.

The Louisiana Purchase was a stunning accomplishment, doubling the size of the nation at a single stroke, but it brought a new threat. New England Federalists had long feared that western expansion would diminish their region's power, and some of them now talked openly of leaving the Union. When Alexander Hamilton refused to support their plan for a separate confederation, the northeastern secessionists turned to Aaron Burr, the ambitious vice-president, who was seeking election as governor of New York. After Hamilton accused Burr of plotting to dismember the nation, Burr killed him in a duel—the preferred aristocratic method for settling personal disputes—and was indicted for murder.

This tragic event propelled Burr into yet another secessionist scheme. After completing his term as vice-president early in 1805, he moved west to avoid prosecution. There he conspired with General James Wilkinson, the military governor of the Louisiana Territory. Their plan remains a mystery, but it is thought to have involved either the capture of Spanish territory in Mexico or a rebellion to establish Louisiana as a separate nation headed by Burr. Whatever their intentions, Wilkinson betrayed his ally, arresting Burr on a charge of treason as the former vice-president led an armed force down the Ohio River.

In a highly publicized and politicized trial presided over by Chief Justice John Marshall, Burr was acquitted. But the verdict in Burr's trial was less important than the dangers to national unity that the trial revealed. The Republicans' expansionist policies had increased sectional tension and party conflict, giving new life to states' rights sentiments and secessionist schemes.

The Road to War

Meanwhile, the outbreak of the Napoleonic Wars in Europe (1802–1815) had begun to draw the new nation into European conflicts. Great Britain and France, the major belligerents, refused to respect American neutrality, claiming the right to board merchant ships and confiscate cargoes destined for each other's ports. While on board, the British often removed sailors they suspected of deserting the Royal Navy and *impressed* them back into military service. Between 1802 and 1811 British officers seized nearly 8,000 sailors, many of whom were American citizens.

Long-simmering American resentment erupted in 1807, when a British warship attacked the U.S. Navy vessel *Chesapeake*, killing or wounding twenty-one men and seizing four alleged deserters. "Never since the battle of

Lexington have I seen this country in such a state of exasperation as at present," Jefferson declared. The president demanded monetary reparations and an end to impressment. To demonstrate his resolve, he barred British warships from American ports, preventing their resupply. The British government apologized and promised compensation but continued to seize French goods from American ships and impress suspected deserters.

To protect American interests while avoiding war, Jefferson pursued a policy of peaceful coercion. Working closely with Secretary of State James Madison, the president devised the Embargo Act of 1807. This legislation prohibited American ships from leaving their home ports until Britain and France repealed their restrictions on U.S. trade. Though the embargo was imaginative—an economic weapon similar to the nonimportation movements between 1765 and 1775—it was also naive. Jefferson and Madison overestimated the belligerents' dependence on American shipping and underestimated resistance from New England merchants, who feared the embargo would ruin them. The embargo crippled American exports, which plunged from $108 million in 1806 to $22 million in 1808, hurting farmers as well as merchants and prompting Federalists to demand its repeal. "Would to God," exclaimed one Federalist, "that the Embargo had done as little evil to ourselves as it has done to foreign nations."

Despite public discontent with the embargo, voters elected James Madison to the presidency in 1808. Madison promptly acknowledged the embargo's failure. He replaced it with the Nonintercourse Act, which permitted trade with all nations except France and Britain, and offered the promise of normal commerce if the belligerents respected America's neutral rights. When Britain and France ignored this overture, Madison bowed to pressure from Congress and accepted an act that reopened legal trade but threatened to cut off trade with any nation interfering with American commerce. But the British ministry refused to alter its policies, and the astute Napoleon exploited the ill-conceived legislation. Publicly exempting American commerce from seizure, the French emperor instructed his customs officials privately to ignore the exemption. "The Devil himself could not tell which government, England or France, is the most wicked," an exasperated congressman declared.

Republicans were pretty sure it was Britain; congressmen from the West accused Governor-General James Craig of Canada of providing military assistance to native Americans in the Ohio River Valley. Bolstered by British goods and guns, the Shawnee chief Tecumseh, assisted by his brother, the Prophet Tenskwatawa, had revived the Western Confederation. The two leaders had constructed a new ideology that blended ancestral religious values with Christian teachings. Like other Indian leaders before them, they called for a ban on liquor, less dependence on European goods, and an end to the cohabitation of Indian women and white men. To symbolize the religious roots of Indian resistance, Tecumseh centered his confederacy in a sacred town at the junction of the Tippecanoe and Wabash rivers. He traveled widely among southern tribes in hopes of winning their support.

**Tenskwatawa, "The Prophet,"
1836**
Although his brother Tecumseh was the greater leader, Tenskwatawa added a spiritual dimension to native American resistance, urging a holy war against white settlers. His religious message transcended differences among Indian peoples, helping to create a formidable political and military alliance.

To prevent further land cessions, Tecumseh revived the doctrine of common tribal ownership of the territory north of the Ohio River and vowed to exclude white settlers. But thousands of white settlers already lived in the West, and their concerns had a decisive impact on American policy. Expansionists in Congress condemned British support of Tecumseh and threatened to retaliate by invading Canada and seizing Florida from Spain, Britain's ally. Urged on by such talk, some Americans living near and in the western (panhandle) region of Florida took up arms and tried to annex it to the United States. Meanwhile, southern planters campaigned for the conquest of eastern Florida to prevent slaves from taking refuge among the Seminole Indians. In 1811, responding to Indian raids in the Indiana Territory, Governor William Henry Harrison marched on Prophetstown, Tenskwatawa's sacred village, fended off the confederation's warriors at the Battle of Tippecanoe, and burned the town to the ground.

Prompted by these events, Henry Clay of Kentucky, the new Speaker of the House of Representatives, and John C. Calhoun, a rising young congressman from South Carolina, pushed Madison toward war with Great Britain. With national elections approaching, Madison bowed to pressure from western and southern War Hawks and abandoned the strategy of economic coercion. He demanded that the British respect American sovereignty in the West and neutral rights on the Atlantic. When the British failed to respond quickly enough, Madison asked Congress for a declaration of war. In June 1812 a sharply divided Senate voted 19 to 13 for war; the House of Representatives concurred, 79 to 49.

The causes of the War of 1812 have been much debated. Officially, the United States went to war because of violations of its neutral rights: the seizure of its ships and the impressment of its sailors. But the patterns of voting in Congress and in the election of 1812 suggest that the war was fought as much for land as for maritime rights. The war was opposed by Federalist congressmen and by a majority of voters in New England and the Middle Atlantic states, who gave 89 electoral votes to the Federalist candidate for president, De Witt Clinton of New York.

Madison amassed 128 electoral votes, mostly in the South and West—regions whose congressmen had heeded the demands of their constituents and voted for war. Western farmers were angry because the British blockade had cut the price of their crops. Settlers in frontier districts demanded war against the Indians and their British allies. War Hawks in Congress eyed new territory in Florida and Canada and hoped war would discredit the Federalists and underscore America's independence from Britain. Many Americans had been enraged by British arrogance; Republicans exploited this anger to mobilize support for the war. As President Madison put it, "National honor is national property of the highest value."

The War of 1812

The War of 1812 was a near disaster for the United States both militarily and politically. Republican congressmen had predicted an easy victory in Canada, but when General William Hull invaded western Canada in the summer of 1812, he was immediately forced to retreat. Nonetheless, American forces stayed on the offensive. Commodore Oliver Hazard Perry defeated a small British flotilla on Lake Erie, and in October 1813 General William Henry Harrison defeated a combined British and Indian force at the Battle of the Thames, killing Tecumseh, who had become a general in the British army. Another American force captured and burned the Upper Canada capital of York (now Toronto) but, lacking men and supplies, quickly withdrew.

Political divisions in the United States prevented a major invasion of Canada. Federalist governors in the New England states opposed the war and prohibited their militias from fighting outside their states. Boston merchants and banks declined to lend money to the federal government—some actually invested in British bonds instead—making the war difficult to finance. In Congress, Daniel Webster, a dynamic young representative from New Hampshire, led Federalist opposition to higher taxes and tariffs. To force a negotiated peace, Webster discouraged enlistment and successfully opposed the conscription of state militiamen into the national army. Having led a divided nation into war, Madison and the Republicans were unable to strike the British in Canada, their weakest point.

In the Atlantic, the small American navy proved no match for the Royal Navy. Although the British lost scores of merchant vessels to American privateers in the first months of the war, thereafter the Royal Navy redeployed its fleet and British commerce moved in relative safety. By 1813 Britain had taken the initiative at sea: a flotilla of warships moved up and down the American coastline, interfering with shipping and threatening seaport cities. In 1814, the fleet sailed up Chesapeake Bay and British army units stormed ashore to attack the District of Columbia. There they set fire to government buildings in retaliation for the destruction of York. The troops advanced on Baltimore where they were finally repulsed by courageous American resistance at Fort McHenry. After two years of sporadic warfare, the United States was stalemated in Canada and on the defensive along the Atlantic, its new capital city in ruins.

Sectional opposition to the war strengthened in 1814. The Massachusetts legislature called for a convention "to lay the foundation for a radical reform in the National Compact." In December New England Federalists gathered in Hartford, Connecticut. Some delegates to the Hartford Convention proposed outright secession by their states, but the majority favored a revision of the Constitution. Their object was to reverse the declining role of the Federalist party—and New England—in the expanding nation. To end the Virginia Dynasty, the delegates proposed a constitutional amendment limiting the presidency to a single four-year term, rotating the office among citizens from different states. Other Federalists suggested amendments restricting commercial embargoes to sixty days and requiring a two-thirds majority in Congress to declare war, prohibit trade, or admit a new state.

A minority in the nation and divided among themselves, the Federalists could hope to prevail only if the war continued to go badly—a very real prospect. In the late summer of 1814 a planned British invasion of the Hudson River Valley had been narrowly averted by an American naval victory at the Battle of Lake Champlain. Then, in December, British transports landed thousands of seasoned veterans at New Orleans, threatening to cut off the West's access to the sea. The United States was under pressure from both north and south. The only hopeful sign was that Britain had finally defeated Napoleon in Europe and wanted peace with the United States.

In August 1814 the British entered into negotiations with an American delegation at Ghent, Belgium. The American commissioners—John Quincy Adams, Albert Gallatin, and Henry Clay—at first demanded territory in Canada and Florida, but British diplomats insisted on a buffer state between the United States and Canada to serve as a refuge for their native American allies. In the end both sides realized that the small concessions they might win at the bargaining table were not worth the cost of prolonging the war. The Treaty of Ghent, signed on Christmas Eve, 1814, restored the prewar borders of the United States and left unresolved disputes to future negotiations.

These results hardly justified three years of fighting and a sharply divided nation. But a final victory in combat lifted Americans' morale. Before news of the Treaty of Ghent reached the United States, newspaper headlines proclaimed

A Kentucky Soldier Describes the Battle of New Orleans

For Americans, the Battle of New Orleans was a glorious victory that brought an upbeat end to an inglorious war. For the British, the clash was a bloody disaster, as this account by a Kentucky soldier makes clear.

The official report said the action lasted two hours and five minutes, but it did not seem half that length of time to me. It was so dark that little could be seen, until just about the time the battle ceased. The morning had dawned to be sure, but the smoke was so thick that everything seemed to be covered up in it. Our men did not seem to apprehend any danger, but would load and fire just as fast as they could, talking, swearing, joking all the time. . . .

When the smoke cleared away and we could obtain a fair view of the field, it looked at first glance like a sea of blood. It was not blood itself which gave it this appearance, but the red coats in which the British soldiers were dressed. Straight out before our position, for about the width of space which we supposed had been occupied by the British column, the field was entirely covered with prostrate bodies. In some places they were lying in piles of several, one on top of the other. . . .

Individuals could be seen in every possible attitude. Some lying quite dead, others mortally wounded, pitching and tumbling about in the agonies of death. Some had their heads shot off, some their legs, some their arms. Some were laughing, some crying, some groaning, and some screaming. . . .

SOURCE: Linda R. Monk, ed., *Ordinary Americans: U.S. History through the Eyes of Everyday People* (Alexandria, VA: Close Up Publications, 1994), pp. 47–48.

"ALMOST INCREDIBLE VICTORY!! GLORIOUS NEWS." On January 8, 1815, General Andrew Jackson's troops had crushed the British forces attacking New Orleans. Jackson's victory made the rugged, slaveowning Tennessee planter a national hero and a symbol of the emerging West. Yet Jackson dominated the battlefield not through the marksmanship of his Kentucky sharpshooters in coonskin caps but through a traditional deployment of regular troops, including a contingent of French-speaking black Americans, the Corps d'Afrique. The Americans fought from carefully constructed breastworks and were amply supplied with cannon, which rained "grapeshot and cannister bombs" on the massed British formations. With 700 Redcoats dead and 2,000 wounded or taken prisoner, the British lost thousands of their finest troops. American casualties totaled only 13 dead and 58 wounded. The victory redeemed the nation's battered pride and, with the coming of peace, undercut the Hartford Convention's demands for a revised Constitution. The young nation's political institutions had survived a divisive war.

The tumultuous era of the early republic thus came to an end. Peace in Europe ended two decades of political conflict over foreign policy and hastened the demise of the Federalists, whose elitist policies garnered little support in an expanding, increasingly democratic nation. "No Federal character can run with success," Gouverneur Morris of New York lamented, and the election results of 1818 bore out his pessimism. Republicans now outnumbered Federalists 37 to 7 in the Senate and 156 to 27 in the House of Representatives.

The decline of the Federalists prompted contemporary observers to dub James Monroe's two terms as president (1817–1825) the Era of Good Feeling. Actually, national political harmony was more apparent than real, for the Republican party—by then home to many former Federalists—soon split into factions that struggled over power, patronage, and, after 1820, economic policy.

REGIONAL DIVERSITY AND NATIONAL IDENTITY

During the colonial period four separate American cultures had emerged: New England, the Middle Atlantic, the Chesapeake, and the Lower South. The political divisions of the War of 1812 showed that regional differences remained strong. As the migrants transplanted their seaboard cultures to the interior, American life became even more diverse.

Atlantic Seaboard Societies

Observers had long noticed the contrast between the race- and class-divided societies of the Chesapeake and the freehold farming regions of the North. A British traveler detected both religious "fanaticism" and "a great strain of industry among all ranks of people" in New England. Visitors to the Chesapeake commented on the rude manners and heavy drinking of white tenant farmers and small freeholders, who had a "passion for gaming at the billiard table, a cock-fight or cards."

These popular stereotypes reflected genuine cultural differences. Because of its Puritan heritage, New England had a strong tradition of primary schooling and Bible reading. As a result, in 1790 most of the men and more than half the women in New England could read and write. By contrast, the slaveholding elite that ruled southern society refused to provide schooling for ordinary whites. Most white women and a third of white men in the Chesapeake could not even write their names and had to sign wills and marriage licenses with a mark such as an "X."

Holidays were another sign of regional differences. In Virginia, South Carolina, and other states with an Anglican religious heritage, Christmas was an occasion for feasting and celebration. Not so in New England, where ministers condemned such celebrations as profane; most churches in that region did not celebrate Christmas until the 1850s. New England's holiday was Thanksgiving, which commemorated the trials and triumphs of the first Pilgrim and Puritan settlers. Indeed, the region's history contributed to its strong sense of identity. By the 1820s most men and women had ties to large clans that could trace their American roots back six or seven generations. No fewer than 281 members of the Newhall clan were living in Lynn, Massachusetts, in the 1820s, along with 259 Breeds, 195 Alleys, and 162 Johnsons. In a very real sense, New England was a society of interrelated families.

The culture of the Middle Atlantic region was more diverse, for the settlers there had consciously maintained their distinct ethnic identities. In Pennsylvania, New Jersey, and western Maryland, Quakers and Scots-Irish had married largely within their own ethnic groups, while Germans had held on to their language and customs, especially in farming towns. As a visitor to Hanover, Maryland, noted around 1820, "The inhabitants are all German. Habits, speech, newspapers, cooking—all German." This diversity within and between regions delayed the emergence of an American national identity.

Political events occasionally reminded isolated farmers and ethnic communities that they were members of a larger nation. During the War of 1812 Americans began to refer to the federal government as "Uncle Sam": "The letters U.S. on government waggons &c are supposed to have given rise to it," reported a newspaper in Troy, New York. War patriotism gave instant popularity to "The Star Spangled Banner," written by Francis Scott Key during the battle at Fort McHenry.

Newspapers brought national news and advertisements to small towns and rural areas. Political parties subsidized some papers in an effort to create a national debate on various legislative issues. The influential *Niles Weekly Register*, established in Baltimore in 1811, and the *North American Review*, founded in Boston in 1815, carried news from Europe and the port cities to every region. But only members of certain elites—merchants, politicians, lawyers—participated fully in the emerging national culture. Most Americans lived out their lives in the local cultures into which they had been born.

The Old Northwest

When Jedidiah Morse published *American Geography* in 1793, he listed three "grand divisions of the United States": northern, middle, and southern. In the 1819 edition he added a new section: "Western States and Territories." Initially this region lacked a culture of its own. When 176 residents of Granville, Massachusetts, moved to Ohio, they transplanted their Congregational church whole, complete with ministers and elders, along with their system of freehold agriculture. Throughout the trans-Appalachian West, most "new" communities were not new; they were old communities that had moved inland.

Cut off from most trade with outside markets, settlers made their own clothes, repaired old tools, and bartered goods and labor with their neighbors.

"A noble field of Indian corn stretched away into the forest on one side," an English visitor to an Ohio farm in the 1820s noted, waxing romantic,

> and immediately before the house was a small potato garden, with a few peach and apple trees. The woman told me that they spun and wove all the cotton and woollen garments of the family, and knit all the stockings; her husband, though not a shoemaker by trade, made all the shoes. She manufactured all the soap and candles they use. All she wanted with money, she said, was to buy coffee, tea, and whiskey, and she could "get enough any day by sending a batch of butter and chickens to market."

Self-sufficiency meant a low standard of living. As late as 1840, per capita income in the Old Northwest was only 70 percent of the national average.

Apart from its relative poverty, the Northwest's distinctiveness lay in the conflict among competing cultural traditions. As New Englander Lucy Maynard wrote home from central Illinois, "Our neighbors are principally from ... Kentucky, some from Virginia, all friendly but very different from our people in their manner and language and every other way." In Indiana these differences sparked a twenty-year struggle between education-conscious migrants from New England and tax-shy yeomen from the southern states. Because of such diverse cultural traditions, the states of the Old Northwest resembled the mixed societies of the Middle Atlantic region.

Slavery Moves into the Old Southwest

While poor whites fled from the Chesapeake, migrating first to Kentucky and then to the Old Northwest, wealthy planters carried slavery into the Old Southwest—the future states of Alabama, Mississippi, and Louisiana. At the Philadelphia convention in 1787 slaveowners from Georgia and South Carolina had preserved the Atlantic slave trade for twenty more years. By 1808, the year Congress ended the trade, Georgia and South Carolina rice growers had imported 250,000 new African workers—as many as had been imported in the entire colonial period. The black population throughout the South also grew through reproduction, increasing from half a million in 1775 to 1.8 million in 1820.

Many Africans and African-Americans still toiled on tobacco and rice plantations. When soil exhaustion lowered tobacco production in the Tidewater region of the Chesapeake, planters took the crop to the Virginia Piedmont, North Carolina, Kentucky, and Tennessee. Simultaneously, white planters in Louisiana—some of them refugees from black-controlled Haiti—established a booming sugar economy. Slaves in Louisiana, like those on the sugar plantations of the West Indies, were brutally exploited and died quickly from disease and overwork.

However, it was a new crop—cotton—that provided the main impetus for the expansion of slavery. For centuries most Europeans had worn clothing made from wool or flax. Although English manufacturers had taken up cotton

A Migrant Recalls the Frontier Experience

Born around 1810, Reuben Davis grew up on the Alabama frontier, where his slaveowning father had migrated to find land and opportunities for his many children.

Both my parents were born in Virginia, and remained there after marriage until ten children were added to their family. They then removed to Tennessee, and settled near Winchester. . . .

When I was about five years of age, my father removed from Tennessee to North Alabama. The land had been recently purchased from the Indians, and many of them yet roamed the dense forests of that section. I well remember how I hunted with these wild companions, and was taught by them to use the bow and arrow. Even now I can recall something of the emotion excited in my youthful breast by the wild yells of a party of drunken savages passing near my father's house. . . .

At that time the country was as wild and unsettled as possible; there were no laws, no schools, and no libraries. Every man did what was right in his own eyes, but in spite of general recklessness and lawlessness, there was a rough code of honor and honesty which was rarely broken. The settlers lived a life of great toil and many privations, but they were eminently social, kindly, and friendly. . . . My brothers and myself, assisted by six colored hands, cultivated the land, and attended school only about three months in the year. . . .

There was this great advantage that, while none were very wealthy, few were poor enough to suffer actual want. . . . The simple habits of the laboring man were not shamed by the ostentation of his more prosperous neighbor; and there was none of that silent, perpetual contrast of luxury and penury, which now adds bitterness to class hatreds.

SOURCE: Reuben Davis, *Recollections of Mississippi and Mississippians* (Boston: Houghton, Mifflin & Company, 1890), pp. 2–4.

spinning and weaving, cotton textiles had remained a minor industry until 1750. Then a European population explosion increased the demand for cloth just as the technological breakthroughs of the Industrial Revolution began to boost production and lower prices. Rising consumer demand generated a huge demand for cotton goods, which manufacturers met with the use of the newly invented water-powered spinning jenny and weaving mule.

Since independence American planters had grown a smooth-seed, long-fiber variety of cotton on the sea islands of the southern Atlantic coast. In the 1790s, Eli Whitney and other inventors developed machines to separate the rough seeds from the fiber of short-staple cotton, which could be grown in most areas of the South. The combination of British demand and American innovation created a new agricultural industry and a massive demand for land and labor. In South Carolina and Georgia, thousands of white planters moved into the interior to grow cotton. After the War of 1812, production spread to Alabama and Mississippi, which entered the Union in 1817 and 1819, respectively. In a single year a government land office in Huntsville, Alabama, sold $7 million of uncleared land. The expression "doing a land-office business"—a metaphor for rapid commercial expansion—dates from this time.

For enslaved blacks, the coming of cotton meant social upheaval. Entire black communities were uprooted from the Chesapeake and Lower South and forced to move west with their masters. Thousands more young women and men were sold by their owners to domestic slave traders, who resold them to planters in the new tobacco regions and booming cotton states. By 1820 whites had relocated more than 250,000 African-Americans. Torn from their loved ones, African-Americans had to rebuild their lives, laboring "from day clean to first dark" on frontier plantations in Alabama and Mississippi. "I am Sold to a man by the name of Peterson a trader," lamented a Georgia slave. "My Dear wife for you and my Children my pen cannot Express the griffe I feel to be parted from you all."

Early antislavery reformers had hoped that the decline of the tobacco economy and the end of the Atlantic slave trade would allow slavery to "die a natural death." Their dream was shattered when Louisiana, Mississippi, and Alabama joined the Union with state constitutions that permitted slavery. When Missouri applied for admission on a similar basis in 1819, antislavery forces rallied. Congressman James Tallmadge of New York proposed a ban on the importation of slaves into Missouri and the gradual emancipation of its black inhabitants, setting off a bitter debate in Congress. When whites in Missouri refused to end slavery, the northern majority in the House of Representatives blocked the territory's admission to the Union. In response, southerners used their power in the Senate, which was equally divided between eleven free and eleven slave states, to withhold statehood from Maine, which was seeking to separate from Massachusetts. Tempers flared in the heat of debate. Senator Thomas W. Cobb of Georgia accused Tallmadge of kindling "a fire which all the waters of the ocean cannot put out and which seas of blood can only extinguish."

The controversy raged for two years before Representative Henry Clay of Kentucky persuaded the House to accept a series of agreements known collectively as the Missouri Compromise. Maine would enter the Union as a free state in 1820 and Missouri as a slave state the following year, a bargain that preserved the sectional balance in the Senate and set a precedent for the admission of states in pairs, one free and one slave. To mollify antislavery sentiment in the House of Representatives, southern congressmen accepted a ban on slavery in the rest of the Louisiana Territory north of latitude 36° 30′, Missouri's southern boundary (see Map 8.2).

In 1821 as in 1787, white leaders in the North and the South gave priority to the Union, finding complex ways to reconcile their regions' interests.

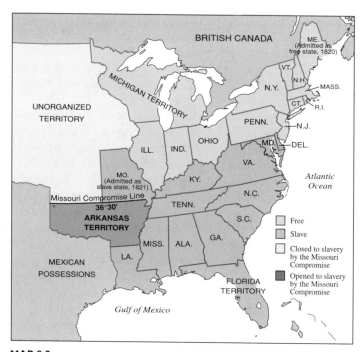

MAP 8.2
The Missouri Compromise, 1820
The Missouri Compromise resolved for a generation the issue of slavery in the lands of the Louisiana Purchase. Slavery was forbidden north of the compromise line, 36° 30′ north latitude, with the exception of Missouri, which entered the Union as a slave state. The compromise provided for the nearly simultaneous admission of Maine, maintaining an equal number of free and slave states in the Senate.

But the task had become more difficult. The delegates at the Constitutional Convention had resolved their sectional differences in two months; Congress took two years to craft the Missouri Compromise, and there was no guarantee that it would work. The fates of the West, the Union, and the black race had become inextricably intertwined. As Thomas Jefferson exclaimed at the time, the Missouri controversy "like a fire-bell in the night, awakened and filled me with terror."

African-American Society and Culture

After 1800 a more unified African-American culture developed in the United States for three reasons. First, the end of the transatlantic slave trade in 1808 made it unnecessary to assimilate newly arrived Africans. Even in South Carolina only about 20 percent of the slaves in 1820 had been born in Africa.

Second, the movement of slavery into the Old Southwest had reduced differences among slaves. For example, the Gullah dialect spoken by slaves from the Carolinas gradually died out on the cotton plantations of Alabama and Mississippi, replaced by the black English spoken by slaves from the Chesapeake. Third, especially in northern cities, free blacks consciously created a distinct African-American community.

African cultural elements found an important place in the lives of American blacks. Descriptions of blacks who "danced the Congo and sang a purely African song" appeared as late as 1890. African-Americans also retained the incest taboos of their homeland. Unlike South Carolina's white elite, which allowed marriage between cousins to keep property in the family, enslaved blacks shunned such marriages. For example, on the Good Hope plantation in South Carolina, where 40 percent of the 175 slave children born between 1800 and 1857 were related by blood to just three slaves from Africa, only one marriage took place between cousins.

Because slaveowners forbade legal marriage between blacks (so that slaves could be sold without breaking a marriage bond), African-Americans devised their own rituals. Young men and women first asked their parents' consent to marry and then sought their owner's permission to live together in their own cabin. Following African custom, many couples jumped over a broomstick together in a public ceremony. Christian blacks were often wed by a white or black preacher, but the rites never ended with the customary phrase "until death do you part."

Although forced separations split many black families, the majority of unions were stable. Among the slaves on the Good Hope plantation, about 70 percent of the women conceived all their children by the same man. Black family life was much more fragile in Louisiana, where labor in the sugar fields killed many men.

To maintain their identity, many recently imported slaves in the Lower South bestowed African names on their children. Males born on Friday were often called Cuffee—the name of that day in several West African languages. Most Chesapeake slaves chose names of British origin and bound one generation to another by naming sons after fathers, uncles, or grandfathers. Daughters often were named after grandmothers. Like incest rules and marriage rituals, African-American naming patterns created order in a harsh and arbitrary world.

After the family, the religious community played the most important role in the lives of enslaved African-Americans. Some blacks maintained African practices, invoking traditional spirits in time of need, but many became Christians, absorbing the religious views of white Baptists and Methodists and adapting them to their needs. Black Christians generally ignored the doctrines of original sin and predestination as well as biblical passages that portrayed the church as a lawgiver and symbol of authority. They preferred to envision God as a warrior who had liberated the Jews, his chosen people. "Their cause was similar to the Israelites'," explained a slave conspirator during a thwarted rebellion in Virginia. Slaves also identified with the persecuted Christ, who had suffered and died so that his followers might gain salvation. Amid the manifest injustice of their lives, African-Americans used Christian principles to affirm their equality with whites in the eyes of God.

As local African-American cultural communities developed, the quality of slave life gradually improved. During the eighteenth century the diverse origins of African-born slaves had enabled white men to take easy advantage of blacks—to rape women and punish defiant men by branding them or cutting off their fingers or ears. Although these abuses did not stop after 1800, they were questioned more often. White politicians condemned rape as an aristocratic vice ill suited to a republican society, while the spread of evangelical Christianity prompted many masters to treat slaves more humanely. Meanwhile, by forming stable families and strong communities, African-Americans were better able to resist the worst forms of oppression. They insisted that work gangs be sold "in families" and defied their masters when they were not. One Maryland slave, faced with transport to Mississippi and separation from his wife, "neither yields consent to accompany my people, or to be exchanged or sold," his owner reported. Masters ignored such resistance at their peril, because a slave's relatives might retaliate with arson, poison, or destruction of crops or equipment.

Blacks in the rice-growing lowlands of South Carolina were particularly successful in gaining the right to labor by the *task* rather than work under constant supervision. Each day a worker would have to complete a precisely defined task—turn over a quarter acre of land, hoe half an acre, or pound seven mortars of rice. By working hard, many lowland slaves finished their tasks "by one or two o'clock in the afternoon," a Methodist preacher reported, and had "the rest of the day for themselves, which they spend in working their own private fields . . . planting rice, corn, potatoes, tobacco &c. for their own use and profit." "Should any owner increase the work beyond what is customary," a rice planter in South Carolina warned around 1800, "he subjects himself . . . to such discontent amongst his slaves as to make them of little use to him."

Still, white masters had virtually unlimited power, both legal and physical, over their slaves. In the upland cotton-growing regions of South Carolina and Georgia and in Alabama and Mississippi, owners forced workers to labor in "gangs" that were supervised by black "drivers" or white overseers. Planters sold slaves who were recalcitrant and punished those they viewed as lazy. Particularly on newly settled plantations, profit-conscious masters used the lash to extract labor from exhausted field workers. A few blacks, such as Gabriel Prosser in Virginia (1799) and Denmark Vesey in South Carolina (1822), plotted mass uprisings and murders. But most blacks realized that a revolt was unlikely to be successful. Flight was also perilous. The northern and western states were hotbeds of racial prejudice, and the Fugitive Slave Law (1793) allowed masters to carry escaped slaves back to bondage. In these circumstances, slaves had no option but to build the best possible lives for themselves where they were. Like the oppressed peasantry of Europe, they worked as dependent agricultural laborers and built close-knit communities based on family, kinship, and religion.

Meanwhile, free African-Americans—about 5 percent of all blacks in the United States by 1820—explored the limits of their liberty. Most free blacks earned low wages as farm workers or city laborers and laundresses. Their lives were circumscribed by prejudice: they were usually forbidden to vote, attend public schools, or sit next to whites in churches. But a few African-Americans who were able to make full use of their talents achieved great distinction. The mathematician and surveyor Benjamin Banneker published an almanac and helped lay out the new national capital. Joshua Johnston won praise for his portraiture, and Robert Sheridan acquired a small fortune from his mercantile enterprises. But more impressive and enduring were the institutions this first generation of free African-Americans created. Hundreds of free blacks pooled their resources and talents to found schools, mutual-benefit and fellowship societies, antislavery organizations, and religious denominations such as the AME (African Methodist Episcopal) Church. Over the years these institutions gave free African-Americans a sense of cultural autonomy.

Mount Bethel African Methodist Episcopal Church
After they were segregated in the gallery of Philadelphia's St. George's Methodist Church, a group of African-American Methodists decided to worship "separate from our white brethren." In 1794 they formed the Methodist Bethel Church. Led by Richard Allen, the congregation won legal recognition as an independent "African" church in 1816. Allen became the first bishop of the African Methodist Episcopal Church.

The Fate of Native Americans

"Next to the case of the black race within our bosom," James Madison remarked as he left the presidency in 1817, "that of the red race on our borders is the problem most baffling to the policy of our country." Political opinion was sharply divided. A few influential Americans advocated extermination: "Cut up every Indian Cornfield and burn every Indian town," proclaimed William Henry Drayton of South Carolina, so that their "nation be extirpated and the lands become the property of the public." Many others, including Henry Knox, Washington's first secretary of war, favored assimilation. As a first step, Knox advocated breaking up commonly owned tribal land and redistributing it to individual Indian families. But that idea was rejected by the Indians, who did not normally possess wealth as individuals and wanted to maintain their clans and tribes.

Nonetheless, until the 1820s the U.S. government generally encouraged assimilation. It instructed territorial governors to purchase huge tracts of native American land, opening them to white pioneers and encouraging Indians to settle in farming communities on their remaining territory. And it welcomed the efforts of missionaries to change the Indians' culture. The object, as one Kentucky minister put it, was to make the Indian "a farmer, a citizen of the United States, and a Christian."

Most native Americans resisted attempts to redefine their identity. "Born free and independent," an observer noted, Indians were "struck with horror at whatever has the shadow of despotic power." Many tribes drove out white missionaries and forced converts to Christianity to participate in traditional native American rites. To justify their ancestral values, native American leaders devised dualistic cultural and religious theories. As a Munsee prophet put it, "there are two ways to God, one for the whites and one for the Indians."

Nevertheless, many tribes broke into hostile religious factions. Among the Seneca of New York, for example, the prophet Handsome Lake promoted traditional agricultural ceremonies—such as the green corn dance and the strawberry festival—in which the celebrants gave thanks to the earth, plants, animals, water, and sun. But Handsome Lake also adopted some Christian precepts, such as a belief in heaven and hell, and used them to discourage his followers from drinking alcohol, gambling, and practicing witchcraft. The more conservative among the Seneca, led by Red Jacket, opposed the innovations suggested by white missionaries, such as expecting men to work in the fields. Traditionally, Indian women had been responsible for growing staple foods and had often controlled the inheritance of cultivation rights. Their economic importance gave Indian women some political power; for example, the Shawnee chose female "war" and "civil" chiefs, who could prevent the dispatch of war parties and save captives from being tortured. Consequently, most Indian women insisted on retaining their role as cultivators. Even Christian Indians would not give up their social identities. To view themselves as individuals, as the Europeans demanded, would have been to repudiate the clan, the essence of Indian life.

Only under special circumstances did native Americans accept European ways. When whites attempted to oust the Cherokee from their ancestral lands in Georgia and the Carolinas in 1806 and again in 1817, a small faction of Cherokee mixed-bloods, the Christian offspring of white fur traders and Indian women, attempted to resist removal by adopting some elements of Anglo-American culture. They organized a national council, developed a written language, and in 1827 promulgated a charter of government modeled on the U.S. Constitution. But most full-blooded Cherokee rejected Anglo-American values; seizing control of the national council, they denounced both cultural assimilation and forced removal. As a chief of the neighboring Creeks declared, "We would not receive money for land in which our fathers and friends are buried. We love our land; it is our mother."

Continental Empire: Spain and the United States

Native Americans were not the only obstacles to America's westward expansion. During the reign of Carlos III (1759–1788) Spanish officials had sought to unite the long-settled territories on New Spain's northern border (present-day Florida, Texas, New Mexico, and Arizona) with new Spanish settlements in California. Under the direction of José de Gálvez, Spanish troops had established military presidios at San Diego, Santa Barbara, Monterey, and San Francisco. There and elsewhere along the California coast between 1769 and 1782, the Franciscan friar Junípero Serra had set up religious missions. Spanish ranchers followed, grazing huge herds of cattle.

To pacify the vast region that stretched from California to Florida, the Spanish attempted to contain or exterminate the war-prone Apache and to make more cooperative peoples dependent on Spanish trade through treaties and gifts, especially arms and alcohol. This policy brought peace to New Spain's northern frontier, allowing more Spanish ranchers and farmers to settle in Texas, New Mexico, and Arizona.

New Spain's borderlands empire quickly came under pressure from the newly independent American republic. To deter American settlement west of the Appalachians, Spanish authorities restricted American trade on the Mississippi River in 1784 and entered into an alliance with the Creek peoples. But American threats and military setbacks in Europe forced Spain to accept Pinckney's Treaty of 1795, which gave Americans access to the Mississippi and voided Spanish land claims in the Ohio River Valley. To prevent further American expansion (and curry favor with Napoleon), Spain ceded Louisiana to France in 1800. When the French emperor sold Louisiana to the United States in 1803, Spanish diplomats reacted strongly. They disputed President Jefferson's claim that Louisiana extended to the Rio Grande and the Rocky Mountains, which would have placed all of

Texas and half of New Mexico under American control. Instead, they argued that Louisiana was limited to the land along the Mississippi River (the present-day states of Louisiana, Arkansas, and Missouri). The issue remained unresolved at the end of the War of 1812, along with the status of West Florida, which had been occupied by American troops during the war (see Map 8.3).

The disputes between Spain and the United States were resolved by John Quincy Adams, son of the Federalist president John Adams. John Quincy had joined the Republican party before the War of 1812. As secretary of state under President Monroe, the younger Adams pursued an expansionist western policy. Exploiting a diplomatic crisis created by an unauthorized military expedition into Florida led by General Andrew Jackson, the secretary negotiated the Adams-Onís Treaty of 1819. Spain gave up its claim to the Oregon country and allowed the United States to annex East Florida; in return, the American government renounced its dubious claim to Spanish Texas and accepted a compromise boundary between New Spain and the Louisiana Territory. Adams also negotiated two

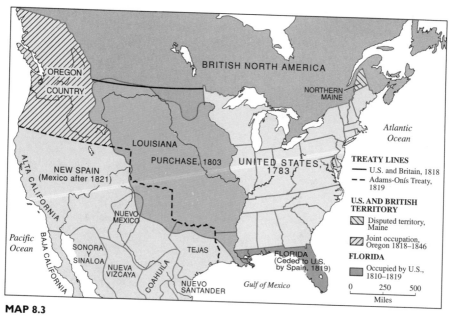

MAP 8.3

Defining the National Boundaries

After the War of 1812, John Quincy Adams negotiated treaties with Great Britain and Spain that made Florida and northern Maine part of the United States and defined the American boundaries with Canada and New Spain (which in 1821 became the independent nation of Mexico). These treaties eliminated the threat of war until the 1840s, providing the young nation with a much needed period of peace.

important agreements with Great Britain. The Rush–Bagot Treaty of 1817 limited naval forces on the Great Lakes, and an agreement in 1818 established the border between the Louisiana Territory and British Canada at the 49th parallel. Adams's diplomacy gave the United States undisputed possession of a vast inland empire.

Secretary Adams and President Monroe had this continental empire in mind when they outlined a new foreign policy that thirty years later became known as the Monroe Doctrine. In an address to Congress in 1823, Monroe warned European powers to stay out of the Western Hemisphere. Monroe's warning was meant for Spain in particular: patriots in Mexico and other Spanish colonies had revolted against Spanish rule and established independent republics, and Monroe was warning Spain not to try to subdue them. Adams and Monroe also hoped to prevent the Russians from extending their fur-trading posts south of Alaska. Thus, Monroe declared that the Americas were not "subject for further colonization" by European nations. In return, he pledged "not to interfere in the internal concerns" of European states. Monroe and Adams had turned their backs on the Old World and were looking westward, envisioning an American empire that would stretch from the Atlantic to the Pacific.

CHAPTER 8 TIMELINE

1790s	White settlers move west; cotton production expands Turnpikes and short canals built
1790–1791	Little Turtle defeats American armies
1792	Kentucky joins Union; Tennessee follows (1796)
1794	Battle of Fallen Timbers; Treaty of Greenville (1795)
1800s	Handsome Lake revival among Seneca
1800	Spain restores Louisiana to France
1801–1807	Gallatin reduces national debt Price of federal land reduced Seizures of American ships and sailors
1803	Louisiana Purchase; Lewis and Clark expedition follows Aaron Burr and western secession
1808	Tecumseh and Tenskwatawa mobilize Indians Congress bans importation of slaves
1810s	Expansion of slavery into Old Southwest Cherokee resist white advance Decline of Federalist party
1811	Battle of Tippecanoe
1812	War of 1812
1815	Battle of New Orleans; Treaty of Ghent
1817	Rush-Bagot Treaty (U.S.–Canadian boundary)
1817–1825	Era of Good Feeling
1819	Adams-Onis Treaty: Florida annexed, Texas boundary defined
1820	Missouri Compromise
1823	Monroe Doctrine

TOWARD A CAPITALIST PROTESTANT REPUBLIC, 1790-1820

- Political Economy: The Capitalist Commonwealth
- Visions of a Republican Social Order
- Protestant Christianity and Women's Lives

For most white Americans July 4, 1826, was a day of celebration. For fifty years they had lived in a self-governing society, free of an arbitrary government that imposed high taxes and an established church that enforced rigid dogma. Not even the deaths of John Adams and Thomas Jefferson on that Independence Day could diminish Americans' optimism. Indeed, for many citizens the timing of the deaths of two former presidents was a sign that God looked with favor on their experiment in self-government. Two of the greatest Founders had died, but the republic lived on.

During that first half-century the nation had matured into a full-fledged "republican" society. It now boasted not only a self-governing polity but also an economic system and a cultural order that reflected many of the values of ordinary citizens. State governments and social reformers had applied republican ideals to traditional institutions such as families, schools, and churches, unleashing a process of change that provided women as well as men with a new social identity. Reflecting the self-confident spirit of the new republic, leading citizens hailed their society as a model for all peoples. "The temperate zone of North America," a Kentucky judge declared in a Fourth of July speech, "already exhibits many signs that it is the promised land of civil liberty, and of institutions designed to liberate and exalt the human race."

POLITICAL ECONOMY: THE CAPITALIST COMMONWEALTH

The American quest for economic independence was longer and more arduous than the struggle for political autonomy. To enhance the prosperity of their citizens, states played a leading role in economic development, creating new legal institutions and providing financial incentives for ambitious entrepreneurs.

A Capitalist Society

Merchants had dominated the economic life of port cities in colonial times; with the departure of the British, they began to set the social and cultural tone as well. America was "a Nation of Merchants," a British visitor reported from Philadelphia in 1798, "always alive to their interests; and keen in the pursuit of wealth in all the various modes of acquiring it." And acquire it they did, especially during the European wars that dragged on from 1792 to 1815. Daring entrepreneurs, such as the fur trader John Jacob Astor and the merchant Robert Oliver, became the nation's first millionaires. Astor migrated from Germany to New York in 1784 and became wealthy by carrying furs from the Pacific Northwest to markets in China. Investing his profits in real estate, he became the largest landowner in New York City. Oliver made his fortune in Baltimore, beginning as an agent for Irish linen merchants and then starting his own mercantile firm. Exploiting the wartime shipping boom, he reaped enormous profits in the West Indian coffee and sugar trade.

To finance the expansion of mercantile enterprises, Americans had to devise an entirely new banking system. Before 1776 economically ambitious colonists were unable to secure loans. Farmers had relied on government-sponsored land banks, pledging their land as security, while merchants such as Oliver had arranged partnerships, borrowed funds from other merchants, or obtained credit from British suppliers. Then, in 1781, several Philadelphia merchants, Robert Morris among them, persuaded the Confederation Congress to charter the Bank of North America to provide short-term commercial loans. Traders in Boston and New York founded similar banks in 1784. Those institutions provided merchants with the credit they needed to finance their transactions, freeing them from dependence on overseas sources of financing.

In 1791, as part of Alexander Hamilton's plan to centralize the expanding American financial system, Congress chartered the Bank of the United States. The bank had the power to issue notes and make commercial loans; although the bank's managers used their lending powers cautiously, profits still averaged a handsome 8 percent annually. By 1805, in response to the continuing demand for commercial credit, the bank had set up branches in eight major cities.

Nonetheless, for political reasons, the First Bank of the United States did not survive. Jeffersonians had long condemned the idea of a national bank, warning that it would produce "a consolidated, energetic government supported by public creditors, speculators, and other insidious men lacking in public spirit of any kind." When the bank's twenty-year charter expired in 1811,

President Madison did not seek its renewal, a decision that forced merchants, artisans, and farmers to turn to their state legislatures. New York chartered the Mechanics' and Farmers' Bank of Albany in 1811, and other states followed suit. By the time Madison chartered the Second Bank of the United States in 1816, there were no fewer than 246 state-chartered banks. Unfortunately, many state banks issued notes without adequate reserves of specie, a shortsighted policy that inhibited commercial growth by undermining the notes' value.

Poorly managed state banks were one cause of the Panic of 1819, a credit crisis sparked by a sharp drop in world agricultural prices. With farm income suddenly cut by a third, many American farmers were unable to pay their creditors, setting in motion successive bankruptcies among local storekeepers, wholesale merchants, and overextended state banks. The economic recession continued for two years, giving many Americans their first taste of the *business cycle*—the periodic expansion and contraction of profits and employment that is an inherent part of a market economy.

The Panic revealed that more and more Americans—artisans and yeomen as well as merchants and southern planters—were dependent on regional or national markets. Before 1790, thousands of artisans in New England and the Middle Atlantic states had handcrafted furniture, tools, wagons, shoes, saddles, clothing, and dozens of other items, but most of those goods had remained within the local community. But some artisans—especially those who worked in large, specialized groups—had an eye on more distant markets. Even before independence, shipbuilders in seacoast towns, iron smelters in Pennsylvania and Maryland, and shoemakers in Lynn, Massachusetts, had sold their products in far-flung markets. During the Revolutionary War, merchants had encouraged rural men and women to make cheese, textiles, paper, and gunpowder. Later, national pride prompted calls for the expansion of *all* domestic handicrafts. "Until we manufacture more," a writer in the *Boston Gazette* declared in 1788, "it is absurd to celebrate the Fourth of July as the birthday of our independence."

Once the war was over, many merchants stopped investing in domestic manufacturing because it was more profitable to sell low-priced British goods. Still, some entrepreneurs continued to develop wider markets for American rural manufactures. For instance, merchants sold goods made on Massachusetts farms not only in Boston but also in other New England seaports. As a Polish traveler in central Massachusetts reported in 1798, "Along the whole road from Boston, we saw women engaged in making cheese."

As rural manufacturing increased, the northeastern regions of the United States took a major step toward a *capitalist* manufacturing economy. At the center of this productive system stood a dynamic group of merchant-entrepreneurs who recruited rural households to manufacture goods in a manner similar to the European *outwork*, or *putting-out*, system (see Chapter 1). At the periphery were hundreds of thousands of farm families that supplied the labor. When a French traveler visited central Massachusetts in 1795, he found "almost all these houses . . . inhabited by men who are both cultivators and artisans; one is a tanner, another a shoemaker, another sells goods, but all are farmers."

This system achieved its greatest success in the shoe and boot trade. In the 1780s merchants and master craftsmen in Lynn, Massachusetts, began buying large quantities of leather, thread, and awls and put thousands of farm families to work. Women and children stitched together the thin leather and canvas uppers; then the half-finished shoes were taken by wagon to Lynn for assembly by journeymen shoemakers. When the Embargo of 1807 cut off competition from British-made shoes, merchants in Lynn and over thirty other Massachusetts towns expanded their output, making millions of shoes.

By the 1820s entrepreneurs had mobilized an enormous work force in the New England countryside. Farm families produced shoes, brooms, palm-leaf hats, and tinware—baking pans, cups, utensils, lanterns. Merchants and peddlers sold those products throughout the United States, creating a *national* market.

These successes stemmed primarily from innovations in organization and marketing rather than in technology. Even as their markets expanded, tinworkers, shoemakers, and other artisans continued to use traditional *preindustrial* manufacturing methods. Power-driven machines—the product of the Industrial Revolution in Britain—were adopted slowly in America, beginning in the

The Household as Factory
The outwork system used the labor of all the members of a rural household. Here the wife spins wool into yarn, which her husband weaves into cloth. One of her children fashions strips of palm leaves into a seat (or perhaps a hat), and the other works at another task. Wage labor increased the incomes of many families and tied them to the emerging market economy.

textile industry. In the 1780s merchants built scores of small mills along the creeks and rivers of New England and the Middle Atlantic states. They installed water-powered machines and hired workers to card and comb wool—and later cotton—into long strands. For several decades, the next steps in the manufacturing process were accomplished under the outwork system rather than in factories. Farm women and children spun the strands into yarn, receiving wages for their work, while men in other households wove the yarn into cloth. In 1810 there were about 2,500 outwork weavers in New England. A decade later more than 12,000 household workers in that region were weaving woolen cloth, which was then taken to water-powered fulling mills to be pounded flat and finished smooth.

The rise of rural manufacturing transformed the agricultural economy. To supply merchants and artisans with raw materials, ambitious farm families switched from mixed-crop agriculture to livestock raising. The shoe business consumed thousands of beef hides each year, the new cheese industry required large herds of dairy cows, and textile mills processed the wool from tens of thousands of sheep. High prices for these raw materials brought prosperity and new businesses to many farming towns. In 1792 Concord, Massachusetts, had one slaughterhouse and five small tanneries; a decade later it had eleven slaughterhouses and six large tanneries. Foul odors from the stockyards and tanning pits drifted over the town, but its residents were able to acquire more goods.

At first, barter transactions were a central feature of the emergent market system, as the records of the book-manufacturing firm of Ebenezer and Daniel Merriam of Brookfield, Massachusetts, demonstrate. When the Merriams began selling books to publishing houses in New York City, Philadelphia, and Boston in the 1810s, they received neither cash nor credit in return but other *books*, which they had to exchange with local storekeepers to get supplies for their business. The Merriams paid their employees on a barter basis; a journeyman printer received the use of a small house, credits at local stores, and a third of his "wages" in books, which he had to peddle for himself to gain more than a literary profit from his labors.

Gradually, a cash economy replaced this complex barter system. Instead of exchanging their surplus crops for household necessities, farm families supplied merchants with specialized goods in return for cash or store credit.

The new capitalist-run market economy had some drawbacks. Rural parents—and their children—now worked longer and harder, making shoes, hats, and cloth during the winter and planting, weeding, and harvesting crops during the warmer seasons. Perhaps more important, they lost some of their economic independence. Instead of working solely for themselves as yeomen farm families, they toiled as part-time wage earners for merchants and manufacturers. The new market system decreased the self-sufficiency of families and communities even as it made them more productive.

But the tide of change was unstoppable and, on the whole, beneficial. Beginning around 1800, per capita income in the United States increased more than 1 percent per year—over 30 percent in each generation. By the 1820s

American Country Furniture
Country artisans, such as the unknown maker of this high chest of drawers from Norwich, Vermont (circa 1780), simplified high-style English designs. Using common woods such as birch and pine rather than expensive mahogany, these rural manufacturers built furniture that was both affordable and elegant. (Shelburne Museum)

the extraordinary increase in output, artisan skills, and merchant capital had laid the foundation for the American Industrial Revolution (see Chapter 10). After half a century of political independence, the nation was beginning to achieve economic independence.

State Governments and Mercantilism: The "Commonwealth" System

Throughout the nineteenth century, the most important political institutions in the United States were the state governments. State legislatures took the lead in regulating social life, abolishing slavery in the North but retaining it in the South. They enacted laws governing criminal and civil affairs, set voting requirements, established taxation systems, and created and oversaw subordinate county, city, and town governments. Beginning in the late 1810s, many states rewrote their constitutions to make them more democratic, decreasing the property requirements for voting, reapportioning legislatures, and increasing the number of elected (rather than appointed) officials. Consequently, state governments had a much greater impact on the day-to-day lives of Americans than did the national government.

As early as the 1790s, many state legislatures attempted to enhance their states' prosperity by devising an American plan of mercantilism known as the "commonwealth" system. Just as the British Parliament had promoted the imperial economy by passing Acts of Trade, state legislatures enacted measures to stimulate commerce and economic development. In particular, they granted hundreds of *corporate charters* to private businesses that were intended, as the act establishing the Massachusetts Bank put it, to be "of great public utility." Chartered companies were not new, of course; English investors had used them to establish the first American colonies. Under English law, however, colonial governments had been discouraged from creating corporations. As a result, American merchants had financed their mills, shipyards, and trading ventures through private partnerships, which lacked some of the economic advantages of government-chartered corporations, such as tax exemptions and monopoly privileges.

Private partnerships also lacked the funds required to build the large-scale transportation projects—the economic infrastructure—that had become a high priority. State legislatures therefore issued numerous charters of incorporation to promote investment in roads, bridges, and canals. In 1794 the Lancaster Turnpike Company received a monopoly charter from the Pennsylvania assembly to lay a graded gravel road between Lancaster and Philadelphia. The success of the venture set off a boom in turnpike construction. Improved roads soon connected dozens of inland market centers to seaport cities.

By 1800 state governments had granted more than 300 corporate charters. Incorporation enhanced the status of private companies in two ways. First, some charters protected investors by granting them *limited liability*; in the event of a business failure, shareholders' personal assets could not be seized to pay the corporation's debts. Second, most transportation charters included the power of *eminent domain*, which enabled turnpike, bridge, and canal corporations to use the judicial system to force the sale of land along their routes. This power—previously available only to the government—permitted private corporations to take land from property owners for a reasonable price, even if the owners did not want to sell. In granting corporations the power of eminent domain, state legislatures promoted the good of the commonwealth at the expense of the property rights of private citizens.

Such uses of state power by private companies were controversial and, in the eyes of some critics, contrary to republicanism, "which does not admit of granting peculiar privileges to any body of men." Charters not only violated the "equal rights" of all citizens, opponents argued, but limited the sovereignty of the people. As a Pennsylvanian put it, "whatever power is given to a corporation, is just so much power taken from the State, in derogation of the original power of the mass of the community."

Nonetheless, state courts consistently upheld the validity of corporate charters. Judges routinely approved grants of eminent domain to private corporations. "The opening of good and easy internal communications is one of the highest duties of government," a New Jersey court declared.

State mercantilism soon encompassed much more than transportation. In the years immediately following the Embargo of 1807, which cut off goods and credit from Europe, New England state governments awarded charters to 200 iron-mining, textile-manufacturing, and banking firms. Over the next few decades the Pennsylvania legislature was even more active, chartering more than 1,100 corporations and authorizing them to hold over $150 million in capital. Corporations, whether in the form of incorporated towns and cities, incorporated churches and charitable institutions, or chartered private businesses, were becoming a central institution in American society. As one contemporary put it, "the whole political system" was "made up of concatenations of various corporations, political, civil, religious, social and economical."

By 1820 the innovative policies of state governments had created a new political economy: the commonwealth system. This system enhanced the public good as well as the economic and political power of capitalist entrepreneurs. The use of state legislation to encourage business enterprise and improve the general welfare would continue for another generation. In 1820 Missouri lawmakers incorporated the concept of the commonwealth system into that state's first constitution, specifying that "internal improvements shall forever be encouraged by the government of this state."

Law and the "Commonwealth": Republicans versus Federalists

Both Federalists and Republicans endorsed the idea of the commonwealth, but in different ways. Federalists looked to the national government for economic leadership and supported Hamilton's program of *national* mercantilism: a funded debt, tariffs, and a central bank. Jeffersonian Republicans generally relied instead on *state* legislatures to promote economic development. After the War of 1812, some Republicans, led by Henry Clay of Kentucky, began to support national economic initiatives, but many more, including President James Monroe, still opposed them. This fundamental disagreement about the role of the national government would shape political debate for the next thirty years (see Chapter 11).

Differing conceptions of law also separated Federalists and Republicans. From the earliest colonial times, American jurisprudence had followed English common law. In deciding cases, judges relied on *precedents*—previous decisions in similar cases—and assumed, as a Maryland lawyer put it, that "the Common Law takes in the Law of Nature, the Law of Reason and the Revealed Law of God." In this view, which was held by many Federalists, law was venerable and unchanging.

The revolutionary republican doctrine of popular sovereignty undermined the intellectual foundations of the old legal order. In the debate over constitutional principles, many Americans recognized that law was a human invention, the product of politics rather than a sacred body of timeless truths. During the 1790s Thomas Jefferson and other Republican party leaders attacked the common-law system, maintaining that law made by judges following common-law precedent was inferior to the statute ("positive") law enacted by representatives of the people. As a Republican jurist put it, a magistrate "should be governed himself by *positive* law" while executing and enforcing "the will of the supreme power, which is the will of THE PEOPLE."

In response, Federalist judges and politicians warned that popular sovereignty had to be curbed. Without safeguards, representative government would result in the "tyranny of the majority"—the passage of statutes that would infringe on the property rights of individual citizens. To prevent state legislatures from overriding property rights, Federalist lawyers asserted that judges had the power to void laws that violated traditional common-law principles or were contrary to "natural law" or "natural rights" (see Chapter 4).

Because common-law precedents had evolved in a relatively static agricultural economy, they often discouraged new modes of enterprise. For example, capitalist entrepreneurs who erected dams to power flour or textile mills often flooded adjacent farmlands; outraged farmers sued, charging that the dams infringed on their property rights, constituted a public "nuisance," and should be pulled down. At first the farmers won most of these cases, as judges used common-law precedents to rule that interfering with the natural flow of a river for nonfarming purposes was illegal.

But when it became clear that such decisions would stifle economic development, republican-minded state legislatures enacted statutes that overrode common law. In Massachusetts, the Mill Dam Act of 1795 allowed mill proprietors to flood adjacent farmland and required farmers to accept "fair compensation" for their lost acreage. Prodevelopment legislators justified the taking of private property by asserting the superior rights of those who made dynamic, rather than static, use of their property.

State judges with Republican leanings accepted the doctrines of popular sovereignty and legislative power and tended to uphold mill acts. To these judges, *social utility*—the greatest good for the greatest number—justified the government's intrusion into individual citizens' property rights. Such rulings shocked the Federalist lawyer and politician Daniel Webster, who considered them no less than a "revolution against the foundations on which property rests." Although both political parties favored economic development, Federalists gave a higher priority to national mercantilism, common law, and a static theory of property rights; Republicans emphasized state activism, statute law, and a dynamic concept of property.

Federalist Law: John Marshall

When he became president in 1801, Thomas Jefferson warned that his Federalist opponents were retreating into the judiciary, from which fortress "all the works of Republicanism are to be beaten down and erased." The legal career of John Marshall confirmed Jefferson's prediction. Appointed chief justice of the Supreme Court by John Adams in 1801, Marshall upheld Federalist principles until his death in 1835. His success stemmed not from a mastery of legal

Chief Justice John Marshall
A Virginia Federalist, Marshall had a commanding personal presence and made over the United States Supreme Court in his image, transforming it from a minor department to a major institution in American legal and political life.

principles and doctrines—indeed, his opinions usually cited very few precedents—but from the power of his logic and the force of his personality. Until 1821 Marshall dominated his colleagues on the Supreme Court, who largely accepted his definition of the meaning of the Constitution.

Three principles shaped Marshall's jurisprudence: a commitment to judicial authority, the supremacy of national over state legislation, and a traditional, static view of property rights. The celebrated case of *Marbury v. Madison* (1803) demonstrated Marshall's commitment to the first principle: the preeminent power of the judiciary. The case arose from President Adams's controversial "midnight" appointments of Federalist judges just as he was leaving office. As secretary of state in Jefferson's incoming Republican administration, James Madison had refused to commission one of those appointees, William Marbury, as a justice of the peace in the District of Columbia. When Marbury asked the Supreme Court to issue a legal writ on his behalf, Marshall ruled that while Marbury had a right to his commission, that right was not enforceable by the Court. This was so, Marshall declared, because the Judiciary Act of 1789 violated the Constitution by expanding the powers given to the Supreme Court in that document. Marshall's decision was politically astute, condemning Madison's action while avoiding a direct confrontation with the Republican administration.

More important, Marshall's decision marked the first time the Supreme Court had overturned a national law. Five years earlier, during the dispute over the Alien and Sedition acts, the Republican-dominated legislatures in Kentucky and Virginia had asserted their authority to determine the constitutionality of national laws. But the Constitution implied that the Supreme Court held the power of *judicial review*, and Marshall claimed it explicitly: "It is emphatically the province and duty of the judicial department to say what the law is." Thereafter, the doctrine of judicial review evolved slowly. During the first half of the nine-teenth century, the Supreme Court and the state courts used it only to overturn *state* laws that conflicted with constitutional principles. Not until the *Dred Scott* decision of 1857 would the Supreme Court void another national law.

Marshall's second principle—nationalism—was most eloquently expressed in the controversial case *McCulloch v. Maryland* (1819). When Congress created the Second Bank of the United States in 1816, it gave that bank the authority to handle the notes of state-chartered banks and thus to monitor their finan-cial reserves. To preserve the independence and competitive position of its state banks, the Maryland legislature passed a statute imposing an annual tax of $15,000 on notes issued by the Second Bank's Baltimore branch. The Second Bank contested the constitutionality of that action, claiming that it infringed on the powers of the national government. In response, lawyers for the state of Maryland adopted Jefferson's argument against the First Bank of the United States, maintaining that Congress lacked the constitutional authority to char-ter a national bank. Even if such a bank could be created, the lawyers argued, Maryland had a right to tax its activities within the state.

Marshall firmly rejected both arguments. The Second Bank was constitu-tional, he declared, because its existence was "necessary and proper," given the national government's responsibility to control currency and credit. Like Alexander Hamilton and other Federalists, Marshall preferred a loose con-struction of the Constitution. "Let the end be legitimate, let it be within the scope of the Constitution and all means which are appropriate, which [are consistent] . . . with the letter and the spirit of the constitution, are constitu-tional," he wrote. As for Maryland's right to tax all institutions within its bor-ders, the chief justice embraced the nationalist position advanced by Daniel Webster, a fellow Federalist and the legal counsel to the Second Bank. "The power to tax involves the power to destroy," Marshall observed, suggesting that Maryland's bank tax would render the national government "dependent on the states"—a situation that "was not intended by the American people" when the Constitution was ratified.

Marshall asserted the dominance of national statutes over state legislation again in *Gibbons v. Ogden* (1824), which struck down a monopoly the New York legislature had granted to Aaron Ogden for steamboat passenger service across the Hudson River. Asserting that the Constitution gave the federal gov-ernment the authority to regulate interstate commerce, the chief justice up-held the claim of Thomas Gibbons, who held a federal coasting license.

Marshall also turned to the Constitution to uphold his third principle: property rights. To protect individuals against government interference with their property, Marshall seized on the *contract clause* of the Constitution

(Article I, Section 10), which prohibits the states from passing any law "impairing the obligation of contracts." Delegates at the Philadelphia convention had included this clause primarily to void state laws that protected debtors from merchants and other creditors. But Marshall expanded the scope of the contract clause by using it to defend other property rights against legislative challenge.

For example, the case of *Fletcher v. Peck* (1810) involved a large grant of land made by the Georgia legislature to the Yazoo Land Company. When a newly elected state legislature canceled the grant, alleging that it had been obtained through fraud and bribery, speculators who had already purchased Yazoo lands appealed to the Supreme Court to uphold their titles. Speaking for the Court, Marshall ruled that the purchasers held valid contracts whose provisions could not be impaired by the state of Georgia. This decision was far-reaching. It not only gave constitutional protection against subsequent legislation to those who purchased state-owned lands but, by upholding the rights of out-of-state speculators, also encouraged the development of a national capitalist economy.

The court extended its defense of property rights even further in *Dartmouth College v. Woodward* (1819), in which the trustees of the college contested the state legislature's attempt to turn it into a public institution. The Court ruled that the school's charter, which dated back to colonial times, constituted a contract that could not be tampered with by the New Hampshire legislature. In Marshall's view, Dartmouth College was private property.

Marshall had difficulty persuading his colleagues to accept this position. Although he was still the dominant member, by 1819 five of the seven Supreme Court justices had been appointed by the Republican presidents Jefferson and Madison. Some of those justices embraced the commonwealth ideal, arguing that a public university would better serve the common good. Other Republican judges hesitated to restrict the powers of state legislatures or expand the broad protection for property rights set forth in *Fletcher v. Peck*. Only after months of deliberation—and the preparation of a precedent-filled decision by Associate Justice Joseph Story, a New England jurist with strong Federalist leanings—did the other justices on the Court follow Marshall and rule in favor of the college. In Story's view, *Dartmouth College v. Woodward* not only upheld a static, or "vested," conception of property rights but extended constitutionally protected property rights from individuals to business corporations. Thereafter, corporations would claim that their state-granted charters were "contracts" that protected them forever from regulation or control by the governments that had created them.

Marshall's triumph seemed complete; he had incorporated Federalist principles into the law of the land. Indeed, many of Marshall's legal principles, such as judicial review and corporate rights, would become central fixtures of American law. But even before the chief justice's death in 1835, jurists who valued the rights of states had begun to qualify his nationalist vision, and state legislators evaded the restrictions of the Dartmouth College decision by granting charters that included clauses allowing the state to alter their terms.

As this tactic indicates, the legal conflict between Marshall and his Republican opponents was primarily over the means, not the ends, of economic development. Both sides strongly supported private ownership of property and the expansion of a market economy. Together they laid the legal and political foundations for the American Economic Revolution (see Chapter 10).

VISIONS OF A REPUBLICAN SOCIAL ORDER

After independence, Americans tried to become "republicans" not just in their laws but also in their political outlook, social behavior, and cultural values. Their pursuit of republican ideals was complex and conflict-ridden. It pitted propertyless men against their social betters, increased the tension between men and women, and generated new theories of child rearing and education.

Social Mobility and Democracy for Men

Between 1780 and 1820 hundreds of well-educated Europeans visited the United States to observe life in a republican society. They came from countries with monarchical governments, established churches, male-dominated families, and profound divisions between social classes. And they wondered—as have successive generations of historians—whether America represented a different and more just social order. The French-born essayist Crèvecoeur had no doubts. In his famous *Letters from an American Farmer* (1782), Crèvecoeur wrote that European society was composed "of great lords who possess everything, and of a herd of people who have nothing." America, by contrast, had "no aristocratical families, no courts, no kings, no bishops." Because they lived in a society without hereditary rulers, another writer argued, Americans should value people not for their "wealth, titles, or connections" but for their "talents, integrity, and virtue."

Republican ideology undermined hierarchical authority by proclaiming that all free men were equal before the law. "The law is the same for everyone both as it protects and as it punishes," noted a European traveler. Legal equality was not the same as social uniformity, however. Foreign visitors were well aware that class divisions existed in the United States, but they saw them as differing from those in Europe. The American colonies had never had—and the republican state and national constitutions prohibited—a legally privileged nobility. The absence of a hereditary aristocracy encouraged enterprising Americans to seek upward social mobility and to justify class divisions on the basis of achievements. "In Europe to say of someone that he rose from nothing is a disgrace and a reproach," remarked an aristocratic Polish visitor. "It is the opposite here. To be the architect of your own fortune is honorable. It is the highest recommendation."

Some Americans from long-distinguished families questioned the moral legitimacy of a social order based primarily on financial success. "The aristocracy of Kingston [New York] is more one of money than any village I have ever seen," complained Nathaniel Booth in 1825. Booth's ancestors had once ruled Kingston, but his family had lost its prominence in the rapidly growing Hudson River town. "Man is estimated by dollars," he lamented; "what he is worth determines his character and his position at once." But Booth spoke for only a minority of Americans. For most white men, republicanism meant the opportunity to advance their interests and those of their families. For them, America was the "best poor man's country."

By the 1820s republicanism had also come to mean voting rights for free white men. With the revision of state constitutions and the advent of political democracy, property ownership and high social status no longer constituted the foundation of citizenship. Increasingly, Americans repudiated the hierarchical ideal of Federalists such as Samuel Stone, who had called for "a *speaking* aristocracy in the face of a *silent* democracy." Rejecting the deferential politics of the eighteenth century, they refused to vote for Federalist politicians who flaunted their high social status, with their "top boots, breeches, and shoe buckles," their hair in "powder and queues." Instead, they elected Republican politicians who dressed simply and advocated extending the franchise.

Republican-dominated state legislatures did enact laws to expand political democracy. Maryland extended the vote to all adult men in 1810, and the new states of Indiana (1816), Illinois (1818), and Alabama (1819) provided for a broad male franchise in their constitutions. By the end of the 1820s, only a few states—North Carolina, Virginia, and Rhode Island—required that voters own freehold property. Others, such as Ohio and Louisiana, limited suffrage to men who paid taxes or served in the militia. But a majority of the states had instituted universal white manhood suffrage (see Map 9.1, following page).

Popular pressure brought other constitutional changes as well. Between 1818 and 1821, reform-minded politicians in Connecticut, Massachusetts, and New York revised their state constitutions, reapportioning their legislatures on the basis of population and instituting more democratic forms of local government, such as the election rather than the appointment of judges and justices of the peace. If such "democratic doctrines" had been advanced ten years earlier, the Federalist Chancellor James Kent of New York protested, they "should have struck the public mind with astonishment and terror."

As the status of ordinary white men rose, that of white women and free blacks actually declined. Increasingly, political rights in the new republic depended on gender and race. Among the new states admitted to the Union between 1790 and 1860, only Vermont and Maine gave the vote to free blacks. Existing states, such as Pennsylvania and New York, took the franchise away from free African-Americans or subjected them to substantial property qualifications. Women, who had been excluded from public life by custom, now were explicitly banned from voting by constitutional provisions that limited full citizenship to men. To justify such discrimination, republican legislators in New Jersey (who excluded property-owning women from the vote in 1807) invoked traditional biological and social arguments. As a letter to the editor of a newspaper put it, "Women, generally, are neither by nature, nor habit, nor education, nor by their necessary condition in society fitted to perform this duty with credit to themselves or advantage to the public."

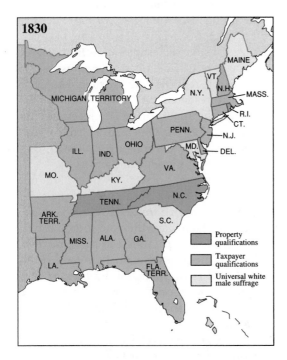

MAP 9.1

The Expansion of Voting Rights for White Men

Between 1800 and 1830 the United States moved steadily toward political democracy. Many states revised their constitutions, replacing property ownership with taxpaying or militia service as a qualification for voting. Some states—both in the East and the West—extended the franchise to all white men. A broader electorate changed the tone of politics, as parties tried to appeal to the interests and values of ordinary people.

Republican Marriage

Despite its limitations republicanism was a revolutionary ideology, which as John Adams lamented, "spread where it was not intended," threatening the husband's control of the family. Both in Europe and in America, husbands had long dominated wives and controlled family property. But in the eyes of some women, subordination to men seemed arbitrary, at odds with their belief in equal natural rights. Patriarchy was not "natural" and could be justified only on pragmatic grounds, "for the sake of order in families," as Mercy Otis Warren put it.

Economic and cultural changes also eroded customary family relations. Landowning parents had long arranged their children's marriages to ensure their own economic well-being during old age. But as land holdings shrank in long-settled rural communities, parents could no longer bequeath substantial farms—the economic incentives they had used to control their children's lives. Young men and women began to choose their own partners, influenced by the new cultural attitude of sentimentalism.

The New Conjugal Family
Grace and Philip Schuyler pose informally with their daughters and encourage their musical and literary talents. The affectionate mood of this early nineteenth-century scene stands in sharp contrast to family portraits painted in earlier eras, which emphasized the authority of the father and the subordinate status of his wife and children. (Collection of the New-York Historical Society)

Originating in Europe during the Romantic movement of the late eighteenth century, *sentimentalism* celebrated the importance of "feeling"—that is, a physical, sensuous appreciation of God, nature, and other human beings. By 1820 sentimentalism had touched all classes of American society. It dripped from the pages of the German and English literary works that were read in educated circles. It fell from the lips of actors in tear-jerking melodramas, which soon became the most popular theatrical entertainments in the United States. And it infused the rhetoric of revivalist preachers, who appealed to the passions of the heart rather than the logic of the mind.

Sentimentalism, in short, encouraged couples to marry for love. Parents had always taken physical attraction and emotional compatibility into account in arranging marriages for their children, but romance in and of itself did not have a high cultural value. Most parents were more concerned with the personal habits and financial resources of a prospective son- or daughter-in-law. A skeptical mother in Virginia remarked that young women should remain single "till they were old enough to form a proper *judgement* of mankind." Wealthy fathers who worried that their resources would be squandered by a free-spending son-in-law often placed funds in legal trusts so that their daughters would not be completely dependent on their husbands. As a Virginia planter wrote to his lawyer, "I rely on you to see the property settlement properly drawn *before the marriage*, for I by no means consent that Polly shall be left to the Vicissitudes of Life." By such means fathers gave up the hope of patriarchal dominance and became paternalists, protecting the interests of children who married for love.

Republicanism made marriage rather than parenthood the fundamental family relationship, and the new youth-run marriage system gave young adults greater freedom. Magazines promoted marriages "contracted from motives of affection, rather than of interest"; this outlook encouraged a young person to seek a spouse who was, as Eliza Southgate of Maine put it, "calculated to promote my happiness." Such freedom had its costs, because young adults often lacked the maturity and experience to choose wisely. Many were disappointed when their spouses failed as providers or faithful companions; a few sought divorces. Before 1800 most petitioners for divorce had charged their spouses with neglect, abandonment, or adultery—serious offenses against the moral order of society—but after that date emotional grounds dominated petitions. One woman complained that her husband had "ceased to cherish her," while a man lamented that his wife had "almost broke his heart." Reflecting these changed cultural values, some states expanded the legal grounds for divorce to include personal cruelty and drunkenness and made divorce available through judicial decree rather than only, as in the past, through a special act of the legislature.

Still, most unions, happy or not, lasted until death and, especially among urban Americans of middling status, were influenced by the republican ideal of a "companionate" marriage. But this noble ideal, in which wives enjoyed "true equality, both of rank and fortune," with their husbands, often foundered in the face of deeply ingrained cultural habits that favored men and laws that placed all

A Companionate Marrige: Mary and Henry Lee

After a financial reverse, Henry Lee went to India as a merchant while Mary Lee raised their daughter, Molly, in Boston. Their letters reveal the personal intimacy, social equality, and shared financial responsibility of the ideal republican marriage.

[India] January 12, 1813
My respected and belov'd wife. . . .
You perhaps do not know that I have a partner in my business upon whose judgment I rely in all difficult cases. . . . Are you at a loss to know who this sage adviser is? No other than yourself, my dear wife, from whom I have rec'd many wise counsels which I ought to have benefited by more than I have, as indeed I should if I had followed all of them. . . .

The letters you have written would do honour to any one. They gratify me now almost as much as when first rec'd—the affectionate concern you take in my welfare touches me most sensibly. . . . I cannot help loving you the better for it.

[Boston] 28th Feb'y, Sunday Evening. . . . Oh, my dear, dear husband, when we do meet I believe I shall hold you fast—for it appears to me that almost any labour, if together, would not be too hard for us. . . . I know not why the wife should not work a *little* as well as the husband *labour so hard*, and did I feel a certainty that you would agree with me upon the subject, I should most certainly act upon the principle.

[Boston] 28th October, 1813. . . . The Indigo consigned to Patrick has sold at a very handsome advance; he . . . said that one speculation had afforded you more than all he had done for ever so long. . . . As for the property consigned *to me*, I cannot give a very good account of my stewardship. . . . I have sold all my goods but the handkerchiefs, and I fear they will sell so badly as to make my sales average very badly. They are in Tuckerman's shop.

SOURCE: Frances Rollins Morse, ed., *Henry and Mary Lee, Letters and Journals . . . 1802–1860* (Boston, privately printed, 1926), pp. 78–81.

property in men's hands. Moreover, because the new marriage system discouraged parents from playing an active role in their children's lives, young wives could no longer rely on their parents for emotional or financial support; they became even more dependent on their husbands than their mothers had been. The marriage contract "is so much more important in its consequences to females than to males," a young man at the Litchfield Law School noted astutely in 1820, "for besides leaving everything else to unite themselves to one man, they subject themselves to his authority. He is their all—their only relative—their only hope."

Republican Mothers

Traditionally, most American women had focused their lives on domestic duties: bearing and raising children and work in the home or on the farm. As the changing political order challenged long-standing customs, a few upper-class women sought a public voice. But most women—and certainly most men—did not assume that the egalitarian logic of republican ideology would affect gender roles. Few demanded or even supported a substantial public role for American women. Instead, many clergymen and political leaders promoted the traditional notion of a *separate sphere* for women, but expanded it. Women had special domestic skills and responsibilities, they argued, and should play a leading role in home and family life.

This enhanced domestic role for women stemmed in part from changes in Christian thought. Traditionally, most religious writers had viewed women as morally inferior to men—as sexual temptresses or witches. By 1800 the clergy had begun to hold men responsible for sexual misconduct instead. Moralists now claimed that modesty and purity were inherent in woman's nature, making women uniquely qualified to educate the spirit. Thus, the cultivation of virtue became part of women's sphere.

Political leaders also called on women to ensure the future of the new American republic. In *Thoughts on Female Education* (1787), Benjamin Rush argued that a young woman should receive intellectual training so that she would be "an agreeable companion for a sensible man"; her responsibility, as another moralist put it, was to ensure "his perseverance in the paths of rectitude." Rush and other men of affairs welcomed the emergence of loyal "republican mothers" who would instruct "their sons in the principles of liberty and government." As the author of a list of "Maxims for Republics" put it, "Some of the first patriots of ancient times were formed by their mothers."

Ministers embraced the idea of republican motherhood, devising new roles for women in moral and religious education. "Preserving virtue and instructing the young are not the fancied, but the real 'Rights of Women,'" the Reverend Thomas Bernard told the Female Charitable Society of Salem, Massachusetts, in 1803. He urged his audience to dismiss the public roles advocated by Mary Wollstonecraft, a British republican who had published the pathbreaking feminist manifesto *A Vindication of the Rights of Women* in 1792. Instead, women should be content to care for their children, a responsibility that gave them "an extensive power over the fortunes of man in every generation." While Bernard wanted women to remain in their traditional domestic sphere, he campaigned to enhance its value.

Many American women from the middling classes accepted this limited revision of their role. As a young New England woman wrote in 1803, "She is still *woman*, with duties prescribed her by the God of Nature essentially different from those of *man*." Some educated women of the upper classes, however, insisted on the equality of the separate male and female worlds. "I will never consent to have our sex considered in an inferior point of light," proclaimed Abigail Adams, the wife of President John Adams, in 1799. And some ministers envisioned a public role for women that was based on their domestic virtues. As Thomas Grimké, a South Carolina minister, asserted, "Give me a host of educated pious mothers and sisters and I will revolutionize a country, in moral and religious taste."

PROTESTANT CHRISTIANITY AND WOMEN'S LIVES

Religion had always been a significant part of American life. But in the decades between 1790 and 1820, a series of revivals planted the values of Protestant Christianity deep in the American national character. In the process, religious revivalism created new public roles for women.

The Second Great Awakening

The revivals that began around 1790 were much more complex than those of the First Great Awakening. In the 1740s most revivals had occurred in existing congregations; fifty years later they took place in frontier camp meetings as well and often involved the creation of new churches and denominations. Even more strikingly, the Second Great Awakening spawned a wide variety of organizations dedicated to social and political reform.

The churches that prospered in the new nation were typically republican in their outlook or organization. Because it was dominated by bishops and priests, the Roman Catholic Church attracted few converts either among Protestants, who embraced Luther's doctrine of the priesthood of all believers, or among the unchurched, who feared clerical power. Few ordinary Americans joined the Episcopal Church, which had a similar hierarchical structure and was dominated by its wealthiest members. The Presbyterian Church was more popular, in part because it was more "republican": ordinary members elected laymen to the synods (congresses) where doctrine and practice were formulated.

Methodism attracted even more adherents. Although bishops took the lead on theological issues and enforced order in the church, the evangelical fervor of early Methodism fostered lay preaching, emotional worship services, and communal singing, which created an egalitarian religious culture. The most democratic forms of church government belonged to Quakers, Baptists, and Congregationalists. No bishops or governing bodies stood above the local congregations, and most decisions—on matters of theology as well as administration—rested with church members. Partly because of their democratic features, Methodist and Baptist churches grew spectacularly; by the early nineteenth century they were the largest religious denominations in the United States.

A continuous wave of revivalism fueled the expansion of Protestant Christianity. Beginning in the 1780s, Baptists and Methodists evangelized the older cities and backcountry of New England. A new sect of Universalists, who repudiated the Calvinist doctrine of predestination and preached universal salvation, attracted thousands of converts, especially in northern New England. After 1800 enthusiastic camp meeting revivals swept the frontier regions of

South Carolina, Kentucky, Tennessee, and Ohio. James McGready, a Scots-Irish Presbyterian preacher, "could so array hell before the wicked," an eyewitness reported, "that they would tremble and Quake, imagining a lake of fire and brimstone yawning to overwhelm them." When frontier preachers got together at a revival meeting, they were electrifying. One young man, James Finley, was so moved by the Cane Ridge, Kentucky, revival of 1802 that he became a Methodist minister:

> The noise was like the roar of Niagara. The vast sea of human beings seemed to be agitated as if by a storm. I counted seven ministers, all preaching at one time, some on stumps, others on wagons. . . . Some of the people were singing, others praying, some crying for mercy. A peculiarly strange sensation came over me. My heart beat tumultuously, my knees trembled, my lips quivered, and I felt as though I must fall to the ground.

Through such revivals, Baptist and Methodist preachers reshaped the spiritual landscape of the South and the Old Southwest. They won over most of the white population and, with the assistance of black ministers, began to implant evangelical Protestant Christianity among African-Americans as well.

Unlike the First Great Awakening, which had split many churches into hostile factions, the Second Awakening brought about friendly competition among Protestant churches to spread the faith to the unconverted. In New England and the Middle Atlantic states, pious women supplemented the work of preachers and lay elders, doubling the amount of organized spiritual energy. In the South and West, Baptist and Methodist preachers traveled constantly. Instead of settling in a congregation, a Methodist cleric followed a circuit, "riding a hardy pony or horse . . . with his Bible, hymn-book, and Discipline." Wherever they went, these "circuit riders" established new churches by searching out devout families, bringing them together for worship, then appointing lay elders to lead the congregation and enforce moral discipline until the circuit rider returned.

Evangelical ministers copied the techniques of George Whitefield and other eighteenth-century revivalists, codifying their intuitive genius in manuals of "practical preaching." To attract converts, preachers were cautioned to emphasize piety over theology; extemporaneous speech was deemed more powerful than a written sermon. "Preach without papers," advised one minister, "seem earnest & serious; & you will be listened to with Patience, & Wonder; both of your hands will be seized, & almost shook off as soon as you are out of the Church."

These missionary innovations attracted converts and shifted the denominational base of American religion toward the Baptists, Methodists, and other evangelical churches. The leading churches of the Revolutionary Era—the Congregationalists, Episcopalians, and Quakers—declined in relative membership. Their leaders and members were content for the most part to maintain their existing congregations or grow slowly through natural increase.

The Second Great Awakening changed the character of American thought—and social action—in dramatic ways. Before the Awakening, the Calvinist preoccupation with human depravity and weakness had shaped the

Peter Cartwright Finds God

As the son of a pious mother, Peter Cartwright was well prepared to respond to the evangelical message. After becoming a minister in the rapidly growing Methodist Church, he spread the Gospel throughout the Mississippi Valley.

In 1801, when I was in my sixteenth year, my father, my eldest half brother, and myself, attended a wedding about five miles from home, where there was a great deal of drinking and dancing, which was very common at marriages in those days. I drank little or nothing; my delight was in dancing. . . .

[That night] I began to reflect on the manner in which I had spent the day and evening. I felt guilty and condemned. I arose and walked the floor. My mother was in bed. It seemed to me, all of a sudden, my blood rushed to my head, my heart palpitated, in a few minutes I turned blind; an awful impression rested on my mind that death had come and I was unprepared to die. I fell on my knees and asked God to have mercy on me.

My mother sprang from her bed, and was soon on her knees by my side, praying for me, and exhorting me to look to Christ for mercy. . . . Three months rolled away, and still I did not find the blessing of the pardon of my sins. . . .

As there was a great waking up among the Churches, from the revival that had broken out at Cane Ridge [Kentucky], many flocked to sacramental meetings. . . . I went, with weeping multitudes, and bowed before the stand, and earnestly prayed for mercy. In the midst of a solemn struggle of soul, an impression was made on my mind, as though a voice said to me, "Thy sins are all forgiven thee." Divine light flashed all round me, unspeakable joy sprung up in my soul. . . . I have never, for one moment, doubted that the Lord did, then and there, forgive my sins and give me religion.

SOURCE: W. P. Strickland, ed., *Autobiography of Peter Cartwright, The Backwoods Preacher* (New York: Hunt & Eaton, 1856), pp. 34–38.

thinking of many writers, teachers, and statesmen. But by the early nineteenth century, ministers—whether or not they were revivalists—had begun to place greater stress on human ability and individual free will. Their view imparted a new optimism to the intellectual culture of the United States.

In New England, the primary source of the new theology, many educated and economically well-off Congregationalists became Unitarians. Rejecting the concept of the Trinity—God the Father, Son, and Holy Spirit—Unitarians worshiped an indivisible and "united" God (hence the name Unitarian). Reacting against the emotionalism of Methodist and Baptist services, they stressed the power of human reason. "The ultimate reliance of a human being is, and must be, on his own mind," argued the famous Unitarian minister William

Ellery Channing, "for the idea of God is the idea of our own spiritual nature, purified and enlarged to infinity." This emphasis on a believer's reason, a legacy of the Enlightenment, gave Unitarianism a humanistic and individualistic cast.

Optimistic ideas affected mainstream Congregational churches as well. Lyman Beecher, the preeminent New England clergyman, accepted the evangelical doctrine of universal salvation. Although he believed humans have a natural tendency to sin, he retreated from the Calvinist doctrine of predestination, declaring that all men and women have the capacity to choose God. In emphasizing choice—the free will of the believer—Beecher testified to the growing confidence in the power of human action.

Reflecting this optimistic outlook, the minister Samuel Hopkins linked individual salvation with social reform through the concept of religious *benevolence*. Benevolence was the practice of disinterested virtue, to be undertaken by those who had received God's sanctifying grace. According to the New York Presbyterian minister John Rodgers, such fortunate individuals had a duty "to dole out charity to their poorer brothers and sisters." Inspired by such arguments, pious merchants founded the New York Humane Society and other charitable organizations. By the 1820s some conservative church leaders were complaining that through their benevolence, lay men and women were devoting themselves to secular reforms—such as the prevention of pauperism—and neglecting spiritual goals. Their criticism was on the mark. It was her belief, the social reformer Lydia Maria Child later recalled, that "the *only* true church organization [is] when heads and hearts unite in working for the welfare of the human-race."

Ideas of benevolence and religious activism spread quickly through the founding of new theological seminaries such as Andover in Massachusetts and Lane in Ohio, two Congregationalist institutions that fostered cooperation among the denominations. As individual clergymen worked together, American Protestant churches became less dogmatic. Many congregations abandoned orthodox books and pamphlets such as the *Watts Hymnal*, which took controversial stances on old theological debates over predestination, and replaced them, a layman explained, with publications that would not give "offense to the serious Christians of any denomination."

Emulating a British innovation, American Protestants founded five interdenominational societies between 1815 and 1826: the American Education Society (1815), the American Bible Society (1816), the American Sunday School Union (1824), the American Tract Society (1824), and the American Home Missionary Society (1826). The new organizations were based in New York, Boston, and Philadelphia, but they ministered to a national congregation. Each year the societies dispatched hundreds of missionaries and distributed tens of thousands of religious pamphlets.

Organization on this scale united the individual energies of thousands of church members in a great collective undertaking, providing the Second Great Awakening with momentum and power. "I want to see our state evangelized," declared one pious New York layman. "Suppose the great State of New York in all its physical, political, moral, commercial, and pecuniary resources should come over to the Lord's side. Why it would turn the scale and could convert the world. I shall have no rest until it is done." For the first time in America, men and women in small villages scattered across the nation saw themselves as part of a large religious movement that could change the course of history.

As a result of the Second Awakening, religion became a central force in American life. On July 4, 1827, the Reverend Ezra Stiles Ely called on the members of the Seventh Presbyterian Church in Philadelphia to begin a "Christian party in politics." In his sermon "The Duty of Christian Freemen to Elect Christian Rulers," Ely set out for the American republic a new religious goal—one Thomas Jefferson and John Adams would have found strange, if not troubling. The two recently deceased presidents had believed that America's mission was to spread political republicanism. In contrast, Ely urged the United States to become an evangelical Christian nation dedicated to religious conversion at home and abroad. As Ely put it, "All our rulers ought in their official capacity to serve the Lord Jesus Christ." The Second Great Awakening had added an intense religious dimension to American politics and the emerging national identity.

Women and Religion

Revivalism created new opportunities for women in the public sphere. In Rhode Island, the preacher Jemima Wilkinson founded a new sect, the Universal Friends. In many Protestant churches, women took advantage of their enhanced moral status by expanding their role in religious and charitable activities. To give but a few examples, in New Hampshire women managed more than fifty local "cent" societies which raised funds for the Society for Promoting Christian Knowledge; evangelical women in New York City founded a charitable institution, the Society for the Relief of Poor Widows; and young Quaker women in Philadelphia ran the Society for the Free Instruction of African Females.

Jemima Wilkinson, the "Universal Friend"
A tall, graceful woman with dark eyes, Jemima Wilkinson had a magnetic personality and a powerful preaching style. Her message blended the Calvinist warning of "a lost and guilty, gossiping, dying World" with a Quaker-inspired social gospel. Like the Shakers, Wilkinson preached celibacy and never married. More controversial, she dressed like a man, wearing a black robe similar to a clergyman's gown.

Women became active in religion and charitable work partly because they were excluded from other spheres of public life and partly because they formed a substantial majority in many denominations. After 1800 no less than 70 percent of the members of New England Congregational churches were women. Some ministers acknowledged their numbers by changing long-standing practices. In many Protestant faiths, men and women had tradition-ally sat on opposite sides of the church during regular Sunday services and ministers had conducted separate prayer meetings for each sex. Now evangel-ical Methodist and Baptist preachers began to encourage mixed praying. Al-though critics condemned the practice as "promiscuous," Presbyterian and Congregational churches in frontier areas achieved impressive results. "Our prayer meetings have been one of the greatest means of the conversion of souls," a minister in central New York reported in the 1820s, "especially those in which brothers and sisters have prayed together."

As women began to transcend traditional gender roles, their religious ac-tivities and organizations became controversial. Many laymen resented the clergy's emphasis on women's moral superiority and the religious and social activism that sprang from it. "Women have a different *calling*," one man argued. "They are neither required nor permitted to be exhorters or leaders in public assemblies. . . . That they *be chaste, keepers at home* is the Apostle's [St. Paul's] di-rection." But many ministers continued to encourage the creation of women's organizations, and women became increasingly conscious of their new social power and public role. By the 1820s, mothers throughout the United States had founded local maternal associations to encourage Christian child raising. Newsletters such as *Mother's Magazine* were widely read in hundreds of small towns and villages, giving women a sense of shared purpose and identity.

In their capacity as moral paragons, women had an immediate and direct impact on social behavior. Imbibing the principle of female virtue, many young women, and the men who courted them, postponed sexual intercourse until after marriage—a form of self-restraint that had not been common in the eighteenth century. In Hingham, Massachusetts, and many other New England towns, about 30 percent of the women who married between 1750 and 1800 had borne a child within eight months of the wedding day. By the 1820s the proportion had dropped to 15 percent.

Religious activism also advanced the education of women. Churches es-tablished scores of seminaries and academies where girls—mostly from the middling classes—received sound intellectual training as well as moral instruc-tion. Emma Willard, the first American to advocate higher education for women, opened the Middlebury Female Seminary in Vermont in 1814 and later founded girls' schools in Waterford and Troy, New York.

Women educated in female academies gradually displaced men from their customary roles as schoolteachers. By the 1820s women were teaching the summer session in many public schools; in the following decade they would work the more demanding winter term as well. Women took over teaching in primary schools because they had few other opportunities and because they would accept lower pay than men would. Women earned $12 to $14 per month with room and board as schoolteachers—less than a farm laborer did. But they benefited from the higher moral status accorded to women and from the imperatives of republican motherhood: they would instruct the young not only at home but also in school. As schoolteachers, women had an acknowledged place in public life that had been beyond their reach in colonial and Revolutionary times. Thus, the Second Great Awakening transformed both the character of American culture and the scope of women's lives.

CHAPTER 9 TIMELINE	
1780s	Rural outwork system, especially shoes and textiles
1781	Philadelphia merchants found Bank of North America
1782	St. Jean de Crèvecoeur, *Letters from an American Farmer*
1787	Benjamin Rush, *Thoughts on Female Education*
1790s	State mercantilism encourages economic development Second Great Awakening Republican motherhood defined
1791	First Bank of the United States founded; dissolved in 1811
1794	Lancaster Turnpike Company
1795	Massachusetts Mill Dam Act
1800s	State-chartered banks proliferate Rise of sentimentalism and republican marriage system Women's religious activism and female academies Spread of evangelical Baptists and Methodists Beginnings of benevolent reform
1801	John Marshall becomes chief justice of the United States
1803	*Marbury v. Madison* states theory of judicial review
1807	New Jersey excludes propertied women from suffrage
1810	*Fletcher v. Peck* expands contract clause
1816	Second Bank of the United States chartered
1819	*McCulloch v. Maryland* enhances power of national government *Dartmouth College v. Woodward* protects corporate property rights
1818–1821	Democratic revision of state constitutions
1820s	Women become schoolteachers Growth of cash-based market economy
1824	*Gibbons v. Ogden* establishes federal authority over interstate commerce

THEMATIC TIMELINE

	ECONOMY Economic Revolution Creates New Social Classes	GOVERNMENT Creating a Democratic Polity	SOCIETY Reforming People and Institutions	SECTIONALISM From Compromise to Civil War and Reconstruction
1820	Waltham textile factory employs women operatives (1814) Erie Canal completed (1825)	Universal white male suffrage Rise of Jackson and Democratic party	American Colonization Society (1817) "Benevolent" Reform Revivalist Charles Finney	Missouri Compromise (1820) Walker's *Appeal to the Colored Race* (1829)
1830	Protective tariffs aid owners and workers Panic of 1837 cripples union movement	Anti-Masonic movement Whig party formed (1834); Second Party System emerges	Joseph Smith founds Mormonism Female Moral Reform Society (1834)	Nullification crisis (1832) Garrison forms American Anti-Slavery Society (1833)
1840	Irish join labor force *Commonwealth v. Hunt* (1842) legalizes unions	Log Cabin campaign mobilizes voters Antislavery parties: Liberty and Free Soil	Fourierist and other communal settlements founded Seneca Falls Convention (1848)	War with Mexico and Wilmot Proviso (1846) increase sectional conflict
1850	Free labor ideology justifies inequality Panic of 1857	Whig party disintegrates Republican party founded (1854): Third Party System	Stowe's *Uncle Tom's Cabin* (1852)	Compromise of 1850 Kansas-Nebraska Act (1854) and "Bleeding Kansas" *Dred Scott* decision (1857)
1860	Republicans enact agenda: Homestead Act, aid to railroads, high tariffs	Thirteenth Amendment (1865) ends slavery; Fourteenth Amendment (1868) extends legal and political rights	U.S. Sanitary Commission and American Red Cross founded	South Carolina secedes (1860) Confederate States of America (1861–65)
1870	Panic of 1873	Fifteenth Amendment extends vote to black men (1870)	Freed African-Americans create schools and institutions	Compromise of 1877 ends Reconstruction

PART 3

ECONOMIC REVOLUTION AND SECTIONAL STRIFE

1820–1877

Between 1820 and 1877 the United States was transformed from a predominantly agricultural society into one of the world's most powerful industrial economies, a change that affected every aspect of American life.

First, the expansion of markets and the growth of industry revolutionized the economy. High-speed machines and a new organization of labor boosted factory output while a new network of canals and railroads helped create a vast national market. A wealthy elite of business owners emerged at the top of the social order, while the urban middle class grew in size and importance. At the bottom of the scale propertyless workers labored for wages in the new factories and businesses.

Second, these changes spurred the development of political parties and a more open, democratic polity. Farmers, workers, and entrepreneurs turned to politics to improve their economic welfare, while Irish and German immigrants entered the political arena to protect their religion and culture from nativists and reformers. The result was a two-party system that engaged the energies of the vast majority of the electorate.

Third, many Americans troubled by the changes sweeping the country joined reform movements, many with religious roots. Dedicated men and women preached the gospel of temperance, Sunday observance, and prison reform. Others sought more radical change—equal rights for women and the abolition of slavery—and a few pursued their vision in utopian communities.

All these changes sharpened sectional divisions: the North became an urbanizing and industrializing society based on free labor while the South remained a rural, slaveholding one. Conflicts over the expansion of slavery in the West led finally to the secession of the South and a bloody civil war to restore the Union and liberate the slaves. But in the Reconstruction Era that followed, the victorious North failed to extend the full benefits of democracy and opportunity to African-Americans.

THE ECONOMIC REVOLUTION, 1820–1840

- The Coming of Industry: Northeastern Manufacturing
- The Expansion of Markets
- A Changing Social Structure

The United States was founded as an agrarian republic and over the next half-century matured into a commercially advanced agricultural society. Then enterprising Americans initiated a century-long process of change that transformed the nation into the world's most powerful industrial economy. The 1820s and 1830s were crucial decades in this transition, for they saw a dramatic acceleration in the growth of its two central components: the system of manufacturing and the market economy. Together, the "industrial revolution" and the "market revolution" created a new economic structure. A major change in manufacturing methods enabled Americans to increase their economic *productivity* (making far more goods per worker), while the building of new transportation networks—turnpikes, canals, and railroads—allowed those products to be sold throughout the land.

The French aristocrat Alexis de Tocqueville captured a key feature of this economic revolution in his treatise *Democracy in America* (1835). "What most astonishes me," he remarked after a two-year stay in the United States, "is not so much the marvelous grandeur of some undertakings, as the innumerable magnitude of small ones." It was the individual efforts of tens of thousands of artisan-inventors, entrepreneurial storekeepers and manufacturers, and commercially minded farmers that propelled the country into a new economic era. As the editor of *Niles Weekly Register* put it, there was an "almost *universal ambition to get forward.*"

Not all Americans embraced the new ethic of enterprise, and many who did failed to share in the new prosperity. Industrial and commercial expansion created a class-divided society that challenged the founders' vision of an agricultural republic with few distinctions of wealth or power. "The invasion of Nature by Trade with its Money, its Credit, its Steam, its Railroad," the philosopher Ralph Waldo Emerson wrote in 1839, "threatens to . . . establish a new, universal Monarchy."

THE COMING OF INDUSTRY: NORTHEASTERN MANUFACTURING

The Industrial Revolution came to the United States after 1790 as American merchants increased productivity by reorganizing work and building factories. These innovations in manufacturing boosted output and living standards to an unprecedented extent; the average per capita wealth of Americans increased by nearly 1 percent per year—30 percent over the course of a generation. Goods that once had been luxury items became part of everyday life.

New Organization and New Technology

This impressive gain in output stemmed primarily from changes in the organization of production. Since the 1790s American merchants had used their profits from commerce to expand the outwork system, which made domestic manufacturing more efficient even without technological improvements (see Chapter 9). For example, during the 1820s and 1830s outwork transformed the shoe industry as merchants and manufacturers introduced the "division of labor" into the system of production. The employers hired journeymen and set them to work in central shops cutting leather into soles and "uppers." Then they sent out the uppers to shoe binders, usually women who worked at home binding the uppers and sewing in fabric linings. Finally, the manufacturers had other journeymen assemble the shoes in small shops and return them to the central shop for inspection and packing. The new system of production made the master a powerful employer, the "shoe boss," and eroded workers' control over the pace and conditions of labor. This division of labor also dramatically increased the output of shoes while cutting their price.

For tasks that were not suited to the outwork system, entrepreneurs created an even more important new organization, the modern *factory*. They concentrated as many of the elements of production as possible under one roof and divided the work into specialized tasks. For example, in the 1830s Cincinnati merchants built slaughterhouses that included "disassembly" lines for butchering hogs. A simple system of overhead rails moved the carcasses past workers who had specific tasks: splitting the animals, removing various organs, and trimming the carcasses before packers stuffed them in barrels and pickled them. The system was efficient and quick; every hour more than sixty hogs were butchered and packed. In the 1840s Cincinnati was disassembling so many hogs that the city became known as "Porkopolis."

Upper Falls of the Genesee River, 1835
Like many early industries, the prosperous flour mills at Rochester, New York, were located to take advantage of natural resources. The Genesee River provided water to transport grain to the mills, and its falls powered the mill machinery. (Collection of the New-York Historical Society)

The new factories boasted impressive new technology. As early as 1782 the prolific Delaware inventor Oliver Evans had built a highly automated labor-saving flour mill driven by water power. His machinery lifted the grain to the top of the mill, cleaned the grain as it fell into hoppers, ground it into flour, conveyed the flour back to the top of the mill, and then cooled the flour during its descent into barrels. Evans's factory, remarked one observer, "was as full of machinery as the case of a watch." It needed only six men to mill 100,000 bushels of grain a year.

The Textile Industry

The most dramatic gains in productivity occurred when manufacturers in the textile industry *combined* these organizational and technological innovations. In the 1760s textile manufacturers in northern England had begun to use water-driven machines to produce huge quantities of inexpensive cloth, and in the 1790s American entrepreneurs tried to duplicate their success. This task was difficult because British law prohibited the export of textile machinery and the emigration of mechanics who knew how to build it. Lured by high wages or offers of partnerships, thousands of British mechanics disguised themselves as ordinary laborers and set sail for the United States. By 1812 there were more than 300 British mechanics at work in the Philadelphia area alone.

The most important was Samuel Slater, who came to America in 1789. He had worked for Richard Arkwright, the inventor and operator of the most advanced machinery for spinning cotton. Having memorized the design of Arkwright's machinery, the young Slater contacted Moses Brown, a wealthy merchant who had been trying to duplicate British spinning technology. Slater took over the management of Brown's cotton mill in Providence, Rhode Island, and replicated Arkwright's machines. The opening of Slater's mill in 1790 marks the advent of the American Industrial Revolution.

In competing with British mills, American manufacturers had one major advantage: an abundance of natural resources. America's rich agriculture produced a wealth of cotton and wool, and from Maine to Delaware its rivers provided a cheap source of energy. As rivers cascaded downhill from the Appalachian foothills to the Atlantic coastal plain, they were easily harnessed to run power machinery. All along this *fall line* industrial villages and towns sprang up.

However, the British producers easily undersold their American competitors. Thanks to cheap shipping and low interest rates in Britain, it was profitable to import raw cotton from the United States, manufacture it into cloth, and then ship the textiles back across the Atlantic. Moreover, because British companies were better established, they could engage in cutthroat competition, cutting prices briefly but sharply to drive the newer American firms out of business. The most important British advantage was cheap labor. Britain had a larger population—about 12.6 million in 1810 compared with 7.3 million Americans—and thousands of landless laborers who were willing to take low-paying factory jobs. Since unskilled American workers could obtain good pay for farm or construction work, American manufacturers had to pay them higher wages.

To offset these British advantages, American entrepreneurs sought assistance from the federal government. In 1816 Congress passed a tariff that gave cotton cloth manufacturers some protection from low-cost imports. New protective legislation in 1824 levied a tax of 35 percent on imported iron products, woolen and cotton textiles, and various agricultural products, and the rate rose to 50 percent in 1828. But in 1833, under pressure from southern planters, western farmers, and urban consumers—all of whom wanted to keep down the price of manufactured goods—Congress began to reduce tariffs (see Chapter 11). Unable to compete with lower-cost British producers, American textile manufacturers often failed.

American producers adopted two strategies to compete with their British rivals. First, they tried to improve on British technology. In 1811 Francis Cabot Lowell, a wealthy Boston merchant, spent a holiday touring British textile mills. A well-educated and charming young man, he flattered his hosts by asking a great many questions, but his easy manner hid a serious purpose. Lowell listened closely and secretly made detailed drawings of power machinery. Paul Moody, an experienced American mechanic, then copied the machines and made improvements. In 1814 Lowell joined two other merchants,

A New England Mill Worker: Sarah Rice

*B*etween 1815 and 1850 tens of thousands of New England farm girls took jobs
in new textile factories. Sarah Rice, who tended looms in a Masonville, Connecticut, mill, explains both the financial advantages of factory labor over work as a
domestic servant and the toll on her health taken by fourteen-hour workdays.

Masonville Feb 23d 1845
Dear Father
   I now take my pen in hand to let you know where I am. I have been waiting perhaps longer than I ought to without leting you know where I am yet I
had a reason for so doing . . . knowing that you was dolefully prejudiced
against a Cotton Factory, and being no less prejudiced myself I thought it best
to wait and see how I prospered. . . .
   To be sure it is a noisy place and we are confined more than I like to be
but I do not wear out my clothes and shoes as I do when I do house work. If
I can make 2 dollars per week beside by board and save my clothes and shoes
I think it will be better than to do housework for nine shillings [$1.12] I mean
for a year or two. I should not like to spend my days in a mill . . . because I
like a Farm to well for that.

Millbury [Massachusetts] Sept 14th 1845
You surely cannot blame me for leaving the factory so long as I realised that it
was killing me to work in it. Could you have seen me att the time or a week
before I came away you would [have] advised me as many others did to leave
immediately. I realise that if I lose my health which is all I possess on earth . . .
that I shall be in a sad condition.

SOURCE: Gary Kulik, Roger Parks, Theodore Z. Penn, eds., *The New England Mill Village, 1790–1860*
(Cambridge, Mass.: MIT Press, 1982), pp. 389–390.

Nathan Appleton and Patrick Tracy Jackson, to form the Boston Manufacturing Company. Raising the staggering sum of $400,000, they built a textile
plant in Waltham, Massachusetts, on the Charles River. The Waltham factory
was the first in America to perform all the operations of cloth making under
one roof. More important, thanks to Moody's improvements, Waltham's
power looms operated at higher speeds than British looms and needed fewer
workers.
   The second American strategy was to find less expensive workers. The
Boston Manufacturing Company took the lead, pioneering a manufacturing
system that became known as the Waltham plan. The company recruited
thousands of farm girls and women, who would work at low wages, as textile

operatives. To attract these workers, the company provided boardinghouses and cultural activities such as evening lectures. The mill owners reassured anxious parents by enforcing strict curfews, prohibiting alcoholic beverages, and requiring regular church attendance. At Lowell (1822), Chicopee (1823), and other sites in Massachusetts and New Hampshire, the Boston Manufacturing Company built new cotton factories on the Waltham plan; other Boston-owned firms quickly followed suit.

By the early 1830s more than 40,000 young women were working in textile mills in New England. Eleven-year-old Lucy Larcom of Lowell, Massachusetts, went to work in a textile mill, she later recalled, so that she could support herself and not be "a trouble or burden or expense" to her widowed mother. Many operatives sent their savings home to help their fathers pay off farm mortgages, defray the cost of schooling for their brothers, or accumulate a dowry for themselves. Women textile operatives often found their work oppressive and took periodic breaks before moving to another mill, but many gained a new sense of freedom and autonomy. "Don't I feel independent!" a mill worker wrote to her sister in the 1840s. "The thought that I am living on no one is a happy one indeed to me."

The owners of the Boston Manufacturing Company were even happier. By using improved technology and cheap female labor, they finally achieved competitive superiority over their British rivals in American markets. They also had an advantage over textile manufacturers in New York and Pennsylvania, where agricultural employment was better paid than in New England and textile wages consequently were higher. Producers in those states pursued a different strategy, modifying traditional technology to produce higher-quality cloth, also with good results. In 1825 Thomas Jefferson, once a critic of industrialization, expressed his pride in the American achievement: "Our manufacturers are now very nearly on a footing with those of England."

American Mechanics and Technological Innovation

By the 1820s American craftsmen had replaced British immigrants at the cutting edge of technological innovation. Although few had a formal education and once had been viewed as "mean" or even "servile" workers, they now claimed respect as "men professing an ingenious art." One such inventor, Richard Garsed, started working in a textile mill when he was eight years old. Ten years later, in 1837, Garsed experimented with improvements on power looms in his father's factory and in three years nearly doubled their speed. By 1846 he had patented a cam and harness device that allowed elaborately figured fabrics such as damask to be woven by machine.

In the Philadelphia region, the most important inventors came from the remarkable Sellars family. Samuel Sellars, Jr., invented a machine for twisting worsted woolen yarn. His son John devised more efficient ways of using water power to run the family's sawmills and gristmills and built a machine to weave wire sieves. John's sons and grandsons built machine shops that turned out a

The Norris Locomotive Works
Founded in 1831, the Norris Works became a prime supplier of locomotives to railroads in the United States and Europe. Its large workshops boasted sophisticated machine tools and could produce three locomotives every six days. (National Museum of American History, Smithsonian)

variety of new products: riveted leather fire hoses, papermaking equipment, and eventually locomotives. In 1824 members of the Sellars family and other mechanics founded the Franklin Institute in Philadelphia. Named after Benjamin Franklin, whom the mechanics admired for his scientific accomplishments and idealization of hard work, the institute fostered a sense of professional identity. The Franklin Institute published a journal; provided high school–level instruction in mechanics, chemistry, mathematics, and mechanical drawing; and organized annual fairs to exhibit the most advanced products. Craftsmen in Ohio and other states soon established their own mechanics institutes, which played a crucial role in diffusing technical knowledge and encouraging innovation. Around 1820 the United States Patent Office issued about 200 patents on new inventions each year; by 1850 it was awarding 1,000 annually, and ten years later over 4,000.

During these years American mechanics pioneered the development of *machine tools*—machines for making other machines. This technical advance was crucial because it facilitated the rapid spread of the Industrial Revolution.

For example, mechanics serving the textile industry invented lathes, planers, and boring machines that made standardized parts. These machine-tooled parts, which required a minimum of filing and fitting, made it possible to manufacture new spinning jennys and weaving looms at a low cost and to repair broken machines. Moreover, this machinery was precise enough in design and construction to operate at higher speeds than British equipment.

Technological innovation swept through the rest of American manufacturing. For example, in 1832 the mechanics employed by Samuel W. Collins in his Connecticut ax-making company built a vastly improved die-forging machine—a device that pressed and hammered hot metal into dies, or cutting forms. Using the improved machine, a skilled worker could increase his production of ax heads from 12 to 300 a day. A few years later mechanics in Massachusetts perfected a power-driven shoe-stitching machine, boosting the output of well-made boots while cutting the cost.

The most important advances in machine building came in the firearms industry. To fill large-scale contracts from the federal government, Eli Whitney and his coworkers in Connecticut developed machine tools that produced parts that were not only interchangeable but also precision-crafted. After Whitney's death this innovative work in machine design was continued by his partner, John H. Hall, an engineer at the federal armory at Harpers Ferry, Virginia. By the 1840s Hall had developed an array of basic machine tools to work metal: turret lathes, milling machines, and precision grinders. Thereafter, manufacturers could use those machine tools to produce complicated machinery with great speed, at low cost, and in large quantities. With this expansion in the availability of machines, the American Industrial Revolution came of age.

Wage Workers and the Labor Movement

As the Industrial Revolution gathered momentum, it changed the economic system and the character of the American social order. Each decade, more and more white Americans lost their economic independence and took work as wage-earning employees, hired by the day, week, or season (or for a specific job). They had no security of employment and little control over their working conditions.

Some wage workers worked in traditional crafts, such as the building trades. These journeymen artisans—carpenters, housepainters, stonecutters, masons, nailers, and cabinetmakers—had valuable skills and a strong sense of craft identity. Consequently, they were able to form unions and bargain with the master artisans who employed them. The journeymen's main concern was the increasing length of the workday, which deprived them of time to spend with their families or use to improve their education. The traditional workday for artisans had averaged out, over the winter and summer seasons, at about twelve hours; they began at first light, took breaks for lunch and dinner, and stopped at dusk. By the 1820s masters were abusing the old work rules—

scheduling more jobs for summer when the workday was longer and charging customers more while paying journeymen the old daily rate. In response, 600 carpenters in Boston went on strike in 1825, demanding a ten-hour day, 6 A.M. to 6 P.M., with an hour each for breakfast and dinner. Although the Boston protest failed, two years later several hundred journeymen carpenters in Philadelphia won a similar strike for a ten-hour day and then helped found the Mechanics' Union of Trade Associations. This citywide organization of fifty unions and 10,000 Philadelphia wage earners articulated a broad reform program, demanding "a just balance of power . . . between all the various classes."

By the mid-1830s skilled workers in the building trades had forced many urban employers to accept ten hours as the standard workday. In 1835 the Philadelphia city council set a ten-hour day for local public works, and the following year President Andrew Jackson established a ten-hour day at the Philadelphia navy yard. These victories were significant; they gave skilled American workers the same hours that British building-trade workers had enjoyed since the 1750s.

Artisans whose occupations were threatened by industrialization were less successful. As machines changed the nature of their work, shoemakers, hatters, printers, furniture makers, and weavers faced declining incomes, unemployment, and loss of status. To avoid the regimentation of factory work, some artisans moved to small towns or set up small, specialized shops that catered to a limited market. For example, in New York City 800 highly skilled cabinetmakers produced fashionable or custom-made products. In status and income they outranked a much larger group of 3,200 semitrained workers—derogatively called "botches"—who turned out cheap, mass-produced furniture.

In many industries less skilled factory workers banded together to form craft unions to seek higher pay and better working conditions. In 1830 in Lynn, Massachusetts, journeymen shoemakers founded a Mutual Benefit Society that quickly grew into a national union and formed local federations with other craft unions. In 1834 federations from Boston to Philadelphia joined to form the National Trades' Union, the first national union of different trades.

Union leaders mounted a critique of the new industrial order. Afraid that workers were becoming "slaves to a monied aristocracy" (their term for commercial middlemen and capitalist employers), they condemned the new organization of production in which "capital and labor stand opposed." To restore a just society, they devised a *labor theory of value,* arguing that the price of a product should reflect the labor required to make it and should be paid primarily to the producer, to "enable him to live as comfortably as others." Appealing to the spirit of the American Revolution, which had destroyed the aristocracy of birth, they called for a new revolution to destroy the aristocracy of capital. Armed with this artisan-republican ideology and pressed by rapidly increasing prices, in 1836 union men organized nearly fifty strikes for higher wages, many of which were temporarily successful.

This agitation for workers' rights inspired women operatives in cotton and woolen textile mills. As competition among cloth producers cut profit margins and threatened bankruptcy, employers reduced the pay of their workers and imposed more stringent work rules. In 1828 women mill workers in Dover, New Hampshire, struck against new rules, winning some relief; six years later more than 800 Dover women walked out to protest wage cuts. That same year 2,000 women in Lowell, Massachusetts, backed up a strike by withdrawing their savings from an employer-owned bank. The *Boston Transcript* reported that "one of the leaders mounted a pump, and made a flaming . . . speech on the rights of women and the iniquities of the 'monied aristocracy.'"

However powerful the rhetoric, most strikes by factory operatives failed. Employers often fired the leaders, and the rest of the workers either returned to work or moved to another factory. Even the more successful strikes by building-trade workers and shoemakers did not alter the inferior position of wage laborers in the new industrial order. They lacked access to financial capital, business know-how, and a broad education, three key ingredients of success in the new society. In these circumstances, a group of Philadelphia workers declared, "liberty is but an unmeaning word, and equality an equal shadow."

THE EXPANSION OF MARKETS

As American factories turned out more manufactures, merchants and legislators sought faster and cheaper ways to get those products to consumers. Beginning in the 1820s, they promoted the construction of a massive system of canals and roads to link eastern manufacturers and markets to the trans-Appalachian West, where hundreds of thousands of farm families had settled.

The West: Farming New Land

In the generation after independence vast numbers of men and women left the seaboard states, taking with them their savings, personal property, and skills. Some families wanted to acquire enough land to settle their children on nearby farms, re-creating traditional rural communities. Others were more entrepreneurial and hoped for greater profits from the fertile soil of the West. By the 1820s the Carolinas, Vermont, and New Hampshire were losing as many people through migration as they gained through natural increase. Abandoned farms and homes dotted the countryside, their owners gone in search of better lands. "It is useless to seek to excite patriotic emotions" and loyalty to one's state of birth, complained an easterner, "when self-interest speaks so loudly." By 1840 about 5 million people—more than a third of the nation's population—lived west of the Appalachians (see Map 10.1).

These pioneers migrated in three great streams. In the South, plantation owners encouraged by the voracious demand of British factories for raw cotton moved their slaves into the Old Southwest. Deserting depleted fields in

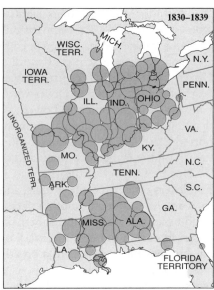

MAP 10.1
Western Land Sales, 1820–1839
In the 1830s hundreds of thousands of migrants settled in the farmlands of the Ohio Valley
and the cotton belt of the Old Southwest. Each circle centers on a government land office,
and the area of each circle represents the relative amount of land sold at that office.

Georgia and the Carolinas, they established the Cotton Kingdom in the new
states of Louisiana (admitted to the Union in 1812), Mississippi (1817), Alabama (1819), Missouri (1821), and Arkansas (1836). "*The Alabama Fever*
rages here with great violence," a North Carolina planter complained, "and
has *carried off* vast numbers of our Citizens."

Small-scale farmers from the Upper South, especially Virginia and Kentucky, created a second stream as they crossed the Ohio River into the Old
Northwest. Some of these migrants were fleeing planter-dominated slave
states. In a free community, thought Peter Cartwright, a Methodist lay
preacher from southwestern Kentucky, "I would be entirely clear of the evil of
slavery ... [and] could raise my children to work where work was not thought
a degradation." These southerners introduced corn and hog farming to Ohio
(admitted in 1803), Indiana (1816), and Illinois (1818).

The third stream of migrants came from the overcrowded farms of New
England. Thousands had poured into upstate New York during the 1790s, and
now thousands more abandoned the rocky soils of Vermont and New Hampshire for the rich lands of the Old Northwest. They wanted to maintain their
traditional life as yeomen farmers and keep their children on the land, sparing
them from industrial work. These settlers established wheat farms throughout
the Great Lakes Basin: northern Ohio, northern Illinois, Michigan (admitted
in 1837), Iowa (1846), and Wisconsin (1848).

To meet the demand for cheap land, in 1820 Congress reduced the price of federal land from $2.00 an acre to $1.25—just enough to cover the cost of surveying and sale. For $100 a farmer could buy 80 acres, the minimum required under federal law. With huge quantities of public land available at that price, the market price for all undeveloped land remained low. Many American families saved enough in a few years to make the minimum purchase and used money from the sale of an old farm to finance the move. By 1840 the population center of American society had shifted significantly to the west.

The Transportation Revolution

Extending the market economy into the interior required a revolution in transportation. Previously, most overland trade had been local, consisting of an exchange of goods between towns and nearby rural areas. For example, Philadelphia merchants and artisans traded their textiles and ironware for farm products grown nearby: flour and corn, dairy products, fruits and vegetables, and wood for heating and cooking. More distant trade was virtually impossible because of the lack of a system of well-maintained roads.

To enhance the "common-wealth" of their citizens, the federal and state governments tried to create a larger market. Beginning in the 1790s, they chartered private companies to build toll-charging turnpikes in well-populated areas and subsidized road construction in the West (see Map 10.2). The most significant feat was the National Road, which started in Cumberland, Maryland, passed Wheeling (then in Virginia) in 1818, crossed the Ohio River in 1833, and reached Vandalia, Illinois, in 1850. At first these interregional highways mostly carried migrants and their heavily loaded wagons to the West and herds of livestock to the East, but gradually they became conduits for manufactured goods and farm products. Merchants in the Northeast exchanged textiles, clothing, boots and shoes, muskets, and farm equipment for wheat, corn, whiskey, and hogs from farms in the Great Lakes Basin and the Ohio Valley.

By facilitating regional specialization, improved transportation greatly increased the overall productivity of the American economy. For example, it allowed western farmers to reap the advantages of cheap land and inexpensive factory-made tools. Farmers throughout the North and the West bought the new cast-iron plow invented in 1819 by Jethro Wood, a farmer in upstate New York. Wood's plow cut cultivating time in half, allowing farmers to till much larger fields, and could easily be repaired with replaceable cast-iron parts. Northeastern factories supplied other low-cost, high-quality products to western farmers: shovels and spades fabricated from rolled iron at the Delaware Iron Works, axes forged in a Connecticut factory, steel horseshoes manufactured in Troy, New York. Indeed, the production of farm implements consumed fully half the nation's output of pig iron. For their part, western farmers contributed to the rapid progress of the American Industrial Revolution by providing low-cost cotton, wool, leather, and other raw materials to

MAP 10.2

The Transportation Revolution: Roads and Canals, 1820–1850
By 1850 the United States had an efficient transportation system based on roads, natural waterways, and canals. Short canals and navigable rivers carried cotton, tobacco, and other products from the upcountry of the seaboard states into the Atlantic commercial system. Major canals—the Erie, Chesapeake and Ohio, and Pennsylvania Mainline—linked major seaport cities to the vast trans-Appalachian region, and a set of regional canals connected most of the Great Lakes region to the Ohio and Mississippi rivers and New Orleans.

eastern manufacturers. In addition, they supplied the abundant and inexpensive grain, meat, vegetables, and fruit that helped maintain the health and vigor of factory workers and urban populations in the Northeast.

To get these goods to market, Americans replaced slow and expensive overland trade with a water-borne transportation system of unprecedented size, complexity, and cost. As early as 1790 entrepreneurs had begun to build canals to connect inland areas with coastal cities and towns, but progress was slow. When the New York legislature began the Erie Canal in 1817, no canal in the United States was longer than 28 miles—a reflection of the huge capital investment canals required and the lack of American engineering expertise. But the New York project had three things in its favor: the vigorous support of New York City merchants, who wanted access to western markets; the backing of New York's governor, DeWitt Clinton, who persuaded the legislature to finance the waterway from tax revenues, tolls, and bond sales to foreign investors; and the relative gentleness of the terrain west of Albany. Even so, the task was enormous. Millions of cubic yards of dirt had to be dug out by hand and hauled away, thousands of tons of rock quarried to build huge locks to raise and lower boats, and vast reservoirs constructed to ensure a steady supply of water. The first great engineering project in American history, the Erie Canal altered the ecology as well as the economy of an entire region.

The Erie Canal was an instant success. The first section, a stretch of 75 miles opened in 1819, immediately generated enough revenue to repay its cost. When the canal was completed in 1825, the 40-foot-wide ribbon of water stretched 364 miles from Albany to Buffalo. The canal carried lightweight

Construction of the Erie Canal
Tens of thousands of workers, primarily poor immigrants from Ireland, built the American canal system. The vast scale of the project and the impressive economic benefits concealed a huge cost in lives. In the marshes near Syracuse a thousand workers fell ill with fever, and many died.

packet boats from New York City to Buffalo in only six days, and 100-ton freight barges pulled by two horses moved along at a steady 24 miles a day, greatly accelerating the flow of goods and cutting transportation costs. (On up-state New York roads, it took four horses to pull a small 1-ton wagon 12 miles in a day.)

The Erie Canal brought prosperity to central and western New York, carrying wheat and meat from farming communities in the interior to eastern cities and foreign markets. In 1818 the mills in Rochester, New York, had processed only 26,000 barrels of flour from the wheat of nearby farmers; ten years later the number soared to 200,000 barrels, and in 1840 to 500,000 barrels. After a trip on the canal, the novelist Nathaniel Hawthorne suggested that its water "must be the most fertilizing of all fluids, for it causes towns with their masses of brick and stone, their churches and theaters, their business and hubbub, their luxury and refinement, their gay dames and polished citizens, to spring up."

The spectacular benefits of the Erie Canal prompted a national canal boom. Civic and business leaders in Philadelphia and Baltimore proposed their own waterways to compete for the trade of the West. Copying New York's fiscal innovations, they persuaded their state governments to allocate tax money to canal projects, making it easier to raise the needed capital. Some state governments invested directly in canal companies or forced state-chartered banks to do so; others offered to guarantee their loans, and this encouraged British and Dutch investors to provide almost three-quarters of the $200 million invested in canals by 1840. Canals quickly became the most important part of the inland American transportation system, connecting the Great Lakes region with the great port cities of New York (via the Erie and Pennsylvania canals) and New Orleans (via the Ohio and Mississippi rivers).

The steamboat, another product of the industrial age, ensured the success of this vast water transportation system. The engineer-inventor Robert Fulton built the first American steamboat, the *Clermont*, which he navigated up the Hudson in 1807. However, the first steamboats were expensive to run because their engines consumed large amounts of wood or coal, and they could not navigate shallow western rivers. During the 1820s engineers broadened the hulls of these boats, and this increased their cargo capacity, speeded loading and unloading, and gave them a shallower draft. This improved design cut the cost of upstream river transport in half, dramatically increasing the flow of goods into the interior. Steam-powered shipping also speeded the transit of people and news. In 1830 a traveler or a letter from New York could go by water to Boston in a day and a half, to Charleston in five days, and to New Orleans or Detroit in two weeks. Thirty years earlier the same journeys, by road or sail, had taken twice as long.

The rapid emergence of this national system of transportation was encouraged by the Supreme Court headed by John Marshall, which struck down state controls over interstate commerce. In the crucial case of *Gibbons v. Ogden* (1824) the Court declared that the federal government had paramount authority over interstate commerce. This decision meant that no local monopolies—or tariffs—would impede the flow of goods and services across the nation.

The Growth of Cities and Towns

Industrialization and the expansion of interregional trade greatly expanded the urban population of the United States. In 1820 there were only 58 towns in the nation with 2,500 to 50,000 people; by 1840 there were 126. During those two decades the number of urban residents grew fourfold, from 443,000 to 1,844,000.

The most rapid growth occurred in the new industrial towns that sprang up along the fall line. In 1822, for example, the Boston Manufacturing Company decided to build a new complex of mills in East Chelmsford, Massachusetts, on the Merrimack River. Within a few years the sleepy river village was transformed into a bustling town, now named Lowell in honor of the company's founder. Hartford, Connecticut, Trenton, New Jersey, and Wilmington, Delaware, also became urban centers as mill owners exploited their water power and recruited workers from the surrounding countryside.

Western commercial cities such as New Orleans, Pittsburgh, Cincinnati, and Louisville grew almost as rapidly. The initial expansion of these cities resulted from their location at points where goods had to be transferred from one mode of transport, such as canal boats or farmers' wagons, to another, such as steamboats or sailing vessels. As the western population grew during the 1830s, St. Louis, Rochester, Buffalo, Cleveland, Detroit, and Chicago emerged as dynamic centers of commerce. Merchants and bankers settled there, developing the marketing, provisioning, and financial services that were essential to farmers and small-town merchants in the hinterland.

The old Atlantic seaports—Boston, New York, Philadelphia, and Baltimore—remained the largest American cities. Traditionally places of commerce, the port cities now became centers of finance and manufacturing. In 1817 New York merchants founded the New York Stock Exchange, which soon became the nation's chief market for securities. The New York metropolis grew at a phenomenal rate, diversifying into small-scale manufacturing and becoming the center of the ready-made clothing industry, which relied on the labor of thousands of low-paid seamstresses. "The wholesale clothing establishments are . . . absorbing the business of the country," a "Country Tailor" complained to the *New York Tribune*, "casting many an honest and hardworking man out of employment [and allowing] . . . the large cities to swallow up the small towns."

New York's growth stemmed primarily from its control of foreign trade. It had the best harbor in the United States, and oceangoing vessels could sail or steam 150 miles up the Hudson River to Albany. The city's merchants exploited these natural advantages. In 1818 four Quaker merchants founded the Black Ball Line as the first transatlantic packet service. Black Ball ships operated on a regular schedule, carrying cargo, people, and mail between New York and European ports such as Liverpool, London, and Le Havre. New York merchants also gained an unassailable lead in commerce with the newly independent Latin American nations of Brazil, Peru, and Venezuela. Finally, they moved into the cotton trade. Their agents in southern ports offered finance, insurance, and shipping to cotton exporters and won for New York a dominant share of the cotton that passed through northern harbors. In their most aggressive stroke New York merchants persuaded the state government to build the Erie Canal, which solidified New York's position as the nation's premier port. By 1840 New York's merchants controlled almost two-thirds of foreign imports and almost half of all foreign trade.

A CHANGING SOCIAL STRUCTURE

The industrial and market revolutions transformed the material lives of many Americans, allowing them to live in larger houses, cook on iron stoves, and wear better-made clothes. But the new economic order also widened social distinctions between a wealthy industrial and commercial elite, a substantial urban middle class, and a mass of propertyless wage earners. By creating a class-divided society, industrialization posed a momentous challenge to American republican ideals.

The Business Elite

Before industrialization, white American society had been divided into various *ranks*, with a group of notables at the top ruling over the "lower orders." But in rural society the different ranks shared a common culture: gentlemen farmers talked easily with yeomen about crop yields and livestock breeds, while their wives conversed with humble farm women about the arts of quilting and preserving food. In the South humble tenants and aristocratic slaveowners shared the same amusements: gambling, cockfighting, and horse racing. Rich and poor attended the same Quaker meetinghouse or sat together in the same Presbyterian or Congregational church. "Almost everyone eats, drinks, and dresses in the same way," a European visitor to Hartford, Connecticut, reported in 1798, "and one can see the most obvious inequality only in the dwellings."

The Industrial Revolution shattered this traditional order and created a society of *classes*, each with its own culture. The new economic system pulled many Americans into cities and made a few of them—merchants, manufacturers, bankers, and landlords—very rich. In 1800 the top 10 percent of the nation's families owned about 40 percent of the wealth; by 1860 the wealthiest 10 percent owned nearly 70 percent. Inequality was greatest in the cities, where the richest 1 percent of the population held more than 40 percent of all tangible property—such as land and buildings—and an even higher share of intangible property—such as stocks and bonds.

Government policies encouraged this accumulation of wealth by placing heavier taxes on the middling and poorer classes than on the rich. The U.S. Treasury raised most of its revenue from tariffs—taxes on imported goods such as textiles that were purchased mostly by ordinary citizens. State and local governments also favored the wealthier classes. They usually taxed real estate and tangible personal property (such as furniture, tools, and machinery) but almost never taxed the stocks and bonds owned by the rich or the inheritances they passed on to their children.

Over time the wealthiest families consciously set themselves apart. Instead of laboring side by side with journeymen and apprentices in small shops, merchants and manufacturers became managers, issuing orders to hundreds of outworkers or factory operatives. Similarly, they chose to live in separate residential areas. Previously many wage earners had lived in the same home or neighborhood as their employers. By the 1830s most employers had stopped providing their workers with housing and moved their families to distinct upper-class enclaves, often at the edge of the city. The desire for greater privacy by privileged families divided many American cities into class-segregated communities for the first time.

The Middle Class

Standing between wealthy owners and entrepreneurs at one end of the social spectrum and nonpropertied wage earners at the other was a growing middle class. In the words of a Boston printer and publisher, the "middling class" was made up of "the farmers, the mechanics, the manufacturers, the traders, who carry on professionally the ordinary operations of buying, selling, and exchanging merchandize." As industry expanded, skilled mechanics were in demand, building contractors and shopkeepers profited as cities grew, commercial-minded farmers benefited from rising prices, and lawyers and surveyors were swamped with clients seeking assistance on legal matters and property boundaries. Middle-class business owners, employees, and professionals were most numerous in the Northeast, where they numbered about 30 percent of the population in 1840, but they could be found in every American town and village, even in the agrarian South.

Increasingly these middling people shared a common style of living that gave them a distinct cultural identity. Husbands had sufficient earnings so that their wives did not have to seek paid work. Typically, middle-class men saved about 15 percent of their income, depositing it in banks and using it to buy a well-built house in a "respectable part of town." They purchased handsome clothes for themselves and their families and drove about town in smart carriages. Their wives and daughters were literate and accomplished; they bought books and pianos as well as commodious furniture for their front parlors. The more affluent among them hired a servant or two to work in the kitchen and the stables. Material comfort became a distinguishing mark of the middle class.

Moral and mental discipline was an equally prominent feature of the middle class. Successful parents wanted to pass their status on to their children. Therefore, they usually provided their offspring with a full high school education (in an era when most white children received only four or five years of elementary education). Ambitious parents were equally concerned with their children's character and stressed discipline, morality, and hard work.

Many middle-class men and women shared the economic and moral values of the business elite, especially a belief in hard work and personal achievement. Puritans and other American Protestants had long believed that work in an earthly "calling" was a duty people owed to God. In the 1820s and 1830s the business elite and the middle class gave this idea a secular twist: they celebrated work as socially beneficial, the key to a higher standard of living for the nation and social mobility for the individual.

Benjamin Franklin gave classical expression to the secular work ethic in his *Autobiography*, which was published in full in 1818 and immediately found a huge audience. Heeding Franklin's suggestion that an industrious man would become a rich one, tens of thousands of young American men worked hard, saved their money, adopted temperate habits, and practiced honesty in their business dealings. Countless magazines, children's books, self-help manuals, and novels taught the same lessons. The ideal of the "self-made man" became a central theme of American popular culture. Just as a rural-producer ethic had united the social ranks in pre-1800 America, this new goal of personal achievement and social mobility tied together the upper and middle classes of the new industrializing society.

The New Urban Poor

As thoughtful members of the business elite and the middle class surveyed the emerging social landscape, they worried that many Americans might never improve their status. A yeomanlike society made up of independent families no longer seemed possible or even advisable. "Entire independence ought not to be wished for," Ithamar A. Beard, the paymaster of the Hamilton Manufacturing Company, told a mechanics' association in 1827. "In large manufacturing towns, many more must fill subordinate stations and must be under the immediate direction and control of a master or superintendent, than in the farming towns."

Beard had a point. By 1840 as many as half the nation's free workers were laboring for others rather than for themselves. The bottom 10 percent of this wage-earning labor force consisted of casual workers—those hired on a short-term basis, often by the day, for the most arduous jobs. Poor women washed clothes, while their husbands and sons carried lumber and bricks for construction projects, loaded ships and wagons, and dug out dirt and stones to build canals. Most casual laborers owned no property except the clothes they wore. During business depressions they bore the brunt of unemployment, and even in the best of times their jobs were unpredictable, seasonal, and dangerous.

Other laborers had greater security of employment, but few were prospering. In Massachusetts in 1825 the daily wage of an unskilled worker was about two-thirds that of a mechanic; two decades later it was less than half as much. The 18,000 needlewomen in New York City in the 1850s were no better off, averaging less than $80 a year. These meager wages did not buy much. While middle-class families spent about one-third of their income on food, poorer urban workers had to spend nearly $2 of every $3 they earned just for sustenance. After paying rent for housing, they were broke—unable to take advantage of the rapidly falling prices of manufactured goods. Only the most fortunate working families could afford to educate their children, pay the fees required for apprenticeship in a trade, or accumulate small dowries so that their daughters could marry men with better prospects. Most had to send their children out to work to help support the family. An economic recession or the death of one of the spouses often threw them into dire poverty. As a charity worker noted, "What can a bereaved widow do, with 5 or 6 little children, destitute of every means of support but what her own hands can furnish (which in a general way does not amount to more than 25 cents a day)."

By the 1830s most urban factory workers, journeymen, and unskilled casual laborers resided in well-defined neighborhoods. Certain blocks were dominated by large, crowded boardinghouses where single men and women lived in unhealthy conditions. Elsewhere landlords converted houses, including the basements and attics, into tiny apartments and used the profits from rentals to build more workers' housing. Often the developers squeezed a number of buildings, interspersed with outhouses and connected by foul-smelling courtyards and dark alleys, onto a single lot.

Living in such distressing conditions, many wage earners turned to the dubious solace of alcohol. Liquor had long been an integral part of American life; beer, wine, and rum had lubricated ceremonies, celebrations, work breaks, barn raisings, and games. But during the 1820s urban wage earners led Americans to new heights of alcohol consumption. Aiding them were western farmers, who distilled corn and rye into gin and whiskey as a low-cost way to get their grain to market. By 1830 the per capita consumption of liquor had risen to more than 5 gallons a year, three times present-day levels.

Drinking patterns changed as well. Workers in many craft unions "swore off" liquor, convinced that it would undermine their skilled work as well as their health and finances. But other workers began to drink on the job—and not just during the traditional 11 A.M. and 4 P.M. "refreshers." Journeymen used apprentices to smuggle whiskey into shops, and then, as one baker recalled, "One man was stationed at the window to watch, while the rest drank." Grogshops and tippling houses appeared on almost every block in working-class districts. The saloons became focal points for urban disorder and crime, including assault, burglary, and vandalism. Fueled by unrestrained drinking, a fistfight among young men one night could turn into a brawl the second night and a full-scale riot the third. The urban police forces, consisting of low-paid watchmen and untrained constables, were unable to contain the lawlessness.

The Benevolent Empire

The disorder and lawlessness among urban wage earners sparked concern among well-to-do Americans. Inspired by the religious ideal of "benevolence," they created a number of reform organizations that historians refer to collectively as the "Benevolent Empire."

During the 1820s Congregational and Presbyterian ministers united with like-minded merchants and their wives to launch a program of social regulation. Their purpose, announced Presbyterian minister Lyman Beecher of Boston, was to restore "the moral government of God." The reformers introduced new forms of moral discipline both into their own lives and into the lives of ordinary working people. They would regulate behavior—by persuasion if possible, by law if necessary.

Although the Benevolent Empire targeted age-old evils such as drunkenness, prostitution, and crime, its methods were new. Instead of relying on church sermons and moral suasion by community leaders, the reformers set out to institutionalize charity and combat evil systematically. They established large-scale organizations—the Prison Discipline Society and the American Society for the Promotion of Temperance, among many others. Each had a managing staff, a network of volunteers and chapters, and a newspaper.

Together, these groups set out to "improve" society. First, they encouraged people to lead well-disciplined and moral lives, campaigning for temperance in drinking habits and the end of prostitution. Beyond that, they persuaded local governments to ban carnivals of drink and dancing, such as the Negro Election Day festivities in New England, which had been enjoyed by whites as well as blacks. Second, they created new institutions for people who were threats to society or were unable to handle their own affairs. Reformers provided homes of refuge for the abandoned children of the poor, removed the insane from isolation in attics and cellars and placed them in newly built asylums, and campaigned for an end of corporal punishment for criminals and their rehabilitation through moral training in penitentiaries.

Women played an increasingly active role in the Benevolent Empire. Since the 1790s upper-class women had sponsored a number of charitable organizations, such as the Society for the Relief of Poor Widows with Small Children, founded in New York in 1797 by Isabella Graham, a devout Presbyterian widow. By the 1820s Graham's society was assisting hundreds of widows and their children in New York City. Her daughter, Joanna Bethune, set up other charitable institutions, including the Orphan Asylum Society and the Society for the Promotion of Industry, which gave subsidized employment as spinners and seamstresses to hundreds of poor women.

Some reformers came to believe that one of the greatest threats to the "moral government of God" was the decline of the traditional Sabbath. As the pace of commercial activity accelerated during the 1820s, merchants and shippers began to conduct business on Sunday, since they did not want their goods and equipment to lie idle one day in every seven. To restore traditional values, in 1828 Lyman Beecher and other ministers formed the General Union for Promoting the Observance of the Christian Sabbath. Union chapters sprang up—usually with women's auxiliaries—from Maine to the Ohio Valley. Seeking a symbolic issue to rally Christians to their cause, the Union focused on a law Congress had enacted in 1810 allowing mail to be transported—though not delivered—on Sunday. To secure its repeal the Union adopted the tactics of a political party, organizing rallies and circulating petitions. Its members also boycotted shipping companies that did business on the Sabbath and campaigned for municipal laws forbidding games and festivals on the Lord's Day.

Not everyone agreed with the program of the Benevolent Empire. Men who labored twelve or fourteen hours six days a week refused to spend their one day of leisure in meditation and prayer. Shipping company managers demanded that the Erie Canal provide lockkeepers on Sundays and joined anti-temperance advocates in arguing that boycotts and laws enforcing morality were "contrary to the free spirit of our institutions." And when the Benevolent Empire proposed to teach Christianity to slaves, white southerners were outraged. Such popular resistance or indifference limited the success of the Benevolent Empire. A different kind of message was required if religious reformers were to do more than preach to the already converted and discipline the already disciplined.

Revivalism and Reform

It was the Presbyterian minister Charles Grandison Finney who brought just such a message to Americans. Finney was not part of the traditional religious elite. Born to poor farmers in Connecticut in 1792, he was determined to join the new middle class as a lawyer. But in 1823 he underwent an intense

Charles Finney, Evangelist
Finney (1792–1875) had a long and influential career after his New York revivals, training a generation of ministers at Oberlin College. This daguerreotype, taken in 1850 while Finney and his second wife, Elizabeth Atkinson, were on a evangelistic tour of Britain, suggests his moral intensity.

conversion experience and decided to become a minister. Beginning in towns along the Erie Canal, Finney conducted emotional revival meetings that ignored deep instruction in church doctrine; what counted for Finney was the will to be saved. God would welcome *any* sinner who submitted to the Holy Spirit, and only an infusion of God's grace, poured into the heart of the believer, made a moral life possible. Finney's ministry drew upon—and greatly accelerated—the Second Great Awakening, the wave of Protestant revivalism that had begun after the Revolution (see Chapter 9).

Finney's message that "God has made man a moral free agent" was particularly attractive to members of the new middle class, who had already chosen to improve their material lives. But he became famous for converting those at the ends of the social spectrum: the haughty rich, who had placed themselves above God, and the abject poor, who seemed lost to drink, sloth, and misbehavior. His goal was to humble the pride of the rich and relieve the shame of the poor by celebrating their common fellowship in Christ. Conversion changed not only people's eternal fate but also their moral standing, identifying them spiritually with earnest, pious middle-class respectability.

Finney's most spectacular triumph came in 1830, when he moved his revivals from small towns to Rochester, New York, a major Erie Canal city. For six months he preached every day and added a new tactic—group prayer meetings in family homes—in which women played an active role. Finney's wife, Lydia, and other pious middle-class wives carried the message to the homes of the unconverted, often while their disapproving husbands were at work. Soon, one convert reported, "You could not go upon the street and hear any conversation, except upon religion."

Finney soon won over the influential merchants and manufacturers of Rochester, who pledged to reform their lives and those of their workers. They would attend church, join the "Cold Water" movement by giving up alcohol, and work steady hours. To encourage their employees to follow suit, wealthy businessmen founded a new Free Presbyterian Church—"free" because members did not have to pay for pew space. This church was specifically designed to serve poor workers: canal laborers, transients, and the settled poor. Other evangelical Protestants soon founded two similar churches. To reinforce the work of those churches, Rochester's business elite established a savings bank to encourage thrift, Sunday schools for poor children, and the Female Charitable Society to provide relief for the families of the unemployed.

The success of the Protestant crusade in Rochester was duplicated by revivalists in cities and towns from New England to the Ohio Valley. Dozens of younger ministers—Baptist and Methodist as well as Congregationalist and Presbyterian—adopted Finney's evangelical message and techniques. In New York City, where Finney established himself after leaving Rochester, the wealthy silk merchants Arthur and Lewis Tappan founded a magazine, *The Christian Evangelist*, to promote his ideas. The success of the revival "has been so general and thorough," concluded a General Assembly of Presbyterians, "that the whole customs of society have changed."

AMERICAN VOICES

The Vice of Intemperance

John Gough's impoverished English parents shipped him off at age twelve to America, where he found work as a bookbinder in New York City—and turned to drink. In 1842 he converted to temperance and used his eloquence as a lecturer to command high fees and persuade thousands to join the movement.

Will it be believed that I again sought refuge in rum? Yet so it was. Scarcely had I recovered from the fright, than I sent out, procured a pint of rum, and drank it all in less than an hour. And now came upon me many terrible sensations. Cramps attacked me in my limbs, which racked me with agony; and my temples throbbed as if they would burst. . . . Then came on the drunkard's remorseless torturer—delirium tremens, in all its terrors, attacked me. . . . I was at one time surrounded by millions of monstrous spiders, that crawled slowly over every limb, whilst the beaded drops of perspiration would start to my brow, and my limbs would shiver until the bed rattled. . . . I was falling—falling swiftly as an arrow—far down into some terrible abyss. . . .

By the mercy of God, I survived this awful seizure; and when I rose, a weak, broken-down man, and surveyed my ghastly features in the glass, I thought of my mother, and asked myself how I had obeyed the instructions received from her lips. . . . Oh! how keen were my rebukes; and, in the excitement of the moment, I resolved to lead a better life, and abstain from the accursed cup.

For about a month, terrified by what I had suffered, I adhered to my resolution; then my wife came home, and, in my joy at her return, I flung my good resolutions to the wind, and . . . I took a glass of brandy. That glass aroused the slumbering demon. . . . The night of my wife's return, I went to bed intoxicated.

SOURCE: David Brion Davis, ed., *Antebellum American Culture: An Interpretive Anthology* (Lexington, Mass.: Heath, 1979), pp. 402–403.

The temperance movement proved to be the most effective arena for evangelical reform on a national scale. In 1832 evangelicals gained control of the American Temperance Society; within a few years it had grown to 2,000 chapters with more than 200,000 members. The society adapted the methods that had worked so well in the revivals—group confession and prayer, a focus on the family and the spiritual role of women, and sudden, emotional conversion—and took them into virtually every town and city in the North. On one day in New York City in 1841, 4,000 people took the temperance "pledge." The average annual consumption of spirits fell from about 5 gallons per person in 1830 to about 2 gallons in 1845.

Evangelical reformers also reinforced the traditional moral foundations of the American work ethic. Laziness, drinking, and other wasteful habits could not be cured by Benjamin Franklin's patient methods of self-discipline, they argued. Instead, people had to experience the profound change of heart achieved only in religious conversion. With God's grace would come the determination to turn from drink, sloth, and sin. Then even the poorest family could look forward to a prosperous new life. Through such means, evangelical Protestantism reinforced the sense of common identity between the business elite and the middle class and implanted a commitment to individual enterprise and moral discipline among many wage earners. Religion and the ideology of social mobility served as a powerful cement, holding society together in the face of the massive changes brought by the spread of industrial enterprise and the market economy.

CHAPTER 10 TIMELINE	
1765	James Hargreaves invents spinning jenny
1782	Oliver Evans develops automated flour mill
1790	Samuel Slater opens a cotton mill in Providence, Rhode Island
1807	Robert Fulton launches the *Clermont*
1810s	Beginning of Cotton Kingdom in Old Southwest
1814	Boston Manufacturing Company opens Waltham cotton mill
1817	Erie Canal begun
1819	Cast-iron plow invented
1820	Minimum price of federal land reduced to $1.25 per acre
1820s	Women become textile operatives Building workers seek ten-hour day Rise of Benevolent Empire
1824	Congress passes major protective tariff *Gibbons v. Ogden* promotes interstate trade
1828	Protective tariff raised
1830s	Expansion of western commercial cities Class-segregated urban neighborhoods Growth of temperance movement Charles Grandison Finney begins Rochester revival
1833	National Road crosses Ohio River

CHAPTER 11

A DEMOCRATIC REVOLUTION, 1820–1844

- Democratizing Politics, 1820–1829
- The Jacksonian Presidency, 1829–1837
- Class, Culture, and the Second Party System

The Economic Revolution transformed the lives of millions of Americans. In the old traditional society most white people had lived and worked together in close-knit communities, and their institutions—the family, the village or urban neighborhood, the artisan's shop, the religious congregation, and the town meeting—had functioned well. But geographic expansion and economic change pushed many people out of those intimate settings and divided society along class lines. The new world was less predictable, less personal, and far more complicated.

To address the problems of the new society, Americans turned not only to evangelical religion but also to democratic politics. In the early years of the nation the slogan had been *republicanism*, rule by property-owning "men of TALENTS and VIRTUE." By the 1820s the watchword had become *democracy*, power exercised by party politicians elected by the people as a whole. "That the majority should govern was a fundamental maxim in all free governments," declared Martin Van Buren, the most talented of the new breed of middle-class professional politicians. By uniting Americans from different classes and regions, the new democratic political parties held together an increasingly fragmented social order.

DEMOCRATIZING POLITICS, 1820–1829

Expansion of the franchise was the most dramatic expression of the democratic revolution. Beginning in the late 1810s, one state after another revised its constitution to remove property qualifications, giving ordinary farmers and wage earners the franchise and laying the foundation for the rise of mass politics. Whatever its flaws, the emerging American political system was the most democratic in the world; nowhere else did ordinary men have so much political power.

The Rise of Popular Politics

In the old agricultural society, wealthy notables—northern landlords, slave-owning planters, and seaport merchants—dominated the political system. As former Supreme Court Justice John Jay put it in 1810, "Those who own the country are the most fit persons to participate in the government of it." The notables managed local elections by building up an "interest": lending money to small farmers, buying supplies from storekeepers and artisans, and treating their workers or tenants to rum at election time. An outlay of £5 for refreshments, an experienced poll watcher told an office seeker, "may produce about 100 votes." As Martin Van Buren, whose father was a tavern keeper, knew from personal experience, this gentry-dominated system excluded men of modest means who lacked land, wealth, and "the aid of powerful family connections."

The first assaults on the old deferential order came in the West. As small-holding farmers and ambitious laborers settled the trans-Appalachian region, they broke free of control by the gentry; "no white man or woman will bear being called a servant," reported a traveler in Ohio. The constitutions of the new states of Indiana (1816), Illinois (1818), and Alabama (1819) prescribed a broad male franchise. Armed with the vote, ordinary citizens usually elected middling men to local and state offices. A well-to-do migrant in Illinois was surprised to find that his plowman "was a colonel of militia, and a member of the legislature." Once in public office, men from modest backgrounds responded to the demands of their constituents, making it easier for farmers to claim "squatters' rights" to unoccupied land, restricting imprisonment for debt, and keeping taxes low.

To deter migration to the West and unrest at home, the elites in most eastern states grudgingly accepted a broader franchise. Responding to reformers who condemned property qualifications as a "tyranny" that endowed "one class of men with privileges which are denied to another," Maryland extended the vote to all adult men in 1810. By the mid-1820s only a few states—North Carolina, Virginia, Rhode Island—required the ownership of freehold property for voting. Others, such as Ohio and Louisiana, limited suffrage to men who paid taxes or served in the militia, but a majority of the states had instituted universal white manhood suffrage.

Popular pressure brought major revisions in the state constitutions of Connecticut, Massachusetts, and New York. Between 1818 and 1821 popularly elected conventions wrote new charters that reapportioned legislatures on the basis of population and instituted more democratic forms of local government, such as the election rather than the appointment of judges and justices of the peace.

The politics of democracy was more complex and contentious than the politics of deference. Newly powerful entrepreneurs and speculators demanded government assistance and protection for their business enterprises and used their wealth to elect friendly candidates and lobby for legislation. Bankers sought charters and opposed limits on interest rates; land speculators petitioned for roads and canals to enhance the value of their holdings and demanded the eviction of squatters. Other Americans entered the political arena for religious and cultural reasons. In 1828 evangelical Presbyterians in Utica, New York, campaigned for town ordinances to restrict secular activities on Sunday; in response, a local Universalist attacked this effort at coercive reform, calling for "Religious Liberty."

The rise of the political party allowed the voices of such ordinary voters to be heard. Political "factions" and "parties" had been condemned as antirepublican by the Founders and had no place in state constitutions or the federal constitution. But as the power of notables declined, the political party emerged as the central element in the American system of government. The new parties were disciplined organizations run by professional politicians from middle-class backgrounds, especially lawyers and journalists. To some observers, they resembled the mechanical innovations of the Industrial Revolution, political "machines" that, like a well-designed textile loom, wove the diverse threads of social groups and economic interests into an elaborate tapestry—a coherent legislative program.

Martin Van Buren of New York was the chief architect—and advocate—of the emerging system of party government. Between 1817 and 1821 Van Buren created the first statewide political machine, the Albany Regency; a few years later the "Little Magician" organized the first nationwide political party, the Jacksonian Democrats. In each case Van Buren repudiated republican principles that disparaged political parties as dangerous to the commonwealth. Indeed, the opposite was true. "All men of sense know that political parties are inseparable from free government," Van Buren argued, because they checked the government's "disposition to abuse power . . . [and] the passions, the ambition, and the usurpations of individuals."

One key to Van Buren's success as a politician was his systematic use of the *Albany Argus* and other party newspapers to promote a *platform* and drum up the vote. *Patronage* was even more important, for the awarding of state jobs gave Van Buren a greater "interest" than any landed aristocrat—some 6,000 appointments to the legal bureaucracy of New York (judges, justices of the peace, sheriffs, deed commissioners, and coroners) carrying salaries and fees worth $1 million. Finally, Van Buren insisted on party *discipline*, requiring state legislators to follow the majority decisions of a party meeting, or *caucus*. On one crucial occasion, Van Buren pleaded with seventeen Republicans to "magnanimously sacrifice individual preferences for the general good" and rewarded their loyalty with patronage and a formal banquet where, an observer wrote, they were treated with "something approaching divine honors."

The Election of 1824

The advance of political democracy disrupted the old system of national politics managed by leading notables. The aristocratic Federalist party virtually disappeared, and the Republican party broke up into competing factions. As the election of 1824 approached, no fewer than five candidates, all calling themselves Republicans, campaigned for the presidency. Three were veterans of President James Monroe's cabinet: Secretary of State John Quincy Adams, the son of John Adams; Secretary of War John C. Calhoun; and Secretary of the Treasury William H. Crawford. The fourth candidate was Speaker of the House Henry Clay from Kentucky, and the fifth was General Andrew Jackson, now a senator from Tennessee. Although Crawford had been selected as the "official" nominee by a poorly attended caucus of the Republicans in Congress, the other candidates refused to accept that result.

Instead, they introduced democracy to national politics by seeking support among ordinary voters. Thanks to democratic reforms, eighteen of the twenty-four states used popular elections (rather than a vote of the state legislature) to choose members of the electoral college. Thus, in three-quarters of the states the struggle for the presidency became literally a "popularity" contest won by the candidate who commanded the most support among the voters and thus among the electors.

The battle was closely fought. Thanks to his diplomatic success as secretary of state, John Quincy Adams enjoyed national recognition. Henry Clay framed his candidacy around the *American System*, a national program of tariffs and internal improvements to promote economic growth. Rejecting Clay's plan for an activist central government, William Crawford of Georgia promised strong support for the rights of the states, a position that enhanced his popularity in the South. Recognizing Crawford's strength in his home region, John C. Calhoun of South Carolina switched to the vice-presidential race and endorsed Andrew Jackson for the presidency.

As the hero of the Battle of New Orleans, Jackson embodied the nationalistic pride that had swelled in the wake of the War of 1812. Born in the Carolina backcountry, Jackson had settled in Nashville, Tennessee, where he had formed ties to influential families through his marriage and his career as an attorney, cotton planter, and slaveowner. His reputation as a man of civic virtue and "plain solid *republican utility*" attracted many voters, and his rise from common origins fit the tenor of the new democratic age. Nominated for the presidency by the Tennessee legislature, Jackson soon commanded nationwide support.

Still, Jackson's strong showing in electoral college surprised most political leaders. He received 99 electoral votes; Adams, 84 votes; Crawford (struck down by a stroke during the campaign), 41; and Clay, 37. Since no candidate had received an absolute majority, the Constitution specified that the House of Representatives would choose the president from among the three leading contenders. This requirement hurt Jackson because many congressmen were horrified at the thought of a rough-hewn westerner and blunt general in the White House; following Henry Clay, they feared Jackson as a "military chieftain." Personally out of the race, Clay resolved to use his powers as Speaker to thwart Jackson's election. By the time the House met in February 1825, Clay had put together a coalition of representatives from New England and the Ohio Valley that voted Adams into the presidency. Adams showed his gratitude by appointing Clay secretary of state, the traditional steppingstone to the highest office.

Clay's appointment was a fatal mistake for both men. John C. Calhoun accused Adams of thwarting the will of the people by using "the power and patronage of the Executive" to select his successor. It was, he wrote, "the most dangerous stab, which the liberty of this country has yet received." Jacksonians in Congress, their numbers increased by the election results, condemned Clay for arranging this "corrupt bargain" and vowed he would never become president.

The Presidency of John Quincy Adams, 1825–1829

As president, Adams called for bold leadership. "The moral purpose of the Creator," he told Congress, was to use the president and every other public official to "improve the conditions of himself and his fellow men." To that end, Adams embraced the American System of national economic development proposed by Henry Clay: (1) a protective tariff to stimulate manufacturing, (2) federally subsidized internal improvements (roads and canals) to aid commerce, and (3) a national bank to provide a uniform currency and control credit.

Adams's policies favored his most loyal supporters, the business elite of the Northeast, and assisted entrepreneurs and commercial farmers in the West. They won little support in the South, which opposed tariffs, and among smallholding farmers, who feared powerful banks. From his deathbed, Thomas Jefferson condemned Adams for promoting "a single and splendid government of [a monied] aristocracy . . . riding and ruling over the plundered ploughman and beggared yeomanry." Other politicians objected on constitutional grounds. In 1817 President Madison had vetoed Calhoun and Clay's Bonus Bill (which would have used federal funds to build projects in various states), arguing that it exceeded the national government's constitutional powers, and Adams's program was even more ambitious. There was little public support for an active national government; most politically aware Americans believed that the state governments should assume the primary responsibility for economic development. A hostile Congress defeated most of Adams's proposals, approving only a

John Quincy Adams (1767–1848)
This famous photograph of Adams, taken about 1843, suggests his tenacity and moral commitment, attributes that hindered his effectiveness as president. Ignoring congressional opposition, Adams tried to implement Clay's American System of national mercantilism, a policy that led to the creation of the Democratic party and his defeat in the election of 1828.

few navigation improvements and a short extension of the National Road from Wheeling, Virginia, into Ohio.

The most far-reaching battle of the Adams administration came over tariffs. In 1824, a new tariff had imposed a protective tax of 35 percent primarily on imported manufactures—iron goods and woolen and cotton cloth—and Adams and Clay wanted even higher duties to protect eastern manufacturers. When Van Buren and his Jacksonian allies took control of Congress in 1827, they supported higher tariffs, but for different reasons. By raising tariffs on raw materials and agricultural imports, they hoped to help smallholding farmers. But Van Buren's main objective was to bolster Jackson's prospects in the Middle Atlantic states, which he needed to carry in the 1828 election. "I fear this tariff thing," warned Thomas Cooper of South Carolina; "by some strange mechanical contrivance . . . it will be changed into a machine for manufacturing Presidents, instead of broadcloths, and bed blankets."

Disregarding southern opposition, northern Jacksonians enacted the Tariff of 1828, which raised duties on raw materials *and* manufactures. To win support for Jackson in New York, Pennsylvania, Ohio, and Kentucky, Van Buren and his allies proposed tariffs on flax, hemp, iron, lead, molasses, and raw wool. But to push those rates through Congress, they had to meet the demand of northeastern representatives for a duty of about 50 percent on imported cloth.

The new tariff enraged the South, which gained nothing from the new legislation. As the world's cheapest producer of raw cotton, the South did not need a protective tariff, and by raising the price of British manufactures, the tariff cost southern planters about $100 million a year. They had to buy either high-cost American manufactures, thus enriching northeastern businesses and workers, or highly taxed British goods, thus paying the cost of the national government. This was "little less than legalized pillage" declared an Alabama legislator; with equal fervor other southern politicians denounced the new legislation as the "Tariff of Abominations."

However, most southerners did not blame their tariff woes on Jackson and refused to vote for Adams, who supported not only high tariffs but also the land rights of native Americans in the South. In 1825 U.S. commissioners and a faction of the Creek people had concluded a treaty that ceded the remaining Creek lands in Georgia. When the Creek National Council repudiated the treaty as fraudulent, Governor George M. Troup vowed to take the lands by force. Defying Adams's efforts to help the Indians, Troup attacked the president as a "public enemy . . . the unblushing ally of the savages," and Congress extinguished Creek land titles in Georgia, forcing most of the Creeks to leave the state.

Elsewhere, Adams's primary weakness was political. He was a patrician, the last notable to serve in the White House, and he acted the part: aloof, haughty, paternalistic. Ignoring his waning popularity, Adams failed to use patronage to reward his supporters; indeed, he allowed hostile politicians to keep their appointed positions as long as they were competent. In 1828 Adams "stood" for reelection, telling supporters, "If my country wants my services, she must ask for them."

Martin Van Buren and the professional politicians handling Jackson's campaign had no reservations about "running" for office. Now a senator from New York, Van Buren created the first national campaign organization. His goal was to re-create the old Jeffersonian coalition, uniting farmers and artisans (the "plain Republicans of the North") with the southern slaveowners who had voted Jefferson, Madison, and Monroe into the presidency. John C. Calhoun, Jackson's semiofficial running mate, brought his South Carolina allies into Van Buren's party, and Jackson's close friends in Tennessee rallied voters in the Old Southwest to the cause. With strong direction from above, state leaders orchestrated a newspaper campaign (in New York, fifty Van Burenite papers declared for Jackson on the same day) and mobilized local groups to run mass meetings, torchlight parades, and barbecues to excite public interest. They celebrated Jackson's frontier origins and rise to wealth and fame without the advantages of birth, education, or political intrigue. Old Hickory—the nickname came from the toughest American hardwood tree—was a "natural" aristocrat, a self-made man.

Initially the Jacksonians called themselves Democratic-Republicans, but as the campaign wore on, they became Democrats. The name conveyed their message. The republic, Jacksonians charged, had been corrupted by "special privilege," which they would root out and replace by the rule of the majority—the democracy. "Equality among the people in the rights conferred by government," Jackson would declare, was the "great radical principle of freedom."

Jackson's message appealed to a variety of social groups. His hostility to special privileges for business corporations and to Clay's American System won support among urban workers and artisans in the Northeast who felt threatened by industrialization. In the Southeast and the West, Old Hickory's well-known animus toward native Americans reassured white farmers who favored Indian removal. On the controversial Tariff of Abominations, Jackson benefited from the financial boost it gave to Pennsylvania ironworkers and western farmers; at the same time, he declared his support for a "judicious" tariff, appealing for southern votes by suggesting that the existing rates were too high.

The Democrats' strategy of seeking votes from a wide variety of social and economic groups worked like a charm. In 1824, only about a fourth of the eligible electorate had voted; in 1828, more than half went to the polls, and they voted overwhelmingly for Jackson. The senator from Tennessee received 178 of 261 electoral votes and became the first president from the West, indeed from any state other than Virginia and Massachusetts. The massive outpouring of popular support for Jackson frightened the northern business elite. When the new president came to Washington, warned ex-Federalist Daniel Webster, he would "bring a breeze with him. Which way it will blow, I cannot tell. . . . My *fear* is stronger than my *hope*." Watching an unruly crowd clamber over the elegant furniture in the White House to shake the hand of the newly inaugurated president, Supreme Court Justice Joseph Story lamented that "the reign of King 'Mob' seemed triumphant."

THE JACKSONIAN PRESIDENCY, 1829–1837

Political democracy—a broad franchise, a disciplined political party, and policies tailored to specific social groups—had carried Andrew Jackson to the presidency. Jackson used that popular mandate to enhance his authority; invoking the sovereignty of the people, he attacked Clay's American System and proposed a different—and more limited—vision of the role of the national government.

Jackson's Political Agenda

To decide policy, Jackson relied primarily on an informal group of advisers, his so-called Kitchen Cabinet. Its most influential members were Francis Preston Blair of Kentucky, who edited the *Washington Globe*; Amos Kendall, also from Kentucky, a Treasury Department official who helped Jackson write many of his state papers; Roger B. Taney of Maryland, who became attorney general and then chief justice of the United States; and, most influential, Secretary of State Martin Van Buren.

Republican Majesty . . . and Mobs

When Andrew Jackson came to Washington in 1829, he threatened the authority of traditional leaders. Writing to her son, the Washington socialite Margaret Bayard Smith revealed her anxiety about popular democracy.

The inauguration . . . was . . . an imposing and majestic spectacle. . . . Thousands and thousands of people, without distinction of rank, collected in an immense mass around the Capitol, silent, orderly, and tranquil. . . . The door from
the Rotunda opens, preceded by the marshall surrounded by the judges of the
Supreme Court, the old man [President Jackson] with his grey hair, that crown
of glory, advances, bows to the people, who greet him with a shout that rends
the air. . . . After reading his speech, the oath was administered to him by the
chief justice. The marshall presented the Bible. The president took it from his
hand, pressed his lips to it, laid it reverently down, then bowed again to the
people. Yes, to the people in all their majesty—and had the spectacle closed
here, even Europeans must have acknowledged that a free people, collected in
their might, silent and tranquil, restrained solely by a moral power, without a
shadow around of military force, was majesty, rising to sublimity, and far sur-
passing the majesty of kings and princes, surrounded with armies and glitter-
ing in gold. . . .

[But at the White House reception] . . . what a scene did we witness!! The
majesty of the people had disappeared, and [instead] a rabble, a mob . . . scrambling, fighting, romping. . . . The president, after having literally been nearly
pressed to death . . . escaped to his lodgings at Gadsby's. Cut glass and bone
china to the amount of several thousand dollars had been broken in the struggle to get refreshments. . . . Ladies and gentlemen only had been expected at
this [reception], not the people *en masse*. . . . [The] rabble in the president's
house brought to my mind descriptions I had read of the mobs in the Tuileries
and at Versailles [during the French Revolution].

SOURCE: M. B. Smith to J. B. H. Smith, March, 1829, Smith Family Correspondence, Library of Congress.

Following Van Buren's practice in New York, Jackson used patronage to
create a loyal and disciplined party. He insisted on rotation in office: when a
new administration came to power, bureaucrats would have to leave government service and return "to making a living as other people do." Dismissing
the argument that forced rotation would eliminate expertise, Jackson suggested that most public duties were "so plain and simple that men of intelligence may readily qualify themselves for their performance." William L.
Marcy, a New York Jacksonian, put it more bluntly, telling a Senate committee
that government jobs were like the spoils of war and that there was "nothing
wrong in the rule that to the victor belong the spoils of the enemy." Using the

policy of rotation as a *spoils system*, Jackson dispensed government jobs to win support for his legislative program.

Jackson's main priority was to block Clay's American System and overthrow laws that had expanded the powers of the national government. Responding to western supporters who argued that the "voice of the people" called for "economy in the expenditures of the Government," Jackson rejected federal support for most internal improvements. In 1830 he vetoed a bill that would have extended the National Road from Maysville, Ohio, to Lexington, Kentucky, arguing that it was "an infringement of the reserved powers of states." Then Jackson turned his attention to two other parts of the American System: protective tariffs and the national bank. Those issues were so complex and politically charged that it took years of effort—and great political skill— for Jackson to emerge triumphant, but by the end of his two terms in office the American System lay in disarray.

The Tariff and Nullification

The Tariff of 1828 had helped Jackson win the presidency, but it saddled him with a major political crisis. The fiercest opposition to the tariff was in South Carolina, whose slaveowners suffered from chronic insecurity. South Carolina was the only state with an African-American majority—56 percent of the population in 1830—which made it more like Jamaica or Barbados than the rest of the South. Like their West Indian counterparts, South Carolina planters lived in fear of slave rebellions and, by the late 1820s, the forced abolition of slavery. The British Parliament was about to end slavery in the West Indies (and did so in August 1833), and South Carolina planters worried that the U.S. government might do the same. To prevent that outcome, that state's leaders tried to limit the power of the federal government, choosing the tariff as their target.

The crisis began in 1832, when Congress ignored southern demands to repeal the Tariff of Abominations and placed high duties on cloth and iron. In November, leading planters and politicians in South Carolina called a state convention, which boldly adopted an Ordinance of Nullification. The Ordinance declared the tariffs of 1828 and 1832 null and void, forbade the collection of those duties in the state after February 1, 1833, and threatened secession if the federal government tried to collect them.

South Carolina's act of nullification rested on the constitutional arguments developed in a tract published in 1828, *The South Carolina Exposition and Protest*. Written anonymously by Vice-President John C. Calhoun, the *Exposition* challenged the proposition that majority rule lay at the heart of republican government. "Constitutional government and the government of a majority are utterly incompatible," Calhoun wrote. "An unchecked majority is a despotism." To devise a mechanism to check congressional majorities, Calhoun turned to the arguments advanced by the Antifederalists of the 1780s and by Jefferson and Madison in the Kentucky and Virginia resolutions of 1798. Developing a constitutional theory that states' rights advocates would use well was "subversive of the rights of the States." Using the vocabulary of the American Revolution, he attacked the Second Bank as "dangerous to the liberties of the people," a nest of special privilege and monopoly power that promoted "the advancement of the few at the expense of the many . . . the farmers, mechanics, and laborers." Finally, the president evoked popular support by stressing the heavy investment in the Bank's stock by British aristocrats; such a powerful institution should be *"purely American,"* he declared.

Jackson's attack on the Bank carried him to victory in the presidential election of 1832. Rejecting Calhoun as a nullifier and a snob (because of his refusal to welcome Mrs. Peggy Eaton, a cabinet wife, into Washington society), Jackson took a new vice-presidential running mate, Martin Van Buren. Together, Old Hickory and the Little Magician overwhelmed Henry Clay, who headed the National Republican ticket, by 219 to 49 electoral votes. Jackson's most fervent supporters were farmers and workers whose lives had been disrupted by price fluctuations or falling wages. But many promoters of economic growth were also Jacksonians. State bankers welcomed the demise of the Second Bank, and thousands of middle-class Americans—lawyers, clerks, shopkeepers, artisans—cheered his attacks on privileged corporations. They wanted equal opportunity to rise in the world.

Immediately after his reelection Jackson launched a new attack on the Second Bank, which still had four years left on its charter. He appointed Roger B. Taney, a strong opponent of corporate privilege, secretary of the Treasury and had him withdraw the government's gold and silver from the Bank and deposit it in state institutions, which critics called his "pet banks." To justify this abrupt (and probably illegal) act, Jackson claimed that the recent election had given him a mandate to destroy the Second Bank. It was the first time a president had claimed that victory at the polls allowed him to act independently of Congress.

The "Bank War" continued to escalate. In March 1834, Jackson's opponents in the Senate passed a resolution written by Henry Clay censuring the president and warning of despotism: "We are in the midst of a revolution, hitherto bloodless, but rapidly descending towards a total change of the pure republican character of the Government, and the concentration of all power in the hands of one man." Nicholas Biddle sharply reduced loans by the Second Bank, creating a brief recession. But Jackson and Taney refused to recharter the Second Bank, and in 1836 it became a state bank in Pennsylvania, still a wealthy institution but one without public responsibilities.

Jackson had destroyed both national banking—the creation of Alexander Hamilton—and the American System of protective tariffs and internal improvements favored by John Quincy Adams and Henry Clay. The result was a profound change in the policies and powers of the national government. "All is gone," observed a Washington newspaper correspondent. "All is gone, which the General Government was instituted to create and preserve."

Not quite all, for in certain respects Jackson enhanced the powers of the national government and the president. He stood firmly for the Union during the nullification crisis, threatening the use of military force, and he greatly expanded the authority of the nation's chief executive, using the rhetoric of popular sovereignty to declare that "the President is the direct representative of the American people." Jackson's legacy as chief executive, like those of other great presidents, was complex and rich.

Indian Removal

The status of the native American peoples was as difficult an issue as the tariff and the Bank, and it also raised issues of federal versus state power. In the late 1820s, white voices throughout the West called for the removal of Indians and their resettlement west of the Mississippi River. Removal was also favored by many eastern whites, including those who were sympathetic to the native American peoples; in their view it was a humane way to protect them from direct competition with a superior race.

Jackson endorsed Indian removal in his first inaugural address in 1829 and soon began to implement it. The Old Southwest was the home of the so-called Five Civilized Tribes: the Cherokee and Creeks in Georgia, Tennessee, and Alabama; the Chickasaw and Choctaw in Mississippi and Alabama; and the Seminole in Florida. During the War of 1812, Jackson's expeditions against the Creeks had forced them to relinquish millions of acres. But Indian peoples still controlled vast tracts of land, and some of them, especially mixed-blood Christian Cherokee, had adopted European institutions and values. By the 1820s the mixed-blood Cherokee had created a centralized political system, a thriving agricultural economy, and a wealthy slaveowning class (see Chapter 8). Neither the mixed-blood Cherokee cotton planters nor the full-blood traditionalists wanted to leave their lands.

Cherokee preferences carried no weight with Jackson, a committed Indian fighter (and alleged Indian hater). In 1827 the Cherokee adopted a constitution and proclaimed themselves a separate nation within the United States. In response, the Georgia legislature declared that the Cherokee were merely a collection of individuals who were tenants on state-owned land. Upon becoming president, Jackson threw his support to Georgia, withdrawing the federal troops that had protected Indian enclaves there and in Alabama and Mississippi; the states, he argued, were sovereign within their borders.

Jackson then pushed through the Indian Removal Act of 1830, which offered native Americans land west of the Mississippi in exchange for their ancestral holdings. To encourage native Americans to accept these terms, Jackson instructed his agents to promise that in the West "their white brothers . . . will have no claim to the land" so that they "can live upon it, they and all their children, as long as grass grows and water runs." Unwilling to fight against well-armed federal troops and land-hungry American settlers, some seventy Indian peoples negotiated treaties; taken together, those agreements exchanged 100 million acres of land in the East for $68 million and 32 million acres in the West.

As Jackson pursued Indian removal, the Cherokee carried their case to the Supreme Court. They had claimed status as a "foreign nation" under the U.S.

Constitution, but in *Cherokee Nation v. Georgia* (1831), Chief Justice John Marshall denied the claim of national independence. Speaking for a majority of the justices, Marshall declared that Indian peoples enjoyed only partial autonomy and defined them as "domestic dependent nations." However, in *Worcester v. Georgia* (1832), Marshall sided with the Cherokee, voiding Georgia's extension of state law over them and holding that Indian nations were "distinct political communities, having territorial boundaries, within which their authority is exclusive . . . [and this is] guaranteed by the United States." But Jackson had no interest in protecting the Cherokee and reputedly responded, "John Marshall has made his decision; now let him enforce it."

Jackson was determined to force removal. In 1832 he dispatched troops to dislodge Chief Black Hawk and his Sauk and Fox followers from rich farmland along the Mississippi River in western Illinois. Rejecting Black Hawk's offer to surrender, the American army pursued him into the Wisconsin Territory. There, on August 3, the pursuit ended in the brutal eight-hour-long Bad Axe Massacre,

Black Hawk (1767–1838)
"It was here that I was born—and here lie the bones of many friends and relatives," Black Hawk declared in 1830. "I . . . could never consent to leave it." To protect his ancestral village in Illinois, Black Hawk mobilized Sauk and Fox warriors and forcibly resisted the Indian Removal Act. (Courtesy of the Gilcrease Institute)

which took the lives of 850 of Black Hawk's 1,000 warriors. During the next five years a combination of diplomatic pressure and military power forced virtually all the remaining Indian peoples to move west of the Mississippi.

The Cherokee and the Seminole mounted the greatest resistance. The Cherokee repudiated a treaty that had been signed by a minority faction and refused to leave their lands. By the treaty deadline in May 1838, only 2,000 of the 17,000 Cherokee had departed. During the summer Martin Van Buren, who had succeeded Jackson as president, ordered General Winfield Scott to enforce the treaty. Scott's army rounded up about 14,000 Cherokee and forcibly marched them 1,200 miles to the new Indian Territory (present-day Oklahoma), an arduous journey they remembered as the Trail of Tears (see Map 11.1). Along the way 3,000 Indians died of starvation and exposure. Only the Seminole remained in the Old Southwest. Aided by runaway slaves, many of whom had married into the tribe, the Seminole in Florida fought a guerrilla war into the 1840s against federal

MAP 11.1

The Removal of Native Americans
Between 1820 and 1840 the U.S. government concluded treaties with native Americans in the East, assigning them lands west of the Mississippi River. During the 1830s the Five Civilized Tribes of the Old Southwest (the Cherokee, Chickasaw, Choctaw, Creeks, and Seminole) were forced to move to reservations in the Indian Territory, the present-day state of Oklahoma; other eastern tribes were settled in Kansas.

troops and the state militia. Using military power, the national government had asserted its control over the Indian peoples and forced their removal to the West.

The Jacksonian Legacy

The Jacksonian Democrats used their newfound political power to infuse American institutions with their principles. The process began in 1835, when, after the death of John Marshall, Jackson appointed his close associate Roger B. Taney as chief justice of the Supreme Court. During his long tenure (1835–1864), Taney persuaded the Court to give constitutional legitimacy to Jackson's policies of antimonopoly and states' rights.

Thus, in the landmark case of *Charles River Bridge Co. v. Warren Bridge Co.* (1837), Taney undermined the legal position of chartered monopolies by ruling that the legislative charter held by the Charles River Bridge Company did not convey an exclusive, monopolistic right, since none was explicitly stated. Instead, the legislature retained the power to charter a competing bridge company. As Taney put it: "While the rights of private property are sacredly guarded, we must not forget that the community also has rights, and the happiness and well-being of every citizen depends on their faithful preservation." This decision qualified John Marshall's interpretation of the contract clause in cases such as *Dartmouth College v. Woodward* (1819), which had emphasized the binding nature of public charters and had limited the power of states to alter or repeal them (see Chapter 9). It also encouraged competitive enterprise, opening the way for legislatures to charter railroads that would compete with existing canal and turnpike companies.

Other decisions by the Taney Court retreated from Marshall's nationalist interpretation of the commerce clause and enhanced the regulatory role of state governments. For example, in *Mayor of New York v. Miln* (1837) the Taney Court ruled that New York State could use its "police power" to inspect the health of arriving immigrants. The Taney Court also restored to the states some of the economic powers they had exercised before 1787. In *Briscoe v. Bank of Kentucky* (1837) the Court approved the issuance of currency by a bank owned and controlled by the state of Kentucky, ruling that it did not violate the provision (in Article I, Section 10, of the U.S. Constitution) that forbade states from issuing "bills of credit."

Jacksonian Democrats mounted their own constitutional revolution in the states. Between 1830 and 1860 twenty states called conventions to revise their basic charters, greatly enhancing their democratic aspects. Most states extended the vote to all white men and reapportioned their legislatures on the basis of population. They brought government "near to the people" by cutting the number of appointed posts and mandating the election of most officials, including sheriffs, justices of the peace, and judges. Most constitutions also implemented Jacksonian ideals by prohibiting states from granting special charters to corporations or extending loans or credit guarantees to private businesses. "If there is any danger to be feared in a republican government," declared a New Jersey Democrat, "it is the danger of associated wealth, with special privileges." Finally, the Jacksonian constitutions protected taxpayers by setting strict limits on state indebtedness and encouraging judges to enforce them. As a New York reformer put it, "We will not trust the legislature with the power of creating indefinite mortgages on the people's property." Just as Jackson had undermined the American System of government subsidies on the national level, his disciples in the states subverted the "commonwealth" philosophy of economic development that depended on chartered monopolies and legislative assistance. Declaring that "the world is governed too much," Jacksonians embraced a small-government, laissez-faire outlook that allowed more decisions to be made by ordinary people acting in the marketplace and the voting booth.

CLASS, CULTURE, AND THE SECOND PARTY SYSTEM

The rise of the Democrats and Jackson's tumultuous presidency sparked the creation in the mid-1830s of a second national party—the Whigs. For the next two decades Whigs and Democrats dominated American politics, forming what historians call the Second Party System. Many evangelical Protestants became Whigs, while most Catholics and nonevangelical Protestants joined the Democrats. The two parties competed fiercely for votes, debating issues of economic policy, class power, and moral reform and offering Americans a clear choice between political programs.

The Whig Persuasion

The Whig party began in Congress in 1834, when opponents of Andrew Jackson banded together to protest his policies and high-handed actions. They took the name *Whigs* to identify themselves with the pre-Revolutionary American and British parties—also called Whigs—that had opposed the arbitrary actions of King George III and previous monarchs. The Congressional Whigs charged that "King Andrew I" had violated the Constitution through "executive usurpation." Led by Senators Webster of Massachusetts, Clay of Kentucky, and Calhoun of South Carolina, the Whigs gradually elaborated their plan for the nation's future. During the election of 1836 they formulated a party platform and sought votes among evangelical Protestants and upwardly mobile middle- and working-class citizens in the North.

The Whigs did not preach a message of economic equality. They believed that it was natural for individuals to have different abilities and acquire different amounts of wealth. They reconciled an economic hierarchy with republican ideals by exalting *equality of opportunity*; pointing to the relative absence of permanent distinctions of class and status among white citizens of the United States, they argued that "this is a country of *self-made men*." Like the Federalists, the Whigs envisioned a political world dominated by men of ability and wealth. Unlike the Federalists, they wanted an elite chosen by talent, not birth.

"BORN TO COMMAND."

OF VETO MEMORY.

HAD I BEEN CONSULTED.

KING ANDREW THE FIRST.

A Whig Cartoon
"Attacking the president as "KING ANDREW THE FIRST," this political cartoon accuses Andrew Jackson of acting like an arbitrary monarch and trampling on the principles of the Constitution. Seeking to turn democratic fervor to the advantage of the Whig party, the caption asked: "Shall he reign over us, or shall the PEOPLE RULE?" (Collection of the New-York Historical Society)

Inspired by a republican Constitution and Christian principles, this select group would govern in the best interests of all the people.

The Whigs also justified elite rule by celebrating the role played by enterprising entrepreneurs and activist governments in increasing the nation's wealth. Suggesting that industrialization had increased social harmony, they welcomed the investments of "moneyed capitalists" as increasing the "chances of improvement to those who had little" and providing "bread, clothing and homes to the poor." As the Whig Congressman Edward Everett told a Fourth of July crowd in Lowell, Massachusetts, there was a "holy alliance" among laborers, owners, and governments. Many workers agreed, especially those holding jobs in the New England textile factories and Pennsylvania iron mills that benefited from state subsidies and protective tariffs. To continue economic progress, Everett and northern Whigs called for a return to the American System of Henry Clay and John Quincy Adams.

Southern Whigs had a different perspective. They condemned Jackson's "executive usurpation" and advocated rapid economic development but opposed the nationalism of the northern Whigs and their belief in high tariffs and social fluidity. Indeed, Calhoun argued that the northern Whig ideal of equal opportunity was contradicted by the reality of slavery and industrial capitalism. "A conflict between labor and capital" was inevitable, he argued, urging southern slaveowners and northern factory owners to unite in a defensive alliance against their common foe: the working class composed of enslaved blacks and propertyless whites.

Most Whig leaders rejected Calhoun's class-conscious vision. "A clear and well-defined line between capital and labor" might fit the slave South or class-ridden Europe, Daniel Webster admitted, but in the North "this distinction grows less and less definite as commerce advances." Webster emphasized the growing importance of the northern middle class, which, attracted by the promise of upward mobility, was becoming the backbone of the Whig party. In the election of 1834 the Whigs won a majority in the House of Representatives by appealing to prosperous farmers, small-town merchants, and skilled industrial workers in New England, New York, and the new communities along the Great Lakes. Those voters were attracted to the Whigs' ideology of individual mobility and commitment to moral reform. Many of them had previously been Anti-Masons, members of a powerful but short-lived political movement directed against the secret Order of Freemasonry. Picking up on Anti-Masonic themes—temperance, equality of opportunity, evangelical religious values—Whigs favored legal curbs on the sale of alcohol and local by-laws that preserved Sunday as a day of worship.

Henry Clay carried the Whig message into the Ohio and Mississippi valleys, where it appealed to farmers, bankers, and shopkeepers who favored public investment in roads, canals, and bridges. But support for the Whigs in the South was fragmentary, resting more on the appeal of specific policies than on agreement with the Whigs' social vision. For example, many nonslaveholding whites in the backcountry voted Whig to break the grip over state politics held by rich planters, most of whom were Democrats. Yet a significant minority of wealthy planters became Whigs, especially those who had invested heavily in railroads, banks, and factories and had close ties to northern markets and New York capitalists. Finally, some states' rights Democrats in Virginia and South Carolina shared former Vice-President Calhoun's anger at Andrew

Jackson's threat to use force to suppress nullification and, like him, joined the Whigs in protest.

In the election of 1836, the Whigs faced Martin Van Buren, the architect of the Democratic party and Jackson's handpicked successor. Van Buren emphasized his and Jackson's opposition to the American System and support for "equal rights." But the Little Magician also promised to preserve American liberty from the coercion implicit in the Whig program of moral reform. He declared himself an "inflexible and uncompromising opponent" of the use of government power to restrict slavery, as many antislavery activists and some Whigs were demanding, and opposed similar plans to enforce temperance or change social mores. The Whigs ran three regional candidates, hoping to garner enough electoral votes to throw the election into the House of Representatives, which they controlled. The plan failed. The Whig tally—73 electoral votes collected by William Henry Harrison of Ohio, 26 by Hugh L. White of Tennessee, and 14 by Daniel Webster—fell far short of Van Buren's 170 votes. Still, the size of the popular vote for Whig candidates—49 percent of the total—showed that the party's message of economic improvement and moral uplift had appealed not only to middle-class Americans but also to farmers and workers with little or no property.

Labor Politics and the Depression of 1837–1843

In seeking the votes of workers, Whigs had to compete with the workingmen's parties that had sprung up in fifteen states between 1827 and 1833. Rising prices and stagnant wages had lowered the standard of living of many urban artisans and wage earners, who feared what they called "the glaring inequality of society." Thus, the Working Men's party in New York City demanded the abolition of private banks, chartered monopolies, and imprisonment for debt. Philadelphia workers demanded higher taxes on the wealthy and a system of universal publicly financed education so that their children could advance into the ranks of the propertied. In 1834 the Working Men's party persuaded the Pennsylvania legislature to authorize free, tax-supported schools.

The ideology underlying the workingmen's parties was artisan republicanism, which called for a society in which (as the radical Democrat Orestes Brownson put it) "instead of one man's working for another and receiving wages thereof, all men will be independent proprietors, working on their own capitals, on their own farms, or in their own shops." This vision led workers to demand "equal rights" and attack legislation that created chartered corporations and monopolistic banks "for the benefit of the rich and the oppression of the poor." "The only safeguard against oppression," argued William Leggett, a leading member of the New York Loco-Foco (Equal Rights) party, "is a system of legislation which leaves to all the free exercise of their talents and industry."

At first the workingmen's parties did well in urban areas, but divisions over policy and voter apathy soon took a toll. By the mid-1830s most politically active

AMERICAN VOICES

New York Seamstresses Organize

W*orking long hours to earn $1.25 a week, most New York City seamstresses lived in poverty. When clothing contractors cut piecework rates in 1831, the seamstresses organized the United Tailoresses Society, adopted a "bill" of wages, and, as this speech by the society's treasurer, Lavinia Waight, indicates, found a common identity as workers and women.*

That females are imposed upon, and oppressed in almost every stage of action to which the circumstances of their existence render them liable, is a fact, that . . . requires only the reiteration of cases. . . .

Are not females in the first place excluded from equal liberality in the circumstances of their education, incapacitated for the duties of legislation and other matters of like importance, in which, you will all allow, they are equally interested? . . . Why should not women be engaged in the duties of trade and legislation? to whom shall I put the question? to those helpless and oppressed beings who are, and have been, blindfolded by a cunning and designing policy, from a fair view of their own interests?

Shall I then question the lords and tyrants of the world, and the monopolizers of all interest? It is unnecessary. Look to the baneful effects that a degraded and major portion of mankind exhibit to your view. Shall I ask *Nature* if the physical inequalities which she has made, furnish a cause for these evils? or shall I argue from her decrees, a total reversion of the present degraded order of things?

These remarks may be thought by some . . . irrelevant to the immediate purposes of this meeting. I have thought them important links in the chain of oppressions against the truly dominated *weaker sex.* . . .

SOURCE: *New York Daily Sentinel*, February 17, 1831, reprinted in Gerda Lerner, *The Female Experience: An American Documentary* (Bloomington: Indiana University Press, 1977). pp. 278–279.

workers had joined the Democratic party, and they continued to agitate against monopolies, banks, and imprisonment for debt. They also condemned protective tariffs, which gave "bounties to particular interests," and supported legislation placing taxes on the personal property of the wealthy: stocks, bonds, machinery, and furniture. At the same time they shifted their attention to the workplace, taking advantage of the shortage of skilled labor to create new unions in small cities and General Trade Union federations in New York City and Philadelphia.

Employers responded to worker agitation by attacking the union movement. In 1836 clothing manufacturers in New York City agreed not to hire workers belonging to the Union Trade Society of Journeymen Tailors and circulated a list—a so-called blacklist—of its members. The employers also brought lawsuits to overturn *closed shop* agreements that required them to hire only union members. They argued that such contracts violated the common law and, in New York State, legislative statutes that prohibited "conspiracies" in restraint of trade.

Judges usually agreed. In 1835, the New York Supreme Court found that a shoemaker's union in Geneva had illegally caused "an industrious man" to be "driven out of employment." "It is important to the best interests of society," the court declared, "that the price of labor be left to regulate itself." When another court upheld a conspiracy verdict against a New York City tailor's union, a crowd of 27,000 people demonstrated outside city hall and tailors circulated handbills proclaiming that the "Freemen of the North are now on a level with the slaves of the South." In 1836 popular demonstrations encouraged local juries to acquit shoemakers in Hudson, New York, carpet makers in Thompsonville, Connecticut, and plasterers in Philadelphia of similar conspiracy charges. The resistance of workers and their supporters had preserved the unions from legal attack.

At this juncture, the Panic of 1837 threw the American economy into disarray. The Panic began early in 1837, when the Bank of England, needing to increase the domestic supply of specie to bolster the British economy, sharply curtailed the flow of money and credit to America. For the previous decade and a half, British manufacturers and investors had stimulated the American economy, providing southern planters with credit to expand cotton production and purchasing millions of dollars of canal bonds in northern

The Panic of 1837
With their once prosperous economy mired in a deep recession, these New Yorkers had little to celebrate on Independence Day in 1837. This cartoon assails Democratic economic policies by illustrating their results (from right to left): sheriffs auctioning off a debtor's property, mechanics clamoring for work, a mother begging, and disheartened laborers turning to the bottle.

states. As the British economy faltered and textile mills cut their purchases, American cotton prices declined sharply, setting off a financial panic. Unable to collect the debts owned by planters, southern banks closed their doors or refused new requests for credit. By late March a number of New York and Philadelphia mercantile firms had declared bankruptcy, undermining faith in paper bank notes. When more and more customers demanded gold and silver, banks suspended specie payments. Deprived of credit, businesses had to cut production, and so trade, manufacturing, and farming slid into decline. "This sudden overthrow of the commercial credit and honor of the nation" had a "stunning effect," observed Henry Fox, the British minister in Washington. "The conquest of the land by a foreign power could hardly have produced a more general sense of humiliation and grief." Soon the crisis engulfed state governments as tax revenues and canal tolls fell. Nine states defaulted on bonds issued to finance canal building; others declared a moratorium on debt payments, undermining British confidence in the American economy and cutting the flow of new investment. Bumper crops during the late 1830s drove down cotton prices even further, bringing more bankruptcies.

The American economy fell into a deep depression. By 1843 canal construction had dropped 90 percent and prices nearly 50 percent; unemployment rose, reaching almost 20 percent of the work force in seaports and industrial centers. From his pulpit, Henry Ward Beecher described a land "filled with lamentation . . . its inhabitants wandering like bereaved citizens among the ruins of an earthquake, mourning for children, for houses crushed, and property buried forever."

By creating a surplus of skilled workers, the depression devastated the labor movement. In 1837, 6,000 masons, carpenters, and other building-trade workers lost their jobs in New York City, depleting the membership of unions and destroying their bargaining power. By 1843 most local unions and all the national labor organizations had disappeared, along with their newspapers and other publications.

However, two events during the depression years improved the long-term prospects of the labor movement. One was a major legal victory. In *Commonwealth v. Hunt* (1842), Chief Justice Lemuel Shaw of Massachusetts upheld the rights of workers to form unions and enforce a closed shop. Shaw, one of the great jurists of the nineteenth century, overturned common-law precedents by making two critical rulings: (1) a union was not an inherently illegal organization, and (2) union members could legally attempt to enforce a closed shop, even by striking. Shaw's opinion was generally accepted by courts in other states, so that unions were free to organize. However, judges (who were mostly Whigs) found other methods, such as court injunctions, to restrict strikes and boycotts. Labor's second success was political. Continuing Jackson's effort to attract workers to the Democratic party, in 1840 President Van Buren signed an executive order establishing a ten-hour day for federal employees. Significantly, this achievement came after the unions had lost their power in the marketplace, underlining the fact that the struggle between labor and capital—like conflicts over tariffs, banks, and internal improvements—had moved into the political arena.

"Tippecanoe and Tyler Too!"

The depression had a major impact on American politics. Because few people understood the workings of the international economy, many Americans blamed the Democrats for the depression. In particular, they derided Jackson for destroying the Second Bank and issuing the Specie Circular of 1836, which required western settlers to use bullion to pay for land purchases and appeared to trigger the financial panic. Van Buren refused to revoke the Specie Circular or take other actions to reverse the downturn. Holding to his philosophy of limited government, he advised Congress that "the less government interferes with private pursuits the better for the general prosperity." As the depression continued, this laissez-faire outlook commanded less and less political support.

Worse, Van Buren's major piece of economic legislation, the Independent Treasury Act of 1840, actually delayed recovery. In 1833 Van Buren had opposed Jackson's decision to place the government's gold and silver in various state banks. Now he condemned the "pet bank" system as corrupt favoritism and, with great difficulty, won approval for a government-run Independent Treasury to handle public funds. However commendable as a political reform, the Independent Treasury cut economic expansion by pulling federal specie out of state banks (which had used it to back loans) and putting it in government vaults (where it did no good at all).

Determined to exploit Van Buren's weakness, the Whigs organized their first national convention and nominated William Henry Harrison of Ohio for the presidency. A military hero of the Battle of Tippecanoe and the War of 1812, Harrison was well advanced in age (he was sixty-eight) and had little political experience. But the Whig leaders in Congress, Clay and Webster, did not want a strong president; they planned to have Harrison rubber-stamp their program for protective tariffs and a national bank. Party strategists such as Thurlow Weed of New York had chosen Harrison primarily because of his military record and western background, promoting him as the Whig version of Andrew Jackson. An unpretentious, amiable man, Harrison warmed to that task, telling voters that Whig policies were "the only means, under Heaven, by which a poor industrious man may become a rich man without bowing to colossal wealth."

The election of 1840 turned more on style than on substance. Whig pamphleteering, songfests, parades, and well-orchestrated mass meetings dominated the campaign, establishing a new political style. Recognizing the importance of women in evangelical churches and reform organizations, Whigs hailed Harrison as "a good Sunday school . . . church going man," invited "the ladies" to political meetings, and called on women to infuse government and society with "pure morality." Whig speakers assailed "Martin Van Ruin" as a manipulative politician with aristocratic tastes—a devotee of fancy wines and elegant clothes, as indeed he was—and praised Harrison (actually the son of a wealthy planter who had signed the Declaration of Independence) as a self-made soldier and statesman who lived in a simple log cabin and enjoyed hard cider, a drink of the common man.

The 1840 election became the great "log-cabin" campaign, the first election in American history in which two national parties competed for the loyalties of a mass electorate. Articles in the Democrat *Washington Globe* and the Whig *National Intelligencer* carried the parties' messages in the nation's capital and the articles were then reprinted in local Jacksonian and Whig newspapers in thousands of crossroads towns. The Democrats relied on party discipline to bring out the vote, while the Whigs drew on the wealth of the business elite to orchestrate their carnival-like campaign. More than 80 percent of the eligible electorate went to the polls in 1840 (up from less than 60 percent in 1832 and 1836). Heeding the Whig slogan "Tippecanoe and Tyler Too," they voted Harrison into the White House and gave the Whigs a majority in Congress.

The Whig triumph was short-lived. One month after his inauguration, Harrison died of pneumonia and the nation got "Tyler Too." Vice-President John Tyler of Virginia, who became president, was not a typical Whig. Tyler had joined the Whig party primarily because he opposed Jackson's stance against nullification; on economic issues he was an Old Republican, sharing Jackson's hostility to the Second Bank and the American System. Acting

The Log-Cabin Campaign, 1840
During the Second Party System, politics became more democratic as ordinary people voted for candidates who shared their values and life styles. The stars in the corner of this homemade campaign flag evoke patriotism, while the central image falsely portrays William Henry Harrison as a poor frontier farmer.

more like a Democrat than a Whig, Tyler vetoed bills that would have raised tariffs and created a new national bank. Also like Jackson, Tyler favored the West and the common man, and he approved the Preemption Act of 1841, which allowed American citizens and immigrants to stake a free claim to 160 acres of federal land. If they built a house on the property and improved the land, they could purchase it later at the standard price of $1.25 an acre. The act helped cash-poor settlers and accelerated the pace of westward expansion.

The split between Tyler and the Whigs gave the Democrats time to regroup. The party vigorously recruited supporters among subsistence farmers in the North and smallholding planters in the South. It cultivated the votes of the urban working class and was particularly successful among Irish and German Catholic immigrants, whose numbers had increased rapidly during the 1830s. Thanks to these recruits, the Democrats remained the majority party: in most parts of the nation, their program of equal rights, states' rights, and cultural liberty was more attractive than the Whig platform of economic nationalism, moral reform, and individual mobility.

The continuing struggle between Whigs and Democrats, each claiming to speak for "the people," completed the democratic revolution. The United States now boasted universal suffrage for white men as well as a highly organized system of representative government that was responsive to ordinary citizens. In their scope and significance for American life, these political innovations matched the economic advances of the industrial and market revolutions.

CHAPTER 11 TIMELINE

1810s	Revision of state constitutions Van Buren creates disciplined party in New York
1825	John Quincy Adams elected president by House; advocates Henry Clay's American System
1827	Philadelphia Working Men's Party organized
1828	Tariff of Abominations Andrew Jackson elected president *The South Carolina Exposition and Protest*
1830	Jackson vetoes extension of the National Road Indian Removal Act
1831	*Cherokee Nation v. Georgia*
1832	Bad Axe Massacre of Sauk and Fox Jackson vetoes rechartering of Second Bank South Carolina nullifies Tariff of 1832
1833	Force Bill and Compromise Tariff
1834	Whig Party formed by Clay, Calhoun, and Webster
1835	Roger Taney named chief justice
1837	*Charles River Bridge Co. v. Warren Bridge Co.* Panic of 1837 begins depression of 1837–1843
1838	Trail of Tears
1840	Log-cabin campaign
1841	Tyler succeeds Harrison as president Preemption Act
1842	*Commonwealth v. Hunt* allows trade unions

CHAPTER 12

THE FERMENT OF REFORM, 1 8 2 0 – 1 8 6 0

- Individualism
- Communalism
- The Women's Movement
- Abolitionism

The whirlwind pace of economic and political change in the 1820s and 1830s transformed the way Americans thought about themselves as individuals and as a society. Increasing opportunities encouraged many men and women in the North to believe that they could improve not just their personal lives but society as a whole. Some dedicated themselves to the cause of reform. Such individuals, the Unitarian minister Henry W. Bellows warned, had committed themselves to the pursuit of "an object, which in its very nature is unattainable—the perpetual improvement of the outward condition."

Many obstacles stood in their way. America's social order was still rigidly divided by race and gender as well as wealth and religious belief. As much as it liberated some individuals, the new industrial and market economy meant new forms of social control for others, such as the strict work discipline imposed on factory operatives. Even the rise of democratic politics brought new forms of social discipline. Party members were "safe if they face the enemy," remarked one of Martin Van Buren's political lieutenants, "but the first man we see *step to the rear*, we *cut down*."

In fact, the first wave of American "improvers," the benevolent reformers of the 1820s, had seized on social discipline as the answer to the nation's ills, championing regular church attendance, temperance, and the strict moral codes of the evangelical churches. Then, in the 1830s and 1840s, a more powerful reform wave spilled out of these conservative channels and washed over

American society, threatening to submerge traditional institutions and values. Mostly middle-class in origin, the new reformers propounded a variety of radical ideals—extreme individualism, communitarianism, sexual equality, the immediate emancipation of slaves—and demanded action to satisfy their visions. The result was a far-reaching intellectual and culture debate that challenged the premises of the American social order.

INDIVIDUALISM

Individualism was a term coined by Alexis de Tocqueville in 1835 following his visit to the United States. He used it to describe people who were "no longer attached to each other by any tie of caste, class, association, or family." Unlike the French political philosopher, who feared the disintegration of society, the New England transcendentalist Ralph Waldo Emerson celebrated this liberation of the individual from the constraints of traditional social ties and institutions. Emerson's vision of individual freedom influenced thousands of ordinary Americans and a generation of important artists and writers.

Emerson and Transcendentalism

Emerson was the leading spokesman for transcendentalism, an intellectual movement rooted in the religious soil of New England. Its first advocates were spiritually inclined young men, often Unitarian ministers from well-to-do New England families, who questioned the constraints imposed by their Puritan heritage. For inspiration they turned to Europe, drawing on a new conception of self and society known as Romanticism. Romantic thinkers, such as the English poet Samuel Taylor Coleridge, rejected the ordered, rational world of the eighteenth-century Enlightenment. Instead they tried to capture the passionate character of the human spirit and sought deeper insights into the mysteries of existence. Drawing on ideas borrowed from the German philosopher Immanuel Kant, English romantics and Unitarian radicals believed that behind the concrete world of the senses was an *ideal* world. To reach this deeper reality, people had to "transcend," or go beyond, the ways in which they normally comprehended the world. By tapping mysterious intuitive powers, people could soar beyond the limits of ordinary experience and gain mystical knowledge of ultimate and eternal things.

Emerson, like his father a Unitarian minister, emerged as the intellectual leader of the transcendentalist movement in 1832 at the age of twenty-nine. After a crisis of conscience he resigned his Boston pulpit, rejecting organized religion in favor of individual moral insight. Emerson moved to Concord, Massachusetts, and turned to writing essays and lecturing, supported in part by a legacy from his first wife. His subject was what he called "the infinitude of the private man," the idea of the radically free individual.

The young philosopher saw people as being trapped in inherited customs and institutions. They wore the ideas of people from earlier times—the tenets of New England Calvinism, for example—as a kind of "faded masquerade" and needed to shed those values and practices. "What is a man born for but to be a Reformer, a Remaker of what man has made?" he asked. For Emerson, an individual's remaking depended on the discovery of his or her own "original relation with Nature," an insight that would lead to a mystical private union with the "currents of Universal Being." The ideal setting for such a discovery was solitude under an open sky, among nature's rocks and trees.

Emerson's genius lay in his capacity to translate vague ideas into examples that made sense to ordinary middle-class Americans. His essays and lectures conveyed the message that all nature was saturated with the presence of God—a pantheistic spiritual outlook that departed from traditional Christian doctrine and underlay his attack on organized religion. Emerson also criticized the new industrial society, predicting that a preoccupation with work, profits, and the consumption of factory-made goods would drain the nation's spiritual energy. "Things are in the saddle," Emerson wrote, "and ride mankind."

The transcendentalist message of inner change and self-realization reached hundreds of thousands of people, primarily through Emerson's writings and lectures. Public lectures had become a spectacularly successful new way of spreading information and fostering discussion among the middle classes. Beginning in 1826, the American Lyceum attempted to "promote the general diffusion of knowledge" by organizing lecture tours by all sorts of speakers—poets, preachers, scientists, reformers—and soon took firm hold, especially in the North. In 1839, 137 local Lyceum groups in Massachusetts invited lecturers to their towns during the fall and winter "season" to speak to more than 33,000 subscribers. Among the hundreds of lecturers on the Lyceum circuit, Emerson was the most popular. Between 1833 and 1860 he gave 1,500 lectures in more than 300 towns in twenty states.

Emerson's celebration of the liberated individual tapped currents that already ran deep in his middle-class audiences. The publication of Benjamin Franklin's *Autobiography* in 1818 had given Americans a down-to-earth model of an individual seeking "moral perfection" through self-discipline. Charles Grandison Finney's account of his conversion experience in 1823 also pointed in Emersonian directions. Finney, the foremost business-class evangelist, pictured his conversion as a mystical union of an individual, alone in the woods, with God. And the great revivalist's message, like that of Emerson, affirmed the importance of individual action. As Finney put it, "God has made man a moral free agent," endowing individuals with the ability to determine their spiritual as well as their worldly fate.

Emerson's Literary Influence

Emerson took as one of his tasks the remaking of American literature. In an address entitled "The American Scholar" (1837) the philosopher issued a literary declaration of independence from the "courtly muse" of old Europe. He urged American writers to celebrate democracy and individual freedom and find inspiration not in the doings and sayings of aristocratic courts but in the "familiar, the low . . . the milk in the pan; the ballad in the street; the news of the boat; the glance of the eye; the form and gait of the body."

A young New England intellectual, Henry David Thoreau (1817–1862), heeded Emerson's call by turning to the American environment for inspiration. Shortly after his graduation from college, Thoreau turned away from society and embraced self-reliance and the natural world, building a cabin at the edge of Walden Pond near Concord, Massachusetts, and living alone there for two years. In 1854 he published *Walden, Or Life in the Woods*, an account of his spiritual search for meaning that went beyond the artificiality of life in a "civilized" society:

> I went to the woods because I wished to live deliberately, confront only the essential facts of life, and see if I could not learn what it had to teach, and not, when I came to die, discover that I had not lived.

Although Thoreau's book had little impact outside transcendentalist circles during his lifetime, *Walden* has become an essential text of American literature and an inspiration to those who reject the dictates of society. Its most famous metaphor provides an enduring justification for independent thinking: "If a man does not keep pace with his companions, perhaps it is because he hears a different drummer." Beginning from this premise, Thoreau became an advocate for social nonconformity and a philosopher of civil disobedience.

As Thoreau sought independence and self-realization for men, Margaret Fuller (1810–1850) explored the possibilities of freedom for women. Born into a wealthy Boston family, Fuller learned to read the classic works of literature in six languages and educated her four siblings. After teaching in a girls' school, she became interested in Emerson's ideas and in 1839 began a transcendental "conversation," or discussion group, for elite Boston women. Soon Fuller was editing the leading transcendentalist journal, the *Dial*, and in 1844 she published *Woman in the Nineteenth Century*, which proclaimed that a "new era" was coming for men and women.

Fuller's philosophy began with the transcendental belief that women, like men, had a mystical relationship with God that gave them identity and dignity. It followed that every woman deserved psychological and social independence—the ability "to grow, as an intellect to discern, as a soul to live freely and unimpeded." Thus, she declared, "We would have every arbitrary barrier thrown down" and "every path laid open to Woman as freely as to Man." Embracing that vision, Fuller became the literary critic of the *New York Tribune* and went to Italy to report on the Revolution of 1848. Her adventurous life brought an early death; returning to the United States at the age of forty, she drowned in a shipwreck. But Fuller's example and writings inspired the rising generation of women reformers.

Another writer who responded to Emerson's call was the poet Walt Whitman (1819–1892). Whitman said that when he first encountered Emerson, he had been "simmering, simmering." Then Emerson "brought me to a boil." Whitman

Margaret Fuller (1810–1850)
This daguerreotype shows Fuller
reading a book and captures her
intense intellectuality and love of
learning. A leading female advocate
of transcendentalism, Fuller used its
doctrines to declare the moral and
intellectual equality of women.

had been a journalist, an editor of the *Brooklyn Eagle* and other newspapers, and an active publicist for the Democratic party. But it was poetry that was the "direction of his dreams." In *Leaves of Grass*, first published in 1855 and constantly revised and expanded for almost four decades afterward, he recorded his attempt to pass a number of "invisible boundaries": between solitude and community, between prose and poetry, and even between the living and the dead.

At the center of *Leaves of Grass* is the individual—the figure of the poet, "I, Walt." He begins alone: "I celebrate myself, and sing myself." But because he has what Emerson called an "original relation" with nature, Whitman claims not solitude but perfect communion with others: "For every atom belonging to me as good belongs to you." Whitman was celebrating democracy as well as himself, arguing that a poet could claim a profoundly intimate, mystical relationship with a mass audience. For Emerson, Thoreau, and Fuller the individual had a divine spark. For Whitman the individual had expanded to *become* divine.

The transcendentalists were not naive optimists. Whitman wrote about human suffering with as much passion as he wrote about everything else. Emerson's accounts of the exhilaration that could come in nature were tinged with anxiety. "I am glad," he said, "to the brink of fear." Thoreau's gloomy judgment of everyday life is well known: "The mass of men lead lives of quiet desperation." Still, such dark murmurings were muted in their work, woven into triumphant and expansive assertions that nothing was impossible for an individual who could break free from tradition, law, and other social restraints.

Emerson's influence also reached two great novelists, Nathaniel Hawthorne and Herman Melville, who had more pessimistic visions. They addressed the opposition between individual transcendence and the legitimate requirements of social order, discipline, and responsibility. Both sounded powerful warnings that unfettered egoism could destroy individuals and those around them. Hawthorne's most brilliant exploration of the theme of excessive individualism appeared in his novel *The Scarlet Letter* (1850). The two main characters, Hester Prynne and Arthur Dimmesdale, challenge their seventeenth-century New England community in the most blatant way—by committing adultery and producing a child. The result of their assertion of individual freedom from social discipline is not liberation but degradation—condemnation by the community.

Melville explored the limits of individualism in even more extreme and tragic terms and emerged as a scathing critic of transcendentalism. He made his most powerful statement in *Moby Dick* (1851), the story of Captain Ahab's obsessive hunt for a mysterious white whale that brings death not only to Ahab but to all but one of his crew. Here the quest for spiritual meaning in nature brings death, not transcendence, to the liberated individual who lacks inner discipline and self-restraint.

Moby Dick was a commercial failure. The middle-class audience that was the primary target of American publishers was unwilling to follow Melville into the dark, dangerous realms of individualism gone mad. Readers also were unenthusiastic about Thoreau's advocacy of civil disobedience and Whitman's boundless claims for a mystical union between the man of genius and the democratic mass. What American readers emphatically preferred were the more modest examples of individualism offered by Emerson.

Brook Farm

To escape the constraints of life in industrializing America, transcendentalists and other radical reformers created ideal communities, or *utopias*. They hoped that these planned societies, which organized life in new ways, would allow members to realize their spiritual and moral potential. The most important communal experiment of the transcendentalists was Brook Farm, founded in 1841. Free from the tension and demands of an urban competitive society, its members hoped to develop their minds and souls and uplift society through inspiration. The Brook Farmers supported themselves by selling milk, vegetables, and hay for cash but organized their farming so that they could remain relatively independent of the market.

The intellectual life at Brook Farm was electric. Hawthorne lived there for a time and later used the setting for *The Blithedale Romance* (1852). All the major transcendentalists, including Emerson, Thoreau, and Fuller, were residents or frequent visitors. A former member recalled that they "inspired the young with a passion for study, and the middle-aged with deference and admiration, while we all breathed the intellectual grace that pervaded the atmosphere." Music, dancing, games, plays, parties, picnics, and dramatic readings filled the leisure hours.

If Brook Farm represented intellectual fulfillment, it faltered in achieving economic self-sufficiency. At first most of its members were ministers, teachers, writers, and students who had few productive skills; to succeed it needed practical men and women. A reorganization in 1844 attracted more farmers and artisans but yielded only marginal economic gains. And these changes resulted in a more disciplined routine that, as one resident put it, suppressed "the joyous spirit of youth." After a devastating fire in 1846, the organizers disbanded and sold the farm.

After the failure of Brook Farm the transcendentalists abandoned their attempts to fashion a new system of social organization. Most accepted the brute reality of industrial society and tried to reform it, especially through the education of workers. However, the passion of the transcendentalists for individual freedom lived on in the movement to abolish slavery, which many of them joined.

COMMUNALISM

Even as Brook Farm faded, thousands of Americans joined other communal settlements during the 1840s, primarily in the Northeast and Midwest (see Map 12.1). Most were ordinary people seeking refuge and security from the seven-year economic depression that had begun with the Panic of 1837. But these rural utopias were also symbols of social protest, explicitly challenging the values of the larger society by organizing themselves along socialist lines with common ownership of property or experimenting with unconventional forms of marriage and family life. In questioning acquisitive capitalist values and traditional gender roles, the communalists pointed to major cultural strains in American society.

The Shakers

The Shakers were the first successful American communal movement and dated back to the era of the Revolution. In 1770 Ann Lee Stanley (Mother Ann), a young cook in Manchester, England, had a vision that she was the second incarnation of Christ; four years later she led a band of eight followers to America, where they established a church near Albany, New York. Because of the ecstatic dances that became part of their worship, the sect became known as "Shaking Quakers" or, more simply, "Shakers." After Mother Ann's death the Shakers decided to withdraw from the evils of the world into strictly run communities of believers. They embraced the common ownership of property, accepted government by the church, and pledged to abstain from alcohol, tobacco, politics, and war. Shakers also eliminated marriage and made a commitment to celibacy, in accordance with Mother Ann's testimony against "the lustful gratifications of the flesh as the source and foundation of human corruption."

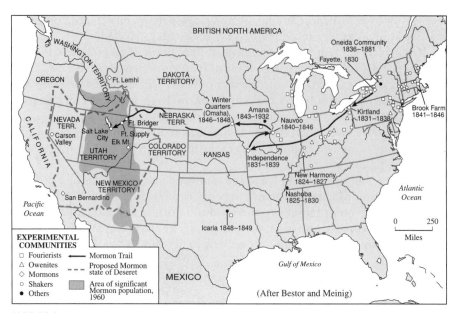

MAP 12.1

Major Communal Experiments before 1860

Some experimental communities sought out frontier locations, but the vast majority simply looked for secluded areas in well-settled regions. The avoidance of the South by these groups is striking. The most successful experimenters by far were the Mormons, who ultimately sought extreme isolation and built an agrarian society in Utah.

The Shakers believed that God was "a dual person, male and female" and that Mother Ann represented God's female element. These doctrines provided the underpinning for their attempt to banish distinctions between the sexes. In practice, Shakers maintained a traditional division of labor between men and women, but they vested the authority for governing each community— in both its religious and its economic spheres—in women and men alike, the Eldresses and Elders.

Beginning in 1787, Shakers founded twenty communities, mostly in New England, New York, and Ohio. Their agriculture and crafts, especially furniture making, acquired a reputation for quality that enabled most of these communities to become self-sustaining and even comfortable. Thanks to this economic success and their ideology of sexual equality, Shaker communities attracted more than 3,000 converts during the 1830s, with women outnumbering men more than two to one. Because Shakers had no children of their own, they had to rely on converts and the adoption of young orphans to replenish their numbers. As these sources dried up in the 1840s and 1850s, the communities stopped growing and eventually began to decline. By the end of the nineteenth century most Shaker communities had disappeared, leaving as their material legacy a distinctive and much-imitated furniture style.

The Fourierist Phalanxes

The rise of the American Fourierist movement in the 1840s was one cause of the Shakers' decline. Charles Fourier (1777–1837) was a French utopian reformer who devised an eight-stage theory of social evolution, predicting the imminent decline of individualism and capitalism. As interpreted by his idealistic American disciple Arthur Brisbane, Fourierism meant "completion of our great political movement of 1776" through new social institutions that would end the "menial and slavish system of Hired Labor or Labor for Wages." In the place of capitalist labor there would be cooperative work and living in groups called *phalanxes*. The members of a phalanx would be its shareholders; they would own all its property in common, including stores and a bank as well as a school and a library. Fourier and Brisbane saw the phalanx as a practical, more humane alternative to the emerging capitalist society and one that would liberate women as well as men. "In society as it is now constituted," Brisbane wrote, "Woman is subjected to unremitting and slavish domestic duties"; in the "new Social Order . . . based upon Associated households," most domestic labor would be eliminated or shared with men.

Brisbane skillfully promoted Fourier's ideas in his influential book *The Social Destiny of Man* (1840), a regular column in Horace Greeley's *New York Tribune*, and hundreds of lectures, many of them in towns along the Erie Canal. These ideas found a receptive audience among educated farmers and craftsmen, who yearned for economic stability and communal solidarity in the wake of the Panic of 1837. In the 1840s Brisbane and his followers started nearly 100 cooperative communities from Massachusetts to Michigan, but almost all were unable to support themselves and quickly collapsed. Despite its failure to establish viable communities, the Fourierist movement was important as an index of both the social dislocation caused by the economic depression and the difficulty of establishing a utopian community in the absence of a charismatic leader or a compelling religious vision.

Noyes and the Oneida Community

The radical minister John Humphrey Noyes was both charismatic and deeply religious. He believed that the Fourierists had failed because their communities lacked the strong religious ethic required for sustained altruism and cooperation and pointed to the success of the Shakers, praising them as the true "pioneers of modern Socialism." Noyes was also attracted by the Shakers' marriageless society and set about creating a community that defined sexuality and gender roles in dramatically new and radical ways.

Noyes was a well-to-do graduate of Dartmouth College who was inspired to join the ministry by the preaching of Charles Finney. When Noyes developed radical doctrines and was expelled from his Congregational Church, he became a leader of "perfectionism." Perfectionism was an evangelical movement that gathered thousands of followers during the 1830s, primarily among religiously minded New Englanders who had settled in New

York. Perfectionists believed that the Second Coming of Christ had already occurred and that people could therefore aspire to perfection in their earthly lives,
attaining complete freedom from sin. Unlike most perfectionists (who lived
conventional personal lives), Noyes believed that the major barrier to achieving
this ideal state was marriage, which did not exist in heaven and should not exist
on earth. "Exclusiveness, jealousy, quarreling have no place at the marriage sup-
per of the Lamb," Noyes wrote. He wanted to reform marriage to liberate individuals from sin, as had the Shakers, but his solution was dramatically different:
instead of Shaker celibacy, Noyes and his followers embraced *complex marriage*—
all the members of his community were married to one another.

Complex marriage was a complex doctrine designed to attain various social goals. Noyes rejected monogamy partly because he wished to free women
from being regarded as the property of their husbands. To give women even
more freedom, he sought to regulate childbirth (urging men to have intercourse without orgasm) and established community nurseries. By freeing
women from endless child bearing and child raising, Noyes hoped to help
them become full and equal members of the community.

In the 1830s Noyes gathered his followers in his hometown of Putney, Vermont, but local opposition to the practice of complex marriage prompted him to
move the community to Oneida, New York, in 1848. By the mid-1850s more
than 200 people were living at Oneida, and it became financially self-sufficient
when the inventor of a highly successful steel animal trap joined the community.
With the profits from the production of traps, Oneida diversified into making sil-
verware with the brand name Community Plate. After Noyes fled to Canada in
1879 to avoid prosecution for adultery, the community abandoned complex
marriage and founded a joint-stock silver manufacturing company, the Oneida
Community, Ltd., which survived well into the twentieth century.

As with the Shakers and Fourierists, the historical significance of Noyes
and his followers lies neither in their numbers nor in their fine crafts but
rather in their effort to create alternative communities that avoided some of
the social and sexual divisions of the emergent capitalist industrial society of
the United States.

The Mormon Experience

Despite their challenge to marriage and family life—two of the most deeply
rooted institutions in American society—neither the Shakers nor the Oneidi-
ans aroused fierce hostility to their social experiments. The case was far different with the Mormons, or the Church of Jesus Christ of Latter-Day Saints,
the most successful by far of all the communal experiments and yet another
alternative to the emerging social order.

The Mormons emerged from the religious ferment that arose among fam-
ilies of Puritan descent who settled along the Erie Canal. The founder of the
Mormon Church was Joseph Smith, a vigorous, powerful individual. Born in
Vermont in 1805, he moved at the age of ten with his very religious but rather

poor farming and shopkeeping family to Palmyra in central New York. In a series of religious experiences that began in 1820, Smith came to believe that God had singled him out to receive a special revelation of divine truth. In 1830 he published *The Book of Mormon*, claiming he had translated it from ancient hieroglyphics on gold plates shown to him by an angel named Moroni. Seeing himself as a prophet to a sinful, excessively individualistic society, Smith organized a church that asserted control over many aspects of life and reaffirmed the primacy of the husband within the family. Like many Protestant ministers, he encouraged his followers to adopt practices central to success in the age of capitalist markets and factories: hard work, saving, and risk taking. Unlike them, Smith placed equal emphasis on a communal framework that would protect the Mormon "New Jerusalem" from outside threats and create a structure for the achievement of human perfection.

Smith struggled for years to establish a sanctuary for his new religion. In the face of persecution in various neighboring settlements, Smith and his growing congregation trekked west, eventually settling in Nauvoo, Illinois, a town they founded on the Mississippi River. By the early 1840s Nauvoo had become the largest utopian community in the United States, with 30,000 inhabitants. But the rigid discipline and secrecy of the Mormons, along with their prosperity, hostility to other sects, and bloc voting in Illinois elections, fueled resentment among their neighbors. Smith turned this resentment into overt hostility when he refused to abide by any Illinois law that he did not approve of personally, asked Congress to turn Nauvoo into a federal territory, and (in 1844) declared himself a candidate for president of the United States.

Moreover, Smith had a new revelation that justified *polygamy*—having more than one wife at the same time. A few Mormon leaders began to practice polygamy, dividing the community from within, while economic and political issues encouraged assaults from without. In 1844 Smith was arrested and charged with treason for allegedly conspiring with foreign powers to create a Mormon colony in Mexico. An anti-Mormon mob stormed the jail where Smith and his brother were being held in Carthage, Illinois, and murdered them.

Now led by Brigham Young, the Mormon elders sought religious independence by leaving the United States to create a new settlement in the western wilderness. In 1846 Young began a phased migration of more than 10,000 people across the Great Plains. (Many of the migrants accepted the practice of polygamy; those who remained in the United States did not. Led by Smith's son, Joseph Smith III, they formed the Reorganized Church of Jesus Christ of Latter-Day Saints, headquartered in Independence, Missouri.) Young's party eventually reached the Great Salt Lake in what was still Mexican territory. Using communal labor and an elaborate irrigation system based on communal water rights, the Mormon pioneers transformed the desert. They quickly spread planned agricultural communities along the base of the Wasatch Range in present-day Utah.

When the United States acquired Utah from Mexico in 1848 (see Chapter 14), Congress rejected a Mormon petition to create a new state, Deseret,

An Illinois "Jeffersonian" Attacks the Mormons

The solidarity of the Mormon community enraged many Illinois residents, who feared the power of the nearly independent city-state at Nauvoo and the 2,000-strong armed "Legion" commanded by Joseph Smith. This letter, probably written by a leading anti-Mormon editor who then published it in his own newspaper, proposes their forcible expulsion from the state.

Mr. Editor,

. . . It is a low pitiable contemptable kind of electioneering, that old Tom Jefferson would have been ashamed of—when a body of men acting under the garb of religion (as the Mormons themselves say they are) shall decide our elections and act together as a body politically, we might as well bid a final farewell to our liberties and the common rights of man.

Now Sir, under all these circumstances, it is high time that every individual should come out and clearly define the position that he occupies. I too am an Anti-Mormon both in principle and in practice. . . . Mr. Editor when I speak harshly of the Mormons . . . I do not mean every individual that advocates the Mormon cause. By no means; that there are some good, law-abiding peaceable citizens belonging to the Mormon profession I verily believe . . . but I am opposed to them because of the unprincipled manner in which the leaders of that fanatical sect, set at defiance the laws of the land . . . (as was the case in Missouri) claiming to be the chosen people of God; not subject to the laws of the state in any respect whatever, and receiving revelations direct from Heaven almost daily commanding them to take the property of the older citizens of the county and confiscate it to the use of the Mormon church. . . .

It was for the commission of such deeds . . . that finally led to their expulsion from that state, and one of the brightest pages in the history of Missouri is that, on which is written "Governor Boggs's exterminating order" directing that the lawless rabble should be driven beyond the limits of the state, or exterminated at their own option. They chose the former, [which was] a most unfortunate thing for the state of Illinois.

SOURCE: David Brion Davis, *Antebellum America: An Interpretive Anthology* (Lexington, Mass.: Heath, 1979), pp. 226–227.

stretching all the way to Los Angeles and San Diego. Instead, it set up the much smaller Utah Territory in 1850, with Young as territorial governor. In 1858 President James Buchanan removed Young from the governorship and, responding to pressure from Christian churches to eliminate polygamy, sent a small army to Salt Lake City. However, the "Mormon War" proved bloodless. Fearing that the forced abolition of polygamy would serve as a precedent for the ending of slavery, Buchanan withdrew the troops. The national govern-

A Mormon Man and His Wives
Only a minority of Mormon men in Utah had more than one wife, and only a few had as
many as this homesteader, who stood to profit from their labor. The cabin, although cramped
for such a large family, is well built with a brick chimney and—a luxury for any pioneer
home—a glass window.

ment did not succeed in pressuring the Utah Mormons to abolish polygamy
until 1890, six years before Utah became a state.

Mormons in both Utah and Missouri had succeeded where other social
experiments and utopian communities had failed. They endorsed the private
ownership of property and encouraged individualistic economic enterprise,
accepting the entrepreneurial spirit of market society. But Mormon leaders
resolutely used strict religious controls to create disciplined communities and
patriarchal families, reaffirming values inherited from the eighteenth century.
This blend of economic innovation, social conservatism, and hierarchical
leadership continued into the twentieth century, creating a prosperous church
with a strong missionary impulse and millions of members.

THE WOMEN'S MOVEMENT

The prominence of gender issues—sexual behavior, marriage, family authority—
among Mormons, Shakers, and Noyesites was the product of a broad shift in
American culture, particularly in the North. After the American Revolution
northern women played a more prominent role in public life, joining religious
revivals and reform movements. Slavery was among the targets of women reformers, and their abolitionist activities created great controversy and made
some of them into feminists. Feminists argued that women had social and political rights as individuals—rights that equaled those of men.

Origins of the Women's Movement

During the American Revolution, upper-class women had demanded greater legal rights for married women and more educational opportunities for their daughters but had been given only a slightly enhanced status as "republican mothers." Subsequently the Economic Revolution presented young farm women with new opportunities for factory labor but imposed new constraints on many middle-class married women, reinforcing their confinement to a "separate sphere" (see Chapter 9). Rather than working as household producers (the traditional roles of the wives of farmers and artisans), middle-class women became full-time providers of household services, such as child care. At the same time, many of these middle-class women achieved greater authority within their families by joining religious revivals and becoming guardians of morality. Such activities bolstered their self-esteem and encouraged them to enlarge their influence over decisions in all areas of family life, including the timing of pregnancies. Publications such as *Godey's Lady's Book* and Catharine Beecher's *Treatise on Domestic Economy* (1841) taught women how to make their homes more efficient and moral and justified a life of middle-class domesticity.

For most middle-class women a greater influence over family life was enough, but some women used their newfound religious authority to increase their involvement outside the home. Moral reform was among the first of their efforts in the public arena. In 1834 a group of middle-class women founded the New York Female Moral Reform Society and elected Lydia Finney, the wife of the evangelical minister Charles Finney, as its president. Its goals were to end prostitution, redeem fallen women, and protect single women from moral corruption. By 1837 the Society had 250 chapters in towns and villages throughout New York State and 15,000 members. Three years later it had grown into a national association, the American Female Moral Reform Society, with 555 chapters throughout the North. Employing only women as its agents, bookkeepers, and staff, the society attempted to provide moral "government" for factory girls, seamstresses, clerks, and servants who lived away from their families. Women reformers even visited brothels, where they sang hymns, offered prayers, searched for runaway girls, and noted the names of clients. They also founded homes of refuge for prostitutes and homeless women and won the passage of laws regulating sexual behavior—including making seduction a crime—in Massachusetts in 1846 and New York in 1848.

Women also turned their energies to the reform of social institutions, working to improve conditions in almshouses, asylums, hospitals, and jails, which grew in number in the 1830s and 1840s. The Massachusetts reformer Dorothea Dix was a leader in these efforts. Outraged that insane women were jailed alongside criminals, Dix persuaded the Massachusetts legislature to expand the state hospital to accommodate the poor and mentally ill. Dix carried her message to other states, persuading legislatures to expand their public hospitals, and nearly secured Congressional legislation that would have set aside 12.5 million acres of public land to support asylums for the insane.

Both as reformers and as teachers, northern women played a major role in education. From Maine to Wisconsin women vigorously supported the movement led by Horace Mann to expand public elementary schools. As secretary of the newly created Massachusetts Board of Education from 1837 to 1848, Mann lengthened the school year; established teaching standards in reading, writing, and arithmetic; and improved instruction by recruiting well-educated women as teachers. The intellectual leader of the new corps of women educators was Catharine Beecher, who founded academies for young women in Hartford and Cincinnati. In a series of publications Beecher argued that "energetic and benevolent women" were the best qualified to impart moral and intellectual instruction to the young. By the 1850s, most teachers were women both because school boards heeded Beecher's arguments and because women could be paid less than men.

Abolitionism and Women

The public accomplishments of moral reformers such as Dix and Beecher inspired other women to assume public roles, and many of them found a cause in the movement to end slavery. During the Revolutionary Era, Quaker women in Philadelphia had established schools for freed slaves, and subsequently many Baptist and Methodist women endorsed religious arguments

The Grimké Sisters
Sarah Moore Grimké (1792–1873) and Angelina Emily Grimké (1805–1879) joined the Philadelphia Female Anti-Slavery Society and began abolitionist lecturing in 1836. They drew crowds of thousands—and scathing criticism for having lost, as some Massachusetts clergymen put it, "that modesty and delicacy . . . which constitutes the true influence of women in society." The Grimké sisters responded with powerful statements protesting male domination of women.

A Feminist Finds Her Voice

In this letter to her friend Lucy Stone, the future feminist leader Antoinette Brown (1825–1921) recounts her confrontation with the president of Oberlin College, the eminent revivalist Charles Grandison Finney, and explores the psychological strain of forging new roles for women.

[June 1848]
Lucy dearest:
The cause of woman is moving on finely here. You know the theological students are required to tell their religious experiences before Prof. Finney. Once or twice when he called for those who had not done so, [James] Tefft mentioned Lettice [Holmes] and me. He looked as though he did not know what to say, and the next time said, "Oh, we don't call upon the ladies." They had all told me we should have to speak, and I felt so badly at what he said that I just began to cry and was obliged to leave the room. . . .

I went over to see him and he certainly seemed to forget that he was talking with a woman. We conversed more than an hour sometimes upon the gravest subjects of philosophy and theology and he expressed himself freely upon the true position of woman . . . that though he did not think she was generally called upon to preach or speak in public because the circumstances did not demand it, still that there was nothing right or wrong in the thing itself and that sometimes she was specially called to speak. . . . A week or two later Professor Finney called upon me to speak in the prayer meeting, and I did so. Told them the exercises of my mind . . . and my determination to preach and speak in public when I was prepared for this. They all seemed surprised and pleased too that I was really expecting to speak.

So, L____, you are going to lecturing, are you? . . . Success to the Truth and to you dearest Lucy so far as you preach it and in the right spirit. I am glad you are going to lecture. . . . Be good, Lucy, be good, and don't be afraid of anybody but speak as though you had a right to.

SOURCE: Nancy Woloch, ed., *Early American Women* (New York: McGraw-Hill, 1997), pp. 273–274. Reproduced with permission of the McGraw-Hill Companies.

against slavery. When William Lloyd Garrison began his radical campaign for *abolition*—the immediate, uncompensated end to slavery—in 1831, a few women rallied to his cause. One of the first Garrisonian abolitionists was Maria W. Stewart, an African-American who spoke to mixed audiences of men and women in Boston in the early 1830s. As the abolitionist movement mushroomed, scores of white women delivered lectures condemning slavery and thousands more conducted home "visitations" to win converts among women and their husbands.

Influenced by abolitionist ideas and their own experience of discrimination, a few women challenged the subordinate status of their sex. The most famous were the abolitionist sisters Angelina and Sarah Grimké. The Grimkés had left their father's South Carolina slave plantation, converted to Quakerism and abolitionism in Philadelphia, and become antislavery lecturers. When some Congregationalist clergymen demanded that they cease speaking to mixed male and female audiences, Sarah Grimké turned to the Christian Bible for justification: "The Lord Jesus defines the duties of his followers in his Sermon on the Mount . . . without any reference to sex or condition," she wrote. "Men and women are CREATED EQUAL! They are both moral and accountable beings and whatever is right for man to do is right for woman." In a debate with Catharine Beecher (who wanted women to exercise power through their domestic activities) Angelina Grimké pushed the argument beyond religion, using Enlightenment principles to claim equal civic rights for women:

> It is a woman's right to have a voice in all the laws and regulations by which she is governed, whether in Church or State. . . . The present arrangements of society, on these points are a *violation of human rights, a rank usurpation of power,* a violent seizure and confiscation of what is sacredly and inalienably hers.

By 1840 the Grimkés were asserting that traditional gender roles amounted to the "domestic slavery" of women. Not all abolitionist women shared that view, but many demanded equality with men within the antislavery movement.

Soon women were using the abolitionist movement as a vehicle to improve the condition of their sex. The most prominent example was the novelist Harriet Beecher Stowe, who in the novel *Uncle Tom's Cabin* (1852) charged that among the greatest moral failings of slavery was its destruction of the slave family and the degradation of slave women. Sojourner Truth, a former slave who lectured to both antislavery and women's rights conventions, hammered home the point that women slaves were denied both basic human rights and the protected separate "sphere" enjoyed by free women. "I have ploughed and planted and gathered into barns, and no man could head me—and ain't I a woman?" she asked. Drawn into public life by abolitionism, thousands of northern women had become firm advocates of greater rights not only for African-Americans but for white women.

The Program of Seneca Falls

The commitment to full civil equality for women emerged during the 1840s as activists devised a pragmatic program of reform. While championing the rights of women, they did not challenge the institution of marriage or even the conventional division of labor within the family. Instead, harking back to the efforts of Abigail Adams and other Revolutionary Era women, they tried to strengthen the legal rights of married women, especially with respect to

The Beecher Family, circa 1859
The Beechers were an impressive family. Lyman (center, seated) was one of the leading Protestant ministers of the nineteenth century, as was his son, Henry Ward (far right). Catharine (second from left) was an influential educator and well-known author who emphasized women's authority within the home. Harriet Beecher (Stowe), pictured at the far left, was an antislavery activist and the author of *Uncle Tom's Cabin*.

property. In 1848 New York adopted legislation giving married women greater control over their own property, and similar laws were enacted in fourteen other states. Affluent men provided crucial support for this legislation. They wanted to protect their spouses' assets in case their businesses went into bankruptcy and to guard against dissolute sons-in-law who might waste their daughters' inheritances.

To push forward the nascent women's movement, Elizabeth Cady Stanton and Lucretia Mott, who had become friends at the World's Anti-Slavery Convention in London in 1840, called a convention in Seneca Falls in upstate New York in 1848. The convention outlined for the first time a coherent program for women's equality. Taking the republican ideology of the Declaration of Independence as a starting point, the delegates declared that "all men and women are created equal" but that "the history of mankind is a history of repeated injuries and usurpations on the part of man toward woman, having in direct object the establishment of an absolute tyranny over her." To persuade

Americans to right this long-standing wrong, they resolved to "use every in-strumentality within our power. . . . We shall employ agents, circulate tracts, petition the State and national legislatures, and endeavor to enlist the pulpit and the press on our behalf." By staking out claims for equality for women in public life, the Seneca Falls convention repudiated the idea that the assign-ment of separate spheres for men and women was the natural order of society.

Although most men dismissed the Seneca Falls Declaration as nonsense, it drew women—and a few radical men—into the movement. During the 1850s conventions of women—at the local, regional, and national levels—hammered out a diverse reform program. They called on churches to revise concepts of female inferiority in their theology and worked for legal changes that would give married women control over their property and earnings, guarantee a mother's custody of her children in the event of divorce or the fa-ther's death, and ensure women's right to sue and testify in court. Finally, and above all else, they began a concerted campaign to win the vote for women. In 1851 a national convention of women declared that suffrage was "the corner-stone of this enterprise, since we do not seek to protect woman, but rather to place her in a position to protect herself."

The struggle for legislation required new tactics and new leaders who had talents as organizers rather than lecturers. The most prominent was Susan B. An-thony. Anthony came from a Quaker family and as a young woman had been an active temperance and antislavery reformer. Her experience in the temperance movement, Anthony explained, had taught her "the great evil of woman's utter dependence on man for the necessary means to aid reform movements." In 1851 she joined the movement for women's rights and forged an enduring friendship with Elizabeth Cady Stanton. Anthony created a network of political "captains," all women, who lobbied the state legislature relentlessly. In 1860 her efforts culminated in a New York law granting women the right to collect and spend their own wages (which fathers or husbands previously could insist on controlling), bring suit in court, and, if widowed, acquire full control of the property they had brought to the marriage. Such successes would provide the basis for more aggressive reform attempts after the Civil War.

ABOLITIONISM

For women as well as men, blacks as well as whites, the dominant American reform movement became the drive to end slavery. In part this focus stemmed from the success of other initiatives: the Second Great Awakening had drawn millions of Americans into churches, temperance was on the rise, hospitals for the sick and mentally ill had been created, and prisons had been reformed. But more important was the new attitude of many northern whites toward the South's "peculiar institution." Early nineteenth-century reformers had criti-cized human bondage as contrary to the tenets of republicanism and liberty. Now abolitionists condemned slavery as a *sin* and saw it as their moral duty to end this violation of God's law.

African Colonization

By 1820 republican-minded reformers had persuaded the northern states to abolish slavery and provide for gradual emancipation. They had also induced Congress to outlaw the importation of enslaved Africans and, in the Missouri Compromise, prohibit slavery in most of the Louisiana Purchase. But the most difficult problem remained untouched: ending slavery in the old South and the border states of Kentucky, Tennessee, and Missouri.

The founders of the American Colonization Society, which included President James Monroe, thought they had the answer. Slaveowners would gradually emancipate their slaves—some 1.5 million people in 1820—and the Society would arrange for their resettlement in Africa. The Society's leaders believed, as Henry Clay put it, that racial bondage had placed Kentucky and the other slaveholding states "in the rear of our neighbors . . . in the state of agriculture, the progress of manufactures, the advance of improvement, and the general prosperity of society."

Slavery had to go, as did the freed slaves. Emancipation without colonization, the influential Kentucky Congressman predicted, "would be followed by instantaneous collisions between the two races, which would break out into a civil war that would end in the extermination or subjugation of the one race or the other." Northerners who joined the Colonization Society had much the same outlook. They regarded the 250,000 free blacks in the northern states as "notoriously ignorant, degraded and miserable, mentally diseased, brokenspirited," as one Society report put it, and hoped they would leave.

However, the American Colonization Society was a dismal failure. Despite appeals to wealthy individuals, churches, and state governments, it raised enough money to purchase freedom for only a few hundred slaves. Most free blacks rejected colonization, agreeing with Bishop Richard Allen of the African Methodist Episcopal Church that "this land which we have watered with our *tears* and our *blood* is now our *mother country.*" Three thousand African-Americans met in Philadelphia's Bethel Church to condemn colonization, declaring that their goal was to advance in American society using "those opportunities . . . which the Constitution and the laws allow to all." In the end, the Society transported only 6,000 African-Americans to Liberia, a colony it established on the west coast of Africa.

Slave Rebellion

Having rejected colonization, free blacks demanded an end to slavery. To build support for emancipation, in 1827 John Russwurm and Samuel D. Cornish began the first African-American newspaper, *Freedom's Journal*, in New York. The Boston agent for the newspaper was David Walker, a free black from North Carolina who made a living selling secondhand clothes. In 1829 Walker published a stirring pamphlet entitled *Appeal . . . to the Colored Citizens* that ridiculed the religious pretensions of slaveholders, justified slave rebellion, and warned white Americans that the slaves would revolt if justice was delayed.

"We must and shall be free. . . . And woe, woe, will be it to you if we have to obtain our freedom by fighting. . . . I do declare that one good black man can put to death six white men." Within a year Walker's *Appeal* had gone through three printings and had begun to reach free blacks in the South.

In 1830 Walker and other African-American activists called a national convention in Philadelphia. The delegates did not adopt Walker's radical position but urged free blacks to use every legal means to improve the condition of their race and asked for divine assistance in breaking "the shackles of slavery."

As Walker was calling for violent black rebellion from Boston, Nat Turner, a slave in Southampton County, Virginia, staged a bloody revolt—a coincidence that had far-reaching consequences. As a child Turner had taught himself to read and had hoped to be emancipated, but a new master forced him into field work and another master separated him from his wife. Turner became deeply spiritual, seeing visions and concluding that he might have been chosen to carry Christ's burden of suffering in a race war. Taking an eclipse of the sun as an omen, Turner plotted with a handful of relatives and close friends to meet the masters' terror with violence of their own. In August 1831, his men killed almost sixty whites, in many cases dismembering and decapitating them. Turner hoped that a vast army of slaves would rally to his cause, but he had mustered only sixty men by the time a white militia dispersed his poorly armed and exhausted followers. Vengeful whites now took slaves' lives at random. One company of cavalry killed forty in two days, putting the heads of fifteen on poles to warn "all those who should undertake a similar plot." Fifty slaves were prosecuted, and twenty were hanged. After hiding for nearly two months, Turner was captured and hanged, still identifying his mission with Christ's.

Deeply shaken by Turner's rebellion, the Virginia legislature debated a bill providing for gradual emancipation and colonization. When the bill was rejected in 1832 by a vote of 73 to 58, the possibility that southern planters would legislate an end to slavery faded forever. Instead, the southern states marched down another path, toughening their slave codes, limiting the movement of slaves, and prohibiting anyone from teaching them to read. They would meet Walker's radical *Appeal* with radical measures of their own.

Evangelical Abolitionism

Frightened by the prospect of a bloody racial revolution and inspired by the antislavery efforts of free blacks, evangelical northern whites launched a moral crusade to abolish slavery. Previously Quakers, along with some Methodists and Baptists, had freed their own slaves and campaigned for gradual emancipation in the North. Now radical Christian abolitionists demanded that southerners free their slaves immediately. The issue was absolute: slaveowners and their supporters were sinning by depriving slaves of their God-given status as free moral agents. If the slaveowners did not repent, the evangelical abolitionists believed, they faced the prospect of revolution in this world and damnation in the next.

The most uncompromising leader of the abolitionist movement during the 1830s was William Lloyd Garrison. A Massachusetts-born printer, Garrison had collaborated in Baltimore during the 1820s with a Quaker, Benjamin Lundy, who published the *Genius of Universal Emancipation*, the leading antislavery newspaper of the decade. In 1830 Garrison went to jail for seven weeks for libeling a New England merchant engaged in the domestic slave trade. Garrison went on to found his own antislavery weekly, *The Liberator*, in Boston in 1831. The next year he spearheaded the formation of the New England Anti-Slavery Society.

From the outset *The Liberator* took a radical stance. Garrison condemned the American Colonization Society, charging that its real aim was to strengthen slavery by removing troublesome African-Americans who were already free. He attacked the U.S. Constitution for its implicit acceptance of racial bondage, labeling it "a covenant with death, an agreement with Hell." And he demanded the immediate abolition of slavery without reimbursement for slaveholders. As time went on, Garrison concluded that slavery was a sign of deep corruption infesting *all* American institutions and called for comprehensive reform of society.

Theodore Dwight Weld, who joined Garrison as a leading abolitionist, came to the movement from the religious revivals of the 1830s. The son of a

William Lloyd Garrison
As this picture suggests, Garrison was an intense and righteous man. In 1854 he publicly burned the Constitution and declared: "So perish all compromises with tyranny." His attack on slavery began a passionate quest to destroy all institutions that prevented individuals—whites as well as blacks, women as well as men—from discovering their full potential.

Congregationalist minister and inspired by Charles Finney, Weld became an advocate of temperance and educational reform. Turning to abolitionism, he worked in northern Presbyterian and Congregational churches, preaching the moral responsibility of all Americans for the denial of liberty to slaves. In 1834 Weld inspired a group of students at Lane Theological Seminary in Cincinnati to form an antislavery society. Weld's crusade gathered force, buttressed by the theological arguments he advanced in *The Bible against Slavery* (1837). Collaborating closely with Weld were Angelina Grimké, whom he married in 1838, and her sister, Sarah.

Weld and the Grimkés provided the abolitionist movement with a mass of evidence in *American Slavery as It Is: Testimony of a Thousand Witnesses* (1839). The book set out to answer a simple question—"What is the actual condition of the slaves in the United States?"—with evidence from southern newspapers and firsthand testimonies. In one account, Angelina Grimké told of a treadmill that slaveowners used for punishment: "One poor girl, [who was] sent there to be flogged, and who was accordingly stripped naked and whipped, showed me the deep gashes on her back—I might have laid my whole finger in them—*large pieces of flesh had actually been cut out by the torturing lash.*" The book sold over 100,000 copies in its first year alone.

In 1833 Weld, Garrison, Arthur and Lewis Tappan, and sixty other delegates, black and white, met in Philadelphia to establish the American Anti-Slavery Society. The Society received financial support from the Tappans, wealthy merchants in New York City. Women abolitionists quickly established their own organizations, such as the Philadelphia Female Anti-Slavery Society, founded by Lucretia Mott in 1833, and the Anti-Slavery Conventions of American Women, formed by a network of local societies in the late 1830s. The women's societies raised money for *The Liberator* and were a major force in the movement, distributing abolitionist literature, collecting tens of thousands of signatures on antislavery petitions, and running schools for free blacks.

Abolitionist leaders developed a two-pronged plan of attack, one part aimed at the general public and the other at politicians. To foster intense public condemnation of slavery, they adopted the tactics of the religious revivalists: large rallies led by stirring speakers, constant agitation by local antislavery chapters, and home visits by agents of the movement. The abolitionists also used the latest techniques of mass communication. Assisted by new steam-powered printing presses, the American Anti-Slavery Society distributed more than 100,000 pieces of literature in 1834. In 1835 the Society launched its "great postal campaign," which flooded the nation, including the South, with a million abolitionist pamphlets. In July 1835 alone abolitionists mailed more than 175,000 items at the New York City post office.

The abolitionists' second strategy was to win support from state and national legislators. In 1835 the American Anti-Slavery Society encouraged local chapters and members to bombard Congress with petitions demanding the abolition of slavery in the District of Columbia, an end to the domestic slave trade, and denial of the admission of new slave states to the Union. By 1838, petitions with nearly 500,000 signatures had arrived in Washington.

This agitation drew thousands of middle-class men and women to abolitionism. During the 1830s the number of local abolitionist societies grew swiftly, from about 200 in 1835 to more than 500 in 1836 and nearly 2,000 by 1840—when they had nearly 200,000 members, including many leading transcendentalists. Emerson condemned the moral failure of a free society that tolerated slavery; Thoreau was even more assertive. In 1846 he protested the Mexican War and slavery by refusing to pay his taxes and submitting to arrest. Two years later he published an anonymous essay entitled "Civil Disobedience" that outlined how individuals, by resisting governments that sanctioned slavery and through loyalty to a higher moral law, could redeem themselves and the state. "A minority is powerless while it conforms to the majority," Thoreau declared, but it becomes "irresistible when it clogs by its whole weight."

Abolitionism Attacked

As Thoreau discerned, the abolitionist crusade had won the wholehearted allegiance of only a small minority—perhaps 10 percent—of white Americans in the North and the sympathy of perhaps twice as many. But men of wealth feared that the abolitionist attack on slave property could turn into a general assault on all property rights. Tradition-minded clergymen warned that the abolitionists threatened the stability of the family by encouraging public roles for women. New York merchants and New England textile producers rallied to the support of their southern customers and suppliers. And many northern wage earners feared that freed slaves willing to work for subsistence wages would pour into northern communities and take their jobs. Moreover, few white northerners believed in civic equality for free blacks. Only five New England states extended suffrage to African-American men, while Connecticut, New Jersey, and Pennsylvania denied them the franchise, as did Ohio, Indiana, and Illinois. Even fewer whites welcomed the prospect of racial mixing and intermarriage.

Moved by such sentiments, northern opponents of abolitionism sometimes turned to violence. Mobs, often led by "gentlemen of property and standing," intimidated free blacks and abolitionists. In 1833 an antiabolitionist mob of fifteen hundred New Yorkers stormed a church in search of Garrison and Arthur Tappan. The next year prominent New Yorkers cheered as a mob of laborers vandalized and set fire to Lewis Tappan's house. Another white mob swept through Philadelphia's African-American neighborhoods, clubbing and stoning residents, destroying homes and churches, and forcing crowds of black women and children to flee the city. In 1835 in Utica, New York, a group of lawyers, local politicians, merchants, and bankers broke up an abolitionist convention and beat several delegates. In the same year a Boston mob dragged Garrison through the streets, threatening to hang him. And two years later in Alton, Illinois, a mob shot and killed an abolitionist editor, Elijah P. Lovejoy.

White southerners reacted to abolitionism with even greater fury. Southern legislatures banned the movement and passed resolutions demanding that northern states follow suit. The Georgia legislature offered a $5,000 reward to anyone who would kidnap Garrison and bring him to the South to be tried for inciting rebellion. In Nashville vigilantes whipped a northern college student for distributing abolitionist pamphlets, and a mob in Charleston attacked the post office and destroyed sacks of abolitionist mail. After 1835, southern postmasters simply refused to deliver mail of suspected abolitionist origin.

Politicians joined the fray. President Andrew Jackson, though a radical on many issues, was a slaveowner and a firm supporter of the southern social order. Jackson privately approved of South Carolina's removal of abolitionist pamphlets from the U.S. mail, and in 1835 he asked Congress to restrict the use of the mails by abolitionist groups. Congress did not comply, but in 1836 the House of Representatives adopted the so-called *gag rule*. Under this rule, which remained in force until 1844, antislavery petitions were automatically tabled when they were received so that they could not become the subject of debate in the House.

Assailed from outside, abolitionists were also divided among themselves. Many antislavery clergymen denounced the public lecturing to mixed audiences by the Grimké sisters and other women as "promiscuous" and immoral. Some male abolitionists left the Anti-Slavery Society because they disagreed with Garrison's broad attack on American institutions.

Garrison grew more radical, supporting pacifism and the abolition of prisons and asylums. Arguing that "our object is *universal* emancipation, to redeem women as well as men from a servile to an equal condition," he demanded that the American Anti-Slavery Society retain a broad platform that supported women's rights. At the convention of the American Anti-Slavery Society in 1840 Garrison precipitated a split with more conservative abolitionists by insisting on equal participation by women and helping to elect Abby Kelley to the organization's business committee. When the movement split, Kelley, Lucretia Mott, and Elizabeth Cady Stanton remained with Garrison in the American Anti-Slavery Society. They recruited new women agents, including Lucy Stone, to proclaim the common interests of enslaved blacks and free women.

Garrison's opponents founded a new organization, the American and Foreign Anti-Slavery Society, which received financial backing from Lewis Tappan. It members worked through their churches to win public support for practical measures against slavery. Other abolitionists turned to electoral politics, establishing the Liberty party and nominating James G. Birney for president in 1840. Birney was a former Alabama slaveowner who had been converted to abolitionism by Theodore Weld and had founded an antislavery newspaper in Cincinnati. Birney and the Liberty party argued that the Constitution did not recognize slavery; that the Fifth Amendment, by barring any

Congressional deprivation of "life, liberty, or property," prevented the federal government from supporting slavery; and that slaves became automatically free when they entered areas of federal authority, such as the District of Columbia and national territories. But Birney won few votes in the election of 1840, and the future of the party and political abolitionism appeared dim.

Coming hard on the heels of popular violence and political suppression, these schisms and electoral failures stunned the abolitionist movement. It had attracted the energies and ideas of thousands of evangelical Protestants, moral reformers, and transcendentalists. But it had aroused the hostility of a substantial majority of the white population, which feared that abolitionism—and the feminist movement that accompanied it—might not reform American society but destroy it. The movement for reform, begun with such confidence in the North in the 1820s, now divided the people of that region and threatened the unity of the nation.

CHAPTER 12 TIMELINE

Year	Event
1817	American Colonization Society founded
1829	David Walker's *Appeal*
1830	Joseph Smith publishes *The Book of Mormon*
1831	William Lloyd Garrison begins publishing *The Liberator* Nat Turner's rebellion
1832	Ralph Waldo Emerson resigns his pulpit New England Anti-Slavery Society founded
1834	New York Female Moral Reform Society established
1836	House of Representatives adopts "gag rule"
1840	Liberty party runs James G. Birney for president
1841	Transcendentalists found Brook Farm Dorothea Dix begins her investigations
1844	Margaret Fuller's *Woman in the Nineteenth Century*
1845	Thoreau withdraws to Walden Pond
1846	Mormons begin trek to Salt Lake
1848	John Humphrey Noyes founds Oneida Community Seneca Falls convention
1851	Herman Melville's *Moby Dick* Susan B. Anthony joins movement for women's rights
1852	Harriet Beecher Stowe's *Uncle Tom's Cabin*
1855	Walt Whitman's *Leaves of Grass*
1858	The "Mormon War"

CHAPTER 13

SECTIONS AND SECTIONALISM, 1840–1860

- The Slave South: A Distinctive Society
- The Northeast: Industry and Culture
- The West: Manifest Destiny

The Economic Revolution increased the wealth of both the North and the South but accentuated long-standing differences between those regions. The North was increasingly industrial and urban, a busy land of movement and markets and individual mobility, while the South remained overwhelmingly agricultural and rural, a vast expanse of white cotton and black slaves. More important, sectional differences were increasingly *felt*, especially in the South. As John C. Calhoun warned in 1850, southerners had come to fear "the long-continued agitation of the slavery question on the part of the North" and the North's growing wealth and political power.

The consciousness of *sectionalism* was more intense and widespread than it had been in the 1790s, when Thomas Jefferson had contested Alexander Hamilton's pronorthern economic program, or the 1830s, when the sections had quarreled over tariffs and the Second Bank. Those were battles over issues. Now the conflict was between different ways of life. By the middle of the nineteenth century northerners and southerners were living in different social systems, with different ways of thinking about the individual and society. Middle-class northerners hailed the new principles of "free labor," individualism, and social mobility; southern slaveowners celebrated the old traditions of slavery, hierarchy, and authority.

Simultaneously, the massive westward migration of Americans shifted the balance of political power to the heartland of the continent, the states of the

337

Mississippi Valley. The emergence of the West as a distinct section created new opportunities—and dangers. Many Americans came to believe that the nation's future lay in the West, that its "Manifest Destiny" was to extend republican institutions to the Pacific Ocean. But whose institutions: those of the North or those of the South? The issue of westward expansion became inextricably entangled with that of slavery and sectional identity.

THE SLAVE SOUTH: A DISTINCTIVE SOCIETY

The South was a complex society based on race and class. White planters grew rich by exploiting the labor of enslaved African-Americans, who numbered one-third of the South's population. Adopting the outlook of a landed gentry, wealthy planters described themselves as natural aristocrats. While yeomen and tenant families contested the dominance of the planter elite, they ultimately stood with it to support "white supremacy."

The Southern Slave Economy

The South's economy grew rapidly between 1830 and 1860. Planters sold more and more tobacco, rice, sugar, and—above all—cotton in Europe. In the 1840s, after the Cotton Kingdom had swept across the Mississippi River into Texas, the South was producing more than two-thirds of the world's cotton and accounted for almost two-thirds of the total value of American exports.

Unlike northern farmers, who profited primarily by selling to domestic consumers and improving farm technology, southern planters grew wealthy by relying on British markets and capital, fresh land, and slavery. The British connection was crucial. The buoyant demand of British textile mills drove up the price of cotton, while British mercantile houses furnished capital for new plantations. The availability of fresh land was equally significant because cotton ruined the soil more quickly than did most other crops. In the early 1850s an observer described Georgia's eastern plantation belt as "red old hills stripped of their native growth and virgin soil, and washed with deep gullies." By 1860 nearly three-fourths of the South's cotton production came from the region's newer plantations—lands stretching from western Georgia to eastern Texas.

Slavery marched west as millions of acres of new land came into production (see Map 13.1). To clear and plant the land quickly and raise the output of their African-American workers, slaveowners devised a new form of work discipline: a gang labor system that resembled factory work. Planters and overseers on plantations with twenty or more slaves organized the hands into disciplined teams, or *gangs*, and assigned them specific tasks. Using the threat of the whip, white overseers and enslaved black drivers worked their gangs at a feverish pace, clearing and plowing the land or hoeing and picking cotton. In 1854 a traveler glimpsed two gangs returning from work on a well-established Mississippi plantation:

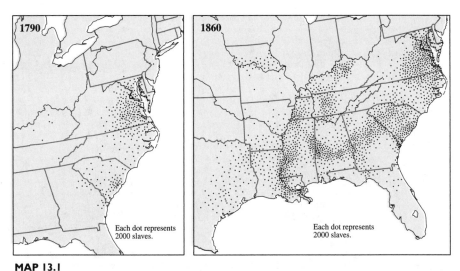

MAP 13.1
Distribution of the Slave Population, 1790–1860
The cotton boom shifted enslaved African-Americans to the Old Southwest. In 1790 most slaves lived and worked on the tobacco plantations of the Chesapeake and in the rice and indigo areas of South Carolina. By 1860 hundreds of thousands were laboring on the cotton and sugar lands of the lower Mississippi Valley and along an arc of fertile cotton land—the "black belt"—sweeping from Mississippi through Georgia.

First came, led by an old driver carrying a whip, forty of the largest and strongest women I ever saw together; they were all in a simple uniform dress of a bluish check stuff, the skirts reaching little below the knee; their legs and feet were bare; they carried themselves loftily, each having a hoe over the shoulder, and walking with a free, powerful swing.

Next marched the plow hands with their mules, "the cavalry, thirty strong, mostly men, but a few of them women."

Thanks to gang labor, fertile western land, and the enormous demand for cotton, slaveowners earned profits on their investments that averaged about 10 percent a year. Even the most successful New England textile mills rarely produced a higher rate of return. But high profits from agriculture created two long-term problems. First, southern investors concentrated their resources in cotton and slaves, so that the percentage of southerners who lived in towns and worked in manufacturing was only half that in the North. The only major cities in the South were the old seaports of Baltimore, Charleston, and New Orleans, which remained predominantly commercial centers.

A second, and more tragic, problem was the low level of education in the South. The wealthy planters who controlled southern society wanted a compliant labor force content with the drudgery of agricultural work. Consequently, they trained most of their slaves as field hands (allowing only a few to learn the arts of the blacksmith, carpenter, and bricklayer) and made little

Harvesting Sugarcane
Growing sugar was arduous work and took the lives of thousands of slaves. In both the West Indies and Louisiana, sugar planters used gang labor to ditch and drain marshlands and plant cane seedlings in long ditches. Harvesting the mature cane and carrying it to the plantation's mill were equally strenuous and, as this watercolor by Franz Holzlhuber shows, were the work of women as well as men.

or no effort to provide blacks, and ordinary whites, with elementary instruction in reading and arithmetic. Some southern states made teaching slaves to read a crime, and no state had a comprehensive system of public schools for whites. As a result, in 1850 most African-Americans and about 20 percent of white southerners were illiterate (compared with less than 1 percent in New England). Lacking cities, factories, and educated workers, the South could not provide a majority of its people with a rising standard of living. In 1860 the per capita income was $141 in the North but only $103 in the South. Enslaved African-Americans and white tenant farmers had little or no property, and landholding yeomen in the back country lacked access to profitable markets. Prosperity was limited primarily to the families—25 percent of the white population—that owned plantations and slaves.

Slaveowning Planters and Yeomen Farmers

Southern society was dominated by planters who owned twenty or more slaves. Making up only 10 percent of all slaveholders (and about 2 percent of whites in the South), they owned about half the slaves. These 10,000 families dominated southern society more completely than the business elite controlled the North. For example, in Alabama in 1850 slaveowners represented only 30 percent of the electorate but 75 percent of the legislators; a fourth of the legislators were large planters who owned fifty or more slaves. Except in the backcountry, most county governments in the South were run by substantial planters, who served as justices of the peace and church vestrymen. The members of this elite married their children to one another, and their sons and daughters became commercial and cultural leaders, working as merchants, lawyers, newspaper editors, and ministers and hosting plantation balls and church fetes.

Wealthy planters marked their success by building splendid mansions and indulging in displays of conspicuous consumption. The Greek Revival mansion on the rural estate of John Henry Hammond, a leading South Carolina planter and politician, boasted a center hall that was 53 by 20 feet, its floor embellished with stylish Belgian tiles and expensive Brussels carpets. "Once a year, like a great feudal landlord," a guest recounted, Hammond "gave a fete or grand dinner to all the country people." To retain the allegiance of ambitious men, Hammond and other planters encouraged them to buy slaves and grow rich.

Like all ruling classes, the planters tried to justify their power by endowing it with moral purpose. Responding to abolitionist attacks in the 1830s, they encouraged politicians, newspaper editors, and clergymen to defend slavery as a "positive good" that raised Africans from their savage condition rather than, as in the past, a "necessary evil" to maintain white living standards and prevent racial warfare. Seeking a religious justification, planters noted that the Hebrews, God's chosen people, had owned slaves and that Christ had never condemned slavery. Many defenders of slavery invoked St. Paul's injunction: "Servants, obey your masters."

Southern apologists also trumpeted the virtues of slavery in comparison to "free labor" in the North. They pointed out that few northern factory owners took any interest in the welfare of their workers, who labored long hours for meager pay and lived in unhealthy slums. In contrast, they praised planters as models of "disinterested benevolence" who ensured that enslaved African-Americans were adequately fed and housed and provided for the sick and elderly who could no longer work.

In fact, because of the prosperity of the mid-nineteenth-century plantation system, most slaves were somewhat better clothed and housed than were the poorest whites in both the South and the North. The slaves' food—particularly when supplemented by greens from their own garden plots and by game and fish—was probably better than that of unskilled workers in the North. And on some large plantations, children, the sick, and the elderly received better care than poor northerners did. But few enslaved African-Americans enjoyed a comfortable standard of living, and, unlike northern workers, slaves did not have the freedom to quit their jobs. And they clearly understood that planters gave them material favors not from benevolence but to protect their investment.

As part of the social defense of slavery, writers praised planters' wives as the managers of large households and lauded their work as nurses, caring for sick African-American children. Many writers especially exalted the sexual purity of white plantation women, contrasting them with stereotypical descriptions of passionately sexual black men and women and defending the brutal punishment of male slaves accused of rape or sexual intimacy with white women. Planters' wives became symbols of the moral superiority of whites over blacks.

The reality of plantation life was far more complex. A few planters' wives did enter into consensual sexual relations with African-Americans, and many planters had sex with their female slaves and fathered children by them. "I cannot tell how much I suffered in the presence of these wrongs," Harriet Jacobs confessed in anguish in her autobiography, *Incidents in the Life of a Slave Girl*. For many enslaved women, sexual assault by their masters was compounded by cruel treatment at the hands of mistresses enraged by their husbands' promiscuity.

In contrast to Brazil and the West Indies, interracial sex in the American South did not lead to the acceptance of a multicolored, mixed-race society. To maintain the loyalty of non-slaveowning whites (and ward off abolitionist attacks), planters increasingly relied on an ideology that asserted the equality of all whites and the inferiority of all blacks, including those of mixed ancestry and light skin color. As William Yancey of Alabama explained to a northern audience, "Your fathers and my fathers built this government on two ideas; the first is that the white race is the citizen and the master race, and the white man is the equal of every other white man. The second is that the Negro is the inferior race."

This rigid racial ideology helped unify a white population divided by property and regional outlook. Three-quarters of white families in the South did not own slaves. Some were tenant farmers, but many more were yeomen who owned farms of 50 to 100 acres in hilly regions or the Appalachian backcountry. Yeomen families grew some cotton but primarily raised corn and livestock, especially hogs. Their goals were modest: to preserve their holdings and secure enough new land or goods to set up all their children as farmers.

Wealthy slaveowners often stood in their way, buying up the best land and forcing yeomen into less fertile regions. Planters used their power in the state legislatures to keep taxes low on slaves and other personal property and tax land by acreage rather than by value so that backcountry farmers paid relatively high taxes on their marginal lands. In addition, planters enacted laws that forced yeomen to "fence in" their livestock (sparing themselves the cost of building fences around their large properties) and prohibited them from hunting on unused private lands. Finally, legislatures forced all white men—whether they owned slaves or not—to serve in patrols and militias that deterred slaves from running away or rebelling.

Few white yeomen or tenants welcomed gentry rule, and some actively opposed it. In 1857 Hinton Helper of North Carolina sought to rouse the

"Non-slaveowners of the South! farmers, mechanics and workingmen," warning that "the slaveholders, the arrogant demogogues whom you have elected to offices of honor and profit, have hoodwinked you . . . used you as mere tools for the consummation of their wicked designs." But Helper was forced into exile in the North by the planter elite, which maintained its rule by cutting some taxes, appointing a few yeomen to patronage positions, and making deals with backcountry leaders. Slaveowners also relied on racial prejudice, warning tenants and yeomen that they had to support slavery or face economic competition and race warfare with freed African-Americans. As John Henry Hammond told his poor white neighbors: "In a slave country every *freeman* is an aristocrat."

Enslaved African-Americans

Custom and law relegated slaves to a thoroughly subordinate social position. By law enslaved individuals were *chattel*—personal property. They could be disciplined at the will of their owners and bought and sold as if they were horses. As Thomas Ruffin, a justice of North Carolina Supreme Court, declared in a court decision in 1829, "The power of the master must be absolute to render the submission of the slave perfect."

The domestic slave trade reflected the brutal reality of the slave system. Few slaves arrived from Africa after 1808, when Congress banned American participation in the Atlantic slave trade. But because their birth rate equaled the high level among rural whites, the African-American population grew rapidly, from 1.1 million in 1810 to 3.9 million in 1860. Although many blacks continued to work on the plantations where they had been born, hundreds of thousands were moved by their owners to the expanding Cotton Kingdom in the Old Southwest. Some migrating slaves—perhaps as many as half—moved with relatives and friends as their owners deserted the Carolinas for the fertile plains of the Mississippi Valley. The rest were "sold South" through a new domestic slave trade that provided tobacco and cotton planters in Maryland, Virginia, and other long-settled regions with a major source of income. By the 1850s slaveowners were shipping 25,000 men and women a year westward, breaking up families and communities. "Dey sole my sister Kate," Anna Harris remembered decades later. "Sole her in 1860, and I ain't seed or heard of her since."

In the face of this internal slave trade, African-Americans nurtured family relationships for protection and support. Because slaves were not allowed to make contracts, their marriages were not legally binding. Nonetheless, many unions were durable. If not broken up by sale, couples usually maintained close nuclear families; in their cabins they loved and quarreled, laughed and suffered, much as free people did. Slaves also developed elaborate kinship networks that included distant relations and even individuals who had no blood or marital ties but shared in the life of the family. Elderly slaves played the role of patriarch, conducting religious services and disciplining

A Child Learns the Meaning of Slavery

Jacob Stroyer, born into slavery in South Carolina, was emancipated and became a minister in Salem, Massachusetts. In My Life in the South *(1855), Stroyer relates a dramatic incident that revealed his parents' subordinate and powerless status.*

Father . . . used to take care of horses and mules. I was around with him in the barnyard when but a small boy; of course that gave me an early relish for the occupation of hostler, and soon I made known my preference to Colonel Singleton, who was a sportsman and had fine horses. . . . Hence I was allowed to be numbered among those who took care of the fine horses, and learned to ride. . . .

It was not long after I had entered my new work before they put me upon the back of a horse which threw me to the ground almost as soon as I reached his back. . . . When I got up there was a man standing near with a switch in hand, and he immediately began to beat me. . . . This was the first time I had been whipped by anyone except Mother and Father, so I cried out in a tone of voice as if I would say, this is the first and last whipping you will give me when Father gets hold of you.

When I got away from him I ran to Father with all my might, but soon my expectation was blasted, as Father very coolly said to me, "Go back to your work and be a good boy, for I cannot do anything for you." But that did not satisfy me, so I went on to Mother with my complaint and she came out to the man who whipped me. He was a groom, a white man whom master hired to train his horses . . . [and] he took a whip and started for her, and she ran from him, talking all the time. . . .

Then the idea first came to me that I, with my dear father and mother and the rest of my fellow Negroes, was doomed to cruel treatment through life and was defenseless. . . .

SOURCE: Linda R. Monk, ed., *Ordinary Americans: U.S. History through the Eyes of Everyday People* (Alexandria, VA: Close Up Publications, 1994), pp. 71–72.

difficult children. Young slaves learned to address their elders by kin titles such as "Aunt" and "Uncle," preparing them for the day when they might be separated from their parents. When parted by sale, members of nuclear and extended families tried to keep track of one another. But the distances were often too great, and many slaves started new families in their new locations. When the Union army registered African-American marriages in Mississippi at the end of the Civil War, officials found that the slave trade had separated about a fourth of the men over forty years old from their first wives.

As migration and the domestic slave trade moved thousands of African-Americans to the Deep South, their working lives became more difficult. The weather was the hottest and conditions the most oppressive in that newly settled region, and the planters were the most brutal because many of them were poor men on the make rather than well-established members of the gentry. Work routines were more demanding as well. Sugar—grown in Louisiana—was the most labor-intensive plantation crop. Work was nearly as strenuous on newly founded cotton plantations in Alabama, Mississippi, Louisiana, Arkansas, and Texas. And the number of enslaved blacks in those states increased from about 500,000 in 1840 to more than 1.5 million in 1860, when they amounted to more than a third of all slaves (see Map 13.1).

To resist gang labor and forced separations, African-Americans used the tactics employed by previous generations of slaves: they feigned illness to slow the pace of work, were deliberately careless with the master's property, losing or breaking tools, and occasionally set fire to houses and barns.

Increasingly, young men resisted by running away. In the 1840s and 1850s tens of thousands of slaves fled from their masters, defying white patrols with bloodhounds, and about 1,000 reached freedom in the North each year. Blacks who lived near a free state had the greatest chance of success. In those areas enslaved women, whose concern for their children often deterred flight, joined the exodus along with their families. The fugitives counted on receiving aid from the "underground railroad," an informal network of white and African-American abolitionists that included free African-Americans in Baltimore, Richmond, Charleston, New Orleans, and other southern cities. In Baltimore, a free African-American sailor lent his identification papers to the future abolitionist Frederick Douglass, who used them to escape to New York and then returned them by mail. Many escaped slaves, such as Harriet Tubman, returned repeatedly to the South, risking reenslavement or death by working with the "railroad."

A few slaves followed the path marked out by David Walker's *Appeal* and Nat Turner's uprising by turning on their masters. But most African-Americans realized that rebellion was more likely to bring death than freedom, and they lacked the strong institutions—such as the communes formed by free peasants or serfs—needed to organize them. Moreover, blacks formed less than half the population in most areas; their southern white adversaries were well armed, unified, and militant; and there were no impenetrable jungles, mountains, and swamps into which they could flee.

In these circumstances, many slaves turned to spiritual resistance derived, especially after 1830, from Protestant Christianity. The Christianity of the slaves repudiated the virtue of obedience: when a white minister urged slaves in Liberty County, Georgia, to obey their masters, he noted that "one half of my audience deliberately rose up and walked off." Black Christianity also downplayed the doctrine of human depravity and developed as a religion of emotional fervor, celebration, and stoic endurance. Religion offered the hope of eventual liberation from life's sorrows and helped many slaves endure their

Harriet Tubman
Harriet Tubman (far left) was born in 1823 and escaped from slavery on a Maryland plantation
in 1849. During the next ten years she became a popular abolitionist speaker and led hundred
of slaves, including those pictured here, to freedom on the underground railroad. Tubman
served as a spy for the Union army during the Civil War and then set up schools for ex-slaves
in North Carolina.

bondage. African-American Protestants took heart from stories of the ancient
Israelites' escape from Egypt and Christ's compassion for the oppressed. Confident of their special relationship with God, slaves prepared themselves spiritually for emancipation, which they saw as deliverance to the Promised Land.

Free Blacks

While nearly 4 million African-Americans were enslaved in 1860, 500,000
were free. About half the free blacks resided in the North, where they lived as
second-class citizens. They were permitted to vote in only four New England
states and New York and could testify against whites in court only in Massachusetts. Virtually all public facilities in the North were segregated, and most
states denied blacks access to public schools. The federal government did not
allow free African-Americans to work for the postal service, claim public
lands, or hold a U.S. passport.

Most free African-Americans in the slave states lived in the Upper South,
where they faced even greater legal restrictions on their liberty, especially after
1840. Free blacks accused of crimes were often denied a jury trial, and those
who lacked work were threatened by vagrancy and apprenticeship laws intended to force them back into slavery. To prove their free status, they had to
carry manumission documents; in some states they needed official permission

just to travel across county lines. Even if they had good papers, free African-Americans had to be careful; kidnapping followed by sale into slavery was a constant threat.

In both the North and the South, free blacks were consigned by custom or law to the most menial and low-paying work. In rural areas they worked as agricultural laborers or tenant farmers; in towns and cities, as domestic servants, laundresses, or day laborers. However, the shortage of skilled workers in southern cities did create opportunities for a few blacks to become carpenters, blacksmiths, barbers, butchers, and shopkeepers. Skilled African-American workers in Baltimore, Richmond, Charleston, and New Orleans formed their own benevolent societies and churches, which became the core of their urban communities, providing education, recreation, and social welfare programs.

As a privileged group among African-Americans, free blacks felt pulled in two directions: loyalty to the welfare of their families, which often meant assimilating white culture, and loyalty to their race, which meant identifying with the great mass of enslaved African-Americans. In some places wealthier free blacks, particularly the mulatto children of white masters and black women, drew apart from common laborers and field hands and adopted the outlook of the planter class. In New Orleans free African-Americans sponsored an opera company and established literary journals. A few owned land and slaves.

Generally, however, free blacks and enslaved African-Americans saw themselves as one people. "We's different [from whites] in color, in talk and in 'ligion and beliefs," as one put it. Knowing that their freedom was not secure as long as slavery existed, free blacks sought to win freedom for their "brothers" and "sisters." A few free blacks in the South—such as Denmark Vesey, a Charleston, South Carolina, carpenter married to an enslaved woman—plotted rebellion, and many more aided fugitive slaves. In the North free African-Americans supported the abolitionist movement, and some—such as David Walker, Frederick Douglass, and Sojourner Truth—rose to positions of leadership. In the rigid caste system of American race relations, free blacks stood as symbols of hope to enslaved African-Americans and omens of danger to the majority of whites.

THE NORTHEAST: INDUSTRY AND CULTURE

As the planter elite carried slavery into the Old Southwest, the business leaders of the Northeast drove mechanization forward at an increasing pace and, in the 1840s and 1850s, began to incorporate the predominantly rural trans-Appalachian West into the expanding industrial economy. The economic results were phenomenal. By 1860 the United States was third in the world in manufacturing, behind only Great Britain and France.

Factories Triumphant

The American population grew from 17 million in 1840 to over 31 million in 1860, nearly doubling the market for industrial goods. This startling increase stemmed in part from a high birth rate (45 births per thousand people per year, compared with 30 per thousand in Europe) and in part from a massive surge in immigration from Western Europe. As the destination of most immigrants, the northeastern and Great Lakes states dominated this demographic surge, accounting for nearly two-thirds of the population increase.

Northern manufacturers easily met the growing demand for goods. They expanded production not only in the industrial towns, where falling water powered mills, but also in the older seaports and, with stunning swiftness, the towns of the interior, where the coal-powered stationary steam engine was used to run other machines. By 1838 there were about 2,000 steam engines in the United States and 133 in Pittsburgh alone, where they were used in the glass industry, sawmills, machine shops, and iron-rolling mills. The use of steam engines enabled manufacturers to build factories in the largest cities, taking advantage of their cheap labor, capital markets, sophisticated trading services, and eager consumers.

Factory production lay at the heart of industrial expansion. Northern manufacturers built hundreds of new factories that used power-driven machines and assembly-line techniques to turn out vast quantities of well-made goods. Cyrus McCormick of Chicago developed power-driven conveyor belts to assemble reapers, and Samuel Colt built an assembly-line factory in Hartford, Connecticut, to produce his invention—the "six-shooter," as it became known. By the late 1850s Colt's factory was turning out 60,000 weapons annually, and five Connecticut clockmakers were using machine tools to make intricate works for half a million clocks a year. As a team of British observers noted with admiration, those products were made "in large factories, with machinery applied to almost every process, the extreme subdivision of labor, and all reduced to an almost perfect system of manufacture."

The sheer volume of output made some products—Remington rifles, Singer sewing machines, Waltham watches, and Yale locks as well as Colt handguns and McCormick reapers—into household words in the United States and abroad. After showing their machine-tooled goods at the Crystal Palace Exhibition in London in 1851, McCormick and Colt built factories in Great Britain that used American machinery and production techniques. Soon their products dominated many European markets.

Steam power and assembly lines had other, less positive effects, such as sharpening conflict between owners and workers. To pay for their new machinery, manufacturers cut wages, and to use it most efficiently, they increased the pace of work, which employees resisted. For example, in 1845 the weaver Sarah G. Bagley and other operatives formed the Female Labor Reform Association to protest wage cuts and a speedup in a Lowell, Massachusetts, textile mill, but the Association was unable to halt the decline in wages and working conditions. As a result, there was an important change in the labor force throughout the textile industry. Few young Yankee women chose to enter the mills, and most older female employees left to marry and raise families; Irish

McCORMICK'S FIRST REAPER

The McCormick Reaper, 1851
The McCormick reaper was a complex piece of machinery, but it was designed to be assembled and repaired by average farmers. Company advertisements informed potential buyers that the reaper's parts were "numbered and marked with paint, showing the connection of the parts with one another so that they can readily be put together by the farmer." By using reapers to harvest ripe grain before it sprouted, farmers could plant many more acres.

and French-Canadian immigrants—more men than women—took their place, working for low wages and foreshadowing the emergence of an all-male system of factory labor (see Chapter 18).

By the 1850s the supply of machine-made goods often exceeded the demand, prompting the laying off or dismissal of workers. One episode of overproduction preceded the Panic of 1857—a financial crisis sparked by excess railroad investments—and resulted in a full-scale depression. Unemployment remained at about 10 percent until the outbreak of the Civil War in 1861, reminding Americans of the social costs of the new—and otherwise very successful—system of industrial production.

The Culture of the Middle Class

Between 1830 and the Panic of 1857, the per capita income of Americans increased by about 2.5 percent a year, a remarkable rate that the United States has never since matched. This prosperity, along with the availability of inexpensive mass-produced goods, allowed the creation of a new material and intellectual culture. A new urban middle class grew in size and self-awareness, and its outlook lent a distinctive character to northern society.

Improvements in housing were one mark of prosperity and middle-class identity. In the 1830s American carpenters devised a faster method to build wooden houses: the balloon frame. Traditional wood construction depended on the careful fitting together of heavy timbers; in the East experienced housewrights fashioned a strong frame with mortise-and-tenon joints, while in the West farmers fitted trimmed logs together. The *balloon frame*, much lighter in weight (as its name implied) but almost as strong, formed a house with a vertical grid of thin wooden studs joined by nails to cross-pieces at the top and bottom. Once the carpenter had thrown up the frame, he simply nailed wood sheathing to the studs to make the walls and then added a layer of clapboard siding. The new technology reduced the cost of housing by 40 percent, and the four-room balloon-frame house quickly became the standard residence, replacing the typical two-room-with-a-loft house of preindustrial society.

The new house design helped change the character of family life. Urban middle-class parents had already begun to have fewer children by using various means of birth control: abstinence, coitus interruptus, animal skin condoms, and abortions induced by herbs. Larger houses allowed family members to avoid close physical contact with one another. To enhance individual privacy, architects published manuals featuring house plans with many bedrooms. Andrew Jackson Downing, the leading architectural philosopher of the era, lauded the new houses in his famous book *The Architecture of Country Houses* (1850). Downing argued they would promote a "refinement of manners" and strengthen the life of the family, which was "the best social form."

Prosperous urban families lived not only in more space but also in greater luxury. Beds with springs of woven rope or iron wire replaced beds with wooden slats, and as mass-produced ticking and sheeting became available in stores, homemade featherbeds, mattresses, and down pillows became standard items. Middle-class residences now boasted furnaces that heated water for bathing and for radiators that warmed entire rooms, eliciting complaints from visiting Europeans that it was impossible to escape hot air: "It meets you the moment the street-door is opened to let you in, rushes after you when you emerge again, half-stewed and parboiled into the wholesome air."

Most affluent urban house owners acquired goods that eased the burden of traditional domestic chores. Stoves with ovens, including broilers and movable grates, replaced inefficient open hearths. Women now had access to a variety of pots, pans, and kettles; mechanical equipment such as grinders and presses; and washboards. Many middle-class households boasted treadle-operated sewing machines and iceboxes, which ice-company wagons filled daily. After the introduction of the Mason jar in 1858, households vastly increased their ability to preserve perishable foods.

No less important, the technology of the Industrial Revolution allowed the realization of Emerson's dream of a democratic audience for American literature. The Napier steam-driven press (1825) and the Hoe rotary press (1847) led to the mass production of cheap books. The northern middle class provided a virtually insatiable market, buying books or borrowing the nearly 13 million volumes available in over 50,000 public libraries. Publishing houses in New York, Philadelphia, and Boston competed with each other, offering discounts to booksellers, sending sales agents into the field, and recruiting popular authors. Between 1820 and 1850 American book publishers such as Harper Brothers and G. P. Putnam's Sons increased their annual sales from about $2.5 million to $12.5 million. The religious press also contributed to the explosion in print. The American Bible Society and dozens of other organizations published more than 1 million Bibles and 6 million books, pamphlets, and magazines each year.

The new book culture was a distinguishing feature of the northern middle class. Fiction constituted a large proportion of literary consumption. One of the first successful American writers of fiction was James Fenimore Cooper. Beginning with *The Pioneers* (1823) and *The Last of the Mohicans* (1826) and ending with *The Deerslayer* (1841), Cooper built an enormous readership for the adventures of his hero, the frontier scout Leatherstocking. Corresponding in popularity was the poetry of Henry Wadsworth Longfellow, who romanticized the American past in *Hiawatha* (1855) and *The Courtship of Miles Standish* (1858).

Women writers were even more popular among middle-class readers, the majority of whom were female. Catharine Maria Sedgwick won wide popularity in the 1820s, as did Caroline Howard Gilman and Caroline Lee Hentz in the next decade. Writers whose names are virtually unknown today—Sara Parton, Augusta Evans Wilson, and Susan Warner—reached even larger audiences in the 1850s. The sentimental melodramas of these women authors, often punctuated by tearful domestic scenes, helped develop the emerging middle-class identity by suggesting that women occupied a "separate sphere" and could achieve their potential only within the context of marriage and the family. In her last novel, *Married or Single* (1857), Sedgwick concluded that marriage was "the great circumstance" of a woman's life where she could form the character of her husband and children.

The most successful woman novelist of the period was Harriet Beecher Stowe. *Uncle Tom's Cabin* (1852), which sold 350,000 copies in its first year, was first and foremost an antislavery novel, but it was also an argument for the superior morality of women and the importance of family life. Stowe gave the home a deep religious meaning, writing in *The Minister's Wooing* (1859) that it was the "appointed sphere for woman, more holy than cloister, more saintly and pure than church and altar."

The commercial success of women novelists gave an ironic twist to their celebration of the private sphere of home, marriage, and family. These writers were actually engaged in a very public—and commercial—enterprise. Bargaining with their publishers, often making their own living, and supporting their families, they were among the first successful professional women in the United States. These talented and energetic women were erasing the contradiction between "domestic" and "public" life and justifying the independent woman. But they did so in a subtle and unthreatening fashion by promoting morality and thus assuming one of the roles of the minister. Indeed, Caroline Lee Hentz described her writing career as "vocation . . . for which God has endowed me."

Indeed, the thousands of middle-class northern women active in religious and reform organizations were living exemplars of the novelists' heroines, as were the multitude of women teachers who were inspired by the writings of Catharine Beecher (see Chapter 12). To Beecher, "moral and religious education must be the foundation of national instruction" and education must be carried out by "energetic and benevolent women." Thus, the cultural world of the new middle class enhanced not only the material lives of American women but also their intellectual and moral authority.

Immigration and Cultural Conflict

Immigrants from Ireland and the German states formed other new cultural worlds in the northeastern states. There was no federal legislation regulating immigration, and state laws, which attempted to set minimum health standards and exclude paupers, were generally ineffective. Consequently, there were no legal barriers to immigrants fleeing poverty and famine or seeking a better life. Between 1820 and 1860 about 2 million Irish men and women poured into the United States, along with 1.5 million Germans and 750,000 Britons. Most avoided the South because they opposed slavery, shunned blacks, or feared competition from enslaved workers and instead settled in the northern states, where they accounted for nearly a third of white adults by 1860.

The economic situation of immigrants varied greatly. The wealthiest were the British, many of whom were professionals, landowning farmers, and skilled workers. The majority of German immigrants came from farming and artisan families and could afford to buy land in America; many of them settled in the West, especially Missouri and Wisconsin. The poorest migrants were peasants and laborers from Ireland, who fled from a famine in the 1840s caused by a devastating blight on the potato crop and English economic policies that encouraged the exportation of scarce grain. The Irish found new homes in the cities of New England and New York, taking low-skilled jobs in factories, construction projects, docks, warehouses, and private homes. Arriving in dire poverty, they were willing to work for long hours, at low wages, and with great intensity. Irish workers gave a competitive edge to industrialists in New York City and Boston, where they numbered nearly one-third of the population by 1850. For example, each of the largest clothing factories in Boston employed about a hundred young Irishwomen.

Many Irish immigrants, like many unskilled native-born day laborers, lived in poverty, unable to afford the food they needed to keep up with the intense pace of factory work. Crowded living conditions threatened their health, for sanitation systems in large cities were primitive. Poorly sealed privies drained into drinking wells, and open sewers ran through the streets. Epidemics of cholera, yellow fever, typhoid, smallpox, diphtheria, and tuberculosis struck with increasing frequency. In the summer of 1849 cholera epidemics hit New York, St. Louis, and Cincinnati. More than 5,000 people, mostly poor immigrants, died in New York alone.

In times of hardship and sorrow, immigrants turned to their churches. French-Canadians, many Germans, and virtually all the Irish were committed Catholics, and they fueled the growth of the Catholic Church. In the 1840s there were 16 Catholic dioceses and 700 churches in the United States, and the number increased to 45 dioceses and 3,000 churches by 1860. With the guidance of their priests and bishops, the Irish built a network of ethnic institutions: charitable societies, orphanages, militia companies, parochial schools, newspapers, social clubs, and political organizations. These community organizations had few equivalents in Ireland, for they had sprung up to help immigrants in their search for housing, jobs, and education. They also reflected the desire of Irish immigrants to maintain their native culture, to which existing American institutions were indifferent or hostile.

The arrival of the first wave of Irish immigrants in the 1830s produced a rash of anti-Catholic publications. One of the most militant critics of Catholicism was Samuel F. B. Morse, who would later make the first commercial adaptation of the telegraph. In 1834 Morse published *Foreign Conspiracy against the Liberties of the United States*, which warned of a Catholic threat to American republican institutions. The "past history" of Roman Catholics, Morse suggested, and "the fact that they everywhere act together, as if guided by one mind, admonish us to be jealous of their influence . . . in relation to our free institutions." He was especially wary of Irish Catholics, who "kept alive their foreign feelings, associations, habits and manners." Morse advocated the formation of an "Anti-Popery Union" to resist the perceived threat.

Morse believed that Irish Catholics would obey the dictates of Pope Pius IX, who strongly opposed republican reformers in Italy and condemned republicanism as a false political ideology based on the sovereignty of the people rather than the sovereignty of God. Republican-minded Protestant ministers of many denominations shared Morse's fears, and *Foreign Conspiracy* became their textbook. Millions of young Americans read it in Protestant Sunday schools.

The social tensions stemming from industrialization intensified anti-Catholic sentiment. Unemployed Protestant mechanics and poorly paid factory workers attacked Catholics, blaming cheap immigrant labor for their economic woes. They organized Native American Clubs, which called for increasing the waiting period for citizenship from five to twenty-one years, restricting public office to native-born Americans, and using only the Protestant version of the Bible in public schools.

Other native-born citizens supported the anti-Catholic movement for reasons of public policy. They wanted a strong system of public schools and therefore opposed proposals from Catholic clergymen and Democratic legislators in many northeastern states that the local taxes paid by Catholics be reserved for parochial (religious) schools. Evangelical ministers and temperance advocates were alarmed by the abuse of alcohol by some Irish men and called for an end to immigration. This cultural warfare among ethnic and religious groups inhibited the development of a strong labor movement. Many Protestant laborers felt they had more in common with their employers than with their Catholic coworkers.

In almost every city with a large immigrant population, religious and cultural conflicts resulted in violence. In 1834, in Charlestown, Massachusetts, a quarrel between Catholic laborers repairing an Ursuline convent and Protestant workers in a neighboring brickyard turned into a full-scale riot. An anti-Catholic mob drove the residents out of the convent and burned it to the ground. Rioting escalated in the 1840s as the Irish began to acquire political influence in northeastern cities. In Philadelphia the violence peaked in 1844 when the Catholic bishop persuaded public school officials to use both Protestant and Catholic versions of the Bible. Anti-Irish rioting incited by the city's Native American Clubs lasted for two months and escalated into open warfare between Protestants and the Penn-

Anti-Catholic Riot in Philadelphia
When riots against Irish Catholics broke out in Philadelphia in 1844, the governor of Pennsylvania called out the militia to protect Catholic churches, including one (pictured in the background) in which young Irish-Americans had stored muskets for self-defense. The Protestant rioters, depicted by the artist as well-dressed gentlemen, exchanged musket fire with the militia, which eventually restored order but not amity to the religiously divided city.

sylvania militia. Ethnicity and religion now split the North in much the same way (although not to the same extent) that race and class had long divided the South.

THE WEST: MANIFEST DESTINY

During the 1840s and 1850s, American settlers and European immigrants filled up the large geographic area that became known as the Midwest and tied it culturally and economically to the Northeast. Captivated by this westward movement, expansionists declared that it was the nation's "Manifest Destiny" to dominate the entire North American continent. A few political leaders realized that this mission would inevitably create conflicts with Mexico and Great Britain and revive the long-simmering conflict between the North and the South over the expansion of slavery, but their reservations were swept aside by the expansionist fervor. The fate of the nation would soon depend on the fate of the West.

The Midwest

By 1860 nearly one-third of the nation's people lived in the Midwest states—Ohio, Indiana, Illinois, Michigan, and Wisconsin, along with Missouri, Iowa, and Minnesota—where they created a complex society and economy that resembled that of the Northeast. Many settlers had come from New England or New York and had carried their culture, churches, and fraternal lodges with them. Tens of thousands more had migrated from Germany and Ireland, and so the ethnic composition of the Midwest was similar to that of the Northeast.

Strong economic bonds tied the two regions. Most midwesterners were wheat farmers who shipped their crops to northeastern markets on the Great Lakes and the Erie Canal. Midwestern inventors and entrepreneurs drew on the industrial technology and mass-production techniques of northeastern manufacturers to produce low-cost labor-saving goods—especially farm machinery. The story of John Deere was typical. As a blacksmith in Grand Detour, Illinois, Deere made his first steel plow out of old saws in 1837; ten years later he opened a factory in Moline that used mass-production techniques. His steel plows, superior in strength to cast-iron models, quickly dominated the midwestern market. Other companies—McCormick, Hussey, Atkins, and Manny—mass-produced reapers that revolutionized the harvesting of grain. Previously, one worker with a cradle scythe had cut 2 to 3 acres a day. With a self-raking reaper, a farmer could cut 12 acres daily. Because their farms were large and laborers were in short supply, midwesterners led the way in using modern agricultural technology, increasing their productivity more than 20 percent during the 1850s.

Another product of industrial technology—the railroad—cemented the union between the Northeast and the Midwest. As late as 1852 canals were

A German Immigrant on Life in Ohio

In 1836 twenty-four-year-old Ernst Stille left his family's overcrowded farm in Prussia and, nearly destitute, settled in Cincinnati. After ten years of hard work, Stille had not achieved his dream of landed independence.

May 20th [1847]
Dearest friends and relatives,
. . . The only people who are really happy here are those who were used to hard work in Germany and with toil and great pains could hardly even earn their daily bread. When people like that come here, even if they don't have any money, they can manage, they rent a room and the husband goes to work, earns his dollar a day and so he can live well and happily with a wife and children. But a lot of people come over here who were well off in Germany but were enticed to leave their fatherland by boastful and imprudent letters from their friends or children and thought they could become rich in America. This deceives a lot of people, since . . . if they want to live in the country and don't have enough money to buy a piece of land that is cleared and has a house then they have to settle in the wild bush and have to work very hard to clear the trees out of the way so they can sow and plant. . . . Here in Cincinnati I know a lot of people who have made it by working hard like Ernst Lots for example he does very well he also owns a brickyard and earns good money. . . . A good worker can do his day's work in 10 hours, earn one dollar and live well on that with a wife and children, and have such good food and drink like the best burgher in Lengerich [Stille's hometown in Germany]. . . .

My plan is if I stay in good health for the next couple of years to buy a piece of land and live there, since from my childhood I've been used to farming, I'd rather do that than stay in the city all of my life, [but] you can't start very well unless you have 300 dollars.

SOURCE: Wolfgang Helbich, Walter Kamphoefner, and Ulrike Sommer, eds., *News from the Land of Freedom: German Immigrants Write Home* (Ithaca, N.Y.: Cornell University Press, 1991), pp. 85–87. © C.H. Beck'she Verlagsbuchhandlung (Oscar Beck), Munich.

carrying twice the tonnage of railroads, but in the next six years track mileage increased dramatically. The new railroads included trunk lines that stretched across New York and Pennsylvania to provide through traffic from New York City and Philadelphia to Cleveland and Chicago (see Map 13.2). More convenient and faster than canals, railroads became the main carriers of freight by 1859. They hastened the settlement of areas that canal and river transport could not serve and made western farming more profitable by lowering the cost of transporting farm goods to market. This *national* market in wheat forced some eastern farmers out of business and prompted others to turn to market gardening.

MAP 13.2
Railroads of the North and South, 1850–1860
In the decade before the Civil War the rapid construction of railroads provided the Northeast and the Midwest with extensive and dense transportation systems that stimulated economic development. The South built a much simpler system. In all regions, railroad lines used different track gauges, hindering the efficient flow of traffic. During the war such problems hampered military operations, especially in the South.

Railroads also promoted the development of commercial and manufacturing cities. Entrepreneurs congregated wherever railroad lines converged or met water transport, establishing grain storehouses, flour mills, packing plants, and docks and providing work for hundreds of artisans and laborers. Shopkeepers and insurance brokers quickly followed, as did manufacturers. In 1846 Cyrus McCormick moved his reaper factory from western Virginia to Chicago to be closer to his midwestern customers. As key railroad junctions and industrial centers, St. Louis and Chicago became boom towns. Thanks in part to the balloon-frame house, which was first developed in Chicago, they grew rapidly into cities. By 1860 St. Louis and Chicago had surpassed Boston and Baltimore in size and had become the nation's third and fourth largest cities, respectively, after New York and Philadelphia.

Railroad construction speeded the modernization of the iron industry, a critical component of northeastern manufacturing. Railroads needed high-quality iron, and so Philadelphia rail mills raised their technical standards. The engineering requirements for train engines had a similar effect on steam engine production in the Northeast and the Midwest, where railroads built a large network of machine shops to service their locomotives. Although separated by geography, the Midwest and the Northeast increasingly resembled each other in ethnic composition, cultural values, and technical skills.

Texas

At the same time that northern farmers and European migrants were settling the Midwest, migrants from the Ohio Valley and the South were claiming the best lands in Arkansas and southern Missouri, pushing just beyond their western boundaries to the 95th meridian of longitude. Beyond this north-south line stretched the semiarid Great Plains. In 1820 an army explorer, Major Stephen H. Long, had described the entire area between the Missouri River and the Rocky Mountains as a Great American Desert, "almost wholly unfit for cultivation." Sharing this assumption, land-hungry American planters looked southward toward Mexican territory, especially the province of Texas.

Texas had long been a zone of conflict between European nations. During the eighteenth century the Spanish had employed Tejas or Texas (so called after the local native American word for "friends") as a buffer against the French. After the Louisiana Purchase in 1803, Texas became Spain's buffer against Americans. Although adventurers from the United States did arrive, the Adams-Onís treaty of 1819 guaranteed Spanish sovereignty over Texas.

After winning independence from Spain in 1821, the Mexican government encouraged its own citizens and colonists from the United States to settle in Texas. To win the allegiance of the Americans, the Mexican government granted them some of the best land in Texas (see Map 13.3). One early grantee was Moses Austin, whose son Stephen F. Austin established a thriving American settlement by offering large land grants at a low cost. By 1830 about 7,000 Americans were living in eastern and central Texas, far outnumbering the 3,000 Mexicans in the southwestern towns of Goliad and San Antonio. The Americans did not assimilate Mexican culture and defied various Mexican laws, including an edict of 1829 ending slavery. By 1835, 27,000 Americans and their 3,000 slaves were living in Texas, raising cotton and cattle.

When the Mexican government tried to assert control over Texas, the resident Americans split into two groups. The "peace party," under the leadership of Stephen Austin, worked to win more self-government for the province within

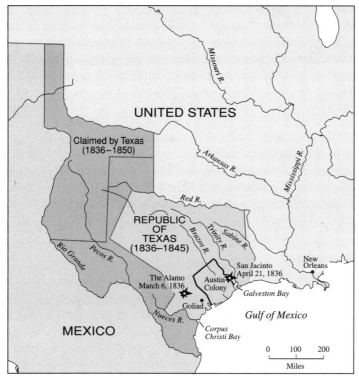

MAP 13.3
American Settlement in Texas
In 1821 Stephen F. Austin established the first organized Anglo-American
settlement in Texas on land granted to his father by the Mexican authorities. By 1834 he had issued land titles to more than 1,000 settlers, who
grew cotton and exported it from Corpus Christi Bay and Galveston Bay.

Mexico, while the "war party" demanded independence. Austin won significant
reforms, but before he could achieve statehood for Texas within Mexico, General Antonio López de Santa Anna became president, appointed a military com-
mandant for Texas, and centralized power in Mexico City. Santa Anna's actions
prompted the American war party to provoke a rebellion that most of the
American settlers ultimately supported. On March 2, 1836, the rebels proclaimed the independence of Texas and adopted a constitution legalizing slavery.

Santa Anna vowed to put down the rebellion. Four days after the declaration of independence, his army wiped out the garrison defending the Alamo
in San Antonio. After capturing the settlement of Goliad, the Mexican chief
ordered the execution of 371 rebel prisoners, whom he regarded as mercenaries rather than Texans because they had just arrived from the United States.
Santa Anna thought he had crushed the rebellion, but the battle of the Alamo
had captured the attention of New Orleans and New York newspapers. Their

correspondents romanticized the heroism of the Texans at the Alamo and the deaths of the folk heroes Davy Crockett and Jim Bowie. Using some of the strongest anti-Catholic rhetoric of the day, the newspapers described the Mexicans as tyrannical butchers in the service of the pope. Thousands of American adventurers, lured by Texan offers of land bounties, set sail from New York, the Gulf states, and the Mississippi Valley. Reinforced by the new arrivals and led by General Sam Houston, the rebels routed the Mexicans in the Battle of San Jacinto on April 21, 1836, establishing de facto independence. The Mexican government refused to recognize the new republic but abandoned efforts to reconquer it.

The Texans immediately voted by plebiscite for annexation by the United States, but Presidents Andrew Jackson and Martin Van Buren refused to act. They knew that adding Texas as a slave state would divide the Democratic party and the nation and almost certainly lead to war with Mexico.

Oregon and California

The annexation of Texas became a more pressing issue in the 1840s as American expansionists developed continental ambitions. Those ambitions were captured by the term Manifest Destiny, coined in 1845 by John L. O'Sullivan, the editor of the *Democratic Review*. As O'Sullivan put it, "Our manifest destiny is to overspread the continent allotted by Providence for the free development of our yearly multiplying millions." Behind the rhetoric of Manifest Destiny was a sense of cultural and even racial superiority; "inferior" peoples—such as native Americans—were to be brought under American dominion, taught about republican forms of government, and converted to Protestantism. O'Sullivan left the geographic scope of Manifest Destiny vague but clearly implied that the United States had a divinely inspired mission to bring the entire West, including parts of Mexico and Canada, into the American republic.

In fact, many residents of the Ohio River Valley were casting their eyes westward to the fertile valleys of the Oregon Country, which was claimed by Great Britain as well as the United States. In 1818 a British-American convention had established the 49th parallel as the Canadian-American boundary up to the Rocky Mountains but no farther, allowing both Britons and Americans to settle anywhere in the disputed region. At that time Oregon stretched from the 42nd parallel in the south (the border with the Mexican province of California) to 54° 40′ in the north (the border with Russian Alaska). Subsequently, the British-run Hudson's Bay Company carried on a lucrative fur trade north of the Columbia River, while several hundred Americans settled to the south, mostly in the Willamette Valley. On the basis of this settlement, the United States established a claim to the zone between the 42nd parallel and the Columbia River.

In 1842 American interest in Oregon increased dramatically. Navy lieutenant Charles Wilkes published glowing reports of the potential harbors he had found in the Strait of Juan de Fuca, Admiralty Inlet, and Puget Sound, which were of great interest to New England merchants plying the China trade. Also in 1842 the first large party, over a hundred people, crossed the Oregon Trail that fur traders and explorers had blazed through the Great Plains and the Rocky Mountains (see Map 13.4). Their reports told of a mild climate and fertile soil.

"Oregon fever" raged. In May 1843 over a thousand men, women, and children gathered in Independence, Missouri, for the trek to Oregon. The migrants were mostly farming and trading families from Missouri and the Ohio Valley: Kentucky, Tennessee, and the southern parts of Indiana and Ohio. They had more than 100 wagons and 5,000 oxen and cattle. With military-style organization and formations, the pioneers overcame flooding streams, dust storms, dying livestock, and encounters with Indians. After a journey of six months, they reached the Willamette Valley, more than 2,000 miles across the continent. During the next two seasons another 5,000 people reached Oregon.

By the Civil War 350,000 Americans, including many from the Midwest, had braved the Oregon Trail. Over 34,000 people died in the effort, mostly from disease and exposure; only 400 deaths came from Indian attacks. The walking migrants wore 3-foot-deep paths, and their wagons carved 5-foot-deep ruts,

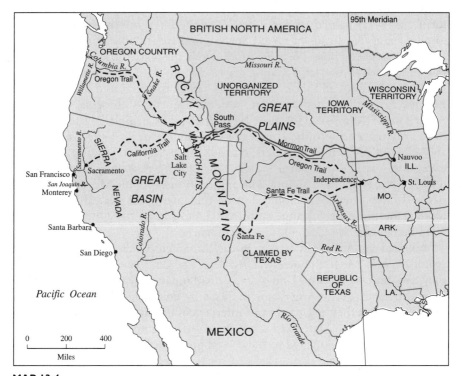

MAP 13.4
Settlement of the Trans-Missouri West
In the 1840s tens of thousands of Americans crossed the Great Plains in huge wagon trains. The Mormons settled in the Salt Lake basin; other pioneers pressed on to Mexican California and the Oregon Country. There was remarkably little crime on these treks because most migrants were deeply religious or were committed to the rule of Anglo-American law, which they enforced through political compacts and self-created institutions.

across sandstone formations in southern Wyoming—tracks that are visible today. Women found the trail especially difficult, for it pulled them away from friends, exaggerated the authority of their husbands, and added to their traditional chores the strenuous work of driving wagons and animals. Some pioneers ended up in the Mexican province of California. They left the Oregon Trail just past Fort Hall on the Snake River and struggled southward down the California Trail, settling in the interior valley of the Sacramento River.

California had been the remotest corner of Spain's American empire, and Spain had established a significant foothold there only in the 1770s, when it built a chain of coastal missions and presidios along the coast (see Chapter 8). New England merchants soon struck up trade with the new California settlements, largely for sea otter pelts that they carried to China. Commerce increased after Mexico won independence from Spain in 1821. To promote the economic development of California, the new Mexican government secularized the California missions, liberating more than 20,000 Indians who had been forced to work for the friars, and promoted large-scale cattle ranching on former mission lands.

The rise of cattle ranching created a new society and economy. While some mission Indians joined native American peoples in the interior of California, many remained in the coastal region. They intermarried with the local *mestizos* (Mexicans of mixed Spanish and Indian ancestry) and worked as laborers and cowboys. New England merchants carried the leather and tallow produced on the large California *ranchos* to customers in the booming Massachusetts boot and shoe industry. To handle the increased business, New England firms dispatched dozens of resident agents to California. Unlike the Americans in Texas, many of those New Englanders assimilated Mexican culture. They married into the families of the elite Mexicans—the *Californios*—and adopted their dress, manners, outlook, and Catholic religion. A crucial exception was Thomas Oliver Larkin, the most successful merchant in Monterey. Larkin established a close working relationship with Mexican authorities and often lent them money, but he remained an American citizen and plotted for the peaceful annexation of California to the United States. In 1843 he became the U.S. consul in California.

Like Larkin, American settlers in the Sacramento Valley had no desire to assimilate into Mexican society. Their legal standing was uncertain because they had received dubious land grants or had squatted without any title. They hoped to emulate the Americans in Texas by colonizing the country, overwhelming what they regarded as an inferior culture, and then seeking annexation by the United States. However, these settlers numbered only about 700 in the early 1840s, compared to the coastal population of 7,000 Mexicans and 300 American traders.

The Election of 1844

The future course of American policy toward California, Oregon, and Texas would be determined by the election of 1844. Since 1836, when Texas first requested annexation to the United States, some southern leaders had favored territorial expansion to protect and extend the slave system. They had been opposed not only by cautious party politicians and northern abolitionists but also (southerners came to think) by British diplomacy. In 1839 Britain and France had intervened in Mexico to force it to pay its foreign debts, and there were rumors that Britain wanted California as payment. Southern leaders also saw evidence that Britain was encouraging Texas to remain independent and had designs on Spanish Cuba, which some southerners wanted to annex as a slave state. It all seemed to add up to a grand scheme concocted by British abolitionists to block American expansion—and the spread of slavery—to the south and west. To thwart this design southern expansionists demanded the annexation of Texas.

Simultaneously, "Oregon fever" and Manifest Destiny altered the political and diplomatic landscape in the North. In 1843 Americans throughout the Ohio Valley and the Great Lakes states called on the federal government to renounce the joint occupation of Oregon and oust the British. Democrats and Whigs jointly organized "Oregon conventions," and in July a bipartisan national convention demanded that the United States seize Oregon all the way to 54° 40′ north latitude, the southern limit of Russian Alaska.

Now that northerners too were demanding expansion, southern Democrats could champion the annexation of Texas without threatening party unity. President John Tyler, disowned by the Whigs because of his opposition to Henry Clay's nationalist economic program, hoped to win reelection in 1844 as a Democrat or as the head of a new political party. To curry favor among expansionists, Tyler proposed both the annexation of Texas and the seizure of Oregon to the 54° 40′ line. In April 1844 Tyler and John C. Calhoun, his new secretary of state, submitted to the Senate a treaty for the annexation of Texas. The treaty was opposed by two other leaders with presidential ambitions: the Democrat Martin Van Buren and the Whig Henry Clay. Each feared alienating northern voters by supporting the annexation of Texas. At their urging, Whigs and northern Democrats united to defeat the treaty.

The annexation of Texas became the central issue in the election. The Democrats passed over Tyler, whom they did not trust, and Van Buren, whom southern Democrats despised for his stance on Texas. Instead, they selected former Governor James K. Polk of Tennessee, a slaveowner who was Andrew Jackson's personal favorite and carried the nickname "Young Hickory." Unimpressive in appearance, Polk was a man of iron will and boundless ambition for the nation. He called for the annexation of Texas and taking all of Oregon. "Fifty-four forty or fight!" became the patriotic cry of his campaign.

The Whigs nominated Henry Clay, who once again championed his American System of internal improvements, high tariffs, and national banking. Throughout the campaign Clay dodged the issue of Texas, finally suggesting that under certain circumstances he might support annexation. His position disappointed thousands of northern Whigs and Democrats who opposed any expansion of slavery. Rather than vote for Clay, some antislavery advocates supported the Liberty party's candidate, James G. Birney of Kentucky. Birney won less than 3 percent of the popular vote but probably took enough votes from Clay in New York to cause him to lose that state by 5,000 votes. By winning New York's 36 electoral votes, Polk won by a margin of 170 to 105 in the electoral college. (Without New York, he would have lost by 141 to 134.)

After Polk's victory, congressional Democrats closed ranks and moved immediately to bring Texas into the Union. Unable to secure a two-thirds majority in the Senate for a treaty with the Texas Republic, they approved annexation by a joint resolution of Congress, which required only a majority vote in each house. Mexico challenged the legality of Congress's action—it had never recognized the independence of the Republic of Texas—and broke off diplomatic relations with the United States. But Polk's strategy of linking Texas and Oregon had been successful. And the continuing dispute with Mexico over Texas would soon give him the opportunity to assert American control over even more territory in the West, fulfilling the dreams of the most ardent advocates of Manifest Destiny.

CHAPTER 13 TIMELINE	
1830s	Slavery defended as a "positive good"
	Expansion of Cotton Kingdom and domestic slave trade
	Growth of cattle ranching in Mexican California
1836	Texas proclaims independence from Mexico
1840s	Spread of factory system to many industries
	Large-scale Irish migration caused by potato famine
1842	Overland migration to Oregon begins
1844	Anti-Catholic rioting in Philadelphia
	Texas and Oregon questions dominate election
1845	Lowell Female Labor Reform Association formed
	John L. O'Sullivan coins term *Manifest Destiny*
	Texas admitted to the Union as a slave state
1849	Cholera epidemics in cities
1850	A. J. Downing's *The Architecture of Country Houses*
1850s	Growth in number of fugitive slaves and underground railroad
	Immigrants replace native-born women as textile operatives
	Rise of middle-class consumer culture
	Chicago and St. Louis become major cities
1857	Hinton Helper attacks slaveowning aristocracy
	Financial panic begins economic depression

CHAPTER 14

THE CRISIS OF THE UNION, 1845–1860

- War, Expansion, and Slavery, 1845–1850
- The End of the Second Party System, 1850–1858
- Abraham Lincoln and the End of Union, 1858–1860

For nearly a generation after the Missouri Compromise of 1820 the two major political parties prevented a confrontation between evangelical abolitionism and the proslavery movement by devising programs that were *national* in appeal. But the compromise worked only so long as the territory of the United States remained unchanged. The annexation of Texas in 1846 and the subsequent war with Mexico prompted a fateful political struggle over the extension of slavery into the West.

As politicians searched desperately for a formula to resolve the status of slavery in the new lands, the nation experienced a decade-long series of crises—first over California and fugitive slaves, then over the settlement of Kansas, and finally over the constitutional status of slavery. "That Union should so long have been preserved in a confederacy which contains an element of discord of such magnitude and of so disturbing a nature as that of Slavery is a wonder," Martin Van Buren reflected in 1856. But even as he spoke, the trust and goodwill that had preserved the Union for nearly three generations were being shattered.

WAR, EXPANSION, AND SLAVERY, 1845–1850

James K. Polk and the Democrats had swept to victory in 1844 by promising the immediate annexation of Texas and laying claim to all of Oregon. But

Polk had even greater territorial ambitions: he wanted all of Mexico west of Texas to the Pacific Ocean and was prepared to go to war to get it. What he was not prepared for, though he should have been, was the major crisis over slavery unleashed by the success of his expansionist dreams.

The War with Mexico, 1846–1848

Mexico had not prospered in the twenty-five years since it won independence from Spain in 1821. Its population remained small at seven million people, and its stagnant economy yielded only modest tax revenue, much of which was eaten up by interest payments on foreign debt and a bloated and often corrupt government bureaucracy. Consequently, the Mexican republic lacked the money and people to settle its distant northern provinces. The Spanish-speaking population of California and New Mexico remained small—about 75,000 in 1840—and contributed little to the national economy. Still, the fledgling Mexican government was determined to retain all its historical territories, and when the breakaway Texas Republic accepted American statehood on July 4, 1845, Mexico broke off diplomatic relations with the United States.

President James Polk viewed that action as a great opportunity. Since taking office in March 1845, Polk had moved quickly to implement Congress's resolution annexing Texas and had devised a secret plan to acquire all Mexico's far northern provinces. To intimidate the Mexican government, he ordered General Zachary Taylor and an American army of 2,000 soldiers to occupy the disputed lands between the Nueces River (the historical boundary of the Mexican province of Texas) and the Rio Grande, which the expansionist-minded Texas Republic claimed as its southern and western border (see Map 14.1). Then Polk launched a diplomatic initiative, dispatching John Slidell on a secret mission to Mexico City. Slidell was instructed to secure Mexico's acceptance of the Rio Grande boundary and buy the Mexican provinces of New Mexico and California, paying as much as $30 million. When Slidell arrived in December 1845, Mexican officials refused to see him, declaring that the American annexation of Texas was illegal.

Anticipating the failure of Slidell's mission, Polk had already embarked on an alternative plan to take California. The president's strategy was to foment a revolution that, as in Texas, would lead to the creation of an independent republic and a request for annexation. In October 1845 he had Secretary of State James Buchanan advise Thomas O. Larkin, the U.S. consul in the major port of Monterey, that the United States would protect Californians if they sought independence from Mexico. Larkin immediately encouraged leading Mexican residents to support a peaceful shift of sovereignty. To add military muscle to any uprising, Polk sent orders to John Sloat, the commander of the U.S. naval squadron in the Pacific, to seize San Francisco Bay and California's coastal towns in the event of war. The president also had the War department dispatch Captain John C. Frémont and an "exploring" party of heavily armed soldiers deep into Mexican territory. By December 1845 Frémont had reached California's Sacramento Valley.

MAP 14.1
The War with Mexico, 1846–1848
American forces easily seized Monterey and San Fransisco but encountered strong Mexican resistance in southern California at San Pascual and San Gabriel. In the heart of Mexico, Santa Anna took advantage of the division of American forces to attack the army of Zachary Taylor at Buena Vista (February 1847). Repulsed by Taylor's smaller force, Santa Anna retreated south to Mexico City, where he was decisively defeated by another American army led by Winfield Scott.

Events now moved quickly toward war. When Polk learned of the failure of Slidell's mission, he ordered General Taylor to build a fort near the Rio Grande, hoping to incite an armed response by Mexico. As Ulysses S. Grant, a young officer serving with Taylor, said much later, "We were sent to provoke a fight, but it was essential that Mexico should commence it." When Mexican and American forces clashed near the Rio Grande in May 1846, Polk delivered the war message he had drafted long before, saying that Mexico "has passed the boundary of the United States, has invaded our territory, and shed American blood upon the American soil." Ignoring Whig pleas for a peaceful resolution of the dispute, the Democratic majority in Congress voted for war with Mexico, unleashing large and almost hysterical demonstrations of popular support. To avoid a simultaneous war with Britain over Oregon, the president retreated from his campaign pledge of "fifty-four forty or fight" and accepted a British proposal to divide the Oregon region at the 49th parallel.

As the Senate ratified the Oregon Treaty with Great Britain in June 1846, fighting broke out in California between American naval forces and Mexican authorities. Commander John Sloat landed 250 marines and seamen in Monterey and declared that California "henceforward will be a portion of the United States." American settlers in the interior staged a revolt and, supported by Frémont's forces, captured the town of Sonoma. To ensure American control of California, Polk ordered army units under General Stephen Kearney to capture Santa Fe in New Mexico (which they did in August) and march to the Pacific Ocean. Despite stiff resistance from the Mexicans, American forces secured control of all of California early in 1847 (see Map 14.1).

Zachary Taylor's army in Texas had been equally successful. In May 1846 the American forces had crossed the Rio Grande, occupied Matamoros, and moved south, using their advantage in artillery to win a series of victories against a larger Mexican army. After a fierce six-day battle in September, Taylor took the interior town of Monterrey. Two months later, a U.S. naval squadron in the Gulf of Mexico seized Tampico, Mexico's second most important port. By the end of 1846 the United States controlled much of northeastern Mexico.

Polk expected that these American victories would prompt the Mexicans to sue for peace, but he had underrated their national pride and strength. Under the newly elected president General Antonio Lopez de Santa Anna, Mexico refused to end the fighting. Instead Santa Anna went on the offensive, attacking the depleted units of Zachary Taylor at Buena Vista in February 1847. Only superiority in artillery enabled Taylor to eke out a victory and hold the American line in northeastern Mexico.

To bring Santa Anna to terms, Polk accepted the plan devised by General Winfield Scott, a veteran army officer, to strike deep into the heart of Mexico. In March 1847 Scott captured the port of Veracruz and began the 260-mile march to Mexico City that the Spanish conquistador Hernando Cortés had taken three centuries earlier. Leading Scott's 14,000 troops was a cadre of talented West Point officers who would become famous in the Civil War: Robert E. Lee, George Meade, and P. G. T. Beauregard. Scott's troops crushed Santa Anna's attempt to block their march at Cerro Gordo, and after inflicting heavy losses on the Mexican army at the Battle of Churubusco, his much-depleted troops seized Mexico City in September 1847. Santa Anna was overthrown, and the new Mexican government agreed to make peace. The war was finally over.

The Wilmot Proviso, Free Soil, and the Election of 1848

Initially many Americans viewed the war with Mexico as a noble struggle to extend American republican institutions across the continent. But the conflict quickly became politically divisive. A few Whigs, such as Charles Francis Adams of Massachusetts and Joshua Giddings of Ohio, had opposed the war from the beginning on moral grounds (becoming known as "conscience Whigs"), viewing it as a conspiracy to add new slave states in the West. They argued that the expansion of slavery would jeopardize the Jeffersonian ideal of a yeoman freeholder society and assure control of the federal government by slaveholding Democrats. These antislavery Whigs grew bolder after the elections of 1846, which gave their party control of Congress. After Taylor's victory at Buena Vista in February 1847, Whigs in the House passed a resolution that congratulated the army but condemned the war, declaring that it had been "unconstitutionally and unnecessarily begun by the President." Whigs grew more vocal as American casualties mounted, particularly during the bloody march to Mexico City.

Whig leaders moved toward an antislavery stance partly because their economic program—especially their support for high tariffs—had lost its appeal. In 1846 Polk and the Congressional Democrats had passed the Walker Tariff, which dramatically reduced duties on imported goods. The Walker Tariff came hard on the heels of Britain's repeal of the Corn Laws (which had placed high duties on imported wheat and corn) and seemed to herald the adoption of free trade throughout the Anglo-American world. American consumers welcomed cheaper prices on imported goods, and their increased purchases pushed up tariff revenues, allowing Polk to finance the war without raising taxes. Given the popularity of free trade, the Whigs could no longer count on winning elections by championing higher tariffs.

As a result of Polk's expansionist policy, the Democrats had even worse problems. In August 1846, David Wilmot, a Democratic representative from Pennsylvania, proposed a simple amendment to a military appropriations bill: slavery would be prohibited in any new territories acquired from Mexico. This provision, known as the Wilmot Proviso, quickly became a rallying point for northerners who feared the expansion of slavery. In the House the Democratic party split as supporters of Martin Van Buren joined forces with antislavery Whigs to pass the Proviso. The Senate, dominated by southerners and proslavery northern Democrats, killed it.

In this heated atmosphere, the most fervent Democrat expansionists became even more aggressive. Polk, Secretary of State Buchanan, and Senators Stephen A. Douglas of Illinois and Jefferson Davis of Mississippi wanted the United States to take at least part of Mexico south of the Rio Grande. But some southerners worried that the United States could not absorb the Mexicans, whom they regarded as an "inferior" people, and feared that a longer war would augment the power of the federal government. John C. Calhoun supported taking only California and New Mexico, the most sparsely populated areas of Mexico. Midwestern Democrats also opposed expansion to the south, in part because of their anger at Polk's compromise with Britain over Oregon.

To reunify the Democratic party before the next election, Polk and Buchanan abandoned their expansionist dreams in Mexico and accepted Calhoun's policy. In February 1848 Polk signed the Treaty of Guadalupe Hidalgo, in which the United States agreed to pay Mexico $15 million in return for more than one-third of its territory: Texas north of the Rio Grande, New Mexico, and California (see Map 14.2). The United States also agreed to assume all the claims of its citizens, totaling $3.2 million, against the Mexican government. The Senate ratified the treaty in March 1848.

The passions aroused by the war dominated the election of 1848. The Wilmot Proviso had energized abolitionists who had been seeking a legislative solution to the problem of slavery, and the Senate's refusal to pass it alarmed them. Antislavery advocates now claimed that southern planters and their northern business allies had entered into a massive "Slave Power" conspiracy to expand the bounds of slavery. To defeat this alleged plan, a significant number of northerners joined a new "free-soil" movement. The free-soilers abandoned the Liberty party's focus on the sinfulness of slavery and the natural rights of African-Americans. Instead, they depicted slavery as a threat to republican institutions and yeoman farming and vowed to prevent its geographic expansion. This shift in emphasis—toward keeping the West open for settlement by white

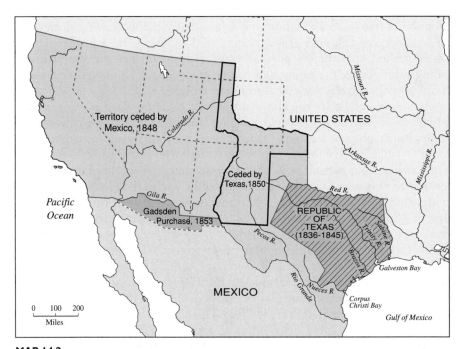

MAP 14.2

The Mexican Cession, 1848

The War with Mexico added a vast territory to the United States: the present states of California, Nevada, Utah, most of Arizona and New Mexico, more than half of Texas, and parts of Wyoming, Colorado, Kansas, and Oklahoma. After Mexico ratified the Treaty of Guadalupe Hidalgo, Polk told Congress that the new territories "constitute of themselves a country large enough for a great empire, and their acquisition is second in importance only to that of Louisiana in 1803."

families and away from freeing slaves—led the radical abolitionist William Lloyd Garrison to denounce free-soil doctrine as racist "whitemanism."

Despite Garrison's hostility, the new political approach worked. The Wilmot Proviso's call for free soil was the first antislavery proposal to attract broad popular support. Hundreds of women in the Great Lakes states joined new female free-soil organizations formed by the American and Foreign Anti-Slavery Society. Frederick Douglass, the foremost black abolitionist, also endorsed free soil, seeing it as the best way to provoke a political struggle between the North and the South that would overthrow slavery. At the same time Douglass urged free-soilers to pay less attention to white demands for land and more attention to the needs of African-Americans, seeking their emancipation in the South and civil rights in the North.

The conflict over slavery took a toll on Polk and the Democratic party. Opposed by free-soilers and exhausted by his rigorous dawn-to-midnight work regime, Polk declined to run for a second term and died three months after leaving office. To maintain unity, the Democrats nominated Senator Lewis Cass of Michigan, an avid expansionist who had advocated buying Cuba, annexing Mexico's Yucatan Peninsula, and taking all of Oregon. Cass campaigned on a platform that was deliberately vague on the question of slavery in the West. He promoted a new idea—*squatter sovereignty*—that would give settlers in each territory the power to determine its status as free or slave.

Cass's political ingenuity failed to hold the party together. Demanding unambiguous opposition to the expansion of slavery, some northern Democrats joined the newly formed Free Soil party, which nominated Martin Van Buren for president. Van Buren's conversion to free soil was genuine, but he also wanted to punish southern Democrats for having denied him the presidential nomination in 1844. To attract Whig votes, the Free Soil party chose a conscience Whig, Charles Francis Adams, as its candidate for vice-president.

To avoid such divisions in their party, the Whigs nominated General Zachary Taylor. Taylor was a southerner and a Louisiana slaveowner, but he had not taken a position on the politically charged issue of slavery in the territories. Equally important, the general's exploits during the War with Mexico had made him a popular hero. Known as "Old Rough and Ready," Taylor possessed a common touch that had won him the affection of his troops. "Our Commander on the Rio Grande," wrote Walt Whitman, "emulates the Great Commander of our revolution"—George Washington.

In 1848, as in 1840, running a military hero worked for the Whigs, but only barely. Taylor took 47 percent of the popular vote against 42 percent for Cass, but the margin in the electoral college was thin: 163 to 127 electoral votes. The Free Soil ticket of Van Buren and Adams made the difference in the election, winning 10 percent of the popular vote and depriving the Democrats of enough votes in New York to cost Cass that state and the presidency. The popularity of the Wilmot Proviso and the rapid growth of the Free Soil party had changed the dynamics of American politics.

1850: Crisis and Compromise

Even before President Taylor took office, events in California had sparked a major political crisis that threatened the Union. In January 1848 (a few months before California formally became part of the United States), workmen building a mill for John A. Sutter discovered flakes of gold in the Sierra Nevada foothills in northern California. Sutter was a Swiss immigrant who arrived in California in 1839, became a Mexican citizen, and established an almost feudal estate in the Sacramento Valley. He tried to keep the discovery a secret, but by May Americans were pouring into the foothills from San Francisco. When President Polk confirmed the discovery in December, the gold rush was on. By January 1849 sixty-one crowded ships had departed from northeastern ports to sail around Cape Horn for San Francisco, and by May 12,000 wagons had crossed the Missouri River, also bound for the goldfields. In 1849 alone more than 80,000 migrants—the "forty-niners"—arrived in California.

The rapid influx of settlers revived the national debate over free soil. The forty-niners, who lived in crowded, chaotic towns and mining camps, demanded the formation of a territorial government to protect their lives and property. To avoid an extended debate over slavery, President Taylor advised the Californians to apply for statehood immediately, and in November 1849 they ratified a state constitution that prohibited slavery. Few of the many southerners who flocked to the goldfields or to San Francisco owed slaves or wanted to; only ranchers in sparsely populated southern California had strongly promoted slavery. For his part, Taylor wanted to attract Free Soilers

California Prospectors
Beginning in 1849, thousands of fortune seekers from all parts of the world converged on the California goldfields. By 1852 the state had 200,000 residents, including 25,000 Chinese, many of whom worked as wage laborers in the goldfields. These prospectors are using a primitive technique—panning—to separate gold from sand and gravel.

The Allure—and Reality—of the Gold Rush

The discovery of gold in California prompted tens of thousands of easterners to head west. Among them were Catherine Haun and her lawyer husband, who, like many others, found adventure but not riches.

Early in January of 1849 we first thought of emigration to California. It was a period of national hard times, and we being financially involved in our business interests near Clinton, Iowa . . . longed to go to the new El Dorado and "pick up" gold enough with which to return and pay off our debts. . . .

Full of the energy and enthusiasm of youth, the prospects of so hazardous an undertaking had no terror for us. Indeed, as we had been married but a few months, it appealed to us as a romantic wedding tour. . . . Some half dozen families of our neighborhood joined us and probably about twenty-five persons constituted our little band. . . .

Eight strong oxen and four of the best horses on the farm were selected to draw our four wagons. . . . Two wagons were filled with merchandise which we hoped to sell at fabulous prices when we should arrive in the "land of gold." The theory of this was good but the practice—well, we never got the goods across the first mountain. . . .

Our caravan had a good many women and children, and although we were probably longer on the journey owing to their presence, they exerted a good influence, as the men did not take such risks with Indians and thereby avoided conflict; . . . more attention was paid to cleanliness and sanitation; and . . . the meals were more regular and better cooked, thus preventing much sickness. . . .

[W]e reached Sacramento on November 4, 1849, just six months and ten days after leaving . . . [but] it was past the middle of January before we reached Marysville—there were only a half dozen houses, all occupied at exorbitant prices. Someone was calling for the services of a lawyer to draw up a will, and my husband offered to do it, for which he charged $150. This seemed a happy omen for success and he hung out his shingle, abandoning all thought of going to the mines.

SOURCE: Diary of Catherine Haun, Huntington Library, San Marino, California (MSS HM 538). Reprinted by permission of The Huntington Library.

and northern Democrats into the Whig party and urged Congress to admit California as a free state.

Southern politicians were alarmed by the swift victory of the antislavery forces in California. Not only had a valuable area been lost to free soil, but the admission of California would threaten the carefully maintained balance in the Senate. In 1845 the entry of Texas and Florida had raised the total of slave states to fifteen, against thirteen free states. However, the entry of Iowa in 1846 and Wisconsin in 1848 had reestablished the balance. Now southern leaders feared that the admission of California would give the North a majority in the Senate as well as the House, placing their section at a political disadvantage from which it would never recover. They were prepared to block the entry of California as a free state unless the federal government guaranteed the future of slavery.

The resulting impasse produced long and passionate debates in Congress. As usual, John C. Calhoun took the most extreme southern position, warning of possible secession by the slave states and civil war. To avoid that outcome, he proposed that slavery be guaranteed in all the territories and that a constitutional amendment be adopted to create a permanent balance of power between the sections. The presidency would become a dual office, with authority divided between executives from the South and the North, each with full veto power.

In making those proposals, Calhoun advanced a radically new constitutional doctrine: Congress had no constitutional authority to regulate slavery in the territories and thus could not exclude slavery from a territory before its admission as a state. This argument ran counter to a half century of practice. Congress had prohibited slavery in the Northwest Territory and, by the Missouri Compromise of 1821, in most of the Louisiana Purchase.

While Calhoun's new doctrine won support in the Deep South, many southerners were prepared to accept a more moderate position with respect to the status of slavery in the West: an extension of the Missouri Compromise line to the Pacific Ocean. This would guarantee slaveowners access to some western territory (in a separate state in southern California, for example) and add more slave states to the Union. Some northern Democrats, including former Secretary of State James Buchanan, also favored this plan as a way to resolve the crisis.

A third alternative was squatter sovereignty, Lewis Cass's platform in the election of 1848, now being championed by Democratic Senator Stephen Douglas of Illinois. Douglas called his plan *popular sovereignty* to emphasize its roots in republican ideology, and it had considerable appeal. Popular sovereignty would place decisions about slavery in the hands of local settlers and their territorial governments rather than in Congress, removing the explosive issue from national politics. However, popular sovereignty was a vague and slippery concept, because it was not clear at what point the people of a territory could legalize or ban slavery—when the territory was first organized or later when it framed a constitution and applied for statehood.

Antislavery advocates were unwilling to accept *any* expansion of slavery, lending credence to Calhoun's warning of the possible breakup of the Union. In 1850 Senator Salmon P. Chase of Ohio, elected by a Democratic–Free Soil coalition, and Senator William H. Seward, a New York Whig, urged federal authorities to contain slavery and then extinguish it completely. Condemning slavery as "morally unjust, politically unwise, and socially pernicious" and invoking "a higher law than the Constitution," Seward demanded bold action to protect freedom, "the common heritage of mankind."

Standing on the brink of disaster, senior Whigs and Democrats desperately sought a compromise. Through a long, complex legislative process, the Whig leaders Henry Clay and Daniel Webster and the Democrat Stephen A. Douglas organized a complex package of six laws known collectively as the Compromise of 1850. To mollify the South, the Compromise included a new Fugitive Slave Act that strengthened a law of 1793 by allowing slaveowners to use federal magistrates to return runaway slaves. To satisfy the North, the Compromise admitted California as a free state, resolved a boundary dispute between New Mexico and Texas in favor of New Mexico through federal assumption of $10 million in unpaid debts of the Republic of Texas, and abolished the slave trade, but not slavery, in the District of Columbia. Finally, the Compromise organized the rest of the lands acquired from Mexico into the territories of New Mexico and Utah on the basis of popular sovereignty.

The Compromise averted a secession crisis in 1850—but only barely. In the midst of the struggle the governor of South Carolina declared that there was not "the slightest doubt" that his state would secede. He and the leaders of Georgia, Mississippi, and Alabama organized special conventions to protect "Southern Rights" and demand secession. Although moderate southern politicians persuaded the convention delegates to support the Compromise, in return they had to agree to support secession in the future if Congress abolished slavery anywhere, failed to recognize slavery in a new territory, or refused to admit a territory with a proslavery constitution into the Union. Lacking the support of other slave states, the "fire-eaters" in South Carolina drew back from secession, averting a constitutional crisis. The fact that the Compromise of 1850 elicited such a passionately negative response throughout the Deep South—and among many northern Whigs and Free Soilers as well—did not augur well for its success.

THE END OF THE SECOND PARTY SYSTEM, 1850–1858

The architects of the Compromise of 1850 hoped that their agreement, like the Missouri Compromise of 1820, would resolve the issue of slavery for another generation. But their hopes were quickly dashed as one conflict after another divided Americans along sectional lines. Demanding freedom for fugitive slaves and free soil in the West, some northerners blocked implementation of the Compromise, while some southerners insisted on the expansion of slavery not just in the West but in the Caribbean. These disputes led to violence and destroyed the Second Party System, deepening the crisis of the Union.

The Fugitive Slave Act

The most controversial element of the Compromise proved to be the Fugitive Slave Act. Under its terms, federal judges or special commissioners in the northern states determined the status of blacks who were accused of being runaway slaves. A commissioner would receive a $10 fee if an alleged fugitive was found to be a runaway but only $5 if he or she was declared a free person—clear encouragement for a slavery verdict. The accused blacks were denied jury trials and even the right to testify; their supporters faced stiff penalties if they defied the law. Because federal marshals were legally required to support slave catchers, the new legislation was effective and many fugitives (as well as some free blacks) were sent to the South and enslaved.

The plight of runaways and the appearance of slave catchers in northern communities aroused popular hostility, and free blacks and abolitionists organized vigilante groups to block enforcement of the act. In October 1850 Theodore Parker and other Boston abolitionists defied the law by helping two slaves escape to freedom and driving a Georgia slave catcher out of town. A year later rioters broke into a courthouse in Syracuse, New York, and freed a fugitive slave. Abandoning pacifism, Frederick Douglass declared that "the only way to make a Fugitive Slave Law a dead letter is to make half a dozen or more dead kidnappers." As if in response, in September 1851 a deadly confrontation took place in the Quaker village of Christiana, Pennsylvania. About twenty African-Americans, including several escaped slaves, exchanged gunfire with a group of slave catchers from Maryland; the slaveowner was killed, and his son was severely wounded. Millard Fillmore, who had become president after the death of Zachary Taylor in 1850, sent troops and federal marshals to arrest thirty-six blacks and four whites and had them indicted for treason. But a jury acquitted one defendant, and northern public opinion forced the government to drop its charges against the rest.

Harriet Beecher Stowe's abolitionist novel, *Uncle Tom's Cabin* (1852), increased northern opposition to the Fugitive Slave Act. The novel tells of a compassionate but weak slaveholder in Kentucky who sells two slaves, Tom and a five-year-old boy, to a slave trader to pay off debts. The beautiful Eliza Harris, the boy's mother, refuses to be separated from her son. With the child in her arms, she crosses the Ohio River on cakes of ice just ahead of the vicious slave trader. Eliza reaches the house of an Ohio politician who, to preserve the Union, had set aside his "private feeling" and voted for a fugitive slave law. His wife persuades him to follow his heart and help Eliza and her child escape to Canada. Meanwhile, Tom has fallen under the control of Simon Legree, a brutal overseer on a southern plantation, who beats Tom to death but never conquers his Christian soul. By translating the moral principles of abolitionism into heartrending personal situations, Beecher's novel evoked a mixture of empathy and outrage throughout the North. More than 300,000 Americans bought copies of *Uncle Tom's Cabin,* and countless families flocked to an emotionally charged stage version produced by local theater companies.

Responding to the growing popular opposition to slave catching, some northern legislatures challenged federal authority by enacting *personal liberty* laws that extended legal rights to accused fugitives. In 1857 the Wisconsin Supreme Court went even further. In *Ableman v. Booth* the Wisconsin judges

Uncle Tom's Cabin
In these illustrations from the original 1852 edition of *Uncle Tom's Cabin*, the engraver portrays Eliza Harris (top panel) as a caring mother and Tom (bottom) as a well-dressed and noble servant. Like the book's text, these images offered whites a sympathetic view of African-Americans, challenging generations of negative stereotypes.

claimed the authority to void federal statutes, ruling that the Fugitive Slave law could not be enforced in their state because it violated the Constitution. Then they contested the power of the federal courts to review their decision, directly challenging a jurisdictional doctrine that had been accepted for more than a generation. When the case was finally considered by the U.S. Supreme Court in 1859, Chief Justice Taney led a unanimous court in affirming the supremacy of federal over state courts—a position that has stood the test of time—and upheld the constitutionality of the Fugitive Slave law. But by that time popular sentiment in many northern states had made it impossible to catch fugitive blacks or secure their conviction. As Douglass had hoped, the act had become a "dead letter."

The Whigs' Decline and the Democrats' Diplomacy

The conflict over fugitive slaves split the Whig party, which went into the election of 1852 weakened by the deaths of Zachary Taylor and Henry Clay, one of its greatest leaders. Passing over Fillmore because of his reputation as an aristocratic snob and vigorous enforcement of the Fugitive Slave Act, the Whigs nominated General Winfield Scott, another hero of the War with Mexico. But about a third of southern Whigs refused to support Scott and, angry over the party's pronorthern economic stance and growing opposition to slavery, threw their support to the Democrats.

The Democrats too were divided. Southerners wanted a candidate who would support Calhoun's position that all territories should be open to slavery, but northern delegates rejected that idea outright. They were committed to the principle of popular sovereignty but were sharply divided among the three candidates—Lewis Cass, Stephen Douglas, and James Buchanan—who supported it. For forty-eight ballots no one could secure the necessary two-thirds majority. Exhausted, the convention settled on a compromise candidate, Franklin Pierce of New Hampshire, a handsome and congenial man reputed to be sympathetic to the South.

The Democrats' cautious strategy paid off, and they swept the election. Pleased by the admission of California as a free state, Martin Van Buren and many other Free Soilers voted for Pierce, reuniting the Democratic party. Conversely, the election fragmented the Whig party. The massive exodus of southerners undermined its status as a national party, and it soon split into sectional wings. The Whigs would never again wage a national campaign.

As president, Pierce pursued an expansionist foreign policy. To assist northern merchants, he supported an ongoing effort to expand trade with Asia by dispatching a mission to Japan that successfully negotiated a commercial treaty. But Pierce was even more solicitous of southern interests. To resolve a dispute over the southern boundary of New Mexico, the president revived Polk's plan to annex Mexican territory south of the Rio Grande. Pierce and his secretary of war, Jefferson Davis, sent James Gadsden to buy a major portion of northern Mexico and Baja (Lower) California. Mexican officials refused to part with those large territories but agreed to the sale of 30,000 square miles of land south of the Gila River. Gadsden, a South Carolina politician and railroad promoter, wanted this territory to expedite the construction of a southern transcontinental railroad to the Pacific. Completed in 1854, the Gadsden Purchase, as it became known, rubbed salt into Mexico's war wounds, reminding it of the power of its northern neighbor.

Pierce's most dramatic foreign policy initiative came in the Caribbean. Southern expansionists had funded three clandestine military expeditions to Spanish Cuba, where they hoped to prod the slaveowning elite into declaring independence. Once Cuba was independent, it would be invited to join the Union as a slave state. In 1853 Pierce covertly supported a new Cuban expedition led by John A. Quitman, a former governor of Mississippi. While Quitman was building up his forces, the Pierce administration threatened war with Spain over the seizure of an American ship, demanding an apology and a large indemnity. But when northern Democrats in Congress refused to support aggressive diplomacy designed to add a new slave state, Pierce and Secretary of State William L. Marcy had to back down.

Still determined to seize Cuba, Marcy instructed the American minister in Madrid "to detach that island from the Spanish dominion" by purchase. When that initiative also failed, Marcy encouraged the minister and the

American diplomats in France and Great Britain to pressure Pierce to seize the island. The result was an inflammatory message to Pierce that became known as the Ostend Manifesto (1854). Invoking the rhetoric of Manifest Destiny, the three American ministers declared that the United States would be justified in seizing Cuba "by every law, human and Divine." Quickly leaked to the press by antiexpansionists, the Ostend Manifesto triggered a new wave of northern resentment against the South and forced Pierce to halt his efforts to acquire Cuba. But the Democrats' policy of expansionism in the Caribbean had already revived northern fears of a "Slave Power" conspiracy.

Kansas-Nebraska and the Rise of New Parties

Almost immediately a new struggle over westward expansion deepened sectional divisions. Because the Missouri Compromise prohibited slavery in the Louisiana Purchase north of 36° 30', southern senators had delayed the political organization of that area, allowing only the admission of Iowa to the Union in 1846 and the formation of the Minnesota Territory. Even though much of the remaining area was in the "Great American Desert," westward-looking residents of the Ohio River Valley and the Upper South demanded that it be organized for settlement. Senator Stephen A. Douglas of Illinois became their foremost spokesman, championing western development and the building of a northern transcontinental railroad from Chicago to California. In 1854 Douglas introduced a bill to extinguish native American rights on the central Plains and organize a large territory to be called Nebraska. Because Nebraska was north of 36° 30', it would be a free territory.

Douglas's bill conflicted with the plans of southern senators, who were determined to extend slavery throughout the Louisiana Purchase and, like James Gadsden, hoped that a city in a slaveholding state—New Orleans, Memphis, or St. Louis—would become the eastern terminus of a transcontinental railroad. To win southern support for the organization of Nebraska, Douglas made two major concessions. First, he amended his bill so that it explicitly repealed the Missouri Compromise, which had prohibited slavery in the northern part of the Louisiana Purchase. The region would be organized on the basis of popular sovereignty. Second, Douglas agreed to the formation of two new territories, Nebraska and Kansas, rather than one, giving slaveholders a chance to dominate the settlement of Kansas, the more southern territory (see Map 14.3). To win northern support for this scheme, Douglas argued that Kansas would be settled primarily by non-slaveholders because its climate and terrain were not suited to plantation agriculture. Supported primarily by southern representatives (along with some northern Democrats), the Kansas-Nebraska Act passed in May 1854.

The Kansas-Nebraska Act proved to be the last nail in the coffin of the Second Party System of Whigs and Democrats. Abolitionists and free-soilers

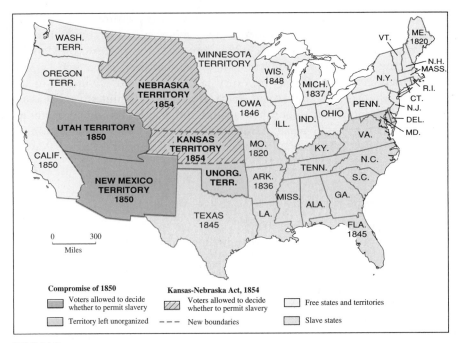

MAP 14.3

The Compromise of 1850 and the Kansas-Nebraska Act, 1854
Vast territories were at stake in the contest over the extension of slavery. The Compromise of 1850 resolved the status of lands in the Far West: California would be a free state, and the settlers of the Utah and New Mexico territories would decide their own fate. The implementation of popular sovereignty in Kansas and Nebraska sparked a local civil war, revealing a fatal flaw in the concept.

denounced the act for opening new territories to slavery, calling it "part of a great scheme for extending and perpetuating supremacy of the slave power." Antislavery northern Whigs and "Anti-Nebraska" Democrats abandoned their respective parties to create a new party, taking the Jeffersonian name *Republican*. Emphasizing uncompromising opposition to the expansion of slavery, the Republicans ran a slate of candidates, primarily in the Midwest, in the congressional election of 1854.

Like most American parties, the Republican party was a coalition of diverse groups—Free Soilers, antislavery Democrats, conscience Whigs—but its founders shared a distinct vision. In the Republican view, slavery produced only two classes of people: masters and slaves. The masters were corrupted by wielding unlimited power, a system of rule that produced habits of subservience, ignorance, and sloth among slaves and poor whites. In contrast, Republicans such as Senator Thaddeus Stevens of Pennsylvania celebrated the virtues of a society based on "the middling classes who own the soil and work it with their own hands." They envisioned communities in which no person would have unlimited power over another and social mobility would prevent the division of society into fixed classes. Abraham Lincoln, an Illinois Whig who became a Republican, articulated the party's vision. "There is no permanent class of hired laborers among us," he argued, and every man had a chance to become an owner. "The man who labored for another last year, this year labors for himself, and next year he will hire others to labor for him." In the face of increasing class divisions in the industrializing North and Midwest, Lincoln and his fellow Republicans asserted the values of republican freedom, individual enterprise, and social mobility.

Competing for Whig and Democratic votes was another new party, the "Know-Nothing," or American, party. The Know-Nothing party had its origins in the anti-immigrant, anti-Catholic passions of the 1840s (see Chapter 13). In 1850 various secret anti-Catholic societies banded together in the Order of the Star-Spangled Banner; a year later they formed the American party. The secrecy-conscious members of the party sometimes answered outsiders' questions by saying "I know nothing," which gave the party its nickname, but its program was far from secret. Know-Nothings attempted to unite northern and southern voters behind a program of nativist opposition to the "alien menace": Irish and German Catholics. Many supported a ban on immigration and advocated literacy tests for voters, which they thought would disfranchise most recent immigrants. In 1854 the Know-Nothings gained control of the state governments of Massachusetts and Pennsylvania and, allied with the Whigs, commanded a majority in the U.S. House of Representatives. The emergence of a new major party led by nativists suddenly became a real possibility.

At that moment the implementation of the Kansas-Nebraska Act created a new political crisis. In 1854 thousands of settlers began to rush into Kansas, putting Douglas's theory of popular sovereignty to the test. On the side of slavery, Senator David R. Atchison of Missouri organized residents of his state to cross into Kansas and vote in crucial elections. Opposing him were agents of the New England Emigrant Aid Society, organized by abolitionists to colonize Kansas with free-soilers. The preference of the Pierce administration was clear. In March 1855 the administration recognized the territorial legislature in Lecompton, Kansas, which had been elected largely by proslavery Missourians who had crossed the border to cast ballots. The territorial legislature declared that questioning the legitimacy of slavery was a felony and aiding a fugitive slave was a capital offense. Pierce assisted the legislature with federal troops and proslavery judicial appointees, but free-soilers rejected the legitimacy of the territorial government.

In May 1856 both sides turned to violence. A proslavery gang, 700 strong, sacked the free-soil town of Lawrence, destroying two newspaper offices, looting stores, and burning down buildings. The attack on Lawrence enraged John Brown, an abolitionist from New York and Ohio, whose free-state militia force arrived too late to save the town. Brown was a complex man with a checkered past. Born in 1800, he had started more than twenty businesses in six states, had fallen into bankruptcy, and had often been sued by his creditors.

Free State Battery, 1856
In Kansas the Civil War began in 1856 as free-soilers from the upper Midwest fought with proslavery forces from Missouri. "[I am using] my utmost endeavors to change the attitude of the Free State settlers from a defensive to an offensive warfare," a young man wrote to his brother in Indiana, but "I found that arms were really scarce." This cannon had seen service in the War with Mexico.

Nonetheless, he had an intelligence and a moral intensity that won the trust of influential people, including leading abolitionists. According to a free-soil minister who knew him, Brown believed "that God had raised him up on purpose to break the jaws of the wicked." Taking vengeance for the sack of Lawrence three days later, he and a few followers murdered and mutilated five proslavery settlers. We must "fight fire with fire" and "strike terror in the hearts of the proslavery people," Brown declared. The "Pottawatomie massacre," as the killings became known, initiated a guerrilla war in Kansas that cost about 200 lives.

The violence that began in Kansas spread within a week to the halls of Congress. In an inflammatory speech, "The Crime against Kansas," Senator Charles Sumner of Massachusetts denounced the Pierce administration, the South, and Senator Andrew P. Butler of South Carolina, who Sumner said had taken "the harlot slavery" as his mistress. Butler's nephew and protégé, Congressman Preston Brooks, took offense at Sumner's attack. Brooks accosted Sumner at his desk and beat him on the head with a walking cane. Severely injured, Sumner did not return to the Senate for two and a half years; Massachusetts venerated him as a martyr, keeping his seat open for him. Southern

"Bleeding Kansas": A Southern View

Early in 1856 Axalla John Hoole and his bride left South Carolina to build a new life in Kansas. These letters show that things did not go well from the start and only got worse; after eighteen months the Hooles returned to South Carolina. A Confederate militia captain, Axalla Hoole died in the Battle of Chickamauga in September 1863.

Kansas City, Missouri, Apl. 3d., 1856

My Dear Brother . . .

The Missourians . . . are very sanguine about Kansas being a slave state & I have heard some of them say it *shall* be . . . but generally speaking, I have not met with the reception which I expected. Everyone seems bent on the Almighty Dollar, and as a general thing that seems to be their only thought. . . .

Lecompton, K.T., Sept. 12, 1856

My dear Mother . . .

I have been unwell ever since the 9th of July. . . . I thought of going to work in a few days, when the Abolitionists broke out and I have had to stand guard of nights when I ought to have been in bed, took cold which . . . caused diarrhea. . . . Betsie is well—

You perceive from the heading of this that I am now in Lecompton, almost all of the Proslavery party between this place and Lawrence are here. We brought our families here, as we thought that we would be better able to defend ourselves. . . .

Lane [and a Free State army] came against us last Friday (a week ago to-day). As it happened we had about 400 men with two cannon . . . but we were acting on the defensive, and did not think it prudent to commence the engagement.

Douglas, K.T., July the 5th., 1857

Dear Sister . . .

I fear, Sister, that [our] coming here will do no good at last, as I begin to think that this will be made a Free State at last. 'Tis true we have elected Proslavery men to draft a state constitution, but I feel pretty certain, if it is put to a vote of the people, it will be rejected, as I feel pretty confident that they have a majority here at this time. The South has ceased all efforts, while the North is redoubling her exertions. . . .

SOURCE: William Stanley Hoole, ed., "A Southerner's Viewpoint of the Kansas Situation, 1856–1857," *Kansas Historical Quarterly* (1934), vol. 3: 43–68, 145–171, passim.

representatives prevented the House from censuring Brooks, and when he resigned, South Carolina voters not only returned him to Congress but also sent
him a batch of new canes to replace the one he had broken in the attack. Passion had replaced compromise as the hallmark of American politics.

Buchanan's Failed Presidency

The violence in Kansas dominated the presidential election of 1856. The Democrats reaffirmed their support for popular sovereignty and the Kansas-
Nebraska Act, but, to counter the impact of "Bleeding Kansas" on northern
voters, turned away from Pierce and nominated James Buchanan of Pennsylvania. A tall, dignified, white-haired figure of sixty-four years, Buchanan was
an experienced but unimaginative and timid politician.

The two-year-old Republican party counted on anger over "Bleeding
Kansas" to boost its fortunes. The party's platform denounced the Kansas-
Nebraska Act and, alleging a "Slave Power" conspiracy to expand slavery, insisted that the federal government prohibit slavery in all the territories. As one
Republican put it, "If we do not exclude slavery from the Territories, it will
exclude us." The platform also called for federal subsidies to transcontinental
railroads, reviving the element of the Whig economic program that was most
popular among midwestern Democrats. For president, the Republicans nominated John C. Frémont, a free-soiler famous for his role in the conquest of
California.

The American party entered the election with high hopes, but it quickly
split into warring factions—North and South—over the struggle in Kansas.
The Republicans cleverly maneuvered the northern faction into endorsing
Frémont and won the support of many Know-Nothing workingmen by
adding anti-Catholic nativism to its program of high tariffs on imported manufactures. As a Pennsylvania congressman declared, "Let our motto be, protection to *everything American, against everything foreign.*" The southern faction of
the American party nominated Millard Fillmore, who ran an effective campaign and won 21 percent of the national vote but only 8 electoral votes.

James Buchanan, the Democrat, won the three-way race. Some southern
Democrats openly threatened secession if Frémont won, and, fearful of such a
cataclysm, enough northern Democrats remained loyal to the party to give
the election to Buchanan, who drew 1.8 million votes (45 percent) to 1.3 million (33 percent) for Frémont. Frémont demonstrated the appeal of the new
Republican party in the North by carrying eleven free states with 114 electoral votes. Buchanan took only five free states, and a small shift of the popular
vote to Frémont in Illinois and Pennsylvania would have won him the
presidency.

The dramatic restructuring of parties was now apparent. The Know-
Nothings had lost their bid to become a major party, and the Republicans had
replaced the Whigs in the contest with the Democrats for national supremacy.
Because the Republicans had no support in the South, the implications for

the sectional crisis were ominous; a victory for the new party might mean the end of the Union. The fate of the Republic hinged on the ability of President Buchanan to achieve a new compromise that would protect free soil in the West and slavery in the South.

Events—and his own values and weaknesses—conspired against Buchanan. Although Congress had long regulated slavery in the territories, its authority to do so had never been subjected to a clear test of constitutionality. In 1856 the case of Dred Scott reached the Supreme Court. Scott was an enslaved African-American who had lived for a time with his master, an army surgeon, in the free state of Illinois and at Fort Snelling in the Wisconsin Territory (later incorporated into the Minnesota Territory), where the Northwest Ordinance (1787) and the Missouri Compromise (1820) prohibited slavery. In his suit, which he filed in Missouri in 1846, Scott claimed that his residence in a free state and a free territory had made him free. In March 1857, only two days after Buchanan's inauguration, the Court announced its decision in *Dred Scott v. Sandford*.

Seven members of the Court concurred on one critical point: Scott remained a slave. But the judges in the majority could not agree on the legal issues raised by the case, and each justice wrote a separate opinion. In the most influential opinion, Chief Justice Roger B. Taney of Maryland declared that blacks, slave *or* free, could not be citizens of the United States and that Scott therefore had no right to sue in federal court. That argument was controversial enough, since free African-Americans could be citizens of a state (which would give them the right to enter federal courts). But Taney went on to make two even more controversial points. First, he repeated John C. Calhoun's argument that because the Fifth Amendment prohibited the taking of property without due process of law, Congress could not prevent southern citizens from taking their slave "property" into the territories or owning it there. Therefore, the chief justice concluded, the Northwest Ordinance and the Missouri Compromise—which prohibited slavery in the territories—had *never* been constitutional, and so Scott's residence at Fort Snelling could not have freed him. Second, Taney declared that Congress could not give to territorial governments any powers that Congress itself did not possess. Since Congress had no authority to prohibit slavery in a territory, neither did a territorial government. Thus Taney also endorsed Calhoun's interpretation of popular sovereignty: only when settlers wrote a constitution and requested statehood could they prohibit slavery.

Five of the seven justices in the majority, including the chief justice, were Democrats from slave states. They and President Buchanan—who privately twisted the arm of his fellow Pennsylvanian, Justice Robert C. Grier, to join the five—intended to make political policy as well as constitutional law. They hoped their decision would be accepted out of respect for the Court and ease the sectional crisis. The result was just the opposite. In a single stroke a Democrat-dominated Supreme Court had declared the Republicans' antislavery platform unconstitutional, a decision the Republicans could never accept.

Led by Senator William H. Seward of New York, they accused the Supreme Court and President Buchanan of participating in the "Slave Power" conspiracy.

Buchanan then made things worse. In early 1858 he recommended the admission of Kansas as a slave state under the constitution written by proslavery forces, the so-called Lecompton constitution. Most observers—including the Democrat Stephen Douglas—believed that constitution had been enacted by fraudulent means. Angered that Buchanan would not permit a referendum in Kansas on the constitution, Douglas broke with the president and his southern allies and mobilized western Democrats and Republicans in the House of Representatives to prevent the admission of Kansas as a slave state. (Kansas would enter the Union as a free state in 1861, after many southern representatives had left Congress.) By pursuing a proslavery agenda—first in the *Dred Scott* decision and then in Kansas—Buchanan had split his party and the nation.

ABRAHAM LINCOLN AND THE END OF UNION, 1858–1860

The crisis of the Union intensified as the national Democratic party fragmented into sectional factions and the Republicans gained the support of a majority of northern voters. During this transition Abraham Lincoln emerged as the pivotal figure in American politics, the only Republican leader whose policies and temperament might have saved the Union. But few southerners trusted Lincoln, and his election threatened to unleash the secessionist movement that had menaced the nation since 1850.

Lincoln's Early Career

The rise of the middle class in the small towns of the Ohio River Valley shaped Lincoln's early career. He came from a farming family of modest means that, searching for prosperity, had moved from Kentucky, where Lincoln was born in 1809, to Indiana and then Illinois. In 1831 Lincoln rejected the life of a farmer and began working as a store clerk in New Salem, Illinois. There he won the admiration of the young men who hung out in local saloons, who elected him captain of a company of militia. A socially ambitious young man, Lincoln also sought entry into the cultured world of the middle class, becoming a member of the New Salem Debating Society. With the help of the local schoolmaster he mastered English grammar and elementary mathematics, and another villager introduced him to Shakespeare.

Lincoln's ambition was "a little engine that knew no rest," as a close associate later remarked. Admitted to the bar in 1837, Lincoln moved to Springfield, the small country town that had become the new state capital. There he met Mary Todd, the daughter of a successful Kentucky businessman and politician; they married in 1842. The couple were a picture in contrasts. Her tastes were aristocratic; his were humble. She was volatile; he was easygoing and deliberate.

Bouts of depression, which plagued Lincoln throughout his life, tried her patience and tested his character. Entering political life, Lincoln served four terms as a Whig in the lower house of the Illinois legislature, where he promoted education, state banking, and internal improvements such as turnpikes, canals, and railroads. An effective speaker, he campaigned actively for William Henry Harrison in 1840 and for his political hero, Henry Clay, in 1844. In 1846 Lincoln won election to Congress.

Abraham Lincoln
Abraham Lincoln was the most photographed man of his time, yet none of the photographs convey his wit, charm, and intelligence. The photography of that day required subjects to stand absolutely still for long periods, causing Lincoln to appear as a formal, rather distant man or, as here, giving him a sad and abstracted air.

As a member of Congress during the War with Mexico, Lincoln had been forced to take a stand on the contentious issue of slavery. He had long felt that slavery was unjust and in 1838 had condemned mob violence against abolitionists. But Lincoln had little sympathy for abolitionism and did not believe that the federal government had the constitutional authority to tamper with slavery in the southern states. Still, he knew that the Whig party had to hold the allegiance of the growing number of people opposed to the expansion of slavery.

Lincoln sought a middle ground. He supported the appropriations bill that sustained Polk's war in Mexico but, to express opposition to the spread of slavery, voted for the Wilmot Proviso. He also proposed the gradual abolition of bondage in the District of Columbia, advancing a plan that would provide compensation to slaveowners and require approval in a referendum of the "free white citizens" of the District. Lincoln argued that such measures—firm opposition to the expansion of slavery, gradual emancipation, and the colonization of freed slaves in Africa and elsewhere—represented the only practical way to address the issue. But his ideas were derided by both sides. Abolitionists assailed him as "the slave hound of Illinois," and proslavery voters in southern Illinois condemned his support for the Wilmot Proviso. Dismayed, Lincoln withdrew from politics and devoted his energies to an increasingly lucrative legal practice representing railroads and manufacturers in Illinois.

Lincoln returned to the political fray after the passage of Stephen Douglas's Kansas-Nebraska Act. Attacking Douglas's position on popular sovereignty in what became known as his Peoria address, Lincoln articulated a clear position on slavery. He would not threaten the institution in areas where it existed, but would use the authority of the national government to exclude it from the territories. Beyond that, Lincoln expressed his conviction that the nation must eventually cut out slavery like a "cancer."

Abandoning the Whig party in favor of the Republicans, Lincoln soon emerged as their leader in Illinois. Campaigning for the U.S. Senate against Stephen Douglas in 1858, Lincoln alerted his audiences to the dangers of the "Slave Power" conspiracy. He warned that the proslavery Supreme Court might soon declare that the Constitution "does not permit a *state* to exclude slavery from its limits," just as it had decided (in *Dred Scott*) that "neither Congress nor the territorial legislature can do it." In that event, he continued, "we shall *awake* to the *reality* . . . that the *Supreme Court* has made *Illinois* a slave state."

The fear that slavery would be extended throughout the nation was widely felt in the North in the wake of the *Dred Scott* decision and informed Lincoln's famous "House Divided" speech. Quoting from the Bible, "A house divided against itself cannot stand," he predicted a constitutional crisis that would bring either the triumph or the demise of slavery:

> I believe this government cannot endure permanently half *slave* and half *free*. I do not expect the Union to be dissolved—I do not expect the house to *fall*—but I do expect it will cease to be divided. It will become *all* one thing, or *all* the other.

Lincoln's Victory and the Nation's Fate

Lincoln's 1858 duel with Stephen Douglas for the U.S. Senate attracted national interest because of Douglas's prominence and Lincoln's reputation as a formidable speaker. To increase his national reputation, Lincoln challenged Douglas to a series of seven debates. During those debates Lincoln attacked slavery as an institution that subverted equality of opportunity. While expressing doubts about the innate abilities of those of African descent and rejecting proposals that would give them social and political equality, he declared that blacks were entitled to "all the natural rights enumerated in the Declaration of Independence." This meant, Lincoln explained, that "in the right to eat the bread, without leave of anybody else, which his own hand earns," the black was "the equal of every living man." Taking the offensive, Lincoln pressed Douglas to explain how he could accept the *Dred Scott* decision (which allowed slaveowners to bring their property into the territories) and at the same time advocate popular sovereignty.

In a debate in Freeport, Illinois, Douglas responded by reformulating popular sovereignty. In what became known as the Freeport doctrine, he asserted that settlers could exclude slavery from a territory simply by not adopting local legislation to protect it. Even if territorial governments lacked the power to prohibit slavery, as Taney had argued in his *Dred Scott* opinion, municipalities could still do so by refusing to support the "peculiar institution." Douglas's Freeport statement upset both proslavery advocates, who feared they would be denied the victory won in the *Dred Scott* decision, and abolitionists, who were not convinced that local regulations would halt the expansion of slavery. Nonetheless the Illinois state legislature reelected the "Little Giant," as Douglas was called, to the Senate. Yet Lincoln had established himself as a national leader, and the Republican party, by winning control of the House of Representatives in the election of 1858, had moved a step closer to national power.

In the wake of Republican gains, southern Democrats divided into two groups. Moderates such as Senator Jefferson Davis of Mississippi, who were known as Southern Rights Democrats, pursued the traditional policy of seeking ironclad commitments to protect slavery in the territories. Radicals such as Robert Barnwell Rhett of South Carolina and William Lowndes Yancey of Alabama abandoned cooperation and actively promoted secession. They proposed extreme measures, such as the reopening of the Atlantic slave trade, in the hope of driving a wedge between the North and the South.

Radical northerners played into their hands. In 1858 William Seward declared that freedom and slavery were locked in "an irrepressible conflict." In October 1859, the militant abolitionist John Brown led eighteen heavily armed black and white men in a raid that seized the federal arsenal at Harpers Ferry, Virginia. Brown's explicit purpose was to provide arms for a slave rebellion that would establish an African-American state in the South. The local militia and U.S. Marines under the command of Colonel Robert E. Lee quickly reclaimed the arsenal, capturing Brown and killing ten of his party. Republican leaders disavowed Brown's raid, but Democrats called his plot, in the words of Stephen Douglas, "a natural, logical, inevitable result of the doctrines and teachings of the Republican party." Fueling the Democratic charges were letters that linked six leading abolitionists to the financing of Brown's raid. The group included two Unitarian ministers, Theodore Parker, who was active in the underground railroad, and Thomas Wentworth Higginson, a free-soiler who would command a regiment of African-American soldiers during the Civil War. Higginson admitted his involvement and declared that Brown's "acquittal or rescue would do half as much good as [his] being executed; so strong is the personal sympathy with him."

Virginia gave the abolitionists the Christian martyr they wanted. Brown was charged with treason, sentenced to death, and hanged. At a church meeting in Concord, Massachusetts, Henry David Thoreau described Brown as "an angel of light," "the bravest and humanest man in all the country." Slaveholders were horrified by northern admiration of Brown and looked toward the future with fear. "The aim of the present black republican organization is the destruction of the social system of the Southern States, without regard to consequences," warned one newspaper.

Nor could the South count on the Democratic party to protect its interests. At the April 1860 party convention, northern Democrats rejected Jefferson Davis's program to protect slavery in the territories, prompting the delegates from eight southern states to leave the hall. When neither Douglas nor anyone else could win the required two-thirds majority for the presidential nomination, the convention adjourned. At a second Democratic convention in Baltimore, northern and western delegates nominated Douglas; southern Democrats met separately and nominated Buchanan's vice-president, John C. Breckinridge of Kentucky. The Democratic party had broken into two sectional pieces.

The Republicans sensed victory. They courted white voters by opposing both slavery and racial equality: "Missouri for white men and white men for Missouri," declared that state's Republican platform. On the national level, the Republican convention chose Lincoln as its presidential candidate. Lincoln's position on slavery was more moderate than that of the best-known Republicans, Senator William H. Seward of New York and Salmon P. Chase of Ohio, who demanded measures that would lead to abolition. Lincoln also conveyed a compelling egalitarian image that appealed to smallholding farmers and wage earners. And Lincoln's home territory—the rapidly growing Midwest—was crucial in the competition between Democrats and Republicans. The Republican platform followed Lincoln's views and struck a moderate tone, upholding free soil in the West and denying the right of states to secede but ruling out direct interference with slavery in the South. In addition, the platform endorsed the old Whig program of economic development, which had gained increasing support in the Midwest, especially after the Panic of 1857.

The Republican strategy was successful. Lincoln received only 40 percent of the popular vote but won every northern and western state except New

Jersey and garnered a majority in the electoral college. Douglas drew support from all regions except the South (taking 30 percent of the total vote) but won electoral votes only in Missouri and New Jersey. Breckinridge captured every state in the Deep South as well as Delaware, Maryland, and North Carolina, while John Bell, a former Tennessee Whig who became the nominee of the Constitutional Union party, carried the Upper South states where the Whigs had been strongest: Kentucky, Tennessee, and Virginia. As the vote indicated, the nation had divided into two antagonistic sections.

The Republicans had united the Northeast, the Midwest, and the Far West behind free soil and had seized national power. To many southerners, it now seemed time to think carefully about the meaning of Lincoln's words of 1858, that the Union must "become all one thing, or all the other."

CHAPTER 14 TIMELINE	
1845	Polk inaugurated
	Texas accepts admission to the Union
	Slidell's mission
1846	United States declares war on Mexico
	Oregon treaty ratified
	Walker Tariff lowers tariffs
	Wilmot Proviso introduced in Congress
1847	Winfield Scott captures Mexico City
1848	Gold discovered in California
	Treaty of Guadalupe Hidalgo
	Free Soil party organized
1850	Compromise of 1850
1851	American party formed
1854	Kansas-Nebraska Act
	Republican party formed
	Ostend Manifesto
	Know-Nothing movement peaks
1856	"Pottawatomie massacre"
	James Buchanan elected president
1857	*Dred Scott v. Sandford*
1858	Buchanan backs Lecompton constitution
	Lincoln-Douglas debates
1859	John Brown's raid on Harpers Ferry
1860	Abraham Lincoln elected president

CHAPTER 15

TWO SOCIETIES AT WAR, 1861–1865

- Secession and Military Stalemate, 1861–1862
- Toward Total War
- The Turning Point: 1863
- The Union Victorious, 1864–1865

For political leaders in the South, the victory of Abraham Lincoln and the Republicans in 1860 presented a clear and immediate danger. They knew that Lincoln regarded slavery as morally wrong and that the Republicans would unite northern society against the "Slave Power." There would be no extension of slavery into the territories. Moreover, unlike any preceding president, Lincoln owed the South not a single electoral vote. Soon, a southern senator warned, "cohorts of Federal office-holders, Abolitionists, may be sent into [our] midst." The result would be waves of bloody slave revolts.

To save slavery, radical southern leaders embarked on the dangerous journey of secession, leading their states out of the Union and establishing their own nation. If Lincoln and the Republicans would not allow them to leave peacefully, they would fight.

And so came the Civil War. Called the "War between the States" by southerners and the "War of the Rebellion" by northerners, the struggle resolved once and for all the great issue of slavery and redefined the character of the Union. The cost was high: more lives lost than in all the nation's subsequent wars put together and a century-long legacy of bitterness between the triumphant North and the vanquished South.

SECESSION AND MILITARY STALEMATE, 1861–1862

After Lincoln's election in November 1860, secessionist fervor swept through the Deep South. In the four months before Lincoln's inauguration in March 1861, political leaders in Washington struggled to forge a new compromise that (like those of 1787, 1820, and 1850) would preserve the Union.

Choosing Sides

The movement toward secession was most rapid in South Carolina—the home of Calhoun, nullification, and the Southern Radical movement. Robert Barnwell Rhett and other South Carolina fire-eaters had been planning for secession since 1850 and called a convention to achieve their goal. On December 20, the convention voted unanimously to dissolve "the union now subsisting between South Carolina and other States."

Moving quickly, fire-eaters in the six cotton states of the Deep South called similar conventions and organized vigilante groups and militia. In early January, in an atmosphere of public celebration, Mississippi enacted a secession ordinance. Within a month Florida, Alabama, Georgia, Louisiana, and Texas had also left the Union (see Map 15.1). In early February the jubilant secessionists met in Montgomery, Alabama, to proclaim a new nation—the Confederate

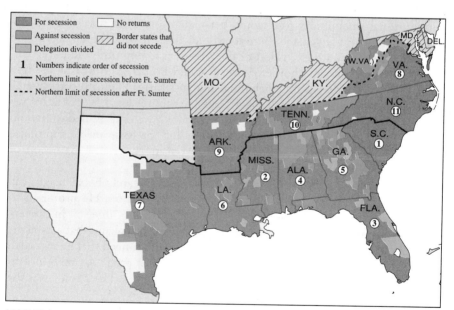

MAP 15.1

The Process of Secession

The states with the highest concentration of slaves (see Map 13.1) led the secessionist movement and, after the attack on Fort Sumter, were joined by the states of the Upper South. Yeoman farmers in Tennessee and the backcountry of Alabama, Georgia, and Virginia opposed secession but, except in the future state of West Virginia, generally supported the Confederate war effort.

States of America. They adopted a provisional constitution and named Jefferson Davis, a former U.S. senator and secretary of war, as provisional president.

Secessionist fervor was less intense in the eight Upper South states (Virginia, Delaware, Maryland, North Carolina, Kentucky, Tennessee, Missouri, and Arkansas). In January 1861 the legislatures of Virginia and Tennessee voted to resist any federal invasion of the seceded states but went no further. Seeking a compromise that would restore the Union, Upper South leaders proposed federal guarantees for slavery in the states where it existed.

Meanwhile, the Union government floundered. In his last message to Congress in December 1860, President Buchanan declared secession illegal but said that the federal government lacked the authority to restore the Union by force. South Carolina immediately claimed that Buchanan's message implied recognition of its independence and demanded the surrender of Fort Sumter, a federal garrison in Charleston harbor. Reluctant to turn over federal property, Buchanan decided to test the secessionists' resolve by ordering an unarmed merchant ship to resupply the fort. When the South Carolinians fired on the ship, Buchanan backed down, refusing to order the navy to escort it into the harbor.

As the crisis continued, Buchanan urged Congress to find a compromise. The proposal that received the most support was submitted by Senator John J. Crittenden of Kentucky, an aging follower of Henry Clay, one of the architects of the Compromise of 1850. Crittenden won congressional approval of a constitutional amendment that would permanently protect slavery from federal interference in any state where it existed. To deal with the territories, he called for the westward extension of the Missouri Compromise line (36° 30′ North) to the California border. Slavery would be barred north of the line and protected to the south, including any territories "hereafter acquired." After consulting with President-elect Lincoln, congressional Republicans rejected Crittenden's plan for the territories. Lincoln was determined to uphold the doctrine of free soil and feared that extending the Missouri Compromise line would encourage the South to embark on an imperialist expansion of slavery into Mexico, the Caribbean, and Latin America.

In his inaugural address on March 4, 1861, Lincoln carefully balanced a call for reconciliation with a firm commitment to the Union. He promised to permit slavery in states where it existed but stood firm for free soil in the territories. Most important, he stated that secession was illegal and that acts of violence in its support constituted insurrection. He announced that he intended to enforce federal law throughout the Union and—of particular relevance to Fort Sumter—hold federal property in the seceded states. The choice was the South's: return to the Union or face war.

The decision came quickly. Within a month of Lincoln's inauguration the garrison at Fort Sumter urgently needed supplies. To maintain his credibility, the new president dispatched a relief expedition, informing South Carolina that it would not land troops or arms unless the delivery of food and medicine was disrupted. Jefferson Davis and his government welcomed Lincoln's decision, believing that a confrontation would turn the wavering Upper South against the North and win foreign support for the Confederate cause. Resolving to take the fort before the arrival of the Union ships, Davis authorized General P. G. T. Beauregard to demand its surrender. When Major Robert Anderson refused to comply, the Confederate forces opened fire, forcing him to surrender on April 14. The next day Lincoln called 75,000 state militiamen into federal service for ninety days to put down an insurrection "too powerful to be suppressed by the ordinary course of judicial proceedings." All talk of compromise was past.

Northern states responded to Lincoln's call to arms with enthusiasm. Asked to provide thirteen regiments of volunteers, Republican Governor William Dennison of Ohio sent twenty. "The lion in us is thoroughly roused," he explained. Many northern Democrats were equally committed to the Union cause. As Stephen Douglas declared six weeks before his death: "Every man must be for the United States or against it. There can be no neutrals in this war, *only patriots—or traitors.*"

The white residents of the Upper South now had to choose between the Union and the Confederacy, and their decision was crucial. Those eight states accounted for two-thirds of the South's white population, more than three-fourths of its industrial production, and well over half its food and fuel. They were home to many of the nation's best military leaders, including Colonel Robert E. Lee of Virginia, a career officer whom General-in-Chief Winfield Scott recommended to Lincoln as field commander of the new Union army. And they were geographically strategic. Kentucky, with its 500-mile border on the Ohio River, was essential to the movement of troops and supplies. Maryland was vital to the Union's security because it surrounded the nation's capital on the north.

The weight of history decided the outcome in Virginia, the original home of American slavery. Three days after the fall of Fort Sumter, a Virginia convention passed an ordinance of secession by a vote of 88 to 55. The dissenting votes came mainly from the yeoman-dominated northwestern counties (see Map 15.1); elsewhere in Virginia whites rallied to the Confederate cause. Refusing Scott's offer to command the Union troops, Robert E. Lee resigned from the army. "Save in defense of my native state," Lee told Scott, "I never desire again to draw my sword." North Carolina, Tennessee, and Arkansas joined Virginia in the Confederacy.

Lincoln moved aggressively to hold the rest of the Upper South. In May he ordered General George B. McClellan to take control of northwestern Virginia, thus securing the railway line between Washington and the Ohio Valley. In October voters there overwhelmingly approved the creation of a new state, West Virginia, which was admitted to the Union in 1863. The Union cause was much less popular in Maryland, where support for slavery was strong. A pro-Confederate mob attacked Massachusetts troops marching between railroad stations in Baltimore, causing the war's first combat deaths: four soldiers and twelve civilians. When other Maryland secessionists destroyed railroad bridges and telegraph lines, Lincoln ordered military occupation of the state and imprisoned suspected secessionists, including members of the state legislature. He released them only in November 1861, after Unionists had gained control of the Maryland legislature.

In Missouri, the key to communications and trade on the Missouri and upper Mississippi rivers, Lincoln mobilized support among the large German-American community. In July a force of German-American militia defeated Confederate sympathizers commanded by the governor. Despite continuing raids by Confederate guerrilla bands led by William Quantrill and Jesse and Frank James, the Union retained control of Missouri.

In Kentucky secessionist and Unionist sentiment was evenly balanced, so Lincoln moved cautiously. Not until August, after Unionists had taken control of the state government, did he order federal troops to cut Kentucky's thriving export trade in horses, mules, whiskey, and foodstuffs to the Lower South. When the Confederacy responded by moving troops into Kentucky, the Unionist legislature asked for federal protection. In September, Illinois volunteers under the command of the relatively unknown brigadier general Ulysses S. Grant crossed the Ohio River and drove the Confederates out. Of the eight states of the Upper South, Lincoln had kept four (Delaware, Maryland, Kentucky, and Missouri) and a portion of a fifth (western Virginia) in the Union.

War Aims and Military Initiatives

After secession, Confederate leaders called on their people to defend the independence of the new nation. At his inauguration in February 1861, Jefferson Davis identified the Confederate cause with that of the American Revolution; like their grandfathers, white southerners were fighting against tyranny and for the "sacred right of self-government." As Davis put it, the Confederacy sought "no conquest, no aggrandizement, no concession of any kind from the states with which we were lately confederated; all we ask is to be let alone." The decision to focus on the defense of the Confederacy (and not to conquer western territories) gave southern leaders a strong advantage: they needed only a military stalemate to guarantee Confederate independence.

Lincoln made his first major statement on Union goals and strategy in a speech to Congress on July 4, 1861. Rejecting General Winfield Scott's plan to use economic sanctions and a naval blockade to persuade the Confederates to return to the Union, Lincoln called for an aggressive miliary strategy to put down the rebellion. He saw secession as an attack on republican government and the rule of law, America's great contribution to world history. The issue was simple: "whether a constitutional republic, or a democracy—a government of the people, by the same people—can or cannot maintain its territorial integrity against its domestic foes." Only by crushing the rebellion could the nation preserve its principles.

The president knew that the northern public wanted a strike toward Richmond, the Confederate capital, and he hoped an early victory would end the rebellion. He therefore dispatched General Irwin McDowell and an army of 30,000 men to attack P. G. T. Beauregard's force of 20,000 troops at Manassas, a major rail junction in Virginia 30 miles southwest of Washington. McDowell attacked strongly on July 21 near Manassas Creek (also called Bull Run), but panic swept through his troops during a Confederate counterattack. For the first time Union soldiers heard the hair-raising rebel yell. "The peculiar corkscrew sensation that it sends down your backbone under these circumstances can never be told," one Union veteran wrote. "You have to feel it." McDowell's troops retreated in disarray to Washington, along with the many civilians who had come to observe the battle. The victorious Confederate troops also dispersed, confused and without the wagons and supplies they needed to pursue McDowell's army.

It was now clear that the rebellion would not be easily crushed. To bolster northern morale, which had been shattered by the rout at Bull Run, Lincoln replaced McDowell with General George B. McClellan and signed bills for the enlistment of a million additional men, who would serve for three years in the newly created Army of the Potomac. A cautious military engineer, McClellan spent the winter of 1861–1862 training raw recruits, and in 1862 he launched the first major offensive of the war, a thrust toward Richmond. In a maneuver that required skillful logistics, the Union general transported about 100,000 troops by boat down the Potomac River and Chesapeake Bay and then up the peninsula between the York and James rivers toward the South's capital. But McClellan failed to anticipate a Confederate counterstroke. In May a Confederate army under Thomas J. ("Stonewall") Jackson marched rapidly north up the Shenandoah Valley, threatening Washington. To head off the danger, Lincoln diverted 30,000 troops from McClellan's army, but Jackson, a brilliant general, defeated three Union armies in the valley. Then Jackson joined the Confederates' formidable commanding general, Robert E. Lee, who had confronted McClellan outside Richmond. Lee launched a ferocious attack that lasted for seven days (June 25–July 1), suffering heavy casualties (20,000 to the Union's 10,000). But McClellan failed to exploit his advantage, refusing to renew the offensive unless he received fresh troops. Lincoln ordered the withdrawal of the Army of the Potomac, and Richmond remained secure.

Lee promptly went on the offensive, hoping for victories that would humiliate Lincoln's government. Joining with Jackson in northern Virginia, Lee routed a Union army in the Second Battle of Bull Run (August 1862) and then struck north through western Maryland, where he met with near disaster. When Lee divided his force—sending Jackson to capture Harpers Ferry in West Virginia—a copy of his orders fell into McClellan's hands. But the Union general again failed to pursue his advantage, delaying his attack until Lee's depleted army had occupied a strong defensive position behind Antietam Creek, near Sharpsburg, Maryland. Outnumbered 87,000 to 50,000, Lee desperately fought off McClellan's attacks. Just as Union regiments were about to overwhelm his right flank, Jackson's troops arrived, saving the Confederates from a major defeat. Appalled by his casualties, McClellan let Lee retreat to Virginia.

The fighting at Antietam was savage. A Wisconsin officer described his men as "loading and firing with demoniacal fury and shouting and laughing hysterically." At a critical point in the battle a sunken road, nicknamed Bloody Lane, was filled with Confederate bodies two and three deep, and the attacking Union troops knelt on "this ghastly flooring" to shoot at the retreating Confederates. The battle at Antietam on September 17, 1862, remains the bloodiest single day in U.S. military history. Together, the Confederate and Union dead numbered 4,800 and the wounded 18,500, of whom 3,000 soon died. (In comparison, 6,000 Americans were wounded or killed on D-Day in World War II.)

In public Lincoln declared Antietam a victory, but privately he believed that McClellan should have fought Lee to the finish. A masterful organizer of men and supplies, McClellan lacked the stomach for a major commitment of his forces. Dismissing McClellan, Lincoln began a long search for an effective replacement. His first choice was Ambrose E. Burnside, who proved to be more daring but less competent. In December, after heavy losses in futile attacks against well-entrenched Confederate forces at Fredericksburg, Virginia, Burnside resigned his command and Lincoln replaced him with Joseph ("Fighting Joe") Hooker. As 1862 ended, the Confederates had some reason to be content: the war in the East was a stalemate.

In the West, Union forces had been more successful. Their goal was to control the Ohio, Mississippi, and Missouri rivers, dividing the Confederacy into isolated pieces and reducing the mobility of its armies. The decision of Kentucky not to join the rebellion had already given the Union dominance in the Ohio River Valley. In 1862 the Union army launched a series of highly innovative land and water operations to gain control of the Tennessee and Mississippi rivers as well. As the northern part of the Union strategy, General Ulysses S. Grant used riverboats clad with iron plates to take Fort Henry on the Tennessee River and Fort Donelson on the Cumberland. Grant then moved south along the Tennessee to seize critical railroad lines. A Confederate army under Albert Sidney Johnston and P. G. T. Beauregard caught Grant by surprise early in April near a small log church named Shiloh. Grant relentlessly threw troops into the battle, forcing a Confederate withdrawal but taking huge casualties. Grant described a large field "so covered with dead that it would have been possible to walk over the clearing in any direction, stepping on dead bodies, without a foot touching the ground." At the cost of many lives Grant had maintained the Union's military momentum in the West.

Three weeks later, Union naval forces commanded by David G. Farragut struck from the south, moving through the Mississippi Delta from the Gulf of Mexico to capture New Orleans. The Union now held the South's financial center and largest city as well as a major base for future naval operations. Union victories in the West had thus significantly undermined Confederate strength in the Mississippi Valley.

TOWARD TOTAL WAR

The carnage at Antietam and Shiloh had made it clear that the war would be long and costly. After Shiloh, Grant later noted, he "gave up all idea of saving the Union except by complete conquest." The conflict now became a *total war*—a struggle that arrayed the entire resources of the two societies against each other and eventually would result in warfare against enemy civilians. Aided by a strong party and a talented cabinet, Lincoln skillfully mobilized the North for all-out war, organizing an effective central government. Jefferson Davis was far less successful in harnessing the resources of the South, because the eleven states of the Confederacy remained deeply suspicious of centralized rule.

Mobilizing Armies and Civilians

Initially, patriotic fervor filled both armies with eager volunteers. The call for soldiers was especially successful in the South, which had a strong military tradition and an ample supply of trained officers. But the initial surge of enlistments fell off as the people saw the realities of war: heavy losses to disease and dreadful battlefield carnage. Soon both governments faced the necessity of forced enlistment.

The Confederacy was the first to act. In April 1862, after the defeat at Shiloh, the Confederate Congress imposed the first legally binding draft in American history. One law extended all existing enlistments for the duration of the war; another required three years of military service from all able-bodied men between the ages of eighteen and thirty-five. In September, after the heavy casualties at Antietam, the age limit was raised to forty-five. The Confederate draft had two loopholes. First, it exempted one white man—either the planter or an overseer—for each twenty slaves, allowing men on large plantations to avoid military service. Second, drafted men could hire substitutes. Before this provision was repealed in 1864, the price for a substitute had risen to $300 in gold, about three times the annual wages of a skilled worker. Laborers and yeomen farmers angrily complained that it was "a rich man's war and a poor man's fight."

Consequently, some southerners refused to serve, and the Confederate government lacked the power to compel them. Because the Confederate constitution vested sovereignty in the individual states, strong governors such as Joseph Brown of Georgia and Zebulon Vance of North Carolina simply ignored Davis's first draft call in early 1862. Elsewhere, state judges issued writs of *habeas corpus* (a legal process designed to protect people from arbitrary arrest and detention) and ordered the Confederate army to release protesting draftees. The Confederate Congress was reluctant to override the judges' authority to free conscripted men, but military need prompted it to suspend habeas corpus for two periods totaling sixteen months. These measures, along with popular enthusiasm and long enlistments, enabled the Confederate government to keep substantial armies in the field well into 1864.

The Union government was able to take a more authoritarian stance toward potential foes and ordinary citizens. To prevent opposition to the war, Lincoln suspended habeas corpus and imprisoned thousands of Confederate sympathizers without trial. The president also extended martial law to civilians who discouraged enlistment or resisted the draft, making them subject to military courts rather than local juries. This firm policy had the desired effect. The Militia Act of 1862 set a quota of volunteers for each state, and enough recruits came forward to satisfy Union needs for a year. As the scale of hostilities increased, Congress passed the Enrollment Act of 1863, which instituted higher quotas but allowed them to be met with volunteers or conscripts. To avoid conscription, northern officials enticed volunteers with cash bounties, prompting the enlistment or reenlistment of almost a million men. As in the South, wealthy men could avoid the draft by providing a substitute or paying a $300 commutation, or exemption, fee.

The Enrollment Act sparked the first significant opposition to the northern war effort, as thousands of recent immigrants refused to serve. Northern Democrats exploited this resentment by charging that Lincoln was drafting

Draft Riots in New York City
The Enrollment Act of 1863 enraged many workers and recent Irish and German immigrants who opposed the war. In July in New York City they took out their anger on free blacks. As the club-waving mob hangs an African-American, three others escape by climbing over a fence. The violence against blacks received wide publicity (this engraving appeared in the *Illustrated London News* on August 8, 1863) and generally strengthened support for the Union war effort.

poor whites in order to free the slaves and flood the cities with black laborers. Some Democrats opposed the war, believing that the South should be allowed to secede; others simply wanted to protect the interests of immigrants, most of whom were Democrats. In July 1863 hostility to the draft and to African-Americans spilled onto the streets of New York City. For five days immigrant Irish and German workers ran rampant, burning the draft office, sacking the homes of important Republicans, and attacking the police. The rioters lynched and mutilated at least a dozen African-Americans, drove hundreds of black families from their homes, and burned down the Colored Orphan Asylum. Lincoln rushed in Union troops, who killed more than a hundred rioters and suppressed the insurrection, but many immigrants continued to oppose conscription.

The Union government's determination to wage total war won greater support among native-born citizens. In 1861 prominent New Yorkers established the United States Sanitary Commission. Its task was to provide medical services and prevent a repeat of the debacle of the recently concluded Crimean War between Britain and Russia, in which disease had accounted for over three-fourths of British casualties. Through its network of 7,000 local auxiliaries, the Sanitary Commission gathered supplies; distributed clothing, food, and medicine to the army; improved the sanitary standards of camp life; and recruited battlefield nurses and doctors for the Union Army Medical Bureau. These efforts were not consistently successful. Diseases—dysentery, typhoid, and malaria as well as childhood viruses such as mumps and measles, to which many rural men had not developed an immunity—killed twice as many Union soldiers (about 250,000) as died in combat. Surgeons inadvertently took more lives by spreading infection than they saved by performing operations. Still, because of better sanitation and high-quality food, the mortality rate among Union troops from disease and wounds was substantially lower than that in other major nineteenth-century wars. Confederate soldiers were less fortunate. Although thousands of white women volunteered as nurses, the Confederate health system was poorly organized. Thousands of southern soldiers contracted scurvy because of the lack of vitamin C in their diets, and they died from camp diseases at higher rates than did Union soldiers.

Women took a leading role in the Sanitary Commission and other wartime agencies. As superintendent of female nurses, Dorothea Dix became the first woman to receive a major federal appointment. Dix used her influence to combat the prejudice against women treating men, opening a new occupation to women. Thousands of educated Union women joined the war effort as clerks in the expanding governmental bureaucracy. In the South women staffed the efficient Confederate postal service. Indeed, in both sections millions of women assumed new economic responsibilities and worked with far greater intensity. They took over many farm tasks previously done by men and went to work in schools and textile, clothing, and shoe factories. A number of women even took on military duties as spies, scouts, and (disguised as men)

The Common Lemon: The Difference between Life and Death

In the Civil War disease took more lives than bullets did, and the northern toll would have been even higher without the work of the doctors and nurses of the United States Sanitary Commission. As this narrative by the volunteer nurse and reformer Jane Swisshelm indicates, public support was also crucial—in this case by providing lemons, which were rich in vitamin C and inhibited a common hospital disease.

About nine o'clock I returned to the man I had come to help. I had sat by him but a few moments when I noticed a green shade on his face. It darkened, and his breathing grew labored—then ceased. I think it was not more than twenty minutes from the time I observed the green tinge until he was gone. I called the nurse, who brought . . . a surgeon [and I knew], by the sudden shadow on his face when he saw the corpse, that he was alarmed; and when he had given minute directions for the removal of the bed and its contents, the washing of the floor and sprinkling with chloride of lime, I went close to his side, and said in a low voice:

"Doctor, is not this hospital gangrene?"

"I am very sorry to say, madam, that it is."

"Then you want lemons!"

"We would be glad to have them!"

"Glad to have them?" I repeated, in profound astonishment, "why, you *must* have them!"

He seemed surprised at my earnestness, and set about explaining: "We sent to the Sanitary Commission last week, and got half a box."

"Seven hundred and fifty wounded men! Hospital gangrene, and half a box of lemons!" . . .

I went to the head nurse . . . who . . . gave me writing materials, and I wrote a short note to the *New York Tribune*:

"Hospital gangrene has broken out in Washington, and we want lemons! *lemons!* LEMONS! LEMONS! No man or woman in health, has a right to a glass of lemonade until these men have all they need; send us lemons!"

I signed my name and mailed it immediately, and it appeared next morning. . . . That day lemons began to pour into Washington, and soon, I think, into every hospital in the land. . . . If there was any more hospital gangrene that season I neither saw nor heard of it.

SOURCE: Jane Swisshelm, *Half a Century* (Chicago: Jansen, McClurg, 1880), pp. 251–253.

soldiers. As the nurse Clara Barton, who later founded the American Red Cross, recalled, "At the war's end, woman was at least fifty years in advance of the normal position which continued peace would have assigned her."

Hospital Nursing
Working as nurses in battlefront hospitals, thousands of Union and Confederate women gained firsthand experience of the horrors of war. Most nurses were unpaid volunteers, cooking and cleaning for their patients as well as tending their wounds. A sense of calm prevails in this behind-the-lines Union hospital in Nashville, where those who survived their wounds were sent to recover.

Mobilizing Resources and Money

Wars usually are won by the side with superior resources and economic organization, and in this regard the Union entered the war with a distinct advantage. With nearly two-thirds of the American people, about two-thirds of the nation's railroad mileage, and nearly 90 percent of American industrial output, the North's economy was far superior to the South's. The North had an especially great advantage in the manufacture of cannon and rifles because many of its arms factories were equipped for mass production.

But the Confederate position was far from weak. Virginia, North Carolina, and Tennessee had substantial industrial capacity. Richmond, with its Tredegar Iron Works, was an important industrial center, and in 1861 the Confederacy transported to Richmond the gun-making machinery captured at the U.S. armory at Harpers Ferry. The production of the Richmond armory, the purchase of Enfield rifles from Britain, and the capture of 100,000 Union rifles enabled the Confederacy to provide every infantryman with a modern weapon by 1863.

Moreover, with 9 million people, the Confederacy could mobilize enormous armies. While one-third of that number were slaves, their masters kept them in the fields, producing food for the armies and cotton for export. The Confederacy counted on "King Cotton" to provide revenue to purchase clothes, boots, blankets, and weapons from abroad. They also counted on cotton as a diplomatic weapon, hoping that the British, who depended on southern cotton to supply their textile factories, would grant diplomatic recognition and provide military and economic aid. Although the British government never recognized the Confederate States of America as an independent nation, it did regard the conflict as a war, and that gave the rebels the status of a belligerent power with the right under international law to borrow money and purchase weapons. Thus the odds did not necessarily favor the Union, despite its superior resources.

The outcome would depend on the success of the two governments in mobilizing the resources of their societies. Lincoln and the Republicans had a clear economic agenda. To build political support for their party and boost industrial output, they enacted virtually the entire program of national mercantilism previously advocated by Henry Clay and the Whig party. First, the Republicans raised tariffs, winning praise from northeastern manufacturers and laborers and farmers who feared competition from cheap foreign labor. Second, Secretary of the Treasury Salmon P. Chase created a national banking system—an important element of every modern centralized government—by linking thousands of local banks. This integrated system was far more effective in raising capital and controlling inflation than earlier efforts by the First and Second banks of the United States had been. Finally, the Lincoln administration devised a far-reaching system of internal improvements. In 1862 Congress fulfilled the Republican promise to build transcontinental railroads, chartering the Union Pacific and Central Pacific railways and subsidizing them lavishly. It gave those railroads 20 square miles of federal land for every mile of track they put down and in 1864 provided a similar subsidy to the Northern Pacific. In addition, the Republicans moved aggressively to provide northern farmers with "free land" in the West. The Homestead Act of 1862 gave heads of families or individuals age twenty-one or older the right to 160 acres of public land after five years of residence and improvement. This economic program sustained the allegiance of a majority of northerners to the Republican party while bolstering the Union's ability to fight the war.

In contrast, the Confederate government had a much less coherent economic policy. True to its states' rights philosophy, the Confederacy left most economic matters in the hands of the state governments. But as the realities of total war became clear, the Davis administration took some extraordinary measures: it built and operated shipyards, armories, foundries, and textile mills; commandeered food and scarce raw materials such as coal, iron, copper, and lead; requisitioned slaves to work on fortifications; and exercised direct control over foreign trade. These coercive measures were resented as the war wore on, because the Confederate leaders failed to explain their wartime needs or cope with misery on the home front. To sustain the war effort they increasingly counted on racial solidarity: Jefferson Davis warned whites that a Union victory would destroy slavery "and reduce the whites to the degraded position of the African race."

For both the North and the South, the cost of fighting a total war was enormous. In the Union, government spending shot up from less than 2 percent of gross national product to about 15 percent. To pay for those expenditures, the Republicans established a powerful modern state that raised money in three ways. First, the government increased taxes by raising tariffs, placing excise duties on consumer goods, and for the first time imposing direct taxes on business corporations, large inheritances, and incomes. These levies paid for about 20 percent of the cost of the war.

The sale of Treasury bonds financed 65 percent of the northern war effort. Following the advice of Jay Cooke, a Philadelphia banker, the Treasury paid interest on the bonds in gold and marketed them widely. Using newspaper advertisements and 2,500 subagents, Cooke persuaded nearly a million northern families to buy war bonds. In addition, the National Banking acts of 1863 and 1864 induced many state banks to purchase Treasury bonds by offering them a national charter, which freed them from certain taxes and offered other economic advantages. By the end of 1865, the number of national banks had tripled and their purchases of U.S. bonds had increased nearly fourfold.

The Union financed most of the remaining cost of the war by printing paper money. As with the "Continentals" issued during the War for Independence, these Treasury notes—known as *greenbacks*—were backed by faith in the government rather than by specie. The Legal Tender Act of 1862 authorized the issue of $150 million in greenbacks and required the public to accept them as legal tender. Unlike the Continentals, this paper money did not depreciate significantly in value because it was issued in limited amounts, funding about 15 percent of wartime expenses. By imposing broad-based taxes, borrowing from the middle class as well as the wealthy, and creating a national monetary system, the Union government created the financial foundations of a modern nation-state, raising huge sums and directly involving millions of citizens in the war effort.

The financial demands on the South were just as great, but it lacked a powerful central government that could tax and borrow. The Confederate Congress fiercely opposed taxes on cotton exports and slaves, the most valuable property of wealthy planters. Taxes fell primarily on urban middle-class and non-slaveholding yeomen farm families, who refused to pay. Consequently, the Confederacy covered less than 5 percent of its expenditures through taxation. The government paid for another 35 percent by borrowing, although many wealthy planters refused to buy large quantities of Confederate bonds and foreign bankers were equally wary.

Thus the Confederacy was forced to finance about 60 percent of its expenses with unbacked paper money. The flood of currency created soaring inflation, which was compounded by counterfeit copies of the poorly printed Confederate notes. As the huge supply of money (and shortages of goods) brought rising food prices, riots broke out in more than a dozen southern cities and towns. In Richmond several hundred women broke into bakeries, crying, "Our children are starving while the rich roll in wealth." Things got worse as the paper money depreciated. By the spring of 1865 prices had risen to ninety-two times their 1861 levels. Inflation not only undermined civilian morale but also caused farmers to refuse to accept Confederate money for their produce. Supply officers had to seize what they needed, offering payment in worthless IOUs. Fearful of a strong government and taxation, the Confederacy was forced to violate the property rights of its citizens to sustain the war.

THE TURNING POINT: 1863

By 1863 the Lincoln administration had mobilized northern society, creating a complex war machine and a coherent economic and financial system. "Little by little," the young diplomat Henry Adams noted at his post in London, "one began to feel that, behind the chaos in Washington power was taking shape; that it was massed and guided as it had not been before." Slowly but surely the tide of battle shifted toward the Union.

Emancipation

From the beginning of the conflict, antislavery Republicans had tried to persuade their party to make abolition a Union war aim. They based their argument not just on morality but on "military necessity," pointing out that slave-grown crops sustained the Confederate war effort. As Frederick Douglass put it, "the very stomach of this rebellion is the Negro in the form of a slave. Arrest that hoe in the hands of the Negro, and you smite the rebellion in the very seat of its life." As war casualties mounted in 1862, Lincoln and some Republican leaders accepted Douglass's argument and began to redefine the war as a struggle against slavery—the cornerstone of southern society.

But it was enslaved African-Americans who forced the issue by seizing freedom for themselves. Exploiting the disorder of wartime, tens of thousands of slaves escaped and sought refuge behind Union lines. The first Union official to confront this issue was General Benjamin Butler. When three slaves reached his camp on the Virginia coast in May 1861, he labeled them "contraband of war" and refused to return them to their owner. His term stuck, and for the rest of the war slaves behind Union lines were known as *contrabands*. Within a few months a thousand contrabands were camping with Butler's army. To define their status and undermine the Confederate war effort, in August 1861 Congress passed the First Confiscation Act, which authorized the seizure of all property—including slaves—used to support the rebellion.

Radical Republicans, who had long condemned slavery, now saw a way to use the war to end it. By the spring of 1862 leading Radicals—Treasury secretary Chase; Charles Sumner, chair of the Senate Committee on Foreign Relations; and Thaddeus Stevens, chair of the House Ways and Means Committee—had pushed moderate Republicans toward abolition. In April Congress enacted legislation ending slavery in the District of Columbia, with compensation for owners. In June it outlawed slavery in the federal territories, finally enacting the Wilmot Proviso and the Republicans' free-soil policy. And in July Congress passed the radical Second Confiscation Act, which, overriding the property rights of Confederate slaveowners, declared "forever free" all fugitive slaves and all slaves captured by the Union army.

Lincoln now seized the initiative from the radicals. In July 1862 he prepared a general proclamation of emancipation and, viewing the battle of Antietam as "an indication of the Divine Will," issued it on September 22, 1862. Based on the president's war powers, the proclamation declared Lincoln's intention to free the slaves in all states still in rebellion on January 1, 1863. The seceding states had a hundred days to preserve slavery by returning to the Union. None chose to do so.

The proclamation was politically astute. Since Lincoln needed to keep the loyalty of the border states still in the Union, he left slavery intact there. He also wanted to win the allegiance of the areas occupied by Union armies— western and central Tennessee, western Virginia, and southern Louisiana, including New Orleans—so he left slavery untouched there. Consequently, because Lincoln's order had no practical effect within the Confederacy, the Emancipation Proclamation did not free a single slave. Yet it dramatically changed the nature of the conflict. The struggle to preserve the Union had become, as Lincoln put it, a war of "subjugation" in which "the old South is to be destroyed and replaced by new propositions and ideas."

As a war aim, emancipation was extremely controversial. During the congressional election of 1862 the Democrats denounced emancipation as unconstitutional, warned of slave uprisings and massive bloodshed in the South, and claimed that a "black flood" would wash away the jobs of northern workers. Democrat Horatio Seymour won the governorship of New York by declaring that if abolition was the purpose of the war, the South should not be conquered. Other Democrats swept to victory in New York, Pennsylvania, Ohio, and Illinois, and the party gained 34 seats in Congress. However, the Republicans still held a 25-seat majority in the House and had gained 5 seats in the Senate. Lincoln refused to retreat. On New Year's Day, 1863, he signed the Emancipation Proclamation. As a gesture to northerners who sympathized with the South and feared race warfare, Lincoln urged slaves to "abstain from all violence." But he now justified emancipation as an "act of justice." "If my name ever goes into history," he said, "it was for this act."

Vicksburg and Gettysburg

The fate of the proclamation would depend on the success of Union armies and the Republicans' ability to win support for their program. The outlook was not encouraging. Not only had Democrats registered gains in the election of 1862, there was increased popular support for Democrats who favored a negotiated peace. Two brilliant victories by Lee, whose army defeated Hooker's forces at Fredericksburg (December 1862) and Chancellorsville, Virginia (May 1863), caused a further erosion of northern support, as did rumors of a new draft.

At this crucial juncture, General Grant mounted a major offensive in the West designed to split the Confederacy in two. Grant drove south along the west

Triumph and Tragedy at Vicksburg

As James K. Newton of the 14th Wisconsin Volunteers celebrated the capture of the Confederate stronghold of Vicksburg on July 4, 1863, he was forced to confront the high cost of victory.

My Dear Parents,
. . . In my opinion I had about as glorious a 4th of July as I could wish to spend. Early in the morning our Reg't was ordered to be in readiness to march at a minutes notice; we fell in, and stacked arms; all of us expecting to spend the day in Vicksburg, and—we were not disappointed. . . .

It looked strange to see Uncle Sam's troops marching through the city, and the Secesh [secessionists] standing in groups at every street corner . . . [those Confederate soldiers] are only too glad to be paroled, and allowed to go home for a while. . . . I presume there are a great many conflicting reports up north, as to what was gained on our side by the surrender of Vicksburg. I should not wonder if the Copperheads [southern supporters] up there made it out to be not much of a victory after all, but notwithstanding what *they say*, and the stories that they circulate, the truth will come out in the end. . . . We have now undisputed possession of the Miss: River. We have taken 31,000 prisoners; 45,000 stand of small arms; over 100 cannon; and nearly 100 stands of Colors. All this we have gained. . . .

I have sad news to write again, and I might as well tell it now as at any other time. Henry Cady is dead: he died on the 1st day of July . . . that makes three of our Comp'y who have died in that hospital, and all for the want of proper care.

"Little Cady"—as we all called him, was universally acknowledged to be the best boy in the Comp'y; . . . The boys all moarn for him, but myself especially, for he was like a brother to me . . . I can but hope that he has gone to that better world where sin, pain, and sorrow can not enter.

SOURCE: Stephen E. Ambrose, ed., *A Wisconsin Boy in Dixie: Civil War Letters of James K. Newton* (Madison: University of Wisconsin Press, 1961), pp. 80–83. Reprinted by permission of The University of Wisconsin Press.

bank of the Mississippi and then moved his troops across the river near Vicksburg, where he defeated two Confederate armies and laid siege to the city. After repelling Union assaults for six weeks, the exhausted and starving Vicksburg garrison surrendered on July 4, 1863. Five days later Union forces took Port Hudson, Louisiana, establishing Union control of the Mississippi. Grant had cut Louisiana, Arkansas, and Texas off from the rest of the Confederacy.

Grant's initial advance down the Mississippi had caused a division over strategy within the Confederate leadership. Davis and other civilian leaders wanted to throw in reinforcements to defend Vicksburg and send troops to

Tennessee to draw Grant out of Mississippi. But Lee, buoyed by his recent victories over Hooker, favored a new invasion of the North. He argued that a military thrust into the free states would relieve the pressure on Vicksburg by drawing the Union armies east. Beyond that, Lee hoped for a major victory that would undermine northern support for the war.

Lee won out. In June 1863 he maneuvered his army north through Maryland into Pennsylvania. The Army of the Potomac moved along with him, positioning itself between Lee and Washington. The two great armies met in an accidental but decisive confrontation at Gettysburg, Pennsylvania (see Map 15.2). On the first day of battle, July 1, Lee drove the Union's advance guard to the south of town. There General George G. Meade, who had just taken over command of the Union forces from Hooker, placed his troops in well-defended hilltop positions and called up reinforcements. By the morning of the second day Meade had 90,000 troops to 75,000 for Lee. Aware that he was outnumbered but bent on victory, Lee attacked both of Meade's flanks but failed to turn them. General Richard B. Ewell, assigned to attack the Union right, was unwilling to risk his men in an all-out assault, and General Longstreet, on the Union left, was unable to dislodge Meade's forces from Little Round Top.

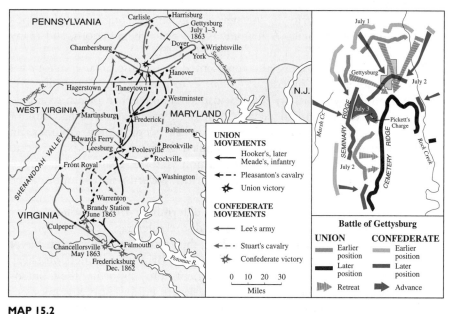

MAP 15.2

The Battle of Gettysburg, 1863

After Lee's victory at Chancellorsville in May, the two armies jockeyed for position as the Confederate forces moved northward. At Gettysburg, the victory of the Union army commanded by General George Meade was primarily the result of superior numbers and its well-fortified position along Cemetery Ridge, which gave its units a major tactical advantage.

On July 3 Lee decided to attempt a frontal assault on the center of the Union lines. He had enormous confidence in his troops and realized that this might be his last chance to inflict a crushing psychological defeat on the North. After the heaviest artillery barrage of the war, Lee ordered 14,000 men under General George E. Pickett to take Cemetery Ridge. But Meade had reinforced the center of his line with artillery and his best troops. When Pickett's men charged across a mile of open terrain, they were met by massive fire and thousands were killed, wounded, or captured. By the end of the battle, Lee had suffered 28,000 casualties, one-third of the Army of Northern Virginia, and Meade had lost 23,000 killed or wounded, making Gettysburg the most lethal battle of the Civil War.

Gettysburg was a great Union victory; never again would a southern army invade the North. But shocked by the bloodletting, Meade allowed the remaining Confederate soldiers to escape, thus losing an opportunity to end the war. "As it is," Lincoln brooded, "the war will be prolonged indefinitely."

Nonetheless, the outcome at Gettysburg and the simultaneous Union victory at Vicksburg amounted to a major turning point in the conflict. In the fall of 1863, Republicans reaped the political gains of those victories by sweeping state and local elections in Pennsylvania, Ohio, and New York. In the South, the military setbacks accentuated war weariness. The Confederate elections of 1863 went sharply against the politicians who supported Jefferson Davis, and a large minority in the new Confederate Congress was outspokenly hostile to his policies. A few advocated peace negotiations, and many more criticized the ineffectiveness of the war effort.

Vicksburg and Gettysburg also represented a great diplomatic victory for the North, ending the Confederacy's chances to gain foreign recognition and acquire advanced weapons. In 1862 British shipbuilders had begun to supply armed cruisers to the Confederacy, and one of them, the *Alabama*, had sunk or captured more than a hundred Union merchant ships. Union diplomats in London despaired of preventing the scheduled delivery of two other ironclad cruisers in mid-1863. But news of the Union victories changed everything, and the American minister persuaded the British government to impound the ships.

Cotton was not "King" and had not determined British policy, as the South had hoped. British manufacturers had stockpiled raw cotton before the war, and when those stocks were depleted, they found new sources in Egypt and India. Equally important, the dependence of British consumers on cheap wheat from the North deterred the government from supporting the Confederacy. Finally, British workers and reformers were enthusiastic champions of abolition, which the Emancipation Proclamation had established as a Union war aim. The results at Vicksburg and Gettysburg confirmed British neutrality by demonstrating the military might of the Union. The British did not want to risk Canada or their merchant marine by provoking a strong, well-armed United States.

THE UNION VICTORIOUS, 1864–1865

The Union victories of 1863 made it clear that the South could not win the war on the battlefield, but the Confederacy still hoped for a stalemate and a negotiated peace. Lincoln and his generals faced the daunting task of winning a quick and decisive military victory; otherwise a majority of northern voters might well desert the Republican party and its policies.

Soldiers and Strategy

Free African-Americans and fugitive slaves had tried to enlist in the Union army as early as 1861, and the black abolitionist Frederick Douglass had embraced their cause: "Once let the black man get upon his person the brass letters, 'U.S.,'. . . a musket on his shoulder and bullets in his pockets, and there is no power on earth which can deny that he has earned the right to citizenship in the United States." Such an outcome frightened many northern whites, who were determined to keep blacks subjugated. Moreover, most Union generals doubted that former slaves would make good soldiers, and so the Lincoln administration initially refused to encourage black aspirations for military service.

The Emancipation Proclamation changed popular thinking and military policy. If blacks were to benefit from a Union victory, some northern whites argued, they should share in the fighting and dying. The valor exhibited by the first African-American regiments also influenced northern opinion. In January 1863 Thomas Wentworth Higginson, the white abolitionist commander of the First South Carolina (Black) Volunteers, wrote a glowing newspaper account of their military prowess: "No officer in this regiment now doubts that the key to the successful prosecution of the war lies in the unlimited employment of black troops." The War department authorized the enlistment of free blacks and contraband slaves, and as white resistance to conscription increased, the Lincoln administration recruited as many African-Americans as it could. Without black soldiers, the president suggested in the autumn of 1864, "we would be compelled to abandon the war in three weeks." By the following spring there were nearly 200,000 African-American soldiers and sailors.

Military service did not end racial discrimination. Black soldiers served under white officers in segregated regiments and were used primarily to build fortifications, garrison forts, and guard supply lines. At first they were paid less than white soldiers ($7 versus $13 per month), and only a few were promoted to higher ranks. Despite such treatment, African-Americans volunteered for military service in disproportionate numbers and diligently served the Union cause. They knew they were fighting for freedom and the possibility of a new social order. "Hello, Massa," said one black soldier to his former master, who had been taken prisoner. "Bottom rail on top dis time." The worst fears of the secessionists had come true: through the agency of the Union army, slaves had risen in a great rebellion.

Black Soldiers in the Union Army
Tens of thousands of African-Americans volunteered for military service and a chance to fight
for the freedom of their people. These soldiers were members of the 107th Colored Infantry.
In January 1865 their regiment participated in the daring capture of Fort Fisher, which protected Wilmington, North Carolina, the last Confederate port open to blockade runners.

As African-Americans enlisted in the ranks, Lincoln finally found a commanding general in whom he had confidence. In March 1864 he put General
Ulysses S. Grant in charge of all the Union armies and approved Grant's plan
to advance simultaneously against all the major Confederate forces. Both the
general and the president wanted a decisive victory before the election of
1864.

As the successful western campaigns of 1863 showed, Grant understood
how to fight a modern war—a war relying on industrial technology and directed at an entire society. At Vicksburg he had besieged an entire city and
forced its surrender. A few months later, in November 1863, he had used the
North's edge in technology to advantage, utilizing railroad transport to charge
to the rescue of a Union army near Chattanooga, Tennessee, and drive an invading army back into Georgia. Moreover, Grant was willing to accept heavy
casualties in assaults on strongly defended positions, abandoning the caution of
earlier Union commanders. "To conserve life, in war," Grant wrote, "is to fight
unceasingly." Grant's aggressive tactics earned him a reputation as a butcher
both of his own men and of enemy armies, which he pursued relentlessly
when they were in retreat. Finally, to crush the South's will to resist, the new
Union commander was willing to terrorize the civilian population.

In May 1864 Grant ordered major new offensives on two fronts. Personally
taking charge of the 115,000-strong Army of the Potomac, he set out to destroy Lee's force of 75,000 troops in Virginia. Simultaneously he instructed

General William Tecumseh Sherman, who shared his views on modern warfare, to invade Georgia and take Atlanta. As Sherman prepared for battle, he wrote that "all that has gone before is mere skirmish. The war now begins."

Grant advanced toward Richmond, hoping to force Lee to fight in open fields, where the Union's superior manpower and artillery could prevail. Lee, remembering Gettysburg, maintained strong defensive positions, attacking only when he held a tactical advantage. He seized such opportunities twice, winning narrow victories in the battles of the Wilderness on May 5–7 and Spotsylvania Court House on May 8–12. Nevertheless Grant drove on toward Richmond. In early June he attacked Lee at Cold Harbor but withdrew after losing 7,000 men in a frontal assault. Grant had severely eroded Lee's forces, which had suffered 31,000 casualties, but Union losses were even higher at 55,000 men.

The fighting took a heavy psychological toll. "Many a man has gone crazy since this campaign began from the terrible pressure on mind and body," complained a Union officer. Previous battles had lasted only a few days and had been separated by long intervals. But in this campaign Grant's relentless advance toward Richmond and Lee's defensive tactics produced sustained fighting and grueling attrition. In June, Grant pulled some of his troops away from Richmond to lay siege to Petersburg, an important railroad center. Protracted trench warfare, which foreshadowed that of World War I, made the spade as important as the sword. Soldiers built complex networks of trenches, tunnels, and artillery emplacements for almost 50 miles around Richmond and Petersburg. An officer described the continuous artillery firing and sniping as "living night and day within the 'valley of the shadow of death.'" The stress was especially great for the outnumbered Confederate troops, who spent months in the muddy, sickening trenches without rotation to the rear. As time passed, Lincoln and Grant felt pressures of their own; the enormous casualties and continued military stalemate threatened Lincoln with defeat in the November election.

The outlook for the Republicans worsened when raids by Jubal Early's cavalry near Washington in early July forced Grant to divert his best troops from the Petersburg campaign. To punish and control the Shenandoah Valley, which provided a base for Early and food for Lee's army, Grant ordered General Philip H. Sheridan to turn the region into "a barren waste." During the fall Sheridan's troops conducted a scorched-earth campaign, destroying grain supplies, barns, farming implements, and gristmills. This terrorism went beyond the military norms of the day, for most officers regarded civilians as noncombatants and feared that a punitive policy against the population would erode military discipline. But Grant's decision to carry the war to Confederate civilians had changed the definition of conventional warfare.

The Election of 1864 and the "March to the Sea"

As the siege at Petersburg dragged on, Lincoln's reelection hopes came to rest on General William Sherman in Georgia. Sherman had gradually penetrated to within about 30 miles of Atlanta, a great railway hub that controlled the heart of the Confederacy. Although his army outnumbered that of General Joseph E. Johnston 90,000 to 60,000, he avoided a direct attack and slowly pried the Confederates out of one defensive position after another. Finally, on June 27, at Kennesaw Mountain, Sherman engaged Johnston in a set battle, in which he suffered 3,000 casualties while inflicting only about 600. By late July the Union general had laid siege to Atlanta, but the next month brought little gain. Like Grant, Sherman seemed bogged down in a hopeless campaign.

Meanwhile, the presidential campaign of 1864 was well under way. In June the Republican convention endorsed Lincoln's war measures, demanded the unconditional surrender of the Confederacy, and called for a constitutional amendment to abolish slavery. To attract Democratic support, the party temporarily renamed itself the National Union party and nominated Andrew Johnson, a Unionist Tennessee Democrat, for vice-president. The Democratic convention met in late August and nominated General George B. McClellan. The delegates declared their opposition to emancipation but were divided over continuing the war. By threatening to bolt the convention, the "Peace Democrats" forced through a platform calling for "a cessation of hostilities" and a convention to restore peace "on the basis of the Federal Union." Although personally a "War Democrat," McClellan promised if elected to recommend an immediate armistice and a peace convention. Rejoicing in "the first ray of real light I have seen since the war began," Confederate Vice-President Alexander Stephens declared that if Atlanta and Richmond held out, Lincoln might be defeated, and northern Democrats then be persuaded to accept the independence of the South.

But on September 2, Atlanta fell. In a stunning move, Sherman pulled his troops from the trenches and swept around the city to destroy its roads and rail links to the rest of the Confederacy, forcing its surrender. In her diary Mary Chestnut, a slaveowning plantation mistress, despaired of victory: "We are going to be wiped off the earth." Amid the 100-gun salutes in northern cities that greeted the news of Sherman's victory, McClellan repudiated the Democratic peace platform. But Republicans charged that he was still a peace candidate and that *Copperheads* (a poisonous snake and the name bestowed on Peace Democrats by Republican newspapers) were hatching treasonous plots in the border states.

Sherman's success in Georgia gave Lincoln a clear-cut victory in November. He took 212 of 233 electoral votes, winning 55 percent of the popular vote in the free and border states and carrying every state except Delaware, Kentucky, and New Jersey. Republicans won 145 of the 185 seats in the House of Representatives and increased their Senate majority to 42 of 52 seats. Many of those victories hinged on the votes of Union troops, most of whom wanted the war to continue until the Confederacy met every Union demand, including emancipation.

Already the pace of legal emancipation had accelerated. In 1864 Maryland and Missouri amended their constitutions to free their slaves, and the three occupied states of Tennessee, Arkansas, and Louisiana followed suit. Abolitionists still worried that the Emancipation Proclamation, based on the president's wartime powers, would lose its force at the end of the war and that southern states would reestablish slavery. Urged on by Lincoln, the new Republican-dominated Congress took the final step toward full legal emancipation. On January 31, 1865, it approved the Thirteenth Amendment, which prohibited slavery throughout the United States. Slavery was nearly dead.

And so was the Confederacy. After the capture of Atlanta, Sherman declined to follow the retreating Confederate army into Tennessee and decided on a bold strategy. Rather than spread his troops dangerously thin by protecting supply lines to the rear, he would "cut a swath through to the sea," living off the land. To persuade Lincoln and Grant to approve this unconventional plan, Sherman pointed out that such a march would devastate Georgia and score a major psychological victory. It would be "a demonstration to the world, foreign and domestic, that we have a power [Jefferson] Davis cannot resist."

Sherman carried out the concept of total war he and Sheridan had pioneered: destruction of the enemy's economic resources and will to resist. "We are not only fighting hostile armies," Sherman wrote, "but a hostile people, and must make old and young, rich and poor, feel the hard hand of war." He

Atlanta in Ruins
As the Confederate army retreated from Atlanta, it blew up factories to keep them out of Union hands. Sherman's forces destroyed the remaining industries, including the roundhouse (on the right) and car repair sheds of the Georgia Central Railroad. The devastation of Atlanta and Georgia during Sherman's "march to the sea" was a severe blow to Confederate morale.

left Atlanta in flames and during his 300-mile march to the sea destroyed railroads, property, and supplies (see Map 15.3). A Union veteran wrote that "[we] destroyed all we could not eat, stole their niggers, burned their cotton & gins, spilled their sorghum, burned & twisted their R.Roads and raised Hell generally." The havoc so demoralized Confederate soldiers that many deserted and fled home to their loved ones. When Sherman reached Savannah, Georgia, in mid-December, the 10,000 Confederate defenders left without a fight.

In February 1865 Sherman invaded South Carolina. He planned to link up with Grant at Petersburg and along the way punish the state where secession had begun. "The truth is," Sherman wrote, "the whole army is burning with an insatiable desire to wreak vengeance upon South Carolina." His troops cut a comparatively narrow swath across the state but ravaged the countryside even more thoroughly than they had in Georgia. By March Sherman had reached North Carolina and was on the verge of linking up with Grant and crushing Lee's army.

Sherman's march exposed an internal Confederate weakness: rising class resentment on the part of poor whites. Long angered by the "twenty-Negro" exemption from military service given to slaveowners and their overseers and fearing that the Confederacy was doomed, ordinary southern farmers increas-

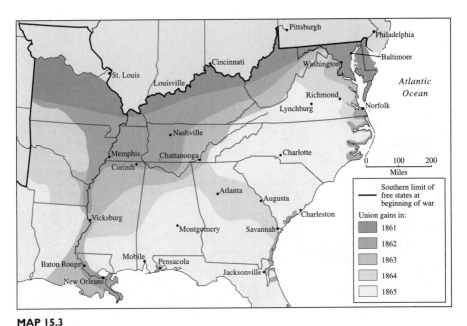

MAP 15.3

The Conquest of the South, 1861–1865

It took four years for the Union army to occupy the territory of the Confederacy, much of which remained under southern control until the last year of the war. Most of the Union's victories came on the western front, where its control of strategic lines of communication allowed it to mount large-scale attacks against Confederate armies.

Lee's Surrender
Lee surrendered to Grant in the parlor of a modest farmer, Wilmer
McLean, who could not escape the war. McLean had fled to Appomattox
for peace and quiet after leaving a Manassas home, which Confederate soldiers had used as a headquarters and Union forces had shelled during the
first major battle of the war.

ingly resisted conscription and desertion became widespread. By early 1865
the Confederacy was experiencing such a severe manpower crisis that its leaders decided to take an extreme measure: arming the slaves. Urged on by Lee,
the Confederate Congress voted to enlist black soldiers; Davis issued an executive order granting freedom to all blacks who served in the Confederate
army. But the war ended too soon to reveal whether any slaves would have
fought for the Confederacy.

The final act of the war took place in Virginia. In April 1865 Grant finally
forced Lee into a showdown by gaining control of the crucial railroad junction at Petersburg and cutting off his supplies. Lee abandoned the defense of
Richmond and turned west, hoping to join up with Confederate forces in
North Carolina. While Lincoln visited the ruins of the Confederate capital,
mobbed by joyful former slaves, Grant cut off Lee's escape route. On April 9,
almost precisely four years after the attack on Fort Sumter, Lee surrendered to
Grant at Appomattox Court House, Virginia. In accepting the surrender of
the impeccably dressed Confederate general, Grant set a tone of egalitarianism
and generosity, wearing an unpressed jacket and muddy trousers and allowing
Lee's men to take their horses home for spring planting. By May 26 all the
Confederate generals had laid down their arms, and the Confederate army
and government simply dissolved.

The armies of the Union had destroyed the Confederacy and much of the South's economy. Its factories, warehouses, and railroads were in ruins, as were many of its farms and some of its most important cities. Almost 260,000 Confederate soldiers had paid for secession with their lives. Most significant, the Union had been preserved and slavery destroyed. But the cost of victory was enormous in money, wasted resources, and lives. Over 360,000 Union soldiers were dead, and hundreds of thousands were maimed and crippled. The hard and bitter war was over, and a reunited nation turned to the tasks of peace, which were to be equally hard and bitter.

CHAPTER 15 TIMELINE

1861	Confederate States of America formed (February 4)
	Abraham Lincoln inaugurated (March 4)
	Confederates fire on Fort Sumter (April 12)
	Virginia convention votes to secede (April 17)
	First Battle of Bull Run (July 21)
	General Benjamin Butler declares runaway slaves "contraband of war"
1862	Congress passes Legal Tender Act
	Homestead Act and federal aid to transcontinental railroads
	Battle of Shiloh (April 6–7)
	Confederacy introduces first draft
	Battle of Antietam (September 17)
	Preliminary Emancipation Proclamation (September 22)
1863	Lincoln issues Emancipation Proclamation (January 1)
	Enrollment Act begins draft in North; riots in New York City (July)
	Battles of Gettysburg (July 1–3) and Vicksburg
1864	Tariffs raised
	Ulysses S. Grant advances on Richmond; siege of Petersburg
	Atlanta falls to William T. Sherman (September 2)
	Lincoln reelected, and Sherman marches through Georgia
1865	Robert E. Lee surrenders (April 9)
	Ratification of Thirteenth Amendment

CHAPTER 16

RECONSTRUCTION, 1865–1877

- Presidential Reconstruction
- Radical Reconstruction
- Redemption

In his second inaugural address, President Abraham Lincoln spoke of the need to "bind up the nation's wounds." No one knew better than Lincoln how daunting a task that would be. Foremost, of course, were the terms for restoring the states in rebellion to the Union. But the war had opened more fundamental questions. Slavery was finished. That much was certain. But what system of labor should replace plantation slavery? What rights should the freedmen be accorded beyond emancipation itself? How far should the federal government go to settle these questions? And who should decide? the president? or the Congress?

While the war was still on, the North began to grope for answers. Relying on his wartime powers, Abraham Lincoln in December 1863 offered a general amnesty to all but high-ranking Confederates willing to pledge loyalty to the Union and accept the abolition of slavery. When 10 percent of a state's 1860 voters had taken this oath, they could organize a new government and apply for restoration to the Union. Only states under military occupation—Louisiana, Arkansas, and Tennessee—took advantage of Lincoln's generous offer, but he hoped Confederates elsewhere might also be induced to abandon the rebellion.

Although it reflected his conciliatory bent, Lincoln's Ten Percent Plan was really aimed at subverting the southern war effort. What it also did was to reveal the rocky road that lay ahead for Reconstruction. Thus, in Louisiana, sugar planters showed little remorse for the crime of slavery. On the contrary, with the aid of the occupying federal forces, they tried to regain control over the freed slaves, buttressed by oppressive curfew and vagrancy regulations. But the Louisiana freedmen fought right back. Led by the free black community of New Orleans, they began to agitate for political rights. No less than their former masters, ex-slaves intended to be actors in the savage drama of Reconstruction.

With Louisiana very much in mind, Republicans in Congress put forth a stricter substitute for Lincoln's Ten Percent Plan. The initiative came from the Radical wing of the party—those bent on a stern peace and full rights for the freedmen—but with broad support among more moderate Republicans. The Wade-Davis bill, passed on July 2, 1864, laid down, as conditions for the restoration of the rebellious states to the Union, an oath of allegiance by a majority of each state's adult white men, new state governments formed and operated only by those who had never carried arms against the Union, and permanent disfranchisement of Confederate civil and military leaders. The Wade-Davis bill served notice that the congressional Republicans were not about to hand reconstruction policy over to the president.

Lincoln was not perturbed. Rather than openly challenging Congress, he executed a "pocket" veto of the Wade-Davis bill by not signing it before Congress adjourned. At the same time he initiated informal talks with congressional leaders aimed at finding a common ground. The last speech he ever delivered, on April 11, 1865, demonstrated Lincoln's cautious realism. Reconstruction, he pleaded, had to be regarded as a practical, not a theoretical, problem. It could be solved only if Republicans remained united, even if that meant compromising, and only if the defeated South gave its consent, even if that meant forgiveness. What the speech showed, above all, was Lincoln's sense of the fluidity of events, of policy toward the South as an evolving, not a fixed, position.

What course Reconstruction might have taken had Lincoln lived is one of the great unanswered questions of American history. On April 14, 1865—five days after Lee's surrender at Appomattox—Lincoln was shot in the head at Ford's Theater in Washington by an unstable actor named John Wilkes Booth. Ironically, Lincoln might have been spared if the war had dragged on longer, for Booth and his Confederate associates had originally plotted to kidnap the president to force a negotiated settlement. Without regaining consciousness, Lincoln died on April 15.

At one stroke John Wilkes Booth had sent Lincoln to martyrdom, hardened many northerners against the South, and handed the presidency to a man utterly lacking in Lincoln's moral sense and political judgment, Vice-President Andrew Johnson.

PRESIDENTIAL RECONSTRUCTION

At the end of the Civil War, a very big constitutional question remained in dispute—whether, on seceding, the Confederate states had legally left the

Union. If so, then these states became conquered territories, and the terms of their readmission demanded the gravest consideration by the Congress. If not, if even in defeat they retained their constitutional status, the initiative for restoring them to the Union might appropriately be taken by the president. This was Andrew Johnson's view, and by an accident of timing, he was free to act on it. For, under leisurely rules that went back to the early republic, the 39th Congress elected in November 1864 was not scheduled to convene until December 1865.

Johnson's Initiative

Andrew Johnson was a self-made man and a former slaveholder from the hills of eastern Tennessee. A Jacksonian Democrat, he saw himself as the champion of the common man. He hated what he called the "bloated, corrupt aristocracy" of the Northeast, and he was just as disdainful of the southern planters, whom he blamed for the poverty of his own yeoman farmers. Johnson's political career had taken him to the U.S. Senate, where he remained when the war broke out, loyal to the Union. After federal forces captured Nashville, Johnson became Tennessee's military governor. The Republicans nominated him for vice-president in 1864 in an effort to promote wartime political unity and to court the support of southern Unionists.

In May 1865, just a month after Lincoln's death, Johnson launched his own plan for restoration. He offered amnesty to all southerners, irrespective of their part in the rebellion, who took an oath of allegiance to the Union, but excluding high-ranking Confederate officials and the wealthier planters, whom

Andrew Johnson
The president was not an easy man. This photograph of Andrew Johnson (1808–1875) conveys some of the personal qualities that contributed so centrally to his failure to reach an agreement with Republicans on a program of moderate reconstruction.

Johnson held responsible for secession. Such persons could be pardoned only by presidential order. He appointed provisional governors for the southern states, and laid down as conditions for their restoration only that they revoke their ordinances of secession, repudiate their Confederate debts, and ratify the Thirteenth Amendment, which abolished slavery. Within months all the former Confederate states had met Johnson's requirements and had functioning, elected governments.

At first Republicans responded favorably. The moderates among them were sympathetic to Johnson's states' rights argument that it was up to the states, not the federal government, to settle questions of the ballot and civil equality for the freedmen. Even the Radicals were optimistic. They liked the stern treatment of Confederate leaders, and they hoped that the new southern state governments would respond positively to Johnson's conciliatory approach and offer the vote at least to African-Americans who were literate and owned property.

Nothing of the sort happened. Instead, the newly seated southern legislatures moved to restore slavery in all but name. They enacted laws—known as Black Codes—designed to drive the freedmen back to the plantations, to restrict their freedom of movement, and to deny them equality before the law. Localities set curfews; insisted that blacks who wanted to live in town obtain white sponsors; and, in an effort to prevent political mobilization, sharply restricted rights of assembly. The new governments had mostly been formed by ex-Whigs and southern Unionists, but when it came to racist attitudes, not a lot distinguished them from the Confederates. The latter, moreover, swiftly filtered back into the corridors of power. It turned out that Johnson, despite his hard words against them, forgave ex-Confederate leaders easily, so long as he got the satisfaction of making them submit to his personal authority. His perceived indulgence of their efforts to restore white supremacy emboldened the ex-Confederates. They packed the delegations to the new Congress with old comrades—nine members of the Confederate Congress; seven former officials of Confederate state governments; four generals and four colonels; and even the vice-president of the Confederacy, Alexander Stephens.

When Congress convened in early December 1865, the Republicans refused to admit the southern delegations, effectively blocking Johnson's reconstruction program. Although relations with the president had already cooled, the Republicans assumed he would work cooperatively with them in formulating the new terms on which the South would be readmitted to Congress. To that end, a House-Senate committee—the Joint Committee on Reconstruction—was formed and began public hearings on conditions in the South. By now, the worst of the Black Codes had been rescinded, but in place of laws aimed specifically at blacks the states brought forth nonracial ordinances that accomplished the same repressive ends. On top of that, a wave of violence erupted across the South, intended to terrorize the freedmen into submission. In Tennessee, a Nashville paper reported in early 1867 that white gangs "are riding about whipping, maiming and killing all negroes who do not obey the orders of their former masters, just as if slavery existed." Listening to the vivid testimony of officials, observers, and victims, Republicans concluded the South had embarked on a concerted effort to circumvent the Thirteenth Amendment. The only possible response was for the federal government to intervene.

Back in March 1865, the previous Congress had established the Freedman's Bureau to provide emergency aid to ex-slaves and refugees during the chaotic transition from war to peace. Now, under the leadership of the moderate Republican Senator Lyman Trumbull, Congress voted to extend the Bureau's life, gave it direct funding for the first time, and authorized its agents to step into cases where blacks were being denied the "civil rights belonging to white persons."

More extraordinary was Trumbull's proposal for a civil rights bill, declaring all persons born in the United States to be citizens and granting them, without regard to race, equal rights of contract, access to the courts, and protection of person and property. Trumbull's bill nullified all state laws depriving citizens of these rights, authorized U.S. attorneys to bring enforcement suits in the federal courts, and provided for fines and imprisonment for anyone, including public officials, guilty of depriving a citizen of civil rights. In response to an unrepentant South, Republicans of the most moderate persuasion concluded that the federal government had to assume responsibility for securing the basic civil rights of the freedmen.

Acting on Freedom

While Congress debated, African-Americans as best they could acted on their own idea of freedom. News of emancipation left them exultant and hopeful. Freedom meant many things. It meant reuniting separated families, the end of punishment by the lash, the ability to move around, the opportunity to establish schools, churches, and social clubs, and, not least, the chance to engage in politics. Across the South, blacks held mass meetings, paraded, and formed organizations. In the cities, where free blacks took the lead, Union Leagues and Equal Rights Leagues worked to give the freedmen a political voice. With the encouragement of Freedmen's Bureau agents, state conventions also began to meet, invariably passing resolutions demanding equality before the law and the right to vote—"an essential and inseparable element of self-government."

First of all, however, came economic independence, which emancipated blacks believed was the basis for true freedom. During the Civil War they had acted on this assumption whenever Union armies drew near. During the final months of the war, when the Union directed its military operations against civilians, freedmen found greater opportunities to win control of land. Most visibly, General William T. Sherman reserved vast tracts of coastal lands in Georgia and South Carolina—the Sea Islands and abandoned plantations within 30 miles of the coast—for liberated slaves, and settled them on 40-acre tracts. Sherman only wanted to relieve the pressure the refugees were placing

AMERICAN VOICES

A Plea for Land

Following is a painfully written letter by the ex-slaves of Edisto Island to President Andrew Johnson, pleading for a reversal of his order that the lands they now worked be returned to the plantation owners.

Edisto Island S.C. Oct 28th, 1865.
To the President of these United States. We the freedmen Of Edisto Island South Carolina have learned . . . with deep sorrow and Painful hearts of the possibility of government restoring These lands to the former owners. . . . Here is where secession was born and Nurtured Here is where we have toiled nearly all Our lives as slaves and were treated like dumb Driven cattle. This is our home, we have made These lands what they are. . . . Shall not we who Are freedmen and have always been true to this Union have the same rights as are enjoyed by Others? Have we broken any Law of these United States? have we forfeited our rights of property In Land?—If not then! are not our rights as A free people and good citizens of these United States To be considered before the rights of those who were Found in rebellion against this good and just Government. . . . And we who have been abused and oppressed For many long years But be subject To the will of these large Land owners? God forbid.

. . . We the freedmen of this Island and the State of South Carolina—Do hereby petition to you as the President of these United States, that some provisions be made by which Every colored man can purchase land. and Hold as his own. We wish to have A home if It be but A few acres. . . . May God bless you in the Administration of your duties as the President Of these United States is the humble prayer Of us all.—

In behalf of the Freedmen
Henry Bram
Committee   Ishmael. Moultrie
yates. Sampson

SOURCE: Eileen Boris and Nelson Lichtenstein, eds., *Major Problems in the History of American Workers: Documents and Essays* (Lexington, MA: Heath, 1990), 137–139.

on his army as it marched across the lower South. But the freedmen assumed that Sherman's order meant that the land would be theirs.

As the war ended, resettlement became the responsibility of the Freedmen's Bureau, which was charged with distributing confiscated land to "loyal refugees and freedmen" and with regulating labor contracts between freedmen and planters. The Freedmen's Bureau also worked with the large number of northern voluntary associations that sent missionaries and teachers to the South to establish schools for former slaves.

With the encouragement of the Freedmen's Bureau, blacks across the South occupied confiscated or abandoned land, including half a million acres of "Sherman" land in Georgia and South Carolina. Many families stayed on their old plantations in the hope that they could claim some of the land after the war. When the South Carolina planter Thomas Pinckney returned home, his freed slaves told him, "We ain't going nowhere. We are going to work right here on the land where we were born and what belongs to us."

Johnson's amnesty plan, entitling pardoned Confederates to recover property seized during the war, brought these hopes to an abrupt halt. In October 1865, Johnson ordered General Oliver O. Howard, head of the Freedmen's Bureau, to tell Sea Island blacks that the land they occupied would have to be restored to the white owners. When Howard reluctantly obeyed, the dispossessed farmers protested: "Why do you take away our lands? You take them from us who have always been true, always true to the Government! You give them to our all-time enemies! That is not right!" In the Sea Islands and elsewhere, former slaves resisted efforts to remove them. Often led by black veterans of the Union army, they fought pitched battles with plantation owners and bands of ex-Confederate soldiers. In this warfare federal troops often backed the local whites, who generally prevailed in recapturing their former holdings.

As returning planters prepared for a new growing season, a great battle began to take shape over the labor system that would replace slavery. Convinced that blacks could not work without supervision, planters insisted on retaining the gang system of plantation labor, only now paying low wages instead of the food, clothing, and shelter their slaves had once received. Many freedmen voted with their feet. Thousands of families abandoned their old plantations, seeking better lives and more freedom in the towns and cities of the South. Those who remained in the countryside refused to work the cotton fields under the hated gang labor or negotiated tenaciously over the terms of their labor contracts. What was freedom all about if not to have a bit more leisure time, to work less intensely than they had as slaves, and to work for themselves and their families? Whatever system of labor finally might emerge, it was clear that the freedmen and their families would never settle for anything resembling the old plantation system.

The efforts of former slaves to control their own lives ran counter to deeply entrenched white attitudes. "The destiny of the black race," asserted one Texan, could be summarized "in one sentence—subordination to the white race." Southern whites, a Freedmen's Bureau official observed, could not "conceive of the negro having any rights at all." When freedmen resisted, white retribution was swift and often terrible. In Pine Bluff, Arkansas, "after some kind of dispute with some freedmen," whites set fire to their cabins and lynched twenty-four of the inhabitants—men, women, and children. The toll of murdered and beaten blacks mounted into untold thousands. The governments established under Johnson's plan only put the stamp of legality on the pervasive efforts to enforce white supremacy. Blacks "would be *just as well* off

Wage Labor of Ex-Slaves
This photograph, taken in South Carolina shortly after the Civil War,
shows former slaves being led from the cotton fields. Although they now
worked for wages, they were probably organized into a gang not far
removed from the earlier slave gangs. Their plug-hatted crew leader is
dressed much as his slave-driving predecessor would have been.

with no law at all or no Government," concluded a Freedmen's Bureau agent,
as with the justice they got under the restored white rule.

In this unequal struggle, blacks turned to Washington. "We stood by the
government when it wanted help," a black Mississippian wrote President
Johnson. "Now . . . will it stand by us?"

Congress versus President

Andrew Johnson was, alas, not the man to ask. In February 1866, he vetoed
the Freedmen's Bureau bill, declaring it unconstitutional because Congress
lacked authority to provide a "system for the support of indigent people" and
because the states most directly affected by its provisions were not yet represented in Congress. The Bureau, said Johnson, was an "immense patronage,"
showering benefits on blacks never granted to "our own people." A month
later, rebuffing the outraged critics of his Freedman's Bureau veto, Johnson
vetoed Trumbull's Civil Rights bill, again arguing that federal protection
of black civil rights constituted "a stride toward centralization." His racism,
hitherto muted, now blazed forth. In his view, granting blacks the privileges of

citizenship was discriminatory, operating "in favor of the colored and against the white race," and threatening all manner of evil consequences, including miscegenation.

Taken by surprise, the Republicans were galvanized into action. They failed, just barely, to override Johnson's veto of the Freedmen's Bureau bill, but in early April, they got the necessary two-thirds majorities in both houses and enacted the Civil Rights bill into law. This was a truly historic event, the first time Congress had prevailed over a presidential veto on a major piece of legislation. In July the Freedmen's Bureau was renewed over a second Johnson veto.

Anxious to consolidate their victory, Republicans moved to enshrine black civil rights in an amendment to the Constitution. They were already upset by the dividend the South had gained from emancipation: a jump in federal representation because, under the Constitution, the slave population had counted as only three-fifths, whereas as free persons blacks counted fully (even if they could not vote). Now this question was bundled with civil rights into what became the Fourteenth Amendment. Section 2 reduced a state's representation in the House of Representatives by the percentage of adult male citizens who were denied the vote. Intended to prod the South toward enfranchising the freedmen, Section 2 was quickly overtaken by events and had no lasting significance, save for the insertion of the word *male* into the Constitution, which, to the outrage of woman suffragists, cast women out from the gathering movement toward universal suffrage. The heart of the Fourteenth Amendment was Section 1, which declared that "all persons born or naturalized in the United States" were citizens. No state could abridge "the privileges or immunities of citizens of the United States," deprive "any person of life, liberty, or property, without due process of law," or deny anyone "the equal protection of the laws." These phrases were vague, intentionally so, but they established the constitutionality of the Civil Rights Act and, more important, the basis on which the courts and Congress could establish an enforceable standard of equality before the law in the states.

For the moment, however, the Fourteenth Amendment was most important for its impact on national politics. With the 1866 congressional elections approaching, Johnson somehow figured he had a winning issue in the Fourteenth Amendment. He denounced it, and urged the states not to ratify it. Months earlier, Johnson had begun to maneuver politically against the Republicans, aiming to build a coalition of white southerners, northern Democrats, and conservative Republicans under the banner of "National Union." For discredited Democrats, Johnson's scheme offered the cloak of respectability, and they eagerly seized it. Any hope of creating a new national party, however, was shattered by Johnson's intemperate behavior and by escalating violence in the South. Sympathetic Republicans and ex-Whigs backed off, a dissension-ridden National Union convention in July ended inconclusively, and Johnson's campaign against the Fourteenth Amendment became, effectively, a campaign for the Democratic party. In late August Johnson embarked on a disastrous "swing around the circle"—a railroad tour from Washington to Chicago and St. Louis and back. It was unprecedented for a president to campaign personally, and Johnson made matters worse by engaging in shouting matches with hecklers and by insulting members of the hostile crowds.

The 1866 congressional elections inflicted a humiliating defeat on Johnson. The Republicans, having won a three-to-one majority in Congress, considered themselves "masters of the situation," free to proceed "entirely regardless of [Johnson's] opinions or wishes." As a referendum on the Fourteenth Amendment, moreover, the election registered strong popular support for the civil rights of the freedmen. The Republican Party emerged with a new sense of unity—a unity coalescing not at the center, but on the left, around the root-and-branch program of the Radical minority.

The Radicals represented the abolitionist strain within the Republican party. Most of them hailed from New England, or from the area of the upper Midwest settled by New Englanders. In the Senate, they were led by Charles Sumner of Massachusetts; in the House, by the redoubtable Thaddeus Stevens from Pennslyvania. For them, Reconstruction was never primarily about restoring the Union; rather, it was about remaking southern society. "The foundations of their institutions . . . must be broken up and relaid," declared Stevens, "or all our blood and treasure will have been spent in vain." Only a handful went as far as Stevens in demanding that the plantations be broken up into small farms for the former slaves. But the Radicals had no qualms about expanding the powers of the national government to protect the civil rights of the freedmen and, more than that, grant them the suffrage. Radicals were aggressively partisan. They regarded the Republican party as the instrument of the Lord, and black votes as the means by which the party could dominate the South and bring about its regeneration.

At first, in the months after the surrender at Appomattox, few but the Radicals themselves imagined they had any chance of putting across so extreme a program. Black suffrage especially seemed beyond reach, since the northern states themselves (excepting in New England) denied blacks the vote at this time. And yet, as fury mounted against the intransigent South, Republicans became ever more radicalized until, in the wake of the smashing victory of 1866, they embraced the Radicals' vision of a reconstructed South.

RADICAL RECONSTRUCTION

Afterward, thoughtful southerners admitted that the South had brought radical Reconstruction on itself. "We had, in 1865, a white man's government in Alabama," remarked the man who had been Johnson's provisional governor, "but we lost it." The state's "great blunder" was not to "have at once taken the negro right under the protection of the laws." Remarkably, the South remained defiant even after the 1866 congressional elections. Every state legislature (except, back in July, Tennessee) rejected the Fourteenth Amendment, mostly by virtual acclamation. It was as if they could not imagine that governments installed under the presidential imprimatur and fully functioning might be swept away. But that, in fact, is just what the Republicans intended to do.

Congress Takes Command

The Reconstruction Act of 1867, enacted in March by the Republican Congress, organized the South as a conquered land, dividing it (with the exception of Tennessee) into five military districts, each under the command of a Union general. The price for reentering the Union was granting the vote to the freedmen and disfranchising the South's prewar leadership class—anyone who had taken an oath of loyalty to the Constitution as an officeholder or a commissioned officer and then had participated in the rebellion. Each military commander was ordered to register all eligible adult males, black as well as white, to supervise the election of state conventions, and to make certain that the new state constitutions contained guarantees of black suffrage. Congress would readmit a state to the Union if its voters ratified the constitution, if that document proved acceptable to Congress, and if the new state legislature approved the Fourteenth Amendment (thus ensuring the needed ratification by three-fourths of the states). Johnson vetoed the act, but Congress overrode the veto. By 1870, all ten of the ex-Confederate states had met the requirements and were readmitted to the Union.

Republicans also checkmated President Johnson. The Tenure of Office Act, a companion to the Reconstruction Act, required Senate consent for the removal of any official whose appointment had required Senate confirmation. Congress chiefly wanted to protect Secretary of War Edwin M. Stanton, a Lincoln holdover and the only member of Johnson's cabinet who favored radical Reconstruction. In his position Stanton could do much to prevent Johnson from frustrating the goals of Reconstruction. Congress also required the president to issue all orders to the army through its commanding general, Ulysses S. Grant.

Seemingly defeated, Johnson appointed generals recommended by Stanton and Grant to command the five military districts in the South. But he was just biding his time. In August 1867, after Congress had adjourned, he "suspended" Stanton and replaced him with Grant, believing that the general would act like a good soldier and follow orders. Next Johnson replaced four of the commanding generals, including Philip H. Sheridan, Grant's favorite cavalry general. Johnson, however, had misjudged Grant, who publicly registered his opposition to the president's machinations. When the Senate reconvened in the fall, it overruled Stanton's suspension. Grant, now an open enemy of Johnson's, resigned so that Stanton could resume his office.

In February 1868 Johnson dismissed Stanton. House Republicans lashed back by using the power granted them by the Constitution to impeach—to charge federal officials with "Treason, Bribery, or other high Crimes and Misdemeanors." The House overwhelmingly (128 to 47) brought eleven counts of criminal misconduct, nine of which dealt with violations of the Tenure of Office Act, against the president.

The case went to the Senate, which the Constitution empowers to act as a court in impeachment cases, presided over by Chief Justice Salmon P. Chase. After an eleven-week trial, thirty-five senators on May 15 voted for conviction, one vote short of the two-thirds majority required. Seven moderate Republicans had broken ranks, voting for acquittal along with twelve Democrats. The reluctant Republicans were overwhelmed by the drastic nature of the attack on Johnson; Congress had removed federal judges from office, but never a president. Even if Johnson had broken the law, they felt, the real issue was a political disagreement between Congress and the president. They feared that a conviction based on a policy dispute would establish a dangerous precedent and undermine the presidency, which seemed too high a price just to punish Johnson.

In any case, even without being convicted, Johnson had been defanged, and he was helpless for the remainder of his term to alter the course of Reconstruction.

The impeachment controversy made Grant, already the North's most popular war hero, a Republican hero as well, and he easily won the party's presidential nomination in 1868. In the fall campaign he supported radical Reconstruction, but he also urged reconciliation between the sections. His Democratic opponent was Horatio Seymour, a former governor of New York and a Peace Democrat who almost declined the nomination, certain that the Democrats could not overcome their identification with the disloyal South. As Seymour feared, the Republicans "waved the bloody shirt," stirring up old wartime emotions against the Democrats to great effect. Grant won about the same share of the northern vote (55 percent) that Lincoln had in 1864, and received 214 of 294 electoral votes. The Republicans also retained two-thirds majorities in both houses of Congress.

In the wake of their smashing victory, the Republicans quickly produced the last major piece of Reconstruction legislation—the Fifteenth Amendment, which forbade either the federal government or the states to deny citizens the right to vote on the basis of race, color, or "previous condition of servitude." Proponents of the amendment were aware that it left open the use of poll taxes and property or literacy tests to discourage blacks from voting. But northern states also valued such qualifications, employing them against immigrants and the "unworthy" poor. A California senator warned that in his state, with its rabidly anti-Chinese sentiment, any restriction on that power would "kill our party as dead as a stone." Despite grumbling by Radical Republicans, the amendment passed without modification in February 1869. Congress required the unreconstructed states of Virginia, Mississippi, Texas, and Georgia to ratify it before they were readmitted to the Union. A year later the Fifteenth Amendment became part of the Constitution.

If the Fifteenth Amendment troubled some proponents of black suffrage, this was nothing as compared to the outrage felt by women's rights advocates. They had fought the good fight for so many years for the abolition of slavery, only to be abandoned by their male allies when the chance finally came to get the vote for women. How could the suffrage be granted to ex-slaves, Elizabeth Cady Stanton demanded to know, but not to them? The Fifteenth Amendment opened up a schism in the ranks of the women's movement. In 1868 a group led by Lucy Stone broke with the American Equal Rights Association, which had declared against the Fifteenth Amendment, and formed the New England Woman Suffrage Association. Its goal was to maintain an alliance with the Republicans in the forlorn hope that, once Reconstruction had been settled, it would be time for woman suffrage.

The South during Radical Reconstruction

Between 1868 and 1871 all the southern states met the congressional stipulations and rejoined the Union. Protected by federal troops and encouraged by northern party leaders, state Republican organizations took hold across the South and won control of the newly established Reconstruction governments. These Republican administrations remained in power for periods ranging from a few months in Virginia to nine years in South Carolina, Louisiana, and Florida (see Map 16.1). African-Americans participated prominently in the Reconstruction governments. In Alabama, Florida, South Carolina, Mississippi,

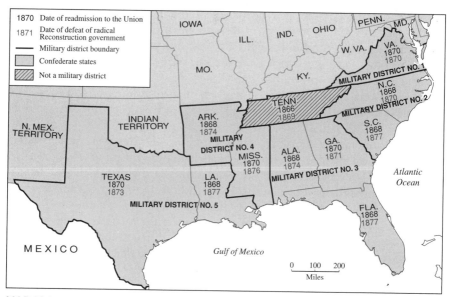

MAP 16.1

Reconstruction

The federal government organized the Confederate states into five military districts during radical Reconstruction. For each state the first date indicates when that state was readmitted to the Union; the second date shows when radical Republicans lost control of the state government. All the ex-Confederate states rejoined the Union from 1868 to 1870, but the periods of radical rule varied widely. Radicals lasted only a few months in Virginia; they held on until the end of Reconstruction in Louisiana, Florida, and South Carolina.

and Louisiana they constituted an outright majority of registered voters. They provided the votes for Republican victories in those states and in Georgia, Virginia, and North Carolina as well, where they accounted for nearly half the registered voters.

Democratic ex-Confederates mocked and scorned black Republican officeholders as ignorant field hands who could only play at politics, and they referred to whites who became Republicans as *scalawags*—an ancient Scots-Irish term for runty, worthless animals. Whites who had come from the North they denounced as *carpetbaggers*—self-seeking interlopers who carried all their belongings in cheap suitcases called carpetbags.

Actually, few southern Republicans conformed to the hostile stereotypes. Some carpetbaggers did come south for personal profit, but they also brought capital and skills. Union army veterans taken with the South—its climate, people, and economic opportunities—also figured heavily among the carpetbaggers. And interspersed with the self-seekers were many idealists anxious to advance the cause of emancipation. The scalawags were even more diverse. Some were former slaveowners, ex-Whigs and even ex-Democrats, drawn to Republicanism as the best way to attract northern capital to southern railroads, mines, and factories. In southwest Texas, the large population of Germans was strongly Republican. They sent to Congress Edward Degener, an immigrant and a San Antonio grocer whom Confederate authorities had imprisoned and whose sons had been executed for treason. Most numerous among the scalawags were yeomen farmers from the back-country districts who wanted to rid the South of its slaveholding aristocracy. Scalawags had generally fought against, or at least refused to support, the Confederacy; they believed that slavery had victimized whites as well as blacks. "Now is the time," a Georgia scalawag wrote, "for every man to come out and speak his principles publickly [*sic*] and vote for liberty as we have been in bondage long enough."

The Democrats' stereotypes of black political leaders were just as false. Until 1867 most African-American leaders in the South came from the elite that had been free before the Civil War. With the formation of the reconstructed Republican governments in 1867, this diverse group of ministers, artisans, shopkeepers, and former soldiers reached out to the freedmen. African-American speakers, some financed by the Republican Congressional Committee, fanned out into the old plantation districts and drew ex-slaves into political leadership. Still, few of the new leaders were field hands; most had been preachers or artisans. The literacy of one ex-slave, Thomas Allen, who was a Baptist minister and shoemaker, helped him win election to the Georgia legislature. "In my county," he recalled, "the colored people came to me for instructions, and I gave them the best instructions I could. I took the *New York Tribune* and other papers, and in that way I found out a great deal, and I told them whatever I thought was right."

Many of the African-American leaders who emerged in 1867 had been born in the North or had spent many years there. They moved south when radical Reconstruction opened up the prospect of meaningful freedom. Like

Hiram R. Revels
In 1870 Hiram R. Revels (1822–1901) was elected to the U.S. Senate from Mississippi to fill Jefferson Davis's former seat. Revels was a free black from North Carolina who had migrated to the North and attended Knox College in Illinois. He recruited blacks for the Union army and as an ordained Methodist minister served as chaplain of a black regiment in Mississippi, where he settled after the war.

white migrants, many were veterans of the Union army. Some had fought in the antislavery crusade, some were employed by the Freedmen's Bureau or northern missionary societies, and a few came from free families and had gone north for an education. Others had escaped from slavery and were returning home, like Blanche K. Bruce, who first taught school in Missouri and then in 1874 became Missisippi's second black U.S. senator.

Although never proportionate to the size of the black population, African-American officeholders held positions of importance throughout the South. In 1868 they constituted a majority in the lower house of the South Carolina legislature. They were heavily represented in the state's executive offices, elected three members of Congress, and won a seat on the state supreme court. Across the South generally, twenty African-Americans served as governor, lieutenant governor, secretary of state, treasurer, or superintendent of education, more than six hundred served as state legislators, and sixteen served in the U.S. House of Representatives. Almost all who became state executives had been free before the Civil War, but in the legislatures most black members had been slaves.

The Republicans who took office had ambitious plans for a reconstructed South. They modernized state constitutions and made more offices elective. They established hospitals, penitentiaries, and asylums for orphans and the insane. Republican governments built roads in areas where roads had never existed. They poured money into rebuilding the region's railroad network. And they did all this without federal financing. Southern Republicans fell far short of making their vision a reality, but they accomplished more than their critics gave them credit for.

To pay for their ambitious programs the Republican governments copied the taxes that northern states had relied on since the Jacksonian period. These were general property taxes applying not only to real estate but to personal wealth as well. The goal was to make planters pay their fair share of taxes and to broaden the tax base by forcing them to sell off uncultivated land. In many plantation counties, especially in South Carolina, Louisiana, and Mississippi, former slaves served as tax assessors and collectors, administering the taxation of their one-time owners.

Increasing tax revenues never managed to overtake the burgeoning obligations assumed by the Reconstruction governments. State debts mounted rapidly, and, as interest payments on bonds fell into arrears, public credit collapsed. On top of that, much of the spending was wasted, especially the aid to railroads, or ended in the pockets of state officials. Corruption was endemic to American politics, of course, present in the southern states before the Republicans came on the scene, and rampant everywhere in this era, not least in the Grant administration itself. But there was no question that, in the free-spending atmosphere of the early Republican regimes, corruption was especially luxuriant or that it was damaging to the cause of radical Reconstruction.

A Freedmen's School
An 1866 sketch from *Harper's Weekly* of a Vicksburg, Mississippi, school run by the Freedmen's Bureau illustrates the desire for education by ex-slaves of all ages. Because most southern blacks were farmers, schools often offered night classes that left students free for field work during the day.

Nothing, however, could dim the achievement in public education. Here the South had lagged woefully; only Tennessee had a system of public schooling. Republican state governments vowed to make up for lost time, viewing education as the foundation for a democratic order. African-Americans of all ages rushed to attend the newly established schools, even when they had to pay tuition. An elderly man in Mississippi explained his desire to go to school: "Ole missus used to read the good book [the Bible] to us . . . on Sunday evenin's, but she mostly read dem places where it says, 'Servants obey your masters.' . . . Now we is free, there's heaps of tings in that old book we is just suffering to learn." By 1875 about half of all the children in Florida, Mississippi, and South Carolina were enrolled in school.

Except in New Orleans, the new schools were segregated. Most African-Americans did not complain. They seemed to agree that integration was an issue for a later day; they shared Frederick Douglass's judgment that separate schools were "infinitely superior" to no schools at all.

The building of schools was part of a larger effort by African-Americans to fortify the institutions that had sustained their spirit during the days of slavery. Most important, they strengthened family life as the cornerstone of new communities. Families moved away from the slave quarters, usually building homes scattered around their old plantations (see Map 16.2, following page). Husbands, wives, and children who had been separated were reunited, sometimes after journeys of hundreds of miles. Couples stepped forward to record marriages that had not been recognized under slavery. Many women refused to work in the fields. Instead, they insisted on tending gardens, managing households, and bringing education and religion to their children. Wives asserted their independence, opening individual bank accounts, refusing responsibility for their husbands' debts at country stores, and bringing complaints of abuse and lack of child support to the Freedmen's Bureau.

Religious belief had deep roots in nineteenth-century slave society. Now, in freedom, the African-Americans buttressed their new communities by founding their own churches. They left their old white-dominated congregations, where they had been relegated to segregated balconies and denied any voice in church governance, and built churches of their own. These churches joined together to form African-American versions of the Southern Methodist and Southern Baptist denominations, including, most prominently, the National Baptist Convention and the African Methodist Episcopal Church. Everywhere the robust black churches served not only as places of worship but as schools, social centers, and political meeting halls.

Black ministers were community leaders and often held political office during Reconstruction. Charles H. Pearce, a Methodist minister in Florida, declared, "A man in this State cannot do his whole duty as a minister except he looks out for the political interests of his people." Calling for the brotherhood of man and the special destiny of the ex-slaves as the new "Children of Israel," black ministers provided a powerful religious underpinning for the Republican politics of their congregations.

MAP 16.2
The Barrow Plantation

Comparing the 1860 map of this central Georgia plantation with the 1881 map reveals the changing patterns of black residence and farming. In 1860 the slave quarters were clustered near the planter's house, which sat on a small hilltop. The free sharecroppers of 1881 built cabins along the spurs or ridges of land between the streams, scattering their community over the plantation. A black church and school were built by this date. A typical sharecropper on the plantation earned most of his income from growing cotton.

HABITATIONS ON THIS PLANTATION	
- Former slaves	Valley floor
● Other black tenant farmers	Gentle slopes
	Higher ground

REDEMPTION

Ex-Confederates were blind to the benefits of radical Reconstruction. Indeed, no amount of achievement could have persuaded them that it was anything but an abomination, undertaken without their consent, and intended to deny them their rightful place in southern society. Led by the planters, ex-Confederates calling themselves the Redeemers staged a massive counterrevolution—one designed to "redeem" the South and restore them to political power under the banner of the Democratic party.

Counterrevolution

Insofar as they could win at the ballot box, the Democrats took that route. They worked hard to get ex-Confederates restored to the rolls of registered voters, they appealed to racial solidarity and southern patriotism, and they attacked black suffrage as a threat to white supremacy. By 1869, the Democrats had enough votes to regain office in Tennessee, and a year later, Virginia. But force was equally acceptable. Throughout the Deep South, especially where black voters were heavily concentrated, ex-Confederate planters and their supporters organized secret societies and waged campaigns of terrorism against blacks and their white allies.

The most widespread of these groups, the Ku Klux Klan, first appeared in 1866 as a Tennessee social club but quickly became a paramilitary force under the ferocious leadership of Nathan Bedford Forrest, the Confederacy's most decorated cavalry general. Forrest was notorious for a wartime incident at Fort Pillow, Tennessee, when his troops massacred African-American soldiers after they had surrendered.

By 1870 the Klan was operating almost everywhere in the South in concert with the Democratic party. The Klan murdered and whipped Republican politicians, burned black schools and churches, and attacked party gatherings. In October 1870 a group of Klansmen assaulted a Republican rally in Eutaw, Alabama, killing four African-Americans and wounding fifty-four. Such terrorist tactics enabled the Democrats to seize power in Georgia and North Carolina in 1870 and to make substantial gains elsewhere. An African-American politician in North Carolina wrote, "Our former masters are fast taking the reins of government."

Congress responded by passing a series of Enforcement Acts in 1870 and 1871, including the Ku Klux Klan Act. These laws authorized President Grant to use federal prosecutions, military force, and martial law to suppress conspiracies to deprive citizens of the rights to vote, to hold office, to serve on juries, and to enjoy equal protection of the law. Federal agents penetrated the Klan and gathered evidence that provided the basis for widespread arrests; federal grand juries indicted more than 3,000 Klansmen. In South Carolina, where the Klan was most deeply entrenched, federal troops occupied nine counties and drove as many as 2,000 Klansmen from the state.

The Grant administration's assault on the Klan raised the spirits of southern Republicans, but it also emphasized how dependent they were on the federal government. If they were to prevail over ex-Confederate terrorism, they needed what one southern Republican described as "steady, unswerving power from without."

Northern Republicans, however, had no stomach for an endless guerrilla war in the South. They grew weary of the financial costs of Reconstruction and the continuing bloodshed it seemed to produce. Although re-elected handily in 1872, Grant did not take his victory as a mandate for holding to his interventionist course. Prosecuting Klansmen under the Enforcement Acts was

White Terror

Although Mississippi remained Republican until 1876, this letter from a party organizer attests to the stubborn white resistance to radical Reconstruction. Without federal bayonets, a town like Brandon would never be secure for the Republicans.

Brandon, Mississippi, June 21, 1868

Dear Sir:

I came here at the most exciting time probably that this place has known since the war. The democrats had a great meeting. . . . After this I learned a paper was circulated for [the colored men] to sign, in which they promised to vote the democratic ticket, and about a 100 names were received. The colored men were induced to do this by threats of being discharged. . . . Supplies have already been stopped from those who would not promise to vote the democratic ticket. One man informs me his horse and wagon, valued at $150, is to be sold to satisfy an attachment for $9, on Saturday next, if not paid before; he has owing him $100 and over from white men; none will pay, nor will the sale be stopped unless he votes democratic; but he is true steel and no signs of backing down. Several colored men have had their lives threatened, and from the best information I can get there will be a row here unless a squad of troops are sent here to keep order. There is not a white republican in town. . . .

Since writing the above, and while out about ten minutes from my room, a K.K.K. warning was put under my door. Below is a copy:

The bloody dagger is drawn; the trying hour is at hand; beware! Your steps are marked; the eye of dark chief is upon you. First he warns; then the avenging dagger flashes in the moonlight.
By order of the Grand Cyclops. . . .

Make a request of the post commander for the troops to be here on election day, or have them sent over on Wednesday, if possible.

Excuse haste, and my scribbling, mistakes, &c.

Respectfully yours,
D. S. Harrison

SOURCE: Stanley I. Kutler, ed., *Looking for America*, 2d ed. (New York: Norton, 1979), 36–37.

an uphill battle. U.S. attorneys usually faced all-white juries, and the Justice department lacked the resources to prosecute effectively. After 1872, prosecutions began to drop off, and many Klansmen received hasty pardons; few served significant prison terms. Moreover, the Supreme Court undercut the Enforcement Acts by ruling that the Fourteenth Amendment protected citizens from

Klan Portrait, 1868
Two armed Klansmen from Alabama pose proudly in their disguises. Northern audiences saw a lithograph based on this photograph in *Harper's Weekly* in December 1868.

actions by the *states*, not by other citizens, so that federal prosecution of private groups like the Klan became legally questionable.

The faltering zeal for Reconstruction in the North, however, had much broader sources. The worst depression in the nation's history struck in 1873, and the North became preoccupied with its own economic problems. Northern business interests complained that the turmoil of Reconstruction retarded the South's economic recovery and harmed their investment opportunities. Sympathy for the freedmen also began to wane. The North was flooded with one-sided, often racist reports, such as James S. Pike's *The Prostrate State* (1873), of extravagant, corrupt Republican rule and a South in the grip of "a mass of black barbarism." In the 1874 elections, the Republicans suffered a crushing defeat, losing control of the House of Representatives for the first time since secession, and also losing seven normally Republican northern states to the Democrats. For Republican party strategists, the political costs in a disillusioned North began to outweigh their hopes for a Republican-dominated South.

In a kind of self-fulfilling prophecy, the unwillingness of the Grant administration to shore up Reconstruction guaranteed that it would fail. Republican

governments that were denied federal help found themselves overwhelmed by
ex-Confederate politicians during the day and by terrorists at night. Democrats overthrew Republican governments in Texas in 1873, in Alabama and
Arkansas in 1874, and in Mississippi in 1875.

The Mississippi campaign showed all too clearly what the Republicans
were up against. As elections neared in 1875, paramilitary groups such as the
Rifle Clubs and the Red Shirts operated openly. Often local Democrats paraded armed, as if they were militia companies. They identified black leaders
in assassination lists called "dead-books"; broke up Republican meetings; provoked rioting that left hundreds of African-Americans dead; and threatened
voters, who still lacked the protection of the secret ballot. Mississippi's Republican governor, Adelbert Ames, a Congressional Medal of Honor winner from
Maine, appealed to President Grant for federal troops, but Grant refused. Ames
then contemplated organizing a state militia but ultimately decided against it,
believing that only blacks would join. Rather than escalate the fighting and
turn it into a racial war, he conceded victory to the terrorists.

By 1877 Republican governments, backed by token U.S. military units, remained in only three states: Louisiana, South Carolina, and Florida. Elsewhere,
the ex-Confederates were back in the saddle.

Sharecropping

In the meantime, the freedmen were locked in a great economic struggle with
their former owners. In 1869, the Republican government of South Carolina
had established a land commission empowered to buy property and resell it on
easy terms to the landless. In this way about 14,000 black families acquired
farms. South Carolina's land distribution plan showed what was possible, but it
was the exception, not the rule. Despite a lot of rhetoric, Republican regimes
elsewhere did little to help the freedmen fulfill their dreams of becoming independent farmers. Federal efforts proved equally feeble. The Southern
Homestead Act of 1866 offered 80-acre grants to settlers, limited for the first
year to freedmen and southern Unionists. The advantage was strictly symbolic, however, since the public land made available to homesteaders was off
the beaten track in swampy, infertile parts of the lower South, and since, in any
case, they lacked the resources to get started. Only about a thousand families
finally succeeded. There was no reversing President Johnson's order restoring
confiscated lands to ex-Confederates, even after the Radical Republicans had
the power to do so. Property rights, it seemed, trumped everything else. The
Freedman's Bureau, which had earlier championed the land claims of the ex-
slaves, now devoted itself to teaching them how to be good agricultural laborers.

So, while they yearned for farms of their own, most freedmen started out
landless, and with no option but to work for their former owners. But not,
they vowed, under the conditions of slavery—no gang work, no overseers, no
fines or punishments, no regulation of their private lives or personal freedom.
They were willing to work for wages, provided the pay was high enough, as it

Sharecropping
This sharecropping family seems proud of its new cabin and crop of cotton, which it planted in every available bit of ground. But the presence of the white landlord in the background suggests that sharecropping was only a limited kind of economic freedom.

was, for example, on the great sugar plantations of Louisiana taken over after the war by northern investors. The problem was that cotton planters lacked the money to pay wages, at least until the crop came in, and sometimes, in lieu of a straight wage, they offered a share of the crop. As a *wage*, sharecropping was a bad deal for the freedmen, but it opened up interesting possibilities. They quickly realized that, if they could be paid in shares for their work, they could pay in those same shares to rent the land they worked. This form of land tenantry, already familiar in parts of the South among white farmers, the freedmen now seized on for the independence it offered them. Planters resisted, believing, as one wrote, that "wages are the only successful system of controlling hands." But, in a battle of wills that broke out all across the cotton South, the planters yielded to "the inveterate prejudices of the freedmen, who desire to be masters of their own time."

Thus there sprang up, quite spontaneously, a distinctively southern system of agricultural labor—*sharecropping*, in which the freedmen worked as renters, exchanging their labor for the use of land, house, implements, and sometimes seed and fertilizer. Typically they turned over between half and two-thirds of their crops to the landlord. The sharecropping system joined laborers and the owners of land and capital in a common sharing of risks and returns. But it was a very unequal relationship, given the force of southern law and custom on the white landowner's side, and given the dire economic circumstances of the sharecroppers. Starting out in poverty, they had no way of making it through the first growing season without borrowing for food and supplies.

Country storekeepers stepped in. Bankrolled by their northern suppliers, they "furnished" the sharecroppers and took as collateral *liens* on their crops. Under laws passed by the new Democratic regimes, crop liens effectively transferred the crops to the storekeeper, leaving sharecroppers only the proceeds that remained after their debts had been paid. Once indebted at one store, the sharecropper was no longer free to shop around, and became an easy target for exhorbitant prices, usurious interest rates, and crooked bookkeeping. As cotton prices declined during the 1870s, more and more sharecroppers failed to settle accounts and fell into permanent debt. And if the merchant was also the landowner, or conspired with the landowner, the debt became a pretext for forced labor, or *peonage*, although evidence now suggests that sharecroppers generally managed to pull up stakes and move on once things became hopeless. Sharecroppers always thought twice about moving, however, because part of their "capital" was being known and well-reputed in their home communities. Freedmen who lacked that local standing generally found sharecropping hard going and likely ended up in the ranks of agricultural laborers.

In the face of so much adversity, black families struggled to better themselves. By the end of Reconstruction, about one-quarter of them had managed to save enough to rent with cash payments. Land ownership was harder to achieve. In many places whites would not sell to blacks or jacked up prices exhorbitantly. For the sake of independence, however, black farmers persevered. Eventually they owned about a third of the land they cultivated, but rarely the best land and usually at a cost greater than its fertility warranted.

For the freedmen, sharecropping was not the worst choice; it certainly beat laboring for their former owners. But for southern agriculture, the costs were devastating. Sharecropping committed the South inflexibly to cotton, the one cash crop capable of satisfying the financial demands of landowners and furnishing merchants. Crop diversification declined, costing the South its self-sufficiency in grains and livestock. And with farms leased year-to-year, neither tenant nor owner had any incentive to improve the property. The crop-lien system lined merchants' pockets with unearned profits—economists estimate the excessive rate of profit at 13.5 percent—that might otherwise have gone into agricultural improvement. The result was a stagnant farm economy, blighting the South's future and condemning it to economic backwardness—a kind of retribution, in fact, for the fresh injustices visited on the people it had once enslaved.

The Political Crisis of 1877

Northerners were scarcely aware of the South's agrarian revolution. National politics had moved on, and other concerns absorbed the voter. Foremost was the stench of scandal that hung over the White House. In 1875 Grant's secretary of the treasury, Benjamin Bristow, exposed the so-called Whiskey Ring, a network of distillers and government agents who had defrauded the Treasury of millions of dollars of excise taxes on liquor. The ringleader was a Grant appointee, and Grant's own private secretary, Orville Babcock, had a hand in the scandal. The others went to prison, but Grant stood by Babcock, possibly perjuring himself to save his secretary from jail. On top of this, the economy had fallen into a severe depression after 1873. Grant's administration responded ineffectually, rebuffing the pleas of debtors for relief by increasing the money supply (see Chapter 19). Among the casualties of the depression was the Freedman's Savings and Trust Company, which had been sponsored by the Freedman's Bureau and held the small deposits of thousands of ex-slaves. When the bank failed in 1874, Congress refused to compensate the depositors, and many lost their life savings. In denying their pathetic pleas, Congress was signaling also that Reconstruction had lost its moral claim on the country.

Abandoning Grant, the Republicans in 1876 nominated Rutherford B. Hayes, governor of Ohio, a colorless figure but untainted by corruption or by strong convictions—in a word, a safe man. His Democratic opponent was Samuel J. Tilden, governor of New York, a wealthy lawyer with ties to Wall Street and a reform reputation for helping to break the grip of the thieving Tweed Ring on New York City politics. The Democrat Tilden, of course, favored "home rule" for the South but so, more discretely, did the Republican Hayes. Reconstruction actually did not figure prominently in the campaign and was mostly subsumed under broader Democratic charges of "corrupt centralism" and "incapacity, waste, and fraud." By now, Republicans had essentially written off the South, and scarcely campaigned there. Not a lot was said about the states still ruled by Reconstruction governments—Florida, South Carolina, and Louisiana.

Once the returns started coming in on election night, however, those three states began to loom very large indeed. Tilden led in the popular vote and, victorious in key northern states, seemed headed for the White House. But sleepless politicians at Republican headquarters realized that if they kept Florida, South Carolina, and Louisiana, Hayes would win by a single electoral vote. The campaigns in those states had been bitterly fought, replicating the Democratic assaults on blacks that had overturned Republican regimes everywhere else in the South. But Republicans still controlled the election machinery in those states, and, citing Democratic fraud and intimidation, they could certify Republican victories. The audacious announcement came forth from Republican headquarters: Hayes had carried the three southern states and won the election. But, of course, newly elected Democratic officials in the three states also sent in electoral votes for Tilden, and, when Congress met in early 1877, it faced two sets of electoral votes from those states.

The Constitution does not provide for this contingency. All it says is that the president of the Senate (in 1877, a Republican) opens the electoral certificates before the House (Democratic) and the Senate (Republican) and that "The votes shall then be counted." For weeks, ever since the November election, an air of crisis had gripped the country. There was wild talk of inside deals, of a new election, even of a violent coup and civil war. Just in case, the commander of the army, General William T. Sherman, deployed four artillery companies in Washington. Finally, Congress decided to appoint an electoral commission to settle the question. The commission included seven Republicans; seven Democrats; and, as the deciding member, David Davis, a Supreme Court justice not known to have fixed party loyalties. But Davis disqualified himself by accepting an Illinois seat in the Senate. He was replaced by Republican Justice Joseph P. Bradley, and by 8 to 7, the commission awarded the disputed votes to Hayes.

Outraged Democrats had one more trick up their sleeves. They controlled the House, and they set about stalling a final count of the electoral votes so as to prevent Hayes's inauguration on March 4. But a week before, secret Washington talks had begun between southern Democrats and Ohio Republicans representing Hayes. Other issues may have been on the table, but the main thing was the situation in South Carolina and Louisiana, where Republican governors physically occupied the statehouses, protected by Union troops. But for the disputed federal election, ironically, the military would not have intervened, and the ex-Confederate Redeemers would already have seized power. Exactly what deal was struck, or how involved Hayes himself was, will probably never be known, but on March 1 the House Democrats suddenly ended their filibuster, the ceremonial counting of votes went forward, and Hayes was inaugurated on schedule. He soon ordered the Union troops back to their barracks, and the Republican regimes in South Carolina and Louisiana fell. Reconstruction had ended.

In 1877 political leaders on all sides seemed ready to say that what Lincoln had called "the work" was complete. But for the freedmen, the work had only begun. Reconstruction turned out to have been a magnificent aberration, a magnum leap beyond what most white Americans actually felt was due their black fellow citizens. Redemption represented a sad falling back to the norm. Still, something real had been achieved—three rights-defining amendments to the Constitution; some elbow room to advance economically; and, not least, a stubborn confidence among blacks that, by their own efforts, they could lift themselves up. Things would, in fact, get worse before they got better, but the work of the Reconstruction was imperishable and could never be effaced.

CHAPTER 16 TIMELINE

1863	Lincoln announces his Ten Percent Plan
1864	Wade-Davis bill passed by Congress Lincoln gives Wade-Davis bill a "pocket" veto
1865	Freedmen's Bureau established Lincoln assassinated; Andrew Johnson succeeds as president Johnson implements his restoration plan
1866	Republicans fail to override Johnson's veto of Freedmen's Bureau bill Civil Rights Act passes over Johnson's veto of Freedmen's Bureau bill Johnson makes disastrous "swing around the circle" Johnson defeated in congressional elections
1867	Reconstruction Acts Tenure of Office Act
1868	Impeachment crisis Fourteenth Amendment ratified Ulysses S. Grant elected president
1870	Ku Klux Klan at peak of power Enforcement Acts passed by Congress Fifteenth Amendment ratified
1871	Ku Klux Klan Act passed by Congress
1872	Grant's re-election as president
1873	Panic of 1873 ushers in depression of 1873–1877
1874	Democrats win majority in House of Representatives
1875	Whiskey Ring scandal undermines Grant administration
1877	Congressional compromise makes Rutherford B. Hayes president after disputed election Reconstruction ends

DOCUMENTS

THE DECLARATION OF INDEPENDENCE

The Unanimous Declaration of the Thirteen United States of America

When in the Course of human events, it becomes necessary for one people to dissolve the political bands which have connected them with another, and to assume among the Powers of the earth, the separate and equal station to which the Laws of Nature and of Nature's God entitle them, a decent respect to the opinions of mankind requires that they should declare the causes which impel them to the separation.

We hold these truths to be self-evident, that all men are created equal, that they are endowed by their Creator with certain unalienable rights, that among these are Life, Liberty, and the pursuit of Happiness. That to secure these rights, Governments are instituted among Men, deriving their just powers from the consent of the governed. That whenever any Form of Government becomes destructive of these ends, it is the Right of the People to alter or to abolish it, and to institute new Government, laying its foundation on such principles and organizing its powers in such form, as to them shall seem most likely to effect their Safety and Happiness. Prudence, indeed, will dictate that Governments long established should not be changed for light and transient causes; and accordingly all experience hath shown, that mankind are more disposed to suffer, while evils are sufferable, than to right themselves by abolishing the forms to which they are accustomed. But when a long train of abuses and usurpations, pursuing invariably the same Object evinces a design to reduce them under absolute Despotism, it is their right, it is their duty, to throw off such Government, and to provide new Guards for their future security.—Such has been the patient sufferance of these Colonies; and such is now the necessity which constrains them to alter their former Systems of Government. The history of the present King of Great Britain is a history of repeated injuries and usurpations, all having in direct object the establishment of an absolute Tyranny over these States. To prove this, let Facts be submitted to a candid world.

He has refused his Assent to Laws, the most wholesome and necessary for the public good.

He has forbidden his Governors to pass Laws of immediate and pressing importance, unless suspended in their operation till his Assent should be obtained; and, when so suspended, he has utterly neglected to attend to them.

He has refused to pass other Laws for the accommodation of large districts of people, unless those people would relinquish the right of Representation in the Legislature, a right inestimable to them and formidable to tyrants only.

He has called together legislative bodies at places unusual, uncomfortable, and distant from the depository of their public Records, for the sole purpose of fatiguing them into compliance with his measures.

He has dissolved Representative Houses repeatedly, for opposing with manly firmness his invasions on the rights of the people.

He has refused for a long time, after such dissolutions, to cause others to be elected; whereby the Legislative powers, incapable of Annihilation, have returned to the People at large for their exercise; the State remaining in the mean time exposed to all the dangers of invasion from without and convulsions within.

He has endeavoured to prevent the population of these States; for that purpose obstructing the Laws of Naturalization of Foreigners; refusing to pass others to encourage their migrations hither, and raising the conditions of new Appropriations of Lands.

He has obstructed the Administration of Justice, by refusing his Assent to Laws for establishing Judiciary powers.

He has made Judges dependent on his Will alone, for the tenure of their offices, and the amount and payment of their salaries.

He has erected a multitude of New Offices, and sent hither swarms of Officers to harass our People, and eat out their substance.

He has kept among us, in times of peace, Standing Armies without the Consent of our legislature.

He has combined with others to subject us to a jurisdiction foreign to our constitution, and unacknowledged by our laws; giving his Assent to their Acts of pretended Legislation:

For quartering large bodies of armed troops among us:

For protecting them, by a mock Trial, from Punishment for any Murders which they should commit on the Inhabitants of these States:

For cutting off our Trade with all parts of the world:

For imposing taxes on us without our Consent:

For depriving us of many cases, of the benefits of Trial by jury:

For transporting us beyond Seas to be tried for pretended offences:

For abolishing the free System of English Laws in a neighbouring Province, establishing therein an Arbitrary government, and enlarging its Boundaries so as to render it at once an example and fit instrument for introducing the same absolute rule into these Colonies:

For taking away our Charters, abolishing our most valuable Laws, and altering fundamentally the Forms of our Governments:

For suspending our own Legislatures, and declaring themselves invested with Power to legislate for us in all cases whatsoever.

He has abdicated Government here, by declaring us out of his Protection and waging War against us.

He has plundered our seas, ravaged our Coasts, burnt our towns, and destroyed the lives of our people.

He is at this time transporting large armies of foreign mercenaries to compleat the works of death, desolation, and tyranny, already begun with circumstances of Cruelty & perfidy scarcely paralleled in the most barbarous ages, and totally unworthy the Head of a civilized nation.

He has constrained our fellow Citizens taken Captive on the high Seas to bear Arms against their Country, to become the executioners of their friends and Brethren, or to fall themselves by their Hands.

He has excited domestic insurrections amongst us, and has endeavoured to bring on the inhabitants of our frontiers, the merciless Indian Savages, whose known rule of warfare, is an undistinguished destruction of all ages, sexes, and conditions.

In every stage of these Oppressions We have Petitioned for Redress in the most humble terms: Our repeated Petitions have been answered only by repeated injury. A Prince, whose character is thus marked by every act which may define a Tyrant, is unfit to be the ruler of a free people.

Nor have We been wanting in attention to our British brethren. We have warned them from time to time of attempts by their legislature to extend an unwarrantable jurisdiction over us. We have reminded them of the circumstances of our emigration and settlement here. We have appealed to their native justice and magnanimity, and we have conjured them by the ties of our common kindred to disavow these usurpations, which, would inevitably interrupt our connections and correspondence. They too have been deaf to the voice of justice and of consanguinity. We must, therefore, acquiesce in the necessity, which denounces our Separation, and hold them, as we hold the rest of mankind, Enemies in War, in Peace Friends.

We, therefore, the Representatives of the United States of America, in General Congress, Assembled, appealing to the Supreme Judge of the world for the rectitude of our intentions, do, in the Name, and by Authority of the good People of these Colonies, solemnly publish and declare, That these United Colonies are, and of Right ought to be FREE AND INDEPENDENT STATES; that they are Absolved from all Allegiance to the British Crown, and that all political connection between them and the State of Great Britain, is and ought to be totally dissolved; and that as Free and Independent States, they have full Power to levy War, conclude Peace, contract Alliances, establish Commerce, and to do all other Acts and Things which Independent States may of right do. And for the support of this Declaration, with a firm reliance on the Protection of Divine Providence, we mutually pledge to each other our Lives, our Fortunes, and our sacred Honor.

John Hancock

Button Gwinnett	George Wythe	James Wilson	Josiah Bartlett
Lyman Hall	Richard Henry Lee	Geo. Ross	Wm. Whipple
Geo. Walton	Th. Jefferson	Caesar Rodney	Saml. Adams
Wm. Hooper	Benja. Harrison	Geo. Read	John Adams
Joseph Hewes	Thos. Nelson, Jr.	Thos. M'Kean	Robt. Treat Paine
John Penn	Francis Lightfoot Lee	Wm. Floyd	Elbridge Gerry
Edward Rutledge	Carter Braxton	Phil. Livingston	Step. Hopkins
Thos. Heyward, Junr.	Robt. Morris	Frans. Lewis	William Ellery
Thomas Lynch, Junr.	Benjamin Rush	Lewis Morris	Roger Sherman
Arthur Middleton	Benja. Franklin	Richd. Stockton	Sam'el Hunington
Samuel Chase	John Morton	Jno. Witherspoon	Wm. Williams
Wm. Paca	Geo. Clymer	Fras. Hopkinson	Oliver Wolcott
Thos. Stone	Jas. Smith	John Hart	Matthew Thornton
Charles Carroll of Carrollton	Geo. Taylor	Abra. Clark	

THE ARTICLES OF CONFEDERATION AND PERPETUAL UNION

Between the states of New Hampshire, Massachusetts Bay, Rhode Island and Providence Plantations, Connecticut, New York, New Jersey, Pennsylvania, Delaware, Maryland, Virginia, North Carolina, South Carolina, Georgia.*

Article 1.

The stile of this confederacy shall be "The United States of America."

Article 2.

Each State retains its sovereignty, freedom and independence, and every power, jurisdiction, and right, which is not by this confederation expressly delegated to the United States, in Congress assembled.

Article 3.

The said states hereby severally enter into a firm league of friendship with each other for their common defence, the security of their liberties and their mutual and general welfare; binding themselves to assist each other against all force offered to, or attacks made upon them, or any of them, on account of religion, sovereignty, trade, or any other pretence whatever.

Article 4.

The better to secure and perpetuate mutual friendship and intercourse among the people of the different states in this union, the free inhabitants of each of these states, paupers, vagabonds, and fugitives from justice excepted, shall be entitled to all privileges and immunities of free citizens in the several states; and the people of each State shall have free ingress and regress to and from any other State, and shall enjoy therein all the privileges of trade and commerce, subject to the same duties, impositions, and restrictions, as the inhabitants thereof respectively; provided, that such restrictions shall

---

*This copy of the final draft of the Articles of Confederation is taken from the *Journals*, 9:907–925, November 15, 1777.

not extend so far as to prevent the removal of property, imported into any State, to any other State of which the owner is an inhabitant; provided also, that no imposition, duties, or restriction, shall be laid by any State on the property of the United States, or either of them.

If any person guilty of, or charged with treason, felony, or other high misdemeanor in any State, shall flee from justice and be found in any of the United States, he shall, upon demand of the governor or executive power of the State from which he fled, be delivered up and removed to the State having jurisdiction of his offence.

Full faith and credit shall be given in each of these states to the records, acts, and judicial proceedings of the courts and magistrates of every other State.

Article 5.

For the more convenient management of the general interests of the United States, delegates shall be annually appointed, in such manner as the legislature of each State shall direct, to meet in Congress, on the 1st Monday in November in every year, with a power reserved to each State to recal its delegates, or any of them, at any time within the year, and to send others in their stead for the remainder of the year.

No State shall be represented in Congress by less than two, nor by more than seven members; and no person shall be capable of being a delegate for more than three years in any term of six years; nor shall any person, being a delegate, be capable of holding any office under the United States, for which he, or any other for his benefit, receives any salary, fees, or emolument of any kind.

Each State shall maintain its own delegates in a meeting of the states, and while they act as members of the committee of the states.

In determining questions in the United States, in Congress assembled, each State shall have one vote.

Freedom of speech and debate in Congress shall not be impeached or questioned in any court or place out of Congress: and the members of Congress shall be protected in their persons from arrests and imprisonments, during the time of their going to and from, and attendance on Congress, *except for treason*, felony, or breach of the peace.

Article 6.

No State, without the consent of the United States, in Congress assembled, shall send any embassy to, or receive any embassy from, or enter into any conference, agreement, alliance, or treaty with any king, prince, or state; nor shall any person, holding any office of profit or trust under the United States, or any of them, accept of any present, emolument, office or title, of any kind whatever, from any king, prince, or foreign state; nor shall the United States, in Congress assembled, or any of them, grant any title of nobility.

No two or more states shall enter into any treaty, confederation, or alliance, whatever, between them, without the consent of the United States, in Congress assembled, specifying accurately the purposes for which the same is to be entered into, and how long it shall continue.

No state shall lay any imposts or duties which may interfere with any stipulations in treaties entered into by the United States, in Congress assembled, with any king, prince, or state, in pursuance of any treaties already proposed by Congress to the courts of France and Spain.

No vessels of war shall be kept up in time of peace by any State, except such number only as shall be deemed necessary by the United States, in Congress assembled, for the defence of such State or its trade; nor shall any body of forces be kept up by any State, in time of peace, except such number only as, in the judgment of the United States, in Congress assembled, shall be deemed requisite to garrison the forts necessary for the defence of such State; but every State shall always keep up a well regulated and disciplined militia, sufficiently armed and accoutred, and shall provide, and constantly have ready for use, in public stores, a due number of field pieces and tents, and a proper quantity of arms, ammunition and camp equipage.

No State shall engage in any war without the consent of the United States, in Congress assembled, unless such State be actually invaded by enemies, or shall have received certain advice of a resolution being formed by some nation of Indians to invade such State, and the danger is so imminent as not to admit of a delay till the United States, in Congress assembled, can be consulted; nor shall any State grant commissions to any ships or vessels of war, nor letters of marque or reprisal, except it be after a declaration of war by the United States, in Congress assembled, and then only against the kingdom or state, and the subjects thereof, against which war has been so declared, and under such regulations as shall be established by the United States, in Congress assembled, unless such State be infested by pirates, in which case vessels of war may be fitted out for that occasion, and kept so long as the danger shall continue, or until the United States, in Congress assembled, shall determine otherwise.

Article 7.

When land forces are raised by any State for the common defence, all officers of or under the rank of colonel, shall be appointed by the legislature of each State respectively, by whom such forces shall be raised, or in such manner as such State shall direct; and all vacancies shall be filled up by the State which first made the appointment.

Article 8.

All charges of war and all other expences, that shall be incurred for the common defence or general welfare, and allowed by the United States, in Congress assembled, shall be defrayed out of a common treasury, which shall be supplied by the several states, in proportion to the value of all land within each State, granted to or surveyed for any person, as such land and the buildings and improvements thereon shall be estimated according to such mode as the United States, in Congress assembled, shall, from time to time, direct and appoint.

The taxes for paying that proportion shall be laid and levied by the authority and direction of the legislatures of the several states, within the time agreed upon by the United States, in Congress assembled.

Article 9.

The United States, in Congress assembled, shall have the sole and exclusive right and power of determining on peace and war, except in the cases mentioned in the 6th article; of sending and receiving ambassadors; entering into treaties and alliances, provided that no treaty of commerce shall be made, whereby the legislative power of the respective states shall be restrained from imposing such imposts and duties on foreigners as their own people are subjected to, or from prohibiting the exportation or importation of any species of goods or commodities whatsoever; of establishing rules for deciding, in all cases, what captures on land or water shall be legal, and in what manner prizes, taken by land or naval forces in the service of the United States, shall be divided or appropriated; of granting letters of marque and reprisal in times of peace; appointing courts for the trial of piracies and felonies committed on the high seas, and establishing courts for receiving and determining, finally, appeals in all cases of captures; provided, that no member of Congress shall be appointed a judge of any of the said courts.

The United States, in Congress assembled, shall also be the last resort on appeal in all disputes and differences now subsisting, or that hereafter may arise between two or more states concerning boundary, jurisdiction or any other cause whatever; which authority shall always be exercised in the manner following: whenever the legislative or executive authority, or lawful agent of any State, in controversy with another, shall present a petition to Congress, stating the matter in question, and praying for a hearing, notice thereof shall be given, by order of Congress, to the legislative or executive authority of the other State in controversy, and a day assigned for the appearance of the parties by their lawful agents, who shall then be directed to appoint, by joint consent, commissioners or judges to constitute a court for hearing and determining the matter in question; but, if they cannot agree, Congress shall name three persons out of each of the United States, and from the list of such persons each party shall alternately strike out one, the petitioners beginning, until the number shall be reduced to thirteen; and from that number not less than seven, nor more than nine names, as Congress shall direct, shall, in the presence of Congress, be drawn out by lot; and the persons whose names shall be so drawn, or any five of them, shall be commissioners or judges to hear and finally determine the controversy, so always as a major part of the judges who shall hear the cause shall agree in the determination; and if either party shall neglect to attend at the day appointed, without shewing reasons which Congress shall judge sufficient, or, being present, shall refuse to strike, the Congress shall proceed to nominate three persons out of each State, and the secretary of Congress shall strike in behalf of such party absent or refusing; and the judgment and sentence of the court to be appointed, in the manner before prescribed, shall be final and conclusive; and if any of the parties shall refuse to submit to the authority of such court, or to appear or defend their claim or cause, the court shall nevertheless proceed to pronounce sentence or judgment, which shall, in like manner, be final and decisive, the judgment or sentence and other proceedings begin, in either case, transmitted to Congress, and lodged among the acts of Congress for the security of the parties concerned: provided, that every commissioner, before he sits in judgment, shall take an oath, to be administered by one of the judges of the supreme or superior court of the State where the cause shall be tried, "well and truly to hear and determine the matter in question, according to the best of his judgment, without favour, affection, or hope of reward:" provided, also, that no State shall be deprived of territory for the benefit of the United States.

All controversies concerning the private right of soil, claimed under different grants of two or more states, whose jurisdictions, as they may respect such lands and the states which passed such grants, are adjusted, the said grants, or either of them, being at the same time claimed to have originated antecedent to such settlement of jurisdiction, shall, on the petition of either party to the Congress of the United States, be finally determined, as near as may be, in the same manner as is before prescribed for deciding disputes respecting territorial jurisdiction between different states.

The United States, in Congress assembled, shall also have the sole and exclusive right and power of regulating the alloy and value of coin struck by their own authority, or by that of the respective states; fixing the standard of weights and measures throughout the United States; regulating the trade and managing all affairs with the Indians not members of any of the states; provided that the legislative right of any State within its own limits be not infringed or violated; establishing and regulating post offices from one State to another throughout all the United States, and exacting such postage on the papers passing through the same as may be requisite to defray the expences of the said office; appointing all officers of the land forces in the service of the United States, excepting regimental officers; appointing all the officers of the naval forces, and commissioning all officers whatever in the service of the United States; making rules for the government and regulation of the said land and naval forces, and directing their operations.

The United States, in Congress assembled, shall have authority to appoint a committee to sit in the recess of Congress, to be denominated "a Committee of the States," and to consist of one delegate from each State, and to appoint such other committees and civil officers as may be necessary for managing the general affairs of the United States, under their direction; to appoint one of their number to preside; provided that no person be allowed to serve in the office of president more than one year in any term of three years; to ascertain the necessary sums of money to be raised for the service of the United States, and to appropriate and apply the same for defraying the public expences; to borrow money or emit bills on the credit of the United States, transmitting, every half year, to the respective states, an account of the sums of money so borrowed or emitted; to build and equip a navy; to agree upon the number of land forces, and to make requisitions from each State for its quota, in proportion to the number of white inhabitants in such State; which requisitions shall be binding; and thereupon, the legislature of each State shall appoint the regimental officers, raise the men, and cloathe, arm, and equip them in a soldier-like manner, at the expence of the United States; and the officers and men so cloathed, armed, and equipped, shall march to the place appointed and within the time agreed on by the United States, in Congress assembled; but if the United States, in Congress assembled, shall, on consideration of circumstances, judge proper that any State should not raise men, or should raise a smaller number than its quota, and that any other State should raise a greater number of men than the quota thereof, such extra number shall be raised, officered, cloathed, armed, and equipped in the same manner as the quota of such State, unless the legislature of such State shall judge that such extra number cannot be safely spared out of the same, in which case they shall raise, officer, cloathe, arm, and equip as many of such extra number as they judge can be safely spared. And the officers and men so cloathed, armed, and equipped, shall march to the place appointed and within the time agreed on by the United States, in Congress assembled.

The United States, in Congress assembled, shall never engage in a war, nor grant letters of marque and reprisal in time of peace, nor enter into any treaties or alliances, nor coin money, nor regulate the value thereof, nor ascertain the sums and expences necessary for the defence and welfare of the United States, or any of them: nor emit bills, nor borrow money on the credit of the United States, nor appropriate money, nor agree upon the number of vessels of war to be built or purchased, or the number of land or sea forces to be raised, nor appoint a commander in chief of the army or navy, unless nine states assent to the same; nor shall a question on any other point, except for adjourning from day to day, be determined, unless by the votes of a majority of the United States, in Congress assembled.

The Congress of the United States shall have power to adjourn to any time within the year, and to any place within the United States, so that no period of adjournment be for a longer duration than the space of six months, and shall publish the journal of their proceedings monthly, except such parts thereof, relating to treaties, alliances or military operations, as, in their judgment, require secrecy; and the yeas and nays of the delegates of each State on any question shall be entered on the journal, when it is desired by any delegate; and the delegates of a State, or any of them, at his, or their request, shall be furnished with a transcript of the said journal, except such parts as are above excepted, to lay before the legislatures of the several states.

Article 10.

The committee of the states, or any nine of them, shall be authorized to execute, in the recess of Congress, such of the powers of Congress as the United States, in Congress assembled, by the consent of nine states, shall, from time to time, think expedient to vest them with; provided, that no power be delegated to the said committee, for the exercise of which, by the articles of confederation, the voice of nine states, in the Congress of the United States assembled, is requisite.

Article 11.

Canada acceding to this confederation, and joining in the measures of the United States, shall be admitted into and entitled to all the advantages of this union; but no other colony shall be admitted into the same, unless such admission be agreed to by nine states.

Article 12.

All bills of credit emitted, monies borrowed and debts contracted by, or under the authority of Congress before the assembling of the United States, in pursuance of the present confederation, shall be deemed and considered as a charge against the United States, for payment and satisfaction whereof the said United States and the public faith are hereby solemnly pledged.

Article 13.

Every State shall abide by the determinations of the United States, in Congress assembled, on all questions which, by this confederation, are submitted to them. And the articles of this confederation shall be inviolably observed by every State, and the union shall be perpetual; nor shall any alteration at any time hereafter be made in any of them, unless such alteration be agreed to in a Congress of the United States, and be afterwards confirmed by the legislatures of every State.

These articles shall be proposed to the legislatures of all the United States, to be considered, and if approved of by them, they are advised to authorize their delegates to ratify the same in the Congress of the United States; which being done, the same shall become conclusive.

THE CONSTITUTION OF THE UNITED STATES

We the People of the United States, in Order to form a more perfect Union, establish Justice, insure domestic Tranquility, provide for the common defence, promote the general Welfare, and secure the Blessings of Liberty to ourselves and our Posterity, do ordain and establish this Constitution for the United States of America.

Article I

Section 1
All legislative Powers herein granted shall be vested in a Congress of the United States, which shall consist of a Senate and a House of Representatives.

Section 2
The House of Representatives shall be composed of Members chosen every second Year by the People of the several States, and the Electors in each State shall have the Qualifications requisite for Electors of the most numerous Branch of the State Legislature.

No Person shall be a Representative who shall not have attained to the Age of twenty-five Years, and been seven Years a Citizen of the United States, and who shall not, when elected, be an Inhabitant of that State in which he shall be chosen.

Representatives and direct Taxes shall be apportioned among the several States which may be included within this Union, according to their respective Numbers, *which shall be determined by adding to the whole Number of free Persons, including those bound to Service for a Term of Years, and excluding Indians not taxed, three fifths of all other Persons.** The actual Enumeration shall be made within three Years after the first Meeting of the Congress of the United States, and within every subsequent Term of ten Years, in such Manner as they shall by Law direct. The Number of Representatives shall not exceed one for every thirty Thousand, but each State shall have at Least one Representative; and *until such enumeration shall be made, the State of New Hampshire shall be entitled to chuse three, Massachusetts eight, Rhode Island and Providence Plantations one, Connecticut five, New-York six, New Jersey four, Pennsylvania eight, Delaware one, Maryland six, Virginia ten, North Carolina five, South Carolina five, and Georgia three.*

Note: The Constitution became effective March 4, 1789. Provisions in italics have been changed by constitutional amendment.

*Changed by Section 2 of the Fourteenth Amendment.

When vacancies happen in the Representation from any State, the Executive Authority thereof shall issue Writs of Election to fill such Vacancies.

The House of Representatives shall chuse their Speaker and other Officers; and shall have the sole Power of Impeachment.

Section 3

The Senate of the United States shall be composed of two Senators from each State, *chosen by the Legislature thereof,*[†] for six Years; and each Senator shall have one Vote.

Immediately after they shall be assembled in Consequence of the first Election, they shall be divided as equally as may be into three Classes. The Seats of the Senators of the first Class shall be vacated at the Expiration of the second Year, of the second Class at the Expiration of the fourth Year, and of the third Class at the Expiration of the sixth Year, so that one-third may be chosen every second Year; *and if Vacancies happen by Resignation, or otherwise, during the Recess of the Legislature of any State, the Executive thereof may make temporary Appointments until the next Meeting of the Legislature, which shall then fill such Vacancies.*[‡]

No person shall be a Senator who shall not have attained to the Age of thirty Years, and been nine Years a Citizen of the United States, and who shall not, when elected, be an Inhabitant of that State for which he shall be chosen.

The Vice President of the United States shall be President of the Senate, but shall have no Vote, unless they be equally divided.

The Senate shall chuse their other Officers, and also a President pro tempore, in the absence of the Vice President, or when he shall exercise the Office of President of the United States.

The Senate shall have the sole Power to try all Impeachments. When sitting for that Purpose, they shall be on Oath or Affirmation. When the President of the United States is tried, the Chief Justice shall preside: And no Person shall be convicted without the Concurrence of two thirds of the Members present.

Judgment in Cases of Impeachment shall not extend further than to removal from Office, and disqualification to hold and enjoy any Office of honor, Trust or Profit under the United States: but the Party convicted shall nevertheless be liable and subject to Indictment, Trial, Judgment and Punishment, according to Law.

Section 4

The Times, Places and Manner of holding Elections for Senators and Representatives, shall be prescribed in each State by the Legislature thereof; but the Congress may at any time by Law make or alter such Regulations, except as to the Places of Chusing Senators.

The Congress shall assemble at least once in every Year, and such Meeting *shall be on the first Monday in December, unless they shall by Law appoint a different Day.*[*]

Section 5

Each House shall be the Judge of the Elections, Returns and Qualifications of its own Members, and a Majority of each shall constitute a Quorum to do Business; but a smaller number may adjourn from day to day, and may be authorized to compel the Attendance of absent Members, in such Manner, and under such Penalties, as each House may provide.

[†]Changed by Section 1 of the Seventeenth Amendment.

[‡]Changed by Clause 2 of the Seventeenth Amendment.

[*]Changed by Section 2 of the Twentieth Amendment.

Each House may determine the Rules of its Proceedings, punish its Members for disorderly Behavior, and, with the Concurrence of two thirds, expel a Member.

Each House shall keep a Journal of its Proceedings, and from time to time publish the same, excepting such Parts as may in their Judgment require Secrecy; and the Yeas and Nays of the Members of either House on any question shall, at the Desire of one-fifth of those Present, be entered on the Journal.

Neither House, during the Session of Congress, shall, without the Consent of the other, adjourn for more than three days, nor to any other Place than that in which the two Houses shall be sitting.

Section 6

The Senators and Representatives shall receive a Compensation for their Services, to be ascertained by Law, and paid out of the Treasury of the United States. They shall in all Cases, except Treason, Felony and Breach of the Peace, be privileged from Arrest during their Attendance at the Session of their respective Houses, and in going to and returning from the same; and for any Speech or Debate in either House, they shall not be questioned in any other Place.

No Senator or Representative shall, during the Time for which he was elected, be appointed to any civil Office under the Authority of the United States, which shall have been created, or the Emoluments whereof shall have been increased, during such time; and no Person holding any Office under the United States, shall be a Member of either House during his Continuance in Office.

Section 7

All Bills for raising Revenue shall originate in the House of Representatives; but the Senate may propose or concur with Amendments as on other Bills.

Every Bill which shall have passed the House of Representatives and the Senate, shall, before it becomes a Law, be presented to the President of the United States; If he approve he shall sign it, but if not he shall return it, with his Objections to that House in which it shall have originated, who shall enter the Objections at large on their Journal, and proceed to reconsider it. If after such Reconsideration two thirds of that House shall agree to pass the Bill, it shall be sent, together with the Objections, to the other House, by which it shall likewise be reconsidered, and if approved by two thirds of that House, it shall become a Law. But in all such Cases the Votes of both Houses shall be determined by Yeas and Nays, and the Names of the Persons voting for and against the Bill shall be entered on the Journal of each House respectively. If any Bill shall not be returned by the President within ten Days (Sundays excepted) after it shall have been presented to him, the Same shall be a Law, in like Manner as if he had signed it, unless the Congress by their Adjournment prevent its Return, in which Case it shall not be a Law.

Every Order, Resolution, or Vote to which the Concurrence of the Senate and the House of Representatives may be necessary (except on a question of Adjournment) shall be presented to the President of the United States; and before the Same shall take Effect, shall be approved by him, or being disapproved by him, shall be repassed by two thirds of the Senate and House of Representatives, according to the Rules and Limitations prescribed in the Case of a Bill.

Section 8

The Congress shall have Power To lay and collect Taxes, Duties, Imposts and Excises, to pay the Debts and provide for the common Defence and general Welfare of the United States; but all Duties, Imposts and Excises shall be uniform throughout the United States;

To borrow money on the credit of the United States;

To regulate Commerce with foreign Nations, and among the several States, and with the Indian Tribes;

To establish an uniform Rule of Naturalization, and uniform Laws on the subject of Bankruptcies throughout the United States;

To coin Money, regulate the Value thereof, and of foreign Coin, and fix the Standard of Weights and Measures;

To provide for the Punishment of counterfeiting the Securities and current Coin of the United States;

To establish Post Offices and post Roads;

To promote the Progress of Science and useful Arts, by securing for limited Times to Authors and Inventors the exclusive Right to their respective Writings and Discoveries;

To constitute Tribunals inferior to the supreme Court;

To define and punish Piracies and Felonies committed on the high Seas, and Offenses against the Law of Nations;

To declare War, grant Letters of Marque and Reprisal, and make Rules concerning Captures on Land and Water;

To raise and support Armies, but no Appropriation of Money to that Use shall be for a longer Term than two Years;

To provide and maintain a Navy;

To make Rules for the Government and Regulation of the land and naval Forces;

To provide for calling forth the Militia to execute the Laws of the Union, suppress Insurrections and repel Invasions;

To provide for organizing, arming, and disciplining the Militia, and for governing such Part of them as may be employed in the Service of the United States, reserving to the States respectively, the Appointment of the Officers, and the Authority of training the Militia according to the discipline prescribed by Congress;

To exercise exclusive Legislation in all Cases whatsoever, over such District (not exceeding ten Miles square) as may, by Cession of particular States, and the acceptance of Congress, become the Seat of Government of the United States, and to exercise like Authority over all Places purchased by the Consent of the Legislature of the State in which the Same shall be, for the Erection of Forts, Magazines, Arsenals, dock-Yards, and other needful Buildings;—And

To make all Laws which shall be necessary and proper for carrying into Execution the foregoing Powers, and all other Powers vested by this Constitution in the Government of the United States, or in any Department or Officer thereof.

Section 9

The Migration or Importation of such Persons as any of the States now existing shall think proper to admit, shall not be prohibited by the Congress prior to the Year one thousand eight hundred and eight but a tax or duty may be imposed on such Importation, not exceeding ten dollars for each Person.

The privilege of the Writ of Habeas Corpus shall not be suspended, unless when in Cases of Rebellion or Invasion the public Safety may require it.

No Bill of Attainder or ex post facto Law shall be passed.

No capitation, or other direct, Tax shall be laid, unless in Proportion to the Census or Enumeration herein before directed to be taken.*

No Tax or Duty shall be laid on Articles exported from any State.

---

*Changed by the Sixteenth Amendment.

No Preference shall be given by any Regulation of Commerce or Revenue to the Ports of one State over those of another: nor shall Vessels bound to, or from, one State, be obliged to enter, clear, or pay Duties in another.

No Money shall be drawn from the Treasury, but in Consequence of Appropriations made by law; and a regular Statement and Account of the Receipts and Expenditures of all public Money shall be published from time to time.

No Title of Nobility shall be granted by the United States: And no Person holding any Office of Profit or Trust under them, shall, without the Consent of the Congress, accept of any present, Emolument, Office, or Title, of any kind whatever, from any King, Prince, or foreign State.

Section 10
No State shall enter into any Treaty, Alliance, or Confederation; grant Letters of Marque and Reprisal; coin Money; emit Bills of Credit; make any Thing but gold and silver Coin a Tender in Payment of Debts; pass any Bill of Attainder, ex post facto Law, or Law impairing the Obligation of Contracts, or grant any Title of Nobility.

No State shall, without the Consent of the Congress, lay any Imposts or Duties on Imports or Exports, except what may be absolutely necessary for executing its inspection Laws: and the net Produce of all Duties and Imposts, laid by any State on Imports or Exports, shall be for the Use of the Treasury of the United States; and all such Laws shall be subject to the Revision and Control of the Congress.

No State shall, without the Consent of the Congress, lay any duty of Tonnage, keep Troops, or Ships of War in time of Peace, enter into any Agreement or Compact with another State, or with a foreign Power, or engage in War, unless actually invaded, or in such imminent Danger as will not admit of delay.

Article II

Section 1
The executive Power shall be vested in a President of the United States of America. He shall hold his Office during the Term of four Years, and, together with the Vice President, chosen for the same Term, be elected, as follows:

Each State shall appoint, in such Manner as the Legislature thereof may direct, a Number of Electors, equal to the whole Number of Senators and Representatives to which the State may be entitled in the Congress; but no Senator or Representative, or Person holding an Office of Trust or Profit under the United States, shall be appointed an Elector.

The Electors shall meet in their respective States, and vote by Ballot for two Persons, of whom one at least shall not be an Inhabitant of the same State with themselves. And they shall make a List of all the Persons voted for, and of the Number of Votes for each; which List they shall sign and certify, and transmit sealed to the Seat of the Government of the United States, directed to the President of the Senate. The President of the Senate shall, in the Presence of the Senate and House of Representatives, open all the Certificates, and the Votes shall then be counted. The Person having the greatest Number of Votes shall be the President, if such Number be a Majority of the whole Number of Electors appointed; and if there be more than one who have such Majority, and have an equal Number of Votes, then the House of Representatives shall immediately chuse by Ballot one of them for President; and if no Person have a Majority, then from the five highest on the List the said House shall in like Manner chuse the President.

But in chusing the President, the Votes shall be taken by States, the Representation from each State having one Vote; a quorum for this Purpose shall consist of a Member or Members from two thirds of the States, and a Majority of all the States shall be necessary to a Choice. In every Case, after the Choice of the President, the Person having the greatest Number of Votes of the Electors shall be the Vice President. But if there should remain two or more who have equal Votes, the Senate shall chuse from them by Ballot the Vice President. *

The Congress may determine the Time of chusing the Electors, and the Day on which they shall give their Votes; which Day shall be the same throughout the United States.

No Person except a natural born Citizen, or a Citizen of the United States, at the time of the Adoption of this Constitution, shall be eligible to the Office of President; neither shall any Person be eligible to that Office who shall not have attained to the Age of thirty five Years, and been fourteen Years a Resident within the United States.

In Case of the Removal of the President from Office, or of his Death, Resignation, or Inability to discharge the Powers and Duties of the said Office, the same shall devolve on the Vice President, *and the Congress may by Law provide for the Case of Removal, Death, Resignation, or Inability, both of the President and Vice President, declaring what Officer shall then act as President, and such Officer shall act accordingly, until the Disability be removed, or a President shall be elected.* [†]

The President shall, at stated Times, receive for his Services a Compensation, which shall neither be increased nor diminished during the Period for which he shall have been elected, and he shall not receive within that Period any other Emolument from the United States, or any of them.

Before he enter on the Execution of his Office, he shall take the following Oath or Affirmation:—"I do solemnly swear (or affirm) that I will faithfully execute the Office of President of the United States, and will to the best of my Ability, preserve, protect and defend the Constitution of the United States."

Section 2
The President shall be Commander in Chief of the Army and Navy of the United States, and of the Militia of the several States, when called into the actual Service of the United States; he may require the Opinion, in writing, of the principal Officer in each of the executive Departments, upon any Subject relating to the Duties of their respective Offices, and he shall have Power to Grant Reprieves and Pardons for Offences against the United States, except in Cases of Impeachment.

He shall have Power, by and with the Advice and Consent of the Senate, to make Treaties, provided two thirds of the Senators present concur; and he shall nominate, and by and with the Advice and Consent of the Senate, shall appoint Ambassadors, other public Ministers and Consuls, Judges of the supreme Court, and all other Officers of the United States, whose Appointments are not herein otherwise provided for, and which shall be established by Law: but the Congress may by Law vest the Appointment of such inferior Officers, as they think proper, in the President alone, in the Courts of Law, or in the Heads of Departments.

The President shall have Power to fill up all Vacancies that may happen during the Recess of the Senate, by granting Commissions which shall expire at the End of their next Session.

---

*Superseded by the Twelfth Amendment.

[†]Modified by the Twenty-Fifth Amendment.

Section 3

He shall from time to time give to the Congress Information of the State of the Union, and recommend to their Consideration such Measures as he shall judge necessary and expedient; he may, on extraordinary Occasions, convene both Houses, or either of them, and in Case of Disagreement between them, with Respect to the Time of Adjournment, he may adjourn them to such Time as he shall think proper; he shall receive Ambassadors and other public Ministers; he shall take Care that the Laws be faithfully executed, and shall Commission all the Officers of the United States.

Section 4

The President, Vice President and all civil Officers of the United States, shall be removed from Office on Impeachment for, and Conviction of, Treason, Bribery, or other high Crimes and Misdemeanors.

Article III

Section 1

The judicial Power of the United States, shall be vested in one supreme Court, and in such inferior Courts as the Congress may from time to time ordain and establish. The Judges, both of the supreme and inferior Courts, shall hold their Offices during good Behaviour, and shall, at stated Times, receive for their Services a Compensation, which shall not be diminished during their Continuance in Office.

Section 2

The judicial Power shall extend to all Cases, in Law and Equity, arising under this Constitution, the Laws of the United States, and Treaties made, or which shall be made, under their Authority;—to all Cases affecting Ambassadors, other public Ministers and Consuls;—to all Cases of admiralty and maritime Jurisdiction;—to Controversies to which the United States shall be a Party;—to Controversies between two or more States;—between a State and Citizens of another State;*—between Citizens of different States;—between Citizens of the same State claiming Lands under Grants of different States, and between a State, or the Citizens thereof, and foreign States, Citizens or Subjects.

In all Cases affecting Ambassadors, other public Ministers and Consuls, and those in which a State shall be Party, the supreme Court shall have original Jurisdiction. In all the other Cases before mentioned, the supreme Court shall have appellate Jurisdiction, both as to Law and Fact, with such Exceptions, and under such Regulations as the Congress shall make.

The trial of all Crimes, except in Cases of Impeachment, shall be by Jury; and such Trial shall be held in the State where said Crimes shall have been committed; but when not committed within any State, the Trial shall be at such Place or Places as the Congress may by Law have directed.

Section 3

Treason against the United States, shall consist only in levying War against them, or in adhering to their Enemies, giving them Aid and Comfort. No Person shall be convicted of Treason unless on the Testimony of two Witnesses to the same overt Act, or on Confession in open Court.

---

*Restricted by the Eleventh Amendment.

The Congress shall have Power to declare the Punishment of Treason, but no Attainder of Treason shall work Corruption of Blood, or Forefeiture except during the Life of the Person attainted.

Article IV

Section 1
Full Faith and Credit shall be given in each State to the public Acts, Records, and judicial Proceedings of every other State. And the Congress may by general Laws prescribe the Manner in which such Acts, Records, and Proceedings shall be proved, and the Effect thereof.

Section 2
The Citizens of each State shall be entitled to all Privileges and Immunities of Citizens in the several States.

A Person charged in any State with Treason, Felony, or other Crime, who shall flee from Justice, and be found in another State, shall on demand of the executive Authority of the State from which he fled, be delivered up, to be removed to the State having Jurisdiction of the Crime.

No Person held to Service or Labour in one State, under the Laws thereof, escaping into another, shall, in Consequence of any Law or Regulation therein, be discharged from such Service or Labour, but shall be delivered up on Claim of the Party to whom such Service or Labour may be due. *

Section 3
New States may be admitted by the Congress into this Union; but no new State shall be formed or erected within the Jurisdiction of any other State; nor any State be formed by the Junction of two or more States, or parts of States, without the Consent of the Legislatures of the States concerned as well as of the Congress.

The Congress shall have Power to dispose of and make all needful Rules and Regulations respecting the Territory or other Property belonging to the United States; and nothing in this Constitution shall be so construed as to Prejudice any Claims of the United States, or of any particular State.

Section 4
The United States shall guarantee to every State in this Union a Republican Form of Government, and shall protect each of them against Invasion; and on Application of the Legislature, or of the Executive (when the Legislature cannot be convened) against domestic Violence.

Article V

The Congress, whenever two thirds of both Houses shall deem it necessary, shall propose Amendments to this Constitution, or, on the Application of the Legislatures of two thirds of the several States, shall call a Convention for proposing Amendments, which, in either Case, shall be valid to all Intents and Purposes, as Part of this Constitution, when ratified by the Legislatures of three fourths of the several States, or by Conventions in three fourths thereof, as the one or the other Mode of Ratification

---

*Superseded by the Twelfth Amendment.

may be proposed by the Congress; Provided that no Amendment which may be made prior to the Year One thousand eight hundred and eight shall in any Manner affect the first and fourth Clauses in the Ninth Section of the first Article; and that no State, without its Consent, shall be deprived of its equal Suffrage in the Senate.

Article VI

All Debts contracted and Engagements entered into, before the Adoption of this Constitution, shall be as valid against the United States under this Constitution, as under the Confederation.

This Constitution, and the Laws of the United States which shall be made in Pursuance thereof; and all Treaties made, or which shall be made, under the Authority of the United States, shall be the supreme Law of the Land; and the Judges in every State shall be bound thereby, any Thing in the Constitution or Laws of any State to the Contrary notwithstanding.

The Senators and Representatives before mentioned, and the Members of the several State Legislatures, and all executive and judicial Officers, both of the United States and of the several States, shall be bound by Oath or Affirmation, to support this Constitution; but no religious Test shall ever be required as a Qualification to any Office or public Trust under the United States.

Article VII

The Ratification of the Conventions of nine States shall be sufficient for the Establishment of this Constitution between the States so ratifying the Same.

Done in Convention by the Unanimous Consent of the States present the Seventeenth Day of September in the Year of our Lord one thousand seven hundred and Eighty seven and of the Independence of the United States of America the Twelfth. In Witness whereof We have hereunto subscribed our Names.

Go.Washington
President and deputy from Virginia

New Hampshire	New Jersey	Delaware	North Carolina
John Langdon	Wil. Livingston	Geo. Read	Wm. Blount
Nicholas Gilman	David Brearley	Gunning Bedford jun	Richd. Dobbs Spaight
	Wm. Paterson	John Dickenson	Hu Williamson
Massachusetts	Jona. Dayton	Richard Bassett	
Nathaniel Gorham		Jaco. Broom	South Carolina
Rufus King	Pennsylvania		J. Rutledge
	B. Franklin	Maryland	Charles Cotesworth Pickney
Connecticut	Thomas Mifflin	James McHenry	Pierce Butler
Wm. Saml. Johnson	Robt. Morris	Dan. of St. Thos. Jenifer	
Roger Sherman	Geo. Clymer	Danl. Carroll	Georgia
	Thos. FitzSimons		William Few
New York	Jared Ingersoll	Virginia	Abr. Baldwin
Alexander Hamilton	James Wilson	John Blair	
	Gouv. Morris	James Madison, Jr.	

AMENDMENTS TO THE CONSTITUTION

Amendment I [1791]*

Congress shall make no law respecting an establishment of religion, or prohibiting the free exercise thereof; or abridging the freedom of speech, or of the press; or the right of the people peaceably to assemble, and to petition the Government for a redress of grievances.

Amendment II [1791]

A well regulated Militia, being necessary to the security of a free State, the right of the people to keep and bear Arms shall not be infringed.

Amendment III [1791]

No Soldier shall, in time of peace, be quartered in any house, without the consent of the Owner, nor in time of war, but in a manner to be prescribed by law.

Amendment IV [1791]

The right of the people to be secure in their persons, houses, papers, and effects, against unreasonable searches and seizures, shall not be violated, and no Warrants shall issue, but upon probable cause, supported by Oath or affirmation, and particularly describing the place to be searched, and the persons or things to be seized.

Amendment V [1791]

No person shall be held to answer for a capital or otherwise infamous crime, unless on a presentment or indictment of a Grand Jury, except in cases arising in the land or naval forces, or in the Militia, when in actual service in time of War or public danger; nor shall any person be subject for the same offence to be twice put in jeopardy of life or limb; nor shall be compelled in any criminal case to be a witness against himself, nor be deprived of life, liberty, or property, without due process of law; nor shall private property be taken for public use, without just compensation.

Amendment VI [1791]

In all criminal prosecutions, the accused shall enjoy the right to a speedy and public trial, by an impartial jury of the State and district wherein the crime shall have been committed, which district shall have been previously ascertained by law, and to be informed of the nature and cause of the accusation; to be confronted with the witnesses against him; to have compulsory process for obtaining witnesses in his favor, and to have the Assistance of Counsel for his defence.

---

*The dates in brackets indicate when the amendments were ratified.

Amendment VII [1791]

In suits at common law, where the value in controversy shall exceed twenty dollars, the right of trail by jury shall be preserved, and no fact tried by a jury, shall be otherwise reexamined in any Court of the United States, than according to the Rules of the common law.

Amendment VIII [1791]

Excessive bail shall not be required, nor excessive fines imposed, nor cruel and unusual punishments inflicted.

Amendment IX [1791]

The enumeration in the Constitution, of certain rights, shall not be construed to deny or disparage others retained by the people.

Amendment X [1791]

The powers not delegated to the United States by the Constitution, nor prohibited by it to the States, are reserved to the States respectively, or to the people.

Amendment XI [1798]

The Judicial power of the United States shall not be construed to extend to any suit in law or equity, commenced or prosecuted against one of the United States by Citizens of another State, or by Citizens or subjects of any foreign state.

Amendment XII [1804]

The Electors shall meet in their respective States and vote by ballot for President and Vice-President, one of whom, at least, shall not be an inhabitant of the same State with themselves; they shall name in their ballots the person voted for as President, and in distinct ballots the person voted for as Vice-President, and they shall make distinct lists of all persons voted for as President, and of all persons voted for as Vice-President, and of the number of votes for each, which lists they shall sign and certify, and transmit sealed to the seat of the government of the United States, directed to the President of the Senate;—the President of the Senate shall, in the presence of the Senate and House of Representatives, open all the certificates and the votes shall then be counted;—The person having the greatest number of votes for President, shall be the President, if such number be a majority of the whole number of Electors appointed; and if no person have such majority, then from the persons having the highest numbers not exceeding three on the list of those voted for as President, the House of Representatives shall choose immediately, by ballot, the President. But in choosing the President, the votes shall be taken by States, the representation from each State having one vote; a quorum for this purpose shall consist of a member or members from two-thirds of the States, and a majority of all the States shall be necessary to a choice. And if the House of Representatives shall not choose a President whenever the right of choice shall devolve upon them, before *the fourth day of March* next following, then the Vice-President shall act as President, as in the case of the death or other constitutional disability of the President.*—The person having the greatest number of votes as Vice-President, shall be the Vice-President, if such number be a majority of the whole number of Electors appointed, and if no person have a majority, then from the two highest numbers on the list, the Senate shall choose the Vice-President; a quorum for the purpose shall consist of two-thirds of the whole number of Senators, and a majority of the whole number shall be necessary to a choice. But no person constitutionally ineligible to the office of President shall be eligible to that of Vice-President of the United States.

Amendment XIII [1865]

Section 1
Neither slavery nor involuntary servitude, except as a punishment for crime whereof the party shall have been duly convicted, shall exist within the United States, or any place subject to their jurisdiction.

Section 2
Congress shall have power to enforce this article by appropriate legislation.

Amendment XIV [1868]

Section 1
All persons born or naturalized in the United States, and subject to the jurisdiction thereof, are citizens of the United States and of the State wherein they reside. No State shall make or enforce any law which shall abridge the privileges or immunities of citizens of the United States; nor shall any State deprive any person of life, liberty, or property, without due process of law; nor deny to any person within its jurisdiction the equal protection of the laws.

Section 2
Representatives shall be apportioned among the several States according to their respective numbers, counting the whole number of persons in each State, excluding Indians not taxed. But when the right to vote at any election for the choice of electors for President and Vice-President of the United States, Representatives in Congress, the Executive and Judicial officers of a State, or the members of the Legislature thereof, is denied to any of the male inhabitants of such State, being twenty-one years of age, and citizens of the United States, or in any way abridged, except for participation in rebellion, or other crime, the basis of representation therein shall be reduced in the proportion which the number of such male citizens shall bear to the whole number of male citizens twenty-one years of age in such State.

Section 3
No person shall be a Senator or Representative in Congress, or elector of President and Vice-President, or hold any office, civil or military, under the United States, or

---

*Superseded by Section 3 of the Twentieth Amendment.

under any State, who, having previously taken an oath, as a member of Congress, or as an officer of the United States, or as a member of any State legislature, or as an executive or judicial officer of any State, to support the Constitution of the United States, shall have engaged in insurrection or rebellion against the same, or given aid or comfort to the enemies thereof. Congress may by a vote of two-thirds of each house, remove such disability.

Section 4
The validity of the public debt of the United States, authorized by law, including debts incurred for payment of pensions and bounties for services in suppressing insurrection or rebellion, shall not be questioned. But neither the United States nor any State shall assume or pay any debt or obligation incurred in aid of insurrection or rebellion against the United States, or any claim for the loss or emancipation of any slave; but all such debts, obligations and claims shall be held illegal and void.

Section 5
The Congress shall have power to enforce, by appropriate legislation, the provisions of this article.

Amendment XV [1870]

Section 1
The right of citizens of the United States to vote shall not be denied or abridged by the United States or by any State on account of race, color, or previous condition of servitude—

Section 2
The Congress shall have power to enforce this article by appropriate legislation.

Amendment XVI [1913]

The Congress shall have power to lay and collect taxes on incomes, from whatever source derived, without apportionment among the several States, and without regard to any census or enumeration.

Amendment XVII [1913]

The Senate of the United States shall be composed of two Senators from each State, elected by the people thereof, for six years; and each Senator shall have one vote. The electors in each State shall have the qualifications requisite for electors of the most numerous branch of the State legislatures.

When vacancies happen in the representation of any State in the Senate, the executive authority of such State shall issue writs of election to fill such vacancies: *Provided*, That the legislature of any State may empower the executive thereof to make temporary appointments until the people fill the vacancies by election as the legislature may direct.

This amendment shall not be so construed as to affect the election or term of any Senator chosen before it becomes valid as part of the Constitution.

Amendment XVIII [1919]

Section 1
After one year from the ratification of this article the manufacture, sale, or transportation of intoxicating liquors within, the importation thereof into, or the exportation thereof from the United States and all territory subject to the jurisdiction hereof for beverage purposes hereby prohibited.

Section 2
The Congress and the several States shall have concurrent power to enforce this article by appropriate legislation.

Section 3
This article shall be inoperative unless it shall have been ratified as an amendment to the Constitution by the legislatures of the several States, as provided by the Constitution, within seven years from the date of submission hereof to the States by the Congress.*

Amendment XIX [1920]

The right of citizens of the United States to vote shall not be denied or abridged by the United States or by any State on account of sex.

Congress shall have power to enforce this article by appropriate legislation.

Amendment XX [1933]

Section 1
The terms of the President and Vice-President shall end at noon on the 20th day of January, and the terms of Senators and Representatives at noon on the 3d day of January, of the years in which such terms would have ended if this article had not been ratified; and the terms of their successors shall then begin.

Section 2
The Congress shall assemble at least once in every year, and such meeting shall begin at noon on the 3d day of January, unless they shall by law appoint a different day.

Section 3
If, at the time fixed for the beginning of the term of the President, the President elect shall have died, the Vice-President elect shall become President. If a President shall not have been chosen before the time fixed for the beginning of his term, or if the President elect shall have failed to qualify, then the Vice-President elect shall act as President until a President shall have qualified; and the Congress may by law provide for the case wherein neither a President elect nor a Vice-President elect shall have qualified, declaring who shall then act as President, or the manner in which one who is to act shall be selected, and such person shall act accordingly until a President or Vice-President shall have qualified.

---

*Repealed by Section 1 of the Twenty-First Amendment.

Section 4

The Congress may by law provide for the case of the death of any of the persons from whom the House of Representatives may choose a President whenever the right of choice shall have devolved upon them, and for the case of the death of any of the persons from whom the Senate may choose a Vice-President whenever the right of choice shall have devolved upon them.

Section 5

Sections 1 and 2 shall take effect on the 15th day of October following the ratification of this article.

Section 6

This article shall be inoperative unless it shall have been ratified as an amendment to the Constitution by the legislatures of three-fourths of the several States within seven years from the date of its submission.

Amendment XXI [1933]

Section 1

The eighteenth article of amendment to the Constitution of the United States is hereby repealed.

Section 2

The transportation or importation into any State, Territory, or possession of the United States for delivery or use therein of intoxicating liquors, in violation of the laws thereof, is hereby prohibited.

Section 3

This article shall be inoperative unless it shall have been ratified as an amendment to the Constitution by conventions in the several States, as provided in the Constitution, within seven years from the date of submission hereof to the States by the Congress.

Amendment XXII [1951]

Section 1

No person shall be elected to the office of President more than twice, and no person who has held the office of President, or acted as President, for more than two years of a term to which some other person was elected President shall be elected to the office of the President more than once. But this Article shall not apply to any person holding the office of President when this Article was proposed by the Congress, and shall not prevent any person who may be holding the office of President, or acting as President, during the term within which this Article becomes operative from holding the office of the President or acting as President during the remainder of such term.

Section 2

This article shall be inoperative unless it shall have been ratified as an amendment to the Constitution by the legislatures of three-fourths of the several States within seven years from the date of its submission to the States by the Congress.

Amendment XXIII [1961]

Section 1
The District constituting the seat of Government of the United States shall appoint in such manner as the Congress may direct:

A number of electors of President and Vice-President equal to the whole number of Senators and Representatives in Congress to which the District would be entitled if it were a State, but in no event more than the least populous State; they shall be in addition to those appointed by the States, but they shall be considered, for the purposes of the election of President and Vice-President, to be electors appointed by a State; and they shall meet in the District and perform such duties as provided by the twelfth article of amendment.

Section 2
The Congress shall have power to enforce this article by appropriate legislation.

Amendment XXIV [1964]

Section 1
The right of citizens of the United States to vote in any primary or other election for President or Vice-President, for electors for President or Vice-President, or for Senator or Representative in Congress, shall not be denied or abridged by the United States or any State by reason of failure to pay any poll tax or other tax.

Section 2
The Congress shall have power to enforce this article by appropriate legislation.

Amendment XXV [1967]

Section 1
In case of the removal of the President from office or of his death or resignation, the Vice-President shall become President.

Section 2
Whenever there is a vacancy in the office of the Vice-President, the President shall nominate a Vice-President who shall take office upon confirmation by a majority vote of both houses of Congress.

Section 3
Whenever the President transmits to the President pro tempore of the Senate and the Speaker of the House of Representatives his written declaration that he is unable to discharge the powers and duties of his office, and until he transmits to them a written declaration to the contrary, such powers and duties shall be discharged by the Vice-President as Acting President.

Section 4
Whenever the Vice-President and a majority of either the principal officers of the executive departments or of such other body as Congress may by law provide, transmit

to the President pro tempore of the Senate and the Speaker of the House of Representatives their written declaration that the President is unable to discharge the powers and duties of his office, the Vice-President shall immediately assume the powers and duties of the office as Acting President.

Thereafter, when the President transmits to the President pro tempore of the Senate and the Speaker of the House of Representatives his written declaration that no inability exists, he shall resume the powers and duties of his office unless the Vice-President and a majority of either the principal officers of the executive department or of such other body as Congress may by law provide, transmit within four days to the President pro tempore of the Senate and the Speaker of the House of Representatives their written declaration that the President is unable to discharge the powers and duties of his office. Thereupon Congress shall decide the issue, assembling within forty-eight hours for that purpose if not in session. If the Congress, within twenty-one days after receipt of the latter written declaration, or, if Congress is not in session, within twenty-one days after Congress is required to assemble, determines by two-thirds vote of both Houses that the President is unable to discharge the powers and duties of his office, the Vice-President shall continue to discharge the same as Acting President; otherwise, the President shall resume the powers and duties of his office.

Amendment XXVI [1971]

Section 1
The right of citizens of the United States, who are eighteen years of age or older, to vote shall not be denied or abridged by the United States or by any state on account of age.

Section 2
The Congress shall have power to enforce this article by appropriate legislation.

Amendment XXVII [1992]

No law varying the compensation for services of the Senators and Representatives, shall take effect, until an election of Representatives shall have intervened.

APPENDIX

TERRITORIAL EXPANSION

Territory	Date Acquired	Square Miles	How Acquired
Original states and territories	1783	888,685	Treaty of Paris
Louisiana Purchase	1803	827,192	Purchased from France
Florida	1819	72,003	Adams-Onís Treaty
Texas	1845	390,143	Annexation of independent country
Oregon	1846	285,580	Oregon Boundary Treaty
Mexican cession	1848	529,017	Treaty of Guadalupe Hidalgo
Gadsden Purchase	1853	29,640	Purchased from Mexico
Midway Islands	1867	2	Annexation of uninhabited islands
Alaska	1867	589,757	Purchased from Russia
Hawaii	1898	6,450	Annexation of independent country
Wake Island	1898	3	Annexation of uninhabited island
Puerto Rico	1899	3,435	Treaty of Paris
Guam	1899	212	Treaty of Paris
The Philippines	1899–1946	115,600	Treaty of Paris; granted independence
American Samoa	1900	76	Treaty with Germany and Great Britain
Panama Canal Zone	1904–1978	553	Hay–Bunau-Varilla Treaty
U.S. Virgin Islands	1917	133	Purchased from Denmark
Trust Territory of the Pacific Islands*	1947	717	United Nations Trusteeship

*A number of these islands have recently been granted independence: Federated States of Micronesia, 1990; Marshall Islands, 1991; Palau, 1994.

THE LABOR FORCE

(thousands of workers)

Year	Agricul-ture	Mining	Manufac-turing	Construc-tion	Trade	Other	Total
1810	1,950	11	75	—	—	294	2,330
1840	3,570	32	500	290	350	918	5,660
1850	4,520	102	1,200	410	530	1,488	8,250
1860	5,880	176	1,530	520	890	2,114	11,110
1870	6,790	180	2,470	780	1,310	1,400	12,930
1880	8,920	280	3,290	900	1,930	2,070	17,390
1890	9,960	440	4,390	1,510	2,960	4,060	23,320
1900	11,680	637	5,895	1,665	3,970	5,223	29,070
1910	11,770	1,068	8,332	1,949	5,320	9,041	37,480
1920	10,790	1,180	11,190	1,233	5,845	11,372	41,610
1930	10,560	1,009	9,884	1,988	8,122	17,267	48,830
1940	9,575	925	11,309	1,876	9,328	23,277	56,290
1950	7,870	901	15,648	3,029	12,152	25,870	65,470
1960	5,970	709	17,145	3,640	14,051	32,545	74,060
1970	3,463	516	20,746	4,818	15,008	34,127	78,678
1980	3,364	979	21,942	6,215	20,191	46,612	99,303
1990	3,186	730	21,184	7,696	24,269	60,849	117,914
1994	3,409	669	20,157	7,493	25,699	65,633	123,060

SOURCE: *Historical Statistics of the United States, Colonial Times to 1970* (1975), 139; *Statistical Abstract of the United States*, 1995, Table 653.

Changing Labor Patterns

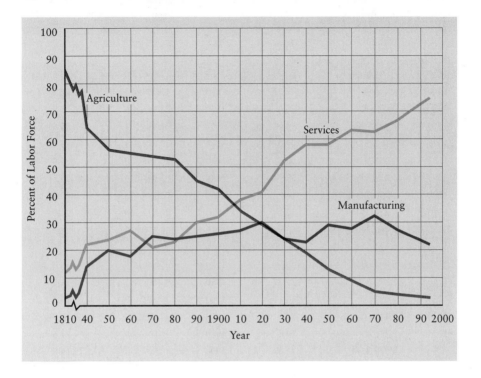

AMERICAN POPULATION

Year	Population	Percent Increase	Year	Population	Percent Increase
1610	350	—	1810	7,239,881	36.4
1620	2,300	557.1	1820	9,638,453	33.1
1630	4,600	100.0	1830	12,866,020	33.5
1640	26,600	478.3	1840	17,069,453	32.7
1650	50,400	90.8	1850	23,191,876	35.9
1660	75,100	49.0	1860	31,443,321	35.6
1670	111,900	49.0	1870	39,818,449	26.6
1680	151,500	35.4	1880	50,155,783	26.0
1690	210,400	38.9	1890	62,947,714	25.5
1700	250,900	19.2	1900	75,994,575	20.7
1710	331,700	32.2	1910	91,972,266	21.0
1720	466,200	40.5	1920	105,710,620	14.9
1730	629,400	35.0	1930	122,775,046	16.1
1740	905,600	43.9	1940	131,669,275	7.2
1750	1,170,800	29.3	1950	150,697,361	14.5
1760	1,593,600	36.1	1960	179,323,175	19.0
1770	2,148,100	34.8	1970	203,235,298	13.3
1780	2,780,400	29.4	1980	226,545,805	11.5
1790	3,929,214	41.3	1990	248,709,873	9.8
1800	5,308,483	35.1	1993	259,383,000	4.3

Note: These figures largely ignore the native American population. Census takers never made any effort to count the native American population that lived outside their political jurisdictions and compiled only casual and incomplete enumerations of those living within their jurisdictions until 1890. In that year the federal government attempted a full count of the Indian population: the Census found 125,719 Indians in 1890, compared with only 12,543 in 1870 and 33,985 in 1880.

SOURCE: *Historical Statistics of the United States, Colonial Times to 1970* (1975); *Statistical Abstract of the United States,* 1995.

SUGGESTED READINGS

CHAPTER 1

One of the few works that cover the history of the various European and native American peoples is Eric Wolf, *Europe and the People without History*. See also Alfred W. Crosby, Jr., *Ecological Imperialism: The Biological Expansion of Europe, 900–1900* (1986); Robert R. Reynolds, *Europe Emerges: Transition toward an Industrial World-Wide Society, 600–1750* (1961); and G. V. Scammell, *The World Encompassed: The First European Maritime Empires* (1981).

Native American Worlds

Brian M. Fagan, *The Great Journey: The People of Ancient America* (1987), synthesizes recent scholarship on the prehistoric Indians of the United States, while his *Kingdoms of Gold, Kingdoms of Jade: The Americas before Columbus* (1991) does the same for the Mesoamerican peoples. See also Stuart J. Fiedel, *Prehistory of the Americas* (1992); Inga Clendinnen, *Aztecs: An Interpretation* (1991); John S. Henderson, *The World of the Maya* (1981); David Carrasco, *Quetzalcoatl and the Irony of Empire* (1982); R. C. Padden, *The Hummingbird and the Hawk* (1962); and R. Tom Zuidema, *Inca Civilization in Cuzco* (1992). Two fine supplements are Michael Coe et al., *Atlas of Ancient America* (1986), and Manuel Lucena Salmoral, *America in 1492* (1991), a photographic survey of dress, artifacts, and architecture.

Alfred W. Crosby, Jr., *The Columbian Exchange: Biological and Cultural Consequences of 1492* (1972), traces the impact of European diseases. See also Russell Thornton, *American Indian Holocaust and Survival: A Population History since 1492* (1987); Henry F. Dobyns, *Their Numbers Became Thinned: Native American Population Dynamics in Eastern North America* (1983); and William M. Denevan, *The Native Population of the Americas in 1492* (1992).

On North America, consult Alvin M. Josephy, Jr., ed., *America in 1492* (1993); Linda S. Cordell, *Ancient Pueblo Peoples* (1994); Bruce D. Smith, ed., *The Mississippian Emergence* (1990); Carl Waldman and Molly Braun, *Atlas of the North American Indian* (1985); and Robert Silverberg, *Mound Builders of Ancient America: The Archaeology of a Myth* (1968). Roger Kennedy, *Hidden Cities* (1994), surveys the early Indian civilizations of the Mississippi Valley.

Traditional European Society in 1450

Barbara W. Tuchman, *A Distant Mirror: The Calamitous Fourteenth Century* (1978), and Johan Huizinga, *The Waning of the Middle Ages* (1947), present vivid portraits of the late medieval world. Two wide-ranging studies of subsequent developments are

George Huppert, *After the Black Death: A Social History of Modern Europe* (1986), and Henry Kamen, *European Society, 1500–1700* (1984). Illuminating specialized studies include Peter Burke, *Popular Culture in Early Modern Europe* (1978); Pierre Goubert, *The French Peasantry in the Seventeenth Century* (1986); Philippe Ariès, *Centuries of Childhood* (1962); B. H. Slicher Van Bath, *The Agrarian History of Western Europe, A.D. 500–1850* (1963); and Emanuel Le Roy Ladurie, *The Peasants of Languedoc* (1974). See also Joel Mokyr, *The Lever of Riches: Technological Creativity and Economic Progress* (1990), and E. P. Thompson, *Customs in Common: Studies in Traditional Popular Culture* (1991).

Europe and the World, 1450–1550

The preconditions for European expansion are treated in James D. Tracy, ed., *Rise of Merchant Empires: Long Distance Trade in the Early Modern World, 1350–1750* (1990). For the southern European background, read selectively in Fernand Braudel's massive and stimulating *The Mediterranean and the Mediterranean World in the Age of Philip II* (1949).

Paul H. Chapman, *The Norse Discovery of America* (1981), and Boies Penrose, *Travel and Discovery in the Renaissance, 1420–1620* (1952), illuminate the growth of geographical knowledge. For the expansion of the Iberian peoples, see Bailey W. Diffie and George Winius, *Foundations of the Portuguese Empire, 1415–1580* (1977), and Henry Kamen, *Crisis and Change in Early Modern Spain* (1993). A good short biography of Columbus and his times is Felipe Fernández-Armesto, *Columbus* (1991).

For the Spanish and Portuguese colonial empires, see Charles R. Boxer, *The Portuguese Seaborne Empire* (1969), and James Lockhard and Stuart B. Schwartz, *Early Latin America: Colonial Spanish America and Brazil* (1984). Fine accounts of the Spanish conquest include the memorable firsthand report by Bernal Diaz del Castillo, *The Discovery and Conquest of Mexico* (ed. by I. A. Leonard, 1956); Leon Portilla, *Broken Spears: The Aztec Account of the Conquest of Mexico* (1962); and Hugh Thomas, *Conquest: Montezuma, Cortés and the Fall of Old Mexico* (1994). The impact on native society in New Spain is portrayed in Daniel T. Reff, *Disease, Depopulation, and Culture Change in Northwestern New Spain, 1518–1764* (1991); for the story north of the Rio Grande, see David J. Weber, *The Spanish Frontier in North America* (1992), and Ramón Gutiérrez, *When Jesus Came, the Corn Mothers Went Away: Marriage, Sexuality, and Power in New Mexico, 1500–1846* (1991).

The Protestant Reformation and the Rise of England, 1500–1630

On the European Reformation, consult William J. Bouwsma, *John Calvin* (1987), and De Lamar Jensen, *Reformation Europe: Age of Reform and Revolution* (1981). For England, see Patrick Collinson, *The Religion of the Protestants: The Church in English Society, 1559–1625* (1982), and Susan Doran and Christopher Durston, *Princes, Pastors, and People: The Church and Religion in England, 1529–1689* (1991).

On the decline of Spain, consult Henry Kamen, *Spain: A Society in Conflict, 1479–1714* (2d ed., 1991), and John Lynch, *The Hispanic World in Crisis and Change, 1598–1700* (1992), which also traces the growing economic independence of New Spain. For a general analysis of economic change in Europe, see T. S. Ashton, ed., *The Brenner Debate* (1987).

A brilliant and forceful portrait of English preindustrial society is offered by Peter Laslett, *The World We Have Lost* (3d ed., 1984). Other important works are

Keith Wrightson, *English Society, 1580–1680* (1982), and two books by Lawrence Stone, *The Crisis of the Aristocracy* (1965) and *Family, Sex, and Marriage in England, 1500–1800* (1977). On the movement of people, see Ida Altman and James Horn, eds., *"To Make America": European Emigration in the Early Modern Period* (1991).

CHAPTER 2

David Weber, *The Spanish Frontier in North America* (1992), and Richard White, *The Middle Ground: Indians, Empires, and Republics in the Great Lakes Region, 1650–1815* (1991), are magisterial studies, while Bernard Bailyn, *The Peopling of British North America* (1986), offers a useful overview of the early English colonies.

Imperial Conflicts and Rival Colonial Models

For Spain's northern empire, see, in addition to Weber, Ramón Gutiérrez, *When Jesus Came, the Corn Mothers Went Away: Marriage, Sexuality, and Power in New Mexico, 1500–1846* (1991). The French threat to its domain is traced by Robert S. Weddle, *The French Thorn: Rival Explorers in the Spanish Sea, 1682–1762* (1991), and Daniel H. Usner, Jr., *Indians, Settlers, and Slaves in a Frontier Exchange Economy: The Lower Mississippi Valley before 1783* (1991).

The best general studies of French Canada are by W. J. Eccles, *The Canadian Frontier, 1534–1760* (1983) and *France in America* (rev. ed, 1990). French interaction with native Americans is covered by Bruce G. Trigger, *The Children of Aataentsic: A History of the Huron People to 1660* (1976); Daniel K. Richter, *The Ordeal of the Long House: The Peoples of the Iroquois League in the Era of European Colonization* (1992); and Patricia O. Dickason, *Canada's First Nations: A History of the Founding Peoples from Earliest Times* (1992).

For English expansion, see Kenneth Andrews, *Trade, Plunder, and Settlement: Maritime Enterprise and the Genesis of the British Empire, 1480–1630* (1984); Nicholas Canny, *Kingdom and Colony: Ireland in the Atlantic World, 1560–1800* (1988); A. L. Rowse, *Sir Walter Raleigh* (1962); David B. Quinn, *England and the Discovery of America, 1481–1620* (1974); and Karen O. Kupperman, *Roanoke* (1984). The interaction of the English and Dutch with native Americans can be followed in Gary B. Nash, *Red, White, and Black: The Peoples of Early America* (1982); Francis Jennings, *The Invasion of America* (1975); and two works by James Axtell, *The European and the Indian* (1981) and *The Invasion Within: The Contest of Cultures in Colonial North America* (1985).

The Chesapeake Experience

Alden Vaughan, *American Genesis: Captain John Smith and the Founding of Virginia* (1975), covers the earliest years, while Edmund S. Morgan, *American Slavery, American Freedom: The Ordeal of Colonial Virginia* (1975), provides a brilliant analysis of the rest of the colonial period. Important essays appear in Thad W. Tate and David L. Ammerman, eds., *The Chesapeake in the Seventeenth Century* (1979), and Lois Green Carr, Philip D. Morgan, and Jean B. Russo, *Colonial Chesapeake Society* (1989). Significant community studies include Carville Earle, *The Evolution of a Tidewater Settlement Pattern: All Hallows Parish, Maryland, 1650–1783* (1975), and Lois Green Carr, et al., *Robert Cole's World: Agriculture and Society in Early Maryland* (1991).

For a discussion of political institutions, see W. F. Craven, *The Southern Colonies in the Seventeenth Century, 1607–1689* (1949), and David W. Jordan, *Foundations of Representative Government in Maryland, 1632–1715* (1988). Contrasting accounts of Bacon's Rebellion can be found in T. J. Wertenbaker, *Torchbearer of the Revolution* (1940), and Wilcomb B. Washburn, *The Governor and the Rebel* (1958).

Puritan New England

For the Puritan migration, see Edmund Morgan, *The Puritan Dilemma: The Story of John Winthrop* (1955); Sumner Chilton Powell, *Puritan Village: The Formation of a New England Town* (1963); David Grayson Allen, *In English Ways: The Movement of Societies and the Transferral of English Local Law and Custom to Massachusetts Bay in the Seventeenth Century* (1981); and David Cressy, *Coming Over: Migration and Communication between England and New England in the Seventeenth Century* (1987).

Puritanism as an intellectual movement is best explored in the works of Perry Miller; see especially *The New England Mind: The Seventeenth Century* (1939). Charles Hambrick-Stowe, *The Practice of Piety: Puritan Devotional Disciplines* (1982), discusses the emotional dimension of Puritanism, while David D. Hall, *World of Wonder, Days of Judgment: Popular Religious Belief in Early New England* (1989), explores its nonrational aspects. See also Andrew Delbanco, *The Puritan Ordeal* (1989).

For a discussion of dissent in early New England, consult Philip Gura, *A Glimpse of Sion's Glory: Puritan Radicalism in New England, 1620–1660* (1984); Edwin S. Gaustad, *Liberty of Conscience: Roger Williams in America* (1991); Amy Schrager Lang, *Prophetic Woman: Anne Hutchinson and the Problem of Dissent in the Literature of New England* (1987); Paul Boyer and Steven Nissenbaum, *Salem Possessed: The Social Origins of Witchcraft* (1974); Carol F. Karlsen, *The Devil in the Shape of a Woman: Witchcraft in New England* (1987); and David D. Hall, ed., *Witch Hunting in Seventeenth-Century New England: A Documentary History, 1632–1691* (1991).

Community studies that reveal the lives of ordinary New England men and women include John Demos, *The Little Commonwealth: Family Life in Plymouth Colony* (1971), and Kenneth A. Lockridge, *A New England Town . . . Dedham, Massachusetts, 1636–1736* (1970). See also John Demos, *The Unredeemed Captive: A Family Story from Early America* (1994).

The Indians' New World

James H. Merrell, *The Indians' New World: Catawbas and Their Neighbors from European Contact through the Era of Removal* (1989), is a pathbreaking study. Douglas Leach, *Flinthawk and Tomahawk: New England in King Philip's War* (1958), is the standard treatment of the conflict. See also Karen Ordahl Kupperman, *Settling with the Indians: The Meeting of English and Indian Cultures in America, 1580–1640* (1981); Bernard Sheehan, *Savagism and Civility: Indians and Englishmen in Colonial Virginia* (1980); and Daniel K. Richter and James H. Merrell, *Beyond the Covenant Chain: The Iroquois and Their Neighbors in Indian North America* (1987). Two illuminating ecological studies are Calvin Martin, *Keepers of the Game: Indian-Animal Relations and the Fur Trade* (1978), and William Cronon, *Changes in the Land: Indians, Colonists, and the Ecology of New England* (1983).

CHAPTER 3

The best short overview of England's empire is Michael Kammen, *Empire and Interest: The American Colonies and the Politics of Mercantilism* (1970), but see also Alison Olson, *Making the Empire Work: London and American Interest Groups, 1690–1790.* On Africa, see Paul Bohannan and Philip Curtin, *Africa and the Africans* (3d ed., 1988). For the mingling of cultures in Virginia, read Mechel Sobel, *The World They Made Together* (1987).

The Politics of Empire, 1660–1713

Robert Bliss, *Revolution and Empire: English Politics and the American Colonies in the Seventeenth Century* (1990), explores the impact of the Puritan Revolution, while Jack M. Sosin, *English America and the Restoration Monarchy of Charles II: Transatlantic Politics, Commerce, and Kinship* (1980), does the same for the restored king. See also Stephen S. Webb, *1676: The End of American Independence* (1984). For the events of 1688–1689, consult David S. Lovejoy, *The Glorious Revolution in America* (1972). A good case study is Lois Green Carr and David W. Jordan, *Maryland's Revolution of Government, 1689–1692* (1974). Ethnic tension in New York can be traced in Robert C. Ritchie, *The Duke's Province: Politics and Society in New York, 1660–1691* (1977); Thomas J. Archdeacon, *New York City, 1664–1710: Conquest and Change* (1976); Donna Merwick, *Possessing Albany, 1630–1710: The Dutch and English Experiences* (1990); and Joyce Goodfriend, *Before the Melting Pot: Society and Culture in Colonial New York City, 1664–1730* (1992). Jack M. Sosin, *English America and Imperial Inconstancy: The Rise of Provincial Autonomy, 1696–1715* (1985), outlines the new imperial system.

The Imperial Slave Economy

For the African background, see John Thornton, *Africa and Africans in the Making of the Atlantic World, 1400–1680* (1992), and Richard Olaniyan, *African History and Culture* (1982). Specialized studies of forced African migration include Philip Curtin, *The Atlantic Slave Trade: A Census* (1969); Paul Lovejoy, ed., *Africans in Bondage: Studies in Slavery and the Slave Trade* (1986); James A. Rawley, *The Transatlantic Slave Trade* (1981); Joseph E. Inikori and Stanley L. Engerman, eds., *The Atlantic Slave Trade* (1992); and Barbara L. Solow, ed., *Slavery and the Rise of the Atlantic System* (1991).

Richard S. Dunn, *Sugar and Slaves: The Rise of the Planter Class in the English West Indies, 1624–1713* (1972), provides a graphic portrait of the brutal slave-based economy, while Sidney W. Mintz, *Sweetness and Power: The Place of Sugar in Modern History* (1985), explores the impact of its major crop. Winthrop D. Jordan, *White over Black, 1550–1812* (1968), remains the best account of Virginia's decision for slavery, but see also Thomas D. Morris, *Southern Slavery and the Law, 1619–1860* (1996). T. H. Breen and Stephen Innes, *"Myne Owne Ground": Race and Freedom on Virginia's Eastern Shore, 1640–1676* (1980), closely examines the lives of the first Africans on Virginia's Eastern Shore. For the creation of African-American society, see Allan Kulikoff, *Tobacco and Slaves: Southern Cultures in the Chesapeake, 1680–1800* (1986); Daniel C. Littlefield, *Rice and Slaves: Ethnicity and the Slave Trade in Colonial South Carolina* (1981); Peter H. Wood, *Black Majority: Negroes in Colonial South Carolina through the Stono Rebellion* (1974); and Marvin L. Michael Kay and Lorin Lee Cary, *Slavery in North Carolina, 1748–1775* (1995). See also Richard Price, ed., *Maroon Societies: Rebel Slave*

Communities in the Americas (1973), and Ira Berlin and Philip D. Morgan, eds., *Cultivation and Culture: Labor and the Shaping of Slave Life in the Americas* (1992).

On white society in the South, read Daniel Blake Smith, *Inside the Great House: Planter Family Life in Eighteenth-Century Chesapeake Society* (1980); Rhys Isaac, *The Transformation of Virginia, 1740–1790* (1982); Timothy H. Breen, *Tobacco Culture* (1985); and a fine older study of political practices, Charles Sydnor, *American Revolutionaries in the Making* (1952). Urban society and trade are explored in Gary B. Nash, *The Urban Crucible* (1979); Gary M. Walton and James F. Shephard, *The Economic Rise of Early America* (1979); and Christine L. Heyrman, *Commerce and Culture: The Maritime Communities of Colonial Massachusetts, 1690–1750* (1984). See also Marcus Rediker, *Between the Devil and the Deep Blue Sea: Merchant Seamen, Pirates, and the Anglo-American Maritime World, 1700–1750* (1987).

The New Politics of Empire, 1713–1750

The appearance of a distinctive American polity is traced in Bernard Bailyn, *The Origins of American Politics* (1968). Studies of various colonies include Jack P. Greene, *The Quest for Power: The Lower Houses of Assembly in the Southern Royal Colonies, 1689–1776* (1963); Patricia U. Bonomi, *A Factious People: Politics and Society in Colonial New York* (1971); A. Roger Ekirch, *"Poor Carolina": Politics and Society in Colonial North Carolina, 1729–1776* (1981); and Richard Bushman, *King and People in Provincial Massachusetts* (1985). John Schutz, *William Shirley* (1961), shows how a competent colonial governor wielded power, while Thomas C. Barrow, *Trade and Empire: The British Customs Service in Colonial America, 1660–1775* (1967), and Alison G. Olson, *Anglo-American Politics, 1660–1775* (1973), explore various aspects of British mercantilism.

Douglas E. Leach, *Roots of Conflict: British Armed Forces and Colonial Americans, 1677–1763* (1986), and Howard H. Peckham, *The Colonial Wars, 1689–1762* (1964), cover the diplomatic and military conflicts of the period, but these Anglo-American perspectives should be balanced by David J. Weber, *The Spanish Frontier in North America* (1992).

CHAPTER 4

A fine collection of important articles can be found in Stanley Katz, John Murrin, and Douglas Greenberg, eds., *Colonial America: Essays in Politics and Social Development* (4th ed., 1993). John J. McCusker and Russell R. Menard, *The Economy of British America, 1607–1783* (1985), survey economic change, while Jon Butler, *Awash in a Sea of Faith: Christianizing the American People* (1990), covers religious developments. Jack P. Greene, *Pursuits of Happiness* (1988), offers a provocative comparative analysis of regional social evolution.

Freehold Society in New England

A good local study is Daniel Vickers, *Farmers & Fishermen: Two Centuries of Work in Essex County Massachusetts, 1630–1830* (1994), while Bruce C. Daniels, *The Fragmentation of New England: Comparative Perspectives on Economic, Political, and Social Divisions in the Eighteenth Century* (1988), and Allan Kulikoff, *The Agrarian Origins of American Capitalism* (1992), offer a wider view. See also Robert Gross, *The Minutemen and Their*

World (1976), and Richard Bushman, *From Puritan to Yankee: Character and the Social Order in Connecticut, 1690–1765* (1967). On women's lives, see Laurel Thatcher Ulrich, *Good Wives: Image and Reality in the Lives of Women of Northern New England, 1650–1750* (1982), and Marylynn Salmon, *Women and the Law of Property in Early America* (1986). For studies of material culture that reveal the character of society, see Robert B. St. George, ed., *Material Life in America, 1600–1860* (1988), and Cary Carson, et al., eds., *Of Consuming Interest* (1994).

The Mid-Atlantic: Toward a New Society, 1720–1765

On Pennsylvania, consult Michael Zuckerman, ed., *Friends and Neighbors: Group Life in America's First Plural Society* (1982), and Barry J. Levy, *Quakers and the American Family* (1988). James T. Lemon, *The Best Poor Man's Country* (1972), pays some attention to ethnicity, as does Marilyn J. Westerkamp, *Triumph of the Laity: Scots-Irish Piety and the Great Awakening, 1625–1760* (1988). On white indentured servants and ethnic migration, see the classic study by Abbot E. Smith, *Colonists in Bondage* (1947); A. G. Roeber, *Palatines, Liberty, and Property: German Lutherans in Colonial British America* (1993); R. J. Dickson, *Ulster Immigration to Colonial America, 1718–1775* (1966); Jon Butler, *The Huguenots in America* (1983); Ned Landsman, *Scotland and Its First American Colony, 1683–1775* (1985); and A. Roger Ekirch, *Bound for America: The Transportation of British Convicts to the Colonies, 1718–1775* (1987). Important studies on mid-Atlantic politics include Patricia U. Bonomi, *A Factious People: Politics and Society in Colonial New York* (1971); Thomas L. Purvis, *Proprietors, Patronage, and Money: New Jersey, 1703–1776* (1986); Alan Tully, *Forming American Politics* (1994); and Benjamin H. Newcomb, *Political Partisanship in the American Middle Colonies, 1700–1776* (1995).

The Enlightenment and the Great Awakening, 1740–1765

Henry F. May, *The Enlightenment in America* (1976), is still the standard treatment, but see also Paul Merrill Spurlin, *The French Enlightenment in America* (1984), and Herbert Leventhal, *In the Shadow of the Enlightenment: Occultism and Renaissance Science in Eighteenth-Century America* (1976). For medical knowledge, consult Richard Shryock, *Medicine and Society in America, 1660–1860* (1960). Brooke Hindle, *The Pursuit of Science in Revolutionary America, 1735–1789* (1956), and John C. Greene, *American Science in the Age of Jefferson* (1984), are also relevant.

Good studies of the Great Awakening include David S. Lovejoy, *Religious Enthusiasm in the New World: Heresy to Revolution* (1985); Patricia U. Bonomi, *Under the Cope of Heaven: Religion, Society, and Politics in Colonial America* (1986); and Harry S. Stout, *The New England Soul: Preaching and Religious Culture in Colonial New England* (1986). Three good biographies of New England revivalists are Patricia Tracy, *Jonathan Edwards, Pastor* (1979); W. G. McLoughlin, *Isaac Backus and American Pietistic Tradition* (1957); and Christopher Jedrey, *The World of John Cleaveland* (1979). Harry Stout, *The Divine Dramatist* (1991), is a biography of George Whitefield. Richard Bushman, ed., *The Great Awakening* (1970), and Rhys Isaac, *The Transformation of Virginia, 1740–1790* (1982), capture the emotions of ordinary participants. William L. Joyce et al., eds., *Printing and Society in Early America* (1983), assesses the impact of books, pamphlets, and newspapers on the American mind.

The Midcentury Challenge: War, Trade, and Land, 1750–1765

Douglas E. Leach, *Roots of Conflict: British Armed Forces and Colonial Americans, 1677–1763* (1986), sets the Great War for Empire in a larger context. See also Edward P. Hamilton, *The French and Indian Wars* (1962); Guy Fregault, *Canada: The War of the Conquest* (1969); George F. G. Stanley, *New France: The Last Phase, 1744–1760* (1968); and Fred Anderson, *A People's Army: Massachusetts Soldiers and Society in the Seven Years' War* (1984). Richard White, *The Middle Ground* (1991), and Francis Jennings, *Empire of Fortune: Crown, Colonies, and Tribes in the Seven Years' War* (1988), describe the crucial role played by Indians in the conflict. See also Richard Aquila, *The Iroquois Restoration: Iroquois Diplomacy on the Colonial Frontier, 1701–1754* (1983), and David H. Corkran, *The Cherokee Frontier: Conflict and Survival, 1740–1762* (1966).

Gary M. Walton and James F. Shepherd, *The Economic Rise of Early America* (1979), trace the growing importance of commerce. See also Paul G. E. Clemens, *The Atlantic Economy and Colonial Maryland's Eastern Shore: From Tobacco to Grain* (1980).

Backcountry political agitation forms the focus of Richard D. Brown, *The South Carolina Regulators* (1963), and some of the essays in Alfred Young, ed., *The American Revolution: Essays in the History of American Radicalism* (1976). See also W. Stitt Robinson, *The Southern Colonial Frontier, 1607–1763* (1979); Richard Beeman, *The Evolution of the Southern Backcountry* (1984); and Rachel N. Klein, *Unification of a Slave State: The Rise of the Planter Class in the South Carolina Backcountry, 1660–1808* (1994).

CHAPTER 5

Jack P. Greene and J. R. Pole, eds., *The Blackwell Encyclopedia of the American Revolution* (1991), illuminates both obscure and well-known aspects of the Revolutionary Era. A good interpretive synthesis is Edward Countryman, *The American Revolution* (1985).

The Reform Movement, 1763–1765

For the state of the empire in 1763, see Alison Gilbert Olson, *Making the Empire Work: London and the American Interest Groups, 1690–1790* (1992), and Jack P. Greene, *Peripheries and Center: Constitutional Development . . .1607–1788* (1986). The impact of the Seven Years' War is traced in the classic study by Lawrence H. Gipson, *The Coming of the Revolution, 1763–1775* (1954), and in the following works: Richard Middleton, *The Bells of Victory: The Pitt-Newcastle Ministry and the Conduct of the Seven Years' War, 1757–1762* (1985); Alan Rogers, *Empire and Liberty: American Resistance to British Authority, 1755–1763* (1974); Howard H. Peckham, *Pontiac and the Indian Uprising* (1947); and Joseph A. Ernst, *Money and Politics in America, 1755–1775* (1973). Marc Egnal, *A Mighty Empire: The Origins of the Revolution* (1988), provides an interpretive synthesis.

British politics and imperial reform can be traced in John Brewer, *Party Ideology and Popular Politics at the Accession of George III* (1976); P. D. G. Thomas, *British Politics and the Stamp Act Crisis . . . 1763–1767* (1975); Thomas C. Barrow, *Trade and Empire: The British Customs Service in Colonial America, 1660–1775* (1967); John L. Bullion, *A Great and Necessary Measure: George Grenville and the Genesis of the Stamp Act, 1763–1765* (1982); Carl Ubbelohde, *The Vice-Admiralty Courts and the American Revolution* (1960); and Philip Lawson, *George Grenville* (1984).

The Dynamics of Rebellion, 1765–1766

For the American response to the British reform laws, see Edmund S. Morgan and Helen M. Morgan, *The Stamp Act Crisis* (1963); Pauline Maier, *From Resistance to Revolution . . . 1765–1776* (1972); and Gary B. Nash, *The Urban Crucible: Social Change, Political Consciousness, and the Origins of the American Revolution* (1979). Merrill Jensen, *The Founding of a Nation . . . 1763–1776* (1968), and Robert Middlekauff, *The Glorious Cause: The American Revolution, 1763–1789* (1982), provide detailed narratives of the struggle.

Studies of individual colonies capture the spirit of the resistance movement. See Paul A. Gilje, *The Road to Mobocracy: Popular Disorder in New York City, 1763–1834* (1986); David Lovejoy, *Rhode Island Politics and the American Revolution* (1958); and Ronald Hoffman, *A Spirit of Dissension: Economics, Politics, and the Revolution in Maryland* (1973). The motives of Patriots are best addressed through biographies. See Francis Jennings, *Benjamin Franklin, Politician* (1996); Pauline Maier, *The Old Revolutionaries: Political Lives in the Age of Samuel Adams* (1980); Milton E. Flower, *John Dickinson, Conservative Revolutionary* (1983); Richard R. Beeman, *Patrick Henry: A Biography* (1974); John R. Alden, *George Washington: A Biography* (1984); Helen Hill Miller, *George Mason: Gentleman Revolutionary* (1975); and Page Smith, *John Adams* (1962).

The most important single study of Patriot ideology is Bernard Bailyn, *The Ideological Origins of the American Revolution* (1967), but see also Robert M. Calhoon, *Dominion and Liberty: Ideology in Anglo-American Political Thought, 1660–1801* (1994). Other works include Caroline Robbins, *The Eighteenth-Century Commonwealthman* (1959); Morton White, *The Philosophy of the American Revolution* (1978); Garry Wills, *Inventing America: Jefferson's Declaration of Independence* (1978); and H. T. Dickinson, *Liberty and Property: Political Ideology in Eighteenth-Century Britain* (1978). For a discussion of the legal tradition, see Charles H. McIlwain, *The American Revolution: A Constitutional Interpretation* (1923), and the various volumes of John Phillip Reid's *Constitutional History of the American Revolution* (1986–1996).

The Growing Confrontation, 1767–1770

Peter D. G. Thomas, *The Townshend Duties Crisis . . . 1767–1773* (1987), is the most comprehensive treatment, but see also Colin Bonwick, *English Radicals and the American Revolution* (1977), and Ian R. Christie and Benjamin W. Labaree, *Empire or Independence, 1760–1776* (1976). On American resistance, consult Richard Alan Ryerson, *The Revolution Is Now Begun: The Radical Committees of Philadelphia, 1765–1776* (1978); Peter Shaw, *American Patriots and the Rituals of Revolution* (1981); and Stanley Godbold, Jr., and Robert W. Woody, *Christopher Gadsden* (1982). The confrontation between Patriots and British authority is covered in John Shy, *Toward Lexington: The Role of the British Army in the Coming of the American Revolution* (1965), and Hiller B. Zobel, *The Boston Massacre* (1970).

The Road to War, 1771–1775

Benjamin Labaree, *The Boston Tea Party* (1964), is comprehensive and stimulating and can be supplemented by Peter D. G. Thomas, *Tea Party to Independence* (1991); Bernard Donoughue, *British Politics and the American Revolution: The Path to War, 1773–75*

(1972); and David Ammerman, *In the Common Cause: American Response to the Coercive Acts of 1774* (1968). A fine study of the resistance movement is Edward F. Countryman, *A People in Revolution: The American Revolution and Political Society in New York* (1983). On prewar Loyalism, see Bernard Bailyn, *The Ordeal of Thomas Hutchinson* (1974), and Janice Potter, *The Liberty We Seek: Loyalist Ideology in Colonial New York and Massachusetts* (1983). For the rising of the countryside, see David Hackett Fischer, *Paul Revere's Ride* (1994); Gregory H. Nobles, *Divisions throughout the Whole: Politics and Society in Hampshire County, Massachusetts, 1740–1775* (1983); Jere R. Daniell, *Experiment in Republicanism: New Hampshire Politics and the Revolution, 1741–1790* (1970); and Richard Bushman, *King and People in Provincial Massachusetts* (1985). The transfer of authority is described in Jerrilyn Greene Marston, *King and Congress: The Transfer of Political Legitimacy, 1774–1776* (1987).

CHAPTER 6

Gordon Wood, *The Radicalism of the American Revolution* (1992), offers a fine overview. For a contrasting interpretation, see the essays in Alfred F. Young, ed., *Beyond the American Revolution: Explorations in the History of American Radicalism* (1993).

Toward Independence, 1775–1776

Jerrilyn Green Marston, *King and Congress: The Transfer of Political Legitimacy, 1774–1776* (1987), and Jack N. Rakove, *The Beginnings of National Politics* (1979), discuss the movement toward independence. See also Eric Foner, *Tom Paine and Revolutionary America* (1976); Jack Fruchtman, Jr., *Thomas Paine: Apostle of Freedom* (1994); and Pauline Maier, *American Scripture: Making the Declaration of Independence* (1997). On Loyalism, read William N. Nelson, *The American Tory* (1961); Robert M. Calhoon et al., *The Loyalist Perception* (1989); and the essays collected in Robert M. Calhoon, Timothy M. Barnes, and George A. Rawlyk, eds., *Loyalists and Community in North America* (1994).

The Perils of War and Finance, 1776–1778

The military history of the war is covered in James L. Stokesbury, *A Short History of the American Revolution* (1991), and Piers Mackesy, *The War for America, 1775–1783* (1964). Don Higginbotham, *George Washington and the American Military Tradition* (1985), and Ronald Hoffman and Peter Albert, eds., *Arms and Independence: The Military Character of the American Revolution* (1984), offer a more analytic perspective. The war in the North can be followed in Ira D. Gruber, *The Howe Brothers and the American Revolution* (1972), and Richard J. Hargrove, Jr., *General John Burgoyne* (1983).

Studies of ordinary soldiers include Rodney Attwood, *The Hessians* (1980); Sylvia R. Frey, *The British Soldier in America* (1981); Robert K. Wright, Jr., *The Continental Army* (1983); Charles P. Neimeyer, *America Goes to War: A Social History of the Continental Army* (1996); and John C. Dann, ed., *The Revolution Remembered: Eyewitness Accounts of the War for Independence* (1980). For the military bureaucracy, see R. Arthur Bowler, *Logistics and the Failure of the British Army in America, 1775–1783* (1975), and E. Wayne Carp, *To Starve the Army at Pleasure: Continental Army Administration and American Political Culture, 1775–1783* (1984).

Local studies include Jean Butenhoff Lee, *The Price of Nationhood: The American Revolution in Charles County* (1994); David Hackett Fischer, *Paul Revere's Ride* (1994); Robert Gross, *The Minutemen and Their World* (1976); Richard Buel, Jr., *Dear Liberty: Connecticut's Mobilization for the Revolutionary War* (1980); and Donald Wallace White, *A Village at War: Chatham, New Jersey, and the American Revolution* (1979).

African–American participation in the war is discussed by Gary A. Puckrein, *The Black Regiment in the American Revolution* (1978); Sidney Kaplan, *The Black Presence in the Era of the American Revolution* (rev. ed., 1989); and Gary B. Nash, *Race and Revolution* (1990).

The native American response is described in Barbara Graymont, *The Iroquois in the American Revolution* (1972); Isabel T. Kelsey, *Joseph Brant, 1743–1807* (1984); and James H. O'Donnell III, *Southern Indians in the American Revolution* (1973).

Two classic discussions of the fiscal problems created by the war are E. James Ferguson, *The Power of the Purse: A History of American Public Finance: 1776–1790* (1961), and Clarence L. Ver Steeg, *Robert Morris, Revolutionary Financier* (1954). A more recent study is William G. Anderson, *The Price of Liberty: The Public Debt of the American Revolution* (1983).

The Path to Victory, 1778–1783

Bradford Perkins, *The Creation of a Republican Empire, 1776–1865* (1993), and Jonathan R. Dull, *A Diplomatic History of the American Revolution* (1985), provide good overviews. More specialized studies include James H. Hutson, *John Adams and the Diplomacy of the American Revolution* (1980); Richard B. Morris, *The Peacemakers: The Great Powers and American Independence* (1965); and Ronald Hoffman and Peter Albert, eds., *Peace and the Peacemakers: The Treaty of 1783* (1986).

For the southern campaign, consult W. Robert Higgins, ed., *The Revolutionary War in the South* (1979); Ronald Hoffman, Thad W. Tate, and Peter J. Albert, eds., *An Uncivil War: The Southern Backcountry during the American Revolution* (1985); and Jeffrey J. Crow and Larry E. Tise, eds., *The Southern Experience in the American Revolution* (1978). Studies of military action include Hugh F. Rankin, *Francis Marion: The Swamp Fox* (1973), and John S. Pancake, *The Destructive War, 1780–1782* (1985).

Republicanism Defined and Challenged

Milton M. Klein et al., *The Republican Synthesis Revisited* (1992), explores the debate over the importance of republican thought. See also Charles Royster, *A Revolutionary People at War: The Continental Army and American Character, 1775–1783* (1979). On women's lives, see Ronald Hoffman and Peter J. Albert, eds., *Women in the Age of the American Revolution* (1989); Mary Beth Norton, *Liberty's Daughters: The Revolutionary Experience of American Women, 1750–1800* (1980); Lynn Withey, *Dearest Friend: A Life of Abigail Adams* (1980); and Joy Day Buel and Richard Buel, Jr., *The Way of Duty: A Woman and Her Family in Revolutionary America* (1984).

On the black experience, consult Sylvia R. Frey, *Water from the Rock: Black Resistance in a Revolutionary Age* (1991); Ira Berlin and Ronald Hoffman, eds., *Slavery and Freedom in the Age of the American Revolution* (1983); Gary B. Nash, *Forging Freedom: The Formation of Philadelphia's Black Community, 1720–1840* (1988); and David Brion Davis, *The Problem of Slavery in the Age of Revolution, 1770–1823* (1975). See also James W. St. G. Walker, *The Black Loyalists: The Search for a Promised Land in Nova Scotia and*

Sierra Leone, 1783–1870 (1976), and Shane White, *Somewhat More Independent:The End of Slavery in New York City, 1770–1810* (1991).

On changes in American religion, see Ronald Hoffman and Peter J. Albert, eds., *Religion in a Revolutionary Age* (1994); Rhys Isaac, *The Transformation of Virginia, 1740–1790* (1982); Fred Hood, *Reformed America 1783–1837* (1980); and Nathan O. Hatch, *The Democratization of American Christianity* (1989).The spiritual roots of a new secular religion are traced by Catharine Albanese, *Sons of the Fathers:The Civil Religion of the American Revolution* (1976), and Ruth Bloch, *Visionary Republic: Millennial Themes in American Thought* (1985).

CHAPTER 7

Jack N. Rakove, *Original Meaning: Politics and Ideas in the Making of the Constitution* (1996), and Richard B. Bernstein and Kym S. Rice, *Are We to Be a Nation? The Making of the Constitution* (1987), are the best recent overviews, while Stanley Elkins and Eric McKitrick, *The Age of Federalism:The Early Republic, 1788–1800* (1993), offers a comprehensive assessment of the 1790s.

Creating New Institutions, 1776–1789

Elisha P. Douglass, *Rebels and Democrats* (1965), documents the struggle for equal political rights. See also Jackson T. Main, *The Sovereign States, 1775–1783* (1973), and Ronald L. Hoffman and Peter Albert, eds., *Sovereign States in an Age of Uncertainty* (1981). Important studies of state constitutions include Willi Paul Adams, *The First American Constitutions* (1980); Edward Countryman, *A People in Revolution:The American Revolution and Political Society in New York, 1760–1790* (1981); Donald Lutz, *Popular Consent and Popular Control:Whig Political Theory in the Early State Constitutions* (1980); and J. R. Pole, *Political Representation in England and the Origins of the American Republic* (1966).

On women and republicanism, see Linda K. Kerber, *Women of the Republic* (1980), and Ronald Hoffman and Peter Albert, eds., *Women in the Age of the American Revolution* (1989). Fine in-depth studies include Rosemarie Zagarri, *A Woman's Dilemma: Mercy Otis Warren and the American Revolution* (1995); Judith Sargent Murray, *The Gleaner*, ed. by Nina Baym (1992); and Lynn Withey, *Dearest Friend: A Life of Abigail Adams* (1982).

Gordon Wood, *The Creation of the American Republic, 1776–1790* (1965), links state and national constitutional development. Other important works on the 1780s include Peter S. Onuf, *The Origins of the Federal Republic:Jurisdictional Controversies in the United States, 1775–1787* (1983); Roger H. Brown, *Redeeming the Republic: Federalists, Taxation, and the Origins of the Constitution* (1993); Richard B. Morris, *The Forging of the Union, 1781–1789* (1987); and Robert A. Gross, ed., *In Debt to Shays* (1993).

The Constitution of 1787

In 1913 two studies initiated the modern analysis of the Constitution: Charles A. Beard, *An Economic Interpretation of the Constitution of the United States*, and Max Farrand, *The Framing of the Constitution*. For critiques of Beard's work, see Leonard Levy, ed., *Essays on the Making of the Constitution* (rev. ed., 1987); for an update of Farrand, read Christopher Collier and James L. Collier, *Decision in Philadelphia* (1987).

Other significant works include Forrest McDonald, *Novus Ordo Seculorum: The Intellectual Origins of the Constitution* (1985); Edmund S. Morgan, *Inventing the People: The Rise of Popular Sovereignty in England and America* (1988); and Michael Kammen, *A Machine That Would Go by Itself: The Constitution in American Culture* (1986). Three fine collections of essays are Richard R. Beeman et al., eds., *Beyond Confederation: Origins of the Constitution* . . . (1987); Ellen Frankel Paul and Howard Dickman, eds., *Liberty, Property and the Foundations of the American Constitution* (1989); and Herman Belz et al., eds., *To Form a More Perfect Union: The Critical Ideas of the Constitution* (1992).

On the Antifederalists and ratification, see Patrick T. Conley and John P. Kaminiski, eds., *The Constitution and the States* (1988); Stephen L. Schechter, *The Reluctant Pillar: New York and the Adoption of the Federal Constitution* (1985); and Herbert Storing, *The Antifederalists* (1985). Two recent studies of the Federalist papers are David F. Epstein, *The Political Theory of "The Federalist"* (1984), and Charles R. Kesler, ed., *Saving the Revolution* (1987).

R. A. Rutland, *The Birth of the Bill of Rights, 1776–1791* (rev. ed., 1983), offers the basic narrative; more analytic treatments include Michael J. Lacey and Knud Haakonssen, *A Culture of Rights* (1991); David J. Bodenhemer and James W. Ely, Jr., *The Bill of Rights in Modern America* (1993); and Joyce Lee Malcolm, *To Keep and Bear Arms: The Origins of an Anglo-American Right* (1993).

The Political Crisis of the 1790s

A good synthesis is James Rogers Sharp, *American Politics in the Early Republic: The New Nation in Crisis* (1993). Studies of important statesmen include Forrest McDonald, *Alexander Hamilton: A Biography* (1979), and James T. Flexner, *George Washington and the New Nation, 1783–1793* (1970) and *George Washington: Anguish and Farewell, 1793–1799* (1972). For Jeffersonian ideology, see Joyce Appleby, *Capitalism and a New Social Order: The Republican Vision of the 1790s* (1984); Drew McCoy, *The Elusive Republic: Political Economy in Jeffersonian America* (1982); Lance Banning, *The Jeffersonian Persuasion: The Evolution of a Party Ideology* (1978); and John R. Nelson, Jr., *Liberty and Property: Political Economy and Policymaking in the New Nation, 1789–1812* (1987).

Richard Hofstadter, *The Idea of a Party System: The Rise of Legitimate Opposition in the United States, 1790–1840* (1969), offers an overview of the subject; see also John F. Hoadley, *Origins of American Political Parties, 1789–1803* (1986). More detailed studies are Thomas P. Slaughter, *The Whiskey Rebellion* (1986), and Richard J. Twomey, *Jacobins and Jeffersonians* (1989). On diplomatic and military history, consult Henry Ammon, *The Genêt Mission* (1973); Jerald A. Combs, *The Jay Treaty* (1970); Richard H. Kohn, *Eagle and Sword* (1975); and Lawrence D. Cress, *Citizens in Arms: The Army and the Military to the War of 1812* (1982).

On Adams's administration, see Ralph Brown Adams, *The Presidency of John Adams* (1975). More specialized studies are William Sinchcombe, *The XYZ Affair* (1980); Leonard Levy, *The Emergence of a Free Press* (1985); and James M. Smith, *Freedom's Fetters: The Alien and Sedition Laws and American Civil Liberties* (rev. ed., 1966).

Good state histories include Patricia Watlington, *The Partisan Spirit: Kentucky Politics, 1779–1792* (1972); Richard R. Beeman, *The Old Dominion and the New Nation, 1788–1801* (1972); and Mary K. Bonsteel Tachau, *Federal Courts in the Early Republic: Kentucky, 1789–1816* (1978).

CHAPTER 8

Gregory Evans Dowd, *A Spirited Resistance: The North American Indian Struggle for Unity, 1745–1815* (1992), presents a fine survey of the Indian peoples, while Donald R. Wright, *African-Americans in the Early Republic, 1789–1831* (1993), provides a good overview of the black population. Donald R. Hickey, *The War of 1812: A Forgotten Conflict* (1989), puts the war in an economic and diplomatic context.

Westward Expansion

For studies of white policy toward native Americans, see Bernard Sheehan, *Seeds of Extinction: Jeffersonian Philanthropy and the American Indian* (1973); Reginald Horsman, *Expansion and American Indian Policy, 1783–1812* (1967); Dorothy Jones, *License for Empire: Colonialism by Treaty in Early America* (1982); and Richard Slotkin, *Regeneration through Violence: The Mythology of the American Frontier* (1973). Works dealing with the impact of Christian missions include Henry Warner Bowden, *American Indians and Christian Missions: Studies in Cultural Conflict* (1981); William W. Fitzhugh, ed., *Cultures in Contact* (1985); William G. McLoughlin, *Cherokees and Missionaries, 1789–1839* (1984); and Earl P. Olmstead, *Blackcoats among the Delaware* (1991). Other analyses of cultural interaction are William G. McLoughlin, *Cherokee Renascence in the New Republic* (1986); J. Leitch Wright, Jr., *Creeks and Seminoles: The Destruction and Regeneration of the Muscogulge People* (1986); Katherine E. H. Braund, *Deerskins and Duffels* (1993); and John Mack Faragher, *Daniel Boone* (1992).

Two fine accounts of settlers and speculators are Alan Taylor, *Liberty Men and Great Proprietors . . . on the Maine Frontier, 1760–1820* (1990) and *William Cooper's Town* (1995). For developments west of the mountains, see Malcolm J. Rohrbough, *The Transappalachian Frontier: Peoples, Societies, and Institutions, 1775–1850* (1978), and John Mack Faragher, *Sugar Creek: Life on the Illinois Prairie* (1986).

Republican Policy and Diplomacy

Two good general accounts are Marshall Smelser, *The Democratic Republic, 1801–1815* (1968), and Ralph Ketcham, *Presidents above Party: The First American Presidency, 1789–1829* (1984). Detailed studies of Jefferson's presidency include Daniel Sisson, *The Revolution of 1800* (1974); Dumas Malone, *Jefferson the President* (2 vols., 1970 and 1974); and Richard E. Ellis, *The Jeffersonian Crisis: Courts and Politics in the New Republic* (1971). For the Louisiana Purchase, see Stephen E. Ambrose, *Undaunted Courage: Meriwether Lewis, Thomas Jefferson, and the Opening of the American West* (1996); Donald Jackson, *The Letters of the Lewis and Clark Expedition* (1963); and James P. Ronda, *Lewis and Clark among the Indians* (1984).

The activities of Aaron Burr are covered in Milton Lomask, *Aaron Burr* (1979), while the Federalists are discussed in David Hackett Fischer, *The Revolution of American Conservatism: The Federalist Party in the Age of Jeffersonian Democracy* (1965); Linda K. Kerber, *Federalists in Dissent: Imagery and Ideology in Jeffersonian America* (1970); and James Banner, *To the Hartford Convention: The Federalists and the Origins of Party Politics in the Early Republic, 1789–1815* (1970).

American attempts to avoid involvement in the Napoleonic Wars are traced in Lawrence Kaplan, *"Entangling Alliances with None": American Foreign Policy in the Age of Jefferson* (1987), and Bradford Perkins, *The First Rapprochement: England and the United*

States, 1795–1805 (1967) and *Prologue to War: England and the United States, 1805–1812* (1963). See also Clifford L. Egan, *Neither Peace nor War: Franco-American Relations, 1803–1812* (1983), and Doron S. Ben-Atar, *The Origins of Jeffersonian Commercial Policy and Diplomacy* (1993). On Madison, see Robert A. Rutland, *The Presidency of James Madison* (1990); J. C. A. Stagg, *Mr. Madison's War: Politics, Diplomacy, and Warfare in the Early Republic, 1783–1830* (1983); and Drew McCoy, *The Last of the Fathers: James Madison and the Republican Legacy* (1989). Native American involvement in the war is discussed by R. David Edmunds, *The Shawnee Prophet* (1983) and *Tecumseh and the Quest for Indian Leadership* (1984), as well as by H. S. Halbert and T. H. Ball, *The Creek War of 1813 and 1814* (1970).

Regional Diversity and National Identity

For life in the northern seaboard states, see Benjamin W. Labaree, *The Merchants of Newburyport, 1764–1815* (1962), and Sean Wilentz, *Chants Democratic: New York City and the Rise of the American Working Class, 1788–1850* (1984). The essays in R. A. Burchell, ed., *The End of Anglo-America* (1991), document various shifts in cultural identity.

A sophisticated analysis of the Old Northwest is Andrew R. L. Cayton and Peter S. Onuf, *The Midwest and the Nation* (1990). More detailed studies include Richard C. Wade, *The Urban Frontier: The Rise of Western Cities, 1790–1840* (1973), and Andrew Cayton, *The Frontier Republic: Ideology and Politics in the Ohio Country, 1789–1812* (1986).

Peter Kolchin, *American Slavery, 1619–1877* (1993), provides a fine overview. On the expansion of slavery, see Ira Berlin and Ronald Hoffman, eds., *Slavery and Freedom in the Age of the American Revolution* (1983); Donald L. Robinson, *Slavery in the Structure of American Politics, 1765–1820* (1971); and Albert Raboteau, *Slave Religion* (1968). Also see Ira Berlin and Philip D. Morgan, eds., *Cultivation and Culture: Labor and the Shaping of Slave Life* (1993), and Dena J. Epstein, *Sinful Tunes and Spirituals: Black Folk Music to the Civil War* (1977). Two good studies of the Carolina region are Joyce E. Chaplin, *Agricultural Innovation and Modernity in the Lower South, 1730–1815* (1993), and Peter A. Coclanis, *The Shadow of a Dream: Economic Life and Death in the South Carolina Low Country, 1670–1920* (1988).

For blacks in the northern states, see Gary B. Nash, *Forging Freedom: Philadelphia's Black Community, 1720–1840* (1988). Glover Moore, *The Missouri Compromise* (1953), provides a detailed analysis of that crisis. See also Merton L. Dillon, *Slavery Attacked: Southern Slaves and Their Allies, 1619–1865* (1990).

Spain's quest for empire is covered in David Weber, *The Spanish Frontier in North America* (1992), while American initiatives are the subject of Walter LaFeber, ed., *John Quincy Adams and American Continental Empire* (1965); Ernest May, *The Making of the Monroe Doctrine* (1976); and Henry Ammon, *James Monroe: The Quest for National Identity* (1971).

CHAPTER 9

Three fine local studies—Alan Taylor, *William Cooper's Town: Power and Persuasion on the Frontier of the Early American Republic* (1995); Christopher Clark, *The Roots of Rural Capitalism* (1990); and Laurel Thatcher Ulrich, *A Midwife's Tale: The Life of Martha Ballard*

(1990)—capture the texture of life in the early republic. Nathan O. Hatch, *The Democratization of American Christianity* (1987), offers an interpretation of religious change.

Political Economy: The Capitalist Commonwealth

Thomas Doerflinger, *A Vigorous Spirit of Enterprise: Merchants and Economic Development in Revolutionary Philadelphia* (1986); John Denis Haeger, *John Jacob Astor* (1991); and Stuart Bruchey, *Robert Oliver: Merchant of Baltimore* (1956), are fine studies of merchant enterprise. The standard history is Curtis R. Nettels, *The Emergence of a National Economy, 1775–1815* (1965). See also Ronald Hoffman, John J. McCusker, and Peter Albert, eds., *The Economy of Revolutionary America* (1987), and Daniel P. Jones, *The Economic and Social Transformation of Rhode Island, 1780–1850* (1992).

On banking, consult the classic study by Bray Hammond, *Banks and Politics in America* (1957), and Richard H. Timberlake, *Monetary Policy in the United States* (1992). Studies of manufacturing include Thomas C. Cochran, *Frontiers of Change: Early Industrialism in America* (1981); David Jeremy, *Transatlantic Industrial Revolution: The Diffusion of Textile Technology* . . . (1981); and Judith A. McGaw, *Early American Technology* (1994).

The classic studies of state mercantilism are Oscar and Mary Handlin, *Commonwealth: A Study of the Role of Government in the American Economy: Massachusetts, 1774–1861* (1947), and Louis Hartz, *Economic Policy and Democratic Thought: Pennsylvania, 1776–1860* (1948). State support for transportation can be traced in Carter Goodrich, *Government Promotion of American Canals and Railroads* (1960); Erik F. Hiates et al., *Western River Transportation: The Era of Early Internal Development, 1810–1860* (1975); and Harry N. Scheiber, *Ohio Canal Era: A Case Study of Government and the Economy* (1969).

The legal implications of commonwealth ideology are analyzed in Leonard Levy, *The Law of the Commonwealth and Chief Justice Shaw* (1955), and Morton Horwitz, *The Transformation of American Law, 1790–1860* (1976). R. Kent Newmyer, *The Supreme Court under Marshall and Taney* (1968), offers a concise treatment. See also Robert K. Faulkner, *The Jurisprudence of John Marshall* (1968); Francis N. Stites, *John Marshall: Defender of the Constitution* (1981); and Thomas C. Shevory, ed., *John Marshall's Achievement* (1989). A fine case study is C. Peter McGrath, *Yazoo: Law and Politics in the New Republic* (1966). William R. Casto, *The Supreme Court in the Early Republic: The Chief Justiceships of John Jay and Oliver Ellsworth* (1995), looks at the pre-Marshall court.

Visions of a Republican Social Order

Warren S. Tryon, *A Mirror for Americans: Life and Manners in the United States, 1790–1870, as Recorded by European Travelers* (3 vols., 1952), suggests the distinctive features of republican society. Clement Eaton, *Henry Clay and the Art of American Politics* (1957), perceptively describes the coming of political democracy. More detailed studies are Ronald Formisano, *The Transformation of Political Culture: Massachusetts Parties, 1790s–1840s* (1983), and Chilton Williamson, *American Suffrage from Property to Democracy* (1960).

Michael Grossberg, *Governing the Hearth* (1985), discusses changing marriage rules. Catherine M. Scholten, *Childrearing in American Society, 1650–1850* (1985), should be supplemented by Philip Greven's pathbreaking analysis, *The Protestant Temperament: Patterns of Childrearing, Religious Experience, and the Self in Early America*

(1977). On sentimentalism, see Shirley Samuels, *The Culture of Sentiment: Race, Gender and Sentimentality in Nineteenth Century America* (1992). Other important works include Daniel Blake Smith, *Inside the Great House: Planter Family Life in Eighteenth-Century Chesapeake Society* (1980); Bernard Wishy, *The Child and the Republic* (1970); and Jan Lewis, *The Pursuit of Happiness: Family and Values in Jefferson's Virginia* (1983).

Protestant Christianity and Women's Lives

Perry Miller, *The Life of the Mind in America* (1966), offers a good overview of the Second Great Awakening. For revivalism, see Stephen A. Marini, *Radical Sects of Revolutionary New England* (1982); Bernard A. Weisberger, *They Gathered at the River* (1958); Jon Butler, *Awash in a Sea of Faith* (1989); P. Jeffrey Potash, *Vermont's Burned Over District* (1991); and Ian H. Murray, *Revival and Revivalism: The Making and Marring of American Evangelicalism, 1750–1858* (1994). The course of religious thought in New England is traced in Daniel Walker Howe, *The Unitarian Conscience* (1970).

Some of the many recent studies touching on evangelical religion include Christine L. Heyrman, *Southern Cross: The Beginnings of the Bible Belt* (1997); Diana Hockstedt Butler, *Standing against the Whirlwind: Evangelical Episcopalians in Nineteenth-Century America* (1995); Randy J. Sparks, *On Jordan's Stormy Banks: Evangelicalism in Mississippi, 1773–1876* (1994); and John G. West, Jr., *The Politics of Revelation and Reason: Religion and Civic Life in the New Nation* (1996).

For women's lives, see Susan Juster, *Disorderly Women: Sexual Politics and Evangelicalism in Revolutionary New England* (1994); Harriet B. Applewhite and Darline G. Levy, eds., *Women and Politics in the Age of Democratic Revolution* (1990); and Linda Kerber, *Women of the Republic: Intellect and Ideology in Revolutionary America* (1980). Specialized studies include Joan M. Jensen, *Loosening the Bonds: Mid-Atlantic Farm Women, 1750–1850* (1986); Nancy F. Cott, *The Bonds of Womanhood: "Women's Sphere" in New England, 1780–1835* (1977); and Jeanne Boydston, *Home and Work* (1990).

Women's religious initiatives are discussed in Mary P. Ryan, *Cradle of the Middle Class* (1981); Barbara Epstein, *The Politics of Domesticity: Women, Evangelism, and Temperance* (1978); and Keith Melder, *Beginnings of Sisterhood: The American Women's Rights Movement, 1800–1850* (1977), which also traces the growth of female academies.

CHAPTER 10

Two important studies of American economic transformation are Stuart Bruchey, *Enterprise: The Dynamic Economy of a Free People* (1990), and Charles G. Sellers, Jr., *The Market Revolution: Jacksonian America, 1815–1840* (1991).

The Coming of Industry: Northeastern Manufacturing

Surveys of the broad economic setting and impact of the Industrial Revolution include W. Elliot Brownlee, *Dynamics of Ascent: A History of the American Economy* (1979); Thomas C. Cochran, *Frontiers of Change: Early Industrialism in America* (1981); and Douglass C. North, *The Economic Growth of the United States, 1790–1860* (1961). Another useful survey is the pioneering work in economic geography, Donald W. Meinig, *The Shaping of America: A Geographical Perspective*, Volume 2: *Continental America, 1800–1867* (1993).

Books on the role of technological change include Gary Cross and Rick Szostak, *Technology and American Society: A History* (1995); H. J. Habakkuk, *American and British Technology in the Nineteenth Century: The Search for Labour-Saving Inventions* (1962); David Freeman Hawke, *Nuts and Bolts of the Past: A History of American Technology, 1776–1860* (1988); Brooke Hindle and Steven Lubar, *Engines of Change: The American Industrial Revolution, 1790–1860* (1986); Donald K. Hoke, *Ingenious Yankees: The Rise of the American System of Manufactures in the Private Sector* (1990); David A. Hounshell, *From the American System to Mass Production, 1800–1932: The Development of Manufacturing Technology in the United States* (1984); Harold C. Livesay, *American Made: Men Who Shaped the American Economy* (1979); Judith A. McGaw, ed., *Early American Technology: Making and Doing Things from the Colonial Era to 1850* (1994); Nathan Rosenberg, *Perspectives on Technology* (1976); and Barbara M. Tucker, *Samuel Slater and the Origins of the American Textile Industry* (1984).

Stanley Lebergott, *Manpower in Economic Growth: The United States Record since 1800* (1964), provides a useful survey of the contribution of labor to the Industrial Revolution. Two in-depth studies of an important group of women workers are by Thomas Dublin, *Women at Work: The Transformation of Work and Community in Lowell, Massachusetts, 1826–1860* (1979) and *Transforming Women's Work: New England Lives in the Industrial Revolution* (1994). Regional studies of the early Industrial Revolution include Peter J. Coleman, *The Transformation of Rhode Island* (1963); Dianne Lindstrom, *Economic Development in the Philadelphia Region, 1810–1850* (1978); and Anthony F. C. Wallace, *Rockdale: The Growth of an American Village in the Early Industrial Revolution* (1978).

The Expansion of Markets

Urban development in this period is best explored in R. G. Albion, *The Rise of New York Port, 1815–1860* (1939); Eric E. Lampard, "The Evolving System of Cities in the United States: Urbanization and Economic Development," in *Issues in Urban Economics* (Harvey S. Perloff and Lowdon Wingo, Jr., eds., 1968); Richard C. Wade, *The Urban Frontier: Pioneer Life in Early Pittsburgh, Cincinnati, Lexington, Louisville, and St. Louis* (1964); and Alan R. Pred, *Urban Growth and the Circulation of Information: The United States System of Cities, 1790–1840* (1973). The best introductions to agricultural expansion in this period are Paul W. Gates, *The Farmer's Age: Agriculture, 1815–1860* (1960), and Lewis C. Gray, *History of Agriculture in the Southern United States to 1860* (1933). The classic history of the role of transportation is George R. Taylor, *The Transportation Revolution, 1815–1860* (1951). On the role of canals, consult Carter Goodrich et al., *Canals and American Economic Development* (1961); Ronald E. Shaw, *Canals for a Nation: The Canal Era in the United States, 1790–1860* (1990); Carol Sherrif, *The Artificial River: The Erie Canal and the Paradox of Progress, 1817–1862* (1996); and Peter Way, *Common Labour: Workers and the Digging of North American Canals* (1993). On the contribution of the law to the economic revolution, see Oscar Handlin and Mary Flug Handlin, *Commonwealth: A Study in the Role of Government in the American Economy, Massachusetts, 1774–1861* (1947); Morton J. Horwitz, *The Transformation of American Law, 1780–1860* (1977); James Willard Hurst, *Law and the Conditions of Freedom in the Nineteenth-Century United States* (1964); and Christopher L. Tomlins, *Law, Labor and Ideology in the Early American Republic* (1993).

A Changing Social Structure

The following works provide a good introduction to the study of the distribution of wealth and income in the early nineteenth century: Frederic C. Jaher, *The Urban Establishment: Upper Strata in Boston, New York, Charleston, Chicago, and Los Angeles* (1982); Edward Pessen, *Riches, Class, and Power before the Civil War* (1973); and Jeffrey G. Williamson and Peter H. Lindert, *American Inequality: A Macroeconomic History* (1980). These studies should be supplemented with analyses of social mobility such as Robert Doherty, *Society and Power: Five New England Towns, 1800–1860* (1977); Don H. Doyle, *The Social Order of a Frontier Community: Jacksonville, Illinois, 1825–1870* (1978); Peter R. Knights, *The Plain People of Boston, 1830–1860* (1976); and Stanley Lebergott, *The American Economy: Income, Wealth, and Want* (1976). Some of the disruptive effects of economic change are addressed in Karen Haltunen, *Confidence Men and Painted Women: A Study of Middle-Class Culture in America, 1830–1870* (1982); Alan Dawley, *Class and Community: The Industrial Revolution in Lynn* (1976); Bruce Laurie, *Working People of Philadelphia* (1980); Jonathan Prude, *The Coming of Industrial Order: Town and Factory Life in Rural Massachusetts* (1983); W. J. Rorabaugh, *The Alcoholic Republic: An American Tradition* (1979); Christine Stansell, *City of Women: Sex and Class in New York, 1789–1860* (1986); and Sam Bass Warner, Jr., *The Private City* (1968). For a stimulating discussion of the effects of markets and manufacturing on the countryside, see Christopher Clark, *The Roots of Rural Capitalism: Western Massachusetts, 1789–1860* (1990).

The concept of the business class is developed in Michael Katz et al., *The Social Organization of Early Industrial Capitalism* (1982). Surveys of reform movements closely linked to the Second Great Awakening include Alice F. Tyler, *Freedom's Ferment: Phases of Social History from the Colonial Period to the Outbreak of the Civil War* (1944), and Ronald G. Walters, *American Reformers, 1815–1860* (1978). Studies of the relationship between religious evangelism and reform are particularly abundant for communities in New York State. See Paul E. Johnson, *A Shopkeeper's Millennium: Society and Revivals in Rochester, New York, 1815–1837* (1978), and Mary Ryan, *Cradle of the Middle Class: The Family in Oneida County, New York, 1790–1865* (1981). On the relationship between religion and labor protest, see Jama Lazerow, *Religion and the Working Class in Antebellum America* (1996). For more general studies of religious ferment in the early republic, see John Butler, *Awash in a Sea of Faith: Christianizing the American People* (1990); Nathan O. Hatch, *The Democratization of American Christianity* (1989); and R. Lawrence Moore, *Selling God: American Religion in the Marketplace of Culture* (1994).

CHAPTER 11

Two fine surveys of the Jacksonian era are Charles Sellers, *The Market Revolution: Jacksonian America, 1814–1846* (1992), and Harry L. Watson, *Liberty and Power: The Politics of Jacksonian America* (1990). See also Daniel Feller, *The Jacksonian Promise: America, 1815–1840* (1995).

Democratizing Politics and the Jacksonian Presidency

Arthur M. Schlesinger, Jr., *The Age of Jackson* (1945), initiated the modern reexamination of Andrew Jackson and his significance. Among the most provocative subsequent studies are: Lee Benson, *The Concept of Jacksonian Democracy: New York as a Test Case* (1961); Marvin Meyers, *The Jacksonian Persuasion: Politics and Belief* (1957); and John William Ward, *Andrew Jackson; Symbol for an Age* (1962). For studies of Jackson and political institutions, see Donald Cole, *The Presidency of Andrew Jackson* (1992), and Leonard D. White, *The Jacksonians: A Study in Administrative History, 1828–1861* (1954). On the politics of the Bank war, see Robert V. Remini, *Andrew Jackson and the Bank War* (1967). On the nullification crisis, see William W. Freehling, *Prelude to Civil War* (1966), and Richard E. Ellis, *The Union at Risk* (1987). Works treating Jackson's Indian policy include Ralph S. Cotterill, *The Southern Indians* (1954); Grant Forman, *Indian Removal* (1953); Michael D. Green, *The Politics of Indian Removal* (1982); William G. McLoughlin, *Cherokee Renascence in the New Republic* (1986); Gary E. Moulton, *John Ross: Cherokee Chief* (1978); Francis P. Prucha, *American Indian Policy in the Formative Years* (1962) and *American Indian Treaties: The History of a Political Anomaly* (1994); and Ronald N. Satz, *American Indian Policy in the Jacksonian Era* (1975). For a comprehensive view of Jackson's life, see Robert V. Remini, *Andrew Jackson and the Course of American Freedom, 1822–1833* (1977), *Andrew Jackson and the Course of American Democracy, 1833–1845* (1984), and *The Life of Andrew Jackson* (1988). For important biographies of other leading politicians, consult Samuel Flagg Bemis, *John Quincy Adams and the Union* (1956); Leonard L. Richards, *The Life and Times of Congressman John Quincy Adams* (1986); John Niven, *Martin Van Buren: The Romantic Age of American Politics* (1983); Robert V. Remini, *Martin Van Buren and the Making of the Democratic Party* (1959); and James C. Curtis, *The Fox at Bay* (1970). For studies of the leading Whigs, see Richard N. Current, *John C. Calhoun* (3 vols., 1944–1951); Irving H. Bartlett, *Daniel Webster* (1978); and Robert V. Remini, *Henry Clay: Statesman for the Union* (1991).

Class, Culture, and the Second Party System

A rich literature describes the emergence of the Whigs in the context of a changing political culture and the creation of the Second Party System. Books that deal broadly with these topics include John Ashworth, *"Agrarians" & "Aristocrats": Party Political Ideology in the United States, 1837–1846* (1983); Richard Hofstadter, *The Idea of a Party System* (1972); Daniel W. Howe, *The Political Culture of the American Whigs* (1979); Robert Kelley, *The Cultural Pattern in American Politics: The First Century* (1979); Lawrence F. Kohl, *The Politics of Individualism: Parties and the American Character in the Jacksonian Era* (1989); Richard P. McCormick, *The Second American Party System: Party Formation in the Jacksonian Era* (1966); and Joel H. Silbey, *The Partisan Imperative: The Dynamics of American Politics before the Civil War* (1985). More specialized studies include Thomas Brown, *Politics and Statesmanship: Essays on the American Whig Party* (1985); Ronald P. Formisano, *The Birth of Mass Political Parties: Michigan, 1827–1861* (1972) and *The Transformation of Political Culture: Massachusetts Parties, 1790's–1840's* (1983); William G. Shade, *Banks or No Banks: The Money Issue in Western Politics, 1832–1865* (1972); Harry L. Watson, *Jacksonian Politics and Community Conflict: The Emergence of the Second Party System in Cumberland County, North Carolina* (1981); and Chilton Williamson, *American Suffrage from Property to Democracy, 1760–1860* (1960). For the presidency of John Tyler, see Robert J. Morgan, *A Whig Embattled* (1954).

An earlier generation of historians of labor emphasized the organization of unions during early industrialization. See Norman Ware, *The Industrial Worker, 1840–1860* (1924), and John R. Commons, *History of Labor in the United States,* Vol. 1 (1918). More recently, historians have explored the political and social context of the labor movement. See Mary H. Blewett, *Men, Women, and Work: Class, Gender, and Protest in the New England Shoe Industry, 1780–1910* (1988); Jeanne Boydston, *Home and Work: Housework, Wages, and the Ideology of Labor in the Early Republic* (1990); Alan Dawley, *Class and Community: The Industrial Revolution in Lynn, 1780–1860* (1976); Paul G. Faler, *Mechanics and Manufacturers in the Early Industrial Revolution* (1981); Paul A. Gilje and Howard B. Rock, eds., *Keepers of the Revolution: New Yorkers at Work in the Early Republic* (1992); Susan E. Hirsch, *Roots of the American Working Class: The Industrialization of Crafts in Newark, 1800–1860* (1978); Bruce Laurie, *Working People of Philadelphia, 1800–1860* (1980); Jonathan Prude, *The Coming of the Industrial Order: Town and Factory Life in Rural Massachusetts, 1810–1860* (1983); Ronald Schultz, *The Republic of Labor: Philadelphia Artisans and the Politics of Class* (1993); and Sean Wilentz, *Chants Democratic, New York City and the Rise of the American Working Class, 1788–1850* (1984). See also Christopher L. Tomlins, *Law, Labor and Ideology in the Early American Republic* (1993).

CHAPTER 12

General surveys of antebellum reform movements include Robert H. Abzug, *Cosmos Crumbling: American Reform and the Religious Imagination* (1994); C. S. Griffen, *The Ferment of Reform, 1830–1860* (1967); Alice F. Tyler, *Freedom's Ferment* (1944); and Ronald G. Walters, *American Reformers, 1815–1860* (1978).

Individualism

The leading study that connects transcendentalism with reform movements is Ann C. Rose, *Transcendentalism as a Social Movement, 1830–1850* (1981). See also Catherine L. Albanese, *Corresponding Motion: Transcendental Religion and the New America* (1977). Studies that link literary developments to reform themes and cultural history include Harold Kaplan, *Democratic Humanism and American Literature* (1972); David S. Reynolds, *Beneath the American Renaissance: The Subversive Imagination in the Age of Emerson and Melville* (1988) and *Walt Whitman's America: A Cultural Biography* (1995); R. Jackson Wilson, *Figures of Speech: American Writers and the Literary Marketplace, from Benjamin Franklin to Emily Dickinson* (1989); and Larzer Ziff, *Literary Democracy: The Declaration of Cultural Independence in America* (1981). On Margaret Fuller, see Paula Blanchard, *Margaret Fuller: From Transcendentalism to Revolution* (1978); Charles Capper, *Margaret Fuller: An American Romantic Life* (1992); and Joan von Mehren, *Minerva and the Muse: A Life of Margaret Fuller* (1995).

Communalism

On communitarian experiments, see Arthur Bestor, Jr., *Backwoods Utopias: The Sectarian and Owenite Phases of Communitarian Life in America* (1970); Lawrence Foster, *Religion and Sexuality: Three American Communal Experiments of the Nineteenth Century* (1981); Jean McMahon Humez, ed., *Gifts of Power: The Writings of Rebecca Jackson, Black Visionary, Shaker Eldress* (1981); Louis J. Kern, *An Ordered Love: Sex Roles and Sexuality in Victorian Utopias—The Shakers, the Mormons, and the Oneida Community* (1981); Spencer Klaw, *Without Sin: The Life and Death of the Oneida Community* (1995); Charles Nordhoff, *The Communistic Societies of the United States* (1875, reprinted 1960); and

Stephen J. Stein, *The Shaker Experience in America* (1992). On the Mormon experience, see James B. Allen and Glen M. Leonard, *The Story of the Latter-Day Saints* (1992); Leonard J. Arrington, *The Mormon Experience: A History of the Latter-Day Saints* (1992); John L. Brooke, *The Refiner's Fire: The Making of Mormon Cosmology, 1644–1844* (1994); Grant Underwood, *The Millennarian World of Early Mormonism* (1993); and Kenneth H. Winn, *Exiles in a Land of Liberty: Mormons in America, 1830–1846* (1989). On the linkages between religion and the utopians, see Paul E. Johnson and Sean Wilentz, *The Kingdom of Matthias: A Story of Sex and Salvation in 19th-Century America* (1995), and Timothy L. Smith, *Revivalism and Social Reform: American Protestantism on the Eve of the Civil War* (1980).

The Women's Movement

The most comprehensive history of women in the United States is Nancy Woloch, *Women and the American Experience* (1992). On the social history of women, see W. Elliot Brownlee and Mary M. Brownlee, *Women in the American Economy: A Documentary History, 1675–1929* (1976); Nancy F. Cott, *The Bonds of Womanhood: "Women's Sphere" in New England, 1780–1835* (1977); Carl N. Degler, *At Odds: Women and the Family in America from the Revolution to the Present* (1980); and Mary P. Ryan, *Cradle of the Middle Class: The Family in Oneida County, New York, 1790–1865* (1981). The most thorough description of the participation of women in benevolence and reform is Keith Melder, *Beginnings of Sisterhood: The American Women's Rights Movement, 1800–1850* (1977). For studies of more specific aspects of women's involvement in reform, see Barbara J. Berg, *The Remembered Gate: Origins of American Feminism: The Woman and the City, 1800–1860* (1978); Estelle B. Freedman, *Their Sisters' Keepers: Women's Prison Reform in America, 1830–1860* (1981); Lori D. Ginzberg, *Women and the Work of Benevolence: Morality, Politics, and Class in the Nineteenth-Century United States* (1990); Nancy A. Hewitt, *Women's Activism and Social Change: Rochester, New York, 1822–1872* (1984); and Jean F. Yellin, *Women and Sisters: The Antislavery Feminists in American Culture* (1989). On Dorothea Dix, see David Gollaher, *Voice for the Mad: The Life of Dorothea Dix* (1995), and Charles M. Snyder, *The Lady and the President: The Letters of Dorothea Dix and Millard Fillmore* (1975). The leading histories of feminists and the early women's rights movement include Kathleen Barry, *Susan B. Anthony—A Biography: A Singular Feminist* (1988); Ellen Du Bois, *Feminism and Suffrage: The Emergence of an Independent Women's Movement, 1848–1869* (1978); and Eleanor Flexner, *Century of Struggle: The Woman's Rights Movement in the United States* (1959).

Abolitionism

Surveys of antislavery reform include Robert H. Abzug, *Passionate Liberator: Theodore Dwight Weld and the Dilemma of Reform* (1980); David Brion Davis, *The Problems of Slavery in the Age of Revolution, 1770–1823* (1975); Louis Filler, *The Crusade against Slavery, 1830–1860* (1960); Stanley Harrold, *The Abolitionists and the South, 1831–1861* (1995); Leon F. Litwack, *North of Slavery: The Negro in the Free States, 1790–1860* (1961); Stephen B. Oates, *To Purge This Land with Blood: A Biography of John Brown* (1970); Lewis Perry, *Childhood, Marriage, and Reform: Henry Clarke Wright, 1797–1870* (1980); Benjamin Quarles, *Black Abolitionists* (1969); James B. Stewart, *Holy Warriors: The Abolitionists and American Slavery* (1976); John L. Thomas, *The Liberator: William*

Lloyd Garrison (1963); and Bertram Wyatt-Brown, *Lewis Tappan and the Evangelical War against Slavery* (1959). For the role of women in the antislavery movement, consult Edmund Fuller, *Prudence Crandall: An Incident of Racism in Nineteenth-Century America* (1971); Blanche Hersh, *The Slavery of Sex: Female Abolitionists in Nineteenth-Century America* (1978); Gerda Lerner, *The Grimké Sisters from South Carolina: Pioneers for Women's Rights and Abolition* (1967); and Alma Lutz, *Crusade for Freedom: Women of the Antislavery Movement* (1968). On northern hostility to abolition, see Leonard L. Richards, *"Gentlemen of Property and Standing": Anti-Abolition Mobs in Jacksonian America* (1970).

CHAPTER 13

Useful books on the social history of sections and sectionalism in the 1840s and 1850s include Stuart M. Blumin, *The Emergence of the Middle Class: Social Experience in the American City, 1760–1900* (1989); David Alan Johnson, *Founding the Far West: California, Oregon, and Nevada, 1840–1890* (1992); James Oakes, *The Ruling Race: A History of American Slaveholders* (1982); and William R. Taylor, *Cavalier and Yankee: The Old South and American National Character* (1961).

The Slave South: A Distinctive Society

The culture of the planter class and non-slaveholding whites can be explored in O. Vernon Burton, *In My Father's House Are Many Mansions: Family and Community in Edgefield, South Carolina* (1985); Drew Gilpin Faust, *Southern Stories: Slaveholders in Peace and War* (1992); Robert W. Fogel, *Without Consent or Contract* (1989); and Eugene Genovese, *The Slaveholder's Dilemma: Freedom and Progress in Southern Conservative Thought, 1820–1860* (1992). The best studies of women in southern slave society are Catherine Clinton, *The Plantation Mistress* (1983), and Elizabeth Fox-Genovese, *Within the Plantation Household: Black and White Women of the Old South* (1988). Catherine Clinton, ed., *Half Sisters of History: Southern Women and the American Past* (1994) is a collection of important articles. Efforts to connect southern culture with southern politics include George M. Frederickson, *White Supremacy: A Comparative Study in American and South African History* (1981), and J. Mills Thornton III, *Politics and Power in a Slave Society: Alabama, 1800–1860* (1978). On the nature of violence in southern society, see John Hope Franklin, *The Militant South 1800–1861* (1956), and Bertram Wyatt-Brown, *Southern Honor: Ethics and Behavior in the Old South* (1982).

On the role of family life and religion in helping African-Americans cope with the oppression of slavery, the pioneering studies were John W. Blassingame, *The Slave Community: Plantation Life in the Antebellum South* (1979); Albert J. Raboteau, *Slave Religion* (1978); Eugene D. Genovese, *Roll, Jordan, Roll* (1974); Herbert G. Gutman, *The Black Family in Slavery and Freedom, 1750–1925* (1976); and Lawrence W. Levine, *Black Culture and Black Consciousness* (1977). More recent studies include Jacqueline Jones, *Labor of Love, Labor of Sorrow: Black Women, Work, and the Family from Slavery to the Present* (1986), and Deborah G. White, *Ar'n't I a Woman? Female Slaves in the Plantation South* (1985).

On slave revolts, see Stephen B. Oates, *The Fires of Jubilee: Nat Turner's Fierce Rebellion* (1975), and Eugene D. Genovese, *From Rebellion to Revolution: Afro-American Slave*

Revolts in the Making of the Modern World (1979). On the ambiguous position of free blacks in a slave society, consult Ira Berlin, *Slaves without Masters: The Free Negro in the Antebellum South* (1974).

The Northeast: Industry and Culture

The economic changes in the North during the 1840s and 1850s can be studied in many of the economic history sources listed in Chapter 10. In addition, see Albert Fishlow, *American Railroads and the Transformation of the Ante-Bellum Economy* (1965).

On European immigration, consult Maldwyn Allen Jones, *American Immigration* (1960), and Philip Taylor, *The Distant Magnet: European Immigration to the U.S.A.* (1971). The most useful introduction to the nature of immigrant communities in the 1840s and 1850s is Oscar Handlin, *Boston's Immigrants: A Study in Acculturation* (1979). See also Kathleen Neils Conzen, *Immigrant Milwaukee, 1836–1860* (1976), and Bruce Laurie, *Working People in Philadelphia, 1800–1850* (1980).

Studies of women and popular literature include Ann Douglas, *The Feminization of American Culture* (1977), and Mary Kelley, *Private Woman, Public Stage: Literary Domesticity in Nineteenth-Century America* (1984). On birth control, see Linda Gordon, *Woman's Body, Woman's Rights: A Social History of Birth Control in America* (1976), and James Reed, *From Private Vice to Public Virtue: The Birth Control Movement and American Society since 1830* (1978). On educational reform, see Lawrence A. Cremin, *American Education: The National Experience, 1783–1876* (1980), and Carl F. Kaestle, *Pillars of the Republic: Common Schools and American Society, 1780–1860* (1983). See also Kathryn Kish Sklar, *Catharine Beecher: A Study in American Domesticity* (1973), a definitive biography.

The West: Manifest Destiny

Historians have recently begun to examine the development of the Midwest as a region. See Stephen Aron, *How the West Was Lost: The Transformation of Kentucky from Daniel Boone to Henry Clay* (1996); Andrew R. L. Cayton and Peter S. Onuf, *The Midwest and the Nation* (1990); and Nicole Etcheson, *The Emerging Midwest: Upland Southerners and the Political Culture of the Old Northwest, 1787–1861* (1996). See also William Cronon, *Nature's Metropolis* (1992).

Manifest Destiny is treated in Norman Graebner, *Empire on the Pacific: A Study of American Continental Expansion* (1955); Reginald Horsman, *Race and Manifest Destiny: The Origins of American Racial Anglo-Saxonism* (1981); and Frederick Merk, *Manifest Destiny and Mission in American History* (1963).

In recent years a number of books have opened up exciting new approaches to the history of western America. Leading examples include Patricia Nelson Limerick, *The Legacy of Conquest: The Unbroken Past of the Unbroken West* (1987); Clyde A. Milner II, *The Oxford History of the American West* (1994); David J. Weber, *The Mexican Frontier, 1821–1846* (1982); and Richard White, *"It's Your Misfortune and None of My Own": A History of the American West* (1991). This newer scholarship presents a more complete view of women in the West. See, for example, Susan Armitage and Elizabeth Jameson, eds., *The Women's West* (1987); John Mack Faragher, *Women and Men on the Overland Trail* (1979); Julie R. Jeffrey, *Frontier Women: The Trans-Mississippi West, 1840–1860* (1979); and Joanna L. Stratton, *Pioneer Women: Voices from the Kansas Frontier* (1981).

On the politics of expansion to the Pacific, see William J. Cooper, *The South and the Politics of Slavery, 1828–1856* (1978), and Charles G. Sellers, *James K. Polk: Continentalist, 1843–1846* (1966).

CHAPTER 14

Histories that discuss the disruption of the Union between the Mexican War and the onset of the Civil War in a comprehensive fashion are rare. The best is David M. Potter, *The Impending Crisis, 1848–1861* (1976).

War, Expansion, and Slavery, 1846–1850

Study of expansionism in the 1840s should begin with Frederick Merk, *The Monroe Doctrine and American Expansion, 1843–1849* (1972). On the coming of the Mexican War, consult Paul H. Bergeron, *The Presidency of James K. Polk* (1987); David Pletcher, *The Diplomacy of Annexation: Texas, Oregon, and the Mexican War* (1973); and Charles G. Sellers, *James K. Polk: Continentalist, 1843–1846* (1966). On the fighting of the war, see K. Jack Bauer, *The Mexican War, 1846–1848* (1974), and Otis A. Singletary, *The Mexican War* (1960). For an analysis of the relationship between the war experience and American culture, see Robert W. Johannsen, *To the Halls of the Montezumas: The Mexican War in the American Imagination* (1985), and John H. Schroeder, *Mr. Polk's War: American Opposition and Dissent* (1973). For the Mexican viewpoint, see Gene M. Brack, *Mexico Views Manifest Destiny, 1821–1846: An Essay on the Origins of the Mexican War* (1975). On congressional politics during the 1840s, see Chaplain Morrison, *Democratic Politics and Sectionalism: The Wilmot Proviso Controversy* (1967); Merrill Peterson, *The Great Triumvirate: Webster, Clay, and Calhoun* (1987); and Joel H. Silbey, *The Shrine of Party: Congressional Voting Behavior, 1841–1852* (1967). On the Compromise of 1850, see Holman Hamilton, *Prologue to Conflict: The Crisis and Compromise of 1850* (1964). For an interpretation stressing the contingency of the South's commitment to the Union, consult William W. Freehling, *The Road to Disunion: Secessionists at Bay, 1776–1854* (1991).

The End of the Second Party System, 1850–1858

General studies of sectional conflict in the 1850s include Avery O. Craven, *The Growth of Southern Nationalism* (1953). On the Fugitive Slave Act, consult Stanley W. Campbell, *The Slave Catchers* (1970). The best study of the politics of southern expansionism is Robert E. May, *The Southern Dream of a Caribbean Empire, 1854–1861* (1973). The leading studies of Frederick Douglass include Nathan I. Huggins, *Slave and Citizen: The Life of Frederick Douglass* (1980), and William S. McFeely, *Frederick Douglass* (1991). Essential sources on Douglass include *The Narrative of the Life of Frederick Douglass, An American Slave* (1845) and *Life and Times of Frederick Douglass, Written by Himself* (1881).

On the development of the Republican party, see Eric Foner, *Free Soil, Free Labor, Free Men: The Ideology of the Republican Party before the Civil War* (1970), and William E. Gienapp, *The Origins of the Republican Party, 1852–1856* (1987). The crisis over Kansas is discussed in James A. Rawley, *Race and Politics: Bleeding Kansas and the Coming of the Civil War* (1969), and Gerald W. Wolff, *The Kansas-Nebraska Bill: Party, Section, and the*

Coming of the Civil War (1977). On the Buchanan administration, see Kenneth M. Stampp, *America in 1857: A Nation on the Brink* (1990). On Dred Scott, see Don E. Fehrenbacher, *The Dred Scott Case: Its Significance in American Law and Politics* (1978). For a biography of Stephen A. Douglas, see Robert W. Johannsen, *Stephen A. Douglas* (1973). The best biography of John Brown is Stephen Oates, *To Purge this Land with Blood: A Biography of John Brown* (1970).

Abraham Lincoln and the End of Union, 1858–1860

The fate of the Democratic party is discussed in Roy F. Nichols, *The Disruption of American Democracy* (1948), and Michael Holt, *The Political Crisis of the 1850s* (1978). Abraham Lincoln has inspired a host of biographies. Classic studies include James G. Randall, *Mr. Lincoln* (1957); Carl Sandburg, *Abraham Lincoln: The Prairie Years* (1929); and Benjamin Thomas, *Abraham Lincoln: A Biography* (1952). The most recent major biography of Lincoln is David Herbert Donald, *Lincoln* (1995). For a stimulating set of essays, see Richard N. Current, *The Lincoln Nobody Knows* (1958). The most valuable book on Lincoln's formative political years is Don E. Fehrenbacher, *Prelude to Greatness: Lincoln in the 1850s* (1962). For other interpretations, see George B. Forgie, *Patricide and the House Divided* (1979); Stephen Oates, *With Malice toward None: A Life of Abraham Lincoln* (1977); and Garry Wills, *Lincoln at Gettysburg* (1992).

CHAPTER 15

The best up-to-date, comprehensive one-volume surveys of the Civil War are James M. McPherson's *Battle Cry of Freedom: The Civil War Era* (1988) and *Ordeal by Fire: The Civil War and Reconstruction* (1993). An excellent brief survey is Charles P. Roland, *An American Iliad: The Story of the Civil War* (1991). For a compelling older survey, see Shelby Foote, *The Civil War: A Narrative,* 3 vols. (1958–1974).

Secession and Military Stalemate, 1861–1863

Classic studies of the secession crisis include Richard N. Current, *Lincoln and the First Shot* (1963); David M. Potter, *Lincoln and His Party in the Secession Crisis, 1860–61* (1950); and Kenneth M. Stampp, *And the War Came: The North and the Secession Crisis, 1860–61* (1950). Histories of the secession of the Deep South include William L. Barney, *The Secessionist Impulse: Alabama and Mississippi in 1860* (1974), and Michael P. Johnson, *Toward a Patriarchal Republic: The Secession of Georgia* (1977). On the Upper South, see Daniel Crofts, *Reluctant Confederates: Upper South Unionists in the Secession Crisis* (1989).

Toward Total War

To study northern society and politics during the war, consult Iver Bernstein, *The New York City Draft Riots* (1990); Gabor S. Boritt, ed., *Lincoln the War President: The Gettysburg Lectures* (1992); George M. Fredrickson, *The Inner Civil War: Northern Intellectuals and the Crisis of Union* (2d ed., 1993); J. Matthew Gallman, *The North Fights the Civil War: The Home Front* (1994); Mary E. Massey, *Bonnet Brigades: American Women and the Civil War* (1966); Mark E. Neely, Jr., *The Fate of Liberty: Abraham Lincoln and Civil Liberties* (1991);

Phillip S. Paludan, *The Presidency of Abraham Lincoln* (1994); Susan M. Reverby, *Ordered to Care: The Dilemma of American Nursing, 1850–1945* (1987); Joel Silbey, *A Respectable Minority: The Democratic Party in the Civil War Era* (1977); Hans Trefousse, *The Radical Republicans* (1969); and Garry Wills, *Lincoln at Gettysburg* (1992). Important biographies of Union leaders include Michael Fellman, *Citizen Sherman: A Life of William Tecumseh Sherman* (1995); William McFeely, *Grant: A Biography* (1981); Stephen B. Oates, *With Malice towards None: The Life of Abraham Lincoln* (1977); Stephen W. Sears, *George B. McClellan: The Young Napoleon* (1988); and the Abraham Lincoln studies cited in Chapter 14.

Among the best histories of the Confederacy are George C. Rable, *The Confederate Republic: A Revolution against Politics* (1994), and Emory M. Thomas, *The Confederate Nation: 1861–1865* (1979). Important biographies of leading Confederates include William C. Davis, *Jefferson Davis, the Man and His Hour: A Biography* (1991), and Thomas E. Schott, *Alexander H. Stephens of Georgia: A Biography* (1988).

Studies of the Confederacy include Paul Escott, *After Secession: Jefferson Davis and the Failure of Southern Nationalism* (1978); Drew Gilpin Faust, *The Creation of Confederate Nationalism: Ideology and Identity in the Civil War* (1988); and Philip S. Paludan, *Victims: A True History of the Civil War* (1981).

The Turning Point: 1863

Studies of wartime emancipation include Herman Belz, *A New Birth of Freedom: The Republican Party and Freedmen's Rights, 1861–1866* (1976); John Hope Franklin, *The Emancipation Proclamation* (1963); Louis S. Gerteis, *From Contraband to Freedom: Federal Policy toward Southern Blacks, 1861–1865* (1973); and James M. McPherson, *The Struggle for Equality: Abolitionists and the Negro in the Civil War and Reconstruction* (1964). The best scholarship on the lives of slaves during the war is found in Ira Berlin et al., eds., *Freedom: A Documentary History of Emancipation, 1861–1867*, Series I, Volume I: *The Destruction of Slavery* (1985), and Series I, Volume III: *The Wartime Genesis of Free Labor: The Lower South* (1990).

The Union Victorious, 1864–1865

The most useful introduction to the military aspects of the war is T. Harry Williams, *The History of American Wars* (1981). On the experiences of Civil War soldiers, see Albert Castel, *Decision in the West: The Atlanta Campaign* (1992); Gerald F. Linderman, *Embattled Courage: The Experience of Combat in the American Civil War* (1987); James M. McPherson, *What They Fought For, 1861–1865* (1994); and Reid Mitchell, *Civil War Soldiers* (1988) and *The Vacant Chair: The Northern Soldier Leaves Home* (1993). On the participation of African-Americans in the war, see Ira Berlin et al., eds., *Freedom: A Documentary History of Emancipation, 1861–1867*, Series II: *The Black Military Experience* (1982), and Joseph T. Glatthaar, *Forged in Battle: The Civil War Alliance of Black Soldiers and White Officers* (1990). On Confederate military tactics, see Grady McWhiney and Perry D. Jamieson, *Attack and Die: Civil War Military Tactics and the Southern Heritage* (1982), and Steven E. Woodworth, *Jefferson Davis and His Generals: The Failure of Confederate Command in the West* (1990). An innovative exploration of the dynamics of violence is found in Charles Royster, *The Destructive War: William Tecumseh Sherman, Stonewall Jackson, and the Americans* (1991). The most graphic account of a single battle is Stephen W. Sears, *Landscape Turned Red: The Battle of Antietam* (1983). On the Civil

War in the Far West, consult Alvin M. Josephy, Jr., *The Civil War in the American West* (1991). For insightful analyses of the war's outcome, see Richard E. Beringer et al., *Why the South Lost the Civil War* (1986); Herman Hattaway and Archer Jones, *How the North Won: A Military History of the Civil War* (1983); and Archer Jones, *Civil War Command and Strategy: The Process of Victory and Defeat* (1992).

CHAPTER 16

The starting point for the study of Reconstruction is Eric Foner's major synthesis, *Reconstruction: America's Unfinished Revolution, 1863–1877* (1988), which is also available in a shorter version. Two older surveys that provide useful introductions are John Hope Franklin, *Reconstruction: After the Civil War* (1961), and Kenneth M. Stampp, *The Era of Reconstruction* (1965). *Black Reconstruction in America* (1935), by the black activist and scholar W. E. B. Du Bois, deserves attention as the first book to challenge traditional racist interpretations of Reconstruction as carpetbagger rule unjustly imposed on the defeated South by Radical Republicans.

Presidential Reconstruction

For important studies of presidential efforts to rebuild the Union, see the books on Abraham Lincoln listed in Chapter 15 and the following works on Andrew Johnson: Albert Castel, *The Presidency of Andrew Johnson* (1979); Eric L. McKitrick, *Andrew Johnson and Reconstruction* (1960); and James Sefton, *Andrew Johnson and the Uses of Constitutional Power* (1979). On the Radical resistance to presidential Reconstruction, see James M. McPherson, *The Struggle for Equality: Abolitionists and the Negro in the Civil War and Reconstruction* (1965). Books that focus on Congress include LaWanda Cox and John H. Cox, *Politics, Principle, and Prejudice, 1865–1867* (1963); David Donald, *The Politics of Reconstruction, 1863–1867* (1965); and William B. Brock, *An American Crisis: Congress and Reconstruction, 1865–1867* (1963). For insight into developments in the South, see Dan T. Carter, *When the War Was Over: The Failure of Self-Reconstruction in the South, 1865–1867* (1985). Michael Perman, *Reunion without Compromise: The South and Reconstruction, 1865–1868* (1973), stresses the South's handling of Johnson. On the freedmen, Willie Lee Rose, *Rehearsal for Reconstruction: The Port Royal Experiment* (1964); Peter Kolchin, *First Freedom: The Responses of Alabama's Blacks to Emancipation and Reconstruction* (1972); Leon F. Litwack, *Been in the Storm So Long: The Aftermath of Slavery* (1979); Ira Berlin et al., eds., *Freedom: A Documentary History of Emancipation, 1861–1867: The Wartime Genesis of Free Labor* (1990); Berlin et al., eds., *Slaves No More: Three Essays on Emancipation and the Civil War* (1992); Julie Saville, *The Work of Reconstruction: From Slave to Wage Laborer in South Carolina, 1860–1870* (1994). Jacqueline Jones, *Labor of Love, Labor of Sorrow: Black Women, Work, and the Family from Slavery to the Present* (1985), is a pioneering work on the impact of emancipation on black women.

Radical Reconstruction

For Congress's role in radical Reconstruction, see Michael Les Benedict, *A Compromise of Principle: Congressional Republicans and Reconstruction* (1974), and Hans L. Trefousse, *Impeachment of a President: Andrew Johnson, the Blacks, and Reconstruction* (1975). William

S. McFeely, *Grant: A Biography* (1981), deftly explains the politics of Reconstruction. Also helpful is Brooks D. Simpson, *Let Us Have Peace: Ulysses S. Grant and the Politics of War and Reconstruction, 1861–1868* (1991). State studies of Reconstruction include Richard Lowe, *Republicans and Reconstruction in Virginia, 1856–1870* (1991), and Otto Olsen, ed., *Reconstruction and Redemption in the South* (1980). The best account of carpetbaggers is Richard N. Current, *Those Terrible Carpetbaggers: A Reinterpretation* (1988). On blacks during radical Reconstruction, see Joel Williamson, *After Slavery: The Negro in South Carolina during Reconstruction, 1861–1877* (1965); Robert Cruden, *The Negro in Reconstruction* (1969); Thomas Holt, *Black over White: Negro Political Leadership in South Carolina during Reconstruction* (1977); and Barry A. Crouch, *The Freedmen's Bureau and Black Texans* (1992). Other studies covering southern race relations over a longer time span include John Blassingame, *Black New Orleans, 1860–1880* (1973); Howard N. Rabinowitz, *Race Relations in the Urban South, 1865–1890* (1977); Barbara Fields, *Slavery and Freedom on the Middle Ground: Maryland during the Nineteenth Century* (1985); and Jonathan M. Bryant, *How Curious a Land: Conflict and Change in Greene County, Georgia, 1850–1885* (1996).

Redemption

The most thorough study of the Ku Klux Klan is Allen W. Trelease, *White Terror: The Ku Klux Klan Conspiracy and Southern Reconstruction* (1972). To survey Reconstruction politics in the South, consult Michael Perman, *The Road to Redemption: Southern Politics, 1869–1879* (1984). On politics in the North, see Eugene H. Berwanger, *The West and Reconstruction* (1981); James Mohr, ed., *The Radical Republicans in the North: State Politics during Reconstruction* (1976); and William Gillette, *Retreat from Reconstruction, 1863–1879* (1979). The emergence of the sharecropping system is explored in Roger L. Ransom and Richard Sutch, *One Kind of Freedom: The Economic Consequences of Emancipation* (1977); Jay Mandle, *The Roots of Black Poverty: The Southern Plantation Economy after the Civil War* (1978); Gavin Wright, *Old South, New South: Revolutions in the Southern Economy since the Civil War* (1986); Edward Royce, *The Origins of Southern Sharecropping* (1993); Harold Woodman, *New South, New Law: The Legal Foundations of Credit and Labor Relations in the Postbellum Agricultural South* (1995). On yeomen farmers, consult Steven Hahn, *The Roots of Southern Populism: Yeoman Farmers and the Transformation of the Georgia Upcountry, 1850–1890* (1983). For the impact of Reconstruction on the national state, see Morton Keller, *Affairs of State: Public Life in Late Nineteenth-Century America* (1977), and Richard F. Bensel, *Yankee Leviathan: The Origins of Central State Authority in America, 1859–1877* (1990). On political corruption, see Mark W. Summers, *The Era of Good Stealings* (1993). On the Compromise of 1877, see C. Vann Woodward's classic *Reunion and Reaction* (1956), and K. I. Polakoff, *The Politics of Inertia: The Election of 1876 and the End of Reconstruction* (1973).

CREDITS

Illustrations

Chapter 1   **p. 4** Robert Knight/Leo de Wys; **p. 7** Amerind Foundation, Dragoon, AZ. Photo by Robin Stancliff; **p. 9** Bailey/Howe Library, University of Vermont; **p. 12** Mathias Grünwald, *Isenheim Altar Piece* (central panel), early 16th c., Musée Unterlinden, Colmar/ Giraudon/Art Resource; **p. 24** *Elizabeth I*, Armada Portrait by Anonymous. Private Collection/Bridgeman Art Library, London.

Chapter 2   **p. 32** Nettie Lee Benson Latin American Collection, University of Texas at Austin, General Libraries; **p. 39** Colonial Williamsburg Foundation; **p. 48** Courtesy, Peabody Essex Museum, Salem, MA; **p. 50** Courtesy, American Antiquarian Society; **p. 53** Shelburne Museum, Shelburne, VT. Photograph by Ken Burris.

Chapter 3   **p. 61** *James II*, by Godfrey Kneller, late 17th c. Courtesy of the National Portrait Gallery, London; **p. 69** Benin Bronze Plaque: Mounted King and Attendants, c. 1550–1680. The Metropolitan Museum of Art, NY The Michael C. Rockefeller Memorial Collection; **p. 74** Courtesy, Georgia Department of Archives and History, Atlanta; **p. 75** Abby Aldrich Rockefeller Folk Art Center, Williamsburg, VA; **p. 80** The Connecticut Historical Society.

Chapter 4   **p. 88** The Connecticut Historical Society, Hartford; **p. 95** Courtesy, Museum of Fine Arts, Boston. Bequest of Maxim Karolik; **p. 99** John Steper and Henry Dawkins, *A Southeast Prospect of the Pennsylvania Hospital*, c. 1761. The Library Company of Philadelphia; **p. 109** Stock Montage, Inc.; **p. 112** *View from Bushango Tavern, 5 miles from York Town on the Baltimore Road, July 1788*, Columbian Magazine. Collection of the New-York Historical Society.

Chapter 5   **p. 120** Print Collection. Miriam and Ira D. Wallach Division of Art, Prints and Photographs. The New York Public Library. Astor, Lenox and Tilden Foundations; **p. 123** Courtesy of the John Carter Brown Library at Brown University, Providence, RI; **p. 128** Courtesy, Peabody Essex Museum, Salem, MA; **p. 133** Anon, *Patrick Henry*, n.d. Shelburne Museum, Shelburne, VT. Photograph by Ken Burris; **p. 137** Courtesy of the John Carter Brown Library at Brown University, Providence, RI.

Chapter 6   **p. 148** Library of Congress; **p. 155** Library of Congress; **p. 160** Virginia Historical Society, Richmond; **p. 162** Anne S. K. Brown Military Collection, Brown University Library, Providence; **p. 166** Woodcut from *A Now Touch on the Times . . . By a Daughter of Liberty, Living in Marblehead*, 1779. Collection of the New-York Historical Society.

Chapter 7   **p. 177** John Singleton Copley, *Judith Sargent (Murray) at age 19*. Private Collection. Photo, courtesy Frick Art Reference Library; **p. 190** Ralph Earl, *Oliver Ellsworth and Abigail Wolcott Ellsworth*, c. 1792, Wadsworth Atheneum, Hartford, CT. Gift of the Ellsworth Heirs; **p. 195** Rembrandt Peale, *Thomas Jefferson*, c. 1800. White House Historical Collection.

Photograph by the National Geographic Society; **p. 195** John Trumbull, *Alexander Hamilton*, n.d., Yale University Art Gallery, New Haven.

Chapter 8   **p. 202** Thomas Birch, *Conestoga Wagon on the Pennsylvania Turnpike*, 1816. Shelburne Museum, Shelburne, VT. Photograph by Ken Burris; **p. 206** Courtesy of the Wethersfield Historical Society, CT; **p. 212** Library Company of Philadelphia; **p. 224** Mount Bethel A.M.E. Church, Philadelphia.

Chapter 9   **p. 233** Print Collection, Miriam and Ira D. Wallach Division of Art, Prints and Photographs. The New York Public Library, Astor, Lenox and Tilden Foundations; **p. 235** Shelburne Museum, Shelburne, VT. Photograph by Ken Burris; **p. 239** Chester Harding, *John Marshall*, c. 1830, Boston Atheneum; **p. 245** Ambrose Andrews, *Schuyler Family*, c. 1824, Collection of The New-York Historical Society; **p. 253** John L. D. Mathies, *Jemima Wilkinson*, c. 1816, Collection of the Yates County Historical Society. Reproduced Courtesy the Village Board, Penn Yan, NY.

Chapter 10   **p. 260** Collection of the New-York Historical Society; **p. 264** Smithsonian Institution; **p. 279** Oberlin College Archives.

Chapter 11   **p. 288** Philip Haas, *John Quincy Adams* (daguerreotype), c. 1843, The Metropolitan Museum of Art, Gift of I. N. Phelps Stokes, Edward S. Hawes, Alice Mary Hawes, Marion Augusta Hawes, 1937; **p. 293** The Gibbes Museum of Art, Carolina Art Association, Charleston, SC; **p. 297** George Catlin, *muk a tah mish o kah kaik, the Black Hawk,* mid 19th c., water color on paper. Courtesy of the Thomas Gilcrease Institute of American History and Art, Tulsa, OK; **p. 301** Collection of the New-York Historical Society; **p. 305** Collection of the New-York Historical Society; **p. 308** Collection of the New-York Historical Society.

Chapter 12   **p. 314** Culver Pictures; **p. 321** Culver Pictures; **p. 325** Library of Congress; **p. 325** Library of Congress; **p. 328** Harriet Beecher Stowe Center, Hartford, CT; **p. 332** Unknown, *William Lloyd Garrison* (daguerreotype), 19th c., The Metropolitan Museum of Art, Gift of I. N. Stokes, Edward S. Hawes, Alice Mary Hawes, Marion Augusta Hawes, 1937.

Chapter 13   **p. 340** Franz Holzlhuber, *Sugarcane Harvest in Louisiana & Texas*, c. 1856–1860, Collection of Glenbow Museum, Calgary, Alberta, Canada.; **p. 346** Sophia Smith Collection, Smith College, Northampton, MA; **p. 349** Culver Pictures; **p. 354** Library of Congress.

Chapter 14   **p. 372** Courtesy of the California History Room, California State Library, Sacramento, CA; **p. 377** Chicago Historical Society; **p. 382** The Kansas State Historical Society, Topeka; **p. 387** The Lincoln Museum, Fort Wayne, IN, a part of the Lincoln National Corporation.

Chapter 15   **p. 400** Culver Pictures; **p. 403** Massachusetts Commandery Military Order of the Loyal Legion and the US Army Military History Institute; **p. 412** Library of Congress; **p. 415** Library of Congress.

Text

Chapter 1 **p. 17** From Bartolomé de Las Casas, *The Journal of Christopher Columbus.* Translated by Cecil Jane, revised and annotated by L. A. Vigneras (London: Hakluyt Society, 1960). Reprinted by permission. **p. 19** Bernardino de Sahagún, *The Florentine Codex: A General History of the Things of New Spain.* Translated by Arthur J. O. Anderson and Charles E. Dibble (Salt Lake City and Sante Fe: The University of Utah Press and The School of American Research, 1975), Bk 12, pp. 17–20, 26, 83. Reprinted courtesy of the University of Utah Press.

Chapter 2 **p. 54** From *The Unredeemed Captive: A Family Story from Early America* by John Demos. Copyright © 1994 by John Demos. Reprinted by permission of Alfred A. Knopf, Inc.

Chapter 3 **p. 76** Reprinted from Hunter Dickinson Farish, ed., *Journal and Letters of Philip Vickers Fithian, 1773–1774: A Plantation Tutor of the Old Dominion*, published by the Colonial Williamsburg Foundation, 1965, pp. 38–39.

Chapter 4 **p. 94** From *Voyagers to the West* by Bernard Bailyn. Copyright © 1986 by Bernard Bailyn. Reprinted by permission of Alfred A. Knopf, Inc.

Chapter 6 **p. 156** Henry Steele Commanger and Richard B. Morris, eds., *The Spirit of Seventy-Six* (New York: Harper & Row, 1967). Reprinted by permission.

Chapter 7 **p. 183** Reprinted by permission of The Putnam Publishing Group from *American Populism* by George McKenna. Copyright © 1974 by George McKenna. **p. 176** J. P. Custis, Letter to George Washington, March 16, 1781, *William and Mary Quarterly*, 3rd ser., 43 (April 1986). Reprinted by permission.

Chapter 8 **p. 215** From *The Louisiana Historical Quarterly* (vol. 9, no. 1, January 1926). Reprinted by permission.

Chapter 9 **p. 247** From Marsha Markman, Jonathon Boe, and Susan Corey, *The American Journey: United States History through Letters and Diaries* (St. James, NY: Brandywine Press, 1995). Reprinted by permission of Brandywine Press.

Chapter 10 **p. 262** From Gary Kulik, Roger Parks, and Theodore Z. Penn, eds., *The New England Mill Village, 1790–1860* (Cambridge, MA: MIT Press, 1982). Reprinted by permission of MIT Press.

Chapter 12 **p. 326** Nancy Woloch, ed., *Early American Women* (New York: McGraw-Hill, 1997). Reprinted with permission of The McGraw-Hill Companies.

INDEX

Note: Italic letters following page numbers refer to illustrations *(i)*, and maps *(m)*.

Ableman v. Booth (1857), 376–377
abolitionism, 329–336
  African colonization and, 330
  Civil War and, 406–407
  evangelical, 331–334
  free-soil movement and, 370–371
  Lincoln and, 388
  opposition to, 334–336
  slave rebellions and, 330–331
  women and, 323, 325–327, 333, 335
Acadia (Nova Scotia), 64, 107
Acoma Indians, 30
Acts of Trade and Navigation (1651–1663), 40–41
Adams, Abigail, 168, 177, 248
Adams, Charles Francis, 369, 371
Adams, Henry, 406
Adams, John, 81, 88*i*, 119, 126, 135, 145, 163, 184, 188, 191, 208, 238, 245, 253
  as president, 197–199, 239
  on republican institutions, 175
Adams, John Quincy, 214, 227*m*, 288*i*, 295
  election of 1824 and, 286, 287
  expansionist western policy of, 227–228
  as president, 287–289
Adams, Samuel, 133–134, 145, 182, 184, 189
Adams-Onís Treaty (1819), 227, 358
Africa, 15
  East, 68
  West, 65–67, 67*m*
African-Americans. *See* blacks
African Methodist Episcopal (AME) Church, 224, 224*i*
agriculture. *See also* farmers; horticulture; *and specific crops*
  in colonial period, 110
    mid-Atlantic colonies, 91
  in Europe, 9–10
  Jefferson's vision and, 195
  native American, 3
    Mississippian civilization, 8
    women, 8, 9*i*
  rise of rural manufacturing and, 234
  sharecropping, 441*i*, 441–442
  technological innovation in, 205, 269
    reapers, 348, 349*i*, 355
  westward expansion and (1790s–1810s), 205–206, 206*i*
Aix-la-Chapelle, Treaty of (1748), 83
Alabama, 268, 431, 440
  secession of, 375, 393

slavery in, 220, 223, 341
  voting rights in, 243, 284
Alamo, battle of the (1836), 359–360
Albany, New York, 35
  American Revolution and, 151
Albany Plan of Union (1754), 107, 137
Albany Regency, 285
alcohol consumption, 277, 354. *See also* temperance
Algonquin Indians, 33, 35, 47, 55, 63
Alien Act (1798), 198, 208
Allen, Richard, 224*i*, 330
AME (African Methodist Episcopal) Church, 224, 224*i*
amendments to the Constitution. *See also specific amendments* (e.g., Fifth Amendment)
  Bill of Rights, 190, 191–192
American and Foreign Anti-Slavery Society, 335, 371
American Anti-Slavery Society, 333–334, 335
American Bible Society, 252, 351
American Colonization Society, 330, 332
American Education Society, 252
American Equal Rights Association, 431
American Female Moral Reform Society, 324
American Home Missionary Society, 252
American Indians. *See* native Americans
American Lyceum, 313
American party (Know-Nothing party), 381, 384
American Philosophical Society, 99
American Revolution, 144–171. *See also* Patriots; Revolutionary Era (1776–1790)
  civilians during, 153–154
  as civil war, 153
  creating new institutions after (1776–1787). *See* republican institutions, creating (1776–1787)
  Declaration of Independence and, 147
  events leading to, 144–149
  financial aspects of, 154
  France and, 153, 154, 160, 161, 162–163
    military alliance, 156–158
  Loyalists, 139–140, 145, 153–154, 158, 160, 163
    exodus of, 167
  military strategies and events, 149–163
    advantages of Patriots, 161–162
    advantages of the British, 149
    Howe's strategy (1776), 150
    in the North, 149–153, 152*m*
    in the South, 158–161, 159*m*
    Valley Forge, retreat to (winter of 1777–1778), 155, 156
    Washington's strategy (1776), 150–151
  militia in, 145, 146, 149, 151, 153, 159, 160, 161, 162, 164
  peace talks and treaties, 162–163